HANDBOOK OF
SENTIMENT ANALYSIS
IN FINANCE

EDITED BY

GAUTAM MITRA

AND

XIANG YU

This edition first published in 2016 by Optirisk Systems
in collaboration with Albury Books

Copyright © 2016 Optirisk Systems

OptiRisk R&D House	Albury Books
One Oxford Road	Albury Court
Uxbridge	Albury
Middlesex	Thame
UB9 4DA	Oxfordshire
United Kingdom	OX9 2LP
www.Optirisk-Systems.com	www.AlburyBooks.com

ISBN: 978-1-910571-57-6

Printed and bound in Turkey

ENDORSEMENTS

The technology of extracting financial sentiment from news feeds and other such sources continues to advance. This volume, an update of the earlier *Handbook of News Analytics in Finance*, describes the current state of the art, illustrating the considerable progress over the past five years. It will provide an indispensible introduction to the area, as well as a comprehensive reference work.

Professor David J. Hand

Emeritus Professor of Mathematics, Imperial College, London

Chief Scientific Advisor, Winton Capital Management

An excellent collection of studies into how market prices respond to the flow of information in the economy. Many sources of information ranging from prominent news stories through to social media discussions are analyzed for their impact on asset pricing, including the development of strategies trading the flow of information. The handbook is a fundamental addition to understanding the origins, processes and pathways of price discovery.

Prof Dilip Madan

Professor of Finance, Robert H. Smith School of Business

Mitra and Yu have done a comprehensive coverage of the sentiment analysis in finance. The handbook is both timely and relevant to the current state of research on news analytics, social media analytics and the impact on financial markets. Finance researchers interested in information transmission, news sentiment and investors' trading behavior, ranging from a high-frequency to a longer-horizon, have a lot to gain from reading this book. This book has the potential to shape the next generation of sentiment analysis in finance.

Andreas Milidonis, Ph.D.,

Assistant Professor in Finance, University of Cyprus.

This book contains amazing insights into the analysis of sentiment. The sentiment that expresses people's emotions reflects what sources they use to obtain new information, what they say, what they write, how they behave as part of crowds including networks, and what decisions they make as individuals. Sentiment is complex and multidimensional, and this book offers systematic, novel approaches for addressing that multidimensional complexity. Readers will find fascinating practical applications to the analysis of news about non-farm payroll, corporate earnings, stock returns, commodities, options, and corporate debt.

Prof Hersh Shefrin
Mario L. Belotti Professor of Finance, Santa Clara University

The effective quantification of non-standard, non-numerical data has opened up vast new avenues of investment signal research. This volume provides a cogent and valuable summary of the current research in this area.

Peter Swank, Ph.D.,
Vice President, Tudor Investment Corporation

TABLE OF CONTENTS

PREFACE

BACKGROUND

As the saying goes every book tells a story; this is true even when it is a scientific "tome". Our journey started with The Handbook of News Analytics in Finance (2011); but we have stayed the course and continued to research this topic, networked with the industry leaders and leading academics who have contributed to this field. For this Handbook research started when my academic colleague Dr Keming Yu suggested to his daughter, Xiang Yu, to join us for PhD research in the summer of 2010. Xiang enthusiastically embraced the research topic, diligently worked at Brunel University and OptiRisk as an industry sponsored PhD researcher holding an EPSRC bursary. So it is with thanks to both Keming and EPSRC that this research has been possible. Since Xiang's research was focused on the topic "Analysis of news sentiment and its application to Finance" it gave us a head start in compiling some of the contents at an early stage of our preparation. Throughout these years, OptiRisk have organised annual conferences dedicated to this topic, further focusing our minds to other facets of research and in the domain of sentiment analysis applied to finance. As a result of this continuous exposure to the problems as well as the technologies and the progress achieved in this domain we have ventured to compile this Handbook and share this knowledge with the practitioners as well as researchers in this field.

WHAT'S NEW?

A tremendous amount of progress has been made in the last 5 years, since we compiled and published our last handbook: T*he Handbook of News Analytics in Finance*. We set out below in a summary form some of the salient aspects:

- The technology of natural language processing (NLP) has been added to earlier approaches to text mining and sentiment classification. has brought improvements to accuracy.
- Many alternative information sources have emerged in the last few years; in particular there has been an explosion of information that arrive through blogs and the net. This has on one hand triggered innovative research on the other hand presented problems of trust. For instance we are faced with two classes of information:
    i.   Curated information:
        - macroeconomic news, company reports and filings
        - Newswires with editorial oversight
    ii.   Un-curated information:
        - Microblogs (Twitter)
        - On-line search information, Google and Wikipedia
        - The research in this domain started with equities. But today a number of other asset classes are also covered by sentiment meta-data. These include: commodities, fixed income and FX.

THE ROAD MAP

As editors we had to make two important decisions, namely, the contributions we solicited and the structure within which we presented these contributions as chapters. We have as editors gave our perspective of progress in sentiment analysis applied to finance in the form of an overview chapter. In this chapter we set the scene and introduce readers to the recent developments made in sentiment analysis. We have covered the salient aspects, that are, the classification process, sources of information and applications of sentiment meta data to finance. This overview chapter we recommend as a starting point for the newcomers who wish to make a quick entry to this field. The rest of the handbook has been structured as follows:

Part I TEXT ANAYTICS AND SENTIMENT CLASSIFICATION:

In this part we have included three chapters which relate to Compositional Sentiment Analysis, Document Sentiment Classification and how sentence structures are used in Sentiment Classification.

Part II ONLINE SEARCH AND SOCIAL MEDIA SOURCES:

This part is made up of four chapters which cover Twitter Sentiment Analysis including lexicon method and machine learning, sentiment information extracted from microblogs, finding patterns before stock market moves by making Wikipedia search and one chapter in which the authors analyse company filings for earnings news, investor attention and thereby determining the equity price.

Part III SENTIMENT ANALYSIS APPLIED TO EQUITIES:

The six chapters in this part concern various aspects of equity pricing and equity trading strategies using sentiment meta-data

Part IV PART IV- SENTIMENT ANALYSIS FOR OTHER ASSET CLASSES:

In this part there are five chapters which cover sentiment analysis applied to bonds (fixed income), commodities, FX and also one chapter discussing global economic activities.

Part V USE OF SENTIMENT ANALYSIS IN AUTOMATED TRADING:

Two chapters in this section are devoted to relatively low frequency automated trading, and one chapter on the topic of high frequency trading.

Part VI APPLICATIONS OF SENTIMENT ANALYSIS: CASE STUDIES:

Two case studies are presented in this part.

Part VII DIRECTORY OF SERVICE PROVIDERS:

Summary information of fourteen active service providers are supplied in this part of the Handbook.

After reading the overview chapter the rest of this book can be read in any order, depending on the reader's interest and job role, as the chapters have all been written independently. There is some referencing between the chapters but this does not hinder the understanding of content within each chapter.

The purpose of this handbook is to invigorate and instigate readers to become active and pursue the exploration of sentiment analysis in finance. There are many applications to be explored, techniques and methods to be tested. Our mission is to motivate and excite the researchers and equally practitioners to participate in the research and development or exploitation of research knowledge in their respective areas of interest.

Gautam Mitra and Xiang Yu,
OptiRisk Systems Ltd, London

ACKNOWLEDGEMENTS

Xiang and I would like to thank the many parties who have contributed in different ways and helped us to compile and publish this Handbook. To start with, we would like to thank (i) Albury Press who have helped us in our bold step of self-publishing. Erik Pordes and his team proposed very reasonable terms and set the ball rolling in the summer of 2015. Hannah Howell has managed the relationship, explained many aspects of soft copy and hard copy dual mode publishing and En Tsao did design of the logo, the jacket and finally the typesetting. Best of all the multiple tasks of pricing, design and printing were all done in a timely fashion whenever there were delays these were embarrassingly on our side. Next (ii) we would like to thank our lead sponsors, namely, Bloomberg, Thompson Reuters and RavenPack. These three major content vendors of sentiment meta data have also sponsored and participated in our last two annual conferences in London and in addition to their financial support they have showcased their ongoing R&D work. We acknowledge their contributions on this technological front and those of many other leading industry researchers and academics in this field. These conferences presented us with great opportunities to exchange knowledge and gain insights into the emerging trends in this topic area. We also thank Northfield Information Services; they have been a long-term partner of OptiRisk, inside and outside the topic of sentiment analysis. From another perspective we would like to stress that (iii) this handbook would not have been possible without the contributors, whom we thank for sharing their research results; it is their common passion for research and development of sentiment analysis in finance that has enabled us to compile this volume. We thank the contributors on another count: most of the contributors to this volume have also acted as a reviewer of the contributions. One of our instructions for the review process has been for the reviewer to make constructive comments and give advice so that the contributions can be enhanced in value. We were indeed impressed how this tactics has worked so well and in many chapters it resulted in considerable value addition. So many thanks to the contributors and the reviewers. Finally (iv) Xiang and I would also like to thank our colleagues at OptiRisk for helping us with many aspects of the Handbook, namely, promotion, compilation of the contents, contacting and liaising with the authors many of whom were also presenters at our past events. The team comprises Julie Valentine, Aqeela Rahman, Kavya Agarwal and Christina Erlwein-Sayer without their support it would have taken us much longer to complete this volume.

Gautam Mitra and Xiang Yu,
OptiRisk Systems Ltd, London

ACKNOWLEDGMENTS

EDITORS AND CONTRIBUTORS

EDITORS

Gautam Mitra is founder and MD of Optirisk Systems. He is internationally renowned research scientist in the field of Operational Research in general and computational optimization and modeling in particular. He is an alumni of UCL and currently a visiting professor at UCL. In 2004 he was awarded the title of 'distinguished professor' by Brunel University in recognition of his contributions in the domain of computational optimization, risk analytics and modeling. Professor Mitra is also the founder and chairman of the sister company UNICOM seminars.

Xiang Yu is a Business Development Techno Executive at Optirisk Systems. She has a PhD in Mathematics from Brunel University. Her research interests are in sentiment analysis and market microstructure and their applications in financial analytics. In Optirisk Systems, she conducts client facing applied research; she is also in charge of all aspects of acquiring market data and news metadata.

CONTRIBUTORS

Saeed Amen is the managing director and co-founder of the Thalesians. He has a decade of experience creating and successfully running systematic trading models at Lehman Brothers, Nomura and now at the Thalesians. Independently, he runs a systematic trading model with proprietary capital. He graduated from Imperial College with a first class honours master's degree in Mathematics and Computer Science.

Cristiano Arbex Valle obtained his PhD in Mathematics at Brunel University, where his main research interests were optimisation techniques and financial modelling. He joined OptiRisk in 2011 as a researcher and a software engineer. He is qualified as a computer scientist and coordinates the development and research of OptiRisk's financial analytics products.

Tomaso Aste is Professor of Complexity Science at UCL where he is also Head of the Financial Computing & Analytics Group, Director of the UCL Centre for Blockchain Technologies, Director of MSc in Financial Risk Management, vice Director of the UK Financial Computing & Analytics Doctoral Centre and a board member of the LSE Systemic Risk Centre. He is recognized as a world-leading scientist in complex system studies and financial big-data analytics.

Adam Avakian is a Quantitative Analyst at Citizens Financial Group. He obtained a PhD in Physics from Boston University where his research interests included lattice QCD and lattice gauge theory and geometrical reformulations of the Standard Model and beyond. Prior to that, he worked as a Risk Analyst at the Bank of America.

Ashok Banerjee is currently the Departmental Head of Finance and Control, at the Indian Institute of Management (IIM) Calcutta. He joined IIM Calcutta as Professor (Finance and Control) in 2004 and has been instrumental in setting up the state-of-the-art Financial Research and Trading Laboratory (Finance Lab) there. He is also the founding member of Indian Finance Association.

Svetlana Borovkova is an Associate professor of Quantitative Finance at the Vrije Universiteit Amsterdam specializing in the applications of mathematical and statistical methods to problems within finance and energy sectors. She is frequently consulted by major financial institutions, most notably for her work in derivatives pricing, futures trading, risk management and market modelling.

Chester Curme is currently a Quantitative Analyst at Loomis, Sayles and Company. Prior to this he was a research assistant at Boston University where he obtained his PhD in Physics. His areas of interest include complex networks, multivariate statistics and interdisciplinary applications of physics.

Gurvinder Brar is Global Head of Quantitative Research at Macquarie Securities. Global Quantitative Group is a core vertical of Macquarie Research with over 20-years of experience servicing Domestic and Global long-only, hedge-fund and quantitative managers as well as Sovereign Wealth Fund investors. The diversity of the team, both academic background and industry experience, is the driver of its success as reflected by its Top-1 rating for the past 17-years. The team regularly publishes thought provoking global research and undertake custom projects.

Asher Curtis has been at the University of Washington since 2012, and is currently an assistant professor who holds the Herbert O. Whitten Endowed Professorship in accounting. Asher's research focuses on how capital markets price accounting information, with a focus on valuation, forecasting and financial statement analysis.

Elijah DePalma, PhD, is a Senior Quantitative Research Analyst for Thomson Reuters Machine Readable News group, working directly alongside the StarMine Quantitative Research group. He is actively working on equity research projects in News Analytics over a range of investment horizons. Elijah also delivers client research presentations, manages external academic and supports product development.

Giuliano De Rossi heads the European Quantitative Research Team at Macquarie Securities. He has worked on a wide range of topics, including pairs trading, low volatility, the tracking error of global ETFs, cross asset strategies and downside risk. He has a PhD in Economics from Cambridge University.

Dan diBartolomeo is President and founder of Northfield Information Services, Inc. He is also a Visiting Professor at Brunel University in London. He regularly lectures at universities such as MIT, Harvard and Northwestern and has been admitted as an expert witness in litigation matters regarding investment management practices and derivatives in both US Federal and state courts.

Wei Dong is a Credit Risk Analyst Lead in AIG Asset Management where he works on credit portfolio modelling and CCAR stress testing. He obtained a PhD in Physics from The Graduate Centre, City University of New York where he developed a high sensitivity indirect nuclear magnetic resonance (NMR) detection method.

Michał Dzieliński is a Researcher at Stockholm Business School since September 2013 and a visiting professor at the Swedish House of Finance. He holds a PhD in finance from the University of Zurich. His research focuses on the empirical analysis of the dissemination and consumption of information in financial markets.

Aleksander Fafula is Chief Data Scientist at MarketPsych. For more than twelve years he has worked on distributed mission critical systems related to data security and the financial markets. He is the author of a methodology to detect human cognitive biases in stock price activity, which is the basis of an experimental stock trading system simulator.

Elisabetta Fersini is currently a postdoctoral research fellow at the University of Milano-Bicocca's Computer Science Department. Her research activity is mainly focused on statistical relational learning with particular interests in supervised and unsupervised classification.

Georg Gottlob is Professor of Computing Science at Oxford University and an Adjunct Professor of Computer Science at the Vienna University of Technology, where he is a member of the Information Systems Institute. He is also a co-founder of Lixto Corporation. His Ph.D. degree from University of Technology Vienna is in computer science.

Peter Hafez is Chief Data Scientist at RavenPack and an award-winning expert in the field of applied news analytics. He has consulted for numerous leading trading and investment firms on how to take advantage of news analytics in financial markets. Peter holds a Master's degree in Quantitative Finance from City University's Cass Business School.

Nilesh Kalamkar is Quantitative Researcher at Macquarie Securities and develops alpha generation techniques, portfolio management and risk management. Prior to this, he worked as a Commodity Strategist at Credit Suisse where he worked on quantitative models for portfolio rebalancing. He has a dual degree in Mechanical Engineering from Indian Institute of Technology, Bombay.

Dror Y. Kenett is an interdisciplinary researcher at the U.S. Department of the Treasury, Office of Financial Research. His research focus is on the structure and dynamics of financial markets. In particular, he is investigating sources of vulnerabilities, contagion and spillover effects within, and between financial markets.

Olga Kolchyna is a PhD Researcher in the Centre of Financial Computing and Business Analytics at the University College London, UK. Olga's research interests include natural language processing, machine learning and agent based modelling. Olga provides research support to Certona - a market leader in delivering personalised customer experiences for omni-channel retailers.

Abby Levenberg is a Research Scientist at WorkFusion. He has a PhD from the School of Informatics, University of Edinburgh, on the topic of online algorithms for data streams. His interest lie in the intersection of large dynamic data streams and scalable statistical inference. Other work includes learning online from streams of textual data for statistical machine translation systems, Bayesian inference for word alignments and dynamic web graphs for online spam site detection.

Bing Liu is Professor of Computer Science at the University of Illinois in Chicago. His research interests include sentiment analysis and opinion mining, data mining, machine learning, fake or deceptive opinion detection, and natural language processing. He received his PhD in Artificial Intelligence from the University of Edinburgh. He is an ACM Fellow and an IEEE Fellow.

Changjie Liu is Chief of Analytics at MarketPsych. He has been involved in sentiment research and trading strategies for the last five years. His prior studies include the impact of sentiment on price during technology product launches and effect of staleness on market sentiment reactions. At MarketPsych he creates quantitative trading models based on sentiment reactions in various asset classes.

Enza Messina is Professor in Operations Research at the Department of Informatics Systems and Communications, University of Milano-Bicocca, where she leads the research Laboratory MIND (Models in decision making and data analysis). Her research activity is mainly focused on decision models under uncertainty and more recently on statistical relational models for data analysis and knowledge extraction.

Helen Susannah Moat is an Associate Professor of Behavioural Science at Warwick Business School. Her work exploits data from sources such as Google, Wikipedia and Flickr, to investigate whether data from the Internet can help us measure and even predict human behaviour. She has acted as an advisor to government and public bodies on the predictive capabilities of big data.

Karo Moilanen is the Co-founder and CTO of TheySay, a spin out from Department of Computer Science, University of Oxford. He specializes in computational sentiment and emotion analysis, and takes interest in ambitious next-generation natural language technologies in and around the areas of Natural Language Processing (NLP), Computational Linguistics, Real-time Text Analytics, Affective Computing, Information Extraction, and others.

Richard Peterson is CEO of MarketPsych Data which produces psychological and macroeconomic data derived from text analytics of news and social media. MarketPsych's data is consumed by the world's largest hedge funds. Dr. Peterson is an award-winning financial writer, an associate editor of the Journal of Behavioral Finance, has published widely in academia, and performed postdoctoral neuroeconomics research at Stanford University.

Tobias Preis is Associate Professor of Behavioral Science and Finance at Warwick Business School. He is a computational social scientist focussing on analysis and prediction of social and financial complexity captured in big data. In 2007, he founded Artemis Capital Asset Management GmbH, a proprietary trading firm that is based in Germany.

Federico Alberto Pozzi is Analytical Consultant at SAS Italy. He received his Ph.D. in Computer Science from the Department of Informatics, Systems and Communications, University of Milano-Bicocca (Italy). His research interests focus primarily on probabilistic relational models, natural language processing and social network analysis, in particular applied to sentiment analysis on social media.

Stephen Pulman is Professor of Computational Linguistics at Oxford University's Department of Computer Science, a Professorial Fellow of Somerville College, Oxford and a Fellow of the British Academy. Prof Pulman co- founded TheySay Ltd, which produces ground-breaking research in computational linguistics and social media sentiment analysis.

Vernon J. Richardson is Professor in accounting at the University of Arkansas. He has served in various positions with the American Accounting Association, and performs expert witness and consulting services. He serves as a Director of Advanced Environmental Recycling Technologies, Inc. He obtained a Ph.D. in accounting from the University of Illinois at Urbana-Champaign.

Stephen Roberts is Professor of Machine Engineering at the Oxford University. His main area of research lies in machine learning approaches to data analysis, particularly for time series analysis and decision theory. He leads the Machine Learning Research Group and is Director of the Oxford-Man Institute of Quantitative Finance and co-Founder of the University spin-out company Mind Foundry.

Tilman Sayer joined OptiRisk in 2015 as a visiting researcher working on the topic of financial analytics. He obtained his PhD in Financial Mathematics at the University of Kaiserslautern in Germany with a thesis on the valuation of American-style derivatives within the stochastic volatility model of Heston.

Roy Schmardebeck is an Assistant Professor at the University of Missouri. He obtained a PhD in Business Administration (Accounting) from the University of Arkansas. He was a Certified Public Accountant and worked as an Auditor in Ernst and Young.

Edwin Simpson is a Postdoctoral Research fellow at the University of Oxford where he also pursued his PhD in Machine Learning. Prior to this, he worked as a research engineer in Hewlett- Packard and a Software Engineer in Artwork Systems. His interests lie in machine learning, human computation and aggregating information from disparate, unreliable sources.

Nitish Sinha is an Economist at the Federal Reserve Board. He received PhD in Finance from University of Maryland. He was awarded the Favourite MBA Professor of the year by UIC Liautaud School of Business in 2012 and the best paper by Chicago Quantitative Alliance and Midwest Finance Association in 2011.

H. Eugene Stanley is an American physicist and Warren Professor at Boston University. He has made seminal contributions to statistical physics and proposed the name of the new field econophysics, which joins the disciplines of economics and physics. One of his current research topics is understanding the anomalous behaviour of liquid water.

Tharsis Souza is a Teaching Assistant in the Department of Computer Science at UCL and is pursuing his PhD in Financial Computing and Analytics. His interests range from quantitative finance and financial risk management to data science, machine learning and complex systems. Before his PhD, he was Senior **Business** Analyst at BM&FBOVESPA.

Eric Tham was Director of Quantitative strategies at iMaibo and now works for Thomson Reuters. He has over 10 years of experience in sentiment analysis, risk management, quantitative development and use of machine learning in Finance. He has a MS in Business Analytics (Big Data) from the National University of Singapore and a MS in Financial Engineering from Columbia University.

Philip Treleaven is Professor of Computer Science and Director of the Financial Computing Centre at UCL. He is also a co-founder of numerous companies, including Bodymetrics and Sizemic. His research interests centre on applied research and its commercialisation in financial services and the creative industries, and in entrepreneurship.

ABBREVIATIONS

ABBREVIATIONS	ACRONYMS
AACs	Adverb-Adjective Combinations
AES	Aggregate Event Sentiment
AEV	Aggregate Event Volume
ANOVA	Analysis of variance
API	Application Program Interface
ARM	Advanced RISC Machine
AS	Absolute Sentiment
ASUM	Aspect and Sentiment Unification Model
BMA	Bayesian Model Averaging
BOW	Bag-of-Words
CAPM	Capital Asset Pricing Model
CAR	Cumulative Abnormal Returns
CCA	Contingent claims analysis
CPI	Consumer Price Index
CRB	Commodity Research Bureau
CRF	Conditional Random Fields
CRSP	Centre for Research in Security Prices
CSV	Comma separated values
DJ-UBS	Dow Jones-Union Bank of Switzerland
DJIA	Dow Jones Industrial Average
ECB	European Central Bank
ECN	Electronic Communications Network
EDGAR	Electronic Data Gathering, Analysis and Retrieval
EM	Expectation Maximization
EMH	Efficient Market Hypothesis
ENS	Event Novelty score
EPR	Earnings Press Releases
ER	Excess of Log-return
ERC	Earnings Response Coefficient
ESRC	Economic and Social Research Council
ESS	Event Sentiment Score
ETFs	Exchange-Traded Funds
GARCH	Generalized AutoRegressive Conditional Heteroskedasticity
GLM	Generalized Linear Model
GSCI	Goldman Sachs Commodity Index

H-BMA	Hierarchical Bayesian Model Averaging
HFT	High Frequency Trading
i.i.d	independent and identically distributed
I/B/E/S	Institutional Brokers' Estimate System
IA	Intelligence Amplification
IBCC	Independent Bayesian Classifier Combination
IDF	Inverse Document Frequency
IPO	Initial public offering
IR	Information Ratio
ISM	Institute of Supply Management
JOLTS	Job Openings and Labor Turnover Survey
JST	Joint Sentiment/Topic
LDA	Latent Dirichlet allocation
LGD	Loss Given Default
LIWC	Linguistic Inquiry and Word Count
MA	Moving Average
MACDs	Moving average crossovers
MCMC	Monte Carlo Markov Chain
MD&A	Management Discussion & Analysis
MI	Mutual Information
MLSLDA	Multi Lingual Supervised Latent Dirichlet Allocation
MPMI	MarketPsych Manufacturing Indexes
MPQA	Multi-Perspective Question Answering
MPQQQ	MarketPsych's NASDAQ 100 index code
MT	Machine Translation
NA	News Analytics
NAS	Networked Aspect-Sentiment
NASDAQ	National Association of Securities Dealers Automated Quotations.
NBESI	News Based Economic Sentiment Indices
NFP	Nonfarm Payrolls
NLP	Natural Language Processing
NOK	Norwegian Krone
NYMEX	New York Mercantile Exchange
OL	Opinion Lexicon
OLS	Ordinary Least Square
OVA	One-Versus-All
PD	Probability of Default
PEAD	Post-Earnings-Announcement Drift
pLSA	Probablistic latent semantic analysis
PMI	Purchasing Managers' Index
POS	Part of Speech
REG FD	Regulation Fair Disclosure

RIC	Reuters Instrument Code
RMSE	Root Mean Squared Error
RNSE	Thomson Reuters NewsScope
ROE/ROA	Return on Equity/ Return on Assets
RPNA	RavenPack News Analytics
RSS	Rich Site Summary
SA	Sentiment Analysis
SCL	Structural Correspondence Learning
SEC	Securities and Exchange Commission
SFA	Spectral Feature Alignment
SLDA	Super- vised Latent Dirichlet Allocation
S2-LAN	Semi-supervised Sentiment Learning by Approval Network
SM- SA	Social Media Sentiment Analysis
SMART	System for the Mechanical Analysis and Retrieval of Text
SMD	Sentiment Meta Data
SO	Sentiment Orientation
SOLID	Streams of Online Lead Indicators
SVD	Singular Value Decomposition
SVM	Support Vector Machines
TF	Term Frequency
TFIDF	Term frequency and inverse document frequency
TRACE	Transaction Reporting and Compliance Engine
TRMI	Thomson Reuters MarketPsych Indices
TRNA	Thomson Reuters News Analytics
TRTS	Thomson Reuters Text Analytics System
TSM	Topic Sentiment Mixture
UST	U.S. Treasurary
VAR	Vector AutoRegression
VECM	Vector Error Correction Model
VS	Vector Space
VWAP	Volume Weighted Average Price
WEKA	Waikato Environment for Knowledge Analysis
XBRL	eXtensible Business Reporting Language

CHAPTER 1

Progress in Sentiment Analysis Applied to Finance: an overview

Gautam Mitra, *Visiting Professor, UCL and CEO, Optirisk Systems*

Xiang Yu, *Researcher, Optirisk Systems*

ABSTRACT

In this overview chapter we first give a summary of the different ways textual information is processed and transformed into quantitative sentiment scores. We define the concept of market sentiment and the polarity of the sentiment scores, namely, positive, negative and neutral. We delve into the roots of sentiment analysis in branding and its applications in the consumer sector. Against the backdrop of efficient market hypothesis (EMH) and the contrarian behavioural finance theories we discuss the advantages of applying sentiment data to financial markets. We consider how news stories actually affect, that is, impact the dynamical behaviour of assets as measured by price, volatility and liquidity. A number of salient meta data sources, namely, Newswires, Social Media and On-Line search results are discussed. In particular, we introduce the major attributes of meta data such that these can be used in automated applications. We also consider the financial applications which can be enhanced by Sentiment Analysis. The challenges of handling financial sentiment meta data is discussed from a statistical and institutional perspective. Finally, the sentiment meta data supplied by the major contents vendors, namely, Bloomberg, Thomson Reuters and RavenPack are explained and presented in a summary form.

1.1 INTRODUCTION

Sentiment analysis in general and the text mining of structured and unstructured sources of text in particular are evolving at an accelerated pace. Disparate areas of knowledge such as machine learning, pattern recognition as well as Natural Language Processing (NLP) are variously explored and brought together. There are a few sectors of professional and business life where sentiment analysis is finding more and more applications. Typical examples amongst others are consumer behaviour, politics and organizational reputation. In particular, the emergence of social media, its growing strength and its impact on our societal life, public as well as private, cannot be either denied or ignored. In this Handbook, however, we focus on the narrow but chosen domain of financial applications; our aim is to gather all relevant aspects of knowledge relating to this topic.

At this point, we feel compelled to point out that most of the knowledge disseminated in the English speaking world are about sentiment as described and processed in English language. Yet there is a vast volume of sentiment analysis work that goes on in other languages, particularly Chinese and Japanese. These two Asian languages encompass 17% of the world's population so the significance of understanding information in Chinese and Japanese is obvious. What is not obvious however, is the method of how to train machines to automatically extract and classify sentiment from Chinese and Japanese language texts. Unlike English, these languages do not contain an alphabet, and so, for the case of Chinese, the task of understanding 50,000 characters and all its possible combinations is a great challenge. Additionally, the strict governmental controls within China means that news and information are not easily accessible to foreign countries. However, researchers within China have experimented with social media data from Weibo, the Chinese equivalent to Twitter, and applied text mining techniques to deduce investors' sentiment (see Chapter 14, Magistry et al., 2016 and Cui et al., 2013).

A salient aspect of using the sentiment meta data (SMD) is that just on its own the SMD does not improve the analytics application in finance; we proceed to set out the reasons. The efficient market hypothesis (EMH) forms the basis of market dynamics as it digests all the available information, (see section 3b for further explanation and references therein). On the other hand, adding SMD as an additional information source to market data definitely achieves enhancements of predictive financial analytics models as reported by Gross-Klussman and Hautsch (2011), Riordan et al. (2013), Sinha (2015)a and many more researchers. A vindication of this argument is justified in the following way. Derwent Capital used only Twitter data to make investment decisions; within 12 months of its launch the fund closed. [Needless to say, the buzz around social media-based hedge funds subsided almost immediately after Derwent's Twitter fund was quietly liquidated. Ref: http://www.hedgethink.com/news/whatever-happened-twitter-fund/]

Yet Thomson Reuters and Bloomberg in their event driven content products have built in Twitter and other Blogs. Thomson Reuters now provide (see Appendix 1.A.3, also Chapter 9): Thomson Reuters Text Analytics System (TRTS) for linguistic processing on news, social media and proprietary content. Bloomberg's event driven SMD feed also includes micro blogs and social media data (see Appendix 1.A). There are now multiple analytic quant teams using SMD from these sources and enhancing their trading, fund management and risk control strategies.

The rest of this chapter is organised in the following way. In section 1.2 we give a summary of the different ways textual information is processed and transformed into quantitative sentiment scores. We define the concept of market sentiment and the polarity of the sentiment scores, namely, positive, negative and neutral. In section 1.3 we discuss the roots of sentiment analysis in branding and its applications in the consumer sector. We then consider the applications of sentiment analysis in the domain of finance by setting out the efficient market hypothesis (EMH) and then contesting it against behavioural finance theories. Additionally, the advantages of applying sentiment data to financial markets are also discussed. We also introduce an important research finding by our group, namely, how news stories actually affect, that is, impact the behaviour of assets. In section 1.4 some aspects of the meta data sources, namely, Newswires, Social Media and on-line search results are discussed. In particular, we introduce the major attributes of meta data such that these can be used in automated applications. In section 1.5 we provide a short overview of the financial analytic applications which can be enhanced by Sentiment Analysis. In section 1.6 the challenges of financial documents are discussed; this section contains a concise summary of the working paper by Sinha of FED System. We conclude the chapter with a summary and concluding remarks. In the Appendices we have described some relevant and essential content information that are supplied by major content vendors.

1.2 FOUNDATIONS OF SENTIMENT ANALYSIS

Defining Sentiment

The definition of "sentiment" has evolved as research progressed. The initial sentiment that was of interest to researchers was the views and opinions of investors specifically **investor sentiment** (DeLong et al., 1990; Niederhofer, 1971). Whether it is their direct response to an announcement or after reading a news article, there was motivation to suggest that stock price movements would be related to such sentiment. Often these opinions do not translate into instant reactions but evaluated over time so that an overall perspective is taken in the long term. Naturally, the majority of the investors' views are reflected in the media, which gives a summary of the general mood and consensus for a given (stock) market. In due course, the contents of the published journal papers captured the perspective and came to be known as **media sentiment** (Tetlock, 2007). In the early days, this was derived directly from the text of news stories and simply analyses the number of positive and negative words to deduce the overall sentiment. Eventually this was refined to news sentiment (Barber and Odean, 2008, Sinha, 2015, Smales, 2012), which was the focus of our earlier "Handbook of News Analytics in Finance" (Mitra and Mitra, 2011). In the present handbook, we extend this to the broader context of sentiment deduced from multiple information sources. The classification methods of such sentiment are now more sophisticated and discussed further in section 1.3.2.

Market sentiment was previously proxied by market indices created by investors. For instance, market sentiment goes beyond news sentiment and includes VIX, market conditions and other factors such as put-call ratio. It is dominated by the viewpoints of informed traders, who receive and digest extra information regarding future prices, and so contrasts with the underlying assumption of the efficient market hypothesis (EMH) that the markets efficiently reflect all available information. This is particularly the case for the strong form of EMH. As research progressed, a more representative indicator for market sentiment was developed in the form of quantitative analytical data, directly from the text of published articles. The range of this numerical data evolved from being only across a positive-negative scale to encompass multiple facets of human emotions, such as greed and anger (see Chapter 12). This takes us into the domain of psychology and is interpreted as a reflection of the **market mood**. Therefore, in this handbook, sentiment score is defined in the following way. Given a news story, a real number is produced as the output that provides insight into the overall sentiment. This number falls within a range where the extremities represent a fully **positive sentiment** (or mood) and a fully **negative sentiment** (or mood), for example 0 – 100 or -1 to +1.

The polarity of the sentiments and their implications require further analysis and discussion. Firstly, the midpoint of the above sentiment scoring range represents **neutral sentiment.** This may seem otherwise of little consequence in deducing the overall effect of a news story; yet it cannot be simply discarded and taken out of financial models because it contributes to the newsflow (volume of news). Newsflow is valuable in calculating the **impact of news** sentiment (see Chapter 13) or further explanations. This is most evident in the analysis of content on social media such as Twitter. The second point is not so obvious; for a given news item both positive and negative sentiments can be assigned if we use probability weightings (see Appendix 1.A.3). Some articles are open to interpretation in respect of its sentiment polarity and furthermore, the sentiment can vary depending on the entity that is in question. This is another instance where newsflow comes into play and can facilitate in determining the **impact of news**.

Besides the categorisation of sentiment into positive, neutral and negative, it may further be considered as a range of emotions, thereby expanding the degree of sentiment into many factors (see Figure 1.1). Benjamin Graham, the father of "Value Investing", describes the emotions of investors as a pendulum that swings between optimism and pessimism (represented by fear and greed in Figure 1.1). This is backed by research from behavioural finance that detects systematically biased trading behaviour when emotional responses are triggered from new information (Bushman 2002; Antweiler and Frank, 2004; Da, Engelberg and Gao, 2011;). Chapter 12 delves deeper into this aspect of emotions and their relationship with news sentiment.

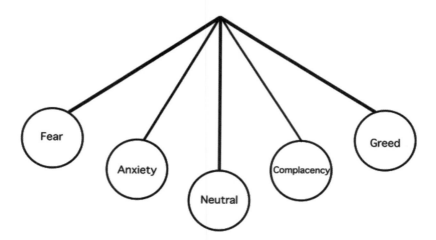

Figure 1.1: A pendulum of investors' emotions between pessimism and optimism.

Extracting Sentiment

Extraction of sentiment can be approached using classifiers and/or natural language processing techniques (NLP). The different classifiers that are used in text mining can be separated into two broad categories: supervised and unsupervised learning methods. Classification algorithms that are based on well-defined input variables belong to supervised learning, whereas in the unsupervised learning methods the latent variables are still to be identified. The former group of methods are well understood and extensively researched but the latter are less explored in comparison, although its popularity is increasing. Examples of unsupervised learning techniques are cluster analysis and community detection, which is where the focus of sentiment analytics is converging. As for the analysis of social media content, Messina, Pozzi and Fersini state that a fully supervised learning technique needs to be applied for the classification of sentiment (see Chapter 6).

With an increase in information sources, new techniques are being explored. The concept of gathering information from relationships within social media structures is considered in Chapter 6. Specifically, social networks and approval networks are discussed as a way to detect polarity alongside social media text. Furthermore, several studies report an improvement on the performance of supervised classifiers when user relationships are considered (Sharara et al., 2011; Fersini and Messina, 2013).

Initial text classification methods merely counted the number of words related to positivity and the words related to negativity within a short piece of text, limited to approximately 50 words. Examples of studies that applied this process are Li (2006), Davis, Piger and Sedor (2006) and Tetlock et al. (2008). In these early research works only two types of sentiment, namely positive and negative were considered; neutral sentiment did not exist. Categorisation of positive and negative words was decided through predetermined databases that had already assigned polarity to a large selection of words, namely, the General Inquirer (GI) of the Harvard Dictionary. The GI is a well-known quantitative content analysis program designed by psychologists spanning 77 categories in total. Tetlock, Saar-Tsechansky and Macskassy (2008) produce document-term matrices filled with frequencies of word appearance relative to a full piece of text; a common scheme known as Bag-of-Words. However, these scoring systems cannot be completely relied upon. Loughran and McDonald (2011) found that three-quarters of words identified as negative in the Harvard Dictionary are not typically considered negative in a financial context. Therefore, there remains a requirement for the presence of human judgement alongside the large databases capable of distinguishing overall sentiment of news stories.

Using dictionaries and databases that assign sentiment based on single words fail to interpret the content in news articles. In more recent work (see Chapter 3 and 4), complete sentences and phrase structures are considered in order to discover the exact context in which words are used. In this way, a more accurate reflection of the news sentiment is deduced. Hence, semantic elements such as negation and adverbs are introduced to the sentiment classification process so that scoring is applied to a string of words and then an average score is taken as the overall sentiment. Now, it is common practice to categorise this step as part of text pre-processing, with Das and Chen (2007) introducing the first negation tagging method.

The techniques mentioned so far are language dependent, that is, domain knowledge is required to carry out tasks. Contrasting to these methods is a group of classifiers that do not require any predefined knowledge, namely, Bayes Classifier and Support Vector Machines. The most widely used classifier in practice is the Bayes classifier, which has many different versions. It uses word-based probabilities and pre-classified text to assign a category to new text. Specifically, a corpus of news is first accurately classified and used as a training data set to identify the prior probabilities, which form the basis for Bayesian analysis. Posterior probabilities of categories are determined by applying the classifier to out-of-sample data, with the assignment of the specific category decided by the highest probability. Alternatively, discriminant-based classifiers have also been introduced, which adjust term weightings to identify the more emotive words.

Similar to these methods and also taken from the field of computer science are machine learning and natural language processing (NLP), where a training set of data is required to initiate the algorithm. The structure of these algorithms involves creating a set of already classified news text by humans to form the training set, classify the news using this information and applying metrics to assess the accuracy and stability of results. See Chapter 2 for more information on how NLP is used in this context. Additionally, machine learning algorithms may also be applied to identify relevant tags for a story. These tags turn the unstructured story texts into a basic machine readable form. The tags are often stored in XML format[1] and reveal the story's topic areas as well as other important properties. For example, they may include information about which company a story is describing. The basic idea behind these technologies is to automate reasoning.

Sentiment deduced from lexicon-based methods are compiled through classification of text to a collection of known and pre-compiled terms – comparable to a dictionary that defines the sentiment of the word rather than the meaning. Machine learning on the other hand explores the grammar, composition and other linguistic features of the text. Chapter 5 by Kolchyna et al contains more details of these two approaches; the authors explore a new method that combines them both.

Excluding humans in the judgement process generates a higher degree of consistency in results because no emotion is involved. Pang, Lee and Vaithyanathan (2002) compare classification results for humans and machine learning techniques and found that indeed machine learning performs better. However, simply applying a singular technique such as naïve Bayes or support vector machines did not beat the performance of topic-based categorization. Hence, modern day classification techniques adopt a combination of new methods, such as Bayes classifier, and existing ones, such as text mining. For a comprehensive overview of text classification techniques see Chapter 3, Chapter 4 and Pang and Lee (2008).

1.3 FOCUS AND PURPOSE OF SENTIMENT ANALYSIS IN FINANCE

Origins in the Branding Industry

The adoption of sentiment analysis started in the branding and marketing industry (Greenfield, 2014). Researchers investigated extensive ways of exploiting the pool of knowledge that can be extracted from textual data. Consumer sentiment, purchasing behaviour and opinions are some of the information that can be deduced from textual data about companies. This information creates useful feedback and insight into the company image and brand without having to hassle consumers directly for their opinion. Textual data is available on social media platforms such as Twitter and blog posts, and identification of companies are made through hashtags or keywords. As technology has developed, even more data has become available about consumers such as geographical locations through "check-in" and network circles. All this data can be monitored and analysed in the brand analytics space. Similarly, this source of information can also be adopted in the financial industry.

Generally, for this application, the more users and comments that are gathered the better, so that a consensus can be generated across the market. For financial applications, however, a set of filters is applied to remove the noise in the data and consider only the relevant content for an individual asset belonging to different asset classes (equities, indices, commodities etc.). See the appendices for typical classification features that allow for such filtering.

Focusing on Finance

News is publicly shared information; it is disseminated to all parties. In the domain of Finance, news sentiment is of great value to the diverse participants of the financial markets. News articles and commentary text covering companies (stocks), countries and regulatory authorities impact and move the financial markets. This information is rapidly digested by markets and a fundamental tenet of the efficient market hypothesis (EMH) is that taking into account all the market participants, it is not possible to achieve returns larger than the average market returns. Indeed this has been the foundation of finance theory for decades, ever since its proponent and now a Nobel Laureate (2013) Professor Eugene Fama developed the hypothesis in 1965 as part of his PhD thesis. The EMH claims that asset prices already reflect all past publicly available information, and change instantly to digest and reflect new public information, even insiders' information. However, as with all landmark theories, there are many studies contesting this frame of thought. Leading psychologists and behavioural scientists have found plenty of instances where EMH is violated, e.g. Shiller et al. (1984) and Basu (1977) find a group of stocks that would outperform others in the form of low price to earnings ratio stocks. This is explained by the argument that market participants (including investors) do not behave rationally and that they are indeed subject to many behavioural biases. By the 1990s, behavioural finance began to be widely accepted, bringing in the opposition to EMH – irrational markets (Kahneman, 2002, Shiller, 2000 and Shefrin, 2008). Postulated by prospect theory (see Kahneman and Tversky, 1979) the argument for irrational traders emerged. Evidence was compiled for over reactions and under reactions to new information, causing excess volatility to appear in the markets. At that time, an explanation for these findings was that they were simply reflecting a complex pattern of compensation for systematic risk, which in classical finance theory is the only determining factor of expected returns. The criticism of EMH is now well accepted and is termed "market anomalies".

Sentiment analysis is now a focal research area of behavioural finance. Sentiment data derived from media sources is entirely extracted from hard facts, unlike the proxies previously mentioned that only give an estimation towards the conditions and mood of the financial markets (e.g. VIX and price earnings ratio). This enables the real (human) factor of text to be captured in the analytics data. Through a combination of market data and sentiment data, a richer dataset of information is created and improvements can be found in four main areas of financial applications, namely:

- Asset allocation (trade signals, daily)
- Portfolio rebalancing (weekly , monthly)

- Regime detection
- Ex-post risk control

How sentiment data is applied to each of these areas is discussed further in Section 5 of this chapter, particularly the data requirements and modelling architecture. It is worth mentioning that due diligence teams in fund of hedge funds are also finding relevance in this dataset.

The ease of accessibility to news and other information sources have become useful parameters for decision making by day traders. With news vendors (Bloomberg, Thomson Reuters, Dow Jones etc.) and brokers' platforms all disseminating news, the trading opportunities become endless. Based on such information making a human judgement and arriving at a decision is what takes up time. Therefore, with an automated procedure of analysing sentiment meta data (SMD), the human decision making process is improved in terms of time and efficiency. The asset classes for which sentiment meta data are produced is also expanding, from only equities in the early days; today such data are available for foreign exchange, commodities and fixed income instruments. Part IV of this book include contributions, which describe in more detail new applications of SMD to these asset classes.

In the low latency applications within the finance industry, namely, in the intraday or high frequency trading (HFT) sentiment analysis is finding increasing acceptance and use. An important aspect of automated execution of strategy is that the ex-ante decisions, that is, positions taken are irreversible. Newsfeeds nowadays appear on traders screens within a matter of milliseconds. This speed of messaging is easily linked to automated trading and HFT; thus all scoring systems set in place electronically, the processing of SMD in general and machine readable news in particular to compute corresponding sentiment scores is commensurate with such trading frequencies. Moreover, it is reasonable to link news analytics to this form of trading, as many studies have shown, since the impact of news on asset prices is already incorporated at lower frequencies such as daily trading.

Unlike other forms of text analytics, the expectation of sentiment analysis performance is shockingly high. For automated HFT to deliver good results a pre-requisite is that computed sentiments and thereby the predicted asset (price) dynamics have to be comparable to that of expert traders, the additional requirement being that of fast processing. The performance criterion of a successful sentiment analysis engine is to process large volumes of incoming news from all around the world. So for equities SMD of 50,000-100,000 different instruments, have to be processed and their sentiment scores have to be computed. Subsequently for subsets of these assets aggregated for different indices and trading venues. The challenging task of automating sentiment calculation was broken down and addressed through many years of work; part I of this handbook is devoted to this topic. After experimenting with lexicon methods and topic separation, just to name a few, the approach of Bayes classifier managed to achieve an accuracy of around 60-70%. This approach is still widely adopted today, however, with human scoring reaching average agreement levels of 82-92%, the hunt for better classifiers continues. Sticking to mathematical methods, the adoption of vector spaces to sentiment analysis became state-of-the-art. Techniques such as support vector machines (SVM) and machine learning bring great hope for this field because they produce a high enough accuracy to compete with human judgement.

Impact of Sentiment

In our research (see Chapter 13), we have separated the **measure of news sentiment** and how news sentiment affects, that is, impacts the behaviour of a given asset in respect of its price, volatility and liquidity. We have therefore introduced the concept of **impact measure**. It is well known from research studies that news flow, that is, the volume of news affects asset behaviour (Patton and Verardo, 2012, Mitra, Mitra and diBartolomeo, 2009). Therefore, accumulation of news items as they arrive is important. Patton and Verardo (2012) noticed decay in the impact of news on asset prices and their betas on a daily timescale and further determine the complete disappearance of news effects within 2-5 days. It was also observed in Arbex-Valle, Erlwein-Sayer et al. (2013). Mitra, Mitra and diBartolomeo (2009) created a composite (sentiment) score in their volatility models after initial experiments revealed no effect on volatility predictions with sentiment alone; the decay period in this study was over 7 days.

News arrives both synchronously and asynchronously and as set out in section 1.2, depending on the nature of sentiment it creates, we classify these into three categories, namely, positive, neutral and negative. For the purpose of deriving impact measures, we only consider those items which lead to positive and negative sentiment.

In order to compute the impact of news events over time we first derive an expression that describes the attenuation of the news sentiment score. The impact of a news item does not solely have an effect on the markets at the time of release; the impact also persists over finite periods of time that follow. To account for this prolonged impact, we have introduced a methodology which reflect the instantaneous impact of news releases and the decay of this impact over a subsequent period of time. The technique combines exponential decay and accumulation of the sentiment score over a given time bucket under observation. We take into consideration the attenuation of positive sentiment to the neutral value and the rise of negative sentiment also to the neutral value and sum these sentiment scores separately. The sum of the positive sentiments and the negative sentiments define **positive impact** and **negative impact** for a given asset. Separation of the positive and negative sums is only logical as this avoids cancellation effects. For instance, cancellation reduces the news flow and an exact cancellation leads to the misinterpretation as if there was no news. The arrival of more news items leads to higher values of accumulation; this therefore takes into account the news intensity, that is, the news flow.

1.4 SOURCES OF METADATA

Since the introduction of news analytics data in the early 2000s, technology of sentiment analysis has progressed substantially. In particular, the rise of social media as the most preferred way of connecting people on-line has led to new models of information communication amongst the peers. Today, printed news is no longer the only form of communicating information. In this handbook, we cover the following sources of information:

i.   **Classical newswires and Macroeconomic announcements**
ii. **Social media**
iii. **Search information**

Besides the first source, the others are newcomers to the application of sentiment to Finance. The value in these sources and some research findings are given in this section.

(i) Classical newswires and Macroeconomic announcements

Classical newswires are still the main-stay of sentiment analysis research. The use of information from this source has been considered in detail in our earlier Handbook (see Mitra and Mitra 2011). A news item is an information event; in unscheduled (asynchronous) news we do not know when the event takes place and the polarity of the sentiment. In contrast, macro-economic announcements are also information events; in this case the timings are scheduled (synchronous) but the polarity of the sentiments is not known. Moreover, the trustworthiness of newswires is strengthened by the fact that all news goes through editorial review and providing output that is factual and reliable.

A consequence of news distribution is that recipients of the news form opinions; this enables investors to make judgements, and take actions in respect of their portfolio of assets or in respect computing and managing their risk exposure.

Returning to the theme of compiling news stories, the steps leading to the public dissemination of news are crucial in sustaining the validity and credibility of news stories. The process involves information gathering through credible sources so that journalists are able to produce a written article, which is then passed through due editorial control. The scrutiny and oversight of this editorial process ensures that only the validated items of information are published to maintain readers' confidence in the trustworthiness of news. Furthermore, this also implies that a process of filtering occurs to determine whether a piece of news is adequate for broadcasting. The reasoning can be explained as follows. The information is exclusively known to a small group of individuals to begin with, which is subsequently passed on to journalists who decide whether it is necessary to be publicised. Thus a selection criterion is imposed to differentiate between news that is suitable for distribution and those that should remain private. In other words, news is a class of information that is deemed noteworthy for market participants (e.g. investors, traders) to see. Naturally this raises the question of who controls such a selection. The intuitive answer would be journalists; upon further reflection it becomes apparent that it is the source that provides the journalist with such information. Hence, there must be some form of motivation driving the source to release it and require it to be shared publicly. Manipulation of such a process occurs when false or misleading information is distributed with the aim of moving markets to produce financial gain for the person. This is known as market manipulation and is illegal. For journalists, their objective is to attract readers' attention and create interest, which may lead to the formation of a common opinion amongst market participants. This is loosely termed as market sentiment.

In general, news articles contain a number of information items, which are required for the automated processing and use in the applied financial models. Typically, timings of news arrival, entity recognition, that is, its link with a given asset, and thereby the relevance of the news item for a given asset (equity) and finally the computed sentiment scores. In order to capture all of these items from the text of a news article, these are supplied as tags. The resulting structured and enhanced (by tags) record is called meta data. Meta data reveals information contained in the text of the news articles, and makes it easy to connect these tags to the applied financial models. A growing number of corporations (content vendors) provide valuable machine readable content to the financial end user community. These vendors have entered this business of sentiment analysis and low latency real time news feed. Thomson Reuters leads the field, and Bloomberg and Dow Jones have followed suit. An overview of these data vendor's analytical products and the structure of the contents are given in Appendix 1.A.

(ii) Social media

As technology evolves, it becomes easier to share information and news with people. The greater the size of the audience, the more potential impact the information is likely to have. In this milieu information is gathered from a range of sources besides classical newswires; for example, social media sites, blogs, forums and online search information. Fund managers have been known to manipulate such meta data to achieve alpha generating strategies. In fact, there is information contained in social media and online activity that is not available in newswires; an example being the pure volume of interest on a particular topic. It must be said, however, that unofficial sources of news are only a fragmentation of the journalism that covers mainstream newswires. This section reviews the value in different sources of information and what data is contained within them.

Goldfish are reported to have an attention span of seven seconds. Nowadays, the average human only has an attention span of eight seconds, according to an article in TIME magazine. The attention span of the average individual is decreasing by the day and as a consequence the top objectives of development in technology are ease of use and ease of interpretation. This is what social media sets out to achieve.

Micro-blogging platforms such as Twitter and Weibo encourage short messages that are restricted in length and utilise tags to highlight the main topics. In turn this increases the speed at which users can create posts, and consequently the volume of posts, often resulting in the first release of particular information, for example economic reports, earnings release and CEO departures. Obviously this advantage in timing compared to classic newswires, is contributed to the fact that information does not have to be verified by multiple sources. But as such, this content can only be referred to as speculation, rumours or opinion, and not, news. The massive volume of content available from social media is also an advantage of social media, as this is synonymous to newsflow. 5 years ago, only one piece of news may be influential to the whole stock market, but nowadays, possibly 10 posts could be influential. Therefore, to capture all this text, computers programmed set to scrape the web and accumulate all this masses of textual data from sources such as Twitter, message boards and blogs (see Appendix 1.A about Bloomberg SMD; Thomson Reuters also have a similar system called Thomson Reuters Text Analytics System (TRTS)). A Swiss start-up named Sentifi (see Directory in Part VII) call this Social listening & financial crowd-intelligence.

The majority of work carried out on social media content has been regarding Twitter, due to the platform being publicly available. Therefore, the data is also much easier to obtain, with time stamps and geographical information all being available. The Chinese equivalent to Twitter is Weibo and chapter 14 sheds some light into this platform.

In a study by Pear Analytics (Ryan, 2009), Twitter conversations were analysed and classified to be 40% "Pointless babble", 38% conversational and the rest is either self-promotion, spam, pass along, or news.

Although Facebook is the most popular form of social media, with 1.6 billion users in the world, it is not widely researched and analysed. This is due to the fact that Facebook is mostly a private network and users can control their own privacy settings. As a result, we do not discuss the use of Facebook as an information source in this book.

(iii) Search information

Returning to the foundations of a market mechanism, whereby a buyer makes an offer and a seller accepts the price and delivers an asset constitutes the basis of a market (micro) structure. In a global market place and the multiple trading venues essentially these market participants, namely buyers and sellers predominantly and also other tertiary participants such as market makers and liquidity providers enable the execution of the market based on information that is exchanged about an asset. This exchange commonly took place over the phone, via printed documents or via word-of-mouth. In today's world these different groups of market participants now gather as well as supply information using the ubiquitous net. Hence, a mountain of data is produced regarding information and topics that are of interest to buyers, sellers and other tertiary participants. Big data of this form contains indicative information on the behaviour of web users, hence, data scientists (Preis et al., 2013) have discovered that collecting data on search words made on Google reveals trends of the overall economy. The role of the participants in this information discovery process is the most important one. Thus there are other ways by which the views of these interested parties are elicited.

Search information such as Wikipedia and Google Trends, produces a massive amount of data and such large quantities of data brings the possibility of testing theories. This is why social scientists love "big data" – it acts as a telescope that could direct theories. From 2010, academics have been scouting through this search information to find indicators of sentiment. Obviously, this sentiment is formed from the entire online community and not just financial investors. Researchers using this form of information have found interesting relationships with stock market movements and the pricing (and mispricing) of earnings news (see Chapter 7 and 8).

1.5 EXPLOITING SENTIMENT ANALYSIS IN FINANCE

Sentiment analysis as in other domains has introduced a new information source in the area of financial applications. In practice this can only add value if this input enhances the established (legacy) as well as emerging applications in the BFSI sectors. The legacy applications comprise trading, fund rebalancing, risk control and retail consumer banking. Since these applications are based on neo-classical economic models or artificial intelligence (AI)/machine learning we first introduce the established taxonomy of models to provide some insights.

The taxonomy of analytic models can be summarised as (Mitra et al., 1989):

Descriptive Models as defined by a set of mathematical relations, which simply describes and thereby in some sense **predicts** how a physical, industrial or a social system may behave.

Normative Models constitute the basis for (quantitative) decision making by a superhuman following an entirely rational that is, **logically scrupulous** set of arguments. Hence quantitative decision problems and idealised decision makers are postulated in order to define these models.

Prescriptive Models involve systematic analysis of problems as carried out by normally intelligent persons who apply intuition and judgement. Two distinctive features of this approach are **uncertainty analysis and preference (or value or utility) analysis.**

Decision Models are in some sense a derived category as they combine the concept underlying the normative models and prescriptive models.

In the Context of Finance

In the domain of finance, trading and fund rebalancing applications are examples of decision modelling whereas risk management provides an example of descriptive modelling. Time and uncertainty play a key role in decision making as they are another important aspect of real world problems, and very much so in the domain of finance. To start with consider the role of "Time"; we observe trading and fund rebalancing are ex-ante decision making activities and risk management is an ex-post performance evaluation activity. Also the decision models are not just based on deterministic optimisation but they are best described as optimisation under uncertainty leading to optimum risk decisions. This slightly complicates the identification of the modelling paradigms. We note that optimisation under uncertainty uses two modelling paradigms, namely, predictive modelling followed by decision modelling. We explain this approach in the following way. The first step is that of predictive modelling such as predicting the asset characteristics followed by an optimum or risk based choice which is a decision modelling step. In Table 5.1 we have set out these financial analytics applications and have provided explanation of (i) the two roles of time, (ii) the data sources and their transactional frequency (iii) the modelling paradigms and (iv) how uncertainty is captured and represented.

Table 1.5.1: *Financial applications of sentiment data and their properties*

Applications		Time		Data Source		Modelling Paradigm	Other Comments
		Frequency	Direction	Market Data	Sentiment Data		
Risk Management (Quantification)		Daily, Monthly, Quarterly or Annual	Ex-post	✓	✓	Descriptive models; parameter values are computed by following a calibration step using historical data	See Mitra et al. (2009) & Arbex-Valle et al. (2014). Reporting normally based on monthly or annual risk exposure.
Fund Rebalancing		Weekly, monthly quarterly	Ex-ante	✓	✓	Predictive models to capture uncertainty via scenarios; followed by a decision model	See Chapter 9 and Chapter 11.
Automated Trading	Daily	Daily	Ex-ante	✓	✓	Predictive Analytics and Execution Algorithms	See Yu et al. (2014).
	Intraday (HF)	Minute bar or less	Ex-ante	✓	✓	Predictive Analytics and Execution Algorithms	
Retail Application (Credit worthiness, Loan and savings advice)		Daily, Monthly, Quarterly or Annual	Ex-ante and Ex-post	✓	✓	Descriptive models; parameter values are computed by following a calibration step using historical data. Also decision models	Expert users: *Kriti Sharma (Barclays, bank) *Sameer Gupta (DBS, bank)

In Table 5.1 we have set out 4 generic financial applications which appear in the left margin. These are listed as (i) risk management through risk quantification: risk computed for exposures of varying time spans, namely, weekly, monthly or annualized, (ii) fund rebalancing on calendar dates : weekly, monthly, yearly (iii) automated trading daily or intraday . There is also a fourth category of newly emerging application (iv) in the area of retail banking. On the top margin we have displayed Time, Data Sources, Modelling Paradigms and general comments.

Time: The frequency in respect of time, and the directional aspect of time, namely, ex-ante or ex-post are indicated in these columns

Data Sources: Market data and news meta-data are indicated in these columns

Modelling Paradigms: These are taken from the taxonomy introduced in the paragraph above. In order to capture uncertainty representation in the optimization or risk based decision models the fund management and trading models require a combination of predictive models of discrete realisations , that is, scenarios followed by decision models. The predictive models by and large use single period density forecast using discrete scenarios. Typical scenario generation methods include MCMC, moment matching and neural networks. Use of sentiment data adds to another important aspect of identifying the market conditions, namely, sentiment reversal. This improves the regime detection in the regime switching models. The decision models are used for ex-ante decision making applications. The risk management models on the other hand are simple descriptive models, which are also based on discrete scenarios; from a directional perspective these are ex-post. The retail application of credit-worthiness is similarly descriptive modelling with ex-post directional perspective. In all these applications, use of sentiment meta-data enhances the quality and the accuracy of these applications in contrast to using only the Market Data.

Modelling and Information Architecture

The modelling architecture for predictive analytics is illustrated in figure 5.1. Multiple information feeds are input variables in the predictive model. The model is then used to predict asset behaviour, namely, price, volatility and liquidity.

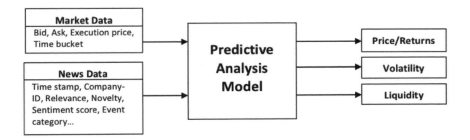

Figure 1.5.1: *Architecture of predictive analysis model*

The structure of the automated trade scheduling application is displayed in Figure 5.2. The end to end process is broken up as two sequences of information and models in tandem. The first is a predictive analytics model which is followed by an ex-ante decision model. This is then followed by an ex-post evaluation model. Another perspective of this process is Pre-Trade Analysis, followed by automated algorithmic trading strategies and finally Post-Trade Analysis.

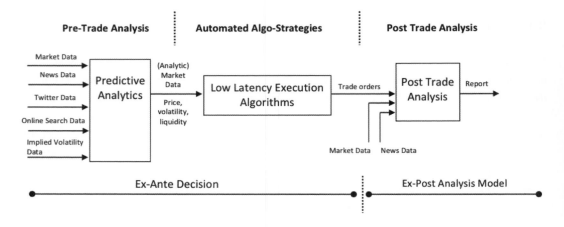

Figure 1.5.2: *Information flow and computational architecture for automated trading*

1.6 CHALLENGES FOR TEXT ANALYSIS OF FINANCIAL DOCUMENTS
This section has been prepared as a summary of the working paper by Nitish Sinha (see Sinha, 2015[b].)

1.6.1 Introduction

As we have set out earlier (Section 1.4, role of SMD), financial markets are moved by 'information'. Therefore, automatic extraction of information is a leading issue and technological innovation of text-mining and transforming it to sentiment is a central aspect in this market moving process. While there are many success stories for text analysis in the finance and economics literature, there are also many challenges that researchers need to embrace as we move forward. Some of these challenges are unique to the text analysis area while others apply to the big data analysis in finance. We classify these challenges in two groups, namely, (i) statistical challenges and (ii) institutional challenges. The rest of this section is organized as follows. In Section 1.6.2 we highlight the statistical challenges and in Section 1.6.3 the institutional challenges. In Section 1.6.4 we set out our conclusions.

1.6.2 Statistical Challenges

We define the sample as:

N... individuals with

K....attributes,

T... time periods.

The sample size is . For example, the sample could be the daily internet searches made by all Americans (N is almost equal to 300 million), with K attributes (home IP address, median income of the neighbourhood, zip code, members in the household, state, profession etc.) and T days (each of the 366 days in 2012).

(i) N = All is compelling but not the biggest challenge in text analysis.

One of the commonly cited appeal and criticism of big data (and textual analysis), such as Harford (2014) center on the premise that , i.e. the data is about all the individuals. For Economics and Finance, it is not as relevant. In these fields we are not only interested in the current state of the world where , if it were possible, is sufficient. Often our interest in data is driven by the needs of prediction. We need to model how the behaviour of individuals is captured by a smaller set of variables so we can predict how the individuals (or the system) will behave in the future or in slightly different economic conditions.

For example, even if we could get all the content of all the newspapers and websites at the time of the financial crisis, we need to be mindful that

1. The data is the content from those who chose to publish it. It does not have content from those who simply acted and not voiced their concerns in text.
2. The data is the content from the recent financial crisis and is not applicable to *all* financial crisis.

(ii) Large K increases the likelihood of spurious results.

For much of the history of empirical economics, economists have worked with a small number of covariates, but with textual data, the data can have potentially as many covariates as there are number of words in the language or higher. Since words individually do not convey the meaning by itself, an economist might want to use combination of two words at a time (bigrams) or n-words at a time (n-grams). The bad news is that with large number of covariates, the probability of stumbling into spurious results increases (see Nyman et al., 2014). The problem of large K is getting worse with cheaper storage technology and growth in the industry of user-data collection on the Internet and social media.

(iii) Getting help from economic models to limit K might not be enough.

In economics, the empirical analysis often does not suffer from too many K problem, partly due to the disciplining effect of economic models. The bad news is that it is only a partial reality. Of course, the researcher has the choice of dropping non-sensible variables, ex-ante, but then with datasets so vast it is also possible that the researcher would inadvertently end up introducing some bias. Sometimes, what appears to be a non-sensible result turns out to be an actual event, and sometimes what appears to be a well-founded result turns out to be a statistical fluke.

(iv) Limiting K, by ex-ante selection of words can also hurt

In finance, literature seems to have settled on using an ex-ante dictionary of positive and negative wordlists created by Loughran and McDonanld (2011) (LM wordlist). The LM wordlist is based on the words used in 10K filings. However, it is possible that the language used in 10 Ks may not be generalizable to all finance documents. A welcome change is that the literature has already recognized this limitation and slowly exploring alternative technologies, for example Hanley and Hoberg (2010) use an alternative dictionary.

(v) Large N provides the illusion of precision.

In econometrics, one learns that with increasing sample size the precision of an estimate increases. Using a sample of New York Times financial articles over nearly 27,500 trading days or nearly 80 years Garcia (2013) shows that a one standard deviation increase in media pessimism implies nearly 9 basis point decline in stock prices the next day. The estimate is statistically significant and is robust to controlling for day of the week effect and whole host of measures. Nevertheless, looking deeper he finds that the effects are concentrated in recessions, Mondays and the day after holidays - nearly one third of his observations were during these volatile times.

(vi) Data might not be representative.

In basic econometrics, one assumes that the sample size increases in an unbiased fashion but many new large datasets in finance might not be representative. One of the emerging areas of research in finance is search behaviour and its impact on stock prices pioneered by Da et. al. (2011). While it is important to understand demand for information from investors, one does need to worry if the internet searches are representative of the investor base that one is attempting to draw conclusion of. For example, are older and wealthier people predominantly using Yahoo instead of Google by force of habit? Similar concerns apply to twitter feeds, another burgeoning area of interest.

(vii) Small number of time buckets T

It is ironic that we are concerned with small sample size – T, while considering textual analysis. Since the financial crisis there has been great interest in text analysis as a potential predictor for crisis, but like recessions, financial crisis do not occur regularly in modern times and research in predicting financial stress using textual data is likely to run in to similar stumbling blocks. Another way this challenge manifests itself is that the textual data today does not resemble the textual data that existed earlier, thereby further reducing T. Words change meaning with usage. For example, the word "awful" was a good word until the middle of the 20th century.

(viii) Text data today does not reflect the textual data that existed earlier.

This challenge is a variant of the bias known in finance literature as the **survivorship bias** as in Brown et al (1992). In 1940, US had over 1,800 newspapers with daily circulation, which chronicled events, information demand and biases of Americans. By 2013, the number of newspapers had declined to 1,382 while the population increased remarkably. While some of the newspapers, have moved completely online and continued reporting in digital format, many have simply ceased operation leaving many localities without a newspaper. If we begin with the current coverage of daily newspapers to arrive at pattern of readership earlier, we are likely to be misled. A related problem is that text data with longer history does not represent the same part of the cross-section of readership.

1.6.3 Institutional Challenges

In an influential and provocative essay, Ioinnidis (2005) asserts that all published research findings are false. The essay notes (emphasis ours) "a research finding is less likely to be true when the studies conducted in a field are smaller; *when effect sizes are smaller; when there is a greater number and lesser preselection of tested relationships; where there is greater flexibility in designs, definitions, outcomes, and analytical modes; when there is greater financial and other interest and prejudice; and when more teams are involved in a scientific field in chase of statistical significance.*"

Unfortunately, for text analysis in finance quite a few of these conditions are ripe. The effect size is small. The area of textual analysis in finance being a nascent line of inquiry has great flexibility in designs, definitions, outcomes and analytic models. Recent interest in textual analysis is likely to aggravate pre-existing conditions for the discovery of false positives. While we have highlighted the statistical challenges earlier, in this section we will outline the institutional challenges that the researchers have to contend with while conducting textual analysis in finance.

(i) Limited access to textual data.

In the US, licenses distinguish between different usages of text , that is, some may only allow viewing but not storage of data. This limits dataset access to a small number of researchers and licensing constraints can make published results hard to replicate. Furthermore, since the interesting findings of earlier papers, textual data has become harder to obtain for researchers.

(ii) Source of the text matters.

Gurun and Butler (2012) show that local firms are able to sway local media to profile them in a better light than the national media. They also show that the sway of local firms is due to advertising dollars. Modern day pressure in the media industry is likely to confound the information content of text. While the concern is shown to exist with the local media, it is unlikely that the online media, twitter or any of the many emerging sources of text are immune to such pressures.

(iii) Much of interesting data exists in almost text format.

Since the quality of text is likely to have suffered in newspapers, it is tempting to look back and be somewhat cautious with newly available sources of text. Also examining older data allows the researcher to increase the time variation in the data. Unfortunately, older data is not in easily digestible textual format. While the text recognition technology has made great strides, research with older text has not gathered much steam due to high set up cost, limited availability of data and finally high cost of acquiring older news archives. There are some promising opportunities, however. The U.S. library of congress has taken up a multiyear project in which they have been digitizing century old newspapers. In due course, this archive is likely to be a treasure trove of textual data. Finance researchers are also likely to look outside newspapers for older text.

(iv) Data-mining is almost a forbidden discipline in finance

Black (1993) expressed his concerns about data mining by finance researchers because "only the models that seem to support his conclusions" may be chosen. Nowadays, finance researchers' attitude to data mining is almost opposite, with the more charitable view held amongst data mining professionals. For example, Hand et al. (2001) note "The science of extracting useful information from large data sets or databases is known as data mining." Since the two disciplines have such different attitudes to data analysis, little exists by the way of interdisciplinary research and perhaps not for lack of demand for such research from the practice of finance. If finance researchers instead acknowledged the lack of power of their traditional tests when it comes down to large textual databases, the analysis would have included some discussion on lack of power to accept or reject a particular hypothesis. The hope is that despite the early resistance from traditional finance, behavioural finance spawned a large literature, textual analysis would achieve likewise in the future.

1.6.4 Conclusions

To summarise, the promise of textual data in finance is almost limitless. While there are many statistical and institutional challenges, they also present opportunities. Large K is a challenge if finance works to give empirical content to economic relations for testing economic theories. In one of the early papers in text analysis in finance, Tetlock (2007) gets around the large K problem by conducting a dimension reduction via principal components analysis. By using historical data in non-traditional textual files such as pdf files of New York Times, Garcia (2013) gets around the problem of small values of T. Often textual data is in an unstructured format, but Automated Entity Extraction can aid the researcher in such cases. To get around the criticism of cherry-picking the choice of words, the literature seems to gravitate to one dictionary. This could be dangerous as words used in textual data seem to differ by the source of text and the authorship of text. There is a welcome trend of examining individual dictionaries such as Loughran and McDonald (2011).

Institutional challenges take longer to surmount but there too we already observe some progress. Textual data is large and new, limiting its acceptance but perhaps this will motivate researchers and libraries to look for new sources of data. We already appear to find usage for newly available free data such as social networks data as in Simon and Heimer (2012). Finally, finance literature is slowly being receptive of new innovative usage of textual data such as Da et al (2011).

1.7   SUMMARY AND CONCLUSION

Since the compilation of our earlier Handbook (see Mitra and Mitra, 2011), sentiment analysis in general and its application to finance in particular has developed in multiple facets. For instance, classification techniques have progressed, data sources have increased and many more use cases of successful applications have been reported. In this chapter we have provided a high level analysis of the current state of the art and where we believe the research developments and applications are heading. We have considered the modelling taxonomy and the information architecture of major financial applications and provided an analysis of how SMD can enhance such applications. We have finally discussed the challenges for text analysis of financial documents.

ACKNOWLEDGEMENTS

We thank Dr Nitish Sinha of the Federal Reserve Board, for providing the contents of the Section 1.6 of this chapter. We also thank Bloomberg, Thomson Reuters and RavenPack, the major content providers of SMD for their help in supplying and where appropriate explaining the manuals and APIs which describe the contents of their products; these are summarised in the Appendix.

Notes

[1] eXtensible Markup Language (XML) – most recent standard for representing text and data.

1.8 REFERENCES

1.   Antweiler, W. and Frank, M. Z. (2004). Is all that talk just noise? The information content of internet stock message boards. *The Journal of Finance*, *59*(3), pp. 259-1294.

2.   Arbex-Valle, C., Erlwein-Sayer, C., Kochendörfer, A., Kübler, B., Mitra, G., Nzouankeu Nana, G. A., Nouwt, B. and Stalknecht, B. (2013). News-Enhanced Market Risk Management. Available at SSRN: http://ssrn.com/abstract=2322668

3.   Barber, B. M. and Odean, T. (2008). All that glitters: The effect of attention and news on the buying behaviour of individual and institutional investors. *Review of Financial Studies, as des*

4.   Basu, S. (1977). Investment performance of common stocks in relation to their price-earnings ratios: A test of the efficient market hypothesis. *The Journal of Finance, 32(3)*, pp. 663–682.

5.   Black, F. (1993). Beta and return. *Journal of Portfolio Management, 20(1)*, pp. 8-18.

6.   Brown, S.J., Goetzmann, W., Ibbotson, R.G. and Ross, S.A. (1992). Survivorship bias in performance studies. *Review of Financial Studies, 5(4)*, pp. 553-580.

7.   Bushman, B.J. (2002). Does Venting Anger Feed or Extinguish the Flame? Catharsis, Rumination, Distraction, Anger and Aggressive Responding. *Personality and Social Psychology Bulletin, 28(6)*, pp. 724-731.

8.   Cui, A., Zhang, H., Liu, Y., Zhang, M. and Ma, S. (2013). Lexicon-based sentiment analysis on topical chinese microblog messages. In *Semantic Web and Web Science*, pp. 333-344. Springer New York.

9.   Da, Z., Engelberg, J. and Gao, P. (2011). In search of attention. *Journal of Finance, 66(5)*, pp. 1461-1499.

10. Das, S.Y. and Chen, M.Y. (2007). Yahoo! for Amazon: Sentiment extraction from small talk on the web. *Management Science, 53(9)*, pp. 1375–1388.

11. Davis, A. K., Piger, J. M. and Sedor, L. M. (2006). Beyond the numbers: An analysis of optimistic and pessimistic language in earnings press releases. *Federal Reserve Bank of St. Louis, Working paper Series,* (2006-005).

12. DeLong, J. B., Shleifer, A., Summers, L. H. and Waldmann, R. J. (1990). Noise trader risk in financial markets. *Journal of Political Economy, 98*, pp. 703–738.

13. Fama, E.F. (1965). The behavior of stock-market prices. *The Journal of Business*, *38*(1), pp. 34-105.

14. Fersini, E. and Messina, E. (2013). Web page classification through probabilistic relational models. *International Journal of Pattern Recognition and Artificial Intelligence, 27(4)*.

15. Garcia, D. (2013). Sentiment during recessions. *The Journal of Finance*, *68*(3), pp. 1267-1300.

16. Greenfield, D. (2014). Social Media in Financial Markets: The Coming of Age. GNIP whitepaper. Available at: http://stocktwits.com/research/social-media-and-markets-the-coming-of-age.pdf.

17. Gross-Klussmann, A. and Hautsch, N. (2011). When machines read the news: using automated text analytics to quantify high frequency news-implied market reactions. *Journal of Empirical Finance, 18*, pp. 321–340.

18. Gurun, U.G. and Butler, A.W. (2012). Don't believe the hype: Local media slant, local advertising, and firm value. *Journal of Finance, 67(2)*, pp. 561-598.

19. Hanley, K.W. and Hoberg, G. (2010). The information content of IPO prospectuses. *Review of Financial Studies, 23(7)*, pp. 2821-2864.

20. Hand, D.J., Mannila, H. and Smyth, P. (2001). *Principles of data mining*. MIT press.

21. Harford, T. (2014). Big data: A big mistake? *Significance, 11(5)*, pp. 14-19.

22. Ioannidis, J. (2005). Why most published research findings are false. *Chance, 18(4)*, pp. 40-47.

23. Kahneman, D. and Tversky, A. (1979). Prospect Theory: An Analysis of Decision under Risk. *Econometrica, 47(2)*, pp. 263 – 292.

24. Kahneman, D. (2002). Maps of bounded rationality: The [2002] Sveriges Riksbank Prize. *[Lecture] in Economic Sciences*. Available at: http://www.nobelprize.org/nobel_prizes/economic-sciences/laureates/2002/kahnemann-lecture.pdf

25. Li, F. (2006). Do stock market investors understand the risk sentiment of corporate annual reports? Available at SSRN: http://ssrn.com/abstract=898181.

26. Loughran, T. and McDonald, B. (2011). When is a liability not a liability? Textual analysis, dictionaries, and 10-Ks. *The Journal of Finance, 66(1)*, pp. 35-65.

27. Magistry, P., Hsieh, S.K. and Chang, Y.Y. (2016). Sentiment detection in micro-blogs using unsupervised chunk extraction. *Lingua Sinica, 2(1)*, pp.1-10.

28. Mitra, G. (1988). Mathematical Models for Decision Support. Invited contribution in Encyclopedia of Computer Science and Technology, Marcel Dekker, 1988, edited by Allen Kent. Also appearing as the review chapter in: Mathematical Models for Decision Support, Editor G. Mitra, in NATO Advanced Study Institute Series, 1988, by Springer Verlag.

29. Mitra, L. and Mitra, G. (2011). *The Handbook of News Analytics in Finance*. John Wiley & Sons.

30. Mitra, L., Mitra, G. and diBartolomeo, D. (2009). Equity portfolio risk (volatility) estimation using market information and sentiment. *Quantitative Finance, 9(8),* pp. 887-895.

31. Niederhoffer, V. (1971). The analysis of world events and stock prices. *The Journal of Business*, 44(2), pp. 193-219.

32. Nyman, R., Ormerod, P., Smith, R. and Tuckett, D. (2014). Big Data and Economic Forecasting: A Top-Down Approach Using Directed Algorithmic Text Analysis. *ECB Workshop on Big Data for Forecasting and Statistics*.

33. Pang, B., Lee, L. and Vaithyanathan, S. (2002). Thumbs up?: Sentiment classification using machine learning techniques. Proceedings of *ACL-02 conference on Empirical methods in natural language processing*. Association for Computational Linguistics, Philadelphia, PA: Vol. 10, pp. 79-86.

34. Pang, B. and Lee, L. (2008). Opinion mining and sentiment analysis. *Foundations and trends in information retrieval, 2(1-2),* pp.1-135.

35. Patton, A. J. and Verardo, M. (2012). Does beta move with news? Firm-specific information flows and learning about profitability. *Review of Financial Studies, 25(9),* pp. 2789-2839.

36. Preis, T., Moat, H. S. and Stanley, H. E. (2013). Quantifying trading behaviour in financial markets using Google Trend. *Scientific Reports, 3*.

37. Riordan, R., Storkenmaier, A., Wagener, M. and Zhang, S. (2013). Public information arrival: Price discovery and liquidity in electronic limit order markets. *Journal of Banking & Finance, 37,* pp. 1148-1159.

38. Ryan, K. (2009). Twitter Study. *Pear Analytics*.

39. Sinha, N. (2015)[a]. Underreaction to news in the US stock market. *The Quarterly Journal of Finance*.

40. Sinha, N. (2015)[b]. Challenges of text analysis for financial documents. Working paper.

41. Sharara, H., Getoor, L. and Norton, M. (2011). Active surveying: A probabilistic approach for identifying key opinion leaders. In IJCAI, pp. 1485–1490.

42. Shefrin, H. (2008). *A Behavioral Approach to Asset Pricing*. Elsevier.

43. Shiller, R. J., Fischer, S. and Friedman, B. M. (1984). Stock prices and social dynamics. *Brookings Papers on Economic Activity, 2*, pp. 457-510.

44. Shiller, R. (2000). *Irrational Exuberance*. Princeton University Press.

45. Simon, D. and Heimer, R. (2012). Facebook finance: How social interaction propagates active investing. In *AFA 2013 San Diego Meetings Paper*.

46. Sinha, N. (2015). Under-reaction to news in the US stock market. *Quarterly Journal of Finance*.

47. Sinha, N. (2015). Challenges for text analysis of financial documents, working paper, Federal Reserve Systems (US)

48. Smales, L. A. (2012). Non-scheduled news arrival and high-frequency stock market dynamics: Evidence from the Australian Securities Exchange. *25th Australasian Finance and Banking Conference 2012*. Available at: http://ssrn.com/abstract=2130193.

49. Tetlock, P. C. (2007). Giving content to investor sentiment: The role of media in the stock market. *Journal of Finance*, 62(3), pp. 1139-1168.

50. Tetlock, P. C., Saar-Tsechansky, M. and Macskassy, S. (2008). More than words: Quantifying language to measure firms' fundamentals. *The Journal of Finance, 63(3),* pp. 1437-1467.

51. Yu, X. (2014). *Analysis of News Sentiment and its Applications to Finance*. PhD. Brunel University.

52. Yu, X., Mitra, G., Arbex-Valle, C. and Sayer, T. (2014). An impact measure for news: Its use in daily trading strategies. Available at: http://ssrn.com/abstract=2702032.

1. A APPENDIX

These appendices provide a summary of the content coverage and data structure of the three leading data vendors in the field of sentiment analysis, namely, Bloomberg, RavenPack and Thomson Reuters. All the information is provided by the companies themselves. For a more extensive list of service providers in financial sentiment analysis, please see Part VII of this book.

1.A.1 Bloomberg Event-Driven Feeds

Bloomberg's Event-Driven Feeds are structured, low-latency news and data feeds delivered in machine-readable format for algorithmic trading, alpha generation, risk management, and compliance activities. Textual news and news analytics are two of a suite of products that also include economic data, company events, and corporate actions.

Textual News

Coverage

Bloomberg textual news draws on a vast and rapidly growing network of more than 100,000 sources, providing approximately 600,000 news items per day. Sources include Bloomberg News, web scrapes (with proprietary technology), third-party content (press releases/other news services), stock exchange news feeds, and social media.

The textual news feed features exhaustive classification and hierarchy of topics, tickers and people—all of which are tied to relevance scores. Content is tagged to more than 75,000 companies and over 10,000 topics. This highly granular approach allows firms to execute strategies with focus and precision. An updated, machine-readable copy of Bloomberg's ticker and topic taxonomy is provided daily.

SOURCE BREAKDOWN

Category	Percentage
Web Scrapes	69.8%
Third Party	17.0%
Social Media	5.4%
Stock Exchange	4.5%
Bloomberg News	3.3%

REGIONAL BREAKDOWN

Region	Percentage
AsiaPac, ANZ	30.4%
North America	29.9%
Europe, Africa, Middle East	28.3%
Latin America	9.9%
Global Macro	1.4%

Point-in-time archives start in November 2008 for Bloomberg News, with a backfill available from 1992. Other sources start between 2009 and 2011. Various backfills exist; typically backfills are generated for customers on request.

Available Fields

Fields are available that provide the unique story reference, time of arrival on Bloomberg's servers, story version, source, language, hot level, headline, story body, slug, story group ID, and metadata

News Analytics

Bloomberg news analytics deliver an informative second layer of processing for our industry-leading textual news feed, enabling firms to gain additional insights and better understand which news stories are significant for executing a given strategy. Analytics provide numerical scores generated from the newswires available through the Bloomberg Professional® service and Event-Driven Feeds. Analytics provided about a news story include sentiment, novelty, and market-moving indicators. At the company level, analytics include sentiment, readership heat, and publication heat. All of these indicators compose the News Analytics package from Bloomberg's Event-Driven Feeds.

Coverage

STORY ANALYTICS

Message Type	Percentage
Social Sentiment	46.7%
Sentiment Score	36.0%
Novelty Score	13.6%
Market-Moving Score	3.7%

COMPANY ANALYTICS

Message Type	Percentage
Publication Heat	39.0%
Sentiment	27.5%
Social Sentiment	23.1%
Readership Heat	10.5%

Approximate number of story analytics messages and company news analytics per day: 130,000. Point-in-time archives start between January 2010 and January 2012 for the different analytics types. Various backfills exist; typically backfills are generated on request for customers.

Available Data Fields

There are two categories of news analytical data: Story-level analytics and Company-level analytics. The former set of fields provide the story headline, unique story reference, news source, time of arrival, company identifier, type of score, score, confidence, and version. The latter set provide the company identifier, type of score, new value, previous value, and time of arrival.

Method and Types of Scores—Story Level

Sentiment: Bloomberg's news sentiment analysis answers the question, "If an investor holding a long position in this security were to read this article, would their confidence in their holdings increase, decrease or remain the same?" Alongside the sentiment score for a company mentioned in a story, we also provide a confidence indicator for that company. Our analyses are based on supervised machine-learning methods such as support vector machines, decision trees, and regression models.

Our algorithms extract and analyze parts of a story that are pertinent to the company under consideration using text summarization methods; they then compare their findings to the average sentiment of the news article as a whole. Features from both the company-specific content and the article overall are combined and evaluated using statistical machine-learning techniques to find the highest-probability class assignment. A novel agglomerative clustering technique is used to provide statistically valid confidence estimates from our ensemble of machine-learning methods, thus maintaining the distributive properties of our underlying models.

Bloomberg provides sentiment analysis on both traditional media sources and Twitter. The model for Twitter uses the same logic but has different training data. Story sentiment is part of the News Analytics package from Bloomberg's Event-Driven Feeds.

Market Impact Score (Predicted): The market impact score identifies, at publication time, news stories that have a high likelihood of causing a significant short-term price move in an equity. The provided score is a true Bayesian estimate for the probability of a short-term market reaction. The article is marked as market moving if the confidence value is above a high threshold. It is calculated by a machine-learning algorithm using features of the story (specific words and phrases, parts of speech, incidence of currency values, dates, etc.) as well as data about the security in question (market cap, etc.).

Market Impact Score (Reactive): A segmented regression algorithm (with some smoothing and normalization) runs on the 24-hour time series of 30-second price bars. It breaks the time series into best-fit line segments ("trends"), thus minimizing errors. The time window and the parameters of the regression vary based on the time of day. An expert system then analyzes the trends and selects anomalies based on differences in the trends' slopes, trading volume and other factors. News stories from the beginning of the trend are retrieved and scored based on a Bayesian model built from confirmed examples of stories that have moved the market.

Novelty: A given article has two types of novelty scores: one that checks the entire headline and article body, and one that puts extra weight on the headline and beginning of the article. Bloomberg designed novelty scores to help identify unique U.S. company news. For example, a press release might be sent on multiple press release wires as well as being posted to the company's website. We calculate the novelty of a story by comparing a story to those seen on other key newswires in the last 7 days. Stories from 67 different wires are compared to and with each other for this calculation.

Method and Types of Scores—Company Level

Sentiment: Company-level sentiment is aggregated from the story sentiment score for a company. Every two minutes (on the even minute), the sentiment aggregation engine computes weighted, time-decayed averages over the past 8 hours of news stories for each company that has received story flow. If the calculated number has an absolute change of at least 0.005, then a new message is issued to the company-level sentiment feed.

Readership: Bloomberg's unique readership score measures the demand for information about a company. The scores take into account both story hits and the number of news searches on a company by users of the Bloomberg Professional service. The final score compares hits/searches over the last hour and the average hourly hits/searches for the past 8 hours. Five possible values for the heat score correlate to the number of standard deviations away from the mean readership of a company.

Publication Heat: Publication Heat measures the supply of news for a given equity by comparing the number of stories per ticker in the current hour against the historical hourly counts for the last 45 days. If the current hour is higher than the historical counts, the publication heat score will be elevated. The score indicates in what percentile the current count falls. A filter is applied so only stories relevant to the company are counted.

Delivery Methods
Real Time

Bloomberg's Event-Driven Feeds can be delivered in real time over the same architecture as all other real-time Bloomberg Enterprise products. Two production delivery points are provided for redundancy as part of a managed service. A third, development instance, is also provided. The data is received through an API that is available for Linux, Oracle Solaris, and Microsoft Windows. C#, C++, Java, and Python programming languages are supported.

End-of-Day

A complete archive of the previous day's messages can be provided as XML files and delivered via SFTP. These can be delivered at a time suitable for the client.

1.A.2 RavenPack News Analytics

Key Information

RavenPack News Analytics delivers sentiment analysis and event data most likely to impact financial markets and trading around the world. The service includes analytics on more than 175,000 entities in over 200 countries and covers over 98% of the investable global market. All relevant news items about entities are classified and quantified according to their sentiment, relevance, topic, novelty, and market impact; the result is a data product that can be segmented into many distinct benchmarks and used in a variety of applications.

Entity Type Coverage
Places: 138,000+
Companies: 34,000+
Organizations: 2,500+
Currencies: 150+
Commodities: 80+

Equity Entity Coverage by Region
Americas: 47.2%
Asia: 25.5%
Europe: 22.4%
Oceania: 4.3%
Africa: 0.6%

Data Field Descriptions
TIMESTAMP_UTC: The Date/Time (YYYY-MM-DD hh:mm:ss.sss) at which the news item was received by RavenPack servers in Coordinated Universal Time (UTC).

RP_ENTITY_ID: A unique and permanent entity identifier assigned by RavenPack. Every entity tracked is assigned a unique identifier comprised of 6 alphanumeric characters.

ENTITY_TYPE: The type of entity associated with a particular RP_ENTITY_ID. Currently RavenPack supports the following 5 entity types:
1. **COMP** (Company): Business organization that may be traded directly on an exchange.
2. **ORGA** (Organization): Non-business organization such as a government, central bank, not-for-profit, terrorist organization, etc.
3. **CURR** (Currency): Currencies of all financial and industrial countries.
4. **CMDT** (Commodity): Exchange traded commodities such as crude oil and soy.
5. **PLCE** (Place): Towns, cities and countries.

RELEVANCE: A score between 0-100 that indicates how strongly related the entity is to the underlying news story, with higher values indicating greater relevance. For any news story that mentions an entity, RavenPack provides a relevance score. A score of 0 means the entity was passively mentioned while a score of 100 means the entity was prominent in the news story. Values above 75 are considered significantly relevant.

ESS – EVENT SENTIMENT SCORE: A granular score between 0 and 100 that represents the news sentiment for a given entity by measuring various proxies sampled from the news. The score is determined by systematically matching stories typically categorized by financial experts as having short-term positive or negative financial or economic impact. The strength of the score is derived from training sets where financial experts classified entity-specific events and agreed these events generally convey positive or negative sentiment and to what degree. Their ratings are encapsulated in an algorithm that generates a score range between 0-100 where higher values indicate more positive sentiment while values below 50 show negative sentiment.

AES – AGGREGATE EVENT SENTIMENT: A granular score between 0 and 100 that represents the ratio of positive events reported on an entity compared to the total count of events (excluding neutral ones) measured over a rolling 91-day window in a particular package (Dow Jones, Web or PR Editions). Only news items that match a RavenPack event category receiving an ESS score are included in the computation of AES. An event with ESS>50 is counted as a positive entry whereas one with ESS<50 is counted as a negative entry. Events with ESS=50 are considered neutral and excluded from the computation.

AEV – AGGREGATE EVENT VOLUME: A value that represents the count of events for an entity (excluding neutral ones) measured over a rolling 91-day window in a particular package (Dow Jones, Web, or PR Editions). Only news items that match a RavenPack event category receiving an ESS score are included in the computation of AEV. Both events with an ESS score above and below 50 are counted by AEV, effectively signaling the volume of highly relevant news on the entity over the past 91 days. Events with ESS=50 are considered neutral and excluded from the computation.

ENS – EVENT NOVELTY SCORE: A score between 0 and 100 that represents how "new" or novel a news story is within a 24-hour time window across all news stories in a particular package (Dow Jones, Web or PR Editions). The first story reporting a categorized event about one or more entities is considered to be the most novel and receives a score of 100. Subsequent stories from the same package about the same event for the same entities receive scores following a decay function whose values are (100 75 56 42 32 24 18 13 10 8 6 4 3 2 2 1 1 1 1 0 ...) based on the number of stories in the past 24-hour window. If a news story is published more than 24 hours after any other similar story, it will again be considered novel and start a separate chain with a score of 100.

1.A.3 Thomson Reuters News Analytics

Powered by a unique processing system from linguistics technology innovator, Lexalytics (formerly Infonic), the Thomson Reuters News Analytics system provides real-time numerical insight into the events in the news, in a format that can be directly consumed by algorithmic trading systems. News Analytics is a resilient server system that performs complex linguistic processing simultaneously on multiple news sources and publishes the calculated scores to multiple consumers via Reuters Market Data System (RMDS).

News Analytics can also read and process archive files to obtain score history, in particular the Thomson Reuters NewsScope Archive files, and publish the calculated scores to file. Each item of news within a feed is scored individually for each asset that is mentioned, specifically equities and commodities. A number of different values are calculated for each asset that broadly fall into the following categories:

1. Relevance: A number of measures of how relevant the news item is to the asset.
2. Sentiment: Whether the news item talks about the asset in a positive, neutral or negative manner.
3. Novelty: A measure of similarity of this item to previously seen news items.
4. Volume: Counts of the number of recent items mentioning the asset.
5. Headline Classification: Specific analysis of the headline.

An output image consists of the calculated News Analytics scores along with news item metadata derived from the input.

DATA FIELD DESCRIPTIONS

There are 81 fields which are common to the News Analytics RMDS image. A few of the most iconic data fields are described below.

IDN TIMESTAMP: The date and time of the news item as timestamped by the IDN and written to the NewsScope Archive. Presented in GMT.
Format: DD MMM YYYY hh:mm:ss.sss

SENTIMENT CLASSIFICATION: News Analytics calculates sentiment scores for each active asset that is mentioned in the news article. The sentiment calculation is at the entity level, so two different assets can have different scores for the same news item. This field indicates the predominant sentiment class for this news item with respect to this asset. The indicated class is the one with the highest probability.

Format: Integer – values:
- "1": Positive
- "0": Neutral
- "-1": Negative

SENT_POS: The probability that the sentiment of the news item was positive for the asset. The three probabilities sum to 1.0.
Format: Real: 0.0-1.0
SENT_NEUT: The probability that the sentiment of the news item was neutral for the asset. The three probabilities sum to 1.0.
Format: Real: 0.0-1.0
SENT_NEG: The probability that the sentiment of the news item was negative for the asset. The three probabilities sum to 1.0.
Format: Real: 0.0-1.0

RELEVANCE: A real valued number indicating the relevance of the news item to the asset. It is calculated by comparing the relative number of occurrences of the asset with the number of occurrences of other organizations and commodities within the text of the item. In addition, if the asset is mentioned in the headline, the relevance is set to 1.0. For stories with multiple assets, the asset with the most mentions will have the highest relevance. An asset with a lower amount of mentions will have a lower relevance score.

Format: Real: 0.0-1.0

NOVELTY: News Analytics calculates the novelty of the content within a news item by comparing it with a cache of previous news items that contain the current asset. The comparison between items is done using a linguistic fingerprint, and if the news items are similar, they are termed as being "linked". There are five history periods that are used in the comparison, by default they are 12 hours, 24 hours, 3 days, 5 days and 7 days prior to the news item's timestamp.

Two sets of scores are given:

Within Feed Novelty: news items are only compared with previous items from the same Feed

Across Feed Novelty: news items are compared across all feeds attached to the system.

VOLUME: News Analytics calculates the volume news for each asset. A cache of previous news items is maintained and the number of news items that mention the asset within each of five history periods is calculated. By default the history periods are 12 hours, 24 hours, 3 days, 5 days and 7 days prior to the news item's timestamp and are the same used in the novelty calculations. Thus direct comparisons between similar and total items within the history periods can be achieved.

HEADLINE CLASSIFICATION: News Analytics analyses the headline of each news item to determine if the article falls into a set of known types. This can aid users in filtering out irrelevant news items.

PART I

Text Analytics and Sentiment Classification

CHAPTER 2

Compositional Sentiment Analysis

Stephen Pulman, *Professor of Computational Linguistics, University of Oxford;*
Co-founder, TheySay Ltd

ABSTRACT

A fundamental principle of natural language semantics is "compositionality", the principle that the meaning of a phrase or sentence is a function of the meanings of the words contained in it and their manner of combination. This is part of the explanation of how, from a finite set of word meanings, it is possible to construct a potentially infinite number of distinct sentence meanings. In Moilanen and Pulman (2007) we argued that the sentiment polarity of a sentence is also largely compositionally derived. In the current chapter we summarise some recent developments in compositional approaches to sentiment analysis, and describe some experiments which suggest that such approaches lead to higher accuracy compared to non-compositional approaches in predicting the direction of the US non-farm payroll. These experiments are described in more detail in chapter 25 by Levenberg et al.

2.1 WHAT IS SENTIMENT ANALYSIS?

The term "sentiment analysis" has been around since about 2000, and has been used to cover a variety of different phenomena. In its most straightforward application, what we might call "sentiment proper", it describes the detection of positive and negative or neutral attitudes expressed in text.

1.   Suffice to say, Skyfall is one of the best Bonds in the 50-year history of moviedom's most successful franchise.
2.   Skyfall abounds with bum notes and unfortunate compromises.
3.   There is a breach of MI6. 007 has to catch the rogue agent.

The first of these examples is an unambiguously positive sentence from a review of the Skyfall movie. The second is an equally unambiguously negative review of the movie. The third is actually neutral, since it does not express an opinion and is simply describing some aspects of the plot. Nevertheless it contains two words that are implicitly rather negative, namely "breach" and "rogue", and it is quite likely that most automated sentiment analysis systems would characterise this neutral review as negative because of this. This example immediately shows us that the task of automated sentiment analysis is by no means trivial. We first need to determine whether or not a sentence in a document expresses an opinion at all, and having determined that it does, decide whether the opinion expressed is positive, negative, neutral or (more likely) a mixture of all three. In fact, the situation is even more complicated because in particular domains, completely factual sentences can imply positive or negative sentiment: "FTSE falls 60 points..."

Sentiment analysis has also been used to describe the detection of emotion in text. I will not have space to go into these issues in detail but a complicating factor in trying to build a system that detects emotion in text is the fact that there is a wide variety of different theories of emotional state. Perhaps the most common is due to the psychologist Paul Ekman (Ekman, 1993), who distinguishes six basic emotions: anger, disgust, fear, happiness, sadness and surprise. These emotions correspond more or less to facial expressions or even emoticons, and with a few reservations they appear to be more or less universal across languages and cultures. In contrast to the Ekman approach there are a variety of multi-dimensional theories that characterise emotions as occupying a point in a three-dimensional space, where the dimensions are described as (approximately) "pleasure" versus "displeasure", "arousal" versus "non-arousal", and "dominance" versus "submissiveness", e.g. Mehrabian (1996). In addition to these two main approaches there is a variety of work in the psychometric literature that purports to measure aspects of mental state like calmness or vitality, activation, valence, potency and intensity, e.g. Pollock et al. (1979).

Whichever approach to emotion detection is taken, we have to start from the assumption that particular words and phrases are reliably associated with expressions of these different emotional categories, since in text we are missing two important signals that we usually have in face-to-face interaction, namely speech and facial expression.

In determining the level of any such reliability, human annotation usually gives an upper limit on what is possible. For the Ekman emotion labels, Strapparava and Mihalcea (2008) found that the results are not particularly good: Table 2.1.1 shows level of agreement between annotators on 1250 news headlines drawn from major news outlets such as *The New York Times*, CNN and BBC News, as well as from the Google News search engine. Performance of various different types of classifiers on a collection of annotated blog posts is shown in the third column.

Table 2.1.1

Emotions	human agreement	best classifier F score
anger	49.55	16.77
disgust	44.51	4.68
fear	63.81	22.8
joy	59.91	32.87
sadness	68.19	23.06
surprise	36.07	14.1

These results, although they show a certain level of agreement between annotators, also show that there is quite wide variation between agreement for different emotions: surprise and sadness, for example. And the results achieved by the classifier trained on this data are too low in accuracy to be of any practical use, although more recent work has achieved higher levels of accuracy that can be used in practical applications.

Various other signals from text are sometimes included under the label "sentiment analysis". Some effort has gone into the detection of expressions of modality and speculation (i.e. distinguishing between what is claimed to be actual, and what is merely possible), particularly in clinical and scientific texts (Agarwal and Yu, 2010). This is a useful dimension to spot, particularly in combination with applications like information extraction, where we might be trying, for example, to mine the biomedical literature for examples of protein interactions. If a particular finding is expressed with a phrase like "this demonstrates that...", or "this proves that...", as opposed to "this suggests that..", or "these results are consistent with..." then we can give it greater weight, and similarly in other cases where a more certain modality is associated with the finding.

More generally, we can see how much a text is regarded as expressing certainty by looking at the number of what are called "hedges", signalled by words like "almost", "nearly", "broadly", etc. These linguistic devices serve to put some distance between the author of the text and the claims made in that text. Some of these acquire a kind of idiomatic status in particular domains, for example in the finance sector if we hear a phrase like "earnings were broadly in line with expectations", that usually means that in fact earnings were rather less than expectations. (Many of the papers in Morante and Sporleder (2012) report recent research in this and the following dimensions.)

Other dimensions of meaning that have been included under the heading of sentiment analysis include "risk", expressions of intent, or more generally "forward-looking" language.[1] It is useful to be able to detect these signals, for example in company reports: typically company reports will be rather positive, but if they also include a large proportion of forward-looking language or expressions of intent, that usually means that there is not really much current basis for the positivity, but rather that people are being optimistic about the future.

Similarly in customer relationship management it is useful to be able to detect the future intent of customers, actual or potential, both to determine where they are in the buying process and on that basis provide further information, or to detect what are known as "intent to churn" signals in blogs or social media sites, whereby a customer signals dissatisfaction with the product or service and declares their intention to move to another provider. ("Terrible service... Paypal should take responsibility for accounts which have been hacked into ... Very disappointed and will never use Paypal again.") Given the high cost of acquiring customers in many industries, there will be an incentive to retain loyalty by responding promptly to these signals and preventing the customer taking their business elsewhere.

2.2 BUILDING A SENTIMENT ANALYSIS SYSTEM

A number of people have commented that it is very easy to do sentiment analysis badly. In this section I outline a series of successively more complex (and successively less bad) ways to do it, concluding with what at the time of writing was the state- of-the-art approach in terms of accuracy.

We can quickly construct a "cheap and cheerful" sentiment analyser by following these steps:

- collect lists of positive and negative words or phrases, from public domain word lists or by mining them from web texts. A simple way to do this is to collect examples of clear positive and negative words, look at the contexts they occur in, and then find other words that also appear in those or similar contexts.
- at run time, given a text, count up the number of positives and negatives, and classify the text based on that proportion. It is surprising how many commercial systems seem to do very little more than this.

There are, however, a number of obvious problems with this approach. To begin with, if the number of positives is the same as the number of negatives, do we say 'neutral'? Surely not: a neutral text is not one that expresses positive sentiment and negative sentiment in equal proportion, it is one that expresses no sentiment at all. But a more serious problem is one posed by the existence of what we will call "compositional sentiment". By this we mean that the sentiment associated with a phrase or sentence is a product not just of the properties of the words themselves or any majority influence, but of the way in which they are combined according to the grammatical structure of the sentence: what linguists call "compositionality". For example, a phrase like "not wonderfully interesting" is negative overall, even though "wonderfully" and "interesting" will be in the list of positive words, and hence a simple counting approach would give the wrong result. Some approaches use "negation tagging" heuristics to solve this problem: look out for a negative, and reverse the polarity of the following words (e.g. Das and Chen, 2007), but while this will work for the present example, it is not a general solution: a phrase like "too clever" is negative, but so is the phrase "not too clever". We will see more complex examples of this phenomenon soon.

A further problem with the simple word counting model – not unique to this approach but less easily addressed within it – is the fact that some words are positive in some contexts, and negative in others: "cold beer" is generally good, whereas "cold coffee" is not.

We can improve on this by using some machine learning techniques. This is in practice what the majority of commercial systems do, in fact. We can construct what is known as a "bag-of-words" classifier, so-called because grammatical structure is ignored and texts are represented as unordered "bags" of words.

To build such a classifier we need to get a training corpus of texts annotated for sentiment. In some cases, we can harvest such a corpus semi-automatically by mining on-line reviews or ratings that have some kind of grading or star system associated with them. We make the assumption that a review that has five stars will be in general rather positive, whereas a review with one star or a small number of stars will be mostly negative. Although it is relatively easy to get such data, there are disadvantages: data acquired in this way is typically specific to a particular limited domain, for example movies, smartphones or cameras. To get high-quality, more general-purpose data, annotated in a more refined way, it is usually necessary to employ some (preferably linguistically trained) human annotators to do the job.

Having obtained such a corpus of annotated data, we represent each text as a vector of counts of n-grams, i.e single words, consecutive pairs (bigrams), triples (trigrams), etc. As n gets bigger, more training data is required, of course, as the longer the sequence, the less likely we are to see it occur in a text. We may also normalise words so that morphological variations are ignored and just the root or stem form is considered: for example "buying", "buys" and "bought" might all be reduced to "buy". This typically makes the classifier more robust, since it will be able to generalise over them instead of regarding them as separate words. (For an overview of stemming and lemmatisation see section 2.2.4 of Manning, Raghavan and Schütze (2008). Having represented our texts as fixed-length vectors of counts we can then proceed to train our favourite classifier on these vectors: common choices are Naive Bayes, Support Vector Machines, Averaged Perceptrons, Neural Networks or other well-known techniques.

Such a sentiment analysis system, at least if it uses bi-grams, should capture some compositional effects: e.g. "very interesting" is a likely signal for positivity, whereas "not very" is a signal for negativity. (Unless using trigrams, it will still not know what to do with "not very interesting", however.)

The great advantage of such automated classification techniques is that they are simple to apply, and will work for any language and domain where you can get accurately labelled training data. However, there remain many problems: the bag-of-words approach means grammatical structure is completely ignored, and so a headline like "Airbus: orders slump but profits rise" will wrongly be regarded as synonymous with "Airbus: orders rise but profits slump". As mentioned, this can be partially overcome by moving to n-grams, but in practice this means a very much larger and expensive corpus annotation effort.

However, equally balanced texts will still be problematic, since the classifier decision will still be based indirectly on (weighted) counts of terms associated with negative and positive annotations. And however large the value of n chosen for n-gram, there will always be richer compositional effects that will be missed: to elaborate on an earlier example, a word like "clever" by default will have positive sentiment. However, "too clever" and, unexpectedly, "not too clever" are both negative in polarity. A word like "kill" is negative by default, and so (in most contexts) is "bacteria"; however "killing bacteria" is usually judged to be a positive thing. We can elaborate such examples: "failing to kill bacteria" is again negative, whereas "never failing to kill bacteria" becomes positive once more. So here we have an example with a sequence of words – "never", "fail", "kill" and "bacteria" – each of which in isolation carries negative connotations but where combined in this grammatical configuration constitute a phrase with overall positive polarity.

It might be objected that this is an artificially constructed example, which it is, but it is the case that quite complex compositional examples like these occur rather frequently in practice:

- The Trout Hotel: This newly refurbished hotel could not fail to impress...
- BT: it would not be possible to find a worse company to deal with...

Furthermore, it is at best clumsy and at worst impossible within such a framework to give sentiment labels accurately to short units like sentences or phrases, or to pick out mixed sentiment: "**The display** is amazingly sharp. However, **the battery life** is disappointing."

2.3 COMPOSITIONAL SENTIMENT ANALYSIS

The best approach to sentiment is to acknowledge and embrace the compositional nature of the phenomenon, and to tackle it head-on using the kind of sophisticated grammatical processing tools that have become available in the last few years. To do this, we do as full a syntactic parse as possible on individual sentences of input texts. This enables us to uncover the essentially hierarchical grammatical structure of sentences: words are grouped into phrases, and phrases grouped into successively larger constituents, up to whole clauses and complete sentences. We can then use this structure to locate subjects, objects etc. – the "who does what to whom" aspect of sentence interpretation. Once given a full syntactic analysis we can use it to guide the application of a set of "sentiment logic" rules to do fully compositional sentiment analysis. Figure 2.3.1 shows our example sentence: "fail" and "kill" are verbs (V), "This product" and "bacteria" are noun phrases (NP), "to kill bacteria" is a verb phrase (VP), and the whole thing is a grammatical sentence (S). (Green nodes represent positive sentiment, and red are negative).

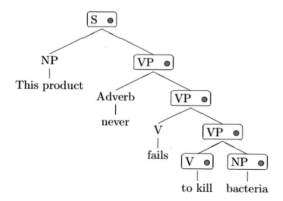

Figure 2.3.1

Sentiment logic rules operating on such structures (Moilanen and Pulman, 2007) can be schematically described as follows:

- kill + negative → positive (kill bacteria)
- kill + positive → negative (kill kittens)
- too + anything → negative (too clever, too red, too cheap)
- etc.

In our example, the word "bacteria" will be classified in the lexicon as being negative by default, and so will "kill". But the first rule will apply to the VP "kill bacteria" and label it as positive. A rule for "fail" will say that when it combines with a positive complement (in this case "kill bacteria", the phrase "fail to kill bacteria" will be labelled negative), and so on, until we have a sentiment value for the whole sentence as well as for all its subconstituents.

In our system (www.theysay.io) we have approaching 70,000 such rules, acquired via manual inspection of corpus and dictionary data, along with some semi-automatic processing. Developing such rules requires both linguistic and computational expertise. They capture the fine-grained behaviour of English words and constructions with respect to sentiment, in a fairly general-purpose setting.

One advantage an approach like this has over the classifier-based approach is that it is very easy to customise some of these rules where needed in a particular application domain, or indeed to fix them if they give the wrong answer. With a classifier, the system is a black box. It is never clear what the source of errors might be – maybe some quirk of the training data – and the only option for domain adaptation is to re-train on different data, with the subsequent annotation costs.

Another major advantage of doing things compositionally is that we now have the entire syntactic structure of sentences at our disposal and so we already automatically have sentiment classifications at every linguistic level: word, phrase, clause, etc. and can assign mixed sentiment to sentences without any extra effort.

Of course, there are still many problems to be solved: some words may be ambiguous and their sentiment polarity can depend on which sense is appropriate in a given context. An example might be "bank", which in its "river" sense is neutral, but which in its financial sense has come to have a rather negative connotation in many settings. We also still need to do some extra work to capture context-dependence: either of the type earlier exemplified by words like "cold", or even more difficult, words like "wicked" or "sick", where usage by certain demographic groups will invert the usual polarity (teenagers in the UK refer to a good night out as a "sick night"). Since we usually have only the text to go on, and have no information about the author of the text, we do not usually have the information that is contextually relevant. Similarly, we do not usually have information about the likely readership of texts, so we cannot deal at all nimbly with reader perspective: "Oil prices are down" is good for me as a motorist and with an oil-guzzling heating system, but probably it is not so good for Chevron or Shell investors, or for governments hoping to collect taxes on sales of oil.

Finally, a problem for every current approach is that we cannot deal well with sarcasm or irony: "Oh, great, they want it to run on Windows". There are a number of reasons that make this a very difficult problem (for people too), including the fact that in text, just as for emotion, we are missing two components of the signal – voice quality and facial expression – and that in the limit we need to know what the beliefs of the speaker really are, since both sarcasm and irony are built on a mismatch between form and content and what the speaker really believes.

2.4 MACHINE LEARNING FOR COMPOSITION

Is it possible to have the best of all worlds? Can we combine the ease and robustness of a machine learning classifier approach with the more fine-grained type of analysis made possible by compositional methods?

In a line of work taking place mostly in Stanford and Oxford, people have been looking at this question. A major "sentiment Treebank" resource for this purpose was developed by Richard Socher and colleagues (Socher et al., 2013), who carried out an annotation exercise on almost 12,000 syntactically analysed sentences from a widely used corpus of movie reviews. The task of the annotators was to assign 5-way sentiment labels at every level – words, phrases (as determined by the parse tree for the sentence) and sentences. The labels were: very negative, somewhat negative, neutral, somewhat positive and very positive. An example tree might look like the tree for the "killing bacteria" example in Figure 2.3.1, or Figure 2.4.1 (simplifying the 5-way labels to just positive, negative, and neutral):

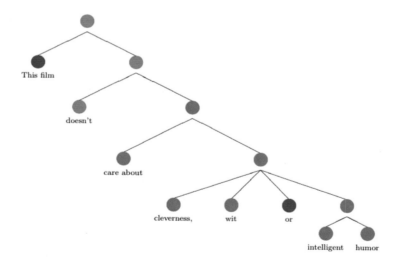

Figure 2.4.1

The compositional aspect is handled using methods derived from neural network or "deep learning" research. I will not attempt to describe the details of these quite complex techniques, but merely to give an intuitive picture of how they work. In the simplest type of neural network, the input is a vector representing properties of the example to be classified. These input values are then multiplied by a matrix of weights representing connections between each element of the input and each element of a "hidden layer", another vector. This multiplication populates the hidden layer vector with values that then have a non-linear function like sigmoid or hyperbolic tangent applied to them. This sequence may be duplicated several times for further hidden layers. The values of the final output layer vector represent the various labels used by the classifier: these are often transformed by a "softmax" function to look like a probability distribution over labels.

Training usually starts with a randomly initialised set of weight matrices. An example with a known label is put into the system and the difference between the observed output and the correct output (the "error") is used to readjust the weights so as to prefer the correct label. The error, intuitively speaking, is pushed back through the network to adjust the values of the weight matrices, a process known as "back-propagation". Examples may be processed singly or in batches, and various parameters ("learning rates") can be changed to accelerate learning. A "deep learning" network is, to a first approximation, any network with more than one hidden layer, according to Yann LeCun, one of the pioneers in the field.

In Socher's approach, sentences are first parsed using an open-source parser to produce a hierarchical grammatical structure like those pictured earlier. Words are represented not as strings but as fixed-length vectors of real number: so-called "word- embeddings" (Turian, Ratinov and Bengio, 2010). These vectors, intuitively speaking, represent the kind of syntactic and semantic contexts that the individual word occurs in in some (large) training corpus of text, and can be learned by standard neural network training methods. The big advantage of using vectors to represent words, rather than atomic symbols, is that they give us an automatic semantic similarity measure between words, which allows us to generalise from a training example with particular words to unseen examples with new words that might have similar meanings to those seen in training. Two vectors can be explicitly compared by a number of similarity measures such as cosine distance. For compositionality, we need to find a way of combining word vectors into phrase vectors and so on recursively until we have analysed the whole sentence:

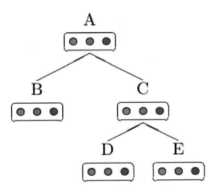

Figure 2.4.2

Figure 2.4.2 immediately suggests a neural network type architecture: to compute C's vector, we concatenate those of D and E ⬚ , and learn from the training data a weight matrix that combines them in the "right" way to form a vector for C: ⬚ . Likewise we combine B and C to find A.

One way of doing this is pictured in Figure 2.4.3, where the phrase vector is derived by multiplying the concatenated word vectors (dimension 2d, where d is the length of the word vector) by a weight matrix (dimension 2d × d) to give a d-dimensional output vector, as required. We apply an element-wise non-linearity to the resulting vector, just as usual. For full compositionality all word and phrase vectors need to be the same length, of course.

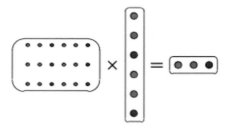

Figure 2.4.3

The weight matrix can be learned via standard neural network methods, and at each level we can if required use a "softmax" function to map from the phrase vectors to a distribution over sentiment labels. Different matrices can be learned for different combinations of words and phrases, given enough training data: the way B and C combine to make A may be different from the way D and E combine to form C.

The most successful version of this kind of architecture, as described by Socher et al. (2013), is one in which the composition function above is replaced by a more complex 2d × 2d × d weight matrix (a "bilinear tensor"), which combines the concatenated vectors with their transpose to yield the output vector (which can then be added to the result of the earlier simpler composition function). Again the weights can be learned by neural network techniques.

This more complex scheme overcomes a problem with the simpler composition function, which was that the two input vectors did not interact with each other except indirectly via the weight matrix. This bilinear tensor operation, by combining the concatenated input vectors with their transpose, captures every possible way in which they could interact, and this pattern of compositional interaction is what the fully-trained weights learn to capture. In the final version of Socher's system, both compositional operators are combined: we add the results of the two together to give the final output vector.

Socher's "Recursive Neural Tensor Network" system, trained and tested on the treebank described earlier, derived from a standard movie review corpus, gives better results on both multi-label and binary sentiment analysis than any earlier non-compositional systems: see Table 2.5.1.

2.5 CONVOLUTIONAL NEURAL NETWORKS

An even more complex architecture is used in Kalchbrenner, Grefenstette and Blunsom (2014), with a similar motivation as in Socher's work, but with the aim of eliminating the explicit prior parsing step used in that model. A "convolutional" neural network is constructed in such a way that rather than learn a single matrix of weights applying to whole vectors, it learns one or more smaller matrices (called "filters" or "feature maps") that apply to overlapping segments of an input vector or matrix. These filters are applied in a sliding window over the input, which in the case of Kalchbrenner, Grefenstette and Blunsom (2014) is a matrix where each column is a word-embedding vector. These filters learn to recognise "features" independently of their position in a sentence, or in the image processing applications from which this architecture is derived, in any region of an image. Multiple feature filters can be applied over the same input if required, which might learn different features from the same data.

In order to capture compositional effects, multiple convolutional layers are stacked, with the output of one acting as the input to the next, after a non-linearity is applied (as with standard neural networks). As with the Recursive Neural Tensor Network architecture, the dimensions of the various filters and layers need to be kept uniform, and to do this a "k-max-pooling" operation is applied, where only the k highest values in any level are passed up as input to the next. The value of k can be fixed, or as here, made – in the lower levels at least – sensitive to the length of the input sentence. Finally, a fully connected layer constitutes the output, to which a soft-max function can be applied to recover a probability distribution over labels. Training again uses variants of neural network techniques.

After suitable training, when analysing a new sentence, the pattern of feature vector activation through the convolutional and pooling layers induces an implicit hierarchical structure (actually a directed acyclic graph), as shown in Figure 2.5.1.

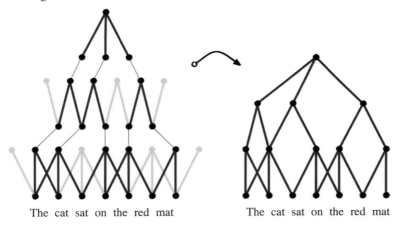

The cat sat on the red mat   The cat sat on the red mat

Figure 2.5.1

This structure represents the contribution of words and phrases to the overall interpretation of the sentence in a compositional-like way, although there is not necessarily direct mapping to a more conventional syntax tree for the sentence. To the extent that this means that compositional analysis can proceed without parsing, that makes the model also applicable to texts that are difficult to parse in a traditional way: for example, ungrammatical, fragmentary or extreme varieties of "Twitterspeak".

The more complex convolutional architecture does significantly better than the Recursive Neural Tensor Network model on the same data, and both outperform non-compositional classifier methods. They can be tested on two subtasks based on the sentiment treebank:

- fine-grained: classify phrases into one of 5 categories (very positive, somewhat positive, neutral, somewhat negative, very negative)
- binary: classify phrases as either positive or negative

The results for both of the neural network-based systems, with a quite strong Naive Bayes and SVM baseline for comparison (from Socher et al., 2013), are shown in Table 2.5.1. The figures report percentage accuracy: clearly the fine-grained 5-way task is much more challenging than the binary task.

Table 2.5.1

System	Fine-grained %	Binary %
1-2gram Naive Bayes	41.9	83.1
1-2gram SVM	40.7	79.4
Stanford: RNTN	45.7	85.4
Oxford: Convolutional NN	**48.5**	**86.8**

2.6 PREDICTING THE US NON-FARM PAYROLL

The results just described establish that compositional sentiment analysis methods of several different types outperform non-compositional methods in terms of accuracy, on at least one large well-known data set. Several questions arise naturally: is the largely rule-based compositional method described earlier better or worse than the compositional neural network methods? We do not have a definitive answer to this, only some anecdotal evidence, unfortunately. We know that in general a method that has been trained on a specific corpus will do better on examples drawn from a similar corpus than a general-purpose system with no special exposure to that corpus. However, the performance of such a corpus-specific system will usually be much worse on text from a different domain and a number of people have reported informally that the Stanford system is much less accurate on financial text than the movie reviews it was trained on. We also know that general-purpose systems like the TheySay one described earlier are usually fairly accurate "straight out of the tin" on any type of text that is reasonably well-behaved, although performance can always be improved by domain customisation. However, what we really need to decide these questions properly is a collection of fine-grained annotated corpora, like the movie review treebank but from a variety of different domains, so that we could carry out a series of controlled trials. Unfortunately we are not in a position to do that at the moment.

A second question that arises is whether any of these actually matters for practical applications. It could be the case that there is a large difference in accuracy between different approaches in a research laboratory setting, but in the context of a specific practical application it actually makes very little difference. Fortunately, in this case we are able to give a definite answer to the question: it **does** matter, and in one area of financial prediction at least, a compositional approach to sentiment analysis demonstrably yields a clear improvement in prediction accuracy over non-compositional methods. The experiments that demonstrate this are described in much more detail in the chapter 2 5 (see also Levenberg et al., 2014), so I will only give a very sketchy description here.

The experiment in question concerned the United States Non-Farm Payroll, a monthly economic index that measures job growth or decay, and which is a "market mover". We were interested in several questions:

- Can we predict the direction (i.e. just "up" or "down") of the Non-Farm Payroll from economic indicators?
- Can we predict the direction of the Non-Farm Payroll from sentiment in text?
- If so, does compositional sentiment perform better than a non-compositional "bag-of-words" classifier?

In order to do this we back-tested on textual and financial data from the years 2000–2012. We mined almost 10m words of text containing keywords assumed relevant to the Non-Farm Payroll, from a variety of sources: Associated Press, Dow Jones, Reuters, Market News and The Wall Street Journal. We also obtained economic time-series data from many different sources, including the Consumer Price Index (CPI), the Institute of Supply Management manufacturing index (ISM) and the Job Openings and Labor Turnover Survey (JOLTS) – all indices widely used in economic forecasting. We processed all the text using the compositional sentiment tools provided by TheySay's API (www.theysay.io), and we also processed the same text using a traditional Support Vector Machine classifier using unigrams and bigrams as features, and trained on whatever public domain annotated texts we could find.

In order to be able to combine signals from both text and numerical streams we used a novel "Independent Bayesian Classifier Combination" method (Simpson et al., 2012) which allows us to do this and also automatically works out the best combination of classifiers to use. Work in ensemble machine learning methods has shown that the results arising from a combination of classifiers are almost always better than those obtained by using any individual classifier, as different classifiers typically pick up different aspects of an underlying signal and the sophisticated statistical technique underlying the Independent Bayesian Classifier Combination method means that even a rather weak classifier may provide a signal that can be usefully combined with others.

The input to the Independent Bayesian Classifier Combination method is a set of outputs from individual logistic regression classifiers trained separately on each different text and numerical stream, divided into temporal "epochs". We would train on data up to epoch t and use this to predict the direction actually taken at epoch $t+1$. For the sentiment text component we used the sentiment distributions per time-slice given by the TheySay API as input features for the logistical regressions classifiers.

In the data, the number of "ups" is the same as the number of "downs" (achieved by subsampling) and so a simple baseline is to always predict "up". An only slightly less simple baseline is just to assume that what happened last time will happen again ("back returns"). Using the signals from the best performing Support Vector Machine classifier – which can only give sentence-level positive or negative decisions – we comfortably beat these baselines: an "area under the curve" (AOC) score of 61%, as shown in Table 2.6.1.

Table 2.6.1

	Area Under Curve
Always up	0.50
Back returns	0.54
Best SVM classifier	0.61

However, the classifier combination method was unable to improve on the performance of this individual classifier: that is, none of the signals from the other streams were able to be combined with it to good effect. This is in contrast to what happens when we use a compositional approach to sentiment analysis. If we simply take the highest scoring label for each sentence (comparable to what we are doing with the SVM classifier), the classifier combination method is still only able to improve a little on the best individual classifier (we only show the best performing independent classifiers) as shown in column A.

However, when we take advantage of the compositional sentiment method's ability to give us both more accurate and more fine-grained analyses below the level of sentences (columns B and C) then the Independent Bayesian Classifier Combination method is able to combine the different signals more effectively to give quite dramatic jumps in accuracy over that obtained by any individual classifier. All the numbers in Table 2.6.2 are AOC measures:

Table 2.6.2

	A	B	C
AP	0.59	0.69	0.37
Market News	0.66	0.70	0.23
Other Sources	0.58	0.63	0.63
Combined classifiers:	0.67	0.81	**0.85**

A = **Percentage** of highest scoring sentence level pos OR neg labels per time slice.
B = **Average percentage** of pos AND neg within each sentence per time slice.
C = **Trends** i.e. differences between B percentages in successive time slices.

This shows quite clearly that using compositional sentiment analysis of text we can achieve an impressive level of accuracy in predicting whether the Non-Farm Payroll will go up or down. Of course, if we also add in the information derived from the economic time-series data we do even better, although here the trends seem to do less well, as shown in Table 2.6.3

Table 2.6.3

Source	AUC
Time Series + Text Averages	**0.94**
Time Series + Text Trends	0.91

2.7 CONCLUSIONS

We have argued that compositional sentiment analysis methods give a substantial improvement in accuracy over simpler word-counting or machine learning classifier methods. There are currently several promising approaches to compositional sentiment analysis: fairly traditional rule-based methods involving full syntactic parsing followed by the application of "sentiment logic" rules; what we might call the "Stanford" approach, where sentences are parsed but the sentiment logic rules are replaced by compositional functions trained on a sentiment treebank corpus using neural network methods; and the (other) Oxford approach, which tries to dispense with explicit parsing and learn all aspects of the compositional structure of sentences relevant to sentiment classification using convolutional neural networks. We can expect rapid advances in the accuracy of these and similar techniques – this is a very "hot" area of computational linguistics and machine learning research.

We have also examined one practical application in the prediction of an important economic indicator, the United States Non-Farm Payroll, and shown that the extra accuracy and the finer-grained analyses delivered by rule-based compositional methods are not just of value in a research laboratory setting, but can yield far more accurate predictions than non-compositional methods in this application. I am confident that this improved prediction accuracy will be found in other applications, too.

ACKNOWLEDGEMENTS

I am grateful to Phil Blunsom, Ed Grefenstette, Karl-Moritz Hermann, Abby Levenberg, Karo Moilanen and Richard Socher for conversations about the material discussed here, and for other inputs to this work.

Notes
[1] Wikipedia says: "In United States business law, a forward-looking statement or safe harbor statement is a statement that cannot sustain itself as merely a historical fact."

2.8 REFERENCES

1. Agarwal, S. and Yu, H. (2010). Detecting hedge cues and their scope in biomedical literature with conditional random fields. *Journal of biomedical informatics*, *43(6)*,953–961.

2. Das, S.R. and Chen, M.Y. (2007). Yahoo! for amazon: Sentiment extraction from small talk on the web. *Manage. Sci.*, *53(9)*, 1375–1388.

3. Ekman, P. (1993). Facial expression and emotion. *American Psychologist, 48(4),* 384–392.

4. Kalchbrenner, N., Grefenstette, E. and Blunsom, P. (2014). A convolutional neural network for modelling sentences. In *Proceedings of the 52nd Annual Meeting of the Association for Computational Linguistics (Volume 1: Long Papers)*, pp 655–665, Baltimore, Maryland, June. Association for Computational Linguistics.

5. Levenberg, A., Pulman, S., Moilanen, K., Simpson, E. and Roberts, S. (2014). Predicting economic indicators from web text using sentiment composition. In *International Journal of Computer and Communication Engineering*, Barcelona, Spain, February. IACSIT Press..

6. Manning, C.D., R aghavan, P. and Schütze, H. (2008). *Introduction to Information Retrieval*. Cambridge University Press, New York, NY, USA.

7. Mehrabian, A. (1996). Pleasure-arousal-dominance: A general framework for describing and measuring individual differences in temperament. In *Current Psychology: Developmental, Learning, Personality, Social*, volume 14, pp 261–292.

8. Moilanen, K. and Pulman, S. (2007). Sentiment composition. In *Proceedings of Recent Advances in Natural Language Processing (RANLP 2007)*, pp 378– 382, September 27–29.

9. Morante, R. and Sporleder, C., editors. (2012). *Proceedings of the Workshop on Extra-Propositional Aspects of Meaning in Computational Linguistics*. Association for Computational Linguistics. ISBN 978-1-937284-34-3.

10. Pollock, V., Cho, D.W., Reker, D. and Volavka, J. (1979). Profile of mood states: the factors and their physiological correlates. *The Journal of Nervous and Mental Disease*, 612–4.

11. Simpson, E., Roberts, S.J., Psorakis, I. and Lintott, C. (2012). Dynamic bayesian combination of multiple imperfect classifiers. In *Decision Making with Imperfect Decision Makers*, Intelligent Systems Reference Library. Springer.

12. Socher, R., Perelygin, A., Wu, J., Chuang, J., Manning, C.D., Ng, A. and Potts, C. (2013). Recursive deep models for semantic compositionality over a sentiment treebank. In *Proceedings of the 2013 Conference on Empirical Methods in Natural Language Processing*, pp 1631–1642, Seattle, Washington, USA, October. Association for Computational Linguistics.

13. Strapparava, C. and Mihalcea, R. (2008). Learning to identify emotions in text. In *Proceedings of the 2008 ACM Symposium on Applied Computing*, SAC '08, pp 1556–1560, New York, NY, USA. ACM.

14. Turian, J., Ratinov, L. and Bengio, Y. (2010). Word representations: A simple and general method for semi-supervised learning. In *Proceedings of the 48th Annual Meeting of the Association for Computational Linguistics*, pp 384–394, Uppsala, Sweden, July. Association for Computational Linguistics. .

CHAPTER 3

Document Sentiment Classification

Bing Liu, *Professor of Computer Science, University of Illinois*

3.1 INTRODUCTION

Starting from this chapter, we discuss the main research topics of sentiment analysis and their state-of-the-art algorithms. *Document sentiment classification* (or *document-level sentiment analysis*) is perhaps the most extensively studied topic in the field of sentiment analysis especially in its early days (see surveys by Pang and Lee, 2008; Liu, 2012). It aims to classify an opinion document (e.g., a product review) as expressing a positive or a negative opinion (or sentiment), which are called *sentiment orientations* or *polarities*. The task is referred to as document-level analysis because it considers each document as a whole and does not study entities or aspects inside the document or determine sentiments expressed about them. Arguably, this is the task that popularized sentiment analysis research. Its limitations also motivated the fine-grained task of aspect-based sentiment analysis (Hu and Liu, 2004) that is widely used in practice today.

Document sentiment classification is considered the simplest sentiment analysis task because it treats sentiment classification as a traditional text classification problem with sentiment orientations or polarities as the classes. Thus, any super-vised learning algorithms can be applied directly to solve the problem. In most cases, the features used in classification are the same as those used in traditional text classification too. Due to its simple problem definition and equivalence to text classification, it has served as the base task of several other research directions adapted from the general text classification, for example, cross-lingual and cross-domain sentiment classification.

To ensure that the task is meaningful in practice, existing literature on document sentiment classification makes the following implicit assumption (Liu, 2010).

Assumption 3.1: Document sentiment classification assumes that the opinion document d (e.g., a product review) expresses opinions on a single entity e and contains opinions from a single opinion holder h.

Thus, strictly speaking, document sentiment classification can only be applied to a special type of opinion documents. We make this assumption explicit in the task definition.

Definition 3.1 (Document sentiment classification): Given an opinion document d evaluating an entity, determine the overall sentiment s of the opinion holder about the entity. In other words, we determine sentiment s expressed on aspect GENERAL in the quintuple opinion definition of:

$$(\_, GENERAL, s, \_, \_),$$

where the entity, opinion holder, and time of opinion are assumed to be either known or irrelevant (Liu, 2015).

There are in fact two popular formulations of document-level sentiment analysis based on the type of values that s takes. If s takes categorical values, for example, positive and negative, it is a classification problem. If s takes numeric values or ordinal scores within a given range, for example, 1 to 5 stars, the problem becomes regression.

On the basis of the preceding discussions, we can see that this task is restrictive because, in general, an opinion document can evaluate more than one entity and the sentiment orientations on different entities can be different. The opinion holder may be positive about some entities and negative about others. In such a case, the task of document sentiment classification becomes less meaningful because it is not so useful to assign one sentiment to the entire document. Likewise, the task is also not so meaningful if multiple opinion holders express opinions in a single document because their opinions can be different too, for example, *"Jane has used this camera for a few months. She said that she loved it. However, my experience has not been great with the camera. The pictures are all quite dark."*

Assumption 3.1 holds well for online reviews of products and services because each review usually focuses on evaluating a single product or service and is written by a single reviewer. However, the assumption may not hold for a forum discussion or blog post because in such a post, the author may express opinions on multiple entities and compare them. That is why most researchers used online reviews to perform the task of classification or regression.

In Sections 3.2 and 3.3, we discuss the classification problem of predicting categorical class labels. In Section 3.4, we discuss the regression problem of predicting sentiment rating scores. Most existing techniques for document-level classification use supervised learning, although there are also unsupervised methods. Sentiment regression has been done mainly using supervised learning. Several extensions to this research have also been attempted, most notably *cross-domain sentiment classification* (or *domain adaptation*) and *cross-language sentiment classification*, which we discuss in Sections 3.5 and 3.6, respectively.

Although this chapter describes several basic techniques in detail, it is mainly written in a survey style because there are a large number of published papers, and most existing techniques are direct applications of machine learning algorithms with feature engineering. No comprehensive and independent evaluation has been conducted to assess the effectiveness or accuracy of these large numbers of proposed techniques.

3.2 SUPERVISED SENTIMENT CLASSIFICATION

Sentiment classification is usually formulated as a two-class classification problem: *positive* and *negative*. The training and testing data used are normally product reviews. Because every online review has a rating score assigned by its reviewer, for example, 1–5 stars, positive and negative classes can be determined easily using the ratings. A review with 4 or 5 stars is considered a *positive* review, and a review with 1 to 2 stars is considered a *negative* review. Most research papers do not use the neutral class (3-star ratings) to make the classification problem easier.

Sentiment classification is basically a text classification problem. However, traditional text classification mainly classifies documents of different topics, for example, politics, science and sport. In such classifications, topic-related words are the key features. In sentiment classification, sentiment or opinion words that indicate positive or negative opinions are more important, for example, *great, excellent, amazing, horrible, bad, worst* and so on.

In this section, we present two approaches: (1) applying a standard supervised machine learning algorithm and (2) using a classification method designed specifically for sentiment classification.

3.2.1 Classification Using Machine Learning Algorithms

Because sentiment classification is a text classification problem, any existing supervised learning method can be directly applied, such as naïve Bayes classification or support vector machines (SVM) (Joachims, 1999; Shawe-Taylor and Cristianini, 2000). Pang et al. (2002) took this approach in classifying movie reviews into positive and negative classes, showing that using unigrams (a bag of words) as features in classification performed quite well with either naïve Bayes or SVM, although the authors also tried a number of other feature options.

In subsequent research, many more features and learning algorithms have been tried by a large number of researchers. Like most supervised learning applications, the key for sentiment classification is the engineering of effective features. Some of the example features are as follows:

Terms and their frequency. These features are individual words (unigram) and their n-grams with associated frequency counts. They are also the most common features used in traditional, topic-based text classification. In some cases, word positions may also be considered. The TFIDF weighting scheme from information retrieval may be applied too. As in traditional text classification, these features have been shown to be highly effective for sentiment classification.

Part of speech. The part of speech (POS) of each word is another class of features. It has been shown that adjectives are important indicators of opinion and sentiment. Thus, some researchers have treated adjectives as special features. However, one can also use all POS tags and their n-grams as features. In this book, we use the standard Penn Treebank POS tags, as shown in Table 3.1 (Santorini, 1990), to denote different parts of speech. The Penn Treebank site is http://www.cis.upenn.edu/~treebank/home.html.

Table 3.1: *Penn Treebank part-of-speech (POS) tags*

Tag	Description	Tag	Description
CC	Coordinating conjunction	PRP$	Possessive pronoun
CD	Cardinal number	RB	Adverb
DT	Determiner	RBR	Adverb, comparative
EX	Existential *there*	RBS	Adverb, superlative
FW	Foreign word	RP	Particle
IN	Preposition or subordinating conjunction	SYM	Symbol
JJ	Adjective	TO	*to*
JJR	Adjective, comparative	UH	Interjection
JJS	Adjective, superlative	VB	Verb, base form
LS	List item marker	VBD	Verb, past tense
MD	Modal	VBG	Verb, gerund or present participle
NN	Noun, singular or mass	VBN	Verb, past participle
NNS	Noun, plural	VBP	Verb, non-3rd person singular present
NNP	Proper noun, singular	VBZ	Verb, 3rd person singular present
NNPS	Proper noun, plural	WDT	Wh-determiner
PDT	Predeterminer	WP	Wh-pronoun
POS	Possessive ending	WP$	Possessive wh-pronoun
PRP	Personal pronoun	WRB	Wh-adverb

Sentiment words and phrases. *Sentiment words* are natural features as they are words in a language for expressing positive or negative sentiments. For example, *good*, *wonderful* and *amazing* are positive sentiment words, and *bad*, *poor*, and *terrible* are negative sentiment words. Most sentiment words are adjectives and adverbs, but nouns (e.g., *rubbish*, *junk*, and *crap*) and verbs (e.g., *hate* and *love*) can also be used to express sentiments. Besides individual words, there are also *sentiment phrases* and *idioms*, for example, *cost someone an arm and a leg*.

Rules of opinion. In addition to sentiment words and phrases, there are many other constructs or language compositions that can be used to express or imply sentiment or opinion.

Sentiment shifters. These are expressions that are used to change sentiment orientations, for example, from positive to negative or vice versa. Negation words are the most important class of sentiment shifters. For example, the sentence "*I don't like this camera*" is negative, although the word *like* is positive. There are also several other types of sentiment shifters. Sentiment shifters also need to be handled with care because not all occurrences of such words mean sentiment changes. For example, *not* in "*not only . . . but also*" does not change sentiment orientation.

Syntactic dependency. Words' dependency-based features generated from parsing or dependency trees are also tried by researchers.

A large number of papers have been published on the topic in the literature. Here we can only briefly introduce some of them.

In Gamon (2004), the authors performed classification of customer feedback data, which are usually short and noisy compared to reviews, and showed that deep linguistic features are beneficial to classification in addition to the surface features of word n-grams. Feature selection is also useful. The deep linguistic features were extracted from the phrase structure tree produced by NLPWin, a NLP system from Microsoft Research. The features included POS trigrams, constituent specific length measures (length of sentence, clause, adverbial/adjectival phrase, and noun phrase), constituent structure in the form of context-free phrase structure patterns for each constituent in the parse tree (e.g., DECL::NP VERB NP, a declarative sentence consisting of a noun phrase, a verbal head, and a second noun phrase), POS information coupled with semantic relations (e.g., "Verb– Subject– Noun" indicating a nominal subject to a verbal predicate), and logical form features provided by NLPWin, such as transitivity of a predicate and tense information.

Mullen and Collier (2004) introduced a set of sophisticated features to combine with n-grams. These new features are categorized into three main classes: (1) features related to sentiment values of words or phrases computed using pointwise mutual information (PMI) (Turney, 2002), (2) values of adjectives for the three factors introduced in Osgood et al. (1957) and (3) sentiment values of words or phrases in 1 and 2 that are near or in the sentence that mentions the entities being reviewed. The three Osgood factors are *potency* (strong or weak), *activity* (active or passive) and *evaluative* (good or bad), with values derived using WordNet relationships (Kamps et al., 2002). These additional features show some, but not a great deal of, improvements over lemmatized unigrams. We discuss PMI in Section 3.3.1.

In Joshi and Penstein-Rosé (2009), *dependency relations* and their generalizations were used as features in addition to word unigrams. The dependency parse for a given sentence is essentially a set of triples, each of which comprises a grammatical relation and a pair of words from the sentence between which the grammatical relation holds: $\{rel_i, w_j, w_k\}$, where rel_i is a dependency relation between words w_j and w_k. Word w_j is usually referred to as the *head word*, and w_k is usually referred to as the *modifier word*. A feature generated from such a dependency relation is of the form RELATION_HEAD_MODIFIER, which is then used as a standard bag-of-words-type of binary or frequency-based feature. For example, "*This is a great car*" has an adjectival modifier (amod) relation between *great* and *car*, which generates the feature amod_car_great. However, this feature is too specific and can only be used for *car*. We can back off or generalize the head word with its POS tag, amod_NN_great, which is a more general feature and can be applied to any noun. In Xia and Zong (2010), this was generalized further by using N to represent NN, NNS, NNP, NNPS or PRP; J to represent JJ, JJS or JJR; R to represent RB, RBS, or RBR; V to represent VB, VBZ, VBD, VBN, VBG or VBP; and O to represent all other POS tags. The rel_i is also discarded so that, for example, amod_car_great is turned into two features, N_great and car_J. The same generalization strategy was also applied to traditional word bigrams. For classification, an ensemble model was proposed, which improved classification. An earlier work in Ng et al. (2006) also used dependency relations (adjective-noun, subject-verb, and verb-object), but no back-off generalization was applied. Their features include unigrams, bigrams, trigrams, sentiment words and objective words. Feature selection based on weighted log-likelihood ratio was performed as well.

Mejova and Srinivasan (2011) compared various feature definitions and selection strategies. They first tested stemming, term frequency versus binary weighting, negation-enriched features, and n-grams or phrases, and then moved to feature selection using frequency-based vocabulary trimming, POS and lexicon selection. Experiments based on three product and movie review data sets of various sizes showed that some techniques were more beneficial for larger data sets than for smaller ones. For large data sets, a classifier trained only on a small number of features that are ranked high by mutual information (MI) outperformed the one trained on all features. However, for small data sets, this did not prove to be true. An earlier work in Cui et al. (2006) described an evaluation using several classification algorithms and high-order n-grams, up to 6-grams. It applied a chi-square-based feature selection algorithm and showed that high-order n-grams help achieve better classification accuracy. High-order n-grams were also utilized successfully in Bespalov et al. (2011), which applied a deep neutral network approach to build a unified discriminative framework for classification. In Abbasi et al. (2008), a genetic-algorithm-based feature selection algorithm was proposed for sentiment classification in different languages. In addition to the usual n-gram features, the authors used stylistic features such as vocabulary richness and function words.

In the context of microblog sentiment classification, Kouloumpis et al. (2011) used four types of features: (1) n-grams; (2) a Multi-Perspective Question Answering (MPQA) subjectivity lexicon (Wilson et al., 2009); (3) counts of the number of verbs, adverbs, adjectives, nouns and any other parts of speech; and (4) binary features that capture the presence of positive, negative, and neutral emoticons, abbreviations, and intensifiers (e.g., all-caps and character repetitions).

Instead of using the full review for classification, Pang and Lee (2004) proposed to apply a machine learning method only to the subjective portions of each review. Such portions are more likely to contain opinions or sentiments. To identify the subjective portions in a review, a simple approach is to use a standard classification algorithm to classify each individual sentence in the review as subjective or objective, treating individual sentences independently. However, neighbouring sentences do have some relationships in a document. Considering proximity relations between sentences enables the algorithm to leverage *coherence*: text spans occurring near each other may share the same subjectivity status (subjective or objective), other things being equal. To consider the proximity relation, the authors represented sentences with a graph. Let the sequence of sentences in a review be $x_1, \ldots, x_n$. Each sentence belongs to one of the two classes C_1 (subjective) or C_2 (objective). The algorithm also has access to the following two types of information:

- *Individual score $ind_j(x_i)$*. A nonnegative estimate of each x_i's preference for being in C_j based on just the features of x_i alone
- *Association score $assoc(x_i, x_k)$*. A nonnegative estimate of how important it is that x_i and x_k are in the same class

Using these pieces of information, an undirected flow graph G is constructed with vertices $\{v_1, \ldots, v_n, s, t\}$, where $v_1, \ldots, v_n$ denote the sentences and s and t denote the *source* and the *sink*, respectively. The algorithm then adds n edges (s, v_i) to the graph, each with weight $ind_1(x_i)$, and n edges (v_i, t), each with weight $ind_2(x_i)$. Finally, it adds $\binom{n}{2}$ edges (v_i, v_k), each with weight $assoc(x_i, x_k)$. The optimization problem for the final classification was set up in such a way that the classification result is the outcome of a *minimum cut* of the graph. The individual score $ind_j(x_i)$ is produced based on a sentence-level subjectivity classifier, for example, naïve Bayes, which will give the probabilities for being in each class, and the probabilities are used as $ind_1(x_i)$ and $ind_2(x_i)$ $(= 1 - ind_1(x_i))$. The association score $assoc(x_i, x_k)$ is computed based on the distance between the two sentences. The final review sentiment classification uses only the subjective sentences produced by the minimum cut algorithm. The classification produced this way was shown to be more accurate than that produced by using the whole review.

Related work along the same lines uses annotator rationales to help classification. A rationale is defined as a text span in a document highlighted by human annotators or an automated system as support or evidence for the document's positive or negative sentiment, which is similar to the subjective portion. In Zaidan et al. (2007), human annotators were used to label the rationales, whereas in Yessenalina et al. (2010a), an automated method based on a sentiment lexicon was employed to label rationales. The technique in Yessenalina et al. (2010b) also tries to identify opinionated or subjective sentences for document sentiment classification. It uses a two-level joint model (sentence level and document level) based on structural SVMs (Yu and Joachims, 2009) and directly optimizes the document-level classification. The sentence-level sentiment is treated as latent, and thus no annotations at the sentence level are needed. The work in McDonald et al. (2007) is similar, but it needs sentence-level annotations.

In Liu et al. (2010), different linguistic features were compared for blog and review sentiment classification. It was found that results on blogs were much worse than on reviews because a review usually focuses on evaluating a single entity, whereas a blog can evaluate multiple entities. Opinions on some entities can be positive, but on some others, they can be negative. The authors then studied two methods to improve the classification accuracy on blogs. The first was an information retrieval method that finds relevant sentences to a given topic in each blog and discards the irrelevant sentences before classification. The second method was a simple domain adaption technique that first trains several classifiers from some review domains and then incorporates the hypotheses of the classifiers on the blog data as additional features for training on the blog data. These argumentations resulted in higher classification accuracy for the blog data.

Becker and Aharonson (2010) showed that sentiment classification should focus on the final portion of the text (e.g., the last sentence in a review) based on psycholinguistic and psychophysical experiments using human subjects. However, no computational studies were carried out to verify the claim.

All existing methods use n-gram (usually unigram) features and assign values to features using various term weighting schemes in information retrieval. In Kim et al. (2009), various combinations of term weighting schemes were tested: PRESENCE (binary indicator for presence), TF (term frequency), VS.TF (normalized TF as in vector space model (VS)), BM25.TF (normalized TF as in BM25; Robert-son and Zaragoza, 2009), IDF (inverse document frequency), VS.IDF (normalized IDF as in VS) and BM25.IDF (normalized IDF as in BM25).

The results showed that PRESENCE did very well. The best combination was BM25.TF·VS.IDF, which needs quite a bit of parameter tuning, and the improvement over PRES-ENCE is minor (about 1.5%).

In Martineau and Finin (2009), a new term weighting scheme called Delta TFIDF was proposed, which produced quite good results. In the scheme, the feature value ($V_{t,d}$) for a term/word t in a document d is the difference of that term's TFIDF scores in the positive and negative training corpora:

$$V_{t,d} = t f_{t,d} \times \log_2 \frac{N^+}{d f_{t,+}} - t f_{t,d} \times \log_2 \frac{N^-}{d f_{t,-}} = t f_{t,d} \times \log_2 \frac{N^+}{d f_{t,+}} \frac{d f_{t,-}}{N^-}, \qquad [3.1]$$

where $t f_{t,d}$ is the number of times term t occurs in document d (term frequency), $d f_{t,+}$ is the number of positive documents in the training set containing term t, N^+ is the total number positive documents in the training set, $d f_{t,-}$ is the number of negative documents in the training set containing term t, and N^- is the total number of negative documents. This term frequency transformation boosts the importance of words that are unevenly distributed between the positive and negative classes and discounts evenly distributed words. This better represents their true importance within the document for sentiment classification.

A comprehensive set of experiments was carried out in Paltoglou and Thelwall (2010) to evaluate the effectiveness of a large number of term weighting schemes. These include those TF and IDF variants in the SMART system (Salton, 1971) and also those variants in BM25 (Robertson and Zaragoza, 2009), their SMART Delta TFIDF versions and their BM25 Delta TFIDF variants. Smoothing was also applied. The results show that the Delta versions with smoothing performed significantly better than other variants.

In Li et al. (2010), personal (I, we) and impersonal ($it, this product$) sentences were exploited to help classification. Specifically, the authors defined a sentence as *personal* if the subject of the sentence is (or represents) a person and *impersonal* if the subject of the sentence is not (does not represent) a person. Three classifiers, f_1, f_2 and f_3, were then constructed by using only the personal sentences, only the impersonal sentences, and all sentences in each review, respectively. The three base classifiers were then combined by multiplying their posterior possibilities, and the multiplied probability was finally used for classification.

Li et al. (2010) explored negations and some other sentiment shifters to help improve document-level sentiment classification. Unlike the lexicon-based approach used in Kennedy and Inkpen (2006), which we discuss in Section 3.3.2, the authors took a supervised learning approach, which does not explicitly identify individual words or phrases that are sentiment shifters. Instead, it separates sentences in a document into sentiment-shifted sentences and sentence-unshifted sentences using classification. This classification required no manually labelled data. It simply exploited the original document-level sentiment labels and a feature selection method. The two types of sentences were then used to build two independent sentiment classifiers, which were combined to produce the final results. Xia et al. (2013) also proposed a method to make good use of negation words in classification.

In Qiu et al. (2009), an integrated approach of lexicon-based and self-learning methods was proposed (the lexicon-based approach is discussed in Section 3.3.2). Briefly, a lexicon-based method uses sentiment words and phrases to determine the sentiment of a document or sentence. The algorithm in Qiu et al. (2009) consists of two phases. The first phase uses a lexicon-based iterative method, in which some reviews are initially classified based on a sentiment lexicon, and then more reviews are classified through an iterative process with a negative/positive ratio control. In the second phase, a supervised classifier is learned by taking some reviews classified in the first phase as training data. The learned classifier is then applied to other reviews to revise the classifications produced in the first phase. The advantage of this approach is that it needs no manually labelled data, so it is essentially an unsupervised method using a supervised technique and can be applied to any domain, unlike the corpus-based classification methods, which need manually labelled positive and negative reviews from every domain to which the algorithm is applied.

Li and Zong (2008) showed how to perform sentiment classification by exploiting training data from multiple domains. Two approaches were proposed. The first approach combines features from multiple training domains. The second approach combines classifiers built from individual domains. Their results showed that the classifier-level combination performed better than single domain classification (using the training data from only its own domain).

In Li et al. (2009), a nonnegative matrix trifactorization model was proposed for sentiment classification. In this model, an $m \times n$ term-document matrix X is approximated by three factors that specify soft membership of terms and documents in one of k classes, that is, $X \approx FSG^T$. F is an $m \times k$ nonnegative matrix representing knowledge in the word space, that is, the ith row of F represents the posterior probabilities of word i belonging to the k classes. G is an $n \times k$ nonnegative matrix representing knowledge in the document space; that is, the ith row of G represents the posterior probabilities of document i belonging to the k classes, and S is a $k \times k$ nonnegative matrix providing a condensed view of X. In the case of two-class classification, $k = 2$. We can obtain G and F matrices through factorization. G gives us the sentiment classification of each document, and F gives us the sentiment association of each term (or word). Without any initial knowledge, this is an unsupervised model. The authors also experimented with some supervision, for example, using a small set of sentiment words and a small set of document labels, to constrain the factorization model. If word i is a positive word, the model sets $(F_0)_{i1} = 1$, and if it is negative, the model sets $(F_0)_{i2} = 1$. Here F_0 is the initial F matrix. The factorization process is iterative, based on three updating rules. Some known document labels can also be used in the same way. That is, $(G_0)_{i1} = 1$ if the ith document expresses a positive sentiment, and $(G_0)_{i2} = 1$ if the ith document expresses a negative sentiment. These semi-supervised options perform classification quite well.

In Bickerstaffe and Zukerman (2010), the authors considered the more general problem of multiway sentiment classification for discrete, ordinal rating scales, focusing on the document level, that is, the problem of predicting the "star" rating associated with each review. Because the classes are ordinal, the algorithm considered interclass similarity in its classification.

Other work on document-level sentiment classification includes using semi-supervised learning and/or active learning (Dasgupta and Ng, 2009; Zhou et al., 2010; Li et al., 2011), labelling features rather than documents (He, 2010), using word vectors to capture latent aspects of words to help classification (Maas et al., 2011), classifying tonality of news article statements (Scholz and Conrad, 2013), and performing word clustering first to reduce feature sparsity and then building models and classifying using the word clusters as features (Popat et al., 2013). In Li et al. (2012), active learning was applied for imbalanced sentiment classification. In Tokuhisa et al. (2008), emotion classification of dialogue utterances was also investigated. It first performed sentiment classification of three classes (positive, negative and neutral) and then classified positive and negative utterances into ten emotion categories. Aly and Atiya (2013) crawled and prepared a large set of Arabic book reviews (63,257). Some initial experiments of sentiment classification and rating prediction were performed on them.

3.2.2 Classification Using a Custom Score Function

Instead of using a standard machine learning method, researchers have proposed customized techniques specifically for sentiment classification of reviews. The score function in Dave et al. (2003) is one such technique. It is based on words in positive and negative reviews. The algorithm consists of two steps:

Step 1. Score each term (unigram or n-gram) in the training set using the following equation:

$$\text{score}(t_i) = \frac{\Pr(t_i|C) - \Pr(t_i|C')}{\Pr(t_i|C) + \Pr(t_i|C')},$$

[3.2]

where t_i is a term, C is a class, C' is its complement, that is, not C, and $\Pr(t|C)$ is the conditional probability of term t_i in class C, which is computed by taking the number of times that a term t_i occurs in class C reviews and dividing it by the total number of terms in the reviews of class C. A term score is thus a measure of the term's bias toward either class ranging from -1 to 1.

Step 2. Classify a new document $d_i = t_1 \ldots t_n$ by summing up the scores of all terms and using the sign of the total to determine the class:

$$\text{class}(d_i) = \begin{cases} C & \text{eval}(d) > 0 \\ C' & \text{otherwise} \end{cases},$$

[3.3]

where

$$\text{eval}(d_i) = \sum_j \text{score}(t_j).$$

[3.4]

Experiments were conducted based on more than thirteen thousand reviews of seven types of products. The results showed that bigrams (two consecutive words) and trigrams (three consecutive words) as terms gave (similar) best accuracies (84.6–88.3%). No stemming or stopword removal was applied.

The authors also experimented with many alternative classification techniques, for example, naïve Bayes, SVM, and several variant score functions, and word substitution strategies to improve generalization, for example,

- replace product names with a token ("_productname")
- replace rare words with a token ("_unique")
- replace category-specific words with a token ("_producttypeword")
- replace numeric tokens with NUMBER

Some linguistic modifications using WordNet, stemming, negation, and collocation were tested too. However, these were not helpful and actually degraded the classification accuracy.

3.3 UNSUPERVISED SENTIMENT CLASSIFICATION

Because sentiment words and phrases are often the dominating factor for sentiment classification, it is not hard to imagine using them for sentiment classification in an unsupervised manner. We discuss two methods here. One, based on the method in Turney (2002), performs classification using some fixed syntactic patterns that are likely to express opinions. The other is based on a sentiment lexicon, which is a list of positive and negative sentiment words and phrases.

3.3.1 Classification Using Syntactic Patterns and Web Search

In Turney (2002), each syntactic pattern is a sequence of POS tags with some constraints (Table 3.2). The algorithm consists of three steps:

Table 3.2: *Patterns of POS tags for extracting two-word phrases*

	First word	Second word	Third word (not extracted)
1	JJ	NN or NNS	anything
2	RB, RBR or RBS	JJ	not NN nor NNS
3	JJ	JJ	not NN nor NNS
4	NN or NNS	JJ	not NN nor NNS
5	RB, RBR, or RBS	VB, VBD, VBN, or VBG	anything

Step 1. Two consecutive words are extracted if their POS tags conform to any of the patterns in Table 3.2. For example, pattern 2 means that two consecutive words are extracted if the first word is an adverb, the second word is an adjective and the third word (not extracted) is not a noun. For example, in the sentence "*This piano produces beautiful sounds,*" *beautiful sounds* will be extracted because it satisfies the first pattern. The reason these patterns are used is that JJ, RB, RBR, and RBS words often express opinions or sentiments. The nouns or verbs act as the contexts because in different contexts, a JJ, RB, RBR, and RBS word may express different sentiments. For example, the adjective (JJ) *unpredictable* may indicate a negative sentiment in a car review, as in "*unpredictable steering,*" but a positive sentiment in a movie review, as in "*unpredictable plot.*"

Step 2. The sentiment orientation (SO) of the extracted phrases is estimated using the PMI (Pointwise Mutual Information) measure:

$$ \text{PMI}(term_1, term_2) = \log_2 \left(\frac{\text{Pr}(term_1 \wedge term_2)}{\text{Pr}(term_1)\,\text{Pr}(term_2)} \right). \tag{3.5} $$

PMI measures the degree of statistical dependence between two terms. Here $\text{Pr}(term_1 \wedge term_2)$ is the actual co-occurrence probability of $term_1$ and $term_2$ and $\text{Pr}(term_1)\text{Pr}(term_2)$ is the co-occurrence probability of the two terms if they are statistically independent. The SO of a phrase is computed based on its association with the positive reference word *excellent* and the negative reference word *poor*:

$$ \text{SO(phrase)} = \text{PMI(phrase, "excellent")} - \text{PMI(phrase, "poor")}. \tag{3.6} $$

The probabilities are calculated by issuing queries to a search engine and collecting the number of *hits*. For each search query, a search engine usually gives the number of relevant documents to the query, called hits. Thus, by searching the two terms together and separately, the probabilities in Equation (3.5) can be estimated. In Turney (2002), the AltaVista search engine was used because it had a NEAR operator to constrain the search to return documents that contain the words within ten words of one another in either order. Let *hits*(*query*) be the number of hits returned. Equation (3.6) can be rewritten as

$$ \text{SO(phrase)} = \log_2 \left(\frac{\text{hits(phrase } NEAR \text{ "excellent")hits("poor")}}{\text{hits(phrase } NEAR \text{ "poor")hits("excellent")}} \right). \tag{3.7} $$

Step 3. Given a review, the average SO score of all phrases in the review is computed, and the review is classified as positive if the average SO value is positive and negative otherwise.

Final classification accuracies on reviews from various domains range from 84% for automobile reviews to 66% for movie reviews.

Feng et al. (2013) compared PMI with three other association measures using different corpora. The three new measures are Jaccard, Dice and Normalized Google Distance. The corpora are Google indexed pages, Google Web IT 5-grams, Wikipedia, and Twitter. Their experimental results show that PMI with the Twitter corpus produces the best results.

3.3.2 Classification Using Sentiment Lexicons

Another unsupervised approach is based on sentiment lexicons and is called the *lexicon-based approach*. The key characteristic of this approach is that it performs classification based on a dictionary of sentiment words and phrases, called a *sentiment lexicon* or *opinion lexicon*, with their associated sentiment orientations and strengths. It may also incorporate intensification and negation to compute a sentiment score for each document (Kennedy and Inkpen, 2006; Taboada et al., 2006, 2011). This approach was used earlier for aspect-level sentiment classification (Hu and Liu, 2004) and for sentence-level sentiment classification (Kim and Hovy, 2004). In the approach, each positive expression (a word or phrase) is assigned a positive SO value, and each negative expression is assigned a negative SO value.

In its base form, to classify a document, the SO values of all sentiment expressions in the document are summed up. The SO of the document is classified positive if the sum is positive, negative if the sum is negative, and neutral if the final sum is 0. There are many variations of this approach, which mainly differ in what value is assigned to each sentiment expression, how negations are handled, and whether additional information is considered. In Hu and Liu (2004) and Kim and Hovy (2004), each positive sentiment expression is given the SO value of +1, and each negative sentiment expression is given the SO value of −1. Negation words (also called *negators*), such as *not* and *never*, reverse the SO value. For example, *good* is +1 and *not good* is −1. It was shown in Polanyi and Zaenen (2004) that other factors in addition to negation words can affect whether a particular expression is positive or negative. These factors are called *sentiment shifters* (or *valence shifters*, as in Polanyi and Zaenen, 2004). Sentiment shifters are expressions that can change the SO value of another expression. There are, in fact, many more sentiment shifters than those identified in Polanyi and Zaenen (2004).

The work in Kennedy and Inkpen (2006) implemented some of the ideas in Polanyi and Zaenen (2004). In addition to negations, which switch or reverse the sentiment of positive or negative expressions, as previously, they considered intensifiers and diminishers, which can alter the SO values of sentiment expressions. Intensifiers and diminishers are expressions that change the degree of the expressed sentiment. An intensifier increases the intensity of a positive or negative expression, whereas a diminisher decreases the intensity of that expression. For example, in the sentence "*This movie is very good,*" the phrase *very good* is more positive than just *good*, whereas in the sentence "*This movie is barely any good,*" the word *barely* is a diminisher that makes this statement less positive. To allow for intensifiers and diminishers, the paper gives all positive sentiment expressions the value of 2. If they are preceded by an intensifier in the same clause, then they are given the value of 3. If the expressions are preceded by a diminisher in the same clause, then they are given the value of 1. Negative sentiment expressions are given the value of −2 by default and −1 or −3 if preceded by a diminisher or an intensifier, respectively.

Taboada et al. (2011) extended this method further by considering finer cases. The SO value for each sentiment expression is assigned a value from the range of −5 (extremely negative) to +5 (extremely positive). The value of 0 is not used. Each intensifier or diminisher is associated with a positive or negative percentage weight respectively. For example, *slightly* is −50, *somewhat* is −30, *pretty* is −10, *really* is +15, *very* is +25, *extraordinarily* is +50, and *(the) most* is +100. If *excellent* has an SO value of 5, *most excellent* would have an SO value of $5 \times (100\% + 100\%) = 10$. Intensifiers and diminishers are applied recursively starting from the closest to the SO-valued expression: if *good* has a SO value of 3, then *really very good* has a SO value of $(3 \times [100\% + 25\%]) \times (100\% + 15\%) = 4.3$. There are two main types of intensifying and diminishing cases: a SO-valued adjective with an adverbial modifier (e.g., *very good*) and a SO-valued noun with an adjectival modifier (e.g., *total failure*). In addition to adverbs and adjectives, other intensifiers and diminishers used in Taboada et al. (2011) are quantifiers (*a great deal of*), all capital letters, exclamation marks, and discourse-connective *but* (to indicate more salient information).

Simply reversing the SO value to handle negation can be problematic in some cases. Consider *excellent*, a +5 adjective: if we negate it, we get *not excellent*, which is a far cry from *atrocious*, a −5 adjective. In fact, *not excellent* seems more positive than *not good*, which would negate to a −3. To capture these pragmatic intuitions, instead of changing the sign, the SO value is shifted toward the opposite polarity by a fixed amount (e.g., 4). Thus a +2 adjective is negated to a −2, but the negation of a −3 adjective (e.g., *sleazy*) is only slightly positive (i.e., +1). Following are a few examples:

a. It's not terrific (5 − 4 = 1) but not terrible (−5 + 4 = −1) either.
b. I have to admit it's not bad (−3 + 4 = 1).
c. This CD is not horrid (−5 + 4 = −1).

The idea is that it is difficult to negate a strongly positive word without implying that a less positive one is to some extent true, and thus the negator becomes a diminisher.

As noticed in Kennedy and Inkpen (2006), lexicon-based sentiment classifiers generally show a positive bias. To compensate for this bias, negative expressions, being relatively rare, are given more weight in Taboada et al. (2011) by increasing the final SO value of any negative expression (after other modifiers have been applied) by 50%.

There are also a number of markers indicating that the words appearing in a sentence might not be reliable for the purpose of sentiment analysis. These usually indicate nonfactual contexts and are referred to as *irrealis* moods. The list of irrealis markers includes modals, conditional markers (*if*), negative polarity items like *any* and *anything*, certain (mostly intensional) verbs (*expect*, *doubt*), questions and words enclosed in quotation marks (which may not be factual but not necessarily reflective of the author's opinion). The SO value of any word in the scope of an *irrealis* marker (i.e., within the same clause) is ignored. This strategy is called *irrealis blocking*. This does not mean that such sentences or clauses express no sentiment. In fact, many such sentences do bear sentiments, for example, "*Anyone know how to repair this lousy car?*" However, it is hard to reliably determine when such sentences express sentiment and when they do not. They are thus ignored. We discuss these issues further when we deal with sentence-level and aspect-level sentiment classification.

In addition to the preceding methods, there are also manual approaches for specific applications. For example, Tong (2001) reported a system that generates sentiment timelines. The system tracked online discussions about movies and displayed a plot of the number of positive and negative messages (*Y*-axis) over time (*X*-axis). Messages were classified by matching specific phrases that indicate the sentiment of the author toward a movie, for example, *great acting*, *wonderful visuals*, *uneven editing* and *highly recommend it*. The phrases were manually compiled as indicating positive or negative sentiments in the application. The lexicon is thus specific to the domain and needs to be compiled anew for each new domain.

We note that if a large amount of labelled training data for a particular domain is available, supervised learning usually gives superior classification accuracy because it can consider domain-dependent sentiment expressions automatically. Lexicon-based methods cannot easily consider domain-dependent sentiment expressions unless there is an algorithm that is able to discover such expressions and determine their orientations automatically. There is already some work on this (Zhang and Liu, 2011a, 2011b), but it is still immature. Supervised learning also has its weaknesses. The main one is that the classifier trained from one domain usually does not work in another domain (see Section 3.5). Thus, for effective classification, training data are required for each application domain. Lexicon-based methods do not need training data and thus have an edge when no training data are available.

3.4 SENTIMENT RATING PREDICTION

Classifying opinion documents only as positive or negative may not be sufficient in some applications, where the user may need the degree of positivity or negativity. For this purpose, researchers have studied the problem of predicting rating scores (e.g., 1–5 stars) of reviews (Pang and Lee, 2005). In this case, the problem is typically formulated as a regression problem because the rating scores are ordinal, although not all researchers solve the problem using regression techniques. Pang and Lee (2005) experimented with SVM regression, SVM multiclass classification using the one-versus-all (OVA) strategy and a meta-learning method called metric labelling and showed that OVA-based classification is significantly poorer than the other two approaches. This is understandable as numerical ratings are not categorical values. Goldberg and Zhu (2006) improved this approach by modelling rating prediction as a graph-based semi-supervised learning problem with both labelled (with ratings) and unlabelled (without ratings) reviews. The unlabelled reviews were the test reviews whose ratings needed to be predicted. In the graph, each node is a document (review) and the link between two nodes is the similarity value between the two documents. A large similarity weight implies that two documents tend to have the same sentiment rating. The authors experimented with several different similarity schemes. They also assumed that, initially, a separate learner had already predicted the numerical ratings of the unlabelled documents. The graph-based method simply improves the initial predictions by revising the ratings through solving an optimization problem to force ratings to be smooth throughout the graph with regard to both the ratings and the link weights.

Qu et al. (2010) modified the traditional bag-of-words representation to introduce a bag-of-opinions representation of documents to capture the strength of n-grams with opinions. Each of the opinions is a triple, a sentiment word, a modifier and a negator. For example, in "*not very good,*" *good* is the sentiment word, *very* is the modifier, and *not* is the negator. For sentiment classification of two classes (positive and negative), opinion modifiers are not crucial, but for rating prediction, they are very important, and so is the impact of negation words. A constrained ridge regression method was developed to learn the sentiment score or strength of each opinion from domain-independent corpora (of multiple domains) of rated reviews. The key idea was to exploit an available opinion lexicon and the review ratings. To transfer the regression model to a newly-given domain-dependent application, the algorithm derives a set of statistics over the opinion scores and then uses them as additional features together with the standard unigrams for rating prediction. Prior to this work, Liu and Seneff (2009) proposed an approach to extracting adverb-adjective-noun phrases (e.g., "*very nice car*") based on the clause structure obtained by parsing sentences into a hierarchical representation. Rather than using learning, they assigned sentiment scores based on a heuristic method that computes the contribution of adjectives, adverbials and negations to the sentiment degree based on the ratings of reviews where these words occurred.

Snyder and Barzilay (2007) studied the problem of predicting the rating for each aspect instead of predicting the rating of each review. A simple approach to this task would be to use a standard regression or classification technique. However, this approach does not exploit the dependencies between users' judgments across different aspects, which are useful for accurate prediction. Thus this article proposed two models: an aspect model (which works on individual aspects) and an agreement model (which models the rating agreement among aspects). Both models were combined in learning. The features used for training were lexical features such as unigram and bigrams from each review.

Long et al. (2010) used a similar approach to that in Pang and Lee (2005) but employed a Bayesian network classifier for rating prediction of each aspect in a review. For good accuracy, instead of predicting for every review, they focused on predicting only aspect ratings for a selected subset of reviews that comprehensively evaluated the aspects because the other reviews did not have sufficient information. The review selection method used an information measure based on Kolmogorov complexity. The aspect rating prediction for the selected reviews used machine learning. The features for training were only from those aspect-related sentences. The aspect extraction was done using a similar method to that in Hu and Liu (2004).

3.5 CROSS-DOMAIN SENTIMENT CLASSIFICATION

It has been shown that sentiment classification is highly sensitive to the domain from which the training data are extracted. A classifier trained using opinion documents from one domain often performs poorly on test data from another domain because words and even language constructs used for expressing opinions in different domains can be quite different. To make matters worse, the same word may be positive in one domain but negative in another. Thus domain adaptation or transfer learning is needed. Existing research is mainly based on two settings. The first setting needs a small amount of labelled training data for the new domain (Aue and Gamon, 2005). The second needs no labelled data for the new domain (Blitzer et al., 2007; Tan et al., 2007). The original domain with labelled training data are often called the *source domain*, and the new domain used for testing is called the *target domain*.

In Aue and Gamon (2005), the authors proposed to transfer sentiment classifiers to new domains in the absence of large amounts of labelled data in these domains. They experimented with four strategies: (1) training on a mixture of labelled reviews from other domains where such data are available and testing on the target domain; (2) training a classifier, as in strategy 1, but limiting the set of features only to those observed in the target domain; (3) using ensembles of classifiers from domains with available labelled data and testing on the target domain; (4) combining small amounts of labelled data with large amounts of unlabelled data in the target domain (this is the traditional semi-supervised learning setting). SVM was used for the first three strategies and expectation maximization (EM) for semi-supervised learning (Nigam et al., 2000) was used for the fourth strategy. Their experiments showed that strategy 4 performed the best because it was able to make use of both the labelled and unlabelled data in the target domain.

In Yang et al. (2006), a simple strategy based on feature selection was proposed for transfer learning for sentence-level classification. Their method first used two fully labelled training sets from two domains to select features that were highly ranked in both domains. These selected features were considered to be domain-independent features. A classifier built using these features was then applied to any target or test domains. Another simple strategy was proposed in Tan et al. (2007), which first trains a base classifier using the labelled data from the source domain and then uses the classifier to label some informative examples in the target domain. On the basis of the selected examples in the target domain, a new classifier is learned, which is finally applied to classify the test cases in the target domain.

Blitzer et al. (2007) used a method called structural correspondence learning (SCL) for domain adaptation, which was proposed earlier in Blitzer et al. (2006). Given labelled reviews from a source domain and unlabelled reviews from both the source and target domains, SCL first chooses a set of m features that occur frequently in both domains and are also good predictors of the source labels (in the article, these were the features with the highest mutual information (MI) values with the source labels). These *pivot features* represent the shared feature space of the two domains. SCL then computes the correlations of each pivot feature with other nonpivot features in both domains. This produces a correlation matrix $\mathbf{W}$, where row i is a vector of correlation values of nonpivot features with the ith pivot feature. Intuitively, positive values indicate that those nonpivot features are positively correlated with the ith pivot feature in the source domain or in the new domain. This establishes a feature correspondence between the two domains. After that, singular value decomposition (SVD) is employed to compute a low-dimensional linear approximation θ (the top k left singular vectors, transposed) of $\mathbf{W}$. The final set of features for training and for testing is the original set of features $\mathbf{x}$ combined with $\theta\,\mathbf{x}$, which produces k real-valued features. The classifier built using the combined features and labelled data in the source domain should work in both the source and target domains.

Pan et al. (2010) proposed a method similar to SCL at the high level. The algorithm works in the setting where there are only labelled examples in the source domain and unlabelled examples in the target domain. It bridges the gap between the domains by using a spectral feature alignment (SFA) algorithm to *align* domain-specific words from different domains into unified clusters, with domain-independent words as the bridge. Domain-independent words are like pivot words in Blitzer et al. (2007) and can be selected similarly. SFA works by first constructing a bipartite graph with the domain-independent words as one set of nodes and the domain-specific words as the other set of nodes. A domain-specific word is linked to a domain-independent word if the words co-occur either in the same document or within a window. The link weight is the frequency of their co-occurrence. A spectral clustering algorithm is then applied on the bipartite graph to co-align domain-specific and domain-independent words into a set of feature clusters. The idea is that if two domain-specific words have connections to more common domain-independent words in the graph, they tend to be aligned or clustered together with a higher probability. Similarly, if two domain-independent words have connections to more common domain-specific words in the graph, they have a higher probability of alignment. For the final cross-domain training and testing, all data examples are represented with the combination of these clusters and the original set of features.

Along the same lines, He et al. (2011) used joint topic modelling to identify opinion topics (which are similar to the earlier clusters) from both domains to bridge them. The resulting topics, which cover both domains, are used as additional features to augment the original set of features for classification. In Gao and Li (2011), topic modelling was used, too, to find a common semantic space based on domain term correspondences and term co-occurrences in the two domains. This common semantic space was then used to learn a classifier, which was applied to the target domain. Bollegala et al. (2011) reported a method to automatically create a sentiment-sensitive thesaurus using both labelled and unlabelled data from multiple source domains to find the association between words that express similar sentiments in different domains. The thesaurus is then used to expand the original feature vectors to train a binary sentiment classifier. Yoshida et al. (2011) devised a method to transfer from multiple source domains to multiple target domains by identifying domain-dependent and -independent word sentiments. Andreevskaia and Bergler (2008) used an ensemble of two classifiers. The first classifier was built using a dictionary, and the second was built using a small amount of in-domain training data.

In Wu et al. (2009), a graph-based method was presented that uses the idea of label propagation on a similarity graph (Zhu and Ghahramani, 2002) to perform the transfer. In the graph, each document is a node and each link between two nodes is a weight computed using the cosine similarity of the two documents. Initially, every document in the old domain has a label score of +1 (positive) or −1 (negative), and each document in the new domain is assigned a label score based a normal sentiment classifier, which can be learned from the old domain. The algorithm then iteratively updates the label score of each new domain document i by finding k nearest neighbours in the old domain and k nearest neighbours in the new domain. A linear combination of the neighbour label scores and link weights is used to assign a new score to node i. The iterative process stops when the label scores converge. The sentiment orientations of the new domain documents are determined by their label scores. Ponomareva and Thelwall (2012) compared graph-based methods with several other state-of-the-art methods and concluded that graph-based representations offer a competitive solution to the domain adaptation problem.

Xia and Zong (2011) found that across different domains, features of some types of POS tags are usually domain dependent, whereas others are domain free. On the basis of this observation, they presented a POS-based ensemble model to integrate features with different types of POS tags to improve the classification performance.

3.6 CROSS-LANGUAGE SENTIMENT CLASSIFICATION

Cross-language sentiment classification is sentiment classification of opinion documents in multiple languages. There are two main motivations for cross-language classification. Firstly, researchers from different countries want to build sentiment analysis systems in their own languages. However, much of the research has been done in English. There are not many resources or tools in other languages that can be used to build good sentiment classifiers quickly in these languages. The natural question is whether it is possible to leverage the automated machine translation capability and existing sentiment analysis resources and tools available in English to help build sentiment analysis systems in other languages. The second motivation is that in many applications, companies want to know and compare consumer opinions about their products and services in different countries. If they have a sentiment analysis system in English, they want to quickly build sentiment analysis systems in other languages through translation.

Several researchers have studied this problem. Much of the current work focuses on sentiment classification at the document level and subjectivity and sentiment classification at the sentence level. Limited work has been done at the aspect level, except that in Guo et al. (2010). In this section, we focus on cross-language document-level sentiment classification. Section 4.7 focuses on the sentence level.

In Wan (2008), sentiment resources in English were exploited to perform classification of Chinese reviews. The first step of the algorithm translates each Chinese review into English using multiple translators, which produce different English versions. It then uses a lexicon-based approach to classify each translated English version. The lexicon consists of a set of positive expressions (words or phrases), a set of negative expressions, a set of negation expressions and a set of intensifiers. The algorithm then sums up the sentiment scores of the expressions in the review considering negations and intensifiers. If the final score is less than 0, the review is negative; otherwise, it is positive. For the final classification of each review, it combines the scores of different translated versions using various ensemble methods (average, max, weighted average, voting, etc.). If a Chinese lexicon is also available, the same technique can be applied to the Chinese version. Its result may also be combined with the results of those English translations. The results show that the ensemble technique is effective. Brooke et al. (2009) also experimented with translation (using only one translator) from the source language (English) to the target language (Spanish) and then used a lexicon-based approach or machine learning for target language document sentiment classification.

In Wan (2009), the author reported a co-training method that uses an annotated English corpus for classification of Chinese reviews in a supervised manner. No Chinese resources were used. In training, the input consisted of a set of labelled English reviews and a set of unlabelled Chinese reviews. The labelled English reviews were translated into labelled Chinese reviews, and the unlabelled Chinese reviews were translated into unlabelled English reviews. Each review was thus associated with an English version and a Chinese version. English features and Chinese features for each review were considered as two independent and redundant views of the review. A co-training algorithm using SVM was then applied to learn two classifiers, which were then combined into a single classifier. In the classification phase, each unlabelled Chinese review for testing was first translated into an English review, and then the learned classifier was applied to classify the review as either positive or negative. In Wan (2013), a co-regression method was presented for cross-language review rating prediction. The method is again based on the co-training idea.

Wei and Pal (2010) used a transfer learning method for cross-language sentiment classification. Because machine translation is still far from perfect, to minimize the noise introduced in translation, they proposed to use the SCL method (Blitzer et al., 2007) to find a small set of core features shared by both languages (English and Chinese). To alleviate the problem of data and feature sparseness, they issued queries to a search engine to find other highly correlated features to those in the core feature set and then used the newly discovered features to create extra pseudo-examples for training.

Boyd-Graber and Resnik (2010) extended the topic modelling method Supervised Latent Dirichlet Allocation (SLDA) (Blei and McAuliffe, 2007) to work on reviews from multiple languages for review rating prediction. SLDA is able to consider the user rating of each review in topic modelling. The extended model MLSLDA creates topics using documents from multiple languages at the same time. The resulting multilanguage topics are globally consistent across languages. To bridge topic terms in different languages in topic modeling, the model used the aligned WordNets of different languages or dictionaries.

In Guo et al. (2010), a topic model–based method was employed to group a set of given aspect expressions in different languages into aspect clusters (categories) for aspect-based sentiment comparison of opinions from different countries.

In Duh et al. (2011), the authors presented their opinions about the research of cross-language sentiment classification. On the basis of their analysis, they claimed that domain mismatch was not caused by machine translation (MT) errors, and accuracy degradation would occur even with perfect MT. They also argued that the cross-language adaptation problem was qualitatively different from other (monolingual) adaptation problems in NLP; thus new adaptation algorithms should be considered.

3.7 EMOTION CLASSIFICATION OF DOCUMENTS

Let us now turn to classification of emotion and mood, which is a considerably harder task because (1) there are many more classes, that is, types of emotions and moods and (2) different types of emotions or moods have many similarities, which makes it difficult to separate them. Note that because in writing, it is not easy to distinguish emotion and mood (Alm, 2008), we will not distinguish them in this section.

Existing approaches to emotion or mood classification at the document level are mainly based on supervised learning. For example, Mishne and de Rijke (2006) performed mood classification on a collection of blog posts from LiveJournal.com. On LiveJournal.com, authors can tag each of their posts with a mood type. Thus its blog posts can be naturally used for supervised classification. The main features used in learning are a set of discriminative terms (words or n-grams) for each mood. These terms are computed as follows: for each mood m, two probability distributions, θ_m and $\theta_{\neg m}$, are produced; θ_m is the distribution of all words in the blog posts tagged with mood m, and $\theta_{\neg m}$ is the distribution of all words in the rest of the blog posts. All words in θ_m are ranked according to their log-likelihood measure, as compared with $\theta_{\neg m}$: this produces a ranked list of "characteristic terms" for mood m. Once this process has been carried out for all moods, a single feature set of "discriminating terms" was created by selecting the terms that appear in the top-N position of the separate rank lists for individual moods. Several other features were also used, for example, the hour of the day when the blog was posted or whether the posting date was a weekend or not. For model building, pace regression (Wang and Witten, 1999) was applied.

Lin et al. (2007) classified news articles provided by Yahoo! Chinese news. Readers had voted on the articles based on the readers' perceived emotions. The algorithm used supervised learning with SVM. Four feature sets were employed. The first set consisted of all Chinese character bigrams. The second set contained all words produced by a Chinese word segmentation tool. The third set was the meta-data of the articles, for example, news reporter, news category, location of the news event, publication time and name of the news agency. The fourth set was the emotion categories of words, which were obtained from an emotion lexicon that has been previously constructed by the authors (Yang et al., 2007).

Supervised learning was also employed in Strapparava and Mihalcea (2008), which used naïve Bayes classification. Another supervised method is based on manifold (Kim et al., 2013). The learning algorithm is different from those used in the preceding articles in that those methods treated mood prediction as a multiclass classification problem with discrete labels. This article assumes a continuous mood manifold and thus involves an inherently different learning paradigm.

Several other studies related to emotions are mainly about emotion lexicon constructions, for example, WordNet-Affect (Strapparava and Valitutti, 2004), which was constructed in the context of WordNet, and the lexicon of Mohammad and Turney (2010), which was constructed using crowdsourcing. Yet, some emotion analysis work (no classification) using different kinds of online texts was also performed in Mihalcea and Liu (2006) and Mohammad (2011).

3.8 SUMMARY

Sentiment classification at the document level detects the overall opinion or sentiment expressed in a document. The problem has been studied extensively by a large number of researchers. However, this level of classification has two main shortcomings:

- It is not concerned with sentiment or opinion targets. Although it is generally applicable to reviews because each review usually evaluates a single entity, it is not easily applicable to nonreviews, such as forum discussions, blogs and news articles, because many such posts evaluate multiple entities and compare the entities using comparative sentences. In many cases, it is hard to determine whether a post actually evaluates the entity in which the user is interested and whether the post expresses any opinion at all because, unlike reviews, a forum post may only give some product descriptions, let alone determine the sentiment about the entity. Document-level sentiment classification does not perform such fine-grained tasks, which require in-depth NLP rather than just text classification. In fact, online reviews do not need sentiment classification because almost every review on the web has a user-assigned star rating. In practice, it is the forum discussions and blogs that really need sentiment classification to determine people's opinions.

- Even if it is known that a document evaluates a single entity, in most applications, the user wants to know additional details, for example, what aspects of the entity are liked and disliked by consumers. In a typical opinion document, such details are provided, but document-level sentiment classification does not extract them for the user. These details can be very important for decision-making. For example, a particular camera got all positive reviews (4 or 5 stars), but some reviewers mentioned the short battery life in their reviews. If a potential buyer wants long battery life, he probably will not buy the camera, although every review is positive about the camera.

3.9 REFERENCES

1.   Andreevskaia, A. and Bergler, S. (2008). When Specialists and Generalists Work Together: Overcoming Domain Dependence in Sentiment Tagging. In *ACL,* pp. 290-298.

2.   Abbasi, A., Chen, H. and Salem, A. (2008). Sentiment analysis in multiple languages: Feature selection for opinion classification in Web forums. *ACM Transactions on Information Systems (TOIS)*, 26(3), p.12.

3.   Aly, M.A. and Atiya, A.F. (2013). LABR: A Large Scale Arabic Book Reviews Dataset. In *ACL, Vol. 2,* pp. 494-498.

4.   Becker, I. and Aharonson, V. (2010). Last but definitely not least: on the role of the last sentence in automatic polarity-classification. In *Proceedings of the ACL 2010 conference Short Papers*. Association for Computational Linguistics, pp. 331-335.

5.   Bespalov, D., Bai, B., Qi, Y. and Shokoufandeh, A. (2011). Sentiment classification based on supervised latent n-gram analysis. In *Proceedings of the 20th ACM international conference on Information and knowledge management*. ACM, pp. 375-382.

6.   Bickerstaffe, A. and Zukerman, I. (2010). A hierarchical classifier applied to multi-way sentiment detection. In *Proceedings of the 23rd international conference on computational linguistics*. Association for Computational Linguistics, pp. 62-70.

7.   Blei, D.M. and Mcauliffe, J.D. (2008). Supervised topic models. *Advances in neural information processing systems*, pp. 121-128.

8.   Blitzer, J., McDonald, R. and Pereira, F. (2006). Domain adaptation with structural correspondence learning. In *Proceedings of the 2006 conference on empirical methods in natural language processing*. Association for Computational Linguistics, pp. 120-128.

9.   Blitzer, J., Dredze, M. and Pereira, F. (2007). Biographies, bollywood, boom-boxes and blenders: Domain adaptation for sentiment classification. In *ACL,* Vol. 7, pp. 440-447.

10. Bollegala, D., Weir, D. and Carroll, J. (2011). Using multiple sources to construct a sentiment sensitive thesaurus for cross-domain sentiment classification. In *Proceedings of the 49th Annual Meeting of the Association for Computational Linguistics: Human Language Technologies, Volume 1*. Association for Computational Linguistics, pp. 132-141.

11. Boyd-Graber, J. and Resnik, P. (2010). Holistic sentiment analysis across languages: Multilingual supervised latent Dirichlet allocation. In *Proceedings of the 2010 Conference on Empirical Methods in Natural Language Processing*. Association for Computational Linguistics, pp. 45-55.

12. Brooke, J., Tofiloski, M. and Taboada, M. (2009). Cross-Linguistic Sentiment Analysis: From English to Spanish. In *RANLP*, pp. 50-54.

13. Cristianini, N. and Shawe-Taylor, J. (2000). *An Introduction to Support Vector Machines and Other Kernel-Based Learning Methods*. Cambridge university press.

14. Cui, H., Mittal, V. and Datar, M. (2006). Comparative experiments on sentiment classification for online product reviews. In *AAAI, Vol. 6*, pp. 1265-1270.

15. Dasgupta, S. and Ng, V. (2009). Mine the easy, classify the hard: a semi-supervised approach to automatic sentiment classification. In *Proceedings of the Joint Conference of the 47th Annual Meeting of the ACL and the 4th International Joint Conference on Natural Language Processing of the AFNLP, Vol. 2*. Association for Computational Linguistics, pp. 701-709.

16. Dave, K., Lawrence, S. and Pennock, D.M. (2003). Mining the peanut gallery: Opinion extraction and semantic classification of product reviews. In *Proceedings of the 12th international conference on World Wide Web*. ACM, pp. 519-528.

17. Duh, K., Fujino, A. and Nagata, M. (2011). Is machine translation ripe for cross-lingual sentiment classification? In *Proceedings of the 49th Annual Meeting of the Association for Computational Linguistics: Human Language Technologies: short papers, Vol. 2*. Association for Computational Linguistics, pp. 429-433.

18. Feng, S., Kang, J.S., Kuznetsova, P. and Choi, Y. (2013). Connotation Lexicon: A Dash of Sentiment Beneath the Surface Meaning. In *ACL (1)*, pp. 1774-1784.

19. Gamon, M. (2004). Sentiment classification on customer feedback data: noisy data, large feature vectors, and the role of linguistic analysis. In *Proceedings of the 20th international conference on Computational Linguistics*. Association for Computational Linguistics, pp. 841.

20. Gamon, M., Aue, A., Corston-Oliver, S. and Ringger, E. (2005). Pulse: Mining customer opinions from free text. In *Advances in Intelligent Data Analysis VI*, pp. 121-132. Springer Berlin Heidelberg.

21. Gao, S. and Li, H. (2011). A cross-domain adaptation method for sentiment classification using probabilistic latent analysis. In *Proceedings of the 20th ACM international conference on Information and knowledge management*. ACM, pp. 1047-1052.

22. Goldberg, A.B. and Zhu, X. (2006). Seeing stars when there aren't many stars: graph-based semi-supervised learning for sentiment categorization. In *Proceedings of the First Workshop on Graph Based Methods for Natural Language Processing*. Association for Computational Linguistics, pp. 45-52.

23. Guo, H., Zhu, H., Guo, Z., Zhang, X. and Su, Z. (2010). OpinionIt: a text mining system for cross-lingual opinion analysis. In *Proceedings of the 19th ACM international conference on Information and knowledge management*. ACM, pp. 1199-1208.

24. Guo, H., Zhu, H., Guo, Z. and Su, Z. (2011). Domain customization for aspect-oriented opinion analysis with multi-level latent sentiment clues. In *Proceedings of the 20th ACM international conference on Information and knowledge management*. ACM, pp. 2493-2496.

25. He, J., Hollink, V. and de Vries, A. (2012). Combining implicit and explicit topic representations for result diversification. In *Proceedings of the 35th international ACM SIGIR conference on Research and development in information retrieval*. ACM, pp. 851-860.

26. Hu, M. and Liu, B. (2004). Mining and summarizing customer reviews. In *Proceedings of the tenth ACM SIGKDD international conference on Knowledge discovery and data mining*. ACM, pp. 168-177.

27. Joachims, T. (1999). Making large scale SVM learning practical. Universität Dortmund.

28. Joshi, M. and Penstein-Rosé, C. (2009). Generalizing dependency features for opinion mining. In *Proceedings of the ACL-IJCNLP 2009 Conference Short Papers*. Association for Computational Linguistics, pp. 313-316.

29. Kamps, J. and Marx, M. (2002). Visualizing wordnet structure. In *Proceedings of the 1st International Conference on Global WordNet*, pp. 182-186.

30. Kennedy, A. and Inkpen, D. (2006). Sentiment classification of movie reviews using contextual valence shifters. *Computational intelligence*, 22(2), pp. 110-125.

31. Kim, S.M. and Hovy, E. (2004). Determining the sentiment of opinions. In *Proceedings of the 20th international conference on Computational Linguistics*. Association for Computational Linguistics, pp. 1367.

32. Kim, J., Li, J.J. and Lee, J.H. (2009). Discovering the discriminative views: measuring term weights for sentiment analysis. In *Proceedings of the Joint Conference of the 47th Annual Meeting of the ACL and the 4th International Joint Conference on Natural Language Processing of the AFNLP, Vol. 1*. Association for Computational Linguistics, pp. 253-261.

33. Kim, M. and Smaragdis, P. (2013). Manifold preserving hierarchical topic models for quantization and approximation. In *Proceedings of the 30th International Conference on Machine Learning*, pp. 1373-1381.

34. He, Y. (2010). Learning sentiment classification model from labeled features. In *Proceedings of the 19th ACM international conference on Information and knowledge management*. ACM, pp. 1685-1688.

35. Kouloumpis, E., Wilson, T. and Moore, J.D. (2011). Twitter sentiment analysis: The good the bad and the omg! *ICWSM, 11*, pp. 538-541.

36. Li, S. and Zong, C. (2008). Multi-domain sentiment classification. In *Proceedings of the 46th Annual Meeting of the Association for Computational Linguistics on Human Language Technologies: Short Papers*. Association for Computational Linguistics, pp. 257-260.

37. Li, T., Zhang, Y. and Sindhwani, V. (2009). A non-negative matrix tri-factorization approach to sentiment classification with lexical prior knowledge. In *Proceedings of the Joint Conference of the 47th Annual Meeting of the ACL and the 4th International Joint Conference on Natural Language Processing of the AFNLP, Vol. 1*. Association for Computational Linguistics, pp. 244-252.

38. Li, S., Lee, S.Y.M., Chen, Y., Huang, C.R. and Zhou, G. (2010). A Sentiment classification and polarity shifting. In *Proceedings of the 23rd International Conference on Computational Linguistics*. Association for Computational Linguistics, pp. 635-643.

39. Li, S., Wang, Z., Zhou, G. and Lee, S.Y.M. (2011). Semi-supervised learning for imbalanced sentiment classification. In *IJCAI Proceedings-International Joint Conference on Artificial Intelligence*. Vol. 22, No. 3, pp. 1826._

40. Li, S., Ju, S., Zhou, G. and Li, X. (2012). Active learning for imbalanced sentiment classification. In *Proceedings of the 2012 Joint Conference on Empirical Methods in Natural Language Processing and Computational Natural Language Learning*. Association for Computational Linguistics, pp. 139-148.

41. Lin, K.H.Y., Yang, C. and Chen, H.H. (2007). What emotions do news articles trigger in their readers? In *Proceedings of the 30th annual international ACM SIGIR conference on Research and development in information retrieval*. ACM, pp. 733-734.

42. Liu, B. (2010). Sentiment Analysis and Subjectivity. In R. Dale, H. Moisl and H. Somers, eds., *Handbook of natural language processing, 2*. CRC Press.

43. Liu, B. and Ding, X. (2010). Resolving object and attribute coreference in opinion mining. In *Proceedings of the 23rd International Conference on Computational Linguistics*. Association for Computational Linguistics, pp. 268-276.

44. Liu, B. (2012). Sentiment analysis and opinion mining. *Synthesis lectures on human language technologies, 5(1)*, pp. 1-167.

45. Liu, B. (2015). *Sentiment Analysis: Mining Opinions, Sentiments and Emotions*. Cambridge University Press.

46. Liu, J. and Seneff, S. (2009). Review sentiment scoring via a parse-and-paraphrase paradigm. In *Proceedings of the 2009 Conference on Empirical Methods in Natural Language Processing, Vol. 1*. Association for Computational Linguistics, pp. 161-169.

47. Long, C., Zhang, J. and Zhut, X. (2010). A review selection approach for accurate feature rating estimation. In *Proceedings of the 23rd International Conference on Computational Linguistics: Posters*. Association for Computational Linguistics, pp. 766-774.

48. Maas, A.L., Daly, R.E., Pham, P.T., Huang, D., Ng, A.Y. and Potts, C. (2011). Learning word vectors for sentiment analysis. In *Proceedings of the 49th Annual Meeting of the Association for Computational Linguistics: Human Language Technologies, Vol. 1*. Association for Computational Linguistics, pp. 142-150.

49. Martineau, J. and Finin, T. (2009). Delta TFIDF: An Improved Feature Space for Sentiment Analysis. *ICWSM, 9*, pp. 106.

50. McDonald, R., Hannan, K., Neylon, T., Wells, M. and Reynar, J. (2007). Structured models for fine-to-coarse sentiment analysis. In *Annual Meeting-Association For Computational Linguistics*. Vol. 45, No. 1, p. 432.

51. Mejova, Y. and Srinivasan, P. (2011). Exploring Feature Definition and Selection for Sentiment Classifiers. In *ICWSM*.

52. Mihalcea, R. and Liu, H. (2006). A Corpus-based Approach to Finding Happiness. In *AAAI Spring Symposium: Computational Approaches to Analyzing Weblogs*, pp. 139-144.

53. Mishne, G. and De Rijke, M. (2006). A study of blog search. In *Advances in information retrieval*, pp. 289-301. Springer Berlin Heidelberg.

54. Mohammad, S.M. and Turney, P.D. (2010). Emotions evoked by common words and phrases: Using Mechanical Turk to create an emotion lexicon. In *Proceedings of the NAACL HLT 2010 workshop on computational approaches to analysis and generation of emotion in text*. Association for Computational Linguistics, pp. 26-34.

55. Mohammad, S. (2011). From once upon a time to happily ever after: Tracking emotions in novels and fairy tales. In *Proceedings of the 5th ACL-HLT Workshop on Language Technology for Cultural Heritage, Social Sciences, and Humanities*. Association for Computational Linguistics, pp. 105-114.

56. Mullen, T. and Collier, N. (2004). Sentiment Analysis using Support Vector Machines with Diverse Information Sources. In *EMNLP, Vol. 4*, pp. 412-418.

57. Nigam, K., McCallum, A.K., Thrun, S. and Mitchell, T. (2000). Text classification from labeled and unlabeled documents using EM. *Machine learning, 39*(2-3), pp.103-134.

58. Ng, V., Dasgupta, S. and Arifin, S.M. (2006). Examining the role of linguistic knowledge sources in the automatic identification and classification of reviews. In *Proceedings of the COLING/ACL on Main conference poster sessions*. Association for Computational Linguistics, pp. 611-618.

59. Osgood, C. E., Succi, G. J. and Tannenbaum, P. H. (1957). The Measurement of Meaning. University of Illinois Press, Urbana IL.

60. Paltoglou, G. and Thelwall, M. (2010). A study of information retrieval weighting schemes for sentiment analysis. In *Proceedings of the 48th Annual Meeting of the Association for Computational Linguistics*. Association for Computational Linguistics, pp. 1386-1395.

61. Pan, S.J., Ni, X., Sun, J.T., Yang, Q. and Chen, Z. (2010). Cross-domain sentiment classification via spectral feature alignment. In *Proceedings of the 19th international conference on World Wide Web*. ACM, pp. 751-760.

62. Pang, B., Lee, L. and Vaithyanathan, S. (2002). Thumbs up?: Sentiment classification using machine learning techniques. In *Proceedings of the ACL-02 Conference on Empirical Methods in Natural Language Processing, Vol. 10*. Stroudsburg: Assocation for Computational Linguistics, pp. 79–86.

63. Pang, B. and Lee, L. (2004). A sentimental education: Sentiment analysis using subjectivity summarization based on minimum cuts. In *Proceedings of the 42nd annual meeting on Association for Computational Linguistics*. Association for Computational Linguistics, pp. 271.

64. Pang, B. and Lee, L. (2005). Seeing stars: Exploiting class relationships for sentiment categorization with respect to rating scales. In *Proceedings of the 43rd Annual Meeting on Association for Computational Linguistics*. Association for Computational Linguistics, pp. 115-124.

65. Pang, B. and Lee, L. (2008). Opinion mining and sentiment analysis. *Foundations and trends in information retrieval, 2(1-2)*, pp. 1-135.

66. Polanyi, L. and Zaenen, A. (2004). Contextual valence shifters. In *Proceedings of AAAI Spring Symposium on Exploring Attitude and Affect in Text*, pp. 106-111.

67. Ponomareva, N. and Thelwall, M. (2012). Do neighbours help?: an exploration of graph-based algorithms for cross-domain sentiment classification. In *Proceedings of the 2012 Joint Conference on Empirical Methods in Natural Language Processing and Computational Natural Language Learning*. Association for Computational Linguistics, pp. 655-665.

68. Popat, B.A. (2013). The haves and the have-nots: Leveraging unlabelled corpora for sentiment analysis.

69. Qiu, G., Liu, B., Bu, J. and Chen, C. (2009). Expanding Domain Sentiment Lexicon through Double Propagation. In *IJCAI*, Vol. 9, pp. 1199-1204.

70. Qu, L., Ifrim, G. and Weikum, G. (2010). The bag-of-opinions method for review rating prediction from sparse text patterns. In *Proceedings of the 23rd International Conference on Computational Linguistics*. Association for Computational Linguistics, pp. 913-921.

71. Robertson, S. and Zaragoza, H. (2009). *The probabilistic relevance framework: BM25 and beyond*. Now Publishers Inc.

72. Salton, G. (1971). *The SMART Retrieval System–Experiments in Automatic Document Processing*. Prentice Hall, NJ, USA.

73. Santorini, B. (1990). Part-of-speech tagging guidelines for the Penn Treebank Project (3rd revision). University of Pennsylvania technical report.

74. Scholz, T. and Conrad, S. (2013). Opinion Mining in Newspaper Articles by Entropy-Based Word Connections. In *EMNLP*, pp. 1828-1839.

75. Snyder, B. and Barzilay, R. (2007). Multiple Aspect Ranking Using the Good Grief Algorithm. In *HLT-NAACL*, pp. 300-307.

76. Strapparava, C. and Mihalcea, R. (2008). Learning to identify emotions in text. In *Proceedings of the 2008 ACM symposium on Applied computing*. ACM, pp. 1556-1560.

77. Strapparava, C. and Valitutti, A. (2004). WordNet Affect: an Affective Extension of WordNet. In *LREC*, *Vol. 4*, pp. 1083-1086.

78. Taboada, M., Anthony, C. and Voll, K. (2006). Methods for creating semantic orientation dictionaries. In *Proceedings of the 5th Conference on Language Resources and Evaluation*, pp. 427-432.

79. Taboada, M., Brooke, J., Tofiloski, M., Voll, K. and Stede, M. (2011). Lexicon-based methods for sentiment analysis. *Computational linguistics*, *37*(2), pp.267-307.

80. Tan, S., Wu, G., Tang, H. and Cheng, X. (2007). A novel scheme for domain-transfer problem in the context of sentiment analysis. In *Proceedings of the sixteenth ACM conference on Conference on information and knowledge management*. ACM, pp. 979-982.

81. Tokuhisa, R., Inui, K. and Matsumoto, Y. (2008). Emotion classification using massive examples extracted from the web. In *Proceedings of the 22nd International Conference on Computational Linguistics-Volume 1*. Association for Computational Linguistics, pp. 881-888.

82. Tong, R.M. (2001). An operational system for detecting and tracking opinions in on-line discussions. Working Notes of the ACM SIGIR 2001 Workshop on Operational Text Classification. New York, NY: ACM, pp. 1-6.

83. Turney, P.D. (2002). Thumbs up or thumbs down?: semantic orientation applied to unsupervised classification of reviews. In *Proceedings of the 40th annual meeting on association for computational linguistics*. Association for Computational Linguistics, pp. 417-424.

84. Wan, X. (2008). Using bilingual knowledge and ensemble techniques for unsupervised Chinese sentiment analysis. In *Proceedings of the conference on empirical methods in natural language processing*. Association for Computational Linguistics, pp. 553-561.

85. Wan, X. (2009). Co-training for cross-lingual sentiment classification. In *Proceedings of the Joint Conference of the 47th Annual Meeting of the ACL and the 4th International Joint Conference on Natural Language Processing of the AFNLP, Vol. 1*. Association for Computational Linguistics, pp. 235-243.

86. Wan, X. (2013). Co-Regression for Cross-Language Review Rating Prediction. In *ACL (2)*, pp. 526-531.

87. Wang, Y. and Witten, I.H. (1999). Pace regression. Department of Computer Science, University of Waikato.

88. Wei, B. and Pal, C. (2010). Cross lingual adaptation: an experiment on sentiment classifications. In *Proceedings of the ACL 2010 Conference Short Papers*. Association for Computational Linguistics, pp. 258-262.

89. Wu, Q., Tan, S. and Cheng, X. (2009). Graph ranking for sentiment transfer. In *Proceedings of the ACL-IJCNLP 2009 Conference Short Papers*. Association for Computational Linguistics, pp. 317-320.

90. Xia, R. and Zong, C. (2010). Exploring the use of word relation features for sentiment classification. In *Proceedings of the 23rd International Conference on Computational Linguistics: Posters*. Association for Computational Linguistics, pp. 1336-1344.

91. Xia, R., Zong, C. and Li, S. (2011). Ensemble of feature sets and classification algorithms for sentiment classification. *Information Sciences*, *181*(6), pp. 1138-1152.

92. Xia, R., Wang, T., Hu, X., Li, S. and Zong, C. (2013). Dual Training and Dual Prediction for Polarity Classification. In *ACL, 2,* pp. 521-525.

93. Yang, H., Callan, J. and Si, L. (2006). Knowledge Transfer and Opinion Detection in the TREC 2006 Blog Track. In *TREC*.

94. Yang, C., Lin, K.H.Y. and Chen, H.H. (2007). Building emotion lexicon from weblog corpora. In *Proceedings of the 45th Annual Meeting of the ACL on Interactive Poster and Demonstration Sessions*. Association for Computational Linguistics, pp. 133-136.

95. Yessenalina, A., Choi, Y. and Cardie, C. (2010)[a]. Automatically generating annotator rationales to improve sentiment classification. In *Proceedings of the ACL 2010 Conference Short Papers*. Association for Computational Linguistics, pp. 336-341.

96. Yessenalina, A., Yue, Y. and Cardie, C. (2010)[b]. Multi-level structured models for document-level sentiment classification. In *Proceedings of the 2010 Conference on Empirical Methods in Natural Language Processing*. Association for Computational Linguistics, pp. 1046-1056.

97. Yoshida, Y., Hirao, T., Iwata, T., Nagata, M. and Matsumoto, Y. (2011). Transfer learning for multiple-domain sentiment analysis—identifying domain dependent/independent word polarity. In *Twenty-Fifth AAAI Conference on Artificial Intelligence*.

98. Yu, C.N.J. and Joachims, T. (2009). Learning structural SVMs with latent variables. In *Proceedings of the 26th annual international conference on machine learning*. ACM, pp. 1169-1176.

99. Zaidan, O., Eisner, J. and Piatko, C.D. (2007). Using" Annotator Rationales" to Improve Machine Learning for Text Categorization. In *HLT-NAACL,* pp. 260-267.

100. Zhou, Z.H. and Li, M. (2010). Semi-supervised learning by disagreement. *Knowledge and Information Systems*, *24*(3), pp.415-439.

101. Zhang, L. and Liu, B. (2011)[a]. Identifying noun product features that imply opinions. In *Proceedings of the 49th Annual Meeting of the Association for Computational Linguistics: Human Language Technologies: short papers-Volume 2*. Association for Computational Linguistics, pp. 575-580.

102. Zhang, L. and Liu, B. (2011)[b]. Extracting Resource Terms for Sentiment Analysis. In *IJCNLP*, pp. 1171-1179.

103. Zhu, X. and Ghahramani, Z. (2002). *Learning from labelled and unlabelled data with label propagation*. Technical Report CMU-CALD-02-107, Carnegie Mellon University.

CHAPTER 4

Sentence Subjectivity and
Sentiment Classification

Bing Liu, *Professor of Computer Science, University of Illinois*

4.1 INTRODUCTION

As discussed in the previous chapter, document-level sentiment classification is too coarse for practical applications. We now move to the sentence level and look at methods that classify sentiment expressed in each sentence. The goal is to classify each sentence in an opinion document (e.g., a product review) as expressing a positive, negative, or neutral opinion. This gets us closer to real-life sentiment analysis applications, which require opinions on sentiment targets. Sentence-level classification is about the same as document-level classification because sentences can be regarded as short documents. Sentence-level classification, however, is often harder because the information contained in a typical sentence is much less than that contained in a typical document because of their length difference. Most document-level sentiment classification research papers ignore the neutral class mainly because it is more difficult to perform three-class classification (positive, neutral and negative) accurately. However, for sentence-level classification, the neutral class cannot be ignored because an opinion document can contain many sentences that express no opinion or sentiment. Note that neutral opinion often means no opinion or sentiment expressed.

One implicit assumption that researchers make about sentence-level classification is that a sentence expresses a single sentiment. Let us start our discussion with an example review:

I bought a Lenovo Ultrabook T431s two weeks ago. It is really light, quiet and cool. The new touchpad is great too. It is the best laptop that I have ever had although it is a bit expensive.

The first sentence expresses no sentiment or opinion as it simply states a fact. It is thus neutral. All other sentences express some sentiment. Sentence-level sentiment classification is defined as follows:

Definition 4.1 (Sentence sentiment classification): Given a sentence x, determine whether x expresses a positive, negative, or neutral (or no) opinion.

As we can see, like document-level sentiment classification, sentence-level sentiment classification also does not consider opinion or sentiment targets. However, in most cases, if the system is given a set of entities and their aspects, the sentiment about them in a sentence can just take the sentiment of the sentence. Of course, this is not always the case. For example, there is no opinion on Chrome in the sentence *"Trying out Chrome because Firefox keeps crashing."* This definition also cannot handle sentences with opposite opinions, for example, *"Apple is doing well in this bad economy."* This sentence is often regarded as containing a mixed opinion. Thus, like document sentiment classification, the problem of sentence sentiment classification is also somewhat restrictive because it is not applicable to many types of sentences due to its ignorance of sentiment (or opinion) targets. It can still be useful, however, because most sentences in practice express a single opinion or sentiment.

Definition 4.1 does not use the quintuple (e, a, s, h, t) notation because sentence-level classification is an intermediate step in the overall sentiment analysis task and is not concerned with the opinion target (entity or aspect), the opinion holder, or the time when the opinion is posted.

Sentence sentiment classification can be solved either as a three-class classification problem or as two separate two-class classification problems. In the latter case, the first problem (also called the first step) is to classify whether a sentence expresses an opinion. The second problem (also called the second step) classifies those opinion sentences into positive and negative classes. The first problem is often called the *subjectivity classification* in the research literature, which determines whether a sentence expresses a piece of subjective information or objective (or factual) information (Hatzivassiloglou and Wiebe, 2000; Riloff and Wiebe, 2003; Yu and Hatzivassiloglou, 2003; Wiebe et al., 2004; Wilson et al., 2004; Riloff et al., 2006; Wilson et al., 2006). Many researchers regard subjectivity and sentiment as the same concept. This is problematic because many objective sentences can imply opinions, and many subjective sentences contain no positive or negative opinions. Thus, it is more appropriate for the first step to classify each sentence as *opinionated* or *not-opinionated* (Liu, 2010), regardless of whether it is a subjective or an objective sentence.

Definition 4.2 (Opinionated): A sentence is opinionated if it expresses or implies a positive or negative sentiment.

Definition 4.3 (Not-opinionated): A sentence is not-opinionated if it expresses or implies no positive or negative sentiment.

However, the common practice is still to use the term *subjectivity classification*. In the following, we first discuss the concept of subjectivity (Section 4.2) and then the existing work on sentence-level subjectivity classification (Section 4.3) and sentiment classification (Section 4.4).

Like Chapter 3, this chapter is written in a survey style owing to there being a large number of published papers, and most of them use supervised machine learning and thus focus on feature engineering. There is still no independent and comprehensive experimental evaluation of the existing techniques and feature sets to assess their effectiveness.

4.2 SUBJECTIVITY

Subjectivity is a concept that has been widely used in sentiment analysis. It has also caused some confusion among researchers. In many papers, being subjective and being sentiment-bearing are regarded as equivalent, but they are not the same. Let us define sentence subjectivity here. Because the concept depends on the definitions of both subjective and objective, we give the dictionary definitions of these two terms first:[1]

Definition 4.4 (Subjective): Proceeding from or taking place in a person's mind rather than the external world.

Definition 4.5 (Objective): Having actual existence or reality.

On the basis of these definitions, we can define sentence subjectivity as follows:

Definition 4.6 (Sentence subjectivity): An *objective sentence* states some factual information, whereas a *subjective sentence* expresses some personal feelings, views, judgments, or beliefs.

An example of an objective sentence is "*The iPhone is an Apple product*." An example of a subjective sentence is "*I like the iPhone*." The task of determining whether a sentence is subjective or objective is called *subjectivity classification* (Wiebe and Riloff, 2005). However, we should note the following:

- A subjective sentence may not express any positive or negative sentiment. Subjective expressions can express opinions, appraisals, evaluations, allegations, desires, beliefs, suspicions, speculations, and stances (Wiebe, 2000; Riloff et al., 2006). Some of these concepts indicate positive or negative sentiments, and some of them do not. For example, "*I think he went home*" is a subjective sentence as it expresses a belief but it does not express or imply any positive or negative sentiment. The sentence "*I want to buy a camera that can take good photos*" is also subjective and even contains a sentiment word *good*, but again it does not give a positive or negative sentiment about anything. It actually expresses a desire or intention.

- Objective sentences can imply opinions or sentiments due to desirable and undesirable facts (Zhang and Liu, 2011b). For example, the following two sentences, which state some facts, clearly imply negative sentiments about the respective products because the facts are undesirable:

  "*The earphone broke in two days*."
  "*I bought the mattress a week ago and a valley has formed in the middle*."

Apart from positive and negative sentiment, many other types of subjectivity have also been studied in various communities, although not as extensively as sentiment, for example, affect, emotion, mood, judgment, appreciation, speculation, hedge, perspective, arguing, agreement and disagreement, and political stances (Lin et al., 2006; Medlock and Briscoe, 2007; Alm, 2008; Ganter and Strube, 2009; Greene and Resnik, 2009; Somasundaran and Wiebe, 2009; Hardisty et al., 2010; Murakami and Raymond, 2010; Neviarouskaya et al., 2010; Mukherjee and Liu, 2012). Many of them may also imply opinions or sentiments.

In summary, the concepts of subjectivity and sentiment are not equivalent, although they have a large intersection. Most people would agree that, psychologically, sentiment is a kind of subjective feeling and that subjectivity is a super-concept of sentiment and sentiment is a subconcept of subjectivity. However, one does not always need to use subjective sentences to express sentiment because our commonsense knowledge and pragmatics in communication can tell us what facts are desirable and what facts are undesirable in a particular context.

4.3 SENTENCE SUBJECTIVITY CLASSIFICATION

Subjectivity classification classifies sentences into two classes, subjective and objective (Wiebe et al., 1999). Early research solved subjectivity classification as a standalone problem, rather than for the purpose of sentiment classification. More recently, researchers and practitioners have treated it as the first step of sentence-level sentiment classification by using it to remove objective sentences that are assumed to express or imply no opinion or sentiment. In this case, as we discussed earlier, *subjective* and *objective* should really mean *opinionated* and *not-opinionated,* respectively.

Most existing approaches to subjectivity classification are based on supervised learning. For example, the early work reported in Wiebe et al. (1999) performed subjectivity classification using the naïve Bayes classifier with a set of binary features, for example, the presence in the sentence of a pronoun, an adjective, a cardinal number, a modal other than *will,* or an adverb other than *not.* Subsequent research used other learning algorithms and more sophisticated features.

In Wiebe (2000), an unsupervised method for subjectivity classification was proposed that simply used the presence of subjective expressions in a sentence to determine the subjectivity of a sentence. Because there was not a complete set of such expressions, it provided some seeds and then used distributional similarity (Lin, 1998) to find similar words, which were also likely to be subjectivity indicators. However, words found this way had low precision and high recall. Then, the method in Hatzivassiloglou and McKeown (1997) and the concept of gradability in Hatzivassiloglou and Wiebe (2000) were applied to filter wrong subjective expressions. *Gradability* is a semantic property that enables a word to appear in a comparative construct and to accept modifying expressions that act as intensifiers or diminishers. Gradable adjectives express properties in varying degrees of strength, relative to a norm either explicitly mentioned or implicitly supplied by the modified noun (for example, a *small planet* is usually much larger than a *large house*). Gradable adjectives were found using a seed list of manually compiled adverbs and noun phrases (such as *a little, exceedingly, somewhat,* and *very*) that are frequently used as grading modifiers. Such gradable adjectives are good indicators of subjectivity.

In Yu and Hatzivassiloglou (2003), Yu and Hatzivassiloglou performed subjectivity classifications using sentence similarity and a naïve Bayes classifier. The sentence similarity method is based on the assumption that subjective or opinion sentences are more similar to other opinion sentences than to factual sentences. They used the SIMFINDER system in Hatzivassiloglou et al. (2001) to measure sentence similarity based on shared words, phrases, and WordNet synsets. For naïve Bayes classification, they used features such as words (unigram), bigrams, trigrams, parts of speech, the presence of sentiment words, the counts of the polarities (or orientations) of sequences of sentiment words (e.g., "++" for two consecutive positively oriented words) and the counts of parts of speech combined with sentiment information (e.g., "JJ+" for positive adjective), as well as features encoding the sentiment (if any) of the head verb, the main subject and their immediate modifiers. They also performed sentiment classification to determine whether a subjective sentence is positive or negative, as we discuss in the next section.

One of the bottlenecks in applying supervised learning is the manual effort involved in annotating a large number of training examples. To save the manual labelling effort, a bootstrapping approach to label training data automatically was proposed in Riloff and Wiebe (2003). The algorithm works by first using two high-precision classifiers (HP-Subj and HP-Obj) to automatically identify some subjective and objective sentences. The high-precision classifiers use lists of lexical items (single words or n-grams) that are good subjectivity clues. HP-Subj classifies a sentence as subjective if it contains two or more strong subjective clues. HP-Obj classifies a sentence as objective if there are no strong subjective clues. These classifiers give very high precision but low recall. The extracted sentences are then added to the training data to learn patterns. The patterns (which form the subjectivity classifiers in the next iteration) are then used to automatically identify more subjective and objective sentences, which are then added to the training set, and the next iteration of the algorithm begins.

For pattern learning, a set of syntactic templates is used to restrict the kinds of patterns to be learned. Some example syntactic templates and example patterns are as follows:

Syntactic template	Example pattern
<subj> passive-verb	<subj> was satisfied
<subj> active-verb	<subj> complained
active-verb <dobj>	endorsed <dobj>
noun aux <dobj>	fact is <dobj>
passive-verb prep <np>	was worried about <np>

Wiebe and Riloff (2005) used the discovered patterns to generate a rule-based method that produces training data for subjectivity classification. The rule-based subjective classifier classifies a sentence as subjective if it contains two or more strong subjective clues; otherwise, it does not label the sentence. In contrast, the rule-based objective classifier looks for the absence of clues: it classifies a sentence as objective if there are no strong subjective clues in the sentence and it meets several other conditions. The system also learns new patterns about objective sentences using the information extraction system AutoSlog-TS (Riloff, 1996), which finds patterns based on some fixed syntactic templates. The data produced by the rule-based classifiers were used to train a naïve Bayes classifier. A related study was also reported in Wiebe et al. (2004), which used a more comprehensive set of features or subjectivity clues for subjectivity classification.

Riloff et al. (2006) studied relationships among different features. They defined subsumption relationships among unigrams, n-grams and lexico-syntactic patterns. If a feature is subsumed by another, the subsumed feature is not needed. This can remove many redundant features.

In Pang and Lee (2004), a mincut-based algorithm was proposed to classify each sentence as being subjective or objective. The algorithm works on a sentence graph of an opinion document, for example, a review. The graph is first built based on local labelling consistencies (which produces an association score of two sentences) and an individual sentence subjectivity score computed based on the probability produced by a traditional classification method (which produces a score for each sentence). Local labelling consistency means that sentences close to each other are more likely to have the same class label (subjective or objective). The mincut approach is able to improve individual sentence-based subjectivity classification because of the local labelling consistencies. The purpose of this work was to remove objective sentences from reviews to improve document-level sentiment classification. In Scheible and Schütze (2013), a similar approach was employed. However, it does not classify based on *subjective* and *objective* classes but *opinionated* and *not-opinionated*, where they are called *sentiment relevance* and *sentiment irrelevance,* respectively. The set of features used is also different.

Barbosa and Feng (2010) classified the subjectivity of tweets (posts on Twitter) based on traditional features with the inclusion of some Twitter-specific clues such as retweets, hashtags, links, uppercase words, emoticons and exclamation and question marks. For sentiment classification of subjective tweets, the same set of features was used.

Interestingly, in Raaijmakers and Kraaij (2008), it was found that character n-grams of subwords rather than word n-grams can also be used to perform sentiment and subjectivity classification well. For example, for the sentence "*This car rocks*," subword character bigrams are th, hi, is, ca, ar, ro, oc, ck, ks. In Raaijmakers et al. (2008) and Wilson and Raaijmakers (2008), word n-grams, character n-grams and phoneme n-grams were all compared for subjectivity classification. BoosTexter (Schapire and Singer, 2000) was used as the learning algorithm. Surprisingly, they showed that character n-grams performed the best and that phoneme n-grams performed similarly to word n-grams.

Wilson et al. (2004) pointed out that a single sentence may contain both subjective and objective clauses. It is useful to pinpoint such clauses. It is also useful to identify the strength of subjectivity. A study of automatic subjectivity classification was presented to classify clauses of a sentence into four levels of strength of subjectivity expressed in individual clauses (*neutral*, *low*, *medium* and *high*). Strength classification thus subsumes the task of classifying a sentence as subjective or objective. For classification, the authors used supervised learning. Their features included subjectivity indicating words and phrases and syntactic clues generated from the dependency parse tree.

Benamara et al. (2011) performed subjectivity classification with four classes, *S*, *OO*, *O*, and *SN*, where *S* means subjective and evaluative (their sentiment can be positive or negative), *OO* means positive or negative opinion implied in an objective sentence or sentence segment, *O* means objective with no opinion, and *SN* means subjective but not evaluative (no positive or negative sentiment). This classification conforms to our discussion in Section 4.2, which showed that a subjective sentence may not necessarily be evaluative (with positive or negative sentiment) and that an objective sentence can imply sentiment as well.

Additional works on subjectivity classification of sentences have also been done in Arabic (Abdul-Mageed et al., 2011) and Urdu languages (Mukund and Srihari, 2010) based on different machine learning algorithms using general and language-specific features.

4.4 SENTENCE SENTIMENT CLASSIFICATION

We now turn to sentence sentiment classification. That is, if a sentence is classified as subjective, or, rather, opinionated, we determine whether it expresses a positive or negative opinion. Supervised learning again can be applied to solve the problem similarly to document-level sentiment classification, as can lexicon-based methods. If an application needs opinions about some desired target entities or entity aspects, the system can simply assign the overall sentiment of each sentence to the target entities and aspects in the sentences. This assignment, however, can be problematic, as we discuss in Section 4.4.1.

4.4.1 Assumption of Sentence Sentiment Classification

As discussed at the beginning of the chapter, sentence-level sentiment classification makes the following important assumption, which is often not explicitly stated in research papers:

Assumption 4.7: A sentence expresses a single opinion or sentiment.

As with document-level analysis, sentence-level analysis does not consider the opinion (or sentiment) target. This assumption also imposes several other restrictions, which make it difficult for sentence-level sentiment classification to be applied to several types of complex sentences:

1. The assumption is only appropriate for simple sentences (subject-verb-object) with one sentiment, for example, "*The picture quality of this camera is amazing*." It is not appropriate for simple sentences with more than one sentiment, for example, "*Lenovo is doing quite well in this poor PC market*." It is often not applicable to compound or complex sentences because they often express more than one sentiment in a sentence. For example, the sentence "*The picture quality of this camera is amazing and so is the battery life, but the viewfinder is a little small for such a great camera*" expresses both positive and negative sentiments. For '*picture quality*' and '*battery life*,' the sentence is positive, but for *viewfinder*, it is negative. It is also positive about the *camera* as a whole. Because of this multiple-sentiment problem, some researchers regard such sentences as having a mixed sentiment and use a separate class called MIXED to represent or label this type of sentences. However, mixed-class sentences are not easy to use in practice.

2. It may detect an overall positive or negative tone from a sentence but ignore the details, which causes problems in applications. For example, many researchers regard the following sentence as positive and expect a sentiment classifier to classify it as such (Neviarouskaya et al., 2010; Zhou et al., 2011): "*Despite the high unemployment rate, the economy is doing well*." It is true that the overall tone of this sentence is positive, as the author emphasizes her positive sentiment on *the economy*, but it does not mean that the sentence is positive about everything mentioned in the sentence. It is actually negative about the *unemployment rate*, which we must not ignore because practical applications often need opinions and their targets. If in an application we simply assign *unemployment rate* the same positive sentiment as the whole sentence, it is clearly wrong. However, if we go to the aspect-level sentiment analysis and consider the opinion target explicitly for each opinion, the problem is solved.

3. Sentence-level sentiment classification can only be applied to sentences expressing regular opinions but not to sentences expressing comparative opinions, for example, "*Coke tastes better than Pepsi*." This example sentence clearly expresses an opinion, but we cannot simply classify the sentence as being positive, negative or neutral. We need different methods to extract and analyse comparative opinions as they have different semantic meanings.

4.4.2 Classification Methods

For sentiment classification of subjective sentences, Yu and Hatzivassiloglou (2003) used a method similar to that in Turney (2002), which we discussed in Section 3.3. Instead of using one seed word for positive and one for negative, as in Turney (2002), this work used a large set of seed adjectives. Furthermore, instead of using PMI, this work used a modified log-likelihood ratio to determine the positive or negative orientation for each adjective, adverb, noun or verb. To assign an orientation to each sentence, it used the average log-likelihood scores of its words. Two thresholds were chosen using the training data and applied to determine whether the sentence has a positive, negative or neutral orientation. The same problem was also studied in Hatzivassiloglou and Wiebe (2000), considering gradable adjectives.

In Hu and Liu (2004), a lexicon-based algorithm was proposed for aspect-level sentiment classification, but the method can determine the sentiment orientation of a sentence as well. It was based on a sentiment lexicon generated using a bootstrapping strategy with some given positive and negative sentiment word seeds and the synonyms and antonyms relations in WordNet. The sentiment orientation of a sentence was determined by summing up the orientation scores of all sentiment words in the sentence. A positive word was given the sentiment score of $+1$ and a negative word was given the sentiment score of -1. Negation words and contrary words (e.g., *but* and *however*) were also considered. In Kim and Hovy (2004), a similar approach was used. Their method for compiling a sentiment lexicon was also similar. However, the sentiment orientation of a sentence was determined by multiplying the scores of the sentiment words in the sentence. The authors also experimented with two other methods of aggregating sentiment scores, but they were inferior. In Kim and Hovy (2004, 2007) and Kim et al. (2006), supervised learning was used to identify several specific types of opinions. In Nigam and Hurst (2004), a domain-specific lexicon and a shallow NLP approach to assessing the sentence sentiment orientation was applied.

In Gamon et al. (2005), a semi-supervised learning algorithm was used to learn from a small set of labelled sentences and a large set of unlabelled sentences. The learning algorithm was based on EM using the naïve Bayes as the base classifier (Nigam et al., 2000). This work performed a three-class classification, positive, negative and "other" (no opinion or mixed opinion).

In McDonald et al. (2007), a hierarchical sequence learning model similar to conditional random fields (CRF) (Lafferty et al., 2001) was proposed to jointly learn and infer sentiment at both the sentence level and the document level. In the training data, each sentence was labelled with a sentiment, and each whole review was also labelled with a sentiment. They showed that learning both levels jointly improved accuracy for both levels of classification. Täckström and McDonald (2011a) further reported a method that learns only from the document-level labelling but performs both sentence-level and document-level sentiment classifications. In Täckström and McDonald (2011b), the authors integrated a fully supervised model and a partially supervised model to perform multilevel sentiment classification.

In Hassan et al. (2010), an algorithm was proposed to identify attitudes about participants in online discussions. Because the authors were only interested in the discussion recipient, the algorithm only used sentence segments with second person pronouns. Its first step finds sentences with attitudes using supervised learning. The features were generated using Markov models. Its second step determines the orientation (positive or negative) of the attitudes, for which it used a lexicon-based method similar to that in Ding et al. (2008), except that the shortest path in the dependence tree was utilized to determine the orientation when there were conflicting sentiment words in a sentence, whereas Ding et al. (2008) used word distance.

In Socher et al. (2013), a deep learning method called Recursive Neural Tensor Network was proposed to perform sentence- and phrase-level sentiment classification. The network basically produces a composition function for phrases represented in parse trees. The training uses the given sentiment label and output of a softmax classifier taking as input the vector generated from the neural network composition function. The softmax classifier is also trained based on the vector of the parse tree node and the given label of the node. The work also produced a labelled movie review data set at the sentence and phrase levels using the review corpus from Pang and Lee (2005). It was shown that the proposed method produces more accurate results than other supervised methods because of its compositionality. For example, it can handle negation of opinions, which is hard to handle based on bag-of-word models.

Finally, many researchers have also studied Twitter post (or tweet) sentiment classification as each tweet is quite short and can be regarded as a sentence. For example, Davidov et al. (2010) performed sentiment classification of tweets using the traditional n-gram features and also hashtags, smileys, punctuation and their frequent patterns. These additional features were shown to be quite effective. Volkova et al. (2013) investigated gender differences in the use of subjective or opinionated languages, emoticons, and hashtags for male and female users. Their experiments showed that gender-aware or gender-dependent classification gives better results than gender-independent classification. Hu et al. (2013) presented a supervised approach to sentiment classification of microblogs by taking advantage of social relations, which are mainly used to tackle the high level of noise in microblogs.

Other interesting recent work includes the study of character-character sentiments towards each other in Shakespeare's plays using a sentiment lexicon (Nalisnick and Baird, 2013) and multimodal sentiment classification of utterances extracted from video reviews of products (Perez-Rosas et al., 2013). Features used in classification include transcribed text of utterances, acoustic signals and facial expressions.

4.5 DEALING WITH CONDITIONAL SENTENCES

Much of the existing research on sentence-level subjectivity classification or sentiment classification focuses on solving the general problem without considering that different types of sentences may need different treatments. Narayanan et al. (2009) argued that it is unlikely to have a one-technique-fits-all solution because different types of sentences express sentiments in very different ways. A divide-and-conquer approach may be needed, that is, focused studies on different types of sentences. Their paper focused on conditional sentences, which have some unique characteristics that make it hard for a system to determine sentiment orientations.

Conditional sentences are sentences that describe implications or hypothetical situations and their consequences. Such a sentence typically contains two clauses that are dependent on each other: the condition clause and the consequent clause. Their relationship has significant impact on whether the sentence expresses a positive or negative sentiment. A simple observation is that sentiment words (e.g., *great*, *beautiful*, *bad*) alone cannot distinguish an opinion sentence from a non-opinion one, for example, "*If someone makes a reliable car, I will buy it*" and "*If your Nokia phone is not good, buy this Samsung phone.*" The first sentence expresses no sentiment towards any particular car, although "*reliable*" is a positive sentiment word, but the second sentence is positive about the Samsung phone and it does not express an opinion about the Nokia phone (although the owner of the Nokia phone may be negative about it). Hence, a method for determining sentiments in nonconditional sentences will not work for conditional sentences. In Narayanan et al. (2009), a supervised learning approach was proposed to deal with the problem using a set of linguistic features, for example, sentiment words or phrases and their locations, POS tags of sentiment words, tense patterns and conditional connectives.

Here we list a set of interesting patterns in conditional sentences that often indicate sentiment. This set of patterns is particularly useful for reviews, online discussions and blogs about products. They are not frequently used in other types of domains. Each of these patterns must appear in the consequent clause. The conditional clause often expresses a conditional intent to buy a particular type of product, for example, "*If you are looking for a great car,*" "*If you are in the market for a good car,*" and "*If you like fast cars.*" The patterns are as follows:

POSITIVE	:: =	ENTITY is for you
	|	ENTITY is it
	|	ENTITY is the one
	|	ENTITY is your baby
	|	go (with | for) ENTITY
	|	ENTITY is the way to go
	|	this is it
	|	(search | look) no more
	|	CHOOSE ENTITY
	|	check ENTITY out
NEGATIVE	:: =	forget (this | it | ENTITY)
	|	keep looking
	|	look elsewhere
	|	CHOOSE (another one | something else)
CHOOSE	:: =	select | grab | choose | get | buy | purchase | pick | check | check out
ENTITY	:: =	this | this ENTITY_TYPE | ENTITY_NAME

POSITIVE and NEGATIVE are the sentiments. ENTITY_TYPE is a product type, for example, car or phone. ENTITY_NAME is a named entity, for example, iPhone or Motorola. Here negation is not included, which should be handled in standard ways. In most cases, the entity names are not mentioned in such sentences; that is, they are either mentioned in earlier sentences or they are actually the product being reviewed. However, the target aspects of opinions are frequently mentioned in the conditional clause, for example, "*If you want a beautiful and reliable car, look no further*," which give positive opinions to both the *appearance* and the *reliability* aspects of the car.

Although these patterns are quite useful for recognizing sentiments in conditional sentences, they can be unsafe for nonconditional sentences. Thus they should not be used for nonconditional sentences. Clearly there are other types of conditional sentences that can express opinions or sentiments, for example, "*If you do not mind the price, this is a great car*." This sentence expressed two opinions, one negative for the *price* and one positive for the *car*. However, most conditional sentences containing sentiment words express no opinions. To recognize them is still very challenging. Incidentally, sentences expressing uncertainty using *if* and *whether* usually express no positive or negative sentiment either, for example, "*I wonder if the new phone from Motorola is good or not*." Here, *wonder* can be replaced by many other words or phrases, for example, *am not sure, am unsure, am not certain, am uncertain, am not clear, am unclear*.

Another type of difficult sentence is the interrogative sentence, that is, the question. For example, "*Can anyone tell me where I can find a good Nokia phone?*" clearly has no opinion about any particular phone. However, "*Can anyone tell me how to fix this lousy Nokia phone?*" has a negative opinion about the Nokia phone. Many rhetorical questions are also opinionated, for example, "*Aren't HP Minis pretty?*" and "*Who on earth wants to live in this building?*" To my knowledge, little work has been done in this area.

To summarize, I believe that for more accurate sentiment analysis, we need to handle different types of sentences differently. Much further research is needed in this direction.

4.6 DEALING WITH SARCASTIC SENTENCES

Sarcasm is a sophisticated form of speech act in which the speakers or the writers say or write the opposite of what they mean. Sarcasm has been studied in linguistics, psychology and cognitive science (Gibbs, 1986; Kreuz and Glucksberg, 1989; Utsumi, 2000; Gibbs and Colston, 2007; Kreuz and Caucci, 2007). In the context of sentiment analysis, it means that when one says something positive, one actually means negative, and vice versa. Sarcastic sentences are very difficult to deal with in sentiment analysis because commonsense knowledge and discourse analysis are often required to recognize them. Some initial attempts have been made to handle sarcasm in recent years (Tsur et al., 2010; González-Ibáñez et al., 2011), but our knowledge about it is still very limited. On the basis of my own experiences, sarcastic sentences are not common in reviews of products and services, but they can be quite frequent in online discussions and commentaries about politics.

In Tsur et al. (2010), a semi-supervised learning approach was proposed to identify sarcasms. The paper also gives a number of nice examples of sarcastic titles of reviews, for example,

1. "[I] Love The Cover" (book)

2. "*Where am I?*" (GPS device)

3. "Be sure to save your purchase receipt" (smart phone)

4. "Are these iPods designed to die after two years?" (music player)

5. "Great for insomniacs" (book)

6. "All the features you want. Too bad they don't work!" (smart phone)

7. "Great idea, now try again with a real product development team" (e-reader)

Example 1 is sarcastic because of the expression *don't judge a book by its cover.* Choosing it as the title of the review reveals that the author is negative about the book. Example 2 requires knowledge of the context (review of a GPS device). Example 3 might seem borderline between suggesting a good practice and a sarcastic utterance, however, like example 1, placing it as the title of the review leaves no doubt about its sarcastic meaning. It implies poor quality of the phone and that one needs to be prepared to return it. In example 4, the sarcasm emerges from the naïve-like question that assumes the general expectation that goods should last. In example 5, the sarcasm requires commonsense knowledge (insomnia → boredom), and in examples 6 and 7, the sarcasm is conveyed by the explicit contradiction. Note that example 7 contains an explicit positive sentiment (*great idea*), whereas the positive sentiment in example 6 is not explicit. From these sentences, we can clearly see the difficulty of dealing with sarcasm.

The sarcasm detection algorithm proposed in Tsur et al. (2010) uses a small set of labelled sentences (seeds) but does not use unlabelled examples. Instead, it expands the seed set automatically through web search. The authors posited that sarcastic sentences frequently co-occur in texts with other sarcastic sentences. An automated web search using each sentence in the seed training set as a query was performed. The system then collected up to fifty search engine snippets for each seed example and added the collected sentences to the training set. This enriched training set was then used for learning and classification. For learning, it used two types of features: pattern-based features and punctuation-based features. A pattern is an ordered sequence of high-frequency words similar to sequential patterns in data mining (Liu, 2006, 2011). Two criteria were also designed to remove too general and too specific patterns. Punctuation-based features include the number of "!," "?," and quotation marks and the number of capitalized or all capital words in the sentence. For classification, a *k*NN-based method was employed. This work, however, did not perform sentiment classification. It only separated sarcastic from nonsarcastic sentences.

González-Ibáñez et al. (2011) studied the Twitter data to distinguish sarcastic tweets and nonsarcastic tweets that directly convey positive or negative opinions (neutral utterances were not considered). Again, a supervised learning approach was taken using SVM and logistic regression. As features, they used unigrams and some dictionary-based information. The dictionary-based features include word categories (Pennebaker et al., 2007),

WordNet-Affect (WNA) (Strapparava and Valitutti, 2004), and a list of interjections (e.g., ah, oh, yeah) and punctuations (e.g., !, ?). Features like emoticons and *ToUser* (which marks if a tweet is a reply to another tweet, signaled by <@user>) were also used. Experimental results for three-way classification (sarcastic, positive and negative) showed that the problem is very challenging. The best accuracy was only 57%. Again, this work did not classify sarcastic sentences into positive and negative classes.

Recently, Riloff et al. (2013) proposed a bootstrapping method to identify a specific type of sarcastic tweets characterized by positive sentiment followed by a negative situation. For example, in "*I love waiting forever for a doctor*," *love* indicates a positive sentiment and *waiting forever* indicates a negative situation. It was found that this type of sarcastic tweet is very common on Twitter. The authors further limited their study to positive sentiments that are expressed as verb phrases or as predicative expressions (predicate adjective or predicate nominal) and negative situation phrases that are complements to verb phrases. The bootstrapping learning process relies on the assumption that a positive sentiment phrase usually appears to the left of a negative situation phrase and in close proximity (usually, but not always, adjacent), that is,

[+ VERB PHRASE] [– SITUATION PHRASE].

The proposed bootstrapping algorithm starts with a single seed positive sentiment verb *love*. Using a manually labelled sarcastic and nonsarcastic tweets corpus, it first finds a set of candidate negative situation phrases that are n-grams following *love* (on the right-hand side) and are verb complement phrases of certain forms, which are defined as some bigram POS patterns. It then scores each candidate phrase based on the manually labelled tweets. Those that pass the score threshold are added to the set of negative situation phrases. The set of negative situation phrases is then used to find the two types of positive sentiment phrases in a similar way. The bootstrapping process alternately learns positive sentiments and negative situations until no more phrases can be found. The resulting sets of positive sentiment phrases and negative situation phrases are then used to identify sarcastic tweets.

4.7 CROSS-LANGUAGE SUBJECTIVITY AND SENTIMENT CLASSIFICATION

Researchers have also studied cross-language subjectivity classification and sentiment classification at the sentence level as well as the document level. Again, the area of research focuses on using the extensive resources and tools available in English and automated translations to help build sentiment analysis systems in other languages that have few resources or tools. Current research proposed three main strategies:

1. Translate test sentences in the target language into the source language and classify them using a source language classifier.
2. Translate a source language training corpus into the target language and build a corpus-based classifier in the target language.
3. Translate a sentiment or subjectivity lexicon in the source language to the target language and build a lexicon-based classifier in the target language.

Kim and Hovy (2006) experimented with strategy 1, translating German e-mails to English and applying English sentiment words to determine sentiment orientation, and with strategy 3, translating English sentiment words into German sentiment words and analyzing German e-mails using German sentiment words. Mihalcea et al. (2007) also experimented with translating English subjectivity words and phrases into the target language. They actually tried two translation strategies for cross-language subjectivity classification. Firstly, they derived a subjectivity lexicon for the target language (in their case, Romanian) using an English subjectivity lexicon through translation. A rule-based subjectivity classifier similar to that in Riloff and Wiebe (2003) was then applied to classify Romanian sentences into subjective and objective classes. The precision was not bad, but the recall was poor. Secondly, they derived a subjectivity-annotated corpus in the target language using a manually translated parallel corpus. They first automatically classified English sentences in the corpus into subjective and objective classes using some existing tools, and then projected the subjectivity class labels to the Romanian sentences in the parallel corpus using the available sentence-level alignment in the parallel corpus. A subjectivity classifier based on supervised learning was then built in Romanian to classify Romanian sentences. In this case, the result was better than the first approach.

In Banea et al. (2008), the authors reported three sets of experiments. Firstly, a labelled corpus in the source language (English) was automatically translated into the target language (Romanian). The subjectivity labels in the source language were then mapped to the translated version in the target language. Secondly, the source language text was automatically labelled for subjectivity and then translated into the target language. In both cases, the translated version with subjectivity labels in the target language was used to train a subjectivity classifier in the target language. Thirdly, the target language was translated into the source language, and then a subjectivity classification tool was used to classify the automatically translated source language text. After classification, the labels were mapped back into the target language. The resulting labelled corpus was then used to train a subjectivity classifier in the target language. The final classification results were quite similar for the three strategies.

Banea et al. (2010) conducted extensive experiments for cross-language sentence-level subjectivity classification by translating from a labelled English corpus to five other languages. Firstly, they showed that using the translated corpus for training worked reasonably well and consistently for all five languages. Combining the translated versions in different languages with the original English version to form a single training corpus can also improve the original English subjectivity classification itself. Secondly, the paper demonstrates that by combining the predictions made by monolingual classifiers using a majority vote, it is possible to generate a high-precision sentence-level subjectivity classifier.

The technique in Bautin et al. (2008) was also to translate documents in the target language into English and use an English lexicon-based method to determine the sentiment orientation for each sentence containing an entity. This technique actually works at the aspect level. The sentiment classification method is similar to that in Hu and Liu (2004).

Kim et al. (2010) introduced a concept called multilingual comparability to evaluate multilingual subjectivity analysis systems. This was defined as the level of agreement in the classification results of a pair of multilingual texts with an identical subjective meaning. Using a parallel corpus, they studied the agreement among the classification results of the source language and the target language using Cohen's kappa. For the target language classification, they tried several existing translation-based cross-language subjectivity classification methods. The results show that classifiers trained on corpora translated from English to the target languages perform well for both subjectivity classification and multilingual comparability.

Lu et al. (2011) tackled a slightly different problem. The paper assumes that there is a certain amount of sentiment-labelled data available for both the source and target languages, and there is also an unlabelled parallel corpus. The method is a maximum entropy-based EM algorithm that jointly learns two monolingual sentiment classifiers by treating the sentiment labels in the unlabelled parallel text as unobserved latent variables and maximizing the regularized joint likelihood of the language-specific labelled data together with the inferred sentiment labels of the parallel text. In learning, it exploits the intuition that two sentences or documents that are parallel (i.e., translations of each another) should exhibit the same sentiment. Their method can thus simultaneously improve sentiment classification for both languages.

4.8 USING DISCOURSE INFORMATION FOR SENTIMENT CLASSIFICATION

Most existing work on both document-level and sentence-level sentiment classification does not use the discourse information either among sentences or among clauses in the same sentence. However, in many cases, such analysis is necessary. For example, in the segment

"I'm not tryna be funny, but I'm scared for this country. Romney is winning."

if there is no intersentential discourse analysis, we will not be able to find out that the author is negative about *Romney*. Current research on discourse analysis is still primitive and cannot handle this kind of case.

Sentiment annotation at the discourse level was studied in Asher et al. (2008) and Somasundaran et al. (2008). Asher et al. (2008) used five types of rhetorical relations: *contrast, correction, support, result* and *continuation,* with attached sentiment information for annotation. Somasundaran et al. (2008) proposed a concept called *opinion frames*. The components of opinion frames are opinions and the relationships with their targets.

In Somasundaran et al. (2009), the authors performed sentiment classification based on the opinion frame annotation using the *collective classification* algorithm in Bilgic et al. (2007). Collective classification performs classification on a graph, in which the nodes are sentences (or other expressions) that need to be classified and the links are relations. In the discourse context, they are sentiment-related discourse relations. These relations can be used to generate a set of relational features for learning. Each node itself also generates a set of local features. The relational features allow the classification of one node to affect the classification of other nodes in the collective classification scheme. In Zhou et al. (2011), the discourse information within a single compound sentence was used to perform sentiment classification of the sentence. For example, the sentence *"Although Fujimori was criticized by the international community, he was loved by the domestic population because people hated the corrupted ruling class"* is a positive sentence, although it has more negative opinion words (see also Section 4.8). This paper used pattern mining to find discourse patterns for classification.

In Zirn et al. (2011), the authors proposed a method to classify discourse segments. Each segment expresses a single (positive or negative) opinion. Markov logic networks were used for classification, which not only can utilize a sentiment lexicon but also the local/neighbouring discourse context.

4.9 EMOTION CLASSIFICATION OF SENTENCES

Like emotion classification at the document level, sentence-level emotion classification is also considerably harder than sentence-level sentiment classification. The classification accuracy of most published works is less than 50% due to many more classes and similarity or relatedness of different emotion types. Emotions are highly subjective, too, which makes it difficult to even manually label them in sentences. Like sentence-level sentiment classification, both supervised learning and lexicon-based approaches have been applied to emotion classification. We discuss some existing works using supervised learning first.

Alm et al. (2005) classified the emotional affinity of sentences in the narrative domain of children's fairy tales using supervised learning. The classification method used was a variation of the Winnow algorithm. The features are not the traditional word n-grams but fourteen groups of Boolean features about each sentence and its context in the document. The classes are only two: neutral and emotional. Additional work was reported in Alm (2008), which used individual types of emotion as class labels. The work in Aman and Szpakowicz (2007) also classifies at the sentence level using only two classes. It experimented with sentiment words, emotional words, and all words as features. It showed that using all words as features gives the best results with SVM.

In Mohammad (2012), a Twitter data set was annotated with emotion types based on emotion word hashtags in Twitter posts and performed classification using SVM with binary features that capture the presence or absence of unigrams and bigrams. In Chaffar and Inkpen (2011), a few classification methods (i.e., decision trees, naïve Bayes, and SVM) were compared on several document-level and sentence-level classification data sets. It was shown that SVM performed consistently better.

In the lexicon-based approach, Yang et al. (2007) first constructed an emotion lexicon and then performed emotion classification at the sentence level using the lexicon. For constructing the emotion lexicon, the proposed algorithm uses only sentences with a single user-provided emoticon. For a word, it computes a collocation (or association) strength of the word with each emoticon using a measure similar to pointwise mutual information (PMI). Those top-scored words are very likely to indicate different types of emotion. For emotion classification of sentences, it experimented with two approaches. The first approach is similar to the lexicon-based approach to sentiment classification. For each sentence, the algorithm uses the emoticon collocation strength scores of the words in the sentence and several voting strategies to decide on the emotion type of the sentence. The second approach uses supervised learning with SVM. The features are only the top k emotion words. The results showed that SVM performed better.

A related method is reported in Liu et al. (2003), which proposed a more sophisticated lexicon-based method. The algorithm first uses a small lexicon of emotion words for six emotion types (viz. *happy*, *sad*, *anger*, *fear*, *disgust*, and *surprise*; from Ekman, 1993) to extract sentences from a commonsense knowledge base called

Open Mind Common Sense (OMCS) (Singh, 2002). The lexicon words and their emotion values in the sentences are then propagated to other related words in the sentences based on some commonsense relation rules. The expanded lexicon and the emotion values of its emotion words are then used with a set of rules (called models in the paper) to classify emotions.

Earlier work in Zhe and Boucouvalas (2002) used a lexicon-based method as well, with a set of accompanied rules for special handling of different types of language constructs and different types of sentences. Yet another similar approach was taken in Neviarouskaya et al. (2009), which used a set of more fine-grained rules to handle constructs at various grammatical levels. Specifically, it followed the compositionality principle and developed a rule-based algorithm for emotion classification. At the individual word level, the algorithm uses an emotion lexicon and a list of emotion-indicating items such as emoticons, abbreviations, acronyms, interjections, question and exclamation marks, repeated punctuations, and capital letters. At the phrase level, rules were designed to deal with emotions expressed in adjective phrases, noun phrases and verb plus adverbial phrases, verb plus noun phrases, and verb plus adjective phrases. At the sentence level, rules are designed to deal with sentence clues indicating no emotions, such as those involving think, believe, may and conditional statements. To classify a sentence into an emotion type, another set of rules was applied to aggregate the emotion scores from the components of the sentence following certain precedence. This technique gave good accuracy in classification of emotions expressed in sentences extracted from blog posts.

4.10 DISCUSSION

Sentence-level subjectivity classification, sentiment classification, and emotion classification go further than document-level classification as they move closer to opinion targets and sentiments about the targets. However, because they are still not concerned with opinion targets, there are several shortcomings for real-life applications, as we mentioned earlier:

- In most applications, the user needs to know what the opinions are about, that is, what entities or aspects of entities are liked and disliked. As at the document level, the sentence-level analysis also does not identify entities and their aspects and opinions about them, which are key to applications.

- Although we might say that if we know the opinion targets (e.g., entities and aspects, or topics), we can simply assign the sentiment orientation of the sentence to the targets in the sentence. However, this is problematic, as we discussed in Section 4.4.1. Sentence-level classification is only suitable for simple sentences with a single opinion in each sentence. It is not applicable to compound and complex sentences such as *"Trying out Chrome because Firefox keeps crashing"* and *"Apple is doing very well in this poor economy"* because in these sentences, the opinions are different for different targets. Even for sentences with a single overall tone, different parts of the sentence can still express different opinions. For example, the sentence *"Despite the high unemployment rate, the economy is doing well "* has an overall positive tone, but it does not have a positive opinion about the *unemployment rate*.

- Sentence-level classification cannot deal with opinions or sentiment in comparative sentences, for example, "*Coke tastes better than Pepsi.*" Although this sentence clearly expresses an opinion, we cannot simply classify the sentence as being positive, negative or neutral. We need different methods to deal with them as they have quite different semantic meanings from regular opinions.

Notes

[1]   http://www.thefreedictionary.com/.

4.11 REFERENCES

1.   Abdul-Mageed, M., Diab, M.T. and Korayem, M. (2011). Subjectivity and sentiment analysis of modern standard Arabic. In *Proceedings of the 49th Annual Meeting of the Association for Computational Linguistics: Human Language Technologies: short papers-Volume 2*. Association for Computational Linguistics, pp. 587-591.

2.   Alm, C.O., Roth, D. and Sproat, R. (2005). Emotions from text: machine learning for text-based emotion prediction. In *Proceedings of the conference on human language technology and empirical methods in natural language processing*. Association for Computational Linguistics, pp. 579-586.

3.   Alm, E.C.O. (2008). *Affect in Text and Speech*. ProQuest.

4.   Aman, S. and Szpakowicz, S. (2007). Identifying expressions of emotion in text. In A. Horak, I. Kopecek and K. Pala, *Text, Speech and Dialogue*, pp. 196-205. Springer Berlin Heidelberg.

5.   Asher, N., Benamara, F. and Mathieu, Y.Y. (2008). Categorizing Opinion in Discourse. In *ECAI*, pp. 835-836.

6.   Banea, C., Mihalcea, R. and Wiebe, J. (2010). Multilingual subjectivity: Are more languages better? In *Proceedings of the 23rd international conference on computational linguistics*. Association for Computational Linguistics, pp. 28-36.

7.   Banea, C., Mihalcea, R., Wiebe, J. and Hassan, S. (2008). Multilingual subjectivity analysis using machine translation. In *Proceedings of the Conference on Empirical Methods in Natural Language Processing*. Association for Computational Linguistics, pp. 127-135.

8.   Barbosa, L. and Feng, J. (2010). Robust sentiment detection on twitter from biased and noisy data. In *Proceedings of the 23rd International Conference on Computational Linguistics: Posters*. Association for Computational Linguistics, pp. 36-44.

9. Bautin, M., Vijayarenu, L. and Skiena, S. (2008). International Sentiment Analysis for News and Blogs. In *ICWSM*.

10. Benamara, F., Chardon, B., Mathieu, Y.Y. and Popescu, V. (2011). Towards Context-Based Subjectivity Analysis. In *IJCNLP,* pp. 1180-1188.

11. Bilgic, M., Namata, G.M. and Getoor, L. (2007). Combining collective classification and link prediction. In *Seventh IEEE International Conference on Data Mining Workshops*. IEEE, pp. 381-386.

12. Chaffar, S. and Inkpen, D. (2011). Using a heterogeneous dataset for emotion analysis in text. In *Advances in Artificial Intelligence*. Springer Berlin Heidelberg, pp. 62-67.

13. Chung, C. and Pennebaker, J.W. (2007). The psychological functions of function words. *Social communication*, pp.343-359.

14. Davidov, D., Tsur, O. and Rappoport, A. (2010). Enhanced sentiment learning using twitter hashtags and smileys. In *Proceedings of the 23rd international conference on computational linguistics: posters*. Association for Computational Linguistics, pp. 241-249.

15. Ding, X., Liu, B. and Yu, P.S. (2008). A holistic lexicon-based approach to opinion mining. In *Proceedings of the 2008 International Conference on Web Search and Data Mining*. ACM, pp. 231-240.

16. Ekman, P. (1993). Facial expression and emotion. *American psychologist*, *48*(4), pp. 384.

17. Gamon, M. and Aue, A. (2005). Automatic identification of sentiment vocabulary: exploiting low association with known sentiment terms. In *Proceedings of the ACL Workshop on Feature Engineering for Machine Learning in Natural Language Processing*. Association for Computational Linguistics, pp. 57-64.

18. Ganter, V. and Strube, M. (2009). Finding hedges by chasing weasels: Hedge detection using Wikipedia tags and shallow linguistic features. In *Proceedings of the ACL-IJCNLP 2009 Conference Short Papers*. Association for Computational Linguistics, pp. 173-176.

19. Gibbs, R.W. (1986). On the psycholinguistics of sarcasm. *Journal of Experimental Psychology: General*, *115*(1), pp. 3.

20. Gibbs, R.W. and Colston, H.L. (2007). *Irony in Language and Thought: A Cognitive Science Reader*. Psychology Press.

21. González-Ibánez, R., Muresan, S. and Wacholder, N. (2011). Identifying sarcasm in Twitter: a closer look. In *Proceedings of the 49th Annual Meeting of the Association for Computational Linguistics: Human Language Technologies: short papers, Vol. 2.* Association for Computational Linguistics, pp. 581-586.

22. Greene, S. and Resnik, P. (2009). More than words: Syntactic packaging and implicit sentiment. In *Proceedings of human language technologies: The 2009 annual conference of the North American chapter of the association for computational linguistics*. Association for Computational Linguistics, pp. 503-511.

23. Hardisty, D.J., Johnson, E.J. and Weber, E.U. (2010) A dirty word or a dirty world? Attribute framing, political affiliation, and query theory. *Psychological Science, 21*(1), pp. 86-92.

24. Hassan, A., Qazvinian, V. and Radev, D. (2010). What's with the attitude?: identifying sentences with attitude in online discussions. In *Proceedings of the 2010 Conference on Empirical Methods in Natural Language Processing*. Association for Computational Linguistics, pp. 1245-1255.

25. Hatzivassiloglou, V. and McKeown, K.R. (1997). Predicting the semantic orientation of adjectives. In *Proceedings of the 35th annual meeting of the association for computational linguistics and eighth conference of the European chapter of the association for computational linguistics*. Association for Computational Linguistics, pp. 174-181.

26. Hatzivassiloglou, V. and Wiebe, J.M. (2000). Effects of adjective orientation and gradability on sentence subjectivity. In *Proceedings of the 18th conference on Computational linguistics, Vol. 1*. Association for Computational Linguistics, pp. 299-305.

27. Hatzivassiloglou, V., Klavans, J.L., Holcombe, M.L., Barzilay, R., Kan, M.Y. and McKeown, K. (2001). Simfinder: A flexible clustering tool for summarization.

28. Hu, M. and Liu, B. (2004). Mining and summarizing customer reviews. In *Proceedings of the tenth ACM SIGKDD international conference on Knowledge discovery and data mining*. ACM, pp. 168-177.

29. Hu, X., Tang, L., Tang, J. and Liu, H. (2013). Exploiting social relations for sentiment analysis in microblogging. In *Proceedings of the sixth ACM international conference on Web search and data mining*. ACM, pp. 537-546.

30. Kim, S.M. and Hovy, E. (2004). Determining the sentiment of opinions. In *Proceedings of the 20th international conference on Computational Linguistics*. Association for Computational Linguistics, pp. 1367.

31. Kim, S.M. and Hovy, E. (2006). Extracting opinions, opinion holders, and topics expressed in online news media text. In *Proceedings of the Workshop on Sentiment and Subjectivity in Text*. Association for Computational Linguistics, pp. 1-8.

32. Kim, S.M. and Hovy, E.H. (2007). Crystal: Analyzing Predictive Opinions on the Web. In *EMNLP-CoNLL,* pp. 1056-1064.

33. Kim, Y.M., Amini, M.R., Goutte, C. and Gallinari, P. (2010). Multi-view clustering of multilingual documents. In *Proceedings of the 33rd international ACM SIGIR conference on Research and development in information retrieval*. ACM, pp. 821-822.

34. Kreuz, R.J. and Glucksberg, S. (1989). How to be sarcastic: The echoic reminder theory of verbal irony. *Journal of Experimental Psychology: General, 118*(4), pp. 374.

35. Kreuz, R.J. and Caucci, G.M. (2007). Lexical influences on the perception of sarcasm. In *Proceedings of the Workshop on computational approaches to Figurative Language*. Association for Computational Linguistics, pp. 1-4.

36. Lafferty, J., McCallum, A. and Pereira, F.C. (2001). Conditional random fields: Probabilistic models for segmenting and labeling sequence data.

37. Lin, D. (1998). Automatic retrieval and clustering of similar words. In *Proceedings of the 17th international conference on Computational linguistics, Vol. 2*. Association for Computational Linguistics, pp. 768-774.

38. Lin, W.H., Wilson, T., Wiebe, J. and Hauptmann, A. (2006). Which side are you on?: identifying perspectives at the document and sentence levels. In *Proceedings of the Tenth Conference on Computational Natural Language Learning*. Association for Computational Linguistics, pp. 109-116.

39. Liu, H. (2003). Unpacking meaning from words: A context-centered approach to computational lexicon design. In P. Brézillon and M. Cavalcanti, *Modeling and Using Context*, pp. 218-232. Springer Berlin Heidelberg.

40. Liu, B. (2010). Sentiment Analysis and Subjectivity. In R. Dale, H. Moisl and H. Somers, eds., *Handbook of natural language processing, 2*, pp.627-666. CRC Press.

41. Liu, B. (2011). Opinion mining and sentiment analysis. In *Web Data Mining*, pp. 459-526. Springer Berlin Heidelberg.

42. Lu, B., Tan, C., Cardie, C. and Tsou, B.K. (2011). Joint bilingual sentiment classification with unlabeled parallel corpora. In *Proceedings of the 49th Annual Meeting of the Association for Computational Linguistics: Human Language Technologies, Vol. 1*. Association for Computational Linguistics, pp. 320-330.

43. McDonald, R., Hannan, K., Neylon, T., Wells, M. and Reynar, J. (2007). Structured models for fine-to-coarse sentiment analysis. In *Annual Meeting-Association For Computational Linguistics, Vol. 45(1)*, pp. 432.

44. Medlock, B. and Briscoe, T. (2007). Weakly supervised learning for hedge classification in scientific literature. In *ACL*, pp. 992-999.

45. Mihalcea, R., Banea, C. and Wiebe, J.M. (2007). Learning multilingual subjective language via cross-lingual projections.

46. Mohammad, S.M. (2012). # Emotional tweets. In *Proceedings of the First Joint Conference on Lexical and Computational Semantics, Vol. 1: Proceedings of the main conference and the shared task, Vol. 2: Proceedings of the Sixth International Workshop on Semantic Evaluation*. Association for Computational Linguistics, pp. 246-255.

47. Mukherjee, A. and Liu, B. (2012). Aspect extraction through semi-supervised modeling. In *Proceedings of the 50th Annual Meeting of the Association for Computational Linguistics: Long Papers, Vol. 1*. Association for Computational Linguistics, pp. 339-348.

48. Mukund, S. and Srihari, R.K. (2010). A vector space model for subjectivity classification in Urdu aided by co-training. In *Proceedings of the 23rd International Conference on Computational Linguistics: Posters*. Association for Computational Linguistics, pp. 860-868.

49. Murakami, A. and Raymond, R. (2010). Support or oppose?: classifying positions in online debates from reply activities and opinion expressions. In *Proceedings of the 23rd International Conference on Computational Linguistics: Posters*. Association for Computational Linguistics, pp. 869-875.

50. Nalisnick, E.T. and Baird, H.S. (2013). Extracting Sentiment Networks from Shakespeare's Plays. In *12th International Conference on Document Analysis and Recognition*. IEEE, pp. 758-762.

51. Narayanan, R., Liu, B. and Choudhary, A. (2009). Sentiment analysis of conditional sentences. In *Proceedings of the 2009 Conference on Empirical Methods in Natural Language Processing, Vol. 1*. Association for Computational Linguistics, pp. 180-189.

52. Neviarouskaya, A., Prendinger, H. and Ishizuka, M. (2009). Sentiful: Generating a reliable lexicon for sentiment analysis. In *3rd International Conference on Affective Computing and Intelligent Interaction and Workshops*. IEEE, pp. 1-6.

53. Neviarouskaya, A., Prendinger, H. and Ishizuka, M. (2010). Recognition of affect, judgment, and appreciation in text. In *Proceedings of the 23rd international conference on computational linguistics*. Association for Computational Linguistics, pp. 806-814.

54. Nigam, K., McCallum, A.K., Thrun, S. and Mitchell, T. (2000). Text classification from labeled and unlabeled documents using EM. *Machine learning, 39*(2-3), pp. 103-134.

55. Nigam, K. and Hurst, M. (2004). Towards a robust metric of opinion. In *AAAI spring symposium on exploring attitude and affect in text*, pp. 598-603.

56. Pang, B. and Lee, L. (2004). A sentimental education: Sentiment analysis using subjectivity summarization based on minimum cuts. In *Proceedings of the 42nd annual meeting on Association for Computational Linguistics*. Association for Computational Linguistics, pp. 271.

57. Pang, B. and Lee, L. (2005). Seeing stars: Exploiting class relationships for sentiment categorization with respect to rating scales. In *Proceedings of the 43rd Annual Meeting on Association for Computational Linguistics*. Association for Computational Linguistics, pp. 115-124.

58. Raaijmakers, S. and Kraaij, W. (2008). A shallow approach to subjectivity classification. In *ICWSM*.

59. Raaijmakers, S., Truong, K. and Wilson, T. (2008). Multimodal subjectivity analysis of multiparty conversation. In *Proceedings of the Conference on Empirical Methods in Natural Language Processing*. Association for Computational Linguistics, pp. 466-474.

60. Riloff, E. (1996). Automatically generating extraction patterns from untagged text. In *Proceedings of the national conference on artificial intelligence,* pp. 1044-1049.

61. Riloff, E. and Wiebe, J. (2003). Learning extraction patterns for subjective expressions. In *Proceedings of the 2003 conference on Empirical methods in natural language processing*. Association for Computational Linguistics, pp. 105-112.

62. Riloff, E., Patwardhan, S. and Wiebe, J. (2006). Feature subsumption for opinion analysis. In *Proceedings of the 2006 Conference on Empirical Methods in Natural Language Processing*. Association for Computational Linguistics, pp. 440-448.

63. Riloff, E., Qadir, A., Surve, P., De Silva, L., Gilbert, N. and Huang, R. (2013). Sarcasm as Contrast between a Positive Sentiment and Negative Situation. In *EMNLP*, pp. 704-714.

64. Rosas, V.P., Mihalcea, R. and Morency, L.P. (2013). Multimodal sentiment analysis of Spanish online videos. *IEEE Intelligent Systems, (3),* pp. 38-45.

65. Schapire, R.E. and Singer, Y. (2000). BoosTexter: A boosting-based system for text categorization. *Machine learning, 39*(2), pp. 135-168.

66. Scheible, C. and Schütze, H. (2013). Sentiment Relevance. In *ACL (1),* pp. 954-963.

67. Singh, P., Lin, T., Mueller, E.T., Lim, G., Perkins, T. and Zhu, W.L. (2002). Open Mind Common Sense: Knowledge acquisition from the general public. In *On the move to meaningful internet systems 2002: Coopis, doa, and odbase*. Springer Berlin Heidelberg, pp. 1223-1237.

68. Socher, R., Perelygin, A., Wu, J.Y., Chuang, J., Manning, C.D., Ng, A.Y. and Potts, C. (2013). Recursive deep models for semantic compositionality over a sentiment treebank. In *Proceedings of the conference on empirical methods in natural language processing, Vol. 1631*, pp. 1642.

69. Somasundaran, S. and Wiebe, J. (2009). Recognizing stances in online debates. In *Proceedings of the Joint Conference of the 47th Annual Meeting of the ACL and the 4th International Joint Conference on Natural Language Processing of the AFNLP, Vol. 1*. Association for Computational Linguistics, pp. 226-234.

70. Somasundaran, S., Ruppenhofer, J. and Wiebe, J. (2008). Discourse level opinion relations: An annotation study. In *Proceedings of the 9th SIGdial Workshop on Discourse and Dialogue*. Association for Computational Linguistics, pp. 129-137.

71. Somasundaran, S., Namata, G., Wiebe, J. and Getoor, L. (2009). Supervised and unsupervised methods in employing discourse relations for improving opinion polarity classification. In *Proceedings of the 2009 Conference on Empirical Methods in Natural Language Processing, Vol. 1*. Association for Computational Linguistics, pp. 170-179.

72. Strapparava, C. and Valitutti, A. (2004). WordNet Affect: an Affective Extension of WordNet. In *LREC, Vol. 4*, pp. 1083-1086.

73. Täckström, O. and McDonald, R. (2011)[a]. Discovering fine-grained sentiment with latent variable structured prediction models. In *Advances in Information Retrieval*. Springer Berlin Heidelberg, pp. 368-374.

74. Täckström, O. and McDonald, R. (2011)[b]. Semi-supervised latent variable models for sentence-level sentiment analysis. In *Proceedings of the 49th Annual Meeting of the Association for Computational Linguistics: Human Language Technologies: short papers-Vol. 2*. Association for Computational Linguistics, pp. 569-574.

75. Turney, P.D. (2002). Thumbs up or thumbs down?: semantic orientation applied to unsupervised classification of reviews. In *Proceedings of the 40th annual meeting on association for computational linguistics*. Association for Computational Linguistics, pp. 417-424.

76. Tsur, O., Davidov, D. and Rappoport, A. (2010). A Great Catchy Name: Semi-Supervised Recognition of Sarcastic Sentences in Online Product Reviews. In *ICWSM*.

77. Utsumi, A. (2000). Verbal irony as implicit display of ironic environment: Distinguishing ironic utterances from nonirony. *Journal of Pragmatics*, *32*(12), pp. 1777-1806.

78. Volkova, S., Wilson, T. and Yarowsky, D. (2013). Exploring Demographic Language Variations to Improve Multilingual Sentiment Analysis in Social Media. In *EMNLP*, pp. 1815-1827.

79. Wiebe, J.M., Bruce, R.F. and O'Hara, T.P. (1999). Development and use of a gold-standard data set for subjectivity classifications. In *Proceedings of the 37th annual meeting of the Association for Computational Linguistics on Computational Linguistics*. Association for Computational Linguistics, pp. 246-253.

80. Wiebe, J. (2000). Learning subjective adjectives from corpora. In *AAAI/IAAI*, pp. 735-740.

81. Wiebe, J., Wilson, T., Bruce, R., Bell, M. and Martin, M. (2004). Learning subjective language. *Computational linguistics*, *30*(3), pp. 277-308.

82. Wiebe, J. and Riloff, E. (2005). Creating subjective and objective sentence classifiers from unannotated texts. In *Computational Linguistics and Intelligent Text Processing*. Springer Berlin Heidelberg, pp. 486-497.

83. Wilson, T., Wiebe, J. and Hwa, R. (2004). Just how mad are you? Finding strong and weak opinion clauses. In *AAAI, Vol. 4,* pp. 761-769.

84. Wilson, T., Wiebe, J. and Hwa, R. (2006). Recognizing strong and weak opinion clauses. *Computational Intelligence, 22*(2), pp. 73-99.

85. Wilson, T. and Raaijmakers, S. (2008). Comparing word, character, and phoneme n-grams for subjective utterance recognition. In *INTERSPEECH,* pp. 1614-1617.

86. Yang, C., Lin, K.H.Y. and Chen, H.H. (2007). Building emotion lexicon from weblog corpora. In *Proceedings of the 45th Annual Meeting of the ACL on Interactive Poster and Demonstration Session.* Association for Computational Linguistics, pp. 133-136.

87. Yu, H. and Hatzivassiloglou, V. (2003). Towards answering opinion questions: Separating facts from opinions and identifying the polarity of opinion sentences. In *Proceedings of the 2003 conference on Empirical methods in natural language processing.* Association for Computational Linguistics, pp. 129-136.

88. Zhang, L. and Liu, B. (2011) [b]. Identifying noun product features that imply opinions. In *Proceedings of the 49th Annual Meeting of the Association for Computational Linguistics: Human Language Technologies: short papers-Vol. 2.* Association for Computational Linguistics, pp. 575-580.

89. Zhe, X. and Boucouvalas, A.C. (2002). Text-to-emotion engine for real time internet communication. In *Proceedings of International Symposium on Communication Systems, Networks and DSPs,* pp. 164-168.

90. Zhou, L., Li, B., Gao, W., Wei, Z. and Wong, K.F. (2011). Unsupervised discovery of discourse relations for eliminating intra-sentence polarity ambiguities. In *Proceedings of the Conference on Empirical Methods in Natural Language Processing.* Association for Computational Linguistics, pp. 162-171.

91. Zirn, C., Niepert, M., Stuckenschmidt, H. and Strube, M. (2011). Fine-Grained Sentiment Analysis with Structural Features. In *IJCNLP,* pp. 336-344.

PART II

Online Search and Social Media Sources

Twitter Sentiment Analysis: Lexicon Method, Machine Learning Method and their Combination

Olga Kolchyna, *PhD Researcher, UCL*

Thársis T. P. Souza, *PhD Researcher, UCL*

Philip C. Treleaven, *Professor of Computer Science, UCL*

Tomaso Aste, *Professor of Complexity Science, UCL*

ABSTRACT

This chapter covers the two approaches for sentiment analysis: i) lexicon based method; machine learning method. We describe several techniques to implement these approaches and discuss how they can be adopted for sentiment classification of Twitter messages. We present a comparative study of different lexicon combinations and show that enhancing sentiment lexicons with emoticons, abbreviations and social-media slang expressions increases the accuracy of lexicon-based classification for Twitter. We discuss the importance of feature generation and feature selection processes for machine learning sentiment classification. To quantify the performance of the main sentiment analysis methods over Twitter we run these algorithms on a benchmark Twitter dataset from the SemEval-2013 competition, task 2-B. The results show that a machine learning method based on SVM and Naive Bayes classifiers outperforms the lexicon method. We present a new ensemble method that uses a lexicon-based sentiment score as input feature for the machine learning approach. The combined method proved to produce more precise classifications. We also show that employing a cost-sensitive classifier for highly unbalanced datasets yields an improvement in sentiment classification performance of up to 7%.

5.1   INTRODUCTION

Sentiment analysis is an area of research that investigates people's opinions towards different matters: products, events, organisations (Bing, 2012). The role of sentiment analysis has been growing significantly with the rapid spread of social networks, microblogging applications and forums. Today, almost every web page has a section for the users to leave their comments about products or services, and share them with friends on Facebook, Twitter or Pinterest – something that was not possible just a few years ago. Mining this volume of opinions provides information for understanding collective human behaviour and it is of valuable commercial interest. For instance, an increasing amount of evidence points out that by analysing sentiment of social-media content it might be possible to predict the size of the markets (Bollen et al., 2011) or unemployment rates over time (Antenucci et al., 2014).

One of the most popular microblogging platforms is Twitter. It has been growing steadily for the last several years and has become a meeting point for a diverse range of people: students, professionals, celebrities, companies and politicians. This popularity of Twitter results in an enormous amount of information being passed through the service, covering a wide range of topics, from people's well-being to opinions about brands, products, politicians and social events. In this context, Twitter becomes a powerful tool for predictions. For example, Asur and Huberman (2010) was able to predict from Twitter analytics the ticket sales at the opening weekend for movies with 97.3% accuracy, higher than the one achieved by the Hollywood Stock Exchange, a known prediction tool for the movies.

In this chapter, we present a step-by-step approach for two main methods of sentiment analysis: the lexicon-based approach (Taboada et al., 2011; Ding et al., 2008) and the machine learning approach (Pak and Paroubek, 2010). We show that the accuracy of sentiment analysis for Twitter can be improved by combining the two approaches: during the first stage a lexicon score is calculated based on the polarity of the words that compose the text; during the second stage a machine learning model is learnt that uses the lexicon score as one of its features. The results showed that the combined approach outperforms the two approaches. We demonstrate the use of our algorithm on a dataset from a popular Twitter sentiment competition SemEval-2013, task 2-B (Nakov et al., 2013). In Chapter 24 of this book our algorithm for sentiment analysis is also successfully applied to 42,803,225 Twitter messages related to companies from the retail sector to predict stock price movements.

5.2   SENTIMENT ANALYSIS METHODOLOGY: BACKGROUND

The field of text categorization was founded a long time ago (Salton and McGill, 1983), but categorization based on sentiment was introduced more recently in (Das and Chen, 2001; Morinaga et al., 2002; Pang et al., 2002; Tong, 2001; Turney, 2002; Wiebe, 2000).

The standard approach for text representation (Salton and McGill, 1983) has been the bag-of-words method (BOW). According to the BOW model, the document is represented as a vector of words in Euclidian space where each word is independent from others. This bag of individual words is commonly called a collection of unigrams. The BOW is easy to understand and can achieve high performance (for example, the best results of multi-label categorization for the Reuters-21578 dataset were produced using the BOW approach (Dumais et al., 1998; Weiss et al., 1999)).

The main two methods of sentiment analysis, the lexicon-based method (unsupervised approach) and machine learning based method (supervised approach), both rely on the bag-of-words. In the machine learning supervised method, the classifiers use unigrams or their combinations (N-grams) as features. In the lexicon-based method, the unigrams found in the lexicon are assigned a polarity score, and the overall polarity score of the text is then computed as the sum of the polarities of the unigrams.

When deciding which lexicon elements of a message should be considered for sentiment analysis, different parts-of-speech were analysed (Pak and Paroubek, 2010; Kouloumpis et al., 2011). Benamara et al. (2007) proposed the Adverb-Adjective Combinations (AACs) approach that demonstrates the use of adverbs and adjectives to detect sentiment polarity. In recent years, the role of emoticons has been investigated (Pozzi et al., 2013a; Hogenboom et al., 2013; Liu et al., 2012; Zhao et al., 2012). In their recent study, Fersini et al. (2016) further explored the use of (i) adjectives, (ii) emoticons, emphatic and onomatopoeic expressions, and (iii) expressive lengthening as expressive signals in sentiment analysis of microblogs. They showed that the above signals can enrich the feature space and improve the quality of sentiment classification.

Advanced algorithms for sentiment analysis have been developed (see Jacobs, 1992; Vapnik, 1998; Basili et al., 2000; Schapire and Singer, 2000) to take into consideration not only the message itself, but also the context in which the message is published, who is the author of the message, who are the friends of the author, what is the underlying structure of the network. For instance, Hu et al. (2013) investigated how social relations can help sentiment analysis by introducing a Sociological Approach to handling Noisy and short Texts (SANT), Zhu et al. (2014) showed that the quality of sentiment clustering for Twitter can be improved by joint clustering of tweets, users and features. In the work by Pozzi et al. (2013b) the authors looked at friendship connections and estimated user polarities about a given topic by integrating post contents with approval relations. You and Luo (2013) improved sentiment classification accuracy by adding a visual content in addition to the textual information. Aisopos et al. (2012) significantly increased the accuracy of sentiment classification by using content-based features along with context-based features. Saiff et al. (2012) achieved improvements by growing the feature space with semantics features.

While many research works focused on finding the best features, some efforts have been made to explore new methods for sentiment classification. Wang et al. evaluated the performance of ensemble methods (Bagging, Boosting, Random Subspace) and empirically proved that ensemble models can produce better results than the base learners (Wang et al., 2014). Fersini et al. (2014) proposed using the Bayesian Model Averaging ensemble method, which outperformed both traditional classification and ensemble methods. Carvalho et al. (2014) employed genetic algorithms to find subsets of words from a set of paradigm words that led to improvement of classification accuracy.

5.3   DATA PRE-PROCESSING FOR SENTIMENT ANALYSIS

Before applying any of the sentiment extraction methods, it is a common practice to perform data pre-processing. Data pre-processing produces a higher quality of text classification and reduces computational complexity. A typical pre-processing procedure includes the following steps:

Part-of-Speech Tagging (POS). The process of part-of-speech tagging allows the automatic tagging of each word in the text in terms of which part of speech it belongs to: noun, pronoun, adverb, adjective, verb, interjection, intensifier, etc. The goal is to extract patterns in the text based on analysis of the frequency distributions of these part-of-speech. The importance of part-of-speech tagging for correct sentiment analysis was demonstrated by Manning and Schütze (1999). The statistical properties of texts, such as adherence to Zipf's law, can also be used (Piantadosi, 2014). Pak and Paroubek (2010) analysed the distribution of POS tagging specifically for Twitter messages and identified multiple patterns. For instance, they found that subjective texts (carrying the sentiment) often contain more pronouns, rather than common and proper nouns; subjective messages often use past simple tense and contain many verbs in a base form and many modal verbs. There is no common opinion about whether POS tagging improves the results of sentiment classification. Barbosa and Feng (2010) reported positive results using POS tagging, while Kouloumpis et al. (2011) reported a decrease in performance.

Stemming and lemmatisation. Stemming is the procedure of replacing words with their stems, or roots. The dimensionality of the BOW is reduced when root-related words, such as "read", "reader" and "reading" are mapped into one word "read". However, one should be careful when applying stemming, since it might increase bias. For example, the biased effect of stemming appears when merging distinct words "experiment" and "experience" into one word "exper", or when words that ought to be merged together (such as "adhere" and "adhesion") remain distinct after stemming. These are examples of over-stemming and under-stemming errors respectively. Over-stemming lowers precision and under-stemming lowers recall. The overall impact of stemming depends on the dataset and stemming algorithm. The most popular stemming algorithm is Porter stemmer (Porter, 1980).

Stop-words removal. Stop words are words that carry a connecting function in a sentence, such as prepositions, articles, etc. (Salton and McGill, 1983). There is no definite list of stop words, but some search machines, are using some of the most common, short function words, such as "the", "is", "at", "which" and "on". These words can be removed from the text before classification since they have a high frequency of occurrence in the text, but do not affect the final sentiment of the sentence.

Negations Handling. Negation refers to the process of conversion of the sentiment of the text from positive to negative or from negative to positive by using special words: *"no","not","don't"* etc. These words are called negations. The example of some negation words is presented in the Table 5.3.1.

Table 5.3.1: *Example Negation Words*

hardly	cannot	shouldn't	doesn't
lack	daren't	wasn't	didn't
lacking	don't	wouldn't	hadn't
lacks	doesn't	weren't	hasn't
neither	didn't	won't	havn't
nor	hadn't	without	haven't

Handling negation in the sentiment analysis task is a very important step as the whole sentiment of the text may be changed by the use of negation. It is important to identify the scope of negation (for more information see Councill et al., 2010). The simplest approach to handle negation is to revert the polarity of all words that are found between the negation and the first punctuation mark following it. For instance, in the text "I don't want to go to the cinema" the polarity of the whole phrase "want to go to the cinema" will be reverted.

Other researchers introduce the concept of the contextual valence shifter (Polanyi and Zaenen, 2006), which consists of negation, intensifier and diminisher. Contextual valence shifters have the impact of flipping the polarity, increasing or decreasing the degree to which a sentimental term is positive or negative.

But-clauses. Phrases like *"but"*, *"with the exception of"*, *"except that"*, *"except for"* generally change the polarity of the part of the sentence following them. In order to handle these clauses, the opinion orientation of the text before and after these phrases should be set opposite to each other. For example, without handling the *"but-type clauses"* the polarity of the sentence may be set as following: *"I don like[-1] this mobile, but the screen has high[0] resolution"*. When "but-clauses" are processed, the sentence polarity will be changed to: "I don't like[-1] this mobile, but the screen has high[+1] resolution". Notice, that even neutral adjectives will obtain the polarity that is opposite to the polarity of the phrase before the "but-clause".

However, the solution described above does not work for every situation. For example, in the sentence "Not only he is smart, but also very kind", the word "but" does not carry contrary meaning and reversing the sentiment score of the second half of the sentence would be incorrect. These situations need to be considered separately.

Tokenisation into N-grams. Tokenisation is a process of creating a bag-of-words from the text. The incoming string gets broken into comprising words and other elements, for example URL links. The common separator for identifying individual words is whitespace, however other symbols can also be used. Tokenisation of social-media data is considerably more difficult than tokenisation of general text since it contains numerous emoticons, URL links and abbreviations that cannot be easily separated as whole entities.

It is a general practice to combine accompanying words into phrases or n-grams, which can be unigrams, bigrams, trigrams, etc. Unigrams are single words, while bigrams are collections of two neighbouring words in a text, and trigrams are collections of three neighbouring words. The n-grams method can decrease bias, but may increase statistical sparseness. It has been shown that the use of n-grams can improve the quality of text classification

(Raskutti et al., 2001; Zhang, 2003; Diederich et al., 2003), however there is no unique solution for the size of an n-gram. Caropreso et al. (2001) conducted an experiment of text categorization on the Reuters-21578 benchmark dataset. They reported that in general the use of bigrams helped to produce better results than the use of unigrams, however while using Rocchio classifier (Rocchio, 1971) the use of bigrams led to a decrease of classification quality in 28 out of 48 experiments. Tan et al. (2002) reported that the use of bigrams on Yahoo-Science dataset improved the performance of text classification using Naive Bayes classifier from 65% to 70% break-even point; however, on Reuters-21578 dataset the increase of accuracy was not significant. Conversely, trigrams were reported to generate poor performances (Pak and Paroubek, 2010).

5.4   SENTIMENT COMPUTATION WITH LEXICON-BASED APPROACH

The lexicon-based approach calculates the sentiment of a given text from the polarity of the words or phrases in that text (Turney, 2002). For this method, a lexicon (dictionary) of words with polarity assigned to them is required. Examples of the existing lexicons include: Opinion Lexicon (Hu and Liu, 2004), SentiWordNet (Esuli and Sebastiani, 2006),

AFINN Lexicon (Nielsen, 2011), LoughranMcDonald Lexicon, NRC-Hashtag (Mohammad et al., 2013), General Inquirer Lexicon[1] (Stone and Hunt, 1963).

The sentiment score *Score* of the text T can be computed as the average of the polarities conveyed by each of the words in the text. The methodology for the sentiment calculation is schematically illustrated in Figure 5.4.1 and can be described with the following steps:

Pre-processing. The text undergoes pre-processing steps that were described in the previous section: POS tagging, stemming, stop-words removal, negation handling, tokenisations into n-grams. The outcome of the pre-processing is a set of tokens or a bag-of-words.

Checking each token for its polarity in the lexicon. Each word from the bag-of-words is compared against the lexicon. If the word is found in the lexicon, the polarity w_i of that word is added to the sentiment score of the text. If the word is not found in the lexicon, its polarity is considered to be equal to zero.

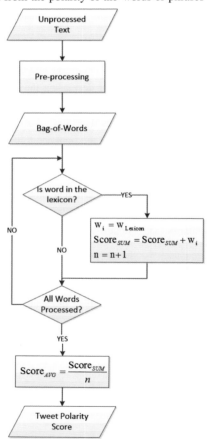

Figure 5.4.1: Schematic representation of methodology for the sentiment calculation

Calculating the sentiment score of the text. After assigning polarity scores to all words comprising the text, the final sentiment score of the text is calculated by dividing the sum of he scores of words caring the sentiment by the number of such words:

$$Score_{AVG} = \frac{1}{m} \sum_{i=1}^{m} W_i. \qquad [5.4.1]$$

The averaging of the score allows to obtain a value of the sentiment score in the range between -1 and 1, where 1 means a strong positive sentiment, -1 means a strong negative sentiment and 0 means that the text is neutral. For example, for the text:

"*A masterful[+0.92] film[0.0] from a master[+1] filmmaker[0.0], unique[+1] in its deceptive[0.0] grimness[0.0], compelling[+1] in its fatalist[-0.84] world[0.0] view[0.0].*"

the sentiment score is calculated as follows:

$$Score_{AVG} = \frac{0.92+0.0+1+0.0+1+0.0+0.0+1-0.84+0.0+0.0}{5} = 0.616.$$

The sentiment score of 0.616 means that the sentence expresses a positive opinion.

The quality of classification highly depends on the quality of the lexicon. Lexicons can be created using different techniques:

Manually constructed lexicons. The straightforward approach, but also the most time-consuming, is to manually construct a lexicon and tag words in it as positive or negative. For example, Das and Chen (2001) constructed their lexicon by reading several thousand messages and manually selecting words that were carrying sentiment. They then used a discriminant function to identify words from a training dataset, which can be used for sentiment classifier purposes. The remained words were "expanded" to include all potential forms of each word into the final lexicon. Another example of hand-tagged lexicon is The Multi-Perspective-Question-Answering (MPQA) Opinion Corpus[2] constructed by Wiebe et al. (2005). MPQA is publicly available and consists of 8,222 subjective expressions along with their POS-tags, polarity classes and intensity.

Another resource is The SentiWordNet created by Esuli and Sebastiani (2006). SentiWordNet extracted words from WordNet[3] and gave them probability of belonging to positive, negative or neutral classes, and subjectivity score. Ohana and Tierney (2009) demonstrated that SentiWordNet can be used as an important resource for sentiment calculation.

Constructing a lexicon from trained data. This approach belongs to the category of the supervised methods, because a training dataset of labelled sentences is needed. With this method the sentences from the training dataset get tokenised and a bag-of-words is created. The words are then filtered to exclude some parts-of-speech that do not carry sentiment, such as prepositions. The prior polarity of words is calculated according to the occurrence of each word in positive and negative sentences. For example, if a word "success" is appearing more often in the sentences labelled as positive in the training dataset, the prior polarity of this word will be assigned a positive value.

Extending a small lexicon using bootstrapping techniques. Hazivassiloglou and McKeown (1997) proposed extending a small lexicon comprising adjectives by adding new adjectives that were conjoined with the words from the original lexicon. The technique is based on the syntactic relationship between two adjectives conjoined with the "AND". It is established that "AND" usually joins words with the same semantic orientation. For example:

"The weather yesterday was nice and inspiring"

Since words "nice" and "inspiring" are conjoined with "AND", it is considered that both of them carry a positive sentiment. If only the word "nice" was present in the lexicon, a new word "inspiring" would be added to the lexicon. Similarly, Hatzivassiloglou and McKeown (1997) and Kim and Hovy (2004) suggested expanding a small manually constructed lexicon with synonyms and antonyms obtained from NLP resources such as WordNet[4]. The process can be repeated iteratively until it is not possible to find new synonyms and antonyms. Moilanen and Pulman (2007) also created their lexicon by semi-automatically expanding the WordNet2.1 lexicon. Other approaches include extracting polar sentences by using structural clues from HTML documents (Kaji and Kitsuregawa, 2007), recognising opinionated text based on the density of other clues in the text (Wiebe and Wilson, 2002). After the application of a bootstrapping technique it is important to conduct a manual inspection of newly added words to avoid errors.

5.5 A MACHINE LEARNING BASED APPROACH

A Machine Learning Approach for text classification is a supervised algorithm that analyses data that were previously labelled as positive, negative or neutral. It extracts features that model the differences between different classes, and infers a function that can be used for classifying new examples unseen before. In the simplified form, the text classification task can be described as follows: given a dataset of labelled data T_{train} = $\{(t_1, l_1), \ldots, (t_n, l_n)\}$, where each text t_i belongs to a dataset T and the label l_i is a pre-set class within the group of classes L, the goal is to build a learning algorithm that receives as an input the training set T_{train} and generates a model that accurately classifies unlabelled texts.

The most popular learning algorithms for text classification are Support Vector Machines (SVMs) (Cortes and Vapnik, 1995; Vapnik, 1995), Naive Bayes (Narayanan et al., 2013); Decision Trees (Mitchell, 1996). Barbosa and Feng (2010) report better results for SVMs while Pak and Paroubek (2010) obtained better results for Naive Bayes. In the work by Dumais et al. (1998) a decision tree classifier was shown to perform nearly as well as an SVM classifier.

In terms of the individual classes, some researchers (Pang et al., 2002) classified texts only as positive or negative, assuming that all the texts carry an opinion. Later Wilson et al. (2005), Pak and Paroubek (2010) and Barbosa and Feng (2010) showed that short messages like tweets and blog comments often just state facts. Therefore, incorporation of the neutral class into the classification process is necessary.

The process of machine learning text classification can be broken into the following steps:

1. **Data Pre-processing.** Before training the classifiers each text needs to be pre-processed and presented as an array of tokens. This step is performed according to the process described in section 5.3.

2. **Feature generation.** Features are text attributes that are useful for capturing patterns in data. The most popular features used in machine learning classification are the presence or the frequency of n-grams extracted during the pre-processing step. In the presence-based representation for each instance, a binary vector is created in which "1" means the presence of a particular n-gram and "0" indicates its absence. In the frequency-based representation, the number of occurrences of a particular n-gram is used instead of a binary indication of presence. In cases where text length varies greatly, it might be important to use term frequency (TF) and inverse term frequency (IDF) measures (Rajaraman and Ullman, 2011). However, in short messages like tweets, words are unlikely to repeat within one instance, making the binary measure of presence as informative as the counts (Ikonomakis et al., 2005).

    Apart from the n-grams, additional features can be created to improve the overall quality of text classification. The most common features that are used for this purpose include:
    *   Number of words with positive/negative sentiment; Number of negations;
    *   Length of a message;
    *   Number of exclamation marks;
    *   Number of different parts-of-speech in a text (for example, number of nouns, adjectives, verbs);
    *   Number of comparative and superlative adjectives.

3. **Feature selection.** Since the main features of a text classifier are n-grams, the dimensionality of the feature space grows proportionally to the size of the dataset. This dramatic growth of the feature space makes it in most cases computationally infeasible to calculate all the features of a sample. Many features are redundant or irrelevant and do not significantly improve the results. Feature selection is the process of identifying a subset of features that have the highest predictive power. This step is crucial for the classification process, since elimination of irrelevant and redundant features reduces the size of the feature space, increasing the speed of the algorithm, avoiding overfitting, and contributing to the improved quality of classification.

    There are three basic steps in feature selection process (Dash and Liu, 1997)
    a. *Search procedure.* A process that generates a subset of features for evaluation. A procedure can start with no variables and add them one by one (forward selection) or with all variables and remove one at each step (backward selection), or features can be selected randomly (random selection).
    b. *Evaluation procedure.* A process of calculating a score for a selected subset of features. The most common metrics for evaluation procedure are: Chi-squared, Information Gain, Odds Ratio, Probability Ratio, Document Frequency, and Term Frequency. An extensive overview of search and evaluation methods is presented in Ladha and Deepa (2011a) and Forman (2003).
    c. *Stopping criterion.* The process of feature selection can be stopped based on: i) a search procedure, if a predefined number of features was selected or predefined number of iterations

was performed; ii) an evaluation procedure, if the change of feature space does not produce a better subset or if an optimal subset was found according to the value of evaluation function.

4. **Learning an Algorithm.** After feature generation and feature selection steps, the text is represented in a form that can be used to train an algorithm. Even though many classifiers have been tested for sentiment analysis purposes, the choice of the best algorithm is still not easy since all methods have their advantages and disadvantages (see Marsland, 2011 for more information on classifiers).

Decision Trees (Mitchell, 1996). A decision tree text classifier is a tree in which non-leaf nodes represent a conditional test on a feature, branches denote the outcomes of the test, and leafs represent class labels. Decision trees can be easily adapted to classifying textual data and have a number of useful qualities: they are relatively transparent, which makes them simple to understand; they give direct information about which features are important in making decisions, which is especially true near the top of the decision tree. However, decision trees also have a few disadvantages. One problem is that trees can easily be overfitted. The reason lies in the fact that each branch in the decision tree splits the training data, thus, the training data available to train nodes located in the bottom of the tree is reduced. This problem can be addressed using tree-pruning. The second weakness of the method is the fact that decision trees require features to be checked in a specific order. This limits the ability of an algorithm to exploit features that are relatively independent of one another.

Naive Bayes (Narayanan et al., 2013) is frequently used for sentiment analysis purposes because of its simplicity and effectiveness. The basic concept of the Naive Bayes classifier is to determine a class (positive, negative, neutral) to which a text belongs using probability theory. In the case of the sentiment analysis, there will be three hypotheses: one for each sentiment class. The hypothesis that has the highest probability will be selected as a class of the text. The potential problem with this approach emerges if some word in the training set appears only in one class and does not appear in any other classes. In this case, the classifier will always classify text to that particular class. To avoid this undesirable effect Laplace smoothing technique may be applied.

Another very popular algorithm is *Support Vector Machines (SVMs)* (Cortes and Vapnik, 1995; Vapnik, 1995). For linearly separable two-class data, the basic idea is to find a hyperplane that not only separates the documents into classes but also for which the Euclidian distance to the closest training example, or margin, is as large as possible. In a three-class sentiment classification scenario, there will be three pair-wise classifications: positive-negative, negative-neutral, positive-neutral. The method has proved to be very successful for the task of text categorisation (Joachims, 1999; Dumais et al., 1998) since it can handle very well large feature spaces. However, it has low interpretability and is very computationally expensive, because it involves calculations of discretisation, normalisation and dot product operations.

5. **Model Evaluation.** After the model is trained using a classifier it should be validated, typically, using a cross-validation technique, and tested on a hold-out dataset. There are several metrics defined in information retrieval for measuring the effectiveness of classification, among them:

    *   *Accuracy*: as described by Kotsiantis (2007), accuracy is "the fraction of the number of correct predictions over the total number of predictions".

- *Error rate*: measures the number of incorrectly predicted instance against the total number of predictions.
- *Precision*: shows the proportion of instances the model classified correctly to the total number of true positive and true negative examples. In other words, precision shows the exactness of the classifier with respect to each class.
- *Recall*: represents the proportion of instances the model classified correctly to the total number of true positives and false negatives. Recall shows the completeness of the classifier with respect to each class.
- *F-score*: Rijsbergen (1979) defined the F1-score as the harmonic mean of precision and recall:

$$F\text{-}Score = \frac{2 * Precision * Recall}{Precision + Recall}.$$ [5.5.1]

Depending on the nature of the task, one may use accuracy, error rate, precision, recall or F-score as a metric, or some mixture of them. For example, for unbalanced datasets, it was shown that precision and recall can be better metrics for measuring classifier performance (Manning and Schütze, 1999). However, sometimes one of these metrics can increase at the expense of the other. For example, in extreme cases, recall can reach 100%, but precision can be very low. In these situations, the F-score may be a more appropriate measure.

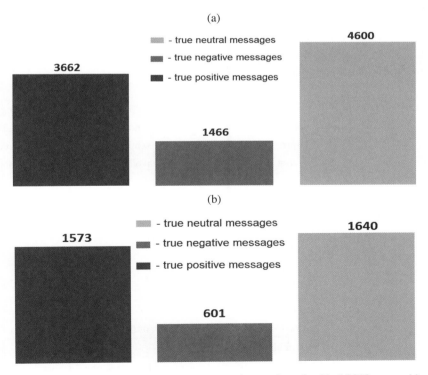

Figure 5.6.1: Statistics of a) training dataset and b) test dataset from SemEval-2013 competition, Task 2-B (Nakov et al., 2013). Dark grey bar on the left represents the proportion of positive tweets in the dataset, grey bar in the middle shows the proportion of negative tweets and light grey bar on the right reflects the proportion of neutral sentences.

5.6   APPLICATION OF LEXICON AND MACHINE LEARNING METHODS FOR TWITTER SENTIMENT CLASSIFICATION

Here we provide an example of the implementation of the lexicon based approach and the machine learning approach on a case study. We use benchmark datasets from SemEval-2013 Competition, Task 2: Sentiment Analysis in Twitter, which included two subtasks: A) an expression-level classification, B) a message-level classification (Nakov et al., 2013). Our interest is in subtask B: "Given a message, decide whether it is of positive, negative, or neutral sentiment. For messages conveying both a positive and a negative sentiment, whichever is the stronger one was to be chosen" (Nakov et al., 2013). After training and evaluating our algorithm on the training and test datasets provided by SemEval-2013, Task-2 (refer to Figure 5.6.1 for statistics on the positive, negative and neutral messages for the training and test datasets), we compare our results against the results of 44 participating teams and 149 submissions.

The second example of an application of our algorithm, to a large dataset of 42,803,225 Twitter messages related to retail companies, is presented in Chapter 24 of this book and investigates the relationship between Twitter sentiment and stock returns and volatility.

5.6.1   Pre-processing

We performed pre-processing steps as described in section 5.3. For the most of the steps we used the machine learning software WEKA[5]. WEKA was developed at the University of Waikato and allows the implementation of many machine learning algorithms. Since it is an open-source tool and has an API, WEKA algorithms can be easily embedded within other applications.

Stemming and lemmatisation. The overall impact of stemming depends on the dataset and stemming algorithm. WEKA contains implementation of a SnowballStemmer (Porter, 2002) and LovinsStemmer (Lovins, 1968). After testing both implementations we discovered that the accuracy of the sentiment classification was reduced after applying both stemming algorithms, so a stemming operation was avoided in the final implementation of the sentiment analysis algorithm.

Stop-words Removal. WEKA provides a file with a list of words, which should be considered as stop-words. The file can be adjusted to one's needs. In our study we used a default WEKA stop-list file.

Table 5.6.1: Example POS tags.

@ Tag	Description
@ at-mentions	Is used to identify the user-recipient of the tweet
U	URL or email address
#	Hashtag to identify the topic of the discussion or a category
~	Discourse marker. Indicates that the message is a continuation of the previous tweet
E	Emoticons, etc.
G	Abbreviations, shortenings of words

Part-of-Speech Tagging (POS). In the current study we tested the performance of multiple existing POS-taggers: Stanford Tagger[6], Illinois Tagger[7], OpenNLP[8], LingPipe POS Tagger[9], Unsupos[10], ArkTweetNLP[11], Berkeley NLP Group Tagger[12]. We finally chose to use the ArkTweetNLP library developed by a team of researchers from Carnegie Mellon University (Gimpel et al., 2011) since it was trained on a Twitter dataset. ArkTweetNLP developed 25 POS tags, with some of them specifically designed for special Twitter symbols, such as hashtags, at-mentions, retweets, emoticons, commonly used abbreviations (see Table 5.6.1 for some tags examples). An example[13] of how ArkTweetNLP tagger works in practice is presented in Table 5.6.2.

Table 5.6.2: Example of ArkTweetNLP (Gimpel et al., 2011) tagger in practice.

Sentence:

ikr smh he asked fir yo last name so he can add u on fb lololol

word tag confidence

ikr ! 0.8143

smh G 0.9406

he O 0.9963

asked V 0.9979

fir P 0.5545

yo D 0.6272

last A 0.9871

name N 0.9998

so P 0.9838

he O 0.9981

can V 0.9997

add V 0.9997

u O 0.9978

on P 0.9426

fb ^ 0.9453

lololol ! 0.9664

"ikr" means "I know, right?", tagged as an interjection.

"so" is being used as a subordinating conjunction, which our coarse tagset denotes P. "fb" means "Facebook", a very common proper noun (^).

"yo" is being used as equivalent to "your"; our coarse tagset has posessive pronouns as D. "fir" is a misspelling or spelling variant of the preposition for.

Perhaps the only debatable errors in this example are for ikr and smh ("shake my head"): should they be G for miscellaneous acronym, or ! for interjection?

As the result of POS-tagging in our study, we filtered out all words that did not belong to one of the following categories: N(common noun), V(verb), A(adjective), R(adverb), !(interjection), E(emoticon), G(abbreviations, foreign words, possessive endings).

Negation Handling. We implemented negation handling using a simple but effective strategy: if a negation word was found, the sentiment score of every word appearing between a negation and a clause-level punctuation mark (.,!?:;) was reversed (Pang et al., 2002). There are, however, some grammatical constructions in which a negation term does not have a scope. Some of these situations we implemented as exceptions:

Exception Situation 1: Whenever a negation term is a part of a phrase that does not carry negation sense, we consider that the scope for negation is absent and the polarity of words is not reversed. Examples of these special phrases include "not only", "not just", "no question", "not to mention" and "no wonder".

Exception Situation 2: A negation term does not have a scope when it occurs in a negative rhetorical question. A negative rhetorical question is identified by the following heuristic: (1) It is a question; and (2) it has a negation term within the first three words of the question. For example:

"Did not I enjoy it?"

"Wouldn't you like going to the cinema?"

Tokenisation into n-grams. We used WEKA tokeniser to extract uni-grams and bi-grams from the Twitter dataset.

5.6.2 Lexicon Approach

Automatic Lexicon Generation. In this study we aimed to create a lexicon specifically oriented for sentiment analysis of Twitter messages. For this purpose we used the approach described in section 5.4: "Constructing a lexicon from trained data" and the training dataset from Mark Hall (Hall, 2012) that comprises 41,403 manually labelled positive Twitter messages and 8552 negative Twitter messages. The method to generate a sentiment lexicon was implemented as follows:

1. Pre-processing of the dataset: POS tags were assigned to all words in the dataset; words were lowered in case; BOW was created by tokenising the sentences in the dataset.
2. The number of occurrences of each word in positive and negative sentences from the training dataset was calculated.
3. The positive polarity of each word was calculated by dividing the number of occurrences in positive sentences by the number of all occurrences:

[5.6.1]

$$positiveSentScore = \frac{\#Positive\ sentences}{(\#Positive\ sentences + \#Negative\ sentences)}.$$

For example, we calculated that the word "*pleasant*" appeared 122 times in the positive sentences and 44 times in the negative sentences. According to the formula, the positive sentiment score of the word "*pleasant*" is

$$positiveSentScore = \frac{122}{(122 + 44)} = 0.73.$$

Similarly, the negative score for the word "*pleasant*" can be calculated by dividing the number of occurrences in negative sentences by the total number of mentions:

$$negativeSentScore = \frac{\#Negative\ sentences}{(\#Positive\ sentences + \#Negative\ sentences)},$$ [5.6.2]

$$negativeSentScore = \frac{44}{(122 + 44)} = 0.27.$$

Based on the positive score of the word, we can make a decision about its polarity: the word is considered positive if its positive score is above 0.6; the word is considered neutral, if its positive score is in the range [0.4; 0.6]; the word is considered negative, if the positive score is below 0.4. Since the positive score of the word "pleasant" is 0.73, it is considered to carry positive sentiment. Sentiment scores of some other words from the experiment are presented in Table 5.6.3.

Table 5.6.3: Example of sentiment scores of words in the automatically generated lexicon.

	GOOD	BAD	LIKE
Positive Score	0.675	0.213	0.457
Negative Score	0.325	0.787	0.543

We can observe from the table that the words "*GOOD*" and "*BAD*" have strongly defined positive and negative scores, as we would expect. The word "*LIKE*" has polarity scores ranging between 0.4 and 0.6, indicating its neutrality. To understand why the "neutral" label for the word "*LIKE*" was assigned we investigate the semantic role of this word in English language:

a.   Being a verb to express preference. For example: "*I like ice-cream*".
b.   Being a preposition for the purpose of comparison. For example: "*This town looks like Brighton*."

The first sentence has positive sentiment, however can easily be transformed into a negative sentence: "*I don't like ice-cream*". This demonstrates that the word "*LIKE*" can be used with equal frequency for expressing positive and negative opinions. In the second example the word "*LIKE*" is playing a role of a preposition and does not affect the overall polarity of the sentence. Thus, the word "*LIKE*" is a neutral word and was correctly assigned a neutral label using the approach described above.

In our study, all words from the Bag-of-Words with a polarity in the range [0.4; 0.6] were removed, since they do not help to classify the text as positive or negative. The sentiment scores of the words were mapped into the range [-1;1] by using the following formula:

$$PolarityScore = 2 * positiveSentScore - 1.$$ [5.6.3]

According to this formula, the word "LIKE", obtained a score 0.446 * 2 - 1 = -0.1, which indicates the neutrality of the word. In a case when the word is extremely positive and had a *positiveSentScore* of 1, the mapped score will be positive: $1 * 2 - 1 = 1$. If the word is extremely negative and has the *positiveSentScore* equal to 0, the mapped score will be negative: $0 * 2 - 1 = -1$.

Lexicon Combinations. Since the role of emoticons for expressing opinion online is continuously increasing, it is crucial to incorporate emoticons into lexicons used for sentiment analysis. Hogenboom et al. (2013) showed that the incorporation of emoticons into lexicon can significantly improve the accuracy of classification. Apart from emoticons, new slang words and abbreviations are constantly emerging and need to be accounted for when performing sentiment analysis. However, most of the existing public lexicons do not contain emoticons or social-media slang; on the contrary, emoticons and abbreviations are often removed as typographical symbols during the first stages of pre-processing.

Table 5.6.4: *Example of tokens from our EMO lexicon along with their polarity. Tokens represent emoticons, abbreviations and slang words that are used in social-media to express emotions.*

Emoticon	Score	Emoticon	Score	Abbreviation	Score	Abbreviation	Score
l-)	1	[-(	-1	lol	1	dbeyr	-1
:-}	1	T T	-1	ilum	1	iwiam	-1
x-d	1	:-((	-1	iyqkewl	1	nfs	-1
;;-)	1	:-[	-1	iwalu	1	h8ttu	-1
=]	1	:(((	-1	koc	1	gtfo	-1

In this study we manually constructed a lexicon of emoticons, abbreviations and slang words commonly used in social media to express emotions (EMO). Examples of tokens from our lexicon are presented in Table 5.6.4. We aimed to analyse how performance of the classic opinion lexicon (OL) (Hu and Liu, 2004) can be improved by enhancing it with our EMO lexicon. We expanded the lexicon further by incorporating words from the automatically created lexicon (AUTO). The process of automatic lexicon creation was described in detail in the previous section.

With opinion lexicon (OL) serving as a baseline, we compared the performance of some lexicon combinations as shown in Table 5.6.5:

Table 5.6.5: *Combinations of lexicons tested*

	Lexicons combinations
1.	OL
2.	OL + EMO
3.	OL + EMO + AUTO

Sentiment Score Calculation. In this study we calculate sentiment scores of tweets as described in section 5.2 using Equation 5.4.1. We also propose an alternative measure based on the logarithm of the standard score. We normalise the logarithmic score in such a way that the values range between [-1; 1] with -1 being the most negative score and 1 being the most positive score (see 5.6.4).

$$ScoreLog10 = \begin{cases} sign(Score_{AVG})Log_{10}(\mid 10Score_{AVG}\mid), & \text{if } \mid Score_{AVG}\mid > 0.1, \quad [5.6.4] \\ 0, & \text{otherwise} \end{cases}$$

Lexicon Performance Results. The analysis of performance of our algorithm was conducted on the test dataset from SemEval-2013, Task 2-B (Nakov et al., 2013) (see Figure 5.6.1b). Figure 5.6.2 presents the results for the three different lexicons using the *Simple Average* as the sentiment score (Equation 5.4.1). The values of the sentiment score range from -1 to 1. The colours of the bars represent the true labels of the tweets: dark grey stands for positive messages, light grey for neutral messages and medium grey stands for negative messages. In the case of perfect classification, we would obtain a clear separation of the colours. However, from Figure 5.6.2 we can see that classification for all three lexicons was not ideal. For example, all lexicons made the biggest mistake in misclassifying neutral messages (we can see that light grey colour is present for the sentiment scores of -1 and 1 in all three histograms, indicating that some of neutral messages were classified as positive or negative). This phenomenon can be explained with the fact that even neutral messages often contain one or more polarity words, which leads to the final score of the message being a value different from 0 and being classified as positive or negative.

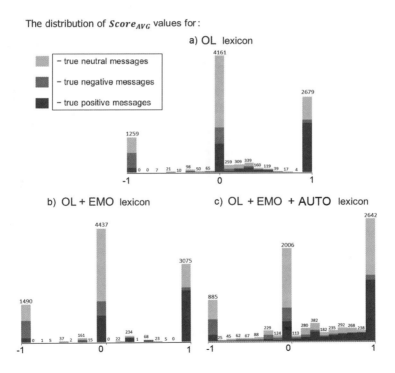

Figure 5.6.2: *Histograms of sentiment scores for different lexicon combinations using the Simple Average Score. The colours of the bars represent the true labels of the tweets: dark grey stands for positive messages, light grey for neutral messages and medium grey stands for negative messages.*

The results based on the logarithmic approach (Equation 5.6.4) reveal that positive, negative and neutral classes became more defined (Figure 5.6.3). Indeed, the logarithmic score makes it easier to set up the thresholds for assigning labels to different classes. Thus we can conclude that using a logarithmic score for calculating sentiment is more appropriate than using a simple average score.

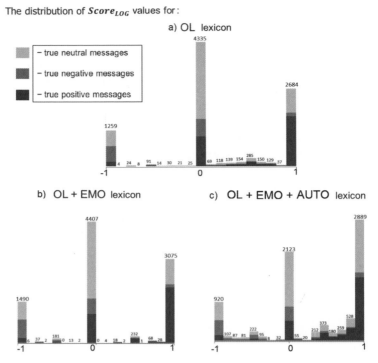

Figure 5.6.3: *Histograms of sentiment scores for different lexicon combinations using the Logarithmic Score. The colours of the bars represent the true labels of the tweets: dark grey stands for positive messages, light grey for neutral messages and medium grey stands for negative messages.*

To compare the performance of three lexicon combinations we need to assign positive, negative or neutral labels to the tweets based on the calculated sentiment scores, and compare the predicted labels against the true labels of tweets. For this purpose we employ a k-means clustering algorithm, using Simple Average and Logarithmic scores as features. The results of K-means clustering for the 3 lexicons and 2 types of sentiment scores are reported in Table 5.6.6.

Table 5.6.6: *Results of K-Means clustering for different lexicon combinations.*

Accuracy	OL	OL + EMO	OL + EMO + AUTO
$Score_{AVG}$	57.07%	60.12%	51.33%
$Score_{Log10}$	58.43%	61.74%	52.38%

As shown in Table 5.6.6 the lowest accuracy of classification for both types of scores corresponded to the biggest lexicon (OL + EMO + AUTO). This result can be attributed to the noisy nature of Twitter data. Training a lexicon on noisy data could have introduced ambiguity regarding the sentiment of individual words. Thus, automatic generation of the lexicon (AUTO) based on Twitter labelled data cannot be considered a reliable technique. The small OL lexicon showed better results since it consisted mainly of adjectives that carry strong positive or negative sentiment that are unlikely to cause ambiguity. The highest accuracy of classification 61.74% was achieved using the combination of OL and EMO lexicons (OL + EMO) and a logarithmic score. This result confirms that enhancing the lexicon for Twitter sentiment analysis with emoticons, abbreviations and slang words increases the accuracy of classification. It is important to notice that the Logarithmic Score provided an improvement of 1.36% over the Simple Average Score.

5.6.3 Machine Learning Approach

We performed Machine Learning-based sentiment analysis. For this purpose we used the machine learning package WEKA[14].

Pre-processing/cleaning the data. Before training, the classifiers the data needed to be pre-processed and this step was performed according to the general process described in section 5.3. Some additional steps had to be performed:

- *Filtering.* Some syntactic constructions used in Twitter messages are not useful for sentiment detection. These constructions include URLs, @-mentions, hashtags and RT-symbols, and they were removed during the pre-processing step.

- *Token replacements.* The words that appeared to be under the effect of the negation words were modified by adding a suffix **NEG** to the end of those words.

For example, the phrase *I don't want.* was modified to *I don't want_NEG*.

This modification is important, since each word in a sentence serves a purpose of a feature during the classification step. Words with **NEG** suffixes increase the dimensionality of the feature space, but allow the classifier to distinguish between words used in the positive and in the negative context.

When performing tokenisation, the symbols ():;, among others are considered to be delimiters, thus most of the emoticons could be lost after tokenisation. To avoid this problem, positive emoticons were replaced with **pos_emo** and negative were replaced with **neg_emo**. Since there are many variations of emoticons representing the same emotions depending on the language and community, the replacement of all positive lexicons by pos_emo and all negative emoticons by neg_emo also achieved the goal of significantly reducing the number of features.

Feature Generation. The following features were constructed for the purpose of training a classifier:

- **N-grams:** we transformed the training dataset into the bag-of-n-grams, taking into account only the presence/absence of uni-grams. Using "n-gram frequency" would not be logical in this particular experiment, since Twitter messages are very short, and a term is unlikely to appear in the same message more than once;

- **Lexicon Sentiment:** the sentiment score obtained during the lexicon based sentiment analysis as described in 5.6.4;

- **Elongated words number**: the number of words with one character repeated more than 2 times, e.g. "soooo";

- **Emoticons**: presence/absence of positive and negative emoticons at any position in the tweet;

- **Last token**: whether the last token is a positive or negative emoticon;

- **Negation**: the number of negated contexts;

- **POS**: the number of occurrences for each part-of-speech tag: verbs, nouns, adverbs, at-mentions, abbreviations, URLs, adjectives and others

- **Punctuation marks**: the number of occurrences of punctuation marks in a tweet;

- **Emoticon number**: the number of occurrences of positive and negative emoticons;

- **Negative token number**: total count of tokens in the tweet with logarithmic score less than 0;

- **Positive token number**: total count of tokens in the tweet with logarithmic score greater than 0;

Feature Selection. After performing the feature generation step described above, a feature space comprising **1826** features was produced. The next important step for improving classification accuracy is the selection of the most relevant features from this feature space. To this purpose we used Information Gain evaluation algorithm and a Ranker search method (Ladha and Deepa, 2011b). Information Gain measures the decrease in entropy when the feature is present vs absent, while Ranker ranks the features based on the amount of reduction in the objective function. We used features for which the value of information gain was above zero. As the result, a subset of **528** features was selected.

Table 5.6.7: *Example of top selected features.*

TOP FEATURES	11. great	22. fun	33. hope
1. LexiconScore	12. posV	23. lastTokenScore	34. thanks
2. maxScore	13. happy	24. i love	35. luck
3. posR	14. love	25. don	36. best
4. minScore	15. excited	26. don't	37. i don't
5. negTokens	16. can't	27. amazing	38. looking forward
6. good	17. i	28. fuck	39. sorry
7. posE	18. not	29 love you	40. didn't
8. posN	19. posA	30. can	41. hate
9. posU	20. posElongWords	31. awesome	42. ...

Some of the top selected features are displayed in Table 5.6.7, revealing that the "Lexicon Sentiment" feature, described in the previous section as a "Lexicon Sentiment", is located at the top of the list. This important result demonstrates that the "Lexicon Sentiment" plays a leading role in determining the final sentiment polarity of the sentence. Other highly ranked features included: minimum and maximum scores, number of negated tokens, number of different parts-of-speech in the message. To validate the importance of the "Lexicon Sentiment" feature and other manually constructed features, we performed cross-validation tests according to two scenarios: i) in the first scenario (Table 5.6.8) we trained three different classifiers using only n-grams as features; ii) in the second scenario (Table 5.6.9) we trained the models using traditional n-gram features in combination with the "Lexicon Sentiment" feature and other manually constructed features: number of different parts-of-speech, number of emoticons, number of elongated words. Tests were performed on a movie review dataset "Sentence Polarity Dataset v 1.0 "[15] released by Bo Pang and Lillian Lee in 2005 and comprised of 5331 positive and 5331 negative processed sentences.

As it can be observed from tables 5.9 and 5.10, the addition of the "Lexicon Senti- ment" feature and other manually constructed features allowed to increase all performance measures significantly for 3 classifies. For example, the accuracy of Naive Bayes classifier was increased by 7%, accuracy of Decision Trees was increased by over 9%, and the accuracy of SVM improved by 4.5%.

Table 5.6.8: *Scenario 1: 5-fold cross-validation test on a movie reviews dataset using only n-grams as features.*

Method	Tokens Type	Folds Number	Accuracy	Precision	Recall	F-Score
Naive Bayes	uni/bigrams	5	81.5%	0.82	0.82	0.82
Decision Trees	uni/bigrams	5	80.57%	0.81	0.81	0.81
SVM	uni/bigrams	5	86.62%	0.87	0.87	0.87

Table 5.6.9: *Scenario 2: 5-fold cross-validation test on a movie reviews dataset using traditional n-grams features in combination with manually constructed features: lexicon sentiment score, number of different parts-of-speech, number of emoticons, number of elongated words, etc.*

Method	Tokens Type	Folds Number	Accuracy	Precision	Recall	F-Score
Naive Bayes	uni/bigrams	5	88.54%	0.89	0.86	0.86
Decision Trees	uni/bigrams	5	89.9%	0.90	0.90	0.90
SVM	uni/bigrams	5	91.17%	0.91	0.91	0.91

Training the Model, Validation and Testing. Machine Learning Supervised approach requires a labelled training dataset. We used a publicly available training dataset (Figure 5.6.1a) from SemEval-2013 competition, Task 2-B (Nakov et al., 2013).

Each of the tweets from the training set was expressed in terms of its attributes. As a result, an n by m binary matrix was created, where n is the number of training instances and m is the number of features. This matrix was used for training different classifiers: Naive Bayes, Support Vector Machines, Decision trees. It is important to note that the training dataset was highly unbalanced, with the majority of neutral messages (Figure 5.6.1a). In order to account for this unbalance we trained a cost-sensitive SVM model (Ling and Sheng, 2007). A Cost-Sensitive classifier minimises the total cost of classification by putting a higher cost on a particular type of error (in our case, misclassifying positive and negative messages as neutral).

As the next step we tested the models on an unseen before test set (Figure 5.6.1b) from SemEval-2013 Competition (Nakov et al., 2013) and compared our results against the results of 44 teams that took part in the SemEval-2013 competition. While the classification was performed for 3 classes (pos, neg, neutral), the evaluation metric was F-score (Equation 5.5.1) between positive and negative classes.

Table 5.6.10: *F-score results of our algorithm using different classifiers. The test was performed on a test dataset from SemEval Competition-2013, Task 2-B (Nakov et al., 2013).*

Classifier	**Naive Bayes**	**Decision Trees**	**SVM**	**Cost SVM**	**Sensitive**
F-SCORE	0.64	0.62	0.66	0.73	

Table 5.6.11: *F-score results of SemEval Competition-2013, Task 2-B (Nakov et al., 2013).*

TEAM NAME	**F-SCORE**
NRC-Canada	0.6902
GUMLTLT	0.6527
teragram	0.6486
AVAYA	
BOUNCE	0.6353
KLUE	0.6306
AMI and ERIC	0.6255
FBM	0.6117
SAIL	
AVAYA	0.6084
SAIL	0.6014
UT-DB	0.5987
FBK-irst	0.5976

Our results for different classifiers are presented in Table 5.6.10. We can observe that the Decision Tree algorithm had the lowest F-score of 62%. The reason may lay in the big size of the tree needed to incorporate all of the features. Because of the tree size, the algorithm needs to traverse multiple nodes until it reaches the leaf and predicts the class of the instance. This long path increases the probability of mistakes and thus decreases the accuracy of the classifier. Naive Bayes and SVM produced better scores of 64% and 66% respectively. The best model was a Cost-sensitive SVM, which achieved an F-measure of 73%. This is an important result, providing evidence that accounting for the unbalance in the training dataset improves model performance significantly. Comparing our results with the results of the competition (Table 5.6.11), we can conclude that our algorithm based on the Cost-sensitive SVM would had produced the best results, scoring 4 points higher than the winner of that competition.

5.7 CONCLUSION

In this chapter we have presented a review of the two main approaches for sentiment analysis: a lexicon-based method and a machine learning method.

In the lexicon-based approach, we compared the performance of three lexicons: i) an Opinion lexicon (OL); ii) an Opinion lexicon enhanced with manually created corpus of emoticons, abbreviations and social-media slang expressions (OL + EMO); iii) OL + EMO further enhanced with automatically generated lexicon (OL + EMO + AUTO). We showed that on a benchmark Twitter dataset, OL + EMO lexicon outperforms both the traditional OL and a larger OL + EMO + AUTO lexicon. These results demonstrate the importance of incorporating expressive signals such as emoticons, abbreviations and social-media slang phrases into lexicons for Twitter analysis. The results also show that larger lexicons may yield a decrease in performance due to ambiguity of word polarity and increased model complexity (agreeing with Ghiassi et al., 2013).

In the machine learning approach we used a lexicon sentiment obtained during the lexicon based classification as an input feature for training classifiers. The ranking of all features based on the information gain scores during the feature selection process revealed that the lexicon feature appeared at the top of the list, confirming its relevance in sentiment classification. We also demonstrated that, in the case of highly unbalanced datasets, the use of cost-sensitive classifiers improves the accuracy of class prediction: on the benchmark Twitter dataset, a cost-sensitive SVM yielded a 7% increase in performance over a standard SVM.

ACKNOWLEDGMENTS

We thank the valuable feedback from the two anonymous reviewers. T.A. acknowledges support of the UK Economic and Social Research Council (ESRC) in funding the Systemic Risk Centre (ES/K002309/1). O.K. acknowledges support from the company Certona Corporation. T.T.P.S. acknowledges financial support from CNPq - The Brazilian National Council for Scientific and Technological Development.

Notes

[1] http://www.wjh.harvard.edu/~inquirer/

[2] http://mpqa.cs.pitt.edu/corpora/mpqa_corpus/

[3] http://wordnet.princeton.edu/

[4] https://wordnet.princeton.edu/

[5] http://www.cs.waikato.ac.nz/ml/weka/

[6] http://nlp.stanford.edu/software/

[7] http://cogcomp.cs.illinois.edu/page/software/

[8] http://opennlp.sourceforge.net/models-1.5

[9] http://alias-i.com/lingpipe/demos/tutorial/posTags/read-me.html

[10] http://wortschatz.uni-leipzig.de/~cbiemann/software/unsupos/

[11] http://www.ark.cs.cmu.edu/TweetNLP

[12] http://nlp.cs.berkeley.edu/software.shtml

[13] http://www.ark.cs.cmu.edu/TweetNLP/

[14] http://www.cs.waikato.ac.nz/ml/weka/

[15] http://www.cs.cornell.edu/people/pabo/movie-review-data/

5.8 REFERENCES

1. Aisopos, F., Papadakis, G., Tserpes, K. and Varvarigou, T. (2012). Content vs. context for sentiment analysis: A comparative analysis over microblogs. In *Proceedings of the 23rd ACM Conference on Hypertext and Social Media*. New York: ACM, pp. 187–196.

2. Antenucci, D., Cafarella, M., Levenstein, M.C., Ré, C. and Shapiro, M.D. (2014). Using social media to measure labor market flows. Available at: http://www.nber.org/papers/w20010. [Accessed 10 April 2015].

3. Asur, S. and Huberman, B. A. (2010). Predicting the future with social media. In *Proceedings of the 2010 IEEE/WIC/ACM International Conference on Web Intelligence and Intelligent Agent Technology - Volume 01*. Washington: IEEE Computer Society, pp. 492–499.

4. Barbosa, L. and Feng, J. (2010). Robust sentiment detection on twitter from biased and noisy data. In *Proceedings of the 23rd International Conference on Computational Linguistics: Posters*. Stroudsburg: Association for Computational Linguistics, pp. 36–44.

5. Basili, R., Moschitti, A., and Pazienza, M. T. (2000). Language-Sensitive Text Classification. In *Proceeding of RIAO-00, 6th International Conference "Recherche d'Information Assistee par Ordinateur"*. Paris: pp. 331–343.

6. Benamara, F., Irit, S., Cesarano, C., Federico, N., and Reforgiato, D. (2007). Sentiment Analysis: Adjectives and Adverbs are better than Adjectives Alone. In *Proceedings of International Conference on Weblogs and Social Media*.

7. Bing, L. (2012). Sentiment analysis: A fascinating problem. In *Sentiment Analysis and Opinion Mining*. Morgan and Claypool Publishers, pp. 7–143.

8. Bollen, J., Mao, H. and Zeng, X. (2011). Twitter mood predicts the stock market. *Journal of Computational Science, 2(1)*, pp. 1–8.

9. Caropreso, M. F., Matwin, S. and Sebastiani, F. (2001). A learner-independent evaluation of the usefulness of statistical phrases for automated text categorization. In: Chin, A. G., ed., *Text Databases and Document Management*. Hershey: IGI Global.pages, pp. 78–102.

10. Carvalho, J., Prado, A. and Plastino, A. (2014). A statistical and evolutionary approach to sentiment analysis. In *Proceedings of the 2014 IEEE/WIC/ACM International Joint Conferences on Web Intelligence (WI) and Intelligent Agent Technologies (IAT) - Volume 02*. Washington: IEEE Computer Society, pp. 110–117.

11. Cortes, C. and Vapnik, V. (1995). Support-vector networks. *Machine Learning, 20(3)*, 273–297.

12. Councill, I. G., McDonald, R. and Velikovich, L. (2010). What's great and what's not: Learning to classify the scope of negation for improved sentiment analysis. In *Proceedings of the Workshop on Negation and Speculation in Natural Language Processing*. Stroudsburg: Association for Computational Linguistics, pp. 51–59.

13. Das, S. and Chen, M. (2001). Yahoo! for amazon: Extracting market sentiment from stock message boards. In *Proceedings of the Asia Pacific Finance Association Annual Conference*. Vol. 35, pp. 43.

14. Dash, M. and Liu, H. (1997). Feature selection for classification. *Intelligent data analysis, 1(3),* 131–156.

15. Diederich, J., Kindermann, J., Leopold, E. and Paass, G. (2003). Authorship attribution with support vector machines. *Applied Intelligence, 19(1-2),* 109–123.

16. Ding, X., Liu, B. and Yu, P. S. (2008). A holistic lexicon-based approach to opinion mining. In *Proceedings of the 2008 International Conference on Web Search and Data Mining*. New York: ACM, pp. 231–240.

17. Dumais, S., Platt, J., Heckerman, D. and Sahami, M. (1998). Inductive learning algorithms and representations for text categorization. In *Proceedings of the seventh international conference on Information and knowledge management*. New York: ACM, pp. 148–155.

18. Esuli, A. and Sebastiani, F. (2006). Sentiwordnet: A publicly available lexical resource for opinion mining. Available at: http://www.bibsonomy.org/bibtex/25231975d0967b9b51502fa03d87d106b/mkroell. [Accessed 7 July 2014].

19. Fersini, E., Messina, E. and Pozzi, F. (2014). Sentiment analysis: Bayesian ensemble learning. *Decision Support Systems, 68,* 26 – 38.

20. Fersini, E., Messina, E., and Pozzi, F. (2016). Expressive signals in social media languages to improve polarity detection. *Information Processing and Management, 52(1),* 20–35.

21. Forman, G. (2003). An extensive empirical study of feature selection metrics for text classification. *The Journal of Machine Learning Research, 3,* 1289–1305.

22. Ghiassi, M., Skinner, J. and Zimbra, D. (2013). Twitter brand sentiment analysis: A hybrid system using n-gram analysis and dynamic artificial neural network. *Expert Systems with Applications, 40(16),* 6266–6282.

23. Gimpel, K., Schneider, N., O'Connor, B., Das, D., Mills, D., Eisenstein, J., Heilman, M., Yogatama, D., Flanigan, J. and Smith, N. A. (2011). Part-of-speech tagging for twitter: Annotation, features, and experiments. In *Proceedings of the 49th Annual Meeting of the Association for Computational Linguistics: Human Language Technologies: Short Papers - Volume 2*. Stroudsburg: Association for Computational Linguistics, pp. 42–47.

24. Hall, M. (2012). Twitter labelled dataset. Available at: http://markahall.blogspot.co.uk/2012/03/sentiment-analysis-with-weka.html. [Accessed 6 February 2013].

25. Hatzivassiloglou, V. and McKeown, K. (1997). Predicting the semantic orientation of adjectives. In *Proceedings of the 35th annual meeting of the Association for Computational Linguistics and eighth conference of the European Chapter of the Association for Computational Linguistics*. Madrid: Association for Computational Linguistics, pp. 174–181.

26. Hogenboom, A., Bal, D., Frasincar, F., Bal, M., de Jong, F. and Kaymak, U. (2013). Exploiting emoticons in sentiment analysis. In *Proceedings of the 28th Annual ACM Symposium on Applied Computing*. New York: ACM, pp. 703–710.

27. Hu, M. and Liu, B. (2004). Opinion lexicon. Available at: https://www.cs.uic.edu/~liub/FBS/sentiment-analysis.html. [Accessed 20 March 2014].

28. Hu, X., Tang, L., Tang, J. and Liu, H. (2013). Exploiting social relations for sentiment analysis in microblogging. In *Proceedings of the Sixth ACM International Conference on Web Search and Data Mining*. New York: ACM, pp. 537–546.

29. Ikonomakis, M., Kotsiantis, S. and Tampakas, V. (2005). Text classification using machine learning techniques. *WSEAS Transactions on Computers, 4*, 966–974.

30. Jacobs, P. S. (1992). Joining statistics with nlp for text categorization. Available at: http://dblp.uni-trier.de/db/conf/anlp/anlp1992.html. [Accessed 7 May 2014].

31. Joachims, T. (1999). Transductive inference for text classification using support vector machines. In *Proceedings of the Sixteenth International Conference on Machine Learning*. San Francisco: Morgan Kaufmann Publishers Inc., pp. 200–209.

32. Kaji, N. and Kitsuregawa, M. (2007). Building lexicon for sentiment analysis from massive collection of html documents. In *EMNLP-CoNLL*, pp. 1075–1083. ACL.

33. Kim, S.M. and Hovy, E. (2004). Determining the sentiment of opinions. In *Proceedings of the 20th International Conference on Computational Linguistics*. Geneva: pp. 1267– 1373.

34. Kotsiantis, S. B. (2007). Supervised machine learning: A review of classification techniques. In *Proceedings of the 2007 Conference on Emerging Artificial Intelligence Applications in Computer Engineering: Real Word AI Systems with Applications in eHealth, HCI, Information Retrieval and Pervasive Technologies*. Amsterdam: IOS Press, pp. 3–24.

35. Kouloumpis, E., Wilson, T. and Moore, J. (2011). Twitter sentiment analysis: The good the bad and the omg! *ICWSM, 11*, 538–541.

36. Ladha, L. and Deepa, T. (2011a). Feature selection methods and algorithms. *International Journal on Computer Science and Engineering*, *3*, 1787–1797.

37. Ladha, L. and Deepa, T. (2011b). Feature selection methods and algorithms, international journal on computer science and engineering. *International Journal on Computer Science and Engineering*, *3*, 1787–1800.

38. Ling, C. X. and Sheng, V. S. (2007). Cost-sensitive Learning and the Class Imbalanced Problem. In Sammut, C., ed., *Encyclopedia of Machine Learning*.

39. Liu, K.L., Li, W.J. and Guo, M. (2012). Emoticon smoothed language models for twitter sentiment analysis. In *Proceedings of the National Conference on Artificial Intelligence*, *volume 2*. pp. 1678–1684.

40. Lovins, J. B. (1968). Development of a stemming algorithm. *Mechanical Translation and Computational Linguistics, 11*, 22–31.

41. Manning, C. D. and Schu¨tze, H. (1999). *Foundations of Statistical Natural Language Processing*. MIT Press, Cambridge, Massachusetts.

42. Marsland, S. (2011). *Machine Learning: An Algorithmic Perspective*. CRC Press. Mitchell, T. M. (1996). *Machine Learning*. McGraw Hill, New York, NY, USA.

43. Mohammad, S. M., Kiritchenko, S. and Zhu, X. (2013). Nrc-canada: Building the state- of-the-art in sentiment analysis of tweets. In *Proceedings of the seventh international workshop on Semantic Evaluation Exercises*.

44. Moilanen, K. and Pulman, S. (2007). Sentiment composition. In *Proceedings of Recent Advances in Natural Language Processing*. pp. 378–382.

45. Morinaga, S., Yamanishi, K., Tateishi, K. and Fukushima, T. (2002). Mining product reputations on the web. In *Proceedings of the Eighth ACM SIGKDD International Conference on Knowledge Discovery and Data Mining*. New York: ACM, pp. 341–349.

46. Nakov, P., Kozareva, Z., Ritter, A., Rosenthal, S., Stoyanov, V., and Wilson, T. (2013). Semeval-2013 task 2: Sentiment analysis in twitter. In *Seventh International Workshop on Semantic Evaluation, volume 2*, pp. 312–320.

47. Narayanan, V., Arora, I. and Bhatia, A. (2013). Fast and accurate sentiment classification using an enhanced naive bayes model. In *Intelligent Data Engineering and Automated Learning – IDEAL 2013*, pp. 194–201. Springer Berlin Heidelberg.

48. Nielsen, F. (2011). A new anew: evaluation of a word list for sentiment analysis in microblogs. In *Proceedings of the ESWC2011 Workshop on 'Making Sense of Microposts': Big things come in small packages 718 in CEUR Workshop Proceedings*, pp. 93–98.

49. Ohana, B. and Tierney, B. (2009). Sentiment classification of reviews using sentiwordnet. Available at: http://
     www.bibsonomy.org/bibtex/2443c5ba60fab3ce8bb93a6e74c8cf87d/bsc.

50. Pak, A. and Paroubek, P. (2010). Twitter as a corpus for sentiment analysis and opinion mining. In
     Proceedings of the Seventh International Conference on Language Resources and Evaluation. Valletta:
     European Language Resources Association.

51. Pang, B., Lee, L. and Vaithyanathan, S. (2002). Thumbs up?: Sentiment classification using machine
     learning techniques. In *Proceedings of the ACL-02 Conference on Empirical Methods in Natural Language
     Processing - Volume 10*. Stroudsburg: Assocation for Computational Linguistics, pp. 79–86.

52. Piantadosi, S. (2014). Zipfs word frequency law in natural language: A critical review and future directions.
     Psychonomic Bulletin and Review, 21, 1112–1130.

53. Polanyi, L. and Zaenen, A. (2006). Contextual Valence Shifters. In *Computing Attitude and Affect in Text:
     Theory and Applications*, pp. 1–10. Springer Netherlands.

54. Porter, M.(2002). Snowball: Quick introduction. Available at: http://snowball.tartarus.org/texts/quickintro.
     html. [Accessed 16 October 2014].

55. Porter, M. F. (1980). An algorithm for suffix stripping. *Program, 14,* 130–137.

56. Pozzi, F.A., Fersini, E., Messina, E. and Blanc, D. (2013a). Enhance polarity classification on social media
     through sentiment-based feature expansion. In *WOA@AI*IA*, pp. 78–84.

57. Pozzi, F. A., Maccagnola, D., Fersini, E. and Messina, E. (2013b). Enhance user-level sentiment
     analysis on microblogs with approval relations. In *AI*IA 2013: Advances in Artificial Intelligence*, pp.
     133–144. Springer.

58. Rajaraman, A. and Ullman, J. D. (2011). *Mining of Massive Datasets*. Cambridge University Press, New
     York, NY, USA.

59. Raskutti, B., Ferrá, H. L. and Kowalczyk, A. (2001). Second order features for maximising text classification
     performance. In *Proceedings of the 12th European Conference on Machine Learning*. London: Springer-
     Verlag, pp. 419–430.

60. Rijsbergen, C. J. V. (1979). *Information Retrieval*. Butterworth-Heinemann, Newton, MA, USA, 2nd edition.

61. Rocchio, J. J. (1971). Relevance feedback in information retrieval. In Salton, G., ed., *The Smart retrieval
     system - experiments in automatic document processing*, pp. 313–323. Englewood Cliffs, NJ: Prentice-Hall.

62. Saif, H., He, Y. and Alani, H. (2012). Semantic sentiment analysis of twitter. In *Proceedings of the 11th International Conference on The Semantic Web - Volume Part I*. Berlin: Springer-Verlag, pp. 508–524.

63. Salton, G. and McGill, M. J. (1983). *Introduction to Modern Information Retrieval*. McGraw Hill Book Co.

64. Schapire, R. E. and Singer, Y. (2000). BoosTexter: A Boosting-based System for Text Categorization. *Machine Learning, 39,* 135–168.

65. Stone, P. J. and Hunt, E. B. (1963). A computer approach to content analysis: Studies using the general inquirer system. In *Proceedings of the May 21-23, 1963, Spring Joint Computer Conference*. New York: ACM, pp. 241–256.

66. Taboada, M., Brooke, J., Tofiloski, M., Voll, K. and Stede, M. (2011). Lexicon-based methods for sentiment analysis. *Computational Linguistics, 37,* 267–307.

67. Tan, C.M., Wang, Y.F. and Lee, C.D. (2002). The use of bigrams to enhance text categorization. *Information processing & management, 38(4),* 529–546.

68. Tong, R. (2001). An operational system for detecting and tracking opinions in on-line discussions. In *Working Notes of the SIGIR Workshop on Operational Text Classification*. New Orleans: pp. 1–6.

69. Turney, P. D. (2002). Thumbs up or thumbs down?: Semantic orientation applied to unsupervised classification of reviews. In *Proceedings of the 40th Annual Meeting on Association for Computational Linguistics*. Stroudsburg: Association for Computational Linguistics, pp. 417–424.

70. Vapnik, V. N. (1995). *The Nature of Statistical Learning Theory*. Springer-Verlag New York, Inc., New York, NY, USA.

71. Vapnik, V. N. (1998). *Statistical Learning Theory*. Wiley, New York, NY, USA.

72. Wang, G., Sun, J., Ma, J., Xu, K. and Gu, J. (2014). Sentiment classification: The contribution of ensemble learning. *Decision Support Systems, 57,* 77 – 93.

73. Weiss, S. M., Apte, C., Damerau, F. J., Johnson, D. E., Oles, F. J., Goetz, T. and Hampp, T. (1999). Maximizing text-mining performance. In *IEEE Intelligent Systems, volume 14*. Piscataway: IEEE Educational Activities Department, pp. 63–69.

74. Wiebe, J. (2000). Learning subjective adjectives from corpora. In *Proceedings of the Seventeenth National Conference on Artificial Intelligence and Twelfth Conference on Innovative Applications of Artificial Intelligence*. AAAI Press, pp. 735–740.

75. Wiebe, J. and Wilson, T. (2002). Learning to disambiguate potentially subjective expressions. In *Proceedings of the 6ᵗʰ Conference on Natural Language Learning, Volume 20*. Taipei: Association for Computational Linguistics, pp. 112–118.

76. Wiebe, J., Wilson, T. and Cardie, C. (2005). Annotating expressions of opinions and emotions in language. *Language Resources and Evaluation, 39,* 164– 210.

77. Wilson, T., Wiebe, J. and Hoffmann, P. (2005). Recognizing contextual polarity in phrase- level sentiment analysis. In *Proceedings of the conference on Human Language Technology and Empirical Methods in Natural Language Processing*. Vancouver: Association for Computational Linguistics, pp. 347–354.

78. You, Q. and Luo, J. (2013). Towards social imagematics: Sentiment analysis in social multimedia. In *Proceedings of the Thirteenth International Workshop on Multimedia Data Mining*. New York: ACM, pp. 3:1–3:8.

79. Zhang, D. (2003). Question classification using support vector machines. In *Proceedings of the 26th annual international ACM SIGIR conference on Research and development in information retrieval*. ACM Press, pp. 26–32.

80. Zhao, J., Dong, L., Wu, J. and Xu, K. (2012). Moodlens: an emoticon-based sentiment analysis system for Chinese tweets. In *The 18th ACM SIGKDD International Conference on Knowledge Discovery and Data Mining*. Beijing, pp. 1528–1531.

81. Zhu, L., Galstyan, A., Cheng, J. and Lerman, K. (2014). Tripartite graph clustering for dynamic sentiment analysis on social media. In *Proceedings of the 2014 ACM SIGMOD International Conference on Management of Data*. New York, pp. 1531–1542.

CHAPTER 6

Sentiment Analysis in Microblogs

Federico Alberto Pozzi, *Analytical Consultant, SAS Italy*

Elisabetta Fersini, *Postdoctoral Research Fellow, University of Milano-Bicocca*

Enza Messina, *Professor in Operations Research, University of Milano-Bicocca*

ABSTRACT

A huge amount of textual data on the Web has built up in the past few years, rapidly creating unique content of massive dimensions that constitute fertile ground for Sentiment Analysis (SA).

In particular, microblogs are a challenging emerging sector where people's natural language expressions can be easily reported in short but meaningful text messages. Since behavioural economics tells us that emotions can profoundly affect individual behaviour and decision-making, this unprecedented content of huge dimensions needs to be efficiently and effectively analysed. A key area of information that can be grasped from social environments relates to the polarity of text messages, i.e. the sentiment (positive, negative or neutral) that the messages convey, which is useful for predicting changes in various economic and commercial indicators. The growing interest in SA is related to the possibility of utilising its results in different tasks, such as: understanding and forecasting the sentiment of financial markets (Mitra and Mitra, 2011), managing business intelligence tasks relating to user feedback (Pang and Lee, 2008) or sounding out public opinion during political campaigns (O'Connor et al., 2010).

In this chapter, the literature review of SA applied to microblogs using supervised and semi-supervised models is presented.

Most work considers text as unique information to infer sentiment and does not take into account that microblogs are actually networked environments. A representation of real world data where instances are considered as homogeneous, independent and identically distributed (i.i.d.) leads us to substantial loss of information and the introduction of a statistical bias. For this reason, the combination of content and relationships is a core task of the recent literature on Sentiment Analysis.

A further and interesting aspect we present concerns models and techniques for sarcasm and irony detection in microposts. In this setting, we present different works which leverage additional features in the bag-of-words model which are symptomatic of greater emphasis in sentiment (Part-Of-Speech, Emoticons Expressive lengthening, etc.).

6.1 INTRODUCTION

The great diffusion of social media and their role in modern society is one of the more interesting novelties in recent years, capturing the interest of researchers, journalists, investors, companies and governments. The dense interconnection that often arises among active users generates a discussion space that is able to motivate and involve individuals of a larger Agora, linking people with common objectives and facilitating diverse forms of collective action. This gives rise to what is called "*individualism on the net*": instead of always relying on a single reference community, with social media it becomes possible to move among often more heterogeneous people and resources.

It therefore appears that social media are creating a digital revolution. The most interesting aspect of this change is not solely related to the possibility of promoting political participation and activism. The real social revolution affects the lives of every single individual. It is the freedom to express oneself, to have one's own space in which to be oneself, or what it would be like to be oneself with few limits or barriers. The social media revolution is about being able to talk about one's emotions and opinions not only to oneself, but especially to those around us, interacting with them, opening a window on other people's worlds, and getting a peak into their lives. One of the most closely related tasks is called Sentiment Analysis (SA), where "What people think" is captured and analyzed by complex models.

More precisely, the aim of SA is to define automatic tools able to extract subjective information, such as opinions, sentiments, evaluations or attitudes, from texts in natural language. We know from psychological research that emotions, in addition to information, play a significant role in human decision-making (Dolan, 2002; Kahneman and Tversky, 1979). Behavioural finance has provided further proof that financial decisions are significantly driven by emotion, mood and sentiment (Nofsinger, 2005).

For this reason, extracting automatically subjective information could help individuals, investors, companies and organizations to make more informed decisions.

We are now able to access the opinions and experiences of a greater pool of people, who might be neither our personal acquaintances nor well-known professional critics. Blogs, microblogs and online social networks are constantly flooded with opinions about a multitude of topics that pop up daily on the news media. This kind of data comes from different sources such as news, editorials and, more generally, user-generated content. Typical examples of the latter are social network contents, which are growing ever vaster and are gaining ever greater popularity. Considering the evolution of the sources where opinions are issued, the strategies available in the current state of the art are no longer effective for mining opinions in this challenging new environment.

In this chapter, a review of the state of the art regarding SA applied to microblogs is presented. In particular, in Section 6.2, the difference between Social Media, Social Networks, Blogs and Microblogs is first discussed, prior to presenting the characteristics, differences and statistics of the most popular platforms. In Section 6.3, the literature review regarding Sentiment Analysis applied to microblogs using supervised and semi-supervised models is presented with particular focus on models and techniques which leverage both content and network structure. In Section 6.4, sarcasm and irony detection in microposts is addressed, while applications are presented in Section 6.5. Conclusions accompanied by future directions are drawn in Section 6.6.

6.2 SOCIAL MEDIA, SOCIAL NETWORK, BLOG OR MICROBLOG?

To better understand the meaning of social media and characterize its different sub-classes, it is useful to begin our discussion by introducing the concept of "social networks".

By **Social Network** we refer to any structure, formal or informal, consisting of a group of people or organizations, together with their respective relationships (Scott, 2000). Usually, a graphical representation of a social network is given by "*nodes*", corresponding to the actors who operate in that network, along with the *connections* among these nodes, which may be more or less dense depending on the intensity of social relations existing among them. These reports can be either *explicit*, as in the case of classmates or family ties, or *implicit*, as with friendships, and may originate and be carried out off-line (i.e. in the real world) and on-line (i.e. in the network). *Facebook[1]* is a better-known example of a social network.

More generally, **Social Media** are virtual platforms that allow one to create, publish and share content, which is generated directly by their users (Yu and Kak, 2012).

In this sense, social media differ from traditional media, such as newspapers, books and television because of their horizontality with respect to the possibility (and faculty) to publish content. While, for example, a newspaper generally only contains news written by its reporters, in the case of social media the entry barrier to the "production" of a text is virtually absent: all that is needed is a computer (or mobile phone) with free internet access.

There are various types of social media. For example, *Wikipedia[2]*, a source of global information of large influence, represents a particular type of social media that goes under the name of "*collaborative project*". In more detail, collaborative projects directly affect users who are called to work together with the aim of producing content that will then become accessible to the whole network. However, Wikipedia is not a social network as social networks must meet three minimal conditions: (1) there must be specific users of the media, (2) these users must be connected each other, and (3) there must be the possibility of interactive communication among the users.

Other types of social media are represented by "*content communities*", i.e. platforms where users can share specific content with other members of the online community, as occurs for videos on *YouTube[3]*.

Moreover, a **blog** in which the writers recount the daily events of their lives or express their own ideas unilaterally (i.e. they do not satisfy any condition of "interactivity"), cannot technically be defined as a social network.

Microblog is blogging, but smaller. *But what is blogging?* "Blog" is short for "web log", and it involves keeping an online journal of writings, pictures and other multimedia, as well as news items and content found on the web.

Some blogs are just places where people write about their feelings and activities so other people can read them. All blogs are simply websites that are updated by their authors fairly frequently around some common theme.

So how does blogging become "micro"? By shrinking it down to its bare essence and relaying the heart of the message, communicating only what is necessary. *How could this be of use?* What if all your colleagues were updating each other about the goings-on at a professional conference so they could decide on the fly which events to attend, and share their experiences, and decide where everyone would be meeting afterward?

Anything that could be helped by contacting an entire group of people quickly with short message could benefit from microblogging. *Twitter*[4] is a better-known example of microblog.

To sum up, Social Networking occurs when you create, build and maintain personal and professional relationships to meet people, find opportunities, and learn new things. While microblogging is a smaller version of blogging, which itself means keeping a "web log" in the form of content (text and/or multimedia) found on the web. The microblog is a blog which been shrunk down to its bare essence and is used for relaying only the bare essentials of a message.

In this chapter, only those social media which have the form of a microblog will be addressed. For this reason, when the wording "social media" is used, this subset is taken into account.

6.2.1 Platform characteristics and differences

One of the most popular social networks is **Facebook**, which is characterized by admitted social interactions. Indeed, a Facebook user must become the"friend" of another user (and be accepted as such by the latter, i.e. the friendship must be two-way) in order to access or share some of the information published by this second user and to be able, for example, to write messages on his timeline. An exception is the profiles or features that users decide to make "public". In this case, the published information becomes freely accessible to all Facebook users (as well as to those who do have not a Facebook account). Finally, a Facebook user can express his/ her pleasure or interest in the activities of other users, initiatives, campaigns, brands or business/institutional accounts through the '*like*' function.

Another very popular social network and microblog is **Twitter**, which was born two years later, in 2006. Unlike Facebook, each user in Twitter can only share short text messages of up to 140 characters, called '*tweets*'. These are updates that are shown in the user's profile page and are automatically forwarded to all those who have registered to receive them (i.e. the user's followers). Thanks to the constant production of ideas and textual content, which may include images, links and short videos, Twitter is considered a social network that generates microblogging.

Unlike Facebook, the "*tacit consent*" rule is applied on Twitter: a user can "follow" another without his/her consensus, unless he/she decides to make a private account. A user can freely direct a public message to any other Twitter user, regardless of their relationship. In Twitter there is also the possibility to spread the entire tweet of another user by sending tweets to all your followers (known as a "*retweet*").

Moreover, messages posted in Twitter can be labelled with the use of one or more "hashtags", i.e. words or combinations of words preceded by the hash sign (#). By labelling a message with a hashtag, a hyperlink to all the other messages which contain the same hashtag is automatically created. Despite the Twitter user base being only a fraction of the size of Facebook's, the former, because of its openness and horizontality, is becoming a source of real-time news that is extremely influential for both the entire network and the traditional media.

Finally, **Google+** is the youngest of the three, having been launched by Google Inc. in June 2011. Compared to other social media, Google+ includes new multimedia content, such as the ability to initiate audio and video sessions through the "hangouts", virtual rooms where it is possible to communicate with multiple

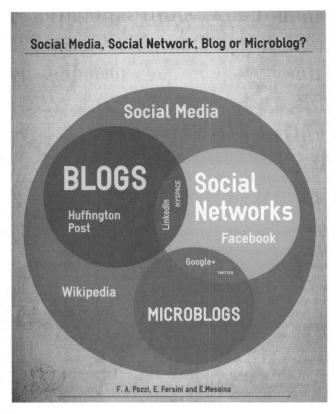

users at the same time. The system of contacts, equivalent to friends on Facebook or followers in Twitter, is organized in "circles". In order to add a new connection to the user's circles, the permission of the user is not requested (as in Twitter), but each user has the ability to customize the information shared with the various connections according to the circle settings. The model of Google+ in this sense is halfway between Facebook and Twitter.

6.3 SENTIMENT ANALYSIS IN MICROBLOGS

Social Media is emerging as a challenging sector in the context of Big Data: the natural language expressions of people can be easily reported through blogs and short text messages, rapidly creating unique content of huge dimensions that must be efficiently and effectively analyzed to create actionable knowledge for decision-making processes. The massive quantity of continuously contributing texts, which should be processed in real time in order to take informed decisions, calls for two main radical progresses: (1) a change of direction in the research through the transition from data-constrained to data-enabled paradigm and (2) the convergence to a multi-disciplinary area that mainly takes advantage of psychology, sociology, natural language processing and machine-learning.

The knowledge embedded in user-generated content has been shown to be of paramount importance from user, investor and company/organization viewpoints alike: people express opinions on any kind of topic in an unconstrained and unbiased environment, while corporations and institutions can gauge valuable information from raw sources.

In order to make qualitative textual data effectively functional for decision processes, the quantification of "what people think" becomes a mandatory step.

This issue is usually approached as a polarity-detection task aimed at classifying texts as positive, negative or neutral. In particular, in the financial domain, intervals such as [-5, 5] or [0, 100] are preferred because of the similarity with market indicator output. Although there is strong literature regarding the analysis of well-formed documents (e.g. newspaper articles, reviews, official news, etc.), there are still many challenges to be faced on social media in order to get a feel for what people think about current topics of interest. In order to make best use of this recent and highly dynamic source of information, we need to be able to distinguish what is important and interesting.

Social media users generate content that is dynamic, rapidly changing to reflect the societal and sentimental fluctuations of the authors as well as the ever-changing use of language. Considering the evolution of the sources where opinions are issued, the strategies available in the current state of the art are no longer effective for mining opinions in this new and challenging environment. In fact, Social Media Sentiment Analysis (SM-SA), in addition to inheriting a multitude of issues from traditional Sentiment Analysis (SA) and Natural Language Processing (NLP), introduces new and complex challenges. Microposts such as tweets are, in one sense, the most challenging text type for text-mining techniques, and in particular for SA, for various reasons:

- **Short messages (microtexts)**: Twitter messages are very short (max 140 characters). Many semantic-based methods supplement this lack with extra information and context coming from embedded URLs and hashtags. For instance, Abel et al. (2011) augment tweets by linking them to contemporaneous news articles, whereas Mendes et al. (2010) exploit online hashtag glossaries to augment tweets.
- **Noisy contents**: Unlike well-formed documents (e.g. news or reviews) which usually have a well-defined linguistic form, Social Media tend to be less grammatical, due to excessive amounts of colloquialism, with hasty spelling (e.g. 2u) and unconventional grammatical quirks. Moreover, social media posts are full of irregular capitalisation (e.g. all capitals or all lowercase letters), emoticons (e.g. :-P), idiosyncratic abbreviations (e.g. ROFL, ZOMG) and "word-lengthening", i.e. replication of letters as if words were screamed in order to emphasize the sentiment (e.g."noooooooo", "I'm haaaappyyyyyyy", etc.). In Gouws et al. (2011), spelling and capitalisation normalisation methods have been developed. Moreover, emoticons are used as strong sentiment indicators coupled with studies of location-based linguistic variations in shortening styles in microtexts.
- **Change over time**: in addition to linguistic analysis, social media content lends itself to analysis along temporal lines, which is a relatively under-researched problem. Addressing the temporal dimension of social media is a pre-requisite for much-needed models of conflicting and consensual information, as well as for modelling change in user interests. Moreover, temporal modelling can be combined with opinion mining, to examine the volatility of attitudes towards topics over time.

- **Metadata**: Since users produce, as well as consume, social media content, there is a rich source of explicit and implicit information about the user, e.g. demographics (gender, location, age, etc.), interests and opinions that can be used to improve classification performance.
- **Multilingual**: Social media content is strongly multilingual. For instance, less than 50% of tweets are in English, with Japanese, Spanish, Portuguese, and German also featuring prominently (Carter et al., 2013). Semantic technology methods have so far mostly focused on English, while low-overhead adaptation to new languages still remains an open issue.
- **Relationships**: A key aspect of several online social networks is that they are rich in content and relationships, and provide unprecedented challenges and opportunities from the perspective of SA, and subsequently knowledge discovery, data-mining, social network analysis and text-mining. Relationships are particularly useful when textual features do not always provide sufficient information to infer sentiment (e.g.*"I agree!"*).

If well handled, these characteristics can form an important part of the meaning. For this reason, although less organized, such information should also be considered as a goldmine which cannot be handled in well-formed documents.

In general, sentiment classification techniques for traditional SA can be roughly divided into **lexicon-based methods** (Taboada et al., 2011) and **Machine Learning methods** (Boiy and Moens, 2009). Lexicon-based methods rely on a sentiment lexicon, a collection of known and pre-compiled sentiment terms. Machine Learning approaches make use of syntactic and/or linguistic features, and hybrid approaches are very common, with sentiment lexicons playing a key role in the majority of methods (Hu and Liu, 2004).

Following the traditional line of standard SA, most of the work regarding SM-SA has predominantly used Machine Learning techniques. One of the reasons for the relative paucity of ad hoc linguistic techniques for SM-SA is most likely due to the difficulties of using NLP on low-quality text, something which machine learning techniques can, to some extent, bypass with sufficient training data.

6.3.1 Learning by supervision

Sentiment classification can be treated as a traditional text classification problem where, instead of classifying documents of different topics (e.g. politics, science and sport), "positive", "negative" and "neutral" classes (or [-5,5], [0,100] intervals) are estimated. Any existing supervised learning method, such as Naive Bayes classifier and Support Vector Machines, can be easily applied.

Although approaches based on supervised learning lead to very high performance, a disadvantage is that by definition they are characterized by tremendous human effort in labelling data which typically grows with the amount of data available. However, supervised learning still remains an active approach for polarity classification, thanks to its ability in predicting sentiment orientations.

In addition to terms, many more features have been tried in the bag-of-words model by a large number of researchers. Some of these features are:

- **Part-of-Speech**: words of different Parts-Of-Speech (POS) may be treated differently (nouns, verbs, pronouns, etc.). For example, it has been shown that adjectives are important indicators of opinions (Whitelaw et al., 2005).

- **Sentiment shifters**: these are expressions that are used to reverse the sentiment orientations, i.e. from positive to negative or vice-versa. Negation words are the most important class of sentiment-shifters. For example, the sentence "*I don't like this camera*" is negative, although 'like' is positive. Please note that not all occurrences of such words mean sentiment inversions (e.g."*not only... but also...*").

- **Pragmatic particles**: pragmatic particles, such as emoticons, emphatic and onomatopoeic expressions, are the linguistic elements typically used in social media to elicit a given message:

    - *Emoticons* are introduced as expressive, non-verbal components into the written language, mirroring the role played by facial expressions in speech (Walther and D'addario, 2001). Instances of positive emoticons are :-), :), =), :D, while examples of negative ones are -(, :(, =(, ;(.

    - *Acronyms for emphatic expressions* are a further pragmatic element used in non-verbal communication in online social media. Although they act as constituent, these emphatic abbreviations play a similar role of emoticons: expressions such as "ROFL" (Rolling On Floor Laughing) clearly represent positive expressions, while abbreviations as "BM" (Bad Manners) denote negative statements.

    - *Onomatopoeic expressions* in online social media can help to convey emotions: some expressions such as "bleh" and "wow" are clear indicators of negative and positive emotional states and therefore can help to distinguish the polarity of a text message.

- **Expressive Lengthening**: word styling (as in bold, italic and underlining) is not always available and often replaced by some linguistic conventions. Moreover, the informal nature of expressions leads social media users to make use of orthographic styles that are actually close to the spoken language. In Pozzi et al. (2013b) and Brody and Diakopoulos (2011) it has been demonstrated that the commonly observed phenomenon of expressive lengthening (usually known as word lengthening or word stretching) is an indication of emphasis that is strongly associated with subjectivity and sentiment. An example of expressive lengthening is "*I loooooove you*".

- **Capital Letters**: as well as the other features, capital letters are symptomatic of a greater emphasis in sentiment (e.g."*I LOVE you!*").

- **Punctuation**: unlike well-formed documents, with a formal style and orthographic conventions, social media posts usually contain a high number of contiguous exclamation and question marks (e.g.,"*Oomf gone have such a lovely summer!!!!!*"). It is clear that it is symptomatic of a greater emphasis in sentiment.

There are several works in the literature which leverage the described features in sentiment classification. Pak and Paroubek (2010) aimed at classifying arbitrary tweets on the basis of positive, negative and neutral sentiment, constructing a classifier which used n-gram and POS features. Also, Agarwal et al. (2011) perform sentiment analysis on Twitter data. They introduce POS-specific prior polarity features and explore the use of a tree kernel to obviate the need for tedious feature engineering. The new features (in conjunction with previously proposed features) and the tree kernel perform approximately at the same level, both outperforming the state-of-the-art baseline. In Pozzi et al. (2013b), three expressive signals typically used in online social media have been explored: (1) adjectives, (2) emoticons, emphatic and onomatopoeic expressions and (3) expressive lengthening.

Their impact in respect of sentiment classification has been investigated by proposing a combination of language normalization and feature expansion of the bag-of-words model. The expressive signals considered have been used to enrich the feature space and train several baseline and ensemble classifiers aimed at polarity classification.

However, most of the existing approaches select the best classification model leading to over-confident decisions that do not take into account the inherent uncertainty of the natural language. In order to overcome this limitation, the paradigm of ensemble learning should be investigated in order to reduce the noise-sensitivity related to language ambiguity and therefore to provide a more accurate prediction of polarity. Through Bayesian Model Averaging (Pozzi et al., 2013a), both the uncertainty and the reliability of each model are taken into account. The classifier selection problem can be addressed by a greedy approach that evaluates the contribution of each model with respect to the ensemble.

Bayesian Ensemble Learning
The most important limitation of existing ensemble methods is that the models to be included in the composition have uniform distributed weights regardless of their reliability.

However, the uncertainty left by data and models can be filtered by considering the Bayesian paradigm.

In particular, all possible models in the hypothesis space could be utilized by considering their marginal prediction capabilities and their reliabilities. Given a message and a set of independent classifiers, the probability of label is estimated by Bayesian Model Averaging (BMA) as follows:

$$P(l(m) \mid C, D) = \sum_{i \in C} P(l(m) \mid i, D) P(i \mid D) \qquad [6.3.1]$$

where $P(l(m) \mid i, D)$ is the marginal distribution of the label predicted by classifier i and $P(i, D)$ denotes the posterior probability of model i. The posterior $P(i, D)$ can be computed as:

$$P(i \mid D) = \frac{P(D \mid i) P(i)}{\sum_{j \in C} P(D \mid j) P(j)} \qquad [6.3.2]$$

where $P(i)$ is the prior probability of i and $P(D \mid \cdot)$ is the model likelihood. In Equation 6.3.1, $\sum_{j \in C} P(D \mid j) P(j)$ is assumed to be a constant and therefore can be omitted. Therefore, BMA assigns . . . the optimal label $l^*(m)$ to s according to the following decision rule:

$$
\begin{aligned}
l^*(m) \quad &= arg \max_{l(m)} P(l(m) \mid C, D) \\
&= arg \max_{l(m)} \sum_{i \in C} P(l(m) \mid i, D) P(i \mid D) \qquad [6.3.3] \\
&= arg \max_{l(m)} \sum_{i \in C} P(l(m) \mid i, D) P(D \mid i) P(i)
\end{aligned}
$$

The implicit measure $P(D \mid i)$ can easily be replaced by an explicit estimate, known as F1-measure, obtained during a preliminary evaluation of the classifier i. In particular, by performing a cross-validation, each classifier can produce an averaged measure stating how well a learning machine generalizes to unseen data. Considering ϕ-folds for cross-validating a classifier i, the measure $P(D \mid i)$ can be approximated as

$$P(D \mid i) \approx \frac{1}{\iota} \sum_{=1} \frac{2 \times P_{\iota\iota}(D) \times R_{\iota\iota}(D)}{P_{\iota\iota}(D) + R_{\iota\iota}(D)} \qquad [6.3.4]$$

where $P_{\iota\iota}(D)$ and $R_{\iota\iota}(D)$ denote precision and recall obtained by classifier i at fold i. The measure $P(D \mid i)$ can be estimated for both positive and negative polarities.

In this way, $P(l(m) \mid i,D)$ in Equation 6.3.3 is tuned according to the ability of the classifier to fit the training data. This approach allows the uncertainty of each classifier to be taken into account, avoiding over-confident inferences. For more details on BMA for polarity detection, see Pozzi et al. (2013a) and Fersini et al. (2014a).

6.3.2 Leveraging content and structure

A key aspect of several online social networks is that they are rich in content and relationships, and provide unprecedented challenges and opportunities from the perspective not only of SA but also of knowledge discovery, data mining, social network analysis and text mining.

Most of the state-of-the-art approaches are consistent with the classical statistical inference problem formulation, in which instances are homogeneous, independent and identically distributed (i.i.d. assumption). In other words, they consider textual information only, not taking into account the fact that Social Media, today's largest and richest source of information, are actually networked environments.

Although the relationship information of social networks has been extensively investigated, the work of incorporating content and relationship information to facilitate polarity detection has not yet been thoroughly studied. This problem is at the heart of the recent literature on SA applied to Online Social Media.

There are mainly three kinds of analysis in the context of social networks and microblogs:

- **Link-based Analysis**: structural relationships are used to simulate and analyze the diffusion model of opinions across the network. For instance, Gatti et al. (2014) presents a method to model and simulate interactive behaviour in microblogs taking into account the users sentiment.
- **Content-based Analysis**: in addition to relationships, social networks contain an extraordinary amount of content which can be leveraged. For example, Message Networks (e.g., Facebook and Twitter) contain tons of unstructured text messages that can be analyzed by Natural Language Processing and Text Mining techniques for SA tasks, while Multimedia Networks (e.g., Flickr and YouTube) allow users to add and share multimedia data coupled with potentially opinionated short

texts. In these contexts, several machine learning approaches have been proposed in the literature (Pang and Lee, 2008).

- **Combining Link-based and Content-based Analysis**: although relationship and content information have been independently investigated in the past, their combination has not been thoroughly studied yet (some exceptions are Hu et al., 2013; Rabelo et al., 2012). This is particularly useful when textual features do not always provide sufficient information to infer sentiment (e.g. "*I agree!*").

Most of the work regarding sentiment classification takes into account text as unique information to infer sentiment (Wang and Manning, 2012; Go et al., 2009; Barbosa and Feng, 2010).

Taking relationships into account could also be useful when dealing with implicit (or implied) opinions, where textual features do not always provide explicit information about sentiment. An implicit opinion is formally an objective statement that implies a regular or comparative opinion that usually expresses a desirable or undesirable fact, e.g."*Saturday night I'll go to the cinema to watch 'Lone Survivor'. I cannot wait to watch it!*" and '*Saving Soldier Ryan' is more violent than 'Lone Survivor'*.

The first example suggests that there are good expectations about the movie, although this is not encoded in words, while the understanding of the hidden opinion in the second example is difficult even for humans. For some people, violence in war movies could be a good characteristic that makes the movie more realistic, while it is a negative feature for others.

Much of the current research has focused on explicit opinions because they are easier to detect and classify than implicit opinions. Less work has been done on implicit opinions (Zhang and Liu, 2011), based on the consideration that textual features do not always provide explicit information about sentiment (e.g. *I cannot wait to watch it!*). Also, in such cases, additional information, such as user network, needs to be considered.

It has been observed that combining content-based and link-based analysis provides more effective results in a wide variety of applications (Fersini et al., 2010; Pozzi et al., 2013c; Mei et al., 2008). The combination of content and relationships is a core task in moving towards novel systems of SA.

Homophily and Constructuralism behind networks

People with different characteristics (e.g. gender, race, age, class background, etc.) usually have very different personalities: educated people are tolerant, women are sensitive and gang members are violent (McPherson et al., 2001). Since people generally have significant contact with others who tend to be like themselves, any personal characteristic tends to converge.

Homophily is the principle stating that *contact among similar people occurs at a higher rate than among dissimilar people*. Homophily implies that differences in terms of social characteristics translate into network distance, i.e. the number of relationships through which a piece of information must travel to connect two individuals. The concept of homophily is extremely ancient. In Aristotle's *Rhetoric* and *Nicomachean Ethics*, he noted that people "love those who are like themselves" (Aristotle, 1934 edition). Plato observed in *Phaedrus* that "similarity begets friendship" (Plato, 1968 edition). However, social scientists only began systematic observation of group formation and network ties in the 1920s (Bott, 1928; Wellman, 1929). They noted that schoolchildren formed friendships and playgroups at higher rates if they were similar in terms of demographic characteristics. The classic and most famous work in sociology is Lazarsfeld and Merton (1954), where the friendship process is studied. They also quote the proverbial expression of homophily, "*birds of a feather flock together*", which is often used to summarize this sociological process.

Lazarsfeld and Merton (1954) distinguished between two types of homophily: **status homophily**, in which similarity is based on informal, formal or ascribed status, and **value homophily**, which is based on values, attitudes and beliefs. Status homophily includes major socio-demographic dimensions such as race, ethnicity, sex and age, and acquired characteristics such as religion, education, occupation or behaviour patterns. Value homophily includes the wide array of internal states presumed to shape our orientation towards future behaviour: attitude, belief and value similarity lead to attraction and interaction. Value homophily is the facet of homophily that is assumed in this paper, where interactions are preferred, compared to static user attributes.

Alongside homophily, Carley (1991) has developed a sociological approach called **constructuralism**, whose core assumption is that *people who share knowledge are more likely to interact* (i.e. form ties).

In particular, constructuralism argues that individual learning from interactions takes place on two levels. Firstly, social interactions allow us to collect new knowledge over time that represents similarity among users better than static socio-demographic dimensions like race, ethnicity, sex or age (i.e. status homophily). Secondly, as humans receive and share knowledge with interaction partners, we "learn" a perception of what we expect them to know. Paired with homophily's assumption that people tend to interact with others similar to themselves, constructuralism explains how social relationships evolve via interaction as the knowledge that two actors share increases (Joseph et al., 2013). This approach to the co-evolution of knowledge and social relationships has considerable explanatory power for the dynamics of social networks and has proved to be an effective tool for social simulation.

Since text does not always provide explicit or sufficient information about sentiment, early studies on sentiment classification (Tan et al., 2011; Hu et al., 2013) overcome this limitation by exploiting the principle of homophily, which is usually modelled through friendships. However, considering the similarity among users on the basis of constructuralism appears to be a much more powerful force than interpersonal influence within the friendship network (Kandel, 1978). In other words, considering friendship connections as a proxy of homophily is a strong assumption: (1) being friends does not necessarily mean agreeing on a particular topic (e.g., there are often opposing political views among friends), (2) dynamic interactions are preferred, compared to static attributes (value homophily): once friendship is established in Online Social Networks, it is rare for it to be interrupted, even when it occurs it changes slowly over time, (3) social interactions allow us to collect new knowledge over time that represents similarity among users better than static socio-demographic dimensions, such as friendship (constructuralism).

For these reasons, a different paradigm to jointly model homophily and constructuralism, called **Approval Network** (Pozzi et al., 2013c), has been proposed.

Approval Network

Approval Network is constructed using approval relations among users. For instance, information can spread in Twitter in the form of *retweets*, which are tweets that have been forwarded by a user to his or her followers. A retweet is identified by the pattern "RT @" followed by the name of the tweet's author and the original tweet (e.g., John tweets "*I like the new iPhone*" and Mary retweets John's tweet: "*RT @John: I like the new iPhone*", i.e. John and Mary positively agree about iPhone). The corresponding approval tool on Facebook is the "Like" tool.

While approving can simply be seen as the act of copying and rebroadcasting, the practice contributes to a conversational ecology in which conversations are composed of a public interplay of voices that give rise to an emotional sense of shared conversational context (Boyd et al., 2010).

The general idea behind Approval Network is that a user who approves (e.g. by 'likes' on Facebook or 'retweets' in Twitter) a given message is likely to hold the same opinion as the message's author. This is because an approval tool does not allow the user to add a comment to the original message to argue against the original post[5]. Thus, "approving" usually means agreeing with the original user: the more the approvals between two users on a particular topic of interest, the higher their agreement on that topic.

Here, the key components that allow us to explicitly use approval relations are formally defined:

DEF. 6.3.1 Given a topic of interest , a **Directed Approval Graph** is a quadruple $DAG_q = \{V_q, E_q, X_q^V, X_q^E\}$, where $V_q = \{v_1, \dots, v_n\}$ represents the set of active users on q; $E_q = \{(v_i, v_j) | v_i, v_j \in V_q\}$ is the set of approval edges, meaning the extent that v_i approved v_j's messages; $X_q^E = \{w_{ij} | (v_i, v_j) \in E_q\}$ is the set of weights assigned to approval edges, indicating that v_i approved w_{ij} messages of v_j on q; $X_q^V = \{k_i | v_i \in V_q\}$; is the set of coefficients related to nodes, where k_i represents the total number of messages of v_i on q.

Given a DAG_q, the Normalized Directed Approval Graph is defined as:

DEF. 6.3.2 Given an Approval Graph $DAG_q = \{V_q, E_q, X_q^V, X_q^E\}$, a **Normalized Directed Approval Graph** is derived as a triple $N - DAG_q = \{V_q, E_q, C_q^E\}$, where $C_q^E = \{c_{ij} | w_{ij} \in X_q^E, k_j \in X_q^V\}$ is the set of normalized weights of approval edges, and c_{ij} is calculated as

$$c_{ij} = \frac{w_{ij}}{max_i w_{ij}} \log_2 \left(1 + \frac{w_{ij}}{k_j}\right)$$ [6.3.5]

Equation 6.3.5 takes into account different aspects.

Firstly, the common characteristic of an approval network is that most of the users usually approve only one message of a target user, and very few users approve two or more messages (Kwak et al., 2010). Thus, for a better approximation, a logarithmic distribution should be used instead of a linear one. Secondly, the number of approvals between two users does not necessarily indicate how much they agree with a particular topic. It could be influenced by the interest and originality of the target user's messages. For example, user A could completely agree with user B but approve only once or twice due to the weak originality of B's messages.

For this reason, the number of approvals from user A to B is normalized considering the maximum number of approvals from any user connected to B. Assuming that approving only one message does not lead to valuable information regarding the agreement among users, $N\text{–}DAG_q$ is able to give a lower weight to edges where the number of approvals is only 1. Moreover, $N\text{–}DAG_q$ penalizes users who approve few tweets of a particular target user if there are other users who approve many tweets of the same target user.

The $N\text{–}DAG_q$ is then extended by defining a heterogeneous graph as a unique representation of both user-user and user-message relationships:

DEF. 6.3.3 Given an $N\text{–}DAG_q$, let $M_q=\{m_1,\cdots, m_m\}$ be the set of nodes representing messages about q and $A_q^M = \{(v_i, m_t)|v_i \in V_q, m_t \in M_q\}$ be the set of arcs that connect the user v_i and the message m_t. A **Heterogeneous Directed Approval Graph** is a quintuple $H - DAG_q = \{V_q, E_q, C_q^E, M_q, A_q^M\}$.

A graphical representation of $H - DAG_q$ is given in Figure 6.3.1. In the following, topic q is intended to be fixed and therefore omitted and $H - DAG$ will be denoted as ϕ.

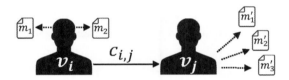

Figure 6.3.1: *H-DAG representing user-message and user-user (approval) dependencies*

User-level Sentiment Analysis with Approval Network: a semi-supervised model

Dealing with sentiment classification in social networks usually requires a fully supervised learning paradigm (Section 6.3.1), where the sentiment orientation of users must be known a priori to derive suitable predictive models. However, this does not reflect the real setting of social networks, where the polarity on a given topic is explicitly available only for some users (black nodes) while for others it could be derived from their posts and relations with other users (white nodes). As black nodes, those users whose bio (description in Twitter) or name clearly states a positive/negative opinion about the studied topic have been considered. For instance, regarding the topic "Obama", a positive user's bio could report "*I love football, TV series and Obama!*" and/or the name could be "*ObamaSupporter*".

In this context, a supervised learning paradigm does not suit the real-life setting. To this end, Pozzi et al. (2013c) propose a semi-supervised sentiment learning approach able to deal both with text and Approval Network: given a small proportion of users already labelled in terms of polarity, it predicts the sentiments of the remaining unlabelled users by combining textual information and Approval Network directly in the probabilistic model.

Semi-supervised Sentiment Learning by Approval Network (S²-LAN)

Given an $H\text{–}DAG_q$, two vectors need to be introduced to tackle the sentiment classification problem at user-level: a vector of labels $L^v=\{l_{v_i}(m_t) \in \{+,-\}| v_i \in V, m_t \in M\}$ that defines each user as either "positive" (+) or "negative"

(-) and an analogous vector of labels $L^M = \{l_{v_i}(m_t) \in \{+,-\}| \; v_i \in V, m_t \in M\}$ that represents the polarity label of each message written by user.

Since the sentiment $l(v_i)$ of the user v_i is influenced by the sentiment labels of his messages and the sentiment labels $l_{v_i}(m_t)$ of the directly connected neighbours $M(v_i)$, the approval model is intended to obey the Markov assumption. The user-message and user-user (approval) relations are combined as follows:

$$\log P(L^V \mid M, \phi)$$

$$= \left(\sum_{v_i \in V} \left[\sum_{m_t \in M} \sum_{\alpha} \sum_{\beta} \mu_{\alpha,\beta} f_{\alpha,\beta} \left(l(v_i), l_{v_i}(m_t) \right) \right. \right.$$

$$\left. \left. + \sum_{v_j \in N(v_i), (v_i, v_j) \in \phi} \sum_{\alpha} \sum_{\beta} \lambda_{\alpha,\beta} g_{\alpha,\beta} \left(l(v_i), l(v_j) \right) \right] \right) \qquad [6.3.6]$$

$$- \log Z$$

where $f_{\alpha,\beta}(\cdot,\cdot)$ and $g_{\alpha,\beta}(\cdot,\cdot)$ are feature functions that evaluate user-message and user-user relations respectively $(\alpha,\beta \in \{+,-\})$, and the weights $\mu_{\alpha,\beta}$ (a user with label α who posts a message with label β), $\lambda_{\alpha,\beta}$ (a user with label α connected to a user with label β) need to be estimated. Z is the normalization factor that enables a coherent probability distribution of $P(L^v)$.

Regarding the estimation of μ, λ and the assignment of user-sentiment labels which maximize $P(L^v)$ see Pozzi et al. (2013c), where a modified version of Sample Rank Algorithm (Wick et al., 2009) is presented.

User-message feature function

A user-message feature function evaluates whether the message polarity agrees (or disagrees) with respect to the user sentiment.

Formally, $f_{\alpha,\beta}(l(v_i), l_{v_i}(m_t))$ is defined as:

$$f_{\alpha,\beta}\left(l(v_i), l_{v_i}(m_t) \right) =$$

$$= \begin{cases} \dfrac{\rho_{T-black}}{|M_{v_j}|} & l(v_i) = \alpha, l_{v_i}(m_t) = \beta, v_i \; black \\[2mm] \dfrac{\rho_{T-white}}{|M_{v_j}|} & l(v_i) = \alpha, l_{v_i}(m_t) = \beta, v_i \; white \\[2mm] 0 & otherwise \end{cases} \qquad [6.3.7]$$

where "v_i black" means that user v_i is initially labelled (i.e. its polarity label is known a priori), and "v_i white" means that user v_i is unlabelled (i.e. its polarity label is unknown a priori). The parameters $\rho_{T-black}$ and $\rho_{T-white}$ represent the different level of confidence in black and white users[6], and $M_{v_i} \subset M$ denotes the set of messages written by user v_i. Every $m_t \in M$ is assumed to have a polarity label. A methodology for automatically labelling messages is described in Section 6.3.1.

User-user feature function

A user-user feature function evaluates whether the polarity of a given user agrees (or disagrees) with his neighbour's sentiment.

Given an H-DAG, $g_{\alpha,\beta}(l(v_i), (v_j))$ is formally defined as follows:

$$
g_{\alpha,\beta}\big(l(v_i), l(v_j)\big)
$$

$$
= \begin{cases} \dfrac{\rho_{neigh} c_{i,j}}{\sum_{v_k \in N(v_i)} c_{i,k}} & l(v_i) = \alpha,\, l_{v_i}(m_t) = \beta,\, v_i\ black \\ 0 & otherwise \end{cases} \qquad [6.3.8]
$$

where ρ_{neigh} represents the level of confidence in relationships among users and denotes the normalized weights of approval edges in ϕ.

Results in Pozzi et al., (2013c) show that the approval relations enclosed in S2-LAN ensure a global improvement of 27% with respect to the text-only method (BMA approach).

Since BMA does not take into account any kind of relationship, the correct prediction of a user does not have any effect on adjoining users. Considering the network, the prediction of each user has impact on all the other nodes by a "propagation" effect, smoothing each predicted label according to adjoining nodes. This investigation finally confirms that the inclusion of relationships in predictive models, as suggested in other studies (Sharara et al., 2011; Fersini and Messina, 2013) leads to improved recognition performance when dealing with non-propositional environments.

Leveraging Network Information in Aspect-Sentiment Modelling: an unsupervised model

This section focuses on simultaneously extracting aspects and classifying sentiments from textual messages, through an unsupervised probabilistic model called Networked Aspect-Sentiment (NAS).

Most of the work in SA (Wang and Manning, 2012; Barbosa and Feng, 2010) is topic-dependent, i.e. they identify the sentiments of documents given a particular topic, which is usually extracted through social tools such as "hashtags" (words or unspaced phrases prefixed with the symbol '#'). But since Social Networks contain highly diverse and often the latest topics, condensed in short messages that make classical text analysis highly inadequate, this is not always sufficient. For example, the above works would assign the topic 'iOS7' to the tweet *"#iOS7 is very good, but they still need to work on battery life and security issues"*.

However, the sentiment behind the above-quoted text distinguishes between the aspects 'battery life' and 'security'. Several works which deal with sentiment classification and topic modelling have been proposed in the literature. *Topic Sentiment Mixture (TSM) model* (Mei et al., 2007) separates topic and sentiment words using an extended pLSA model. Further models based on the LDA principle can be found in He et al. (2011) and Jo and Oh (2011), where the *Joint Sentiment/Topic (JST)* model and the *Aspect and Sentiment Unification Model (ASUM)* are proposed respectively. The main advantage of the joint modelling of sentiments and aspects comes from its ability to reciprocally reduce the noise of both tasks. However, these techniques consider textual information only.

Networked Aspect-Sentiment (NAS) model

In this section, an unsupervised probabilistic model called Networked Aspect-Sentiment (NAS) is presented. It incorporates approval relations to perform the sentiment classification and aspect extraction tasks simultaneously. We present the generative process of NAS and show how the H-DAG (ϕ) is used in the model inference.

Generative Process:

The generative process is stated as follows (see notations in Table 6.3.1):

1. For each sentiment s and aspect z, draw a per-sentiment, per-aspect distribution of words, $\phi_{s,z} \sim$ Dirichlet (β) .

2. For each message m:
    a. Draw a per-message distribution of sentiments, $\pi_m \sim$ Dirichlet (γ) .
    b. For each sentiment s:
        i. Draw a per-message, per-sentiment distribution of aspects, $\theta_{m,s} \sim$ Dirichlet (α) .
    c. For each word w_t in message m:
        i. Choose a sentiment $s_t \sim \pi_m$.
        ii. Choose an aspect $z_t \sim \theta_{m,s_t}$
        iii. Emit $w_t \sim \phi_{s_t,z_t}$.

We also set the hyper-parameter β asymmetric since some positive words are less probable in negative expressions and vice versa. Its entries corresponding to generally positive sentiment words have small values for negative aspect-sentiment pairs, and vice versa.

Table 6.3.1: *Meaning of the notations*

Symbol	Descriptions
v_i	User
(v_i, v_j)	directed edge from user v_i to user v_j
V, E	set of users and approval edges
$M(v_j)$	set of messages of user v_j
$c_{i,j}$	normalized weight of edge (i, j)
T, S, W	number of topics, sentiments and distinct terms
m, z, s, w	message, aspect, sentiment and word
z_{-t}, s_{-t}	vector of assignments of aspects and sentiments for all the words in the corpus, except for the t-th word
π, θ, φ	multinomial distribution over sentiments, aspects and words
α, β, γ	Dirichlet prior vectors for θ, ϕ and π
$N_{w_t,k,l}^{-t}$	number of times that word w_t appeared in aspect k with sentiment l, except for the t-th word
$N_{k,l}^{-t}$	number of times that words are assigned sentiment l and aspect k, except for the t-th word
$N_{k,l,m}^{-t}$	number of times that word w_t is assigned sentiment l and aspect k in message m, except for the t-th word
$N_{l,m}^{-t}$	number of times that sentiment l isassigned to message m, except for the t-th word
N_m^{-t}	total number of words in the corpus, except for the t-th word

Inference:

Collapsed Gibbs sampling (Griffiths and Steyvers, 2004) is a standard inference procedure to obtain a Markov chain over the latent variables in topic models. In the NAS model, we jointly sample latent variables s and z, which gives us a blocked Gibbs sampler. The benefits of the Approval Networks arise from the stronger sentiment agreement on specific aspects between users. Thus, the probability of assigning a sentiment to a message should also be influenced by the sentiments of those users who share the edges in the Approval Network.

Following this rationale, the corresponding conditional distribution is defined below (see notations in Table 6.3.1):

$$P(z_t = k, s_t = s \mid w, z_{-t}, s_{-t}, \alpha, \beta, \gamma, \phi) \propto$$

$$\propto \frac{N_{w_t,k,s}^{-t} + \beta}{N_{k,s}^{-t} + W\beta} \times \frac{N_{k,s,m}^{-t} + \alpha}{N_{s,m}^{-t} + T\alpha} \times \frac{N_{s,m}^{-t} + \gamma}{N_m^{-t} + S\gamma}$$

$$\times \frac{\sum_{(v_i,v_j) \in E} c_{i,j} \frac{1}{|M(v_j)|} \sum_{m' \in M(v_j)} \frac{N_{s,m'}^{-t} + \gamma}{N_{m'}^{-t} + S\gamma}}{\sum_{(v_i,v_j) \in E} c_{i,j}}$$

[6.3.9]

The above conditional distribution takes into consideration both content (**A**) and the information provided by H-DAG (**B**) (See *DEF. 6.3.3*). The weight of the relationship that links the source user v_i and the target user v_j is applied to smoothing the probability. In particular, (**B'**) represents the average probability that the terms of messages m' of v_j (excluding term t) belong to sentiment c_{ij}. This averaged probability is further regularized by weight. The entire smoothing process is based on a projection of weights c_{ij} between users and their corresponding messages (see Figure 6.3.2).

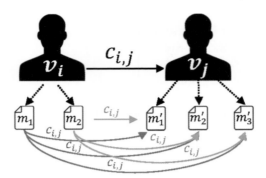

Figure 6.3.2: *Given two users connected by an edge with weight c_ij, all the messages of the source user are connected with the messages of the target user by a projection of the weight c_ij.*

Results show that NAS outperforms existing state-of-the-art models markedly from both the sentiment classification and aspect extraction perspectives. This is because the joint modelling of sentiments and aspects has the ability to reciprocally reduce the noise of both tasks. In particular, NAS achieves a gain of up to 42% in F1-measure in sentiment classification.

6.4 SARCASM AND IRONY DETECTION IN SHORT MESSAGES

As defined in Corbett (1971), a figure of speech is any artful deviation from the ordinary mode of speaking or writing. One of the most problematic figures of speech that Natural Language Processing (NLP) techniques try to detect is sarcasm, which is commonly used to convey implicit criticism with a particular victim as its target, saying or writing the opposite of what the author means. Therefore it is clear that sarcasm and irony highly influence the sentiment classification task. Although sarcasm is a well-studied phenomenon in linguistics, psychology and cognitive science (Gibbs and Colston, 2007), its automatic detection in NLP is still in its infancy because of its complexity. However, some work has been done. In Davidov et al. (2010), a semi-supervised learning approach was proposed to automatically expand the initial seed set of labelled messages through Web search. A supervised approach has been proposed in González-Ibáñez et al. (2011). The authors used unigrams, word categories, interjections (e.g. ah, yeah), and punctuation as features. In addition, emoticons, and ToUser (which marks whether a tweet is a reply to another tweet) were also used. However, the general trend of the research focuses on finding ever more varied additional features, paying little attention to the classification process, often addressed by baseline classifiers. For this reason, although feature expansion still remains a valuable and important step, we want to shift the focus to the classification phase, proposing a voting mechanism based on Bayesian Model Averaging (BMA), reported in Section 6.3.1.

6.4.1 Feature Expansion

The traditional feature vector representing a message (used to train a given classifier) only includes terms that belong to a common vocabulary of terms derived from a message collection:

$$\vec{m} = (w_1, w_2, \ldots, w_{|V|}, l)$$

[6.4.1]

where w_t denotes the weight of term t belonging to m with label l.

It is proposed to enhance the traditional feature vector by including indications about some expressive signals of sarcasm. The expanded feature vector of a message is defined as:

$$\vec{m}_{new} = (w_1, w_2, \ldots, w_{|V|}, f_1, f_2, \ldots, f_n, l)$$

[6.4.2]

where $f_1, f_2, \ldots, f_n$ represent the n additional features discussed in Section 6.3.

Although both pragmatic particles and POS tags independently lead to an increment of accuracy for BMA, when pragmatic particles and POS tags are considered together, the performance is even higher. However, sarcasm and irony detection tasks should not be investigated alone. Since there are multiple ties between *subjectivity*, *polarity* and *sarcasm/irony* detection, they should be jointly addressed. However, these tasks have been often considered in the literature as independent.

Different works have usually treated subjectivity and polarity classification as a two-stage binary classification process, where the first level distinguishes between subjective and objective (neutral) statements, and the second level then further distinguishes subjectivity into: subjective-positive / subjective-negative (Refaee and Rieser, 2014).

The results proposed in Wilson et al. (2009) support the validity of this process, indicating that the ability to recognize neutral classes in the first place can greatly improve the performance in distinguishing between positive and negative utterances at a later time. However, as briefly introduced, irony can also provide a contribution to improving the classification performance.An ironic message involves a shift in evaluative valence, which can be treated in two ways: it could be a shift from a literally positive to an intended negative meaning, or a shift from a literally negative to an intended positive evaluation.

According to the above-mentioned considerations, a hierarchical framework able to jointly address subjectivity, polarity and irony detection is proposed in Fersini et al. (2014b). An overview of the working system, named *Hierarchical Bayesian Model Averaging* (H-BMA), is presented in Figure 6.4.1.

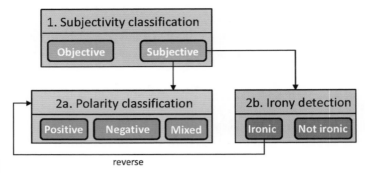

Figure 6.4.1: Hierarchical BMA

Since subjectivity classification is usually the highest-performing task in Sentiment Analysis, the first level distinguishes between subjective and objective statements (neutral is supposed to be objective), and the second level then distinguishes subjectivity into: subjective-positive / subjective-negative / subjective-mixed (a sentence which is subjective, positive and negative at the same time). Jointly with polarity classification, irony detection is also performed. If a given sentence is detected as ironic, then its positive or negative polarity is reversed. On the other hand, if the sentence is ironic but its polarity has been classified as mixed, then it is switched to negative. Thus a message , identified as mixed by the polarity classification layer and ironic (denoted as *iro*) by the irony detection layer, is finally labelled as negative (-) due to the conditional distribution

$$P(s = -| s = iro) \gg P(s = + | s = iro)$$ [6.4.3]

The uncertainty about which model is the optimal one in different contexts has been overcome in this work by Bayesian Model Averaging (Pozzi et al., 2013a), a novel ensemble learning approach able to exploit the potential of several learners when predicting the labels for each task (subjectivity, irony and polarity) of the hierarchical framework.

6.5 APPLICATIONS

Due to all the possible applications, a comprehensive and clear review is needed.

The Sentiment Analysis field is well-suited to various types of intelligence applications. Indeed, business intelligence seems to be one of the main factors behind corporate interest in the field. One of the most important needs of businesses and organizations in the real world is to find and analyse consumer or public opinion about their products and services (e.g., Why aren't consumers buying our laptop?). Sentiment Analysis paves the way for several interesting applications in almost every possible domain. For example, summarizing user reviews is a relevant task of analytics. Moreover, opinions matter a great deal in politics. Some work has focused on understanding what voters are thinking (Goldberg et al., 2007; Hopkins and King, 2007). For instance, US president Barack Obama used Sentiment Analysis to gauge the feelings of core voters during the 2008 presidential elections. A further task is augmenting recommendation systems, where the system might not recommend items that receive several cases of negative feedback (Pang and Lee, 2008). However, Sentiment Analysis can also be applied to more ethical principles. For example, based on observations of Twitter's role in civilian response during the recent 2009 Jakarta and Mumbai terrorist attacks, Cheong and Lee (2011) propose a structured framework to harvest civilian sentiment and response on Twitter during terrorism scenarios.

Sentiment Analysis is also applied to the medical field. Cobb et al. (2013) applied Sentiment Analysis to examine how exposure to messages about the cessation of drug varenicline (used to treat nicotine addiction) affects smokers' decision-making about its use.

In recent years, microblogs have emerged as potential sources of information for Sentiment Analysis in the financial domain. Si et al. (2013) uses financial tweets to predict short-term movements in the S&P100 index, while Bollen et al. (2011) leverage the Twitter mood to predict the stock market. In particular, the authors investigated whether measurements of collective mood states derived from large scale Twitter feeds are correlated to the value of the Dow Jones Industrial Average (DJIA) over time. Ruiz et al. (2012) collect messages relating to a number of companies and search for correlations between stock-market events for those companies and features extracted from microblogging messages.

Although most work investigates the predictive power of stock microblog sentiment to forecast future stock price directional movements, some work has also been published with other aims. Bar-Haim et al. (2011) show that it is beneficial to distinguish expert users from non-experts. They propose a general framework for identifying expert investors, and use it as a basis for several predictive models. Regarding reputation management, Seebach et al. (2012) provide an empirical example of how firms might improve corporate reputation management by sensing social media.

6.6 CONCLUSION AND FUTURE DIRECTIONS

Sentiment Analysis has grown to be one of the most active research areas in NLP only since early 2000, for various reasons. Firstly, it has a wide array of applications in almost every domain. Secondly, it offers many challenging research problems, which have never been studied before. Thirdly, for the first time in human history, we now have a huge volume of opinionated data recorded and easily accessible in digital forms on the Web. Without it, a lot of research would not have been possible.

However, considering the differences between well-formed documents (e.g., news or reviews) and Social Media, where opinions are full of hasty spelling and unconventional grammatical quirks, the strategies available in the current state of the art are no longer effective for mining opinions in this new and challenging environment.

Although most of the work regarding polarity classification considers text as unique information to infer sentiment, Social Networks and Microblogs are actually networked environments. A representation of real-world data where instances are considered as homogeneous, independent and identically distributed (i.i.d.) leads us to substantial loss of information and to the introduction of a statistical bias.

For this reason, starting from the classical state-of-the-art methodologies where text alone is used to infer the polarity of social media messages, this chapter presented novel probabilistic relational models on both the document and the aspect level which integrate this structural information to improve classification performance. Incorporating networks can lead to significant improvements on the performance for complex supervised classifiers based only on textual features.

Sarcasm and irony are still very strong issues in Sentiment Analysis (and more generally NLP) applications. However, in recent years huge strides have been made. The positive results achieved make researchers optimistic that future systems will be able to handle sarcasm and irony detection with very good performance.

Notes

[1] www.facebook.com

[2] en.wikipedia.org

[3] www.youtube.com

[4] www.twitter.com

[5] Note that for this reason Facebook's '*Share*' tool does not belong to approval tools.

[6] Note that $P_{T-black}$, $P_{T-white}$ and P_{neigh} are empirically estimated.

6.7 REFERENCES

1.   Abel, F., Gao, Q., Houben, G.J. and Tao, K. (2011). Semantic Enrichment of Twitter Posts for User Profile Construction on the Social Web. In *Proceedings of the 8th Extended Semantic Web Conference on The Semantic Web: Research and Applications - Volume Part II* . Springer-Verlag, pp. 375–389.

2.   Agarwal, A., Xie, B., Vovsha, I., Rambow, O. and Passonneau, R. (2011). Sentiment Analysis of Twitter Data. In *Proceedings of the Workshop on Language in Social Media*, pp. 30–38.

3.   Aristotle. (1934). Rhetoric. Nicomachean ethics. In *Aristotle in 23 Volumes*, Vol. 19, pp. 1371, translated by H. Rackman. Cambridge: Harvard University Press.

4.   Bar-Haim, R., Dinur, E., Feldman, R., Fresko, M. and Goldstein, G. (2011). Identifying and Following Expert Investors in Stock Microblogs. In *Proceedings of the Conference on Empirical Methods in Natural Language Processing*. Association for Computational Linguistics, pp. 1310–1319.

5.   Barbosa, L. and Feng, J. (2010). Robust Sentiment Detection on Twitter from Biased and Noisy Data. In *Proceedings of the 23rd International Conference on Computational Linguistics: Posters*. Association for Computational Linguistics, pp. 36–44.

6. Boiy, E. and Moens, M.F. (2009). A machine learning approach to sentiment analysis in multilingual Web texts. Information Retrieval, *12(5)*, pp. 526–558.

7. Bollen, J., Mao, H. and Zeng, X. (2011). Twitter mood predicts the stock market. *Journal of Computational Science, 2(1)*, pp. 1–8.

8. Bott, H. (1928). Observation of play activities in a nursery school. *Genetic Psychology Monographs, 4(1)*, pp. 44–88.

9. Boyd, D., Golder, S. and Lotan, G. (2010). Tweet, Tweet, Retweet: Conversational Aspects of Retweeting on Twitter. In *Proceedings of the 2010 43rd Hawaii International Conference on System Sciences*. IEEE Computer Society, pp. 1–10.

10. Brody, S. and Diakopoulos, N. (2011). Cooooooooooooooooollllllllllllllll!!!!!!!!!!!!!!! Using Word Lengthening to Detect Sentiment in Microblogs. In *Proceedings of the Conference on Empirical Methods in Natural Language Processing*, pp. 561–570.

11. Carley, K.M. (1991). A Theory of Group Stability. *American Sociological Review, 56(3)*, pp. 331–354.

12. Carter, S., Weerkamp, W. and Tsagkias, M. (2013). Microblog Language Identification: Overcoming the Limitations of Short, Unedited and Idiomatic Text. *Language Resources and Evaluation, 47(1)*, pp. 195–215.

13. Cheong, M. and Lee, V.C.S. (2011). A microblogging-based approach to terrorism informatics: Exploration and chronicling civilian sentiment and response to terrorism events via twitter. *Information Systems Frontiers, 13(1)*, pp. 45–59

14. Cobb, N.K., Mays, D. and Graham, A.L. (2013). Sentiment analysis to determine the impact of online messages on smokers' choices to use varenicline. *Journal of the National Cancer Institute. Monographs, 2013(47)*, pp. 224–230

15. Corbett, E.P.J. (1971). *Classical Rhetoric for the Modern Student*. 2nd ed., Oxford University Press.

16. Davidov, D., Tsur, O. and Rappoport, A. (2010). Semi-supervised recognition of sarcastic sentences in twitter and amazon. In *Proceedings of the Fourteenth Conference on Computational Natural Language Learning*. Association for Computational Linguistics, pp. 107–116.

17. Dolan, R.J. (2002). Emotion, cognition, and behavior. *Science, 298(5596)*, pp. 1191–1194.

18. Fersini, E. and Messina, E. (2013). Web page classification through probabilistic relational models. *International Journal of Pattern Recognition and Artificial Intelligence, 27(4)*.

19. Fersini, E., Messina, E. and Archetti, F. (2010). Web page classification: A probabilistic model with relational uncertainty. In *Proceedings of the Computational Intelligence for Knowledge-based Systems Design,* and *13th International Conference on Information Processing and Management of Uncertainty.* Springer-Verlag, pp. 109–118.

20. Fersini, E., Messina, E. and Pozzi, F.A. (2014).Sentiment analysis: Bayesian ensemble learning. *Decision Support Systems, 68(0),* pp. 26–38.

21. Fersini, E., Messina, E. and Pozzi, F.A. (2014). Subjectivity, polarity and irony detection: A multi-layer approach. In *Proceedings of the First Italian Conference on Computational Linguistics* and *the Fourth International Workshop EVALITA 2014.*

22. Gatti, M., Cavalin, P., Neto, S., Pinhanez, C., dos Santos, C., Gribel, D. and Appel, A. (2014). Large-scale multi-agent based modeling and simulation of microblogging-based online social network. In *Multi-Agent-Based Simulation XIV,* Lecture Notes in Computer Science, pp. 17–33. Springer Berlin Heidelberg.

23. Gibbs, R.W. and Colston, H.L. (2007). *Irony in Language and Thought: A Cognitive Science Reader.* Lawrence Erlbaum Associates.

24. Go, A., Bhayani, R. and Huang, L. (2009). Twitter sentiment classification using distant supervision. Technical report, Stanford.

25. Goldberg, A.B., Zhu, X. and Wright, S.J. (2007). Dissimilarity in graph-based semi-supervised classification. In *AISTATS,* Vol. 2, pp. 155–162.

26. González-Ibáñez, R., Muresan, S. and Wacholder, N. (2011). Identifying sarcasm in twitter: A closer look. In *Proceedings of the 49th Annual Meeting of the Association for Computational Linguistics: Human Language Technologies: Short Papers - Volume 2.* Association for Computational Linguistics, pp. 581–586.

27. Gouws, S., Metzler, D., Cai, C. and Hovy, E. (2011). Contextual bearing on linguistic variation in social media. In *Proceedings of the Workshop on Languages in Social Media.* Association for Computational Linguistics, pp. 20–29.

28. Griffiths, T.L. and Steyvers, M. (2004). Finding scientific topics. *Proceedings of the National Academy of Sciences 101,* pp. 5228–5235.

29. He, Y., Lin, C. and Alani, H. (2011). Automatically extracting polarity-bearing topics for cross-domain sentiment classification. In *Proceedings of the 49th Annual Meeting of the Association for Computational Linguistics: Human Language Technologies - Volume 1.* Association for Computational Linguistics, pp. 123–131.

30. Hopkins, D. and King, G. (2007). Extracting systematic social science meaning from text. Manuscript available at: http://gking.harvard.edu/files/words.pdf

31. Hu, M. and Liu, B. (2004). Mining and summarizing customer reviews. In *Proceedings of the Tenth ACM SIGKDD International Conference on Knowledge Discovery and Data Mining*, pp. 168–177. ..

32. Hu, X., Tang, L., Tang, J. and Liu, H. (2013). Exploiting social relations for sentiment analysis in microblogging. In *Proceedings of the sixth ACM international conference on Web search and data mining*. ACM, pp. 537–546.

33. Jo, Y. and Oh, A.H. (2011). Aspect and sentiment unification model for online review analysis. In *Proceedings of the Fourth ACM International Conference on Web Search and Data Mining*, pp. 815–824.

34. Joseph, K., Morgan, G.P., Martin, M.K. and Carley, K.M. (2013). On the coevolution of stereotype, culture, and social relationships: An agent-based model. *Social Science Computer Review*.

35. Kahneman, D. and Tversky, A. (1979). Prospect theory: An analysis of decision under risk. *Econometrica: Journal of the Econometric Society*, pp. 263–291.

36. Kandel, D.B. (1978). Homophily, selection, and socialization in adolescent friendships. *The American Journal of Sociology, 84(2)*, pp. 427–436.

37. Kwak, H., Lee, C., Park, H. and Moon, S. (2010). What is twitter, a social network or a news media? In *Proceedings of the 19th international conference on World Wide Web*, pp. 591–600.

38. Lazarsfeld, P.F. and Merton, R.K. (1954). Friendship as a social process: A substantive and methodological analysis. *Freedom and Control in Modern Society*, pp. 18–66.

39. McPherson, M., Smith-Lovin, L. and Cook, J.M. (2001). Birds of a feather: Homophily in social networks. *Annual review of sociology*, pp. 415–444.

40. Mei, Q., Cai, D., Zhang, D. and Zhai, C. (2008). Topic modeling with network regularization. In *Proceedings of the 17ʰᵗ International Conference on World Wide Web*, pp. 101–110.

41. Mei, Q., Ling, X., Wondra, M., Su, H. and Zhai, C. (2007). Topic sentiment mixture: Modeling facets and opinions in weblogs. In *Proceedings of the 16th International Conference on World Wide Web*, pp. 171–180.

42. Mendes, P.N., Passant, A., Kapanipathi, P. and Sheth, A.P. (2010). Linked open social signals. In *Proceedings of the 2010 IEEE/WIC/ACM International Conference on Web Intelligence and Intelligent Agent Technology -Volume 01*. IEEE Computer Society, pp. 224–231.

43. Mitra, G. and Mitra, L. (2011). *The Handbook of News Analytics in Finance*. Wiley Finance

44. Nofsinger, J.R. (2005). Social mood and financial economics. *The Journal of Behavioral Finance, 6(3)*, pp. 144–160.

45. O'Connor, B., Balasubramanyan, R., Routledge, B.R. and Smith, N.A. (2010). From tweets to polls: Linking text sentiment to public opinion time series. *ICWSM 11*, pp. 122–129.

46. Pak, A. and Paroubek, P. (2010). Twitter based system: Using twitter for disambiguating sentiment ambiguous adjectives. In *Proceedings of the 5th International Workshop on Semantic Evaluation*. Association for Computational Linguistics, pp. 436–439.

47. Pang, B. and Lee, L. (2008). Opinion mining and sentiment analysis. *Foundations and trends in information retrieval, 2(1-2)*, pp. 1–135.

48. Plato (1968). Laws. In *Plato in Twelve Volumes*, Vol. 11, pp. 837. Translated by Bury. Cambridge: Harvard University Press.

49. Pozzi, F.A., Fersini, E. and Messina, E. (2013). Bayesian model averaging and model selection for polarity classification. In *Proceedings of the 18th International Conference on Application of Natural Language to Information Systems*, pp. 189–200.

50. Pozzi, F.A., Fersini, E., Messina, E. and Blanc, D. (2013). Enhance polarity classification on social media through sentiment-based feature expansion. In *WOA@ AI* IA*, pp. 78–84.

51. Pozzi, F.A., Maccagnola, D., Fersini, E. and Messina, E. (2013). Enhance user-level sentiment analysis on microblogs with approval relations. In *AI*IA 2013: Advances in Artificial Intelligence*, Lecture Notes in Computer Science, Vol. 8249. Springer International Publishing, pp. 133–144.

52. Rabelo, J.C., Prudêncio, R.C. and Barros, F.A. (2012). Leveraging relationships in social networks for sentiment analysis. In *Proceedings of the 18th Brazilian Symposium on Multimedia and the Web*, pp.181–188.

53. Refaee, E. and Rieser, V. (2014). Subjectivity and sentiment analysis of Arabic twitter feeds with limited resources. In *Proceedings of the 9th edition of the Language Resources and Evaluation Conference*, pp. 16–21.

54. Ruiz, E.J., Hristidis, V., Castillo, C., Gionis, A. and Jaimes, A. (2012). Correlating financial time series with microblogging activity. In *Proceedings of the Fifth ACM International Conference on Web Search and Data Mining*, pp. 513–522.

55. Scott, J.G. (2000). *Social Network Analysis: A Handbook*. SAGE Publications Ltd.

56. Seebach, C., Beck, R. and Denisova, O. (2012). Sensing social media for corporate reputation management: A business agility perspective. In *20th European Conference on Information Systems*, pp. 140–140.

57. Sharara, H., Getoor, L. and Norton, M. (2011). Active surveying: A probabilistic approach for identifying key opinion leaders. In *IJCAI*, pp. 1485–1490.

58. Si, J., Mukherjee, A., Liu, B., Li, Q., Li, H. and Deng, X. (2013). Exploiting topic based twitter sentiment for stock prediction. In *ACL*, pp. 24–29.

59. Taboada, M., Brooke, J., Tofiloski, M., Voll, K. and Stede, M. (2011). Lexicon-based methods for sentiment analysis. *Computational Linguistics, 37(2)*, pp. 267–307.

60. Tan, C., Lee, L., Tang, J., Jiang, L., Zhou, M. and Li, P. (2011). User-level sentiment analysis incorporating social networks. In *Proceedings of the 17th ACM SIGKDD international conference on Knowledge discovery and data mining*, pp. 1397–1405.

61. Walther, J.B. and D'addario, K.P. (2001). The impacts of emoticons on message interpretation in computer-mediated communication. *Social Science Computer Review, 19*, pp. 324–347.

62. Wang, S. and Manning, C.D. (2012). Baselines and bigrams: simple, good sentiment and topic classification. *In Proceedings of the 50th Annual Meeting of the Association for Computational Linguistics: Short Papers -Volume 2*, pp. 90–94.

63. Wellman, B. (1929). The school child's choice of companions. *The Journal of Educational Research, 14(2)*, pp. 126–32.

64. Whitelaw, C., Garg, N. and Argamon, S. (2005). Using appraisal groups for sentiment analysis. In *Proceedings of the14th ACM International Conference on Information and Knowledge Management*, pp. 625–631.

65. Wick, M., Rohanimanesh, K., Culotta, A. and McCallum, A. (2009). Sample rank: Learning preferences from atomic gradients. In *NIPS Workshop on Advances in Ranking*, pp. 69-73.

66. Wilson, T., Wiebe, J. and Hoffmann, P. (2009). Recognizing contextual polarity: An exploration of features for phrase level sentiment analysis. *Computational Linguistics, 35(3)*, pp. 399–433.

67. Yu, S. and Kak, S. (2012). A Survey of Prediction Using Social Media. ArXiv e-prints.

68. Zhang, L. and Liu, B. (2011). Identifying noun product features that imply opinions. In *Proceedings of the 49th Annual Meeting of the Association for Computational Linguistics: Human Language Technologies: Short Papers- Volume 2*. Association for Computational Linguistics, pp. 575–580.

CHAPTER 7

Quantifying *Wikipedia* Usage Patterns
Before Stock Market Moves

Helen Susannah Moat, *Associate Professor of Behavioural Science,*
Warwick Business School, The University of Warwick

Chester Curme, *Quantitative Analyst, Loomis, Sayles and Company*

Adam Avakian, *Quantitative Analyst, Citizens Financial Group*

Dror Y. Kenett, *Interdisciplinary Researcher, U.S. Department of the Treasury,*
Office of Financial Research

H. Eugene Stanley, *Warren Professor, Boston University*

Tobias Preis, *Associate Professor of Behavioural Science and Finance, Warwick Business*
School, The University of Warwick

Reprinted with permission from: "*Quantifying Wikipedia usage patterns before stock market moves*" by
Helen Susannah Moat, Chester Curme, Adam Avakian, Dror Y. Kenett, H. Eugene Stanley and Tobias Preis,
2013. Scientific Reports, Volume 3:1801

ABSTRACT

Financial crises result from a catastrophic combination of actions. Vast stock market datasets offer us a window into some of the actions that have led to these crises. Here, we investigate whether data generated through Internet usage contain traces of attempts to gather information before trading decisions were taken. We present evidence in line with the intriguing suggestion that data on changes in how often financially related *Wikipedia* pages were viewed may have contained early signs of stock market moves. Our results suggest that online data may allow us to gain new insight into early information gathering stages of decision making.

7.1 INTRODUCTION

The complex behaviour of our society emerges from decisions made by many individuals. In certain combinations, these numerous decisions can lead to sudden catastrophe, as demonstrated during crowd disasters and financial crises. Stock market data provide extremely detailed records of decisions that traders have made, in an area in which disasters have a widespread impact. As a result, these stock market records have generated considerable scientific attention (Fehr, 2002; Lillo, Farmer and Mantegna, 2003; Gabaix et al., 2003; Preis et al., 2012; Preis, Schneider and Stanley, 2011; Podobnik et al., 2009; Mantegna and Stanley, 2002; Farmer, Patelli and Zovko, 2005; Feng et al., 2012; Hommes, 2002; Lux and Marchesi, 1999; Sornette and von der Becke, 2011; Johnson, Jefferies and Hui, 2003; Kenett, 2011).

Human decision making does not, however, consist solely of the final execution of a chosen action, such as a trade recorded at a stock exchange. Instead, within the constraints of available resources, we often begin by gathering information to help us identify what the consequences of possible actions might be (Simon, 1955).

With Internet provision becoming so widespread, online resources have become the first port of call in many quests for new information. As a rule, providers of such online resources collect extensive data on their usage, adding to a range of new large-scale measurements of collective human behavior (King, 2011; Vespignani, 2009; Lazer, 2009; Silver 2012; Perc, 2012; Petersen, 2012). In this way, the ubiquity of the Internet in everyday life has not only changed the way in which people collect information to make decisions, but has opened up new avenues for scientists to investigate the early information gathering stages of decision making processes.

Previous studies have demonstrated that analysis of search data can provide insight into current or even subsequent behaviour in the real world. For example, changes in the frequency with which users look for certain terms on search engines such as *Google* and *Yahoo!* have been correlated with changes in the numbers of reports of flu infections across the USA (Ginsberg, 2009), the popularity of films, games and music on their release (Goel et al., 2010), unemployment rates (Askitas and Zimmermann, 2009; Choi and Varian, 2012), tourist numbers (Choi and Varian, 2012), and trading volumes in the US stock markets (Preis, Reith and Stanley 2010; Bordino, 2012). A recent study showed that Internet users from countries with a higher per capita gross domestic product (GDP) search for proportionally more information about the future than information about the past, in comparison with Internet users from countries with a lower per capita GDP (Preis et al., 2012).

In work most closely related to the study presented here, Preis, Moat and Stanley outline an analysis of historic data which suggests that changes in search volume for financially relevant search terms can be linked to stock market moves (Preis, Moat and Stanley, 2013). A further study analysed data from *Twitter* and considered the emotions of traders, rather than their information gathering processes, suggesting that changes in the calmness of *Twitter* messages could be linked to changes in stock market prices (Bollen, Mao and Zeng, 2011).

In this study, we investigate whether data on the usage of the popular online encyclopaedia *Wikipedia* (Capocci, 2006; Muchnik, 2007; Yasseri, Kornai and Kertész, 2012) can be linked to subsequent decisions made in the stock markets. Specifically, can we find any evidence that changes in the numbers of views or edits to articles relating to companies and other financial topics on *Wikipedia* may provide insight into the information gathering process of investors?

7.2 RESULTS

To investigate the relationship between changes in large-scale information gathering behaviour on Wikipedia and market participants' trading decisions, we consider data on how often pages on the English language Wikipedia have been viewed, and how often pages on the English language Wikipedia have been edited. Wikipedia entries can be both viewed and edited by any Internet user. Data on Wikipedia page views were downloaded from the online service stats.grok.se, and data on Wikipedia page edits were obtained by parsing the Wikipedia "Revision history" page associated to the article. We analyse data generated between 10th December 2007, the earliest date for which Wikipedia views data are available from stats.grok.se, and 30th April 2012.

We calculate two measures of *Wikipedia* user activity: the average number of page views and the average number of page edits that have taken place for a given *Wikipedia* page in week t, where we define weeks as ending on a Sunday. All names of *Wikipedia* pages used and further details on data pre-processing are provided in the Supplementary Information. To quantify changes in information gathering behaviour, we choose one measure of *Wikipedia* user activity $n(t)$, either page view or page edit volume, and calculate the difference between the page view or page edit volume for week t, to the average page view or page edit volume for the previous Δt weeks: $\Delta n(t, \Delta t) = n(t) - N(t - 1, \Delta t)$ with $N(t - 1, \Delta t) = (n(t - 1) + n(t - 2) + ... + n(t - \Delta t) / \Delta t$, where t is measure in units of weeks.

We begin our comparison of changes in *Wikipedia* usage to subsequent stock market movements in this historic data by implementing a hypothetical investment strategy that uses data on either *Wikipedia* page views or *Wikipedia* page edits to trade on the Dow Jones Industrial Average (DJIA), following the approach introduced by Preis, Moat, and Stanley (2013). In this hypothetical strategy, we sell the DJIA at the closing price $p(t + 1)$ on the first trading day of week $t + 1$ if the volume of views or edits has increased in week t such that $\Delta n(t, \Delta t) > 0$. We then close the position by buying the DJIA at price $p(t + 2)$ at the end of the first trading day of the following week $t + 2$. Note that mechanisms exist which make it possible to sell stocks on a financial market without first owning them. If instead the volume of views or edits has decreased or remained the same in week t such that $\Delta n(t, \Delta t) \le 0$, then we buy the DJIA at the closing price $p(t + 1)$ on the first trading day of week $t + 1$, and sell the DJIA at price $p(t + 2)$ at the end of the first trading day of the coming week $t + 2$ to close the position.

We calculate the cumulative return R of a strategy by taking the natural log of the ratio of the final portfolio value to the initial portfolio value. If we take a short position—selling at the closing price $p(t + 1)$ and buying back at price $p(t + 2)$—then the change in the cumulative return R for a strategy is $log(p(t + 1)) - log(p(t + 2))$. If we take a long position—buying at the closing price $p(t + 1)$ and selling at price $p(t + 2)$—then the change in the cumulative return R is $log(p(t + 2)) - log(p(t + 1))$. In this way, buy and sell actions have symmetric impacts on the cumulative return R of a strategy. In addition, we neglect transaction fees, since the maximum number of transactions per year when using this strategy is only 104, allowing one closing and one opening transaction per week. We note that inclusion of transaction fees would of course diminish any profit if this hypothetical strategy were to be used in the real world. However, this assumption does not have consequences for conclusions about the relationship between user activity on *Wikipedia* and movements in the DJIA.

We compare the returns from the *Wikipedia* data based strategies to the returns from a random strategy. In the random strategy, a decision is made each week to buy or sell the DJIA. The probability that the DJIA will be bought rather than sold is always 50%, and the decision is unaffected by decisions in previous weeks. This random strategy leads to no significant profit or loss. For the statistical comparisons reported in the following sections, we use 10,000 independent realisations of this random strategy for the period between 10th December 2007 and 30th April 2012. We find no evidence that the overall return from these 10,000 realisations is significantly positive or significantly negative (mean return $= 0.0002$, $V = 25012353$, $p = 0.97$, $a = 0.05$, two-tailed one-sample Wilcoxon signed rank test of symmetry of distribution of returns around 0). We use a non-parametric test to check this point, as the distribution of returns deviates significantly from the normal distribution ($D = 0.1716$, $p < 0.001$, $a = 0.05$, Kolmogorov-Smirnov test). Similarly, the remainder of the analyses of return distributions reported here also use non-parametric tests. Throughout the rest of the results, the cumulative returns R of all non-random strategies are stated in terms of standard deviations above or below the mean cumulative return of the random strategy.

Views and edits of Wikipedia articles about companies listed in the DJIA. Figure 7.2.1 shows the distributions of returns from two portfolios of 30 hypothetical strategies, trading weekly on the DJIA. These trading strategies are based on changes in how often the 30 *Wikipedia* pages describing the companies in the DJIA were viewed (*blue*) and edited (*red*) during the period December 2007 – April 2012, with $\Delta t = 3$ weeks. The distribution of returns from 10,000 independent realisations of a random strategy is also shown (*grey*).

We find that there are significant differences between these three distributions ($\chi^2 = 10.21$, $df = 2$, $p = 0.006$, $a = 0.05$; Kruskal-Wallis rank sum test). Our analysis shows that the returns of *Wikipedia* page view based strategies for this period are significantly higher than the returns of the random strategies (mean $R = 0.50$; $W = 199690$, $p = 0.005$, $a = 0.05$, two-tailed two-sample Wilcoxon rank-sum test, Bonferroni correction applied). There is however no statistically significant difference between the returns from the *Wikipedia* edit based strategies and the random strategies (mean $R = 20.09$; $W = 140781$, $p > 0.9$, $a = 0.05$, two-tailed two-sample Wilcoxon rank-sum test, Bonferroni correction applied).

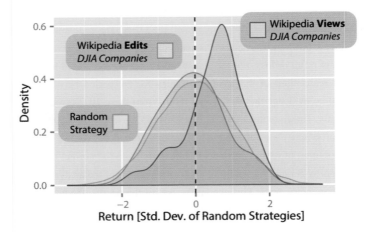

Figure 7.2.1: *Returns from trading strategies based on Wikipedia view and edit logs for articles relating to the companies forming the Dow Jones Industrial Average (DJIA).*

The distributions of returns from two portfolios of 30 hypothetical strategies, trading weekly on the DJIA, based on changes in how often the 30 Wikipedia articles describing the companies listed in the DJIA were viewed (blue) and edited (red) during the period December 2007 – April 2012, with $\Delta t = 3$ weeks. The distribution of returns from 10,000 independent realisations of a random strategy is also shown (grey). Data is displayed using a kernel density estimate and the ggplot2 library (Wickham, 2009), with a Gaussian kernel and bandwidth calculated using Silverman's rule of thumb (Silverman, 1986). Whereas we show in the text that random strategies lead to no significant profit or loss, we find that the returns of Wikipedia article view based strategies for this period are significantly higher than the returns of the random strategies (mean $R = 0.50$; $W = 199690$, $p = 0.005$, $a = 0.05$, two-tailed two-sample Wilcoxon rank-sum test, Bonferroni correction applied). There is however no statistically significant difference between the returns from the Wikipedia edit based strategies and the random strategies (mean $R = -0.09$; $W = 140781$, $p > 0.9$, $a = 0.05$, two-tailed two-sample Wilcoxon rank-sum test, Bonferroni correction applied).

Views and edits of Wikipedia articles about financial topics. We investigate whether these results extend to Wikipedia articles on more general financial topics. To address this question, we make use of the fact that Wikipedia contains lists of pages relating to specific topics. Here, we examine view and edit data for 285 pages relating to general economic concepts, as listed in the subsection "*General economic concepts*" on the English language Wikipedia page "*Outline of economics*".

Figure 7.2.2 shows the results of an analysis of the distribution of returns from two portfolios of 285 hypothetical strategies, trading weekly on the DJIA. These strategies are based on changes in how often these 285 financially related Wikipedia pages were viewed (*blue*) and edited (*red*) during the same period, again with $\Delta t = 3$ weeks. As before, we find that there is a significant difference between the returns generated by the random strategies, the Wikipedia view based strategies and the Wikipedia edit based strategies ($\chi^2 = 307.88$, $df = 2$, $p < 0.001$, $a = 0.05$; Kruskal-Wallis rank sum test). As before, the returns of Wikipedia page view based strategies are significantly higher than the returns of random strategies for this period (mean $R = 1.10$; $W = 2286608$, $p < 0.001$, $a = 0.05$, two-tailed two-sample Wilcoxon rank-sum test, Bonferroni correction applied). Once again however, we find no evidence of a statistically significant difference between the returns from the *Wikipedia* edit based strategies, and the random strategies (mean $R = 0.12$; $W = 1516626$, $p = 0.19$, $a = 0.05$, two-tailed two-sample Wilcoxon rank-sum test, Bonferroni correction applied).

The lack of relationship found for the data on *Wikipedia* edits may simply reflect the substantial difference in the volume of data available for views and for edits, despite the much larger number of pages considered in this second analysis. For example, across the whole period, the *Wikipedia* articles on financial topics had an average of 1,351,796 views each, but only 431 edits. Of these pages, the most viewed page had 14,449,973 views, in comparison to 4832 edits. The least viewed page had 2,033 views, whereas 43 of the 285 pages in question had no edits at all. For the purposes of this study, we therefore do not consider edit data further.

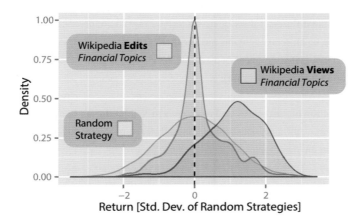

Figure 7.2.2: *Returns from trading strategies based on Wikipedia access and edit logs for pages relating to finance.*

Parallel analysis of the distribution of returns from two much larger portfolios of 285 hypothetical strategies, based on changes in how often a set of 285 financially related Wikipedia pages were viewed (blue) and edited (red) during the same period as Figure 7.2.1, again with Δt = 3 weeks. Our analysis shows that the returns of Wikipedia page view based strategies are significantly higher than the returns of random strategies for this period (mean R = 1.10; W = 2286608, p < 0.001, a = 0.05, two-tailed two-sample Wilcoxon rank-sum test, Bonferroni correction applied). Once again however, we find no evidence of a statistically significant difference between the returns from the Wikipedia edit based strategies, and the random strategies (mean R = 0.12; W = 1516626, p = 0.19, a = 0.05, two-tailed two-sample Wilcoxon rank- sum test, Bonferroni correction applied).

Strategy returns in different years. The period of time we investigate here includes a particularly large drop in the DJIA in 2008. We therefore investigate what the returns from these trading strategies would have been for each individual year in our study period. Again, we consider the returns of strategies based on changes in views of the 285 financially related *Wikipedia* pages, again with Δt = 3 weeks. In Figure 7.2.1, the distribution of returns from the trading strategies are shown for each of the four years for which we have full *Wikipedia* page view data (*blue*) alongside returns from random strategies for that year (*grey*).

We find that returns do differ from year to year (mean return for each year in standard deviations of random strategy returns for the given year: $2008, 0.89$; $2009, 0.19$; $2010, 0.19$; $2011, 0.55$; $\chi^2 = 129.49, df = 3, p < 0.001$; Kruskal-Wallis rank sum test). For every 12 month period however, we find returns significantly above those of the random strategy (2008: $W = 2156094, p < 0.001$; 2009: $W = 1584915, p = 0.001$; 2010: $W = 1585336$, $p = 0.001$; 2011: $W = 1915511, p < 0.001$; $a = 0.05$; all two-tailed two-sample Wilcoxon rank sum tests, using comparisons to the distribution of random strategy returns for the given year).

The effect of Δt. We investigate the effect of changes in Δt on the returns from the trading strategies. Again, we consider portfolios of trading strategies based on changes in views of the 285 financially related *Wikipedia* pages. The mean return from trading strategies, expressed in standard deviations of random strategy returns, is shown in Figure S1 (see Supplementary Information) for $\Delta t = 1$ to 10 weeks. We find that the mean return of the strategies does differ significantly for the different values of Δt we tested ($\chi^2 = 93.26, df = 9, p < 0.001$; Kruskal-Wallis rank sum test). However, the mean return remains greater than 0 for all values of Δt between 1 and 10 weeks (all Ws > 1950000, all ps < 0.001; all two-tailed two-sample Wilcoxon rank sum tests, using comparisons to the random strategy distribution for the whole period).

Mean return of the DJIA following increases and decreases in Wikipedia views. To complement the trading strategy analysis, we carry out a further analysis of weekly DJIA returns following increases and decreases in views of *Wikipedia* articles on financial topics.

For each of the 285 *Wikipedia* articles on financial topics, we identify all weeks t within our study period in which the volume of page views increased in week Δt such that $n(t, \Delta t) > 0$, using $\Delta t = 3$. Across this set of weeks, we calculate the mean return of the DJIA during week $t + 1$, $log(p(t + 2)) - log(p(t + 1))$. Similarly, we calculate the mean return of the DJIA during week $t + 1$ for the set of weeks in which the volume of page views decreased in week t such that $\Delta n(t, \Delta t) < 0$.

Between these two sets of weeks, we find a significant difference in the mean return of the DJIA during week $t + 1$ ($W = 78012, p < 0.001, a = 0.05$, two-tailed two-sample Wilcoxon rank-sum test). Following a decrease in views of *Wikipedia* pages relating to financial topics, we find a mean DJIA weekly return of 0.0027 – a return significantly greater than 0 ($V = 39592, p < 0.001, a = 0.05$, two- tailed one-sample Wilcoxon signed rank test). In contrast, following an increase in views of *Wikipedia* pages relating to financial topics in week t, we find a mean DJIA weekly return of 20.0021, significantly less than 0 ($V = 2222, p < 0.001, a = 0.05$, two-tailed one-sample Wilcoxon signed rank test). The results of this analysis are therefore in line with the relationship between changes in views of *Wikipedia* articles on financial topics and subsequent movements in the DJIA suggested by the trading strategy analysis.

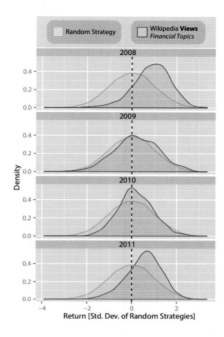

Figure 7.2.3: *Yearly returns from trading strategies based on Wikipedia access logs for pages relating to finance.*
We investigate how returns from the trading strategies based on changes in views of the 285 financially related
Wikipedia pages differ across time. The distribution of returns from the trading strategies, again with $\Delta t = 3$
weeks, are shown for each of the four years for which we have full Wikipedia page view data (blue) alongside
returns from random strategies for that year (grey). Whilst returns differ from year to year (mean return for
each year in standard deviations of random strategy returns for the given year: 2008, 0.89; 2009, 0.19; 2010,
0.19; 2011, 0.55; $\chi^2 = 129.49$, df = 3, p < 0.001; Kruskal-Wallis rank sum test), we find returns significantly
greater than those of the random strategy for every 12 month period (2008: W = 2156094, p < 0.001; 2009: W
= 1584915, p = 0.001; 2010: W = 1585336, p = 0.001; 2011: W = 1915511, p < 0.001; a = 0.05; all two-tailed
two-sample Wilcoxon rank sum tests, using comparisons to the random strategy distributions for the given year).

Views and edits of Wikipedia articles about actors and film-makers. Our assumption so far has been
that only *Wikipedia* usage data relating to pages with financial connotations would provide any insight into
information gathering processes before trading decisions, and therefore future changes in the DJIA. To verify
this assumption, we carry out a further analysis of view data relating to 233 *Wikipedia* pages describing actors
and filmmakers, as listed in the two subsections "*Featured articles*" and "*Good articles*" on the English
language Wikipedia page "*Wikipedia: WikiProject Actors and Filmmakers*". We suggest that such pages have
less obvious financial connotations.

We analyse the distribution of returns for a portfolio of 233 hypothetical trading strategies based on changes in
how often these pages were viewed, trading weekly on the DJIA with $\Delta t = 3$ weeks for the same period as in
previous analyses. We ensured that this set of pages, of similar size to the set of pages relating to financial topics,
had at least equivalent traffic during the period of investigation, to ensure that any failure to find a relationship
was not due to power issues caused through lack of data on *Wikipedia* views. Across the whole period, the actors

and filmmakers pages had an average of 5,440,304 views each (in comparison to 1,351,796 for the financially related pages), where the least popular page had 2,261 views (in comparison to 2,033 views for the least popular financially related page) and the most popular page had 63,629,258 views (in comparison to 14,449,973 views for the most popular financially related page).

In Figure 7.2.4, we show the returns from these 233 strategies based on changes in the number of views of *Wikipedia* articles on actors and filmmakers (*blue*), alongside returns from the random strategies (*grey*). We find that there is no significant difference between the returns generated by the random strategies and the *Wikipedia* view based strategies (mean $R = 0.04$; $W = 1189114$, $p = 0.59$, $a = 0.05$, two-tailed two-sample Wilcoxon rank-sum test).

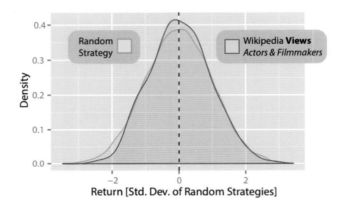

Figure 7.2.4: *Returns from trading strategies based on Wikipedia access logs for pages relating to actors and filmmakers.*
Parallel analysis of the distribution of returns for another portfolio of 233 hypothetical strategies based on changes in how often a set of 233 Wikipedia pages relating to actors and filmmakers were viewed (blue). Here, we find that there is no significant difference between the returns generated by the random strategies and the Wikipedia view based strategies (mean R = 0.04; W = 1189114, p = 0.59, a = 0.05, two-tailed two-sample Wilcoxon rank-sum test).

Similarly, for each of the 233 *Wikipedia* articles on actors and filmmakers, we calculate the return of the DJIA during week $t + 1$ for all weeks t where views of the article increased in comparison to views in the previous $\Delta t = 3$ weeks such that $\Delta n(t, \Delta t) > 0$, and separately for all weeks t where views of the article decreased in comparison to views in the previous $t = 3$ weeks such that $\Delta n(t, \Delta t) < 0$. We find no significant difference in the mean return of the DJIA during week $t + 1$ for these two sets of weeks ($W = 28186, p = 0.47, a = 0.05$, two-tailed two-sample Wilcoxon rank-sum test).

To summarise, neither an analysis based on the hypothetical trading strategy nor a complementary analysis of weekly DJIA returns find any evidence that changes in views of *Wikipedia* articles related to actors and filmmakers bear relation to future changes in the DJIA.

7.3 DISCUSSION

In summary, our results are consistent with the hypothesis that historic usage data from the online encyclopaedia *Wikipedia* between December 2007 and April 2012 may have provided some insight into future trends in the behaviour of financial market actors. In our analysis, we find evidence of increases in the number of page views of articles relating to companies or other financial topics before stock market falls. We do not, however, find any such relationship for changes in the weekly number of views of *Wikipedia* articles on the subject of actors and filmmakers, pages with less obvious financial connotations.

We propose one potential explanation in line with these results. We first suggest that *Wikipedia* records may provide a proxy measurement of the information gathering process of a subset of investors for the investigated period. We further note that previous studies in behavioural economics have demonstrated that humans are loss averse (Tversky and Kahneman, 1991): that is, they are more concerned about losing £5 than they are about missing an opportunity to gain £5. By this logic, it could be argued that the trading decision of greatest consequence for a trader would be to sell a stock at a lower price than they had previously believed it was worth. If we assume that investors may be willing to invest more efforts in information gathering before making a decision which they view to be of greater consequence, then it would follow that increases in information gathering would precede falls in stock market prices, in line with our results.

Our results suggest that Internet usage data may offer a window into the information gathering processes which precede actions captured in real world behaviour data sets. By combining these large data sets, we may be able to gain new insight into different stages of collective decision making.

ACKNOWLEDGMENTS

This work was supported by the Intelligence Advanced Research Projects Activity (IARPA) via Department of Interior National Business Center (DoI/NBC) contract number D12PC00285. The U.S. Government is authorized to reproduce and distribute reprints for Governmental purposes notwithstanding any copyright annotation thereon. Disclaimer: The views and conclusions contained herein are those of the authors and should not be interpreted as necessarily representing the official policies or endorsements, either expressed or implied, of IARPA, DoI/NBC, or the U.S. Government. In addition, this work was partially supported by the German Research Foundation Grant PR 1305/1-1 (to T.P.) and by the Research Councils UK Grant EP/K039830/1 (to H.S.M. and T.P.).

Author contributions
H.S.M. and T.P. designed the study; H.S.M., C.C. and T.P. collected and analysed the data; and H.S.M., C.C., A.A., D.Y.K., H.E.S. and T.P. discussed the results and contributed to the text of the manuscript.

Additional information

Supplementary information accompanies this paper at http://www.nature.com/ scientificreports

7.4 REFERENCES

1.   Askitas, N. and Zimmermann, K.F. (2009). Google econometrics and unemployment forecasting. *Applied Economics Quarterly, 55,* pp. 107–120.

2.   Bollen, J., Mao, H. and Zeng, X. (2011). Twitter mood predicts the stock market. *Journal of Computational Science, 2,* pp. 1–8 .

3.   Bordino, I., Battiston, S., Caldarelli, G., Cristelli, M., Ukkonen, A. and Weber, I. (2012). Web search queries can predict stock market volumes. *PLoS One 7,* pp. e40014.

4.   Capocci, A., Servedio, V.D., Colaiori, F., Buriol, L.S., Donato, D., Leonardi, S. and Caldarelli, G. (2006). Preferential attachment in the growth of social networks: The Internet encyclopedia Wikipedia. *Physical Review E, 74(3),* pp. 036116.

5.   Choi, H. and Varian, H. (2012). Predicting the present with Google trends. *The Economic Record, 88,* pp. 2–9.

6.   Farmer, J. D., Patelli, P. and Zovko, I. I. (2005). The predictive power of zero intelligence in financial markets. *Proceedings of the National Academy Sciences of the U.S.A., 102(6),* pp. 2254–2259.

7.   Fehr, E. (2002). Behavioural science - The economics of impatience. *Nature, 415,* pp. 269–272.

8.   Feng, L., Li, B., Podobnik, B., Preis, T. and Stanley, H. E. (2012). Linking agent-based models and stochastic models of financial markets. *Proceedings of the National Academy Sciences of the U.S.A., 109,* pp. 8388–8393.

9.   Gabaix, X., Gopikrishnan, P., Plerou, V. and Stanley, H. E. (2003). A theory of power-law distributions in financial market fluctuations. *Nature, 423,* pp. 267–270.

10.   Ginsberg, J., Mohebbi, M.H., Patel, R.S., Brammer, L., Smolinski, M.S. and Brilliant, L. (2009). Detecting influenza epidemics using search engine query data. *Nature, 457(7232),* pp. 1012–1014.

11.   Goel, S., Hofman, J. M., Lahaie, S., Pennock, D. M. and Watts, D. J. (2010). Predicting consumer behavior with Web search. *Proceedings of the National Academy Sciences of the U.S.A., 107,* pp. 17486–17490.

12.   Hommes, C. H. (2002). Modeling the stylized facts in finance through simple nonlinear adaptive systems. *Proceedings of the National Academy Sciences of the U.S.A., 99,* pp. 7221–7228.

13. Johnson, N. F., Jefferies, P. and Hui, P. M. (2003). *Financial Market Complexity.* Oxford University Press, Oxford.

14. Kenett, D. Y., Shapira, Y., Madi, A., Bransburg-Zabary, S., Gur-Gershgoren, G. and Ben-Jacob, E. (2011). Index cohesive force analysis reveals that the US market became prone to systemic collapses since 2002. *PLoS ONE,* 6, pp. e19378.

15. King, G. (2011). Ensuring the data-rich future of the social sciences. *Science,* 331, pp. 719–721.

16. Lazer, D., Pentland, A.S., Adamic, L., Aral, S., Barabasi, A.L., Brewer, D., Christakis, N., Contractor, N., Fowler, J., Gutmann, M. and Jebara, T. (2009). Computational Social Science. *Science,* 323, pp. 721–723.

17. Lillo, F., Farmer, J. D. and Mantegna, R. N. (2003). Econophysics - Master curve for price- impact function. *Nature,* 421, pp. 129–130.

18. Lux, T. and Marchesi, M. (1999). Scaling and criticality in a stochastic multi-agent model of a financial market. *Nature,* 397, pp. 498–500.

19. Mantegna, R. N. and Stanley, H. E. (2002). Scaling behaviour in the dynamics of an economic index. *Nature,* 376, pp. 46–49.

20. Muchnik, L., Itzhack, R., Solomon, S. and Louzoun, Y. (2007). Self-emergence of knowledge trees: Extraction of the Wikipedia hierarchies. *Physical Review E, 76,* pp. 016106.

21. Perc, M. (2012). Evolution of the most common English words and phrases over the centuries. *Journal of the Royal Society Interface,* 9, pp. 3323–3328.

22. Petersen, A. M., Tenenbaum, J. N., Havlin, S., Stanley, H. E. and Perc, M. (2012). Languages cool as they expand: Allometric scaling and the decreasing need for new words. *Scientific Reports,* 2, pp. 943.

23. Preis, T., Reith, D. and Stanley, H. E. (2010). Complex dynamics of our economic life on different scales: insights from search engine query data. *Philosophical Transactions of the Royal Society of London A, 368,* pp. 5707–5719.

24. Preis, T., Schneider, J. J. and Stanley, H. E. (2011). Switching processes in financial markets. *Proceedings of the National Academy Sciences of the U.S.A., 108,* pp. 7674–7678.

25. Preis, T., Moat, H. S. and Stanley, H. E. (2013). Quantifying trading behavior in financial markets using Google trends. *Scientific Reports, 3,* pp. 1684.

26. Preis, T., Moat, H. S., Stanley, H. E. and Bishop, S. R. (2012). Quantifying the advantage of looking forward. *Scientific Reports, 2,* pp. 350.

27. Preis, T., Kenett, D. Y., Stanley, H. E., Helbing, D. and Ben-Jacob, E. (2012). Quantifying the behavior of stock correlations under market stress. *Scientific Reports, 2*, pp. 752.

28. Podobnik, B., Horvatic, D., Petersen, A. M. and Stanley, H. E. (2009). Cross-correlations between volume change and price change. *Proceedings of the National Academy Sciences of the U.S.A., 106*, pp. 22079–22084.

29. Silver, N. (2012). *The signal and the noise*. Penguin Group, London.

30. Silverman, B. W. (1986). *Density Estimation*. Chapman and Hall, London.

31. Simon, H. A. (1955). A behavioral model of rational choice. *Quarterly Journal of Economics, 69*, pp. 99–118.

32. Sornette, D. and von der Becke, S. (2011). Complexity clouds finance-risk models. *Nature, 471*, pp. 166.

33. Tversky, A. and Kahneman, D. (1991). Loss aversion in riskless choice: a reference-dependent model. *The Quarterly Journal of Economics, 106*, pp. 1039–1061.

34. Vespignani, A. (2009). Predicting the behavior of techno-social systems. *Science, 325*, pp. 425–428.

35. Wickham, H. (2009). *ggplot2: Elegant Graphics for Data Analysis*. Springer, New York.

36. Yasseri, T., Kornai, A. and Kerte ́sz, J. (2012). A practical approach to language complexity: a Wikipedia case study. *PLoS ONE* 7, pp. e48386.

37. Yasseri, T., Sumi, R. and Kerte ́sz, J. (2012). Circadian patterns of Wikipedia editorial activity: a demographic analysis. *PLoS ONE* 7, pp. e30091.

CHAPTER 8

Investor Attention and the Pricing
of Earnings News

Asher Curtis, *Assistant Professor in Accounting, University of Washington*

Vernon J. Richardson, *Professor in Accounting, University of Arkansas*

Roy Schmardebeck, *Assistant Professor, University of Missouri*

ABSTRACT

We investigate whether investor attention is associated with the pricing (and mispricing) of earnings news where investor attention is measured using social media activity. We find that high levels of investor attention are associated with greater sensitivity of earnings announcement returns to earnings surprises, with the effect being strongest for firms that beat analysts' forecasts. This appears to be appropriate pricing, on average, as only firms with low levels of attention are associated with significant post-earnings-announcement drift. Our results are distinct from other information sources including traditional media outlets, financial blogs and internet search engine activity. Our results are consistent with investor attention observed in social media activity having distinct effects on the pricing and mispricing of earnings news.

8.1 INTRODUCTION

We investigate whether investor attention is associated with the pricing of earnings news, where investor attention is measured using social media activity. The exponential growth of social media has changed how individuals gather and share financial information by providing a platform to observe the collective attention and opinions of millions of individual investors and commentators. Our primary goal is to assess the extent to which investor attention affects the sensitivity of market prices to earnings news. Our analysis provides an initial step towards understanding whether the primary role of social media activity – a possible proxy for investor attention – is associated with more or less efficient pricing of earnings information.[1]

The level of activity on online social media platforms, such as Twitter and StockTwits, provides a measure of the attention, or interest, about the events occurring in real-time for a given stock. Twitter has over 500 million registered users, including individuals, celebrities, traditional news providers and firms.[2] These users share information by posting a 140-character or less "tweet", which is pushed to the followers of that individual and possibly "retweeted" by their followers, further extending the reach of the original posters' interests. Whether the sharing of information using online social media enhances market efficiency, however, is contentious.

On one hand, access to a vast social network facilitates the gathering and sharing of information of interest to individuals, providing an avenue through which news is instantaneously disseminated to a large audience. Shiller and Pound (1989) provide survey evidence consistent with individuals making investment decisions based on the advice of their physical social networks, suggesting that online social networks could potentially influence investment decisions. Caskey et al. (2011) highlight in their model of information diffusion that networks potentially provide the mechanism that links the disclosure of information to the processing and pricing of that information by investors. That is, networks allow investors to become aware of new information. Social media extends the reach and spread of information through word of mouth, providing widespread dissemination of new information. At the same time, investors have access to many sources of information available to them including traditional financial media, newswires, news aggregators such as Yahoo! Finance, financial blogs and message boards. Given this strong pre-existing information environment, empirical tests are required to better understand the impact of social media activity on this information environment and equity prices.

We test whether social media activity is associated with the pricing of earnings information by examining returns around, and following, earnings announcements. We measure investor attention using a recently available database of social media activity provided by Market IQ. Market IQ makes "sense of the web's most powerful real-time unstructured dataset and provides dynamic insights for today's financial professionals" (see www.themarketiq.com) using this data. Specifically, Market IQ runs patented analytics in real time on unstructured data that appears on social networks (including Twitter and StockTwits) to provide insights into social media activity for the financial services industry. Market IQ provided us with two unique dynamic analytics, which they label "Smart Velocity" and "Smart Sentiment". We focus primarily on Smart Velocity (hereafter, *Activity*): a measure of buzz in the marketplace pertaining to a company, calculated on a continuous relative scale using Market IQ's patented algorithms. Market IQ baselines *Activity* at 1X, hence

Activity over 1X indicates elevation of interest relative to the average level of interest for the same firm in the previous 30 days, and *Activity* below 1X reflects vice-versa. As such, Market IQ's metrics provide qualitative measures of the underlying unstructured social media data.

We focus primarily on social media activity as it may measure attentiveness and traditional asset pricing models typically assume that all investors are attentive and undertake trading actions immediately upon receipt of value relevant information. When investors have limited attention, the lower attention will lead to a lower reaction to earnings news (e.g., Hirshleifer and Teoh, 2003). If investor attention varies in the cross-section, then we expect that the response to earnings news will be positively associated with the level of investor attention, and based on the above, the changes in the levels of interest in a firm, or *Activity*, on the day of the earnings announcement will provide a proxy for how much increased attention investors are paying to earnings.

Using Market IQ's measure of social media activity, we find that abnormally high levels of investor attention are associated with significantly higher sensitivity of market returns to earnings news.[3] This effect is evident for both positive and negative earnings news, but the effect is much stronger for positive news. Specifically, for negative news, high levels of *Activity* are associated with approximately 91% higher sensitivity of returns to earnings news. In contrast, the sensitivity of returns to positive earnings news is approximately 234% stronger for the high *Activity* group. Firms with low levels of *Activity*, in contrast, are associated with significant post-earnings-announcement drift (*PEAD*), with no evidence of *PEAD* for portfolios of firms with moderate to high levels of *Activity*. Our results suggest that investor attention, at least as reflected by *Activity*, is associated with an increase in the market responsiveness to earnings news and a lack of investor attention is associated with an under-reaction to earnings news. Our results are not subsumed by traditional measures of attention to earnings announcements, such as the market-to-book, dispersion of analysts' forecasts, size and prior returns.

We also provide further analyses, which investigate the robustness of our findings. As high-attention stocks are also likely to be growth stocks, we examine whether our results are distinct from the market-to-book (e.g. Skinner and Sloan, 2002). We find evidence to suggest that social media activity is distinct from the growth stock characteristic. We next investigate Market IQ's proprietary Smart Sentiment metric (hereafter, *Sentiment*), which provides a refined measure of the relative level of optimism or pessimism observed in the discussions, or "tweets", on social networks about a company[4]. Specifically, Market IQ's *Sentiment* metric takes into consideration several qualitative measures of the underlying unstructured social media data, including but not limited to: contextual analysis, content propagation and user reliability.[5] *Sentiment* is also provided on a real-time basis along with related indicators of inflection thresholds that serve as a leading indicator to potential sentiment-related price movements.

Using *Sentiment*, we find that the group with the highest optimism on the day of the earnings announcement has higher market returns. We also find that *Activity* increases the sensitivity of returns to earnings for firms that announce earnings prior to the opening of the market, and decreases *PEAD*. *Activity* is lower for firms reporting after the market closes, and similar to DellaVigna and Pollet (2009) we find that *PEAD* is higher for firms that report after the market closes. Finally, our results are robust to the inclusion of information about earnings provided by traditional media outlets using the Dow Jones Newswires, financial blogs and Google searches, suggesting that *Activity* provides a distinct proxy for attention to earnings.

We make the following contributions to the literature. First, we contribute to the recent literature on the effect of social networks on capital market outcomes. Online social networks are becoming an increasingly important part of society due to technological advancements in the past decade. We provide novel empirical evidence consistent with social media activity, as a proxy for investor attention, leading to increased sensitivity of market returns to earnings news. More broadly, our evidence complements the recent literature examining how technology aids investors in gathering information, such as via Google search (e.g., Da et al., 2010; Drake et al., 2010; Chi and Shanthikumar, 2014), and highlights that technology enables investors to also play an important dissemination role. Second, we contribute to the large body of accounting research that suggests investors underreact to earnings news (e.g., Lev, 1989; Bernard and Thomas, 1990). Prior studies have examined both the magnitude of the earnings response coefficient relative to expectations (Kormendi and Lipe, 1987) along with evidence of a post-earnings-announcement drift (e.g., Bernard and Thomas, 1989; 1990). Our evidence shows that the under-reaction is concentrated in firms with the lowest levels of investor attention on the day of the earnings announcement.

8.2 INSTITUTIONAL BACKGROUND AND HYPOTHESIS

8.2.1 Institutional background

Online social media has seen an exponential increase in activity in the past ten years. There are at least 12 social media platforms with more than 100 million users each, with over 5.7 billion (overlapping) profiles on these pages (Waite, 2014). Online social networks are generally either micro-blogging websites, such as Twitter, which limit the posts to 140-character "tweets" or more traditional message board or blog-like interactions, the latter often requiring reciprocation between the individual users in the network to allow for the sharing of content. Online social networking is a recent phenomenon, with Twitter one of the largest social networking sites. Twitter was launched on 21 March 2006, and by 2012, it was broadcasting an average of 175 million "tweets" per day. Unlike other online social networks, Twitter facilitates open sharing of information through a social network as "following" another Twitter user requires no reciprocation.[6] In addition, Twitter allows for users to choose to "retweet" content they have received, allowing for information to be near-instantly shared to users outside of the original audience.[7]

Historically, the primary use of data from online social networks was brand analytics, i.e., used for marketing and brand management purposes. Third-party brand analytics began as early as 2006 through Twitter which allowed for the real-time assessment of consumer thoughts and preferences. Gathering and sharing information over Twitter and similar websites has the benefit of having "hashtags", which allow for the grouping of messages by their content. Specifically, the hashtag is a metadata tag using the prefix # allowing users identify the content of their post, such as #investing to group their post into any topic area. StockTwits, an online social media platform that focuses on the sharing of information in the investment and trading community, was founded in 2008. StockTwits uses the same interface as Twitter and introduced the "cashtag" prefix, which organises the online conversations around a company ticker, for example $AAPL identifies the stock ticker for Apple Inc.[8] StockTwits has roughly 230,000 users, while Twitter has over 500 million. In July of 2012, the use of cashtags was also officially adopted by Twitter (Meredith, 2012). The cashtag feature of StockTwits allows for the identification of investors' and other commentators' thoughts on individual stocks in real time.

A recent example of a social media conversation is provided in Appendix 8.A.1. In this example, the cashtags link the discussion about Citigroup ($C). Some of the posts are informative, providing a hyperlink to additional material, in this case analysis of Citigroup's earnings press release. Other comments express either a bullish or bearish opinion of the stock along with a short comment related to their position. Clearly these posts express interest by various individuals and media participants about a company's earnings, but it is clear that the posts are also subjective and are not always in agreement.

More generally, the usefulness of the content of posts made on social media networks is contentious. On the positive side, prior to the advent of social media, Shiller and Pound (1989) survey individual investors and find that word-of-mouth suggestions influence investors' portfolio choices, consistent with social influence affecting the portfolio choices of individual traders. As such, online social networks could act as a natural extension of the influence of word-of-mouth suggestions. On the negative side, in a study by Pear Analytics, Twitter conversations were analysed over a two-week window in August of 2009, with the authors concluding that Twitter posts are 40% "Pointless babble" and 38% conversational, with the remainder being split between self-promotion, spam, pass along and news (Ryan, 2009). In addition, commentators on Twitter highlight that "Trending topics" can often be the result of concerted efforts of users, often the fan base of certain celebrities,[9] rather than due to an event that has influenced the attention of individuals.

Whereas the use of social media is still nascent when compared to traditional news sources, such as the Dow Jones Newswire, Reuters and Bloomberg, which have a long history in financial markets, it represents an interesting intersection of finance and technology. Information from social media, however, is being used with increasing frequency in the financial services industry. High-profile investors and company executives are also increasingly using social media and the content posted by these individuals is often associated with high market volatility and investment decisions. For example, Carl Icahn, an influential activist investor, used his Twitter account to announce a significant purchase of Apple stock last year; this tweet was largely seen as the reason for the $17 billion increase in the market value of Apple over the following hour.[10]

In sum, social media activity provides a measure of the attention of individuals, which could potentially influence investment decisions. Whether the attention of individuals is associated with more or less efficient pricing of earnings information is an open empirical question. In the following section, we discuss how social media activity, as a proxy for investor attention might affect market efficiency.

8.2.2 Investor attention and the pricing of earnings

Prior literature provides a large body of evidence suggesting that investors underreact to earnings announcements. Collectively, the evidence is extensive and is based on both evidence of low responses around the date of the earnings announcements and evidence of a significant post-earnings-announcement drift following earnings announcements. Kormendi and Lipe (1987) analytically derive the expected earnings response coefficient (ERC) based on a stylised time-series model and estimate the expected ERC using estimates of the time-series properties of earnings. They find that the expected ERC for their sample is between nine and ten. They then provide empirical estimates of the ERC based on market returns and find it is approximately two to three. They find that the two ERC measures are correlated but fail to find evidence of equality. Their results suggest that the market responds in the correct direction to what is expected, but the reaction is much smaller than expected.

Ball and Brown (1968) provide initial evidence of a drift following earnings announcements. Bernard and Thomas (1989; 1990) provide evidence that this post-earnings-announcement drift is associated with an under-reaction to the time-series properties of earnings. Taken together these studies suggest that investors are reacting in the correct direction to the news in earnings announcements, and that their reaction is systematically too low.

Traditional asset pricing models typically assume that 1) all investors receive publicly available information instantaneously upon its disclosure, and that 2) investors undertake trading actions immediately upon receipt of this information. That is, for an earnings announcement, when all investors pay attention to earnings announcements, these investors will react to the news in the earnings announcement by trading until the price reflects this information. When investors have limited attention, as suggested by Hirshleifer and Teoh (2003), these assumptions are unlikely to be descriptive for all stocks in the cross-section. Instead, variation in investor attentiveness is likely to be inversely related to variation in the reaction to earnings news. As abnormal social media activity on the day of the earnings announcement measures the amount of increased discussion and posts about a firm, it provides a measure of investor attention to earnings announcements. As such, we predict that high levels of investor attention will be associated with prices that are more sensitive to earnings news. As a hypothesis:

> H_1: Investor attention is positively associated with the earnings response coefficient.

To test Hypothesis 1, we estimate a regression of short-run stock returns on earnings news, with the association between these variables being the measure of the earnings response coefficient (similar to the design in Easton and Zmijewski, 1989), and include an interaction term between high levels of social media activity with earnings news to identify the incremental effect of high levels of social media activity on the earnings response coefficient. In H_1, we predict that high levels of investor attention are associated with incrementally higher earnings response coefficients. Our prediction in H_1 also has implications for post earnings announcement drift. If *PEAD* is based on under-reaction to earnings news, then as high levels of attention reduce the under-reaction to earnings news, we expect *PEAD* to be inversely related to investor attention. As such, we expect that *PEAD* will be higher for firms with lower attention.

8.3 DATA AND SAMPLE

8.3.1 Data

Market IQ provided their data to us for the period January 2012 to July 2013. In addition to other financial analytics, Market IQ provides daily measures of social media activity (*Activity*) and social media optimism (*Sentiment*). By processing millions of unstructured data streams, from social media sources, Market IQ keeps track of "investor attention" with the *Activity* metric. As activity on Social channels fluctuates, Market IQ quantifies the *Activity* metric in real time to measure true "investor attention". As such, *Activity* is provided in the form of a multiple such as "1.50x", which would suggest that the number of mentions of the stock is 1.50 times the average level of mentions of the stock. Market IQ uses a rolling 30-day window to estimate the average level of tweets.

We obtain financial data from the Quarterly Compustat File, analyst forecasts and reported actual earnings from the I/B/E/S Unadjusted Summary File, and market data from the CRSP daily stock and index files. To be included in the sample, we require that each firm is covered by Market IQ and can be identified on Compustat, CRSP and I/B/E/S. We also require that sample firms have end of the quarter stock price of at least $5 per share. Our final sample includes 15,486 firm-quarter observations (from 2,684 unique companies)

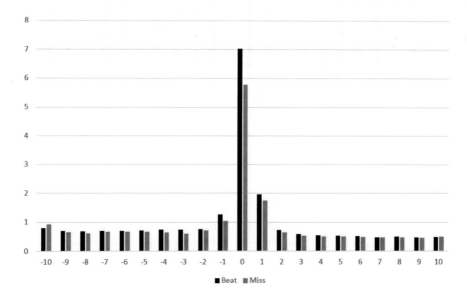

Figure 8.3.1: Social media activity around earnings announcements
Notes: *This graph displays social media activity using Market IQ's velocity measure in the 21-day window surrounding the earnings announcements firms that beat the consensus analyst forecast are displayed as the solid bars, and firms that miss the consensus analyst forecast are displayed as the shaded bars.*

In Figure 8.3.1, we highlight the increase in *Activity* on the days surrounding the earnings announcement. We plot *Activity* for both firms that beat the earnings forecast and those that miss the earnings forecast. On the day of the earnings announcement, firms that beat the consensus analyst forecast have an elevated amount of social media activity, at 7.028 times their base level of *Activity*. The amount of social media activity for firms that miss the consensus analyst forecast is also elevated at 5.787 times their base level of *Activity*. In a test of differences in means, we find that *Activity* for firms that beat the consensus analyst forecast is significantly higher than *Activity* for firms that miss the consensus analyst forecast (p-value for the test of differences < 0.001, untabulated). Overall, the increased level of social media activity is short-lived, as activity reverts back towards the baseline within the first two days. We also see some anticipation in the day before an earnings announcement, with elevated levels of *Activity* in day t-1. In sum, the level of social media activity increases significantly on the day of the earnings announcement.

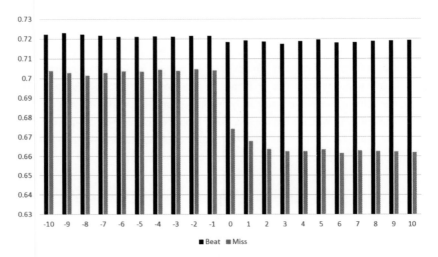

Figure 8.3.2: *Social media optimism around earnings announcements*
Notes: This graph displays social media optimism using Market IQ's sentiment measure in the 21-day window surrounding the earnings announcements. Firms that beat the consensus analyst forecast are displayed as the solid bars, and firms that miss the consensus analyst forecast are displayed as the shaded bars.

In Figure 8.3.2, we plot the average level of optimism for firms in our sample, based on Market IQ's *Sentiment* measure. We plot *Sentiment* over the 21-day window centred on the day of the earnings announcement for firms that beat the analyst forecast and for firms that miss the analyst forecast. Figure 8.3.2 shows that the social media posts are generally optimistic, with both firms that beat the forecast and firms that miss the forecast having a level of optimism above 0.5. The level of optimism on the day before the earnings announcement is statistically higher for firms that beat their forecast (0.722) than for firms that miss (0.704), based on a p-value of less than 0.001 for the differences (not tabulated). The level of optimism drops statistically for firms that miss the analyst forecast (p-value of less than 0.001) but, on average, remains optimistic at 0.674. In sum, social media posts are generally optimistic, but are significantly less optimistic for firms that miss the earnings benchmark.

8.3.2 Descriptive statistics

Table 8.3.1:Means of earnings news and market returns sorted by social media activity

Notes: Activity is Market IQ's velocity measure, where 1x is the baseline effect, CAR is cumulative abnormal returns surrounding the window of the earnings announcement [0,+1], based on the firm's return less the return on the firm's size decile, Ferror is the forecast error scaled by the price at the end of the quarter, HiAct is an indicator variable set to one for observations in the highest decile of investor social media activity on the day of the earnings announcement (Activity) sorted by year and quarter, and zero otherwise, Size is the log of total assets, M/B is the market-to- book ratio, $\int AF$ is the standard deviation of analyst forecasts, Mom is stock return momentum in the month before the earnings announcement.

*** p<0.010, ** p<0.050, * p<0.10

Variable	Full Sample	Q1	Q2	Q3	Q4	Q5	Q5-Q1	t-test	p-value
Activity	6.429	0.126	1.926	3.770	7.331	19.335			
Ferror	0.018	0.011	0.010	0.016	0.024	0.029	0.019	5.617	0.000
%Good	0.587	0.543	0.547	0.571	0.620	0.655	0.112	9.360	0.000
Sentiment	0.705	0.712	0.712	0.711	0.706	0.691	-0.020	-2.882	0.004
CAR	0.001	-0.001	-0.003	0.000	0.002	0.007	0.008	4.048	0.000
PEAD	0.005	0.008	0.006	0.005	0.007	0.001	-0.007	-2.163	0.031
Fullret	0.011	0.007	0.015	0.009	0.011	0.014	0.007	1.769	0.007
M/B	2.945	2.309	2.921	2.947	3.136	3.526	1.217	13.796	0.000
%Pre-open	0.454	0.358	0.334	0.439	0.545	0.590	0.232	18.688	0.000
Size	9,959.089	3,027.993	6,834.664	9,963.548	14,430.430	16,249.520	13,221.520	20.784	0.000
Mom	0.017	0.010	0.018	0.020	0.020	0.016	0.006	2.926	0.003
σAF	0.045	0.043	0.050	0.047	0.045	0.039	-0.003	-2.362	0.018
#Forecasts	10.104	6.102	9.154	10.388	11.780	13.661	7.559	49.321	0.000
Leverage	0.199	0.175	0.223	0.219	0.205	0.183	0.007	1.615	0.106

In Table 8.3.1, we provide descriptive statistics of our dependent and independent variables along with control variables. We report the averages for all firms in the sample as well as for each quintile based on the level of social media activity on the day of the earnings announcement. The average level of *Activity* on the day of the earnings announcement for all firms in the sample is 6.429 (column 1). The average of the lowest group is 0.126 and the average of the highest group is 19.335. These results suggest that there is significant variation in *Activity* on the day of the earnings announcement across the firms in the sample.

We find that the variation in *Activity* is associated with the return on the day of the earnings announcement, *CAR*, with the lowest *Activity* group having an average *CAR* of -0.1% whereas the average returns among the highest *Activity* group is 0.7% with the difference being statistically significant (*p*-value < 0.001); we will condition on the magnitude of the earnings news in the next table as well as in our multivariate analysis. We also find evidence of a statistically significant difference (*p*-value < 0.05) in *PEAD* between the highest and lowest activity groups; firms in the lowest social media activity group display higher returns of 0.8% (column 2) relative to firms in the highest social media activity group, which display returns of 0.1% (column 6). We also report higher positive forecast errors (*%Good*) for the firms in the highest activity group relative to those in the lowest activity group, with similar results for the proportion of firms beating the analyst forecast (*p*-value < 0.001), consistent with individual traders' preference for taking long positions at earnings announcements (Hirshleifer et al., 2008). Sentiment is higher for the lower activity stocks suggesting lower levels of optimism for stocks with the largest amount of activity (*p*-value < 0.01).

Social media activity on the day of the earnings announcement is also positively associated with analyst following and the number of analyst forecasts. The standard deviation of analysts' forecasts is smaller for firms with the highest activity relative to the lowest activity (p-value < 0.05). We also find that higher activity stocks are higher momentum stocks, are larger in size (p-value < 0.01), and have a higher market-to-book ratio (p-value < 0.001), on average. We also find that firms with earnings announcements prior to the market open have a higher level of *Activity* (*p*-value < 0.001).

8.3.3 Market returns around earnings announcements

We next provide descriptive evidence as to whether market returns are more sensitive to earnings news when investor attention is higher. In Table 8.3.2 we present the mean cumulative abnormal return sorted by forecast error quintiles in rows and by *Activity* quintiles in columns. Where *CAR* is cumulative abnormal returns surrounding the window of the earnings announcement [0,+1], based on the firm's return less the return on the firm's size decile, *Ferror* is the forecast error scaled by the price at the end of the quarter and *Activity* is Market IQ's velocity measure sorted into quintiles by year and quarter. In column 1, we document the well-observed positive association between *Ferror* and *CAR*. As expected, the most negative forecast errors are associated with negative returns (average = -3.3%), while the most positive forecast errors are associated with positive returns (average = 3.1%) and this difference is statistically significant (p-value < 0.001).

Within each of the *Activity* groups, we find that the differences between the highest and lowest forecast errors are U-shaped. These results are documented in the row labelled FE5-FE1. For example, the average difference in *CAR* for the low activity group (Q1) is 6.0% versus 4.6% for the median group (Q3) and 10.4% for the highest attention group (Q5). In all cases, however, the differences are positive and significant as expected. The sorts by social media activity highlight that social media activity matters for both the most positive and most negative earnings surprises. For example, the average *CAR* for the most negative earnings surprises for the low activity group is -3.1% versus -5.1% for the highest attention group (p-value < 0.001). Similarly, for the most positive earnings surprises, the average *CAR* is 2.9% for the lowest activity group and 5.3% for the highest activity group (p-value < 0.001).

Table 8.3.2: *CAR sorted by forecast error and social media activity*

Note: FE1 through FE5 represents quintiles of Ferror, with FE1 representing firms with the lowest Ferror and FE5 representing firms with the highest Ferror. Q1 through Q5 represent quintiles of Activity, with Q1 representing the lowest level of Activity and Q5 representing the highest level of Activity. We perform this double sort by ranking CAR by Ferror quintile and within each Ferror quintile we perform a quintile rank by Activity.

Variable	(1) Full Sample	(2) Q1	(3) Q2	(4) Q3	(5) Q4	(6) Q5	(7) Q5-Q1	t-test	p-value
FE1	-0.033	-0.031	-0.028	-0.022	-0.034	-0.051	-0.020	-5.080	0.000
FE2	-0.014	-0.013	-0.013	-0.014	-0.008	-0.022	-0.008	-2.152	0.032
FE3	0.006	0.006	0.005	0.003	0.005	0.012	0.006	1.642	0.101
FE4	0.019	0.019	0.008	0.017	0.024	0.026	0.007	1.793	0.075
FE5	0.031	0.029	0.018	0.024	0.030	0.053	0.024	5.317	0.000
FE5-FE1	0.065	0.060	0.046	0.046	0.065	0.104	0.084		
t-stat	35.437	19.690	11.873	11.795	16.943	19.334		19.725	
P-value	0.000	0.000	0.000	0.000	0.000	0.000			0.000

These results provide some descriptive evidence in support of Hypothesis 1. Specifically, within forecast error deciles, social media activity matters most for the extreme deciles. We next provide descriptive evidence on whether social media activity is associated with *PEAD*.

8.3.4 Market returns subsequent to earnings announcements

Prior literature provides evidence that *PEAD* has been declining over time (Chordia et al., 2009). In Table 8.3.3, Column 1, we report the cumulative returns over 58 days (from day t+2 to day t+60) following the earnings announcement for the full sample. Based on the difference between the highest and lowest earnings surprise groups, we find marginal evidence of a difference in PEAD (p-value < 0.10). In Column 2, however, we report evidence of *PEAD* within the firms with the lowest level of *Activity*. In this case, the portfolio with the lowest earnings surprises underperforms the group with the highest earnings surprises by 2.6% or approximately 57% of the original earnings response (6.0% in Column 1 of Table 2).

Table 8.3.3: *Post-earnings announcement returns sorted by forecast error and social media activity*
Note: FE1 through FE5 represents quintiles of Ferror, with FE1 representing firms with the lowest Ferror
and FE5 representing firms with the highest Ferror. Q1 through Q5 represent quintiles of Activity, with Q1
representing the lowest level of Activity and Q5 representing the highest level of Activity. We perform this double
sort by ranking PEAD by Ferror quintile and within each Ferror quintile we perform a quintile rank by Activity.

Variable	(1) Full Sample	(2) Q1	(3) Q2	(4) Q3	(5) Q4	(6) Q5	(7) Q5-Q1	t-test	p-value
FE1	0.003	-0.005	0.015	0.008	0.002	0.002	0.007	0.891	0.373
FE2	0.000	0.001	-0.002	0.004	0.002	-0.005	-0.006	-0.841	0.400
FE3	0.007	0.015	0.001	0.006	0.009	0.004	-0.011	-1.701	0.089
FE4	0.007	0.012	0.013	0.001	0.008	0.003	-0.009	-1.224	0.221
FE5	0.009	0.021	0.008	0.005	0.010	0.002	-0.019	-2.635	0.009
FE5-FE1	0.006	0.026	-0.007	-0.003	0.008	0.000	0.007		
t-stat	1.683	3.692	-0.730	-0.316	0.920	0.015		0.9436	
p-value	0.092	0.000	0.466	0.752	0.358	0.988			0.346

We do not find statistically significant evidence of *PEAD* in any of the other social media groupings (Columns 3–6). In Column 7, we report the differences between the highest and lowest activity portfolios within each forecast error grouping. In general, the results do not provide compelling evidence of a difference in *PEAD* within each forecast error grouping, although we find some evidence of differences within the middle and top forecast error quintiles, which is driven primarily by the positive returns in the lowest activity group.

In sum, our descriptive analysis of *PEAD* suggests that *PEAD* is only observed in the lowest activity quintile, consistent with Hirshleifer and Teoh (2003), suggesting that firms with moderate to high levels of social media activity on average have no evidence of *PEAD* in our sample period.

8.4 MULTIVARIATE ANALYSIS

8.4.1 Tests of Hypothesis 1

To test our first hypothesis, we first examine whether increased investor attention increases the sensitivity of market returns to earnings news. Specifically, we estimate the association between earnings news and market returns by estimating a regression of short-window returns around the earnings announcement on the consensus analyst forecast error divided by stock price at the end of the quarter (*Ferrorq*). As negative earnings news is expected to have a differential response, we separate positive and negative earnings surprises (e.g. Skinner and Sloan, 2002). Our independent variable of interest is the interaction between an indicator variable for the highest level of *Activity* (*HiAct*) and the scaled forecast error (*Ferror*).

According to Hypothesis 1, we predict that the interaction will be positive and significant. We also include control variables for other firm characteristics which could be correlated with both our variable of interest and the market response; size, market-to-book, momentum, analyst dispersion and leverage. Specifically we estimate the following regression:

$$CAR_q = a_o + b_1\,Ferror_q^+ + b_2 Ferror_q + b_3\,HiAct_q + b_4\,Ferror_q^+ \times HiAct_q + b_5\,Ferror_q \times HiAct_q + controls_q \quad [8.4.1]$$

Where CAR_q is the two-day cumulative abnormal returns to the quarter q earnings announcement on the day of and day following the announcement (i.e., over the window [0,+1]), based on the firm's return less the return on the firm's size decile, $Ferror_q^+$ is the positive forecast error scaled by the price at the end of the quarter, and zero otherwise, $Ferror_q$ is the negative forecast error scaled by the price at the end of the quarter, and zero otherwise, $HiAct_q$ is an indicator variable set to one for observations in the highest quintile of *Activity* sorted by year and quarter, and zero otherwise. Our prediction is that b_4 and b_5 will be positive and significant.

We also include the following controls: *LoAct* is an indicator for the lowest quintile of social media activity, which we also interact with positive and negative forecast errors, *Size* is the log of total assets, *M/B* is the market-to-book ratio, which we also interact with the positive and negative forecast errors based on Skinner and Sloan (2002), *ϭAF* is the standard deviation of analyst forecasts, *Mom* is stock return momentum in the month before the earnings announcement, and *Leverage* is the firm's debt-to-asset ratio.

Table 8.4.1: Multivariate tests with CAR and PEAD
Note: Please see Appendix 8.A.2 for variable definitions, *** p<0.010, **p<0.050, *p<0.10

	(1) CAR			(2) CAR			(3) PEAD		
	coef	p-value		coef	p-value		coef	p-value	
Intercept	-0.002	0.047	**	0.001	0.730		0.001	0.886	
Ferror$^+$	1.912	0.000	***	1.573	0.000	***	1.015	0.150	
Ferror$^-$	1.514	0.000	***	1.151	0.000	***	-0.753	0.093	*
HiAct	-0.000	0.935		-0.001	0.782		-0.006	0.051	*
Ferror$^+$ *x HiAct*	4.469	0.000	***	4.658	0.000	***	0.645	0.556	
Ferror$^-$ *x HiAct*	1.371	0.017	**	1.455	0.012	**	-0.798	0.509	
LoAct				-0.002	0.232		0.001	0.725	
Ferror$^+$ *x LoAct*				0.958	0.062	*	1.532	0.045	**
Ferror$^-$ *x LoAct*				0.294	0.273		1.248	0.060	*
M/B				0.000	0.007	***	0.001	0.128	
Ferror$^+$ *x M/B*				0.145	0.363		-0.431	0.141	
Ferror$^-$ *x M/B*				0.196	0.111		0.380	0.100	
Size				-0.001	0.157		-0.000	0.964	
ϭAF				-0.015	0.214		0.008	0.755	
Mom				0.007	0.411		-0.029	0.109	
Leverage				0.004	0.197		0.011	0.067	*
Number of observations	15,468			15,468			15,468		
Adjusted R^2	0.073			0.075			0.004		

We report the results of this regression in Columns 1 and 2 of Table 8.4.1. In the first column, we present results for a restricted model, which excludes control variables. Consistent with prior research, we find that the coefficient on the analyst forecast error is positive and highly significant for both positive (b_1 = 1.912, p<0.001) and negative earnings surprises (b_2 =1.514, p<0.001). Consistent with our main prediction, we find evidence of a significant positive association between social media activity on the day of the earnings announcement and the sensitivity of market prices to positive earnings news (b_4 = 4.469, p<0.001) and negative earnings news (b_5 = 1.371, p<0.05). The incremental effect of high levels of social media activity on the sensitivity of earnings news is much stronger for positive earnings news at approximately 234% (4.469/1.912) versus 90.6% (1.371/1.514).[11]

In Column 2, we report the model including control variables and find that the effects of high levels of social media activity are not subsumed by other firm characteristics. When including controls, we find that the interactions between *LoAct* and *Ferror*$^+$ is positive and significant, however, the economic magnitude of the results is much smaller than for the high activity interactions. In sum, our results provide support for Hypothesis 1, that increased investor attention is associated with market prices that are more sensitive to earnings.

In Column 3, we report the association between returns following the earnings announcement over the period [+2, +60] and the interactions between social media activity and forecast errors. Based on Hypothesis 1, if investor attention increases the reaction to earnings news on the day of the earnings announcement, we expect less under-reaction to earnings news in the period after the announcement. As such, we expect that post earnings returns will only be associated with earnings surprises for firms with low levels of *Activity*. Consistent with Hypothesis 1, we find evidence consistent with this prediction for both the positive and negative earnings surprise groups.

8.5 FURTHER ANALYSIS

8.5.1 Social media activity and growth stocks

Skinner and Sloan (2002) show that the sensitivity of market returns to earnings news is more sensitive to growth firms relative to value firms; in this section we reconcile with their findings and identify that social media activity is incremental to their sort on growth. This analysis is important as it is possible that growth firms are more actively followed on Twitter.

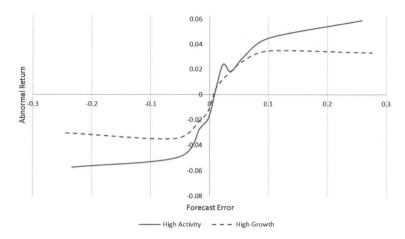

Figure 8.5.1: *Earnings surprise response functions for firms with high levels of social media activity*

Notes: This figure plots cumulative abnormal returns (CAR) surrounding the two-day window of the earnings announcement [0,+1] for high attention and high growth stocks as a function of the quarterly earnings forecast error. The solid line represents high activity firms, which are those firms in the highest quintile based on Market IQ's velocity measure on the day of the earnings announcement. The dashed line represents growth firms, which are those firms in the highest quintile sorted on market-to-book ratios. Each plot is formed by dividing the stocks into ten portfolios based on the magnitude of the forecast error, and then plotting the mean portfolio abnormal returns and forecast errors. The resulting points are connected for illustrative purposes.

Figure 8.5.1 plots the cumulative abnormal returns (*CAR*) surrounding the two-day window of the earnings announcement [0,+1] for high attention and high growth stocks as a function of the quarterly earnings forecast error. In Figure 8.5.1, the returns to high activity firms, which are those firms in the highest quintile based on Market IQ's velocity measure on the day of the earnings announcement, are more sensitive to earnings news than the growth firms, which are those firms in the highest quintile sorted on market-to-book ratios.

Models of investor sentiment, such as Shiller (1984) and DeLong et al. (1990), predict that investors do not optimally trade on fundamental information but rather on "sentiment" or "fads". If investors are on average overly optimistic, then sentiment trading may dampen the effect of earnings news. We use Market IQ's sentiment measure to investigate this possibility.[12] In Table 8.5.1, we examine the relation between high levels of *Activity* and *Sentiment* and the quarterly return (*Fullret*). In this section, we follow Skinner and Sloan (2002) and use the entire quarter return due to the possibility of bad news being pre-announced. In Column 1, we find the interactions of *HiAct* and *Ferror*⁺ and *HiAct* and *Ferror* ⁻ are both positive and significant. In Column 2, we examine how investor sentiment influences the relation between earnings news and *Fullret*. We find *HiSent* is positively related to *Fullret*, suggesting that *HiSent* firms have positive quarterly returns on average.[13] We also find the interaction between *HiSent* and *Ferror* ⁻ is negative and significant, which suggests that firms with high investor sentiment at the earnings announcement and miss analyst earnings expectations have less negative abnormal returns. In Column 3, we continue to find the interactions of *HiAct* and *Ferror*⁺ and *HiAct* and *Ferror* ⁻ to be positive and significant. We also continue to find a positive relation between *HiSent* and *Fullret* and a negative relation between the interaction of *HiSent* and *Ferror* ⁻ and *Fullret*. These results are consistent with a dampened response to negative earnings news due to investor optimism.[14]

8.5.2 Robustness to earnings announcement timing

Table 8.5.2: Pre-open versus post-close announcements

Note: Please see Appendix 8.A.2 for variable definitions, ***p<0.010, **p<0.050, *p<0.10

	CAR				PEAD			
	(1) Pre-Open		(2) Post-Close		(3) Pre-Open		(4) Post-Close	
	coef	p-value	coef	p-value	coef	p-value	coef	p-value
Intercept	-0.000	0.976	-0.003	0.623	-0.010	0.407	0.008	0.411
Ferror$^+$	1.021	0.012 **	2.156	0.000 ***	1.198	0.302	0.791	0.213
Ferror$^-$	0.797	0.043 **	1.337	0.000 ***	-2.007	0.009 ***	-0.652	0.289
HiAct	-0.002	0.521	-0.002	0.570	-0.007	0.091 *	-0.010	0.092 *
Ferror$^+$ *x HiAct*	7.011	0.000 ***	2.089	0.116	1.570	0.251	0.441	0.775
Ferror$^-$ *x HiAct*	1.795	0.002 ***	1.406	0.234	-1.067	0.516	0.227	0.864
LoAct	-0.000	0.925	-0.003	0.222	0.007	0.194	-0.002	0.592
Ferror$^+$ *x LoAct*	1.219	0.132	0.474	0.472	0.140	0.898	3.480	0.000 ***
Ferror$^-$ *x LoAct*	0.467	0.276	0.046	0.919	1.566	0.137	2.032	0.027 **
M/B	0.000	0.348	0.001	0.014 **	0.001	0.289	0.000	0.627
Ferror$^+$ *x M/B*	0.153	0.371	0.337	0.125	-0.275	0.519	-0.648	0.079 *
Ferror$^-$ *x M/B*	0.088	0.624	0.367	0.016 **	0.578	0.087 *	0.052	0.842
Size	-0.000	0.383	-0.000	0.739	0.002	0.168	-0.001	0.320
σAF	-0.017	0.371	-0.009	0.610	-0.021	0.549	0.004	0.918
Mom	0.017	0.205	-0.010	0.457	0.008	0.771	-0.056	0.035 **
Leverage	0.004	0.370	0.007	0.068 *	-0.005	0.640	0.023	0.009 ***
Number of observations	6,310		7,285		6,310		7,285	
Adjusted R^2	0.113		0.062		0.005		0.006	

Patell and Wolfson (1984) document that announcements made after the market close tend to have negative earnings news. DellaVigna and Pollet (2009) suggest that timing is associated with variation in investor attention. We find that social media activity appears to have different effects based on whether the firm announces prior to the market open or after the market closes.[15] In Table 8.5.2, we report evidence suggesting the effect of social media activity is higher for firms reporting prior to the market opening than for firms reporting after the market closes. We observe a significant interaction effect between positive forecast errors and social media activity for firms reporting before the market opens. We also find that the effects of low activity on *PEAD* are observed for firms announcing positive or negative earnings news after the market.

8.5.3 Robustness to other information intermediaries

In Table 8.5.3, Panels A and B, we document that our primary results are robust to the inclusion of information about earnings provided by traditional media outlets using the Dow Jones Newswires, financial blogs and Google searches, suggesting that social media activity provides a distinct proxy for attention to earnings. Li et al. (2011) find that traditional newswires enhance the market pricing of value relevant information in SEC filings and Da et al. (2011) highlight that investor demand for information can be gathered from Google search trends. Finally, Drake et al. (2012) find that when investors perform more

Google searches in the days prior to the earnings announcement there is a lower price reaction when earnings are announced and Chi and Shanthikumar (2014) document that contemporaneous Google search is associated with an increase in the market's response to earnings news, which is higher when the individuals searching are geographically dispersed. As such, we investigate the robustness of social media activity to the inclusion of these traditional proxies for the information environment.

Table 8.5.3 Panel A: *Robustness to the inclusion of alternative sources of online information*

	(1) CAR			(2) CAR			(3) CAR		
	coef	p-value		coef	p-value		coef	p-value	
Intercept	-0.008	0.291		0.000	0.978		-0.009	0.282	
$Ferror^+$	1.334	0.147		1.557	0.000	***	2.392	0.002	***
$Ferror^-$	1.587	0.014	**	0.921	0.007	***	1.104	0.237	
HiAct	-0.000	0.910		-0.001	0.628		0.000	0.963	
$Ferror^+$ x HiAct	4.229	0.000	***	4.225	0.000	***	3.905	0.001	***
$Ferror^-$ x HiAct	2.813	0.011	**	0.665	0.325		1.211	0.310	
LoAct	-0.000	0.769		0.000	0.026	**	0.000	0.986	
$Ferror^+$ x LoAct	1.180	0.002	***	0.355	0.043	**	1.345	0.001	***
$Ferror^-$ x LoAct	-0.004	0.991		0.315	0.082	*	0.044	0.893	
M/B	-0.001	0.800		-0.001	0.534		-0.000	0.929	
$Ferror^+$ x M/B	1.069	0.411		0.826	0.198		0.515	0.697	
$Ferror^-$ x M/B	1.112	0.295		0.638	0.088	*	1.767	0.151	
Pre-AbSearch	0.006	0.120					0.004	0.305	
$Ferror^+$ x Pre-AbSearch	1.217	0.210					1.988	0.122	
$Ferror^-$ x Pre-AbSearch	-0.281	0.862					-1.205	0.453	
HiDJN				0.001	0.762		0.001	0.776	
$Ferror^+$ x HiDJN				0.380	0.631		-1.523	0.192	
$Ferror^-$ x HiDJN				2.092	0.001	***	1.676	0.175	
HiBlog				-0.003	0.312		-0.003	0.518	
$Ferror^+$ x HiBlog				1.268	0.184		0.764	0.552	
$Ferror^-$ x HiBlog				-0.618	0.461		1.075	0.396	
Size	0.001	0.440		-0.000	0.305		0.001	0.492	
sAF	-0.047	0.073	*	-0.009	0.547		-0.040	0.124	
Mom	-0.055	0.014	**	0.000	0.990		-0.055	0.016	**
Leverage	-0.000	0.992		0.004	0.255		-0.002	0.825	
Number of observations	2,866			13,266			2,687		
Adjusted R^2	0.083			0.083			0.096		

In Table 8.5.3, Panel A, in Column 1, after controlling for investor demand for information through Google searches, we find a larger market reaction to positive and negative earnings news when there are high levels of social media activity (*HiAct*). We also find a larger market reaction to positive news when there are low levels of social media activity (*LoAct*). However, we do not find evidence of an association between the earnings response coefficient and Google searches prior to the earnings announcement.[16]

In Column 2, after controlling for information from other sources (i.e., blogs and the Dow Jones Newswire), we continue to find a larger market response to positive earnings news in the presence of high and low levels of social media activity and for negative earnings news in the presence of low levels of social media activity. We also find that increased coverage of the earnings announcement through the Dow Jones Newswire leads to increased sensitivity of market returns to negative earnings information. In Column 3, after including both Google searches and other sources of information, we continue to find a larger market response to positive earnings in the presence of high and low social media activity.

Table 8.5.3 Panel B: *Robustness to the inclusion of alternative sources of online information*
Note: Please see Appendix 8.A.2 for variable definitions, ***p<0.010, **p<0.050, *p<0.10

	(1) PEAD			(2) PEAD			(3) PEAD		
	coef	p-value		coef	p-value		coef	p-value	
Intercept	-0.020	0.145		0.006	0.454		-0.019	0.187	
Ferror⁺	-0.173	0.872		0.808	0.122		-1.534	0.197	
Ferror⁻	-0.483	0.685		-1.131	0.072	*	-0.870	0.649	
HiAct	-0.014	0.037	**	-0.006	0.070	*	-0.008	0.275	
Ferror⁺ x HiAct	-0.656	0.785		-0.086	0.935		-1.370	0.557	
Ferror⁻ x HiAct	-0.624	0.808		-0.051	0.964		2.297	0.377	
LoAct	-0.003	0.006	***	0.001	0.197		-0.002	0.026	**
Ferror⁺ x LoAct	0.353	0.581		-0.308	0.283		1.060	0.064	*
Ferror⁻ x LoAct	0.356	0.651		0.235	0.520		0.445	0.577	
M/B	-0.015	0.046	**	0.003	0.398		-0.014	0.074	*
Ferror⁺ x M/B	3.853	0.003	***	1.206	0.111		4.874	0.000	***
Ferror⁻ x M/B	1.803	0.408		2.710	0.003	***	1.214	0.638	
Pre-AbSearch	0.004	0.716					0.010	0.224	
Ferror⁺ x Pre-AbSearch	0.367	0.932					-3.596	0.230	
Ferror⁻ x Pre-AbSearch	3.994	0.376					7.461	0.092	*
HiDJN				0.001	0.806		-0.006	0.361	
Ferror⁺ x HiDJN				0.405	0.679		-0.330	0.777	
Ferror⁻ x HiDJN				1.283	0.193		-0.076	0.972	
HiBlog				-0.001	0.772		-0.011	0.125	
Ferror⁺ x HiBlog				1.130	0.311		3.793	0.046	**
Ferror⁻ x HiBlog				-2.955	0.055	*	-3.656	0.301	
Size	0.003	0.090	*	-0.001	0.517		0.003	0.108	
sAF	0.110	0.050	*	-0.001	0.982		0.091	0.119	
Mom	-0.033	0.456		-0.029	0.131		-0.022	0.611	
Leverage	0.059	0.000	***	0.015	0.028	**	0.065	0.000	***
Number of observations	2,866			13,266			2,687		
Adjusted R²	0.024			0.005			0.028		

In Table 8.5.3 Panel B, we examine the relation between attention and *PEAD* after controlling for alternative sources of online information. In Column 1, we find a negative relation between low levels of social media activity (*LoAct*) and *PEAD* after controlling for Google searches. In Column 2, we do not find a significant relation between social media activity and *PEAD* after controlling for news from traditional media outlets. However, in Column 3, we find *LoAct* negatively related to *PEAD* and the interaction between

Ferror[+] and *LoAct* positively related to *PEAD* after controlling for both Google searches and news from traditional media outlets.

8.5.4 Caveats

Our results should be interpreted with the important caveat that our data span is short – we are only able to measure social media activity over the period January 2012 through July 2013. In part, this is due to the nature of social media networks, which have only recently experienced significant growth. For example, GNIP (2014) reports that "cashtagging" – the way in which investors communicate the ticker symbol of the company – has increased 550% between 2011 and 2014. Additionally, it is important to note that even regulatory bodies such as the SEC have recently embraced the use of social media channels to broadcast market-moving corporate news, which will potentially result in continued high levels of growth in the use of social media by firms and investors over time. Hence, our results should be considered as providing preliminary evidence on the role of social networks on the pricing of earnings news. Our results are also limited to periods that are out-of-sample to the prior literature, which provides many of the predictions that we test. In some senses this caveat is also a strength of the findings, as our time period shares many empirical regularities highlighted by the prior literature.

8.6 CONCLUSION

The purpose of this paper is to investigate whether investor attention through online social media networks is associated with the pricing, and mispricing, of earnings news. Social media is a relatively new feature of financial markets, and have become an increasingly large channel through which the discussions and preferences of individuals can be measured. We focus primarily on the role of social media activity, which we predict will be associated with an increase in the sensitivity of market returns to earnings news. We find that a firm's social media activity increases significantly on the day of the earnings announcement for firms with positive and negative earnings news.

We find evidence in support of our hypothesis – the prediction that high levels of abnormal social media activity are associated with increased sensitivity of earnings announcement returns to earnings surprises. The effects associated with increased social media activity are greatest for firms that beat analysts' forecasts. We also document evidence of a significant post-earnings-announcement drift for the portfolio of firms with the lowest levels of social media attention to earnings announcements. Our results are based on a direct proxy for investor attention and are consistent with investor attention to earnings announcements being inversely associated with the under-reaction to earnings news.

Our results are incremental to, and larger than, the value-growth partition, and are robust to the timing of earnings announcements and to the inclusion of additional online information proxies. Our results provide implications for future research, especially research that examines variation in investor attention and investor sentiment. Specifically, social media appears to provide observable proxies for these theoretical constructs.

ACKNOWLEDGEMENTS

We appreciate the comments of Nicole Cade, Sabrina Chi, Mirko Heinle, Scott Johnson, Russell Lundholm, Sarah McVay, James Myers, Linda Myers, Rafael Rogo, and workshop participants at the University of Arkansas and the University of British Columbia as well as the discussions about the measurement of data from Fahad Kamr, Haani Bokhari and especially from Adil Kalani of Market IQ, we also thank Sabrina Chi for sharing her Google SVI data. All errors remain our responsibility.

Notes

[1] As we later discuss in more detail, we measure the efficiency of price responses to earnings news by the strength of the initial price reaction to earnings news at the earnings announcement coupled with an examination of post-earnings-announcement drift to identify over- or under-reaction to the news.

[2] Blankespoor et al. (2014) investigate a sample of technology firms that use Twitter to disclose information. They find that these firms have lower bid ask spreads, consistent with firms' use of Twitter lowering information asymmetry between investors.

[3] To measure "earnings news" we use the median EPS forecast computed over the set of the analysts' most recent forecasts that are no earlier than two weeks before the quarterly earnings release date. This procedure avoids the problem of stale analyst forecasts. We use the unadjusted I/B/E/S forecasts to avoid losing the precision in the decimal places of the forecasts due to the I/B/E/S adjustments of prior forecasts for subsequent stock splits (Baber and Kang, 2002; Payne and Thomas, 2003). Actual earnings realisations are obtained from the unadjusted I/B/E/S actual file.

[4] Sentiment is measured on a continuous scale between zero and one, which is increasing in optimism, where 0.5 is considered neutral. The sentiment measure provided is relative to the average sentiment for a given firm over the prior seven days.

[5] Market IQ is able to identify influential users within the social media networks they cover, allowing for a finer partition of the sentiment associated with news from the noise associated with social media conversations.

[6] For example, social networking sites such as Facebook require that both parties agree to the social connection. Note that this feature of Twitter allows for influential users, such as Mad Money / CNBC's Jim Cramer to have significantly larger reach on Twitter, relative to other social networking sites.

[7] Kwak et al. (2010) provide a follower-following topology analysis of Twitter and find that interactions on Twitter deviate significantly from the known characteristic of human social networks. They conclude that this structure is an effective medium for the diffusion of information.

[8] Cashtags help alleviate concerns over common word ticker symbols such as "CAT" making the target of social media conversations less ambiguous than google searches.

1.   [9] The celebrities Katy Perry and Justin Bieber have the two most followed accounts on Twitter, both with over 50 million followers. In Contrast CNN's breaking news is ranked number 32, with 16 million followers (http://twittercounter.com/pages/100) retrieved 4/27/2014.

[10] Carl Icahn's Multibillion-Dollar Tweet Boosts Apple Stock (https://finance.yahoo.com/blogs/the-exchange/carl-icahn-multibillion-dollar-tweet-boosts-apple-stock-205938760.html).

[11] Fischer et al. (2014) provide a model of exaggerated earnings sensitivity where rational investors trade heavily on earnings news in the expectation that future investors will do so as well. The much higher coefficient on the interaction of attention and positive earnings surprises could be a rational response to expected future attention being higher for current attention to good news.

[12] Note that not all firms have available data on sentiment we exclude those with missing values from this analysis.

[13] Similar results are found at the time of the earnings announcement using the short-window returns in Table 8.4.1. We leave to future research whether this effect is due to sentimental investors "ignoring" earnings warnings and other negative news prior to the earnings announcement, or for some other reason.

[14] Our results are consistent with Burger and Curtis (2014) who provide evidence of the increase in margin debt in recent years being associated with a lower sensitivity of aggregate prices to aggregate accounting fundamentals.

[15] We leave day of the week effects to future research. Doyle and Magilke (2009) and DeHaan et al. (2014) provide evidence on the effect of announcing earnings on Fridays versus other days of the week.

[16] To perform this test, we use weekly Google search data as this is the highest frequency data available during our sample period and limit the sample to observations where the end of the Google search period is within seven days of the earnings announcement. Additionally, the sample size is small because we are only able to obtain Google search data for 2012 and the data excludes many companies with ticker symbols that are also common words (e.g., CAT). As such the results should be interpreted with these caveats and is not directly comparable to daily Google search data used in Drake et al. (2012).

8.7 REFERENCES

1.   Baber, W. and Kang, S. (2002). The impact of split adjusting and rounding on analysts' forecast error calculations. *Accounting Horizons*, 16, 277–289.

2.   Ball, R. and Brown, P. (1968). An empirical evaluation of accounting income numbers. *Journal of Accounting Research*, 6(2), 159–178.

3.   Bernard, V. L. and Thomas, J.K. (1990). Evidence that stock prices do not fully reflect the implications of current earnings for future earnings. *Journal of Accounting and Economics, 13(4)*, 305–340.

4.   Bernard, V. L. and Thomas, J.K. (1989). Post-earnings-announcement drift: delayed price response or r isk premium. *Journal of Accounting Research, 27(3)*, 1–36.

5.   Blankespoor, E., Miller, G. S. and White, H. D. (2013). The role of dissemination in market liquidity: e vidence from firms' use of TwitterTM. The Accounting Review, 89(1), 79–112.

6.   Burger, M. A. and Curtis, A. (2014). Aggregate noise trader risk, mispricing, and accounting fundamentals. Available at SSRN http://ssrn.com/abstract=2426573 .

7.   Caskey, J., Minnis, M. and Nagar, V. (2011). Disclosure drifts in investor networks. Available at SSRN: http://ssrn.com/abstract=1848323.

8.   Chi, S. and Shanthikumar, D.M. (2014). The geographic dispersion of Google Search and the market reaction to earnings announcements. Available at SSRN: http://ssrn.com/abstract=2324391.

9.   Chordia, T., Goyal, A., Sadka, G., Sadka, R. and Shivakumar, L. (2009). Liquidity and the post-earnings announcement drift. *Financial Analysts Journal,* 18–32.

10. Da, Z., Engelberg, J. and Gao, P. (2011). In Search of Attention. *The Journal of Finance, 66(5)*, 1461– 1499.

11. DeHaan, E., Shevlin, T. and Thornock, J. (2014). Market (in)attention and earnings announcement timing. Working paper, Stanford University, University of California at Irvine, and University of Washington.

12. DeLong, J. B., Shleifer, A., Summers, L. H. and Waldmann, R. J. (1990). Noise trader risk in financial markets. *Journal of Political Economy*, 98, 703–738.

13. DellaVigna, S. and Pollet, J.M. (2009). Investor inattention and Friday earnings announcements. *The Journal of Finance*, 64(2), 709–749.

14. Doyle, J. T. and Magilke, M.J. (2009). The timing of earnings announcements: an examination of the s trategic disclosure hypothesis. *The Accounting Review,* 84(1), 157–182.

15. Drake, M. S., Roulstone, D.T. and Thornock, J.R. (2012). Investor information demand: evidence from Google Searches around earnings announcements. *Journal of Accounting Research, 50(4)*, 1001– 1040.

16. Easton, P. D. and Zmijewski, M.E. (1989). Cross-sectional variation in the stock market response to accounting earnings announcements. *Journal of Accounting and Economics, 11(2)*, 117–141.

17. Fischer, P., Heinle, M.S. and Verrecchia, R.E. (2014) Projected earnings sensitivity. Working paper, University of Pennsylvania.

18. Henderson, R. (2014) Institutions Reluctant to Twitter Trade Despite Offerings. *The Trade News*. Available at:http://www.thetradenews.com/news/Asset_Classes/Equities/Institutions_reluctant_to_Twitter_trade_despite_offerings.aspx [Accessed 28 February 2014].

19. Hirshleifer, D. A., Myers, J. N., Myers, L. A. and Teoh, S. H. (2008). Do individual investors cause post- earnings announcement drift? Direct evidence from personal trades. *The Accounting Review, 83(6)*, 1521–1550.

20. Hirshleifer, D. and Teoh, S.H. (2003). Limited attention, information disclosure, and financial reporting. *Journal of Accounting and Economics, 36(1*, 337–386.

21. Meredith, J. (2012) *Will Twitter's Cashtag Help Predict the Stock Market?* [Blog] SalesForce. Available at: http://www.salesforcemarketingcloud.com/blog/category/mktgcloud/page/24/

22. Kormendi, R. and Lipe, R. (1987). Earnings innovations, earnings persistence, and stock returns. *Journal of Business,* 323–345.

23. Kwak, H., Lee, C., Park, H. and Moon, S. (2010). What is Twitter, a Social Network or a News Media? *In Proceedings of the 19th International Conference on World Wide Web* (April): 591–600.

24. Lev, B. (1989). On the usefulness of earnings and earnings research: lessons and directions from two decades of empirical research. *Journal of Accounting Research*, 153–192.

25. Li, E. X., Ramesh, K. and Shen, M. (2011). The role of newswires in screening and disseminating value-relevant information in periodic SEC reports. *The Accounting Review*, 86(2), 669–701.

26. Mackintosh, J. (2013). Traders Tap Twitter for Top Stock Tips. *Financial Times*. Available at: http://www.ft.com/cms/s/0/e1335c66-3284-11e3-91d2-00144feab7de.html [Accessed 11 October, 2013].

27. Patell, J. M. and Wolfson, M. A. (1984). The intraday speed of adjustment of stock prices to earnings and dividend announcements. *Journal of Financial Economics,* 13(2), 223–252.

28. Payne, J. and Thomas, W. (2003). The implications of using stock-split adjusted I/B/E/S data in empirical research. *The Accounting Review,* 78, 1049–1067.

29. Ryan, K. (2009) Twitter Study. [Blog] PearAnalytics. Available at: http://web.archive.org/web/20110715062407/www.pearanalytics.com/blog/wp-content/uploads/2010/05/Twitter-Study-August-2009.pdf [Accessed August 2009].

30. Shiller, R. J. (1984). Stock prices and social dynamics. *Brookings Papers on Economic Activity*, 2, 457– 498.

31. Shiller, R. J. and Pound, J. (1989). Survey evidence on diffusion of interest and information among investors. *Journal of Economic Behavior & Organization*, 12(1), 47–66.

32. Skinner D. and Sloan, R. (2002). Earnings surprises, growth expectations and stock returns or don't let an earnings torpedo sink your portfolio. *Review of Accounting Studies*, 7, 289–312.

33. Waite J. (2014) Which Social Networks matter in 2014. [Blog] Adobe. Available at: http://blogs.adobe.com/digitaleurope/2014/01/03/social-networks-care-2014/

8.A   APPENDIX

8.A.1   Example of Social Media Activity from MarketIQ for Citi (Cashtag $C)

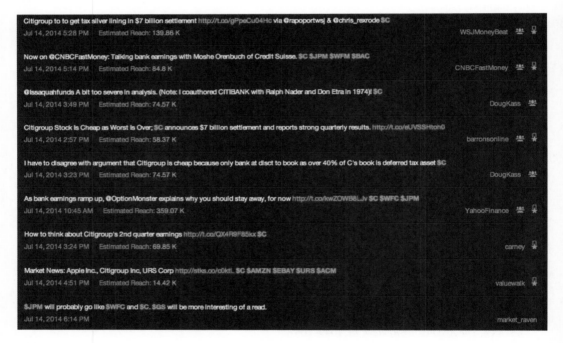

Notes: The above figure displays a typical social media conversation reported on MarketIQ's social media feed about an earnings announcement. The above was collected from MarketIQ. Retrieved 16/7/2014.

8.A.2 Variable Definitions

VARIABLE NAME	DESCRIPTION
Activity	Measure of social media activity from Market IQ, where 1x is the baseline effect that is measured over a 30 day rolling window;
HiAct	An indicator variable set to one for the highest quintile of social media activity, zero otherwise;
LoAct	An indicator variable set to one for the lowest quintile of social media activity, zero otherwise;
Ferror+	Positive forecast error, scaled by end of the quarter price. Measured as the actual earnings realisation from the I/B/E/S unadjusted actuals file minus the median analyst consensus forecast from the I/B/E/S unadjusted summary file;
Ferror-	Negative forecast error, scaled by end of the quarter price. Measured as the actual earnings realisation from the I/B/E/S unadjusted actuals file minus the median analyst consensus forecast from the I/B/E/S unadjusted summary file;
%Good	The percentage of observations that report earnings that beat the median analyst consensus;
Sentiment	Measure of firms-specific investor social media sentiment from Market IQ, measured as a seven-day rolling average;
HiSent	An indicator variable set to one for the highest quintile of social media sentiment, zero otherwise;
LoSent	An indicator variable set to one for the lowest quintile of social media sentiment, zero otherwise;
CAR	Cumulative abnormal returns, measured as the firm's return less the return on the firm's size decile over the two-day window surrounding the earnings announcement [0,+1];
PEAD	Post earnings announcement drift, measured as the firm's return less the return on the firm's size decile over the window [+2,+60] relative to the earnings announcement;
Fullret	The quarterly return, measured as the firm's buy and hold return less the return on the firm's size decile over the period starting 2 days after the previous quarter's earnings announcement to 1 day after the current quarter's earnings announcement;
M/B	Market-to-book, measured as the market value of equity divided by common equity at the end of the quarter;

%Pre-open	The percentage of firms reporting earnings before the market opens;
Pre-AbSearch	Abnormal Google SVI in the week before the earnings announcement;
Size	The natural log of total assets;
Mom	Momentum, measured as the firm's buy and hold return in the month prior to the earnings announcement;
σAF	The standard deviation of analyst forecasts, taken from the I/B/E/S unadjusted summary file;
#Forecasts	The number of analysts issuing forecasts, taken from the I/B/E/S unadjusted summary file;
HiDJN	Indicator variable set to one if the number of Dow Jones Newswire articles on the day of the earnings announcement is greater than the sample median, zero otherwise;
HiBlog	Indicator variable set to one if the number of blog posts on the day of the earnings announcement is greater than the sample median, zero otherwise;
Leverage	The ratio of long-term debt to total assets.

PART III

Sentiment Analysis Applied To Equities

CHAPTER 9

Predicting Stock Returns using Text Mining Tools

Gurvinder Brar, *Global Head of Quantitative Research, Macquarie Securities Group*

Giuliano De Rossi, *Head of European Quantitative Research Team, Macquarie Securities Group*

Nilesh Kalamkar, *Quantitative Researcher, Macquarie Securities Group*

ABSTRACT

This paper documents the research undertaken by the Macquarie Global Quantitative Research Group utilising text mining tools applied to "unstructured text" to predict stock returns. We focus on announcements relating to publication of company reports and earnings press releases. Moreover, we discuss directions for future research that are likely to be of particular relevance for practitioners. Our main conclusion is that investors should utilise text mining tools within their investment process. These tools can help extract information embedded within corporate filing data and the slower decay of the predictive ability of the resulting signal makes them particularly suitable for investors with longer investment horizons.

9.1 INTRODUCTION

Active managers in their thirst for new sources of alpha, both to improve and differentiate their investment processes, have started to search for non-traditional sources of data which may be difficult to access or process but offers alpha opportunities. The popularity of "big-data" or "unstructured text", in our opinion, is an example of this phenomenon and offers significant opportunities to investors with medium- to longer-term investment horizons.

Our paper documents the research undertaken by the Macquarie Global Quantitative Research Group utilising text mining tools applied to "unstructured text" to predict stock returns. Specifically we will focus on announcements relating to publication of company reports and earnings press releases.

9.1.1 Data Sources

We have sourced the data from EDGAR (the SEC's online database) and Factset. The challenge investors have faced in the past has been finding a reliable source from where they can access data in a timely and reliable manner. Both SEC EDGAR and Factset provide tools for investors to be able to systematically download the company filing data in a timely manner. The advantage of using Factset is that its platform offers company filing data for a global universe.

9.1.2 Prior Academic Research

Analysing corporate filing data has been a rich area of research within academia. Earlier work by Baker and Kare (1992), Subramanian et al. (1993) and Li (2010) looked at corporate filings and argued that managers will use the complexity feature, i.e. make it difficult for investors to interpret the company filings, to their advantage when a firm's performance starts to deteriorate. Demers and Vega (2008) find the level of optimism in earnings press releases is positively associated with the market's short-term response to announcements. Larcker and Zakolyukina (2012) analysed the Question and Answer section of earnings conference calls and found their method applied to CEO and CFO narratives is successful in detecting deception.

Research analysing corporate disclosures has mainly used the "bags-of-words" approach. That is, researchers have used dictionaries to count the number of positive or negative words within the text. Loughran and McDonald (2011) argued that the approach employed by standard dictionaries cannot be applied to financial statements because, for example, of the presence of words like "liability" which are frequently used within financial statements but have a negative connotation within standard financial dictionaries. This creates a negative bias and misleading outcomes. The authors have built a custom dictionary with a greater relevance in a financial sense which is commonly used for analysing structured or unstructured text. Our work shows that their dictionary offers advantages relative to off-the-shelf dictionaries like Dicton and Linguistic Inquiry and Word Count (LIWC) and our analysis documents results using the Loughran and McDonald (2011) dictionary.

Despite the "bags-of-words" approach being relatively simple and arguably a naive method, prior research shows that it does works in discriminating between out and under-performers in the cross-section. Loughran and McDonald (2015) survey the recent literature applying textual analysis to finance and accounting and find support for the "bags-of-words" approach and also highlight the nuances investors need to keep in mind when applying such tools.

9.2   CASE STUDY 1: COMPLEXITY OF COMPANY 10-K REPORTS AND STOCK RETURNS

In *Quantamentals: Camouflaged in Complexity* we applied textual analysis to annual US company reports (i.e. 10-K) to uncover accounting manipulations or signals related to future operating performance. Our approach was to analyse the "complexity" of the Management Discussion & Analysis (MD&A) section of 10-K filings. Our prior is that companies with deteriorating financials will attempt to make their financial statements difficult to interpret, i.e. increase 'complexity', which should lead to weaker future performances. That is, increasing "complexity" should be negatively correlated with stocks returns.

How do you measure "complexity"? Li (2010) used the "Fog Index" which is a weighted function of average sentence length and complex words. Our approach was to use a combination of number of words, words per sentence and complex words per sentence to build the "complexity" score. Complexity, however, will be a function of company size as larger companies will be more complex or can arise as part of normal operations. Thus we create a complexity score by stripping out the effects of size, asset growth and sector classification.

$$C_{i,t} = c + \beta_1 \text{Log Total Assets}_{i,t} + \beta_3 \text{Asset Growth}_{i,t} + \sum_{s=1}^{S-1} \beta_s \text{Sector}_{si,t} + \varepsilon_{i,t} \qquad [9.2.1]$$

Where is the complexity of stock i at time t, S is the total number of sectors and is the residual complexity of stock i at time t which is used as the stock signal.

To analyse the efficacy of the complexity scores, we follow the standard backtesting methodology whereby we create five portfolios and measure the equally-weighted performances over a one, three, six, nine and twelve-month holding periods. The rationale for extending the holding periods was to assess the information decay of this signal and whether the signal could be used by investors who have a longer investment horizon.

Figures 9.2.1 and 9.2.2 plot the performances over a one and twelve-month holding period and support Li's (2010) observations that companies whose reports are difficult to read / interpret underperform. Two further observations can be made on the results.

Firstly, only companies with high level of complexity underperform, which would make this a good signal for identifying "short" candidates. The returns asymmetry persists both over short and longer investment horizons. Secondly, this signal works well over both short and longer-horizons, which makes it applicable to investors with both short and longer-holding periods. This is important as investors, especially those with longer investment horizons, traditionally would not have used text mining tools and our results show that they should indeed leverage these insights within their investment process.

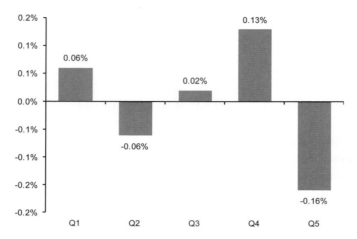

Figure 9.2.1: Average Quintile Returns (1 Month).

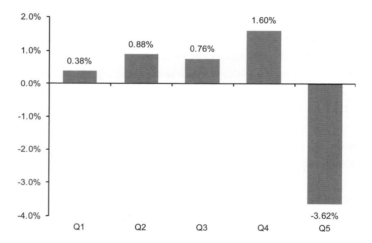

Figure 9.2.2: Average Quintile Returns (12 Months).

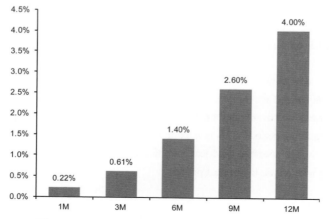

Figure 9.2.3: Average spread Returns.

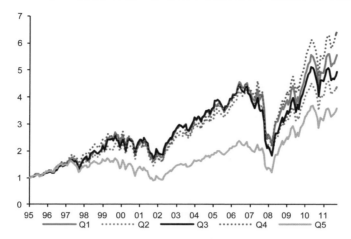

Figure 9.2.4: Cumulative Quintile Returns (1 Month). Source for Figures 9.2.1-4: Securities and Exchange Commission, Russell, Compustat, Macquarie Capital (USA), February 2013.

Why do companies with complex financial statements perform poorly? To answer this question, we link complexity with company fundamentals like ROE/ROA. To do so, we compute the median ROE/ROA for each complexity portfolio and analyse the progression from years FY0 to FY4. Figures 9.2.5 and 9.2.6 show that across both measures, companies with poor scores have weaker operating performance. This is reassuring as the results suggest that the returns are being driven by weakening operating performance and not an artefact of data mining.

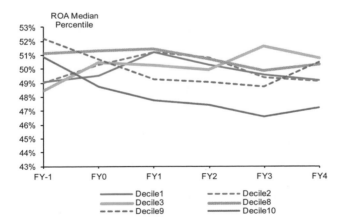

Figure 9.2.5: ROE profile partitioned on complexity.

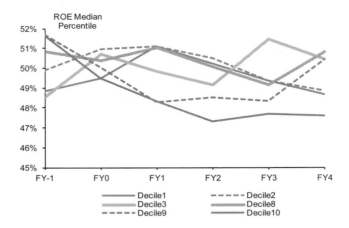

Figure 9.2.6: *ROA profile partitioned on complexity. Source for Figures 9.2.5-6: Securities and Exchange Commission, Russell, Compustat, Macquarie Capital (USA), February 2013.*

Do these results hold across global regions? In a recent paper we analysed the company filing data across a global sample of companies and the results support our earlier observations that increasing "complexity" is negatively correlated with future stock returns.

9.3   CASE STUDY 2: IMPROVING EARNINGS SURPRISE STRATEGIES BY INCORPORATING THE SOFT INFORMATION EMBEDDED IN COMPANY EARNINGS PRESS RELEASES

Earnings surprise signals are commonly used by investors within their investment process and, in line with prior academic research, our analysis also shows that companies that beat (miss) investor expectations out (under) perform, and these effects are stronger for US Small than Large-Caps (see Figures 9.3.1 and 9.3.2).

At the time of earnings announcements, companies also issue a press release which discusses the company's operational performance and is used by investors to assess its quality. In *Quantamentals: A Surprising Tone* we assess whether the soft information contained in quarterly Earnings Press Releases (EPR) complements the hard information contained in reported earning numbers. Can investors combine these two sources of information to improve the efficacy of earnings surprise strategies?

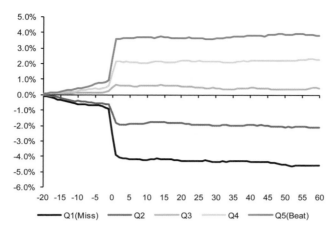

Figure 9.3.1: *Performance with percent beat/miss (Russell 1000).*

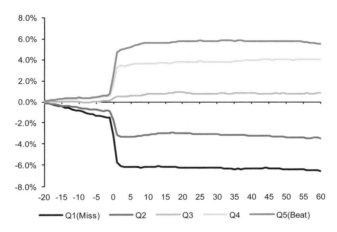

Figure 9.3.2: *Performance with percent beat/miss (Russell 2000). Source for Figures 9.3.1-2: Russell, IBES, Compustat, Macquarie Capital (USA), July 2014.*

Since a company reports hard information, earnings in this instance, and soft information, i.e. EPR, alike, the information content from these two sources is likely to be correlated. That is, companies beating consensus expectations will most likely have a positive bias in their EPR and vice versa. This is indeed what we find when we compute correlations between the two signals. Thus to control for systematic biases, we compute abnormal tone whereby we regress tone of EPR on earnings surprises and use the residual as our "abnormal tone" signal.

$$Tone_{i,t} = \alpha + \beta_{i,t} Percent\ Beat/\ Miss_{i,t} + \epsilon_{i,t} \qquad [9.3.1]$$

In unreported results we also built an "abnormal tone" signal after controlling for prior earnings revisions, twelve-month price momentum and cumulative price reaction one-day around the reporting date. The results were qualitatively similar and interested readers should contact the authors.

We use an event study methodology to assess whether additional information present in abnormal tone can be used to differentiate between companies beating or missing consensus investor expectations. Since we are using quarterly data, we analyse the performance over a three-month holding period. We measure portfolio performance from day 2 to day 60 to avoid the strategy performance being impacted upon by announcement-day effects.

Figures 9.3.3-6 plot the relative performances of companies with positive or negative earnings surprises conditioned on positive or negative tone. What we observe is that "abnormal tone" of EPR helps discriminate between companies that beat expectations whilst having no impact on the stocks that miss street expectations. What is equally interesting is that the signal is more effective over longer (i.e. 3-months) than shorter (i.e. under 1-month) horizons.

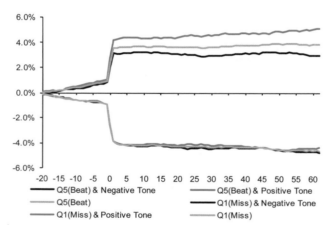

Figure 9.3.3: *Abnormal net tone – Most positive/Most negative earnings (Russell 1000)*

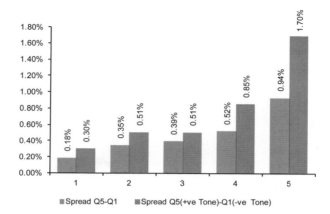

Figure 9.3.4: *Spread returns with tone comparison (Russell 1000).*

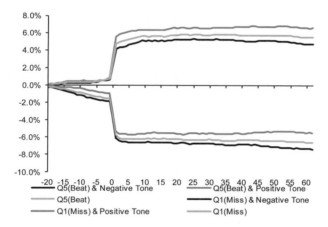

Figure 9.3.5: *Abnormal net tone – Most positive/Most negative earnings (Russell 2000)*

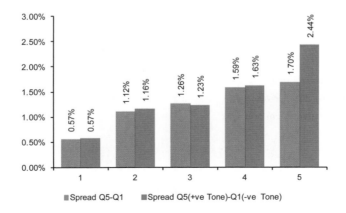

Figure 9.3.6: *Spread returns with tone comparison (Russell 2000). Source: SEC Edgar, Russell, IBES, Compustat, Macquarie Capital (USA), July 2014.*

To assess the performance of a trading strategy in more realistic settings we build a systematic trading strategy whereby we go long (short) stock with positive (negative) earnings surprises and positive (negative) "abnormal tone" and rebalance the portfolio on a quarterly basis. Figures 9.3.7-8 show that within US large-caps, combining EPR with reported numbers leads to an increase in both returns and risk-adjusted returns.

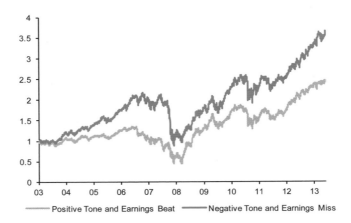

Figure 9.3.7: Cumulative Strategy Returns. Source: Russell, IBES, Compustat, Macquarie Capital (USA), July 2014.

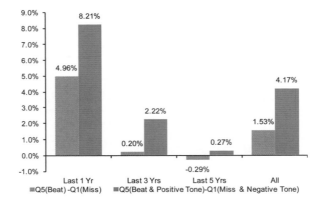

Figure 9.3.8: Recent performance. Source: Russell, IBES, Compustat, Macquarie Capital (USA), July 2014.

The analysis above shows that investors can use the soft information embedded within the tone of the EPR documents to improve the performance of earnings surprise signals. Moreover, these signals are suitable for investors with longer investment horizons.

9.4 DISCUSSION AND DIRECTIONS FOR FUTURE RESEARCH

As we have argued in the previous sections, the application of text mining techniques to stock return prediction has attracted considerable attention in recent years. We believe that it is an exciting new field of finance, which is particularly promising as a means to develop signals that can be used over relatively long investment horizons. In this section we shall examine some aspects of this topic that are likely to be particularly relevant in future research, particularly from the perspective of a practitioner applying the tools to his or her investment process.

9.4.1 Methodology

As the survey by Kearney and Liu (2013) shows, the majority of studies that have appeared in the academic literature use a very simple *count of words* approach. The limitations of such a crude approach are apparent: as it does not attempt to identify the role of each word in the sentence, it is not able to correctly process negations (e.g. "the figure is not encouraging") and other features of the human language. From a purely methodological point of view, the main criticism of the "bag-of-words" approach concerns its subjectivity, as discussed by Li (2010). Words are typically included in the positive or negative list based on a subjective assessment which may be affected by previous empirical results. As a consequence, it may be difficult to obtain genuine out of sample evidence on the performance of this approach. Nevertheless, it is very easy to implement with little or no computational requirements.

Machine learning is one of the methods that might see increasing application in text mining for finance. The naïve Bayes approach, arguably one of the simplest forms of classification, has already been adopted in a handful of papers. Antweiler and Frank (2004) and Das and Chen (2007) used it to analyse social media sentiment and internet postings about individual stocks. Li (2010) analysed financial statements, while Huang et al. (2014) deal with the language in analyst reports.

In our paper *Quantamentals: I just called to say I'm bullish* we have applied the naïve Bayes approach to a set of global analyst conference call transcripts. Our approach consists of manually scoring a subsample of the text (a set of 10,000 sentences) randomly derived from the entire sample. We then tokenise each sentence into single words and create a term matrix with rows representing sentences and columns representing all unique words in sentences so as to record the occurrence of words sentence by sentence. In the last step we then build a simple model of the probability that, given that certain words appear in the sentence, the sentence is positive, negative or neutral.

The classification model is then applied to all the documents that make up our sample, by classifying each sentence as positive, negative or neutral according to which outcome has the highest conditional probability. Scores are then aggregated at the document level as a ratio of positive sentences to the total number. We measure tone by calculating the difference between the ratio of positive and the ratio of negative sentences.

When the signal is used to predict returns we find no evidence that the naïve Bayes approach improves significantly on the "bag-of-words" alternatives (Table 9.4.1). In particular, the signal is derived as the change in tone from the previous available call. Cumulative abnormal returns are calculated over the average return of stocks in the same sector and geographic region. Stocks are sorted in terciles by tone, using thresholds that are calculated based on the information available at the time of the call. Furthermore, we double sort on earnings surprises (sourced from I/B/E/S) and tone and report the average drift after correcting for the well-known post earnings announcement drift.

Table 9.4.1: *Drift between the returns on the top and bottom tercile of stocks sorted by change in tone measured from the Q&A session. Source: Factset, I/B/E/S, Macquarie Capital, April 2015.*

	T (+1,+21) Drift	T (+1,+63) Drift	T (+21,+63) Drift
LM	72	174	102
Diction	17	121	104
LIWC	63	130	67
All dictionaries	68	210	142
Naïve Bayes LM	42	119	77
Naïve Bayes	61	125	64

Drifts are calculated over alternative horizons where, for example, $t+1$ refers to the closing price one trading day after the call has taken place.

LM stands for the dictionary advocated by Loughran and McDonald (2011). Diction and LIWC provide alternative dictionaries. "All dictionaries" is the union of all word lists. Of the two naïve Bayes implementations, "Naïve Bayes" LM uses the word list from Loughran and McDonald (2011) while "Naïve Bayes" is based on a shorter word list obtain by optimising the list of features. In line with the results discussed in Loughran and McDonald (2015), we find no evidence that the drift in the last two rows (naïve Bayes approach) is larger than the drift obtained through the simple *count of words* approach.

9.4.2 International evidence

Most of the evidence presented in the existing literature is based on US data. One of the obvious directions for future research is to extend those analyses to countries outside the US and check the robustness of the current findings.

In our work on conference call transcripts we analysed global data and compared returns predictability across regions. Given the limited availability of data for Japan and the Asia Pacific region, we focused on the comparison between Europe and the US. As Tables 9.4.2 and 9.4.3 show, the drifts generated by our change in tone signal are larger in Europe than in the US. The difference is both economically and statistically significant. It is also interesting to note that for both regions, the drift continues to accrue even 21 trading days after the call has taken place.

Table 9.4.2: *Drift between the returns on the top and bottom tercile of stocks sorted by change in tone measured from the Q&A session in North America. Source: Factset, I/B/E/S, Macquarie Capital, April 2015.*

	T (+1,+21) Drift	T (+1,+63) Drift	T (+21,+63) Drift
Diction	10	87	78
LIWC	60	136	75
All dictionaries	47	176	129
Naïve Bayes LM	10	76	66
Naïve Bayes	36	119	82

Table 9.4.3: Drift between the returns on the top and bottom tercile of stocks sorted by change in tone measured from the Q&A session in Europe. Source: Factset, I/B/E/S, Macquarie Capital, April 2015.

	T (+1,+21) Drift	T (+1,+63) Drift	T (+21,+63) Drift
LM	153	210	57
Diction	-22	243	265
LIWC	50	134	84
All dictionaries	96	314	219
Naïve Bayes LM	125	314	189
Naïve Bayes	173	285	112

9.4.3 Beyond expected returns

Our analysis is centred on the task of predicting stock returns from signals derived from text mining. However, several papers in the existing literature focus on other aspects of the investing process, e.g. Borochin et al. (2015); Wang et al. (2013) and Kogan et al. (2009) try to measure risk from textual disclosures. In particular, Borochin et al. (2015) derive a measure of abnormal tone in conference calls and show that it is negatively related to market perception of risk as measured from the prices of single stock options. Both Wang et al. (2013) and Kogan et al. (2009) show how to derive accurate predictions of return volatility by analysing the tone in corporate disclosures (10-K forms).

Buehlmaier and Zechner (2014) work with a sample of 130,000 articles appearing in the financial press about potential mergers. Their approach is to directly calculate the media-implied likelihood of merger completion by analysing the words used in a given press article and the article's length. Their conclusion is that the stock market systematically underreacts to media content.

9.4.4 New media

The techniques described in this paper have been applied to a variety of textual disclosures: news, message board posts and social media, financial disclosures, press releases, conference call transcripts, IPO prospectuses. Recent work has analysed SEC comment letters (Ryans, 2014) and microblogging about individual stocks (Sprenger et al., 2014).

Which other sources will be used in the future to extract information about stock returns from text mining? While it is difficult to answer this question directly, we highlight the fact that in the existing literature, each signal has been examined in isolation. A promising avenue for future research is the combination of separate sources of predictability from text mining. What is the optimal way to derive a measure of sentiment based, for example, on company reports, earnings press releases and conference call transcripts for the same company? Would such a combined signal achieve significantly better results compared to the individual components taken separately?

9.5 SUMMARY

Our research shows that investors should utilise text mining tools within their investment process. These tools can help extract information embedded within corporate filing data and their slower decay will be attractive to investors with longer investment horizons.

9.6 REFERENCES

1.   Antweiler, W. and Frank, M. (2004). Is All That Talk Just Noise? The Information Content of Internet Stock Message Boards. *Journal of Finance, 59,* pp. 1259-1294.

2.   Baker, H.E. and Kare, D.D. (1992). Relationship between annual report readability and corporate financial performance. *Management Research News, 15,* pp. 1–4.

3.   Borochin, P., Cicon, J., DeLisle, J. and Price, M. (2015). The Effects of Conference Call Content on Market Perceptions of Firm Risk. Working paper.

4.   Buehlmaier, M. and Zechner, J. (2014). Slow-Moving Real Information in Merger Arbitrage. Working paper.

5.   Das, S. and Chen, M. (2007). Yahoo! for Amazon: Sentiment Parsing from Small Talk on the Web. *Management Science, 53,* pp. 1375-1388.

6.   Demers, E. and Vega, C. (2008). Soft Information in Earnings Announcements: News or Noise? *Board of Governors of the Federal Reserve System International Finance Discussion Papers 951.*

7.   Huang, A.H., Zang, A.Y. and Zheng, R. (2014). Evidence on the Information Content of Text in Analyst Reports. *Accounting Review, 89,* pp. 2151-2180.

8.   Kearney, C. and Liu, S. (2013). Textual Sentiment in Finance: A Survey of Methods and Models. *International Review of Financial Analysis, 33,* pp. 171-185.

9.   Kogan, S., Levin, D., Routledge, B., Sagi, J. and Smith, N. (2009). Predicting Risk from Financial Reports with Regression. Working paper.

10. Larcker, D.F. and Zalkolyukina, A.A. (2012). Detecting deceptive discussions in conference calls. *Journal of Accounting Research, 50,* pp. 495-540.

11. Li, F. (2010). The Information Content of Forward-looking Statements in Corporate Filings - A Naive Bayesian Machine Learning Approach. *Journal of Accounting Research, 48,* pp. 1049-1102.

12. Loughran, T. and McDonald, B. (2011). When is a Liability not a Liability? Textual Analysis, Dictionaries, and 10-Ks. *Journal of Finance, 66,* pp. 35-65.

13. Loughran, T. and McDonald, B. (2015). Textual Analysis in Accounting and Finance: A Survey. Working paper.

14. Ryans, J. (2014). Textual Classification of SEC Comment Letters. Berkeley Haas Working Paper Series.

15. Sprenger, T.O., Tumasjan, A., Sandner, P.G. and Welpe, I.M (2014). Tweets and Trades: the Information Content of Stock Microblogs. *European Financial Management, 20,* pp. 926–957.

16. Subramanian, R., Insley, R. G. and Blackwell, R. D. (1993). Performance and readability: A comparison of annual reports of pro table and unprofitable corporations. *Journal of Business Communication, 30,* pp. 50-61.

17. Wang, Ch., Tsai, M., Liu, T. and Chang, Ch. (2013). Financial Sentiment Analysis for Risk Prediction. Working paper.

CHAPTER 10

Sentiment & Investor Behaviour

Elijah DePalma, *Senior Quantitative Research Analyst, Thomson Reuters*

ABSTRACT

Thomson Reuters News Analytics provides automated sentiment and linguistic analytics on financial news. Using Thomson Reuters News Analytics we construct a US market sentiment index from corporate Reuters news sentiment.

Following recent literature identifying the pervasive influence of market sentiment on market anomalies and on the pricing of risk factors, we use this US market sentiment index to demonstrate the influence of market sentiment on the post-earnings announcement drift anomaly, the accruals anomaly and market risk premium.

We show that the classic risk-return trade-off of the Capital Asset Pricing Model (CAPM) holds following negative market sentiment periods, whereas the underperformance of high-risk securities known as the low-volatility anomaly holds following positive market sentiment periods. Thus, we propose a dynamic methodology that accepts the risk-return relationship of either the CAPM or the low-volatility anomaly following periods of negative or positive market sentiment, respectively.

We further demonstrate the influence of market sentiment on the earnings revisions anomaly. As an application we present a monthly quant factor timing strategy driven by market sentiment, and improve upon this strategy by implementing the above, proposed dynamic methodology.

10.1 INTRODUCTION

On Asset Price Drivers

"[Asset price] drivers must be high-frequency changes in privately-held market <u>perceptions</u> of pervasive macro-economic conditions. Perceptions could include (a) rational anticipations of change in macro conditions that are truly pervasive such as real output growth, real interest rates, inflation, energy, etc., and (b) behaviour-driven pervasive shocks in confidence or risk perceptions such as panics, liquidity crises, etc."
Pukthuanthong and Roll (2014)

Understanding the influence of market sentiment is at the forefront of research identifying drivers of asset prices. Recent literature demonstrates both the influence of market sentiment on investor reactions to events and on the pricing of risk factors.

Livnat and Petrovits (2009) present evidence that the overall level of investor sentiment can influence investor reactions to earnings surprises and accruals. They suggest that if the existence of the post-earnings announcement drift and accruals anomalies is due to investor under-reactions and over-reactions, respectively, then these reactions may be sensitive to the level of investor sentiment.

Antoniou et al. (2015) present evidence that a standard CAPM beta is strongly positively priced during periods of pessimistic sentiment, but not during periods of optimistic sentiment. Shen and Yu (2013) obtain similar conclusions for additional macro factors, suggesting that during low-sentiment periods markets tend to be rational and support a classic risk-return tradeoff.

We qualitatively reproduce findings in the above literature, conditioning the post-earnings announcement drift anomaly, the accruals anomaly, and market risk premium on the level of market sentiment. However, while the above literature uses a market sentiment index constructed by Baker and Wurgler (2006), we construct a market sentiment index from financial news sentiment.

We demonstrate that the classic risk-return trade-off of the CAPM holds following negative market sentiment periods. Following positive market sentiment periods, however, we show that high-beta portfolios deliver poor risk-adjusted return performance, in accordance with the low-volatility anomaly. Thus, we propose a dynamic methodology that accepts either the CAPM or the low-volatility anomaly, conditional on the level of trailing market sentiment.

Furthermore, we extend the above literature by conditioning the earnings revisions anomaly on the level of market sentiment, and our results provide evidence that investors respond strongly to earnings revisions following periods of positive market sentiment.

As an application we present a market sentiment-based quant factor timing strategy that constructs portfolios using either an accruals earnings quality factor or an earnings revisions factor following negative or positive market sentiment periods, respectively. We improve both the risk-adjusted and total return performance of the quant factor timing strategy by implementing the above, proposed dynamic methodology. Specifically, following negative market sentiment periods we treat market beta as a systematic risk factor by neutralizing portfolios against market beta, whereas following positive market sentiment periods we treat market beta as an alpha factor by screening out high-beta securities.

We calculate all security and index returns as total returns adjusted for corporate actions.

10.2 MARKET-WIDE NEWS SENTIMENT

News Analytics generally refers to the automated application of computational linguistic analysis to measure qualitative and quantitative attributes of textual news. Thomson Reuters News Analytics (TRNA) provides real-time linguistic analytics on corporate news, such as:

- Identification of companies in a news story
- Sentiment of the author towards a company
- Relevance of a company to the news story
- Novelty or uniqueness of a news story (to identify breaking news)

For each company mentioned in a news article, TRNA provides a *relevance score (0–1)* indicating how relevant the news article is to the company, and *sentiment probabilities, ppos, pneut, pneg (0–1)* indicating the likelihood that the sentiment of the author towards the company is positive, neutral and negative, respectively. If we associate positive, neutral and negative sentiment with the values $1, 0$ and -1, respectively, then we can use TRNA sentiment probabilities to calculate the expected value of sentiment for each company in a news article:

$$Sentiment = 1*ppos + 0*pneut + (-1)*pneg \qquad [10.2.1]$$

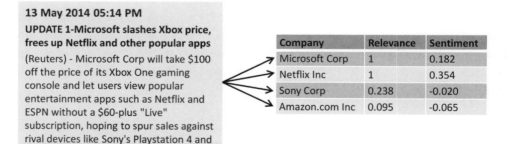

13 May 2014 05:14 PM

UPDATE 1-Microsoft slashes Xbox price, frees up Netflix and other popular apps

(Reuters) - Microsoft Corp will take $100 off the price of its Xbox One gaming console and let users view popular entertainment apps such as Netflix and ESPN without a $60-plus "Live" subscription, hoping to spur sales against rival devices like Sony's Playstation 4 and Amazon's Fire TV ...

Company	Relevance	Sentiment
Microsoft Corp	1	0.182
Netflix Inc	1	0.354
Sony Corp	0.238	-0.020
Amazon.com Inc	0.095	-0.065

Figure 10.2.1: *Thomson Reuters News Analytics provides entity-specific linguistic analysis for each company mentioned in a news article.*

Literature utilizing TRNA has studied market reactions to firm-level news sentiment, demonstrating significant responses over short-term time horizons. For example, Gross-Klussmann and Hautsch (2011) find significant, intra-day market reactions in trading volume and volatility from firm-specific news. In addition, they confirm the positive and negative price impact around relevant, positive and negative firm-level news sentiment, respectively.

Firm-level news sentiment strategies applicable to longer-term investment horizons are found in Meixler (2014), where they conclude that firm-level news sentiment signals improve their ability to predict future analyst revisions and quarterly earnings surprises.

However, we do not consider firm-level news sentiment scores, but instead construct a US market-wide sentiment index by aggregating all TRNA firm-level news sentiment scores over a trailing time period.

To construct a US market sentiment index we calculate the average TRNA sentiment score over all S&P 1500 companies in Reuters articles[1] over a trailing one-month (30-calendar day) period. In Figure 10.2.2 we graph the market sentiment index, and note that the market sentiment index exhibits significant mean-stationarity (time-series mean is constant)[2] centred close to zero, reflecting the objective reporting style of Reuters journalists.

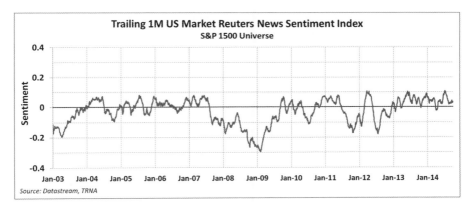

Figure 10.2.2: US market sentiment index constructed as the trailing one-month average of TRNA news sentiment scores for all S&P 1500 companies in Reuters news articles.

We would like to note that large companies receive more media exposure, as 82% of the TRNA scores used to construct the market sentiment index are for S&P 500 (large-cap) companies, 11% are for S&P 400 (mid-cap) companies, and 7% are for S&P 600 (small-cap) companies.

Furthermore, the market sentiment index is not significantly correlated with market returns, as shown in Figure 10.2.3. The six extreme negative market sentiment months (with market sentiment less than -0.2) all occurred during the market crash between September 2008 and February 2009, and we do find that five of these six months are coincident with large negative market return. However, excluding these six months the contemporaneous correlation between market sentiment and market return is only 0.08.

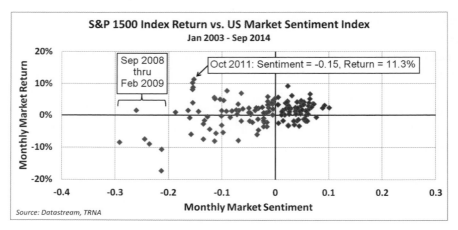

Figure 10.2.3: *Scatter plot of monthly market return versus market sentiment, demonstrating the lack of significant contemporaneous correlation between market return and market sentiment. Market sentiment is the value of the US market sentiment index (viz. Figure 10.2.2.) at the end of each calendar month, and market return is the S&P 1500 index return over the same month.*

In Figure 10.2.3 we highlight a specific example to demonstrate the lack of significant contemporaneous correlation between market sentiment and market return.

Since 2003 the largest monthly market return of 11.3% occurred in October 2011, coincident with a negative monthly market sentiment value of -0.15 in the bottom 10th percentile. During this month Apple, Inc. and JPMorgan Chase & Co. received significant negative sentiment media exposure due to the death of Steve Jobs and the targeting of top executive homes by anti-Wall Street protesters, respectively. However, during this same month the primary shares of those two companies generated returns of 6.2% and 16.4%, respectively.

In the following sections we demonstrate a behavioural influence on investors' reactions due to trailing market sentiment. We emphasize that a behavioural influence due to trailing market return is not observed. Furthermore, no behavioural influence is observed due to the month-to-month change in market sentiment.

10.3 POST-EARNINGS ANNOUNCEMENT DRIFT ANOMALY

Markets react strongly immediately after a large earnings surprise. In addition, stock prices continue to drift in the direction of the surprise for weeks or months after the earnings announcement, known as the post-earnings announcement drift (PEAD) anomaly.

In Figure 10.3.1 we provide evidence of the PEAD anomaly following an earnings surprise, with average buy-and-hold abnormal return drifts of around 100 bps following a ±25% earnings surprise[3] announcement.

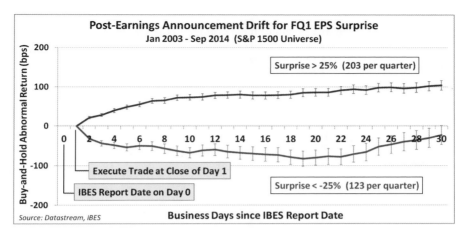

Figure 10.3.1: *Mean buy-and-hold abnormal returns following a ±25% earnings surprise. Buy-and-hold abnormal returns are calculated as excess cumulative returns over a size-specific benchmark index, S&P 500 (large-cap), S&P 400 (mid-cap) or S&P 600 (small-cap), and the error bars are standard-error-of-the-mean (SEM) bars, σ/√n.*

The PEAD anomaly is generally attributed to investors' under-reaction to earnings surprises, and Livnat and Petrovits (2009) find that PEAD is significantly greater when market sentiment is opposite to the direction of the earnings surprise. They suggest that during periods of high (low) sentiment investors generally expect good (bad) news, and if a firm reports earnings contrary to these expectations then investors' under-reaction to the earnings surprise may be magnified.

We obtain similar results in Figure 10.3.2 where we condition earnings surprise events on the level of trailing market sentiment (viz. Figure 10.2.2) on the day prior to the earnings announcement. We find that upward (downward) post-earnings announcement drift for positive (negative) earnings surprises is significantly greater following negative (positive) market sentiment periods than positive (negative) market sentiment periods.

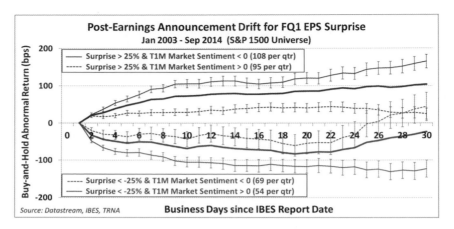

Figure 10.3.2: *PEAD following a positive (negative) earnings surprise is significantly larger following a negative (positive) market sentiment period than a positive (negative) market sentiment period, demonstrating investors' increased under-reaction to the earnings surprise due to the behavioural influence of market sentiment. The thick lines are the unconditional mean buy-and-hold abnormal returns (identical to the lines in Figure 10.3.1), and the thin lines with SEM bars are the mean buy-and-hold abnormal returns conditional on trailing market sentiment.*

10.4 ACCRUALS ANOMALY

The accruals anomaly refers to the outperformance of low accruals firms relative to high accruals firms. The accruals anomaly is generally attributed to investors' failure to distinguish accrual earnings from cash earnings, combined with the tendency of accrual earnings to be a weaker predictor of firm profitability than cash earnings.

The StarMine Accruals Component is a global stock selection factor differentiating between sustainable and unsustainable sources of earnings, and is one component in the StarMine Earnings Quality Model (Gaumer et al., 2009). Monthly portfolios constructed from the StarMine Accruals Component provide significant evidence of the accruals anomaly in the US over the last decade, as shown in Figure 10.4.1.

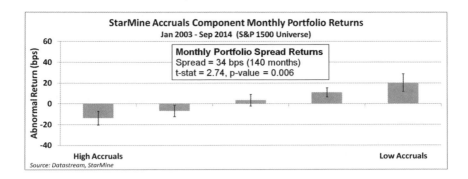

Figure 10.4.1: Abnormal returns and SEM bars for equal-weighted, monthly quintile portfolios constructed using the StarMine Accruals Component, demonstrating the significant outperformance of low versus high accruals firms. Each month we neutralize against firm size by allocating 1/3 of our capital to each of the three S&P 1500 size groups. Within each size group we rank securities by the StarMine Accruals Component factor and construct equal-weighted portfolios from quintiles of factor-ranked securities. Abnormal returns are calculated as excess returns over an equal-weighted size-specific benchmark.

Livnat and Petrovits (2009) find that low accruals firms earn significantly higher abnormal returns following pessimistic sentiment periods versus optimistic sentiment periods. We hypothesize that investors focus on growth strategies following optimistic sentiment periods and value strategies following pessimistic sentiment periods. Thus, if the accruals anomaly is due to investors over-valuing high accruals firms and under-valuing low accruals firms, then this anomaly may be more pronounced following pessimistic sentiment periods when investors focus more on firm earnings (value) but still fail to account for accruals.

In Figure 10.4.2 we condition on the level of trailing market sentiment (viz. Figure 10.2.2) prior to constructing accruals portfolios, and confirm that low accruals firms earn significantly higher returns following negative market sentiment periods than following positive market sentiment periods.

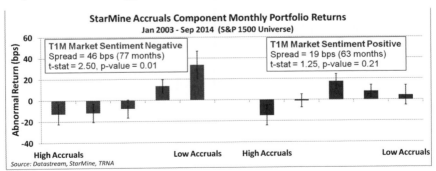

Figure 10.4.2: Monthly portfolios of low accruals firms earn significantly higher abnormal returns following negative market sentiment periods than following positive market sentiment periods, resulting in significantly larger portfolio spread returns. Portfolios are constructed as in Figure 10.4.1, but conditional on trailing market sentiment.

10.5 MARKET BETA

On Market Sentiment

"… time variation in sentiment can lead to conditional deviations from familiar models of risk pricing …
our paper suggests the novel notion that the validity of rational pricing in the cross-section is not a static
concept but varies dynamically over time …"
Antoniou, Doukas and Subrahmanyam (2015)

Market beta is a measure of the systematic risk to a security or portfolio from general market movements. Under a classic risk-return framework, investments in higher-beta securities should, on average, earn higher returns than lower-beta securities.

This paradigm has been challenged for decades, beginning with the seminal research demonstrating a flat risk-return relationship after controlling for size (Fama and French, 1992), and culminating in work on the low-volatility anomaly (Baker et al., 2011).

However, the body of research challenging the classic risk-return relationship has not accounted for the dynamic behavioural influence of market sentiment on risk pricing.

Antoniou et al. (2015) show that, following periods of pessimistic investor sentiment, market beta is strongly priced and supports a classic risk-return relationship. Their research controls for firm size, value and momentum, includes robustness checks against various firm characteristics, and is also robust to two different measures of investor sentiment. They propose that periods of optimism attract equity investment by unsophisticated and overconfident traders in riskier assets. Similarly, research by Shen and Yu (2013) confirms the strong pricing of various macro factors following low sentiment periods.

In Figure 10.5.1 we construct market beta portfolios conditional on the level of trailing market sentiment (viz. Figure 10.2.2) and confirm that market beta is strongly priced following periods of negative market sentiment. Each month we estimated security market betas by regressing trailing monthly security returns against trailing monthly S&P 1500 index returns over a trailing 24–36 month period (as available)[4].

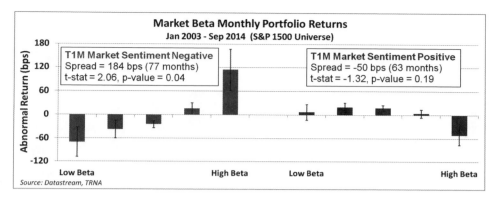

Figure 10.5.1: *Abnormal returns and SEM bars for equal-weighted, monthly quintile portfolios constructed using market beta, demonstrating that market beta is strongly priced following periods of negative market sentiment. Market beta portfolios are neutralized against firm size, as described in the caption for Figure 10.4.1.*

Following negative market sentiment periods, Figure 10.5.1 demonstrates that market beta is systematically priced and that market beta quintile spread portfolios generate a significant, average return of 184 basis points. Furthermore, there is a large correlation of 0.82 between market beta quintile spread returns and market returns, consistent with the classical view of a market risk factor. If we restrict to S&P 500 (large-cap) securities then the Information Ratios[5] of the individual market beta quintile portfolios range from -0.56 to 0.80, whereas an equal-weighted average of the same market beta quintile portfolios has a superior Information Ratio of 0.81. All of these findings support the classic risk-return relationship of the CAPM, and suggest that portfolios should be neutralized against market beta to optimize active risk-adjusted returns.

Following positive market sentiment periods, however, Figure 10.5.1 demonstrates that high-beta securities generate negative abnormal returns. This finding is consistent with recent literature on the low-volatility anomaly. For example, Li et al. (2014) cite literature suggesting that the low-volatility anomaly should more accurately be referred to as the *high-risk anomaly* since the anomaly is explained by the underperformance of high-volatility securities and not the outperformance of low-volatility securities.

Baker et al. (2011) refer to the low-volatility anomaly as "perhaps the greatest anomaly in finance." In their concluding remarks they assert that investors seeking to maximize returns relative to total risk should focus on maximizing the benchmark-free Sharpe Ratio and not the commonly used Information Ratio. However, investors seeking to maximize total risk-adjusted returns would nonetheless find that low-volatility portfolios outperform high-volatility portfolios only following periods of positive market sentiment.

To see this, in Figure 10.5.2 we plot Sharpe Ratios[6] of the same market beta quintile portfolios graphed in Figure 10.5.1, which are conditional on trailing market sentiment (viz. Figure 10.2.2). Following positive market sentiment periods our results support the low-volatility anomaly, i.e., we confirm that high-beta portfolios generate lower Sharpe Ratios than low-beta portfolios. Following periods of negative market sentiment, however, our results do not support the low-volatility anomaly.

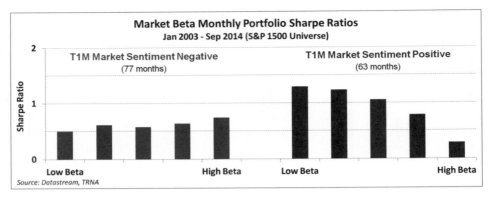

Figure 10.5.2: *Sharpe Ratios (annualized) for equal-weighted, monthly quintile portfolios constructed using market beta, supporting the low-volatility anomaly following positive sentiment periods, but not following negative sentiment periods. Market beta portfolios are identical to the portfolios in Figure 10.5.1, which are neutralized against firm size.*

We remark that our results in Figures 10.5.1 and 10.5.2 demonstrate robustness to the time period chosen, as we obtain qualitatively similar results if we restrict our sample time period to the years prior to the market crash (2003–2007) or following the market crash (2009–2014).

In summary, Figure 10.5.1 suggests that market beta represents a source of systematic risk only following negative market sentiment periods. Thus, following negative market sentiment periods we propose to reject the low-volatility anomaly and accept the CAPM, treating market beta as a risk factor by neutralizing portfolios against market beta.

Following positive market sentiment periods, however, Figures 10.5.1 and 10.5.2 demonstrate that high-beta securities generate lower abnormal returns and lower Sharpe Ratios. Thus, following positive market sentiment periods we propose to reject the CAPM and accept the low-volatility anomaly, treating market beta as an alpha factor by screening out high-beta securities.

We refer to the above, proposed dynamic methodology as the Dynamic CAPM/Low-Vol Methodology, and we apply this methodology to the quant factor timing strategy presented in Section 10.7.

10.6   EARNINGS REVISIONS ANOMALY

The *earnings revisions anomaly* refers to the observation that trailing changes in analyst estimates and recommendations are positively correlated with future returns.Bonne et al. (2007) show that trailing changes in analyst estimates are positively correlated with future changes in analyst estimates, the latter driving stock prices during periods when investors respond strongly to analyst revisions. Based on these findings they developed the StarMine Analyst Revisions Model (StarMine ARM), a stock-selection factor designed to predict future changes in analyst sentiment.

In a literature review and call for further research, Grigaliuniene (2013) document how the influence of market-wide sentiment on investors' reactions to information events remains largely unexplored. However, they do identify literature that suggests that investors' responses to analyst revisions (both upgrades and downgrades) are significantly stronger in optimistic versus pessimistic sentiment periods. Under this premise, the earning revisions anomaly (as well as the performance of StarMine ARM as an indirect predictor of stock returns) will be stronger following optimistic sentiment periods.

In Figure 10.6.1 we condition on trailing market sentiment (viz. Figure 10.2.2) and confirm that StarMine ARM portfolios generate significant spread returns following periods of positive market sentiment, but not following periods of negative market sentiment.

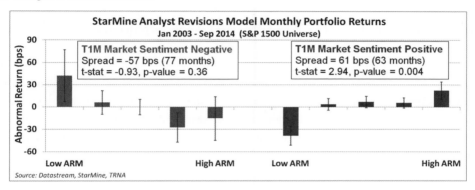

Figure 10.6.1: *Abnormal returns and SEM bars for equal-weighted, monthly quintile portfolios constructed using the StarMine Analyst Revisions Model (ARM), demonstrating the significant spread performance of the revisions-based factor following periods of positive market sentiment. StarMine ARM portfolios are neutralized against firm size, as described in the caption for Figure 10.4.1.*

We reiterate that StarMine ARM directly predicts future changes in analyst sentiment, and thus indirectly predicts future stock returns during periods when investors respond strongly to analyst revisions. Hence, the results in Figure 10.6.1 suggest that investors respond strongly to analyst revisions only following periods of positive market sentiment.

We suspect that following periods of positive market sentiment investors are susceptible to both overconfidence effects and analyst revisions affect heuristics, where *affect heuristics* refers to investors' dependence on feelings to demarcate the positive or negative quality of information (Slovic et al., 2007). Furthermore, these two effects may be complementary, as the influence on investors' judgments due to the affective impressions from analyst revisions may be more pronounced for overconfident investors.

10.7   APPLICATION: QUANT FACTOR TIMING

In the preceding sections we demonstrated the significant spread performance of an accruals quality factor (StarMine Accruals Component) and a revisions-based factor (StarMine ARM) following periods of negative and positive market sentiment, respectively. As an application, we present results of a market sentiment factor timing strategy using these two factors.

In Figure 10.7.1 we graph the cumulative return profiles of various long-only, equal-weighted, monthly quintile strategies constructed from the StarMine Accruals Component (Accruals) and StarMine ARM (ARM) factors. We restrict an S&P 1500 universe to all securities with at least 24 trailing months of returns history, so that market beta may be computed for each security (see Section 10.5). All strategies are neutralized against firm size and market beta, as described in the caption for Figure 10.7.1. Additional performance metrics are provided in Table 10.7.1.

We include the strategies constructed entirely from either the Accruals or ARM factors, as well as the strategy constructed from the static linear combination of Accruals and ARM factors which maximizes Information Ratio over the entire time period (IR-Optimal)[7]. In particular, note that the IR-Optimal strategy is constructed with complete look-ahead bias over the entire time period, and provides an upper bound for active risk-adjusted return performance over all static linear combinations of the two factors.

The market sentiment factor timing strategy (Sentiment Timing) is constructed entirely from the Accruals factor following periods of negative market sentiment, and entirely from the ARM factor following periods of positive market sentiment. Notably, the Sentiment Timing strategy achieves the same Information Ratio as the IR-Optimal strategy, and even outperforms the IR-Optimal strategy on a total return basis (see Table 10.7.1).

Finally, we apply the dynamic methodology proposed in Section 10.5 to the Sentiment Timing strategy (Sentiment Timing with Dynamic CAPM/Low-Vol Methodology) by neutralizing against market beta only following periods of negative market sentiment, and by excluding securities in the top market beta quintile following periods of positive market sentiment.

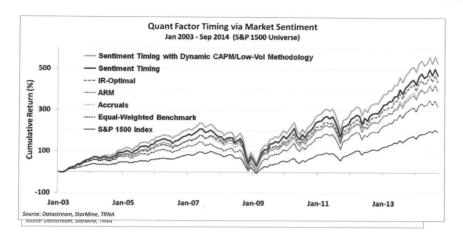

Source: Datastream, StarMine, TRNA

Figure 10.7.1: *Cumulative returns for various long-only, equal-weighted, monthly strategies. Each strategy is neutralized against firm size and market beta, as follows. Each month we allocate 1/3 of our capital to each of the three S&P 1500 size groups. We further partition each size group into quintile bins based on security market beta, and equally divide our capital within each size group among the beta quintile bins. Within each size-beta bin we rank securities by the selected factor, and construct equal-weighted portfolios from the top quintile of factor-ranked securities. The performance of strategies and factors are represented according to the key provided on the chart. Equal-Weighted Benchmark shows the performance of a benchmark strategy that is equal weighted over all securities in our universe. IR-Optimal shows the performance of the strategy constructed form the static linear combination of Accruals and ARM factors which optimizes Information Ratio (IR) over the entire time period. Sentiment Timing shows the performance of a market sentiment factor timing strategy, which is constructed entirely from either the Accruals factor or the ARM factor following negative or positive market sentiment period, respectively.*

Table 10.7.1: *Performance metrics for the strategies presented in Figure 10.7.1.*

Strategy	Ann Ret	IR	T-Stat	Sharpe	ex-Post β	No.Stocks	Turnover
Sentiment Timing with Dynamic CAPM/Low-Vol Methodology	17.1%	0.90	3.07	0.80	1.31	271	41%
Sentiment Timing	16.1%	0.79	2.70	0.76	1.32	299	40%
IR-Optimal	15.5%	0.79	2.69	0.75	1.28	284	26%
ARM	14.8%	0.71	2.43	0.75	1.21	301	42%
Accruals	14.6%	0.64	2.20	0.70	1.32	297	20%
Equal-Weighted Benchmark	13.2%	0.55	1.89	0.67	1.28	1482	4%
S&P 1500 Index	9.8%	-	-	0.64	1.00	-	-

- *Ann Ret* is the annualized return (CAGR)
- *IR* is the Information Ratio relative to the S&P 1500 Index
- *T-Stat* is the (two-tailed) t-statistic for active returns over S&P 1500 Index returns
- *Sharpe* is the Sharpe Ratio
- *ex-Post* β is the realized market beta from a regression of returns against S&P 1500 Index returns
- *No Stocks* is the average number of stocks held each month
- *Turnover* is the average % of equity rebalanced each month

In Table 10.7.1 we show that implementing the Dynamic CAPM/Low-Vol Methodology improves total return, Information Ratio and Sharpe Ratio performance.

Moreover, the Dynamic CAPM/Low-Vol Methodology also improves total return and Sharpe Ratio performance on long-short strategies. For example, an equal-weighted, long-short, monthly market sentiment factor timing decile strategy on the Accruals and ARM factors (with ~150 long and short positions each month) achieves an annualized return of 6.2% and a Sharpe ratio of 1.05, with spread returns having a low correlation of 0.11 with market returns. Implementing the Dynamic CAPM/Low-Vol Methodology increases the annualized return to 6.7% and the Sharpe ratio to 1.12, while maintaining the same low correlation of spread returns with market returns.

10.8   FUTURE DIRECTIONS

We constructed a US market sentiment index by averaging Thomson Reuters News Analytics (TRNA) sentiment scores over all S&P 1500 companies in Reuters news articles over a trailing one-month period.

We provided evidence that trailing market sentiment exerts a significant influence on investor behaviour, and based on these findings we proposed a dynamic methodology that accepts either the CAPM or the low-volatility anomaly, conditional on the level of trailing market sentiment.

As an application we presented a market sentiment factor timing strategy on two traditional quant factors that outperforms all strategies constructed from static linear combinations of the two factors. We demonstrated the improved performance of this market sentiment factor timing strategy by implementing our proposed dynamic methodology. In future research we aim to extend these results to a broader quant factor timing framework.

A value in constructing market sentiment indices from news sentiment is the ability to construct custom sentiment indices by filtering to specific news stories. For example, we have extended the results on market beta presented in this paper to UK markets by constructing a sentiment index from TRNA sentiment scores over all FTSE 350 companies. We further hypothesize that market sentiment is driven more strongly by corporate news on select sectors that generate strong media interest, such as the Technology and Financials sectors.

We also plan to extend the construction of news sentiment indices beyond corporate news. For example, TRNA is a component of the broader Thomson Reuters Text Analytics System (TRTS) for linguistic processing on news, social media and proprietary content. Using TRTS we constructed a sentiment index over all US Treasury Reuters news articles. We found that market beta is strongly priced following high US Treasury news sentiment periods, similar to the results we presented in this paper following negative US corporate news sentiment periods. However, the Treasury and corporate news sentiment indices are not totally correlated, and combining the two sentiment indices yielded stronger results than either sentiment index alone. We further plan to investigate sentiment indices constructed from political and macroeconomic news.

In conclusion, our future research efforts aim to identify how to best filter and aggregate news sentiment to construct market sentiment indices, driven by fundamental research with strong, underlying economic and behavioural hypotheses. We hope to uncover relevant principles and fundamental hypotheses in the active fields of behavioural macroeconomics and neuroeconomics, to better understand how events reflected in financial news drive market sentiment and influence investor behaviour.

Notes

[1]   We exclude auto-generated stock exchange alerts and news link-redirects (see Appendix for details).

[2]   An Augmented Dickey-Fuller (ADF) test rejects a non-stationary unit root with p-value < 0.01.

[3]   We calculate earnings surprise as a percentage by calculating the actual reported EPS less the consensus estimate EPS divided by the absolute value of the consensus estimate EPS. Following Meixler (2014), we adjust for small consensus estimates by placing a lower bound of 10 cents per share on the absolute value of the consensus estimate EPS.

[4]   The results in this section (Figures 10.5.1 and 10.5.2) are robust to estimating market beta over longer trailing time periods (trailing 24–72 months) or to using alternative measures of security risk such as trailing security volatility.

[5]   We compute Information Ratio relative to the S&P 1500 index as the ratio of average active return to the standard deviation of active returns, annualized by multiplying by $\sqrt{12}$.

[6]   We compute Sharpe Ratio as the ratio of average return to volatility, and do not include a risk-free rate.

[7]   The Accruals and ARM factors provide 1–100 scores for each security, and in this study the IR-Optimal linear combination of the two factors is 0.752*Accruals + 0.248*ARM.

10.9 REFERENCES

1.   Antoniou, C., Doukas, J. A. and Subrahmanyam, A. (2015). Investor sentiment, beta, and the cost of equity capital. *Management Science*.

2.   Baker, M. and Wurgler, J. (2006). Investor sentiment and the cross-section of stock returns. *The Journal of Finance, 61(4),* 1645–1680.

3.   Baker, M., Bradley, B. and Wurgler, J. (2011). Benchmarks as limits to arbitrage: understanding the low-volatility anomaly. *Financial Analysts Journal, 67(1).*

4.   Bonne, G., Jahansouz, A., Lichtblau, D. and Malinak, S. (2007). StarMine Analyst Revisions Model (ARM): Global performance. *StarMine white paper*.

5.   Fama, E. F. and French, K. R. (1992). The cross-section of expected stock returns. *The Journal of Finance, 47(2), 427–465*.

6.   Gaumer, T., Malinak, S., Bonne, G., Bae, P. and Sargent, D. (2009). The StarMine EQ Model: Introduction and Global Results. *StarMine white paper*.

7.   Grigaliuniene, Z. (2013). Investor sentiment, overreaction and underreaction in stock market. *Studies in Modern Society, 4(1)*.

8.   Gross-Klussmann, A. and Hautsch, N. (2011). When machines read the news: using automated text analytics to quantify high frequency news-implied market reactions. *Journal of Empirical Finance, 18(2), 321–340*.

9.   Li, X., Sullivan, R. N. and Garcia-Feijóo, L. (2014). The limits to arbitrage and the low-volatility anomaly. *Financial analysts journal, 70(1), 52–63*.

10. Livnat, J. and Petrovits, C. (2009). Investor sentiment, post-earnings announcement drift, and accruals. AAA.

11. Meixler, N. (2014). Improving the Power of Predicted Surprise with TRNA News Sentiment. *StarMine white paper*.

12. Pukthuanthong, K. and Roll, R. (2014). A Protocol for Factor Identification. Working Paper, UCLA.

13. Slovic, P., Finucane, M. L., Peters, E. and MacGregor, D. G. (2007). The affect heuristic. *European Journal of Operational Research, 177(3), 1333–1352*.

14. Shen, J. and Yu, J. (2013). Investor Sentiment and Economic Forces. Working Paper, University of Minnesota.

10.A APPENDIX

We historically identify S&P 1500 companies using point-in-time monthly constituent history from Datastream, and construct the US market sentiment index as the simple average of TRNA sentiment scores over all S&P 1500 companies in Reuters articles over a trailing 30-calendar day time period.

Over all Reuters articles we exclude auto-generated stock exchange alerts related to market imbalances, trading suspensions and NYSE pre-opening indications. We also exclude Reuters articles with no headline, which are primarily auto-generated news messages directing a user to click on a link to access news content (news link-redirects).

Table 10.A.1: Specific filters on TRNA fields used to construct the US market sentiment index (viz. Figure 10.2.2). The TRNA field BCAST_TEXT refers to the headline of the news article.

Filter Description	TRNA Field Filter
Reuters news sources	*ATTRIBTN* = 'RTRS'
News articles	*ITEM_TYPE* = 'ARTICLE'
Exclude imbalance messages	*ITEM_GENRE* ≠ 'IMBALANCE'
Exclude trading halts	*BCAST_TEXT* does not contain 'NYSE|NASDAQ|OTC HALT'
Exclude trading resumes	*BCAST_TEXT* does not contain 'NYSE|NASDAQ|OTC RESUMED'
Exclude NYSE pre-opening indications	*BCAST_TEXT* does not contain 'NYSE INDICATION'
Exclude news link-redirects	*BCAST_TEXT* is not blank

Aside from excluding the auto-generated news items listed in Table 10.A.1, the US market sentiment index is constructed as a simple average of all TRNA scores over all English-language Reuters articles. In particular, we do not weight or filter the sentiment scores using other TRNA fields, such as *relevance, novelty, body size*, etc. However, such adjustments are useful, and we obtain stronger research results (not presented here) by imposing high *relevance* filters, low *novelty* filters, and overweighting for small *body size*.

CHAPTER 11

Thematic Alpha Streams Improve
Performance of Equity Portfolios

Peter Hafez, *RavenPack*

ABSTRACT

In this paper, we propose a robust methodology for equity portfolio construction using news-based thematic alphas. These alphas are the result of our previous research (Hafez and Guerrero-Colón, 2015), where we took advantage of RavenPack's event taxonomy to build a set of theme-based sentiment indicators.

Now, we develop the idea further and combine a large set of thematic alpha streams into an overall equity portfolio. In general, we find that employing our methodology in a long/short strategy yields strong return and turnover improvements, versus treating sentiment as one-dimensional, over our 8-year backtesting period, across both region (Europe and US) and size (small, mid and large market capitalization stocks).

- The use of a thematic alpha approach allows us to treat each alpha stream individually in terms of holding period, in addition to making use of *internal crossing*. Together they provide an effective way of reducing turnover.
- With an average holding period of 2–3 days, our strategy yields Information Ratios of 2.0 for the Russell 1000 and 4.3 for the Russell 2000. For our European equivalent portfolios, the Information Ratios are 2.3 and 3.7.

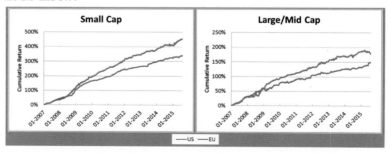

Figure 11.1 *EQUITY PORTFOLIO PERFORMANCE, JAN 2007 TO AUG 2015. This figure shows the cumulative dollar-neutral return of the portfolios across EU and US for both Small and Large/Mid Cap. Source: RavenPack, September 2015*

11.1 INTRODUCTION

The emergence of "big data" in finance, as a result of technological advances in storage and processing power, means portfolio managers have become, or employed, data scientists to deal with not only thousands, but potentially millions of alpha streams within a portfolio.

In this study, we try to show the benefits of an alpha stream approach to using sentiment data. Besides the obvious *diversification* improvements, turnover can be significantly reduced as long as alpha streams can be *crossed internally* on the same alpha platform, assuming they are "not-too-correlated" (Kakushadzexy and Tulchinsky, 2015). This is as opposed to considering sentiment as a one-dimensional *signal* (Hafez and Xie, 2014; Hafez and Xie, 2013).

The concept of *alpha streams* is very well known in the investment community, and there has been a fair amount of research into combining alpha streams (Menchero and Lee, 2014; Kakushadzexy, 2014; Kakushadzexy, 2015), but little research exists on actual alpha creation. Such know-how is usually kept secret by portfolio managers to maintain their edge.

Our recent research focus has been into the non-uniformity of price reaction to different corporate events reported in the news. Our last paper (Hafez and Guerrero-Colón, 2015) described a methodology to create thematic alpha streams based on RavenPack News Analytics corporate event groups. We analysed these alphas as stand-alone signals, and showed promising results. This paper takes this concept forward to present a simple yet robust framework to portfolio construction from the different alpha streams.

We consider an alpha stream to be a time series of returns representing the outcome of a particular trading strategy. As such, an alpha stream can be constructed by combining individual securities into a synthetic asset – with full constituent level visibility. This has the benefit of being able to reduce turnover through internal crossing among the alpha streams that conform to the final portfolio or "super-alpha".

Our methodology relies on a simple combination rule based on the historical Information Ratio of the alpha streams. We show that the constructed portfolios provide attractive performance across different universes. In addition, thanks to its simplicity, we avoid the common problems of optimization methods (collinearity), making the framework robust and easily scalable.

In the paper, Section 2 describes the generation of our building blocks – thematic alpha streams using sentiment of corporate news; Section 3 describes the framework to construct portfolios using these alphas; Section 4 looks into the behavior of different portfolios with regard to holding periods and theme contribution; Section 5 shows the main results across the universes under study; finally, Section 6 summarizes the key conclusions.

11.2 ALPHA STREAM GENERATION

In this section, we provide an overview of the RavenPack data and our previous research. In particular, we describe RavenPack's event taxonomy. We show how to create a set of thematic indicators based on the event taxonomy, which when applied as stand-alone signals, or alpha streams, form the building blocks of the equity portfolios.

11.2.1 Data Source

For this study we only use the Dow Jones Edition of RavenPack News Analytics Version 4.0, which structures relevant information from *Dow Jones Newswires*, *The Wall Street Journal*, *MarketWatch* and *Barron's*. A schematic view of the structured data is shown in Figure 11.2.1. For each record in the dataset, a set of analytics are produced, including information on:

- **Entities:** Relevant company details like name, country of domicile and RavenPack's identifier, among others.
- **Events:** Information about the type of event that occurred based on RavenPack´s event Taxonomy.
- **Scoring:** A set of scores rating different aspects of the event in relation to the entity. Among them we highlight Novelty, Relevance and Sentiment scores.

To evaluate our framework, we consider a backtesting period of nearly 10 years, covering January 2006 to August 2015. Our point-in-time sensitive company universe spans the Russell 1000 and Russell 2000 constituents for the US, as well as the Russell Europe equivalents (i.e. Large/Mid cap vs Small cap).

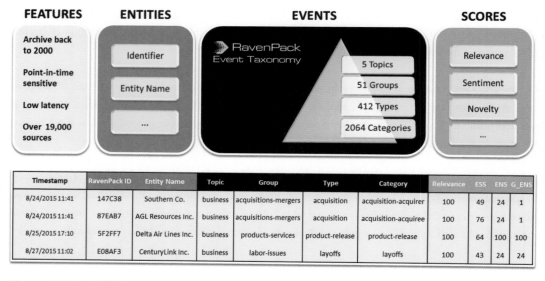

Timestamp	RavenPack ID	Entity Name	Topic	Group	Type	Category	Relevance	ESS	ENS	G_ENS
8/24/2015 11:41	147C38	Southern Co.	business	acquisitions-mergers	acquisition	acquisition-acquirer	100	49	24	1
8/24/2015 11:41	87EAB7	AGL Resources Inc.	business	acquisitions-mergers	acquisition	acquisition-acquiree	100	76	24	1
8/25/2015 17:10	5F2FF7	Delta Air Lines Inc.	business	products-services	product-release	product-release	100	64	100	100
8/27/2015 11:02	E08AF3	CenturyLink Inc.	business	labor-issues	layoffs	layoffs	100	43	24	24

Figure 11.2.1: RAVENPACK'S NEWS ANALYTICS SCHEMA. *This figure presents a schematic view of RavenPack's News Analytics 4.0. Source: RavenPack, September 2015*

11.2.2 Thematic Sentiment Indicators

We use *RavenPack's Event Sentiment Score (ESS) to* create thematic sentiment indicators. The ESS is a granular score between 0 and 100 that represents the entity-specific sentiment for one of the events defined in the RavenPack event taxonomy. The score is determined by systematically matching stories typically categorized by financial experts as having short-term positive or negative financial or economic impact. We only consider entities receiving a *RavenPack Relevance Score* of 100. The Relevance Score measures how important an entity is within any given news article and can range from 0 to 100, where 100 is most relevant[2].

The indicators (S_t) are constructed as simple daily averages of ESS per event group, or theme, rescaled to take values between -1 and 1. We exclude events that do not contain sentiment (i.e. = 50). The resulting formula is as follows:

$$S_t = \frac{1}{|I|} \sum_{i=1}^{|I|} \frac{(ESS_i - 50)}{50}$$
[11.2.1]

Where ESS_i is the event sentiment score for news event $i \in I$ with I representing the set of news events within a given event group (theme) on day t. The daily sentiment snapshot is taken 30 minutes before the market close in New York and London - depending on whether we trade US or European stocks.

11.2.3 Creating Alpha Streams

We generate a set of alpha streams by combining 33 different themes[3], 10 different holding periods (from 1 to 10 days), and 6 strategy types, which are described in Table 11.2.1.

Table 11.2.1: Strategy Type Description. In this Table we describe the 6 different strategies used to create (dollar-neutral) alpha streams. Source: RavenPack, September 2015

Strategy Types	Ranked	Not Ranked
Long Only	Long Top 20% Sentiment-wise	Long those with Positive Sentiment
Short Only	Short Bottom 20% Sentiment-wise	Short those with Negative Sentiment
Long/Short (Spread)	Spread of the above	Spread of the above

Hence there are 1,980 potential alpha stream candidates (33 x 10 x 6) that could, potentially, belong to the final portfolio. To ensure *dollar neutrality*, for each *alpha* we take an opposite market position[4]. Sentiment is measured over a 24-hour period up until 30 minutes before market close, and positions are entered at the following close price and kept for the corresponding holding period (up to 10 trading days[5]).

11.3 EQUITY PORTFOLIO CONSTRUCTION

In this section, we present the methodology used to select and combine the alpha streams described in the previous section into a set of equity portfolios, which can be considered "super-alphas". We also detail the way in which the framework parameter is selected, showing its robustness across both *region* and *size*.

11.3.1 Methodology

To prevent overfitting, we propose a daily rebalancing procedure using a temporal sliding window. This simple, yet effective, methodology involves the following steps:

- **Initial Pruning:** In order to reduce the number of alpha streams, we independently evaluate whether they provide statistically significant performance (return-wise). To that end, a simple t-test is performed over the defined temporal window. Alphas are selected if their corresponding p-values are below 5%.
- **Alpha Combination:** In this step, alpha streams that qualified in the previous step based on statistical significance are evaluated in terms of Information Ratio (IR). We select alpha streams with positive IR and use their IR level to provide the relative weight on each of the alphas. Obviously, more advanced techniques to combine alpha streams could be applied that would more directly take into account the co-variance between alphas – likely using some non-trivial algorithmic approach, see for instance Kakushadzexy (2015). In this paper, however, we take a more simplistic approach for future benchmarking purposes.
- **Internal Crossing:** Combining the constituent weights (equal weighting) within each alpha stream and the IR-based alpha weights from the previous step, we are able to calculate the final constituent (net) weights of the overall portfolio.
- **Rebalancing:** For easier interpretation of our turnover statistics, we normalize the daily weights to a 100% gross exposure level.

11.3.2 Parameter Selection

The proposed methodology relies on just one parameter – the length of the sliding temporal window[6]. To select this parameter, we evaluate the performance of portfolios constructed using different sliding temporal windows. Specifically, we consider 3 months, 6 months and 1 year and define our selection criteria as:

$$IR_{Stability} = \frac{mean(IR_{Rolling252})}{var(IR_{Rolling252})} \qquad [11.3.1]$$

Where $IR_{Rolling252}$ is the rolling Information Ratio of the return series using a sliding window of 252 days. This metric favours the stability of the results rather than the overall IR value itself.

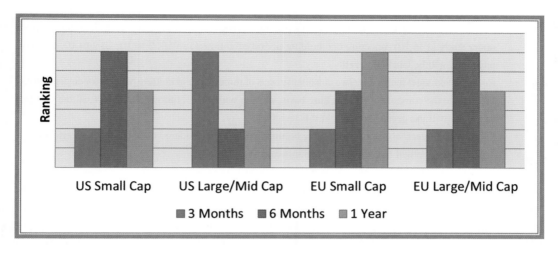

Figure 11.3.1: *RANKING OF THE DIFFERENT LOOKBACK WINDOWS. This figure presents the ranking of the different lookback windows based on a metric that favours stability over time. Results are shown for Small & Large/Mid Cap across both regions (US and EU). Source: RavenPack, September 2015*

Figure 11.3.1 shows a ranking of the different lookback windows (based on our stability measure) across the four universes under study. As can be observed, if we focus on regions, US requires shorter windows than EU for the same cap size. Similar behaviour is noted for size, where, for a given region, small caps require longer windows than large/mid caps. These patterns can be explained by the amount of news we typically see for large cap vs small cap stocks and for US vs EU. The more news there is, the shorter the window needed to achieve a reasonable number of statistically significant alpha streams.

11.4 PORTFOLIO ANALYSIS

In this section, we aim for a better understanding of the contribution of each alpha theme as it relates to the combined portfolios. In particular, we are interested in evaluating:

- How the holding period of the alphas impacts performance.
- Which themes contribute most to the constructed portfolios.

11.4.1 Exploring Holding Periods

To explore the impact of the alphas' holding period on the constructed portfolios, we conduct experiments, varying the method by which we determine the holding period, as follows:

- *Increasing* technique: Incremental sets of holding periods are considered each time. We start from a stand-alone holding period of 1 day, introducing additional days each time (1, 1 to 2, 1 to 3 ... 1 to 10). This will be labelled in blue in the following figures.

- *Decreasing* technique: In contrast to the increasing technique, we start by including all holding periods under study (1 to 10), rejecting one holding period each time (1 to 10, 2 to 10, … 9 to 10, 10). This technique will be labelled in red.
- *Rolling* technique: In this case, we consider subsets of three different holding periods for each portfolio. We change the components on a rolling basis, starting with 1 to 3, followed by 2 to 4, all the way to 8 to 10. We will use green to highlight this technique.
- *Single* technique: Only alphas with same holding period are considered to construct the portfolios (i.e. 1, 2, …, 10). We will be using purple in this case.

In Figure 11.4.1 we show a performance comparison between the described techniques as measured by the Information Ratio. The *Increasing* technique clearly outperforms consistently across region and size. This shows the strong power of keeping the 1-day holding period alphas within the portfolios. Another key fact extracted from the results is that our sentiment signal decays at a similar pace (4 to 5 days) across all universes under study.

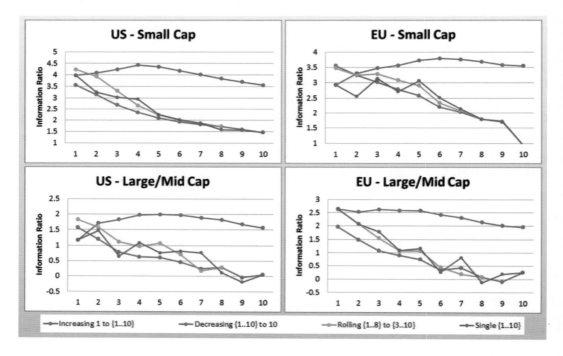

Figure 11.4.1: COMPARING PORTFOLIOS PERFORMANCE IN TERMS OF INFORMATION RATIO. In this figure we show an Information Ratio comparison of portfolios constructed using different restrictions on alpha holding periods (see text for details). Results are shown across region (EU & US) and across size (Small & Large/Mid Cap). All portfolios are dollar-neutral. Source: RavenPack, September 2015

In Figure 11.4.2, we compare the same set of experiments in turnover terms. The shapes of the curves are very similar across region and size – with turnover falling as holding periods increase. The *decreasing* technique provides the lowest turnover, as opposed to the IR comparison, exposing a trade-off between IR and turnover levels when selecting the portfolio constituents.

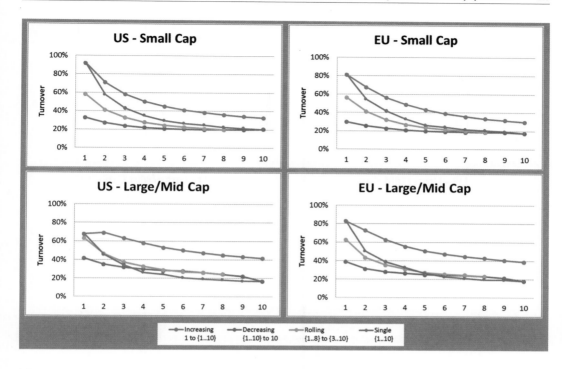

Figure 11.4.2:*Comparing portfolios performance in terms of turnover. This figure shows turnover comparison of portfolios constructed using different restrictions on alpha holding periods (see text for details). Results are shown for Small & Large/Mid Cap across US and EU. Source: RavenPack, September 2015*

The trade-off between IR and turnover becomes more apparent after transaction costs, as shown by Figure 11.4.3, where we repeated the experiments on Information Ratio after trading costs[7].

Again, portfolios built using the *Increasing* technique outperform the rest, meaning that including the 1-day holding period still provides a better performance. Meanwhile the *optimal* holding period moves one day out to 5–6 days, consistently across region and size, with periods beyond 5 days providing no significant additional decay, at least for small cap stocks.

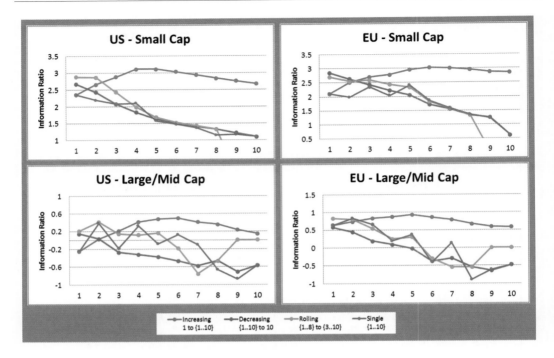

Figure 11.4.3: Comparing portfolios performance in terms of IR after trading costs. This figure shows an Information Ratio comparison of portfolios constructed using different restrictions on alpha holding periods (see text for details). In contrast to Figure 3, we take trading costs into consideration (10 bps roundtrip). Results are shown for Small & Large/Mid Cap across US and EU. All portfolios are dollar-neutral. Source: RavenPack, September 2015

11.4.2 Exploring Alpha Themes

Portfolio Theme Contribution

To evaluate the contribution toward our portfolios from each theme, we aggregate the alpha weights across all alphas matching a particular theme, i.e. across holding period and strategy type. For clarity, we will only consider themes with 5% contribution or more on any single portfolio. Note, once a theme has qualified within a certain portfolio, we include the theme across all portfolios of all regions and sizes, even if they do have less than 5% contribution.

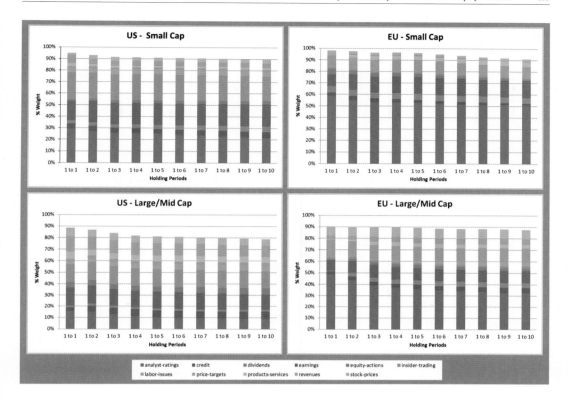

Figure 11.4.4: Portfolio Theme Contribution. These bar charts show the contribution of themes to portfolios constructed using different sets of holding periods (Increasing technique). Results are shown for both US and EU across Small & Large/Mid Cap. Source: RavenPack, September 2015

In Figure 11.4.4, we show the contribution of each theme to the portfolios using our Increasing technique. This allows us to visualize the theme distribution across region and size. The bar charts show the consistency of the theme-contribution across portfolios built under different restrictions (holding periods). Interestingly, we find that 11 themes account for 85–95% of the total portfolio theme allocation. If we focus on region, the US performance seems to be more distributed by theme than the EU, which relies significantly on analyst-ratings.

Alpha Theme Marginal Contribution

We also evaluate the marginal contribution of each theme on portfolio performance, i.e. what is the performance impact of removing particular alphas? Based on our previous results, we only look at alpha streams with holding periods ranging from 1 to 5 days.

Figure 11.4.5 shows a bar chart with the Information Ratio of our four portfolios with a particular theme removed. All results are compared against the benchmark (all themes included) and only those negatively affecting the performance by more than 1% are shown.

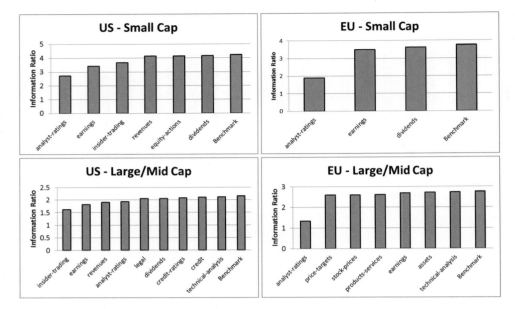

Figure 11.4.5: *THEME MARGINAL CONTRIBUTION. This figure shows bar charts with the Information Ratio of the (dollar-neutral) portfolio after dropping a particular theme. Results are compared against the benchmark (red bars), which includes all themes with holding periods ranging between 1 to 5 days. Results are shown for both US and EU across Small & Large/Mid Cap. Source: RavenPack, September 2015*

As can be observed, the results are consistent with the ones highlighted in Figure 11.4.4. The EU is impacted more than the US when dropping important themes, suggesting that the US is more robust in this regard. Note that these experiments are conducted without taking trading costs into account and doing so could impact our conclusions in terms of marginal contribution.

In any case, which themes to include or exclude would not only depend on your trading cost assumptions, but also on whether the alphas are considered on a standalone basis or in combination with other non-news-based alpha streams that could further reduce the overall allocation and portfolio turnover.

11.5 PORTFOLIOS PERFORMANCE

11.5.1 Experimental Setup

In this section, we show the performance of the four portfolios created using the proposed methodology. We focus on two different regions (EU and US) and two market capitalization groups (small vs mid/large cap stocks). The experimental setup of the portfolio construction is as follows:

- Alpha holding period ranging from 1 to 5 days[8].
- Lookback window is chosen following the criteria described in Section 11.3.2, which yields:

- US Small Cap: 3-month rolling window
- US Large/Mid Cap & EU Small Cap: 6-month rolling window
- EU Large/Mid Cap: 1-year rolling window

Our backtest covers the period January 2006 to August 2015, but we use the first year to initiate our signal[9], i.e. we only report portfolio performance starting from January 2007. To evaluate the impact of trading costs, we consider two different round trip cost levels, i.e. 5 and 10 basis points (bps). Such analysis only becomes relevant, however, when the signal is traded as a standalone, rather than as part of an even larger alpha platform.

11.5.2 Results

Figure 11.5.1 shows the cumulative return series for the different portfolios. Again, we find the results are stable across region and size. Regionally, the EU clearly outperforms the US, while the small cap portfolios outperform their large/mid cap counterparts.

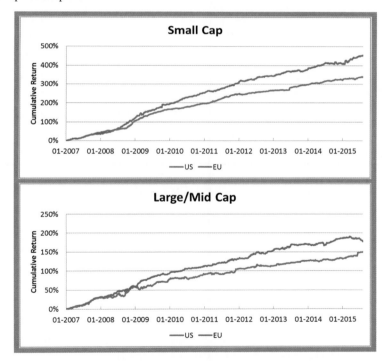

Figure 11.5.1: CUMULATIVE RETURN SERIES ACROSS REGIONS AND SIZES. This figure show cumulative returns of the equity portfolios constructed using holding periods from 1 to 5. Results are shown for Small and Large/Mid Cap across US and EU. Source: RavenPack, September 2015

This behaviour was expected to some extent, since the US region is considered more efficient than the EU and market efficiency is normally higher for larger market capitalization groups. These effects are also reflected in our Annualized Returns and Hit Ratios before trading costs (Table 11.5.1). But note the larger portfolio size for US small-cap provides additional diversification that results in a better risk-return trade-off due to its lower volatility.

Table 11.5.1: *PORTFOLIO STATISTICS. In this table we show the statistics of the constructed (dollar-neutral) portfolios across US and EU, both for Small and Large/Mid Cap. Results are organized in 3 main sections, showing the stats for different transaction cost levels (No trading cost, 5 bps and 10 bps). Turnover and Avg. portfolio size are shown at the bottom row, as it is common to all trading cost levels. Source: RavenPack, September 2015*

STATS		Small Cap		Large/Mid Cap	
		US	EU	US	EU
NO TRADING COSTS	**Annualized Return**	39.5%	51.4%	17.6%	19.9%
	Annualized Volatility	9.1%	13.8%	8.8%	7.7%
	Information Ratio	4.35	3.73	1.99	2.58
	Hit Ratio	64.2%	61.1%	56.3%	58.2%
5 BPS TRADING COST	**Annualized Return**	33.9%	46.0%	10.9%	13.6%
	Annualized Volatility	9.1%	13.8%	8.8%	7.7%
	Information Ratio	3.73	3.34	1.23	1.75
	Hit Ratio	62.1%	59.1%	52.8%	54.7%
10 BPS TRADING COST	**Annualized Return**	28.2%	40.6%	4.2%	7.2%
	Annualized Volatility	9.1%	13.8%	8.9%	7.7%
	Information Ratio	3.11	2.95	0.47	0.93
	Hit Ratio	60.1%	57.6%	49.5%	51.8%
	Turnover	44.9%	42.9%	53.3%	50.5%
Average Portfolio Size (Constituents)		410	90	145	120

We see that both small cap portfolios have turnover levels around 43–45% and the large/mid-cap portfolios have turnover levels around 50–53%[10]. This, coupled with the strong levels of annualized return, makes these portfolios profitable after trading costs – as shown in the second and third sections of Table 11.5.1. As previously mentioned, however, further turnover reduction benefits can be achieved by adding additional orthogonal alpha streams into the portfolio construction process.

Portfolio size also varies by size and region. For our small cap portfolios, we get an average number of constituents of 410 and 90 for the US and EU respectively, while for large/mid-cap the averages are 145 and 120. It is worth mentioning, though, that these numbers could easily be increased, by using longer holding periods (e.g. 1 to 10 days), without a significant drop in performance (as shown in Figures 11.4.1 and 11.4.3).

11.5.3 Portfolios Correlation
To evaluate the potential diversification benefits of investing across size and region, we compute the correlation matrix for the four time series of returns. These results are shown in Table 11.5.2. Perhaps surprisingly, we find almost no correlation between the portfolios. This can be explained by the fact that we are selecting different themes, investment horizons, and strategy types across the four portfolios. This means, by combining the different portfolios we could improve the Information Ratio of our final strategy.

Table 11.5.2: *CORRELATION MATRIX FOR THE FOUR UNIVERSES UNDER STUDY. In this Table we show the correlation among EU & US, both small and large/mid cap. Source: RavenPack, September 2015*

CORRELATION MATRIX	US Small	US Large/Mid	EU Small	EU Large/Mid
US Small	1.00	0.03	0.04	0.05
US Large/Mid	0.03	1.00	-0.02	0.07
EU Small	0.04	-0.02	1.00	0.04
EU Large/Mid	0.05	0.07	0.04	1.00

To add more colour to this finding, we analyse the performance of a set of mixed portfolios. We combine them in the following ways:

- Region-wise: We consider an equally weighted scheme (50/50) across size to provide a regional view, represented in Figure 11.5.2 as *"EU Only"* vs *"US Only"*.

- Size-wise: In this case, we equally weight across regions, to get a size view, represented in Figure 11.3.2 as *"Large/Mid Only"* vs *"Small Only"*.

- All combined: A weighted average (25% each) of all the portfolios under study, represented in Figure 11.5.2 as *"All"*.

The cumulative return series, together with performance statistics are shown in Figure 11.5.2. As found previously, the EU outperforms the US, whereas small caps outperform large/mid cap. Given the overall statistics, these strategies are perfectly tradable, even under conservative trading cost assumptions.

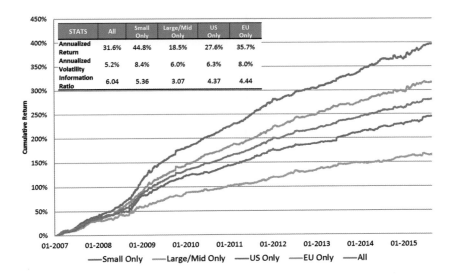

Figure 11.5.2: *CUMULATIVE RETURN SERIES OF PORTFOLIO COMBINATIONS. This figure shows cumulative returns of (dollar-neutral) portfolios combined in different ways: Region-wise ("US Only" vs "EU Only"); Size-wise ("Small Only" vs "Large/Mid Only") and in both dimensions ("All"). Equal weighting is used in all cases. Source: RavenPack, September 2015*

11.6 CONCLUSION

We set out to create a trading strategy (or "super-alpha") that would take advantage of a set of thematic alpha streams, based on corporate news analytics and sentiment data. We hoped to demonstrate an improvement in overall performance and reduced turnover versus treating sentiment as a one-dimensional signal.

We find that by tailoring the holding period to each theme, we not only improve the overall Information Ratio, but also reduce our daily turnover from around 95%[11] to about 43–53% - depending on *size*. With average holding periods of 2–3 days, our US strategies yield Information Ratios around 2.0 and 4.3 for the Russell 1000 and 2000, respectively. For the European equivalent portfolios, the Information Ratios are around 2.6 and 3.7. Interestingly, we find that our size and regional portfolios are almost orthogonal. This allows for additional diversification by trading a combined portfolio, resulting in a pre-trading-cost Information Ratio of around 6.0 - with an IR of 3.1 across large/mid cap and 5.4 for small cap.

From a theme perspective, we find very consistent results across our four portfolios, with 11 themes accounting for about 85–95% of total allocations. We find that a larger set of themes contribute towards performance in the US, while our European portfolios rely, to a greater extent, on just a few themes, including analyst-ratings and price-targets. Our simple methodology has shown strong robustness across both size (Small Cap vs Large/Mid Cap) and region (US vs EU), significantly reducing the chances of being exposed to overfitting. Thanks to its simplicity, the framework doesn't suffer from collinearity issues, making the model easily scalable.

In future research, we plan to further sophisticate our "alpha platform", allowing for a more non-uniform theme selection process – moving from a time to a frequency domain. In addition, we plan to apply different classification techniques to create alpha clusters that can be used as input in a more elaborate portfolio construction process. The main objective is to allocate more capital towards orthogonal alphas rather than to focus on their relative Information Ratios. Finally, we want to expand our source coverage beyond Dow Jones News to include the more than 19,000 web sources tracked by RavenPack – this will lead to the creation of additional "web-based" alpha streams that should bring further value to our portfolio.

Notes

[1] Which we have referred to in our work.

[2] For more details on Relevance or ESS data, please refer to 11.A Appendix.

[3] Using the group-layer of the RavenPack Event Taxonomy,

[4] In this case, the market is considered as the equal weighted return for the given universe, e.g. Russell 1000, Russell 2000, and Russell Europe equivalents.

[5] As an example, the 10-day return is calculated as the return from the "close" of Day 0 to "close" on Day 10.

[6] For simplicity, parameter selection is conducted over the entire sample. However, we plan to apply a more dynamic approach as part of future research.

[7] We apply 10 bps roundtrip.

[8] With alpha streams only considered if they hold a p-value of less than 5% (based on t-stats).

[9] As we need 1 year of data to measure alpha stream performance in the worst case.

[10]   This level is an "out-of-the-box" turnover after a daily naive rebalancing. We could reduce this even further by applying a rebalance algorithm that favours turnover reduction.

[11]   For a strategy with a 1-day holding period.

11.7 REFERENCES

1.   Hafez, P. and Guerrero-Colón, J.A. (2015). Using Sentiment to Create Theme-based Alphas. RavenPack Data Science.

2.   Hafez, P. and Xie, J.Q. (2014). Exploring Global Variations in News Impact on Equities. RavenPack Data Science.

3.   Hafez, P. and Xie, J.Q. (2013). Enhancing Short Term Stock Reversal Strategies with News Analytics. RavenPack Data Science.

4.   Kakushadzexy, Z. (2014). Combining Alpha Streams with Costs. Quantigic Solutions Research.

5.   Kakushadzexy, Z. (2015). Notes on Alpha Stream Optimization. Quantigic Solutions Research.

6.   Kakushadzexy, Z. and Tulchinsky, I. (2015). Performance v. Turnover: A Story by 4,000 Alphas. Quantigic Solutions Research.

7.   Menchero, J. and Lee, J.H. (2014). Efficiently Combining Multiple Sources of Alpha in Portofolio Construction. MSCI Research.

11.A APPENDIX

ESS – EVENT SENTIMENT SCORE

A granular score between 0 and 100 that represents the news sentiment for a given entity by measuring various proxies sampled from the news. The score is determined by systematically matching stories typically categorized by financial experts as having short-term positive or negative financial or economic impact. The strength of the score is derived from training sets in which financial experts classified entity-specific events and agreed that these events generally convey positive or negative sentiment and to what degree. Their ratings are encapsulated in an algorithm that generates a score range between 0–100 where higher values indicate more positive sentiment while lower values below 50 show negative sentiment.

ESS probes many different sentiment proxies typically reported in financial news and categorized by RavenPack. The algorithm produces a score for more than 1,200 types of business, economic and geopolitical events, ranging from earnings announcements to terrorist attacks. The algorithms can dynamically assign an ESS score based on fixed scores assigned by experts or by performing analysis and computation when figures or ratings are disclosed in the story.

For example, the algorithm is capable of interpreting actual figures, estimates, ratings, revisions, magnitudes and recommendations disclosed in news stories. It can compare actual vs estimated figures about earnings, revenues and dividends, and produce an ESS score based on comparisons. It calculates percentage differences between financial figures and reads and interprets stock and credit ratings disclosed by analysts. The ESS algorithms can factor in information such as the Richter scale in the case of an earthquake or the number of casualties in a suicide bombing event. The use of emotionally charged language by authors is also factored in when shaping the strength component of ESS.

The ESS algorithm has embedded information on ratings scales from all major brokerage firms, investment banks and credit rating agencies. It uses this information to differentiate and assess the various actions taken by analysts. For example, the algorithm generates a lower (more negative) ESS score for stories about an analyst downgrade from a "Strong Buy to a Strong Sell" than from a "Buy to a Neutral". In the case of stories about financial results or economic indicators, it computes the percentage change between the disclosed actual figures vs the street consensus or any other benchmarks disclosed in the story. For example, a company beating earnings by 70% will receive a higher (more positive) ESS score than a company exceeding a benchmark by 1%.

ESS leverages RavenPack's event detection technology and produces an entity-specific sentiment score every time an event category is matched. ESS is based on RavenPack's Expert Consensus and Event Score Factors methodologies.

Relevance

A score between 0–100 that indicates how strongly related the entity is to the underlying news story, with higher values indicating greater relevance. For any news story that mentions an entity, RavenPack provides a relevance score. A score of 0 means the entity was passively mentioned while a score of 100 means the entity was predominant in the news story. Values above 75 are considered significantly relevant. Specifically, a value of 100 indicates that the entity identified plays a key role in the news story and is considered highly relevant. RavenPack's analysis is not limited to keywords or mentions when calculating relevance. Automated classifiers look for meaning by detecting the roles entities play in specific events like acquisitions or legal disputes or when announcing corporate actions, executive changes, product launches or recalls, among many other categories. An entity will be assigned a high mark of 100 if it plays a main role in these types of stories (context-aware). If an entity is referenced in the headline or story body, it will receive a value between 0 and 99 (context-unaware). The score is assigned by a proprietary text-positioning algorithm based on where the entity is first mentioned (i.e. headline, first paragraph, second paragraph, etc.), the number of references in the text, and the overall number of entities mentioned in the story. Usually, a relevance value of at least 90 indicates that the entity is referenced in the main title or headline of the news item, while lower values indicate references further down the story body.

CHAPTER 12

The Psychology of Markets:
Information processing and the impact on asset prices

Richard Peterson, *CEO, MarketPsych Data LLC*

ABSTRACT

Crowds move markets. Crowds are made up of individuals - individuals who invest, trade or manage portfolios. They are moved not only by what they read and hear, but often more by their emotional reactions to such information. Behavioural economics researchers have demonstrated that when new information provokes emotional responses such as joy, fear, anger and gloom, individual trading behaviours are systematically biased. And since individuals combine to form a market, their collective emotions manifest in observable market behaviour. This chapter reviews the literature on how specific psychological stimuli impact on information processing and trading behaviour. The chapter uses a cross-sectional rotation model to demonstrate empirical evidence of the possibility of information arbitrage in equity markets, with an emphasis on the value of anger and leadership trust.

12.1 INTRODUCTION

Crowds move markets. Crowds are made up of individuals - individuals who invest, trade, or manage portfolios. The decisions of these individuals are affected by the ebb and flow of news and rumour (Engelberg and Parsons, 2011; Engelberg et al., 2010). They are moved not only by what they read and hear, but often more by their emotional reactions to such information.

Behavioural economics researchers have demonstrated that when new information provokes emotional responses such as joy, fear, anger and gloom, individual trading behaviours are systematically biased (Lerner and Keltner, 2000; Loewenstein and Lerner, 2003). And since individuals combine to form a market, their collective emotions manifest in observable market behaviour. Indeed, financial researchers have demonstrated that news-derived sentiment metrics can be used to predict price movements (Tetlock, 2007). Importantly, information predictably alters the way investors transact in markets.

If investors could understand the perceptions, preoccupations and concerns of market participants, perhaps they could have a better lead on how market prices will respond. This chapter demonstrates how these factors predictably influence prices.

Numerous proxies that represent investor sentiment exist such as consumer and investor surveys, equity fund flow data, closed-end fund discounts and put-call ratios. Each of these proxies has significant limitations compared to text-derived sentiment. These limitations vary by sentiment source and include fewer assets covered, less frequent updating, self-report bias (surveys) and lagging characteristics (market data). Sentiment derived from media analytics has numerous weaknesses including sparseness for some assets, imperfect accuracy of sentiment analysis (usually ranging from 75 to 80%), and source and author biases, among others. This chapter demonstrates how media sentiment data may hold predictive power for some asset prices over various time horizons.

A basic depiction of the predictive relationship between sentiment and asset prices is evident in charts of sentiment averages. When the net sentiment of the news about the S&P 500 companies is plotted against the value of the S&P 500 itself, a simple relationship is evident. Media sentiment is broadly predictive of the S&P 500 over the lifetime of the sentiment data described in this chapter. One simple moving average crossover strategy depicted in Figure 12.1 is: (1) Buy when the short-term (200-day) average of media sentiment is above the longer-term (500-day) average - indicating that news flow and social media is increasingly positive - and (2) Sell short when the 90-day is below the 200-day average - when average media sentiment is turning negative. This simple strategy earned 314% from January 1, 2000 (when the 500-business-day average was fully populated and the trading began) until July 31, 2015 with a maximum drawdown of 33%. The S&P 500 itself, adjusted for dividends, earned 91% over that period with a maximum peak-to-trough drawdown of 57%. Importantly, investors would have been short stocks during the drawdowns associated with the 2000-2002 tech stock crash and the 2007-2009 financial crisis.

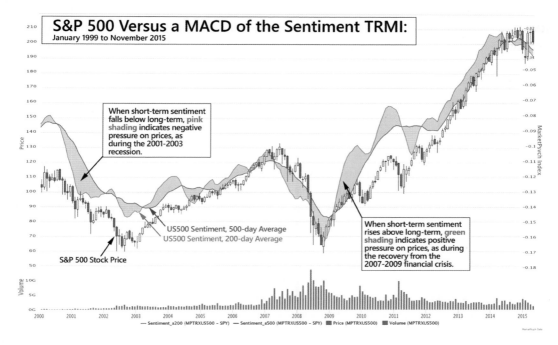

Figure 12.1: *S&P 500 prices versus sentiment, January 2007 to January 2015.*

Researchers wondered why this relationship occurred and whether it was statistically robust. Can investors reliably predict market prices using sentiment?

This chapter opens with a discussion of information known to impact on trader psychology and risk taking. In particular, it examines research indicating that the level of media emotionality, arousal and specific topics in the information flow is predictive of trader behaviour. The second section describes the sentiment data used in this research: the Thomson Reuters MarketPsych Indices (TRMI). The TRMI were constructed in order to capture important nuances of the information flow. In the third section, simple cross-sectional rotation models are used to demonstrate how information predictably impacts on prices. In the conclusion, future directions for research are discussed.

12.2   MARKET PSYCHOLOGY

12.2.1   How Emotions Move Traders

Traditional textual sentiment analysis typically yields only one bipolar index. Sentiment-laden references are scored on a valence scale ranging from positive to negative, with additional consideration for neutrality. Yet humans experience a broad range of emotions and psychological research has demonstrated that more than just positive-negative valence has predictable effects on investor behaviour.

One common classification system of human emotion plots emotions on dimensions (axes) called valence and arousal. Humans can experience high or low levels of both valence and arousal. Pleasantness and exuberance are positive in valence, while boredom and fury are of negative valence. As for arousal, pleasantness and boredom are low arousal states, while exuberance and fury are high arousal states. Researchers represent the valence and arousal dimensions in the affective circumplex model of sentiment (Russell, 1980).

12.2.2 Arousal and Stress

One's arousal level significantly impacts on decision-making. Most people make significantly different decisions when sleepy versus when buzzing with caffeine. In a classic representation of the differential effects of arousal, stress levels map to cognitive performance in an inverse-U curve called the Yerkes-Dodson Law (Yerkes and Dodson, 1908; Diamon et al., 2007).

When stress levels are very high, complex problem-solving performance drops and reliance on pre-existing habits increases (Schwabe, 2009). On the other hand, low stress levels also lead to sub-par performance in complex decision-making environments due to inattention and slow reaction times. Thus decision-makers typically perform with optimal cognition when arousal is in the middle of its range.

In text, arousal can be captured in specific references to Stress (slightly negative valence) and Urgency (neutral valence). High Stress and Urgency scores are expected to correlate with decreased trader cognitive performance. One effect among traders could be incomplete arbitrage of short-term price anomalies. Both high and low levels of arousal may predispose markets to exhibit price patterns such as momentum during low-arousal regimes and mean reversion during high-arousal regimes (Hirshleifer and Subrahmanyam, 1999).

Valence and arousal are only two dimensions out of many possible for describing emotions. The following sections describe research on how other important emotions drive buying and selling decisions among traders.

12.2.3 Anger and Fear

Research has shown that strongly negative emotions such as Anger, Fear and Gloom have a unique and consistent effect in biasing how individuals set bid and ask prices in an experimental market (Winkielman et al., 2007; Winkielman et al., 2005). Much of the modern research on this subject has been led by Professor Jennifer Lerner, now at Harvard University.

In a series of experiments, Professor Lerner induced emotional states of sadness, fear and disgust in subjects using short movie clips (Lerner et al., 2004; Lerner and Keltner, 2001). She then studied how the subjects placed bids and offers in a simulated marketplace.

Lerner found that participants in a disgusted emotional state were emotionally driven to "expel" or "get rid" of items they owned. They also had no desire to accumulate new possessions. As a result, they reduced both their bid and offer prices for consumer items.

The Anger index encompasses angry sentiments ranging in intensity from disgust (low-level anger) to rage (intense anger). Based on Lerner's results, high anger readings are expected to increase selling and reduce buying in affected assets. Expressions of anger in media often relate to a loss of trust, and the anger and trust TRMI are inversely correlated across assets. Results based on the Trust TRMI are described below.

Professor Lerner also studied the effects of fear. Compared to anger, fear is characterized by the combination of lower bid prices, higher ask prices and pessimism about the future (Lerner et al., 2004; Lerner and Keltner, 2001). Fearful investors avoid transacting, paralyzed as prices slide until fear reaches an extreme level, marked by panic. Panic drives a purge of assets, an event which is termed "capitulation" colloquially and "over-reaction" in the behavioural finance literature (Hirshleifer and Subrahmanyam, 1999).

12.2.4 Uncertainty

"The future is never clear, and you pay a very high price in the stock market for a cheery consensus. Uncertainty is the friend of the buyer of long-term values."
~Warren Buffett (Buffet, 1979)

In the first half of the twentieth century Frank Knight developed the concept of Knightian uncertainty to differentiate between two types of uncertainty (Knight, 1921). Knight noted that when potential future outcomes can be expressed probabilistically, they are called risk. When there is a lack of knowledge about potential probabilities, the outcomes are described as uncertain or ambiguous. The Uncertainty index measures expressions of the latter type of uncertainty, a lack of knowledge about outcome probabilities.

Academic researchers identified a psychological process called *ambiguity aversion* that leads investors to mistakenly discount asset prices. Specifically, researchers found that high-uncertainty equities and country indices on average outperform their less ambiguous peers (Erbas and Abbas, 2007). While high uncertainty typically creates discounted valuations (as Warren Buffett notes above), in speculative bubbles uncertainty magnifies the prevailing positive sentiment. During speculative bubbles, companies with valuation uncertainty outperform peers before earnings (Trueman et al., 2003) and during IPOs (Bartov et al., 2002).

Anticipation

Such emotions as fear and excitement are anticipatory. They help people prepare for threats or opportunities, and they are fundamental to the coordination of action either away from danger or toward opportunity. When a threat becomes reality, resulting in immediate danger, then we are compelled to flee, freeze in terror or fight, giving rise to the colloquial expression: "the fight or flight" response. This is a reaction to danger. If one is anticipating danger, fear is experienced, but if one is reacting to danger, then the "fight or flight" response is provoked.

This distinction between anticipatory and reactive emotions is important. Amateur investors often buy stocks based on excitement about an expected price change in their favour. What they don't realize is that their excitement biologically diminishes their ability to detect potential dangers, preventing adequate due diligence.

Excitement decreases fear through a neural feedback mechanism. Excited investors are physically incapable of thoroughly processing information about potential risks.

12.2.5 The Dimensions of Sentiment

Authors describing an asset may reference an event (topic), positive or negative impact (sentiment), outcome ambiguity (uncertainty), the importance of the event (magnitude), its immediacy (urgency), surprise and specific emotions relating to it (emotive sentiments). Thus far, this chapter has addressed the research rationale for studying sentiments such as Stress, Anger, Trust, Fear and Uncertainty. The indexes measure additional emotions and states. Indexes such as governmentAnger and marketRisk encapsulate the relationship between sentiments and specific topics.

Table 12.1 below summarizes the market research on a sample of sentiment-based indexes.

Table 12.1: *Academic and professional research measuring market responses for various TRMI sentiments.*

TRMI COMMON NAME	ANTICIPATED MARKET IMPACT
Sentiment	There are several important research findings related to sentiment and price movement. Based on academic research on Thomson Reuters News Analytics sentiment scores, positive and negative sentiment in the news about individual stocks extend price momentum (Sinha, 2010), which is supported by additional evidence that traders collectively under-react to negative sentiment in news reports (Tetlock et al., 2007). Another study finds that market sentiment improves factor weighting in some models (Stambaugh et al., 2011). In foreign exchange, news sentiment was found to influence volatility (Anderson et al., 2002).
Optimism	There is empirical evidence that proxies for optimism correlate with positive price behaviour (Doukas et al., 2012) and that bullish comments in financial social media precede higher trading volume (Frank and Antweiler, 2001). Optimism in earnings press releases was found correlated with future stock price activity (Davis et al., 2011).
Fear	Academic researchers who aggregated search terms they deemed reflective of economic fear found short-term mean reversion in prices when fear-related search terms spiked in volume (Das et al., 2011). In experimental markets, fear was found to decrease bid and increase ask prices, leading to less overall trading activity (Lerner et al., 2004). As a result, wider bid-ask spreads may be expected when fear is high.

Joy	Joy is a marker of exuberance. Experimental markets demonstrate higher price peaks and larger collapses during bubble simulations if traders watched a positively exciting movie clip before trading begins (Odean et al., 2012).
Trust	Trust was designed specifically for nations and banking and financial groups. Economists have found that national interpersonal Trust levels correlate with future economic growth (Zak and Knack 2001; Bjørnskov 2012).
Conflict	The Conflict TRMI, which is intended to capture disagreement and dispute, is anticipated to correlate with price volatility. A study of international markets found that global conflicts significantly impact asset prices (Guidolin and La Ferrara, 2005).
Stress[*] and Urgency	Urgency and Stress are high-arousal indices that vary in valence. Based on evidence that arousal drives cognitive performance in an inverse-U shaped curve, we infer that pricing anomalies are more likely to emerge at low or high arousal values, as seen with both high positive and high negative arousal during research into experimental market bubbles (Odean et al., 2012).
Uncertainty	Researchers found that high-uncertainty equities and country indices on average outperform their low-uncertainty peers (Erbas and Mirakhor, 2007). In contrast, during speculative bubbles uncertainty amplifies the price momentum of positive sentiment (Bartov et al., 2002). In emerging fixed income markets, releases of macroeconomic data decrease future volatility (Andritzky et al., 2007).
Gloom	Traders in an experimental market offered lower ask and high bid prices when "sadness" was induced prior to trading, leading to increased transaction volume (Lerner et al., 2004). If this result transfers into larger market behaviour, we expect increased trading volume during periods of high Gloom (Lerner et al., 2004). Researchers speculate that identified semi-annual variations in country stock index returns - which scale by latitude and reverse from northern to southern hemispheres - may be caused by seasonal changes in affect (the "winter blues") among local traders (Garretta et al., 2005).
Anger	Traders induced to feel anger in an experimental market decrease both average ask and bid prices (Lerner et al., 2004). As a result, we speculate that higher TRMI Anger readings should lead to increased selling and reduced buying in associated assets, leading to downward pressure on prices during high Anger periods.

Figure 12.2 below depicts several of the above sentiments plotted on the affective circumplex model of sentiment. Each dot corresponds to the emotion's location on the circumplex in Figure 12.1 above, noting that some of the indexes that studied are a hybrid of multiple emotions in the circumplex. Note in Figure 12.2 that indexes representing an emotion and its opposite are plotted with a thin grey line connecting the positive and negative poles.

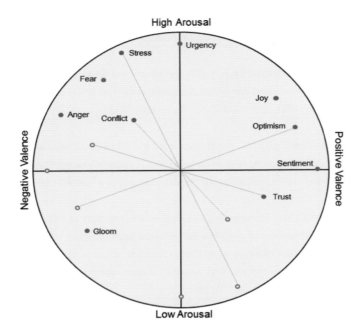

Figure 12.2: The sentiment-derived Thomson Reuters MarketPsych Indices plotted on the affective circumplex.

The next section describes how the text analytics process turns media content into numerical indices.

12.3 DATA

12.3.1 The Thomson Reuters MarketPsych Indices

The Thomson Reuters MarketPsych Indices (TRMI) are based on over 2 million business and finance-related articles received daily from news and social media. In this chapter the TRMI are referred to as sentiment data, but the breadth of coverage is much wider than traditional bipolar positive/negative sentiment. For one, the TRMI score sentiment along with dimensions including specific emotions, expectations, uncertainty and urgency. In addition, the TRMI include an array of one- and two-directional scores on asset-specific topics. Examples of TRMI include Litigation and Layoffs about equities, inflation and BudgetDeficit about countries, ProductionVolume for commodities and PriceForecast for currencies. Given its coverage of issues spanning topics, macroeconomics and sentiments, this data might be used for understanding and modelling price moves and economic activity.

The data set is uniquely interesting to researchers in three key ways:

    1.   The sentiment data is highly dimensional, including scores on more than sixty sentiments, macroeconomic themes and complex fundamentals.

2.   A broad range of entities are tracked. As of this publication, the TRMI deliver sentiments on over 8,000 equities, 52 equity indices, 32 currencies, 34 commodities and 130 countries.
3.   The TRMI content collection includes thousands of social media and news sources dating from 1998.

The remainder of this section delves deeper into the mechanism of extracting emotion and complex meaning from text.

12.3.2 Source Type Customization

There is a vast difference in communication styles between social and news media. Compared to news, social media contain significant levels of sarcasm and irony, incomplete thoughts, misplaced or excessive punctuation, misspellings, non-standard grammar, case insensitivity and crude language. Additionally, in social media many common words are used with colloquial meanings. A statement such as "That trade was the bomb!" with reference to a successful trade is very different from a reference to warfare, as would be interpreted by a historically-trained linguistic analysis engine.

Another significant difference between social and news media lies in how viewpoints are conveyed. In social media there is typically less editorial oversight and more leeway for a passionate author to unreservedly express his or her opinion or emotional state. In contrast, journalists are trained to offer multiple perspectives on the underlying story. In the news, emotion is typically conveyed by journalists whose role is to describe the emotional states of those they are reporting on. As a result, information obtained from social media is typically less inclusive of contrary viewpoints and more emotionally expressive from the first-person perspective than news information.

Direct expressions of emotion in news and social media also vary. In social media authors may utilize a complex array of emoticons (e.g., ">:-(") and acronyms (e.g., "LOL") that developed organically, with regional, industrial and national differences. Furthermore, word context is much more important in social media than in news media for interpreting intended meaning.

As a result of all these differences between news and social media, sentiment scoring accuracy is improved by text analytic models calibrated to source type. MarketPsych currently uses differentiated models for news, social media forums, tweets, SEC filings and earnings conference call transcripts.

12.3.3 Lexical Analysis

There are a variety of approaches used in sentiment analysis. The most common technique is called lexical analysis, and this approach is used in several recent academic studies of sentiment and stock returns (Tetlock, 2007). Lexical analysis identifies explicit words and phrases in a body of text. Relevant content is organized and scored according to a hard-coded ontology. The simplest example of a lexical approach is called "bag of words". In the "bag of words" technique all words are counted according to their frequency, and no additional grammatical or relational post-processing is performed.

There are several known limitations to a purely lexical approach. The most significant one, for the purposes of producing TRMI, is that most lexical approaches are focused only on extracting one-dimensional sentiment. In cases where a variety of sentiment dimensions may be scored using lexical analysis, such as when using the Harvard General Inquirer dictionary, the word tokens representing specific sentiments are occasionally incongruent with meanings in contemporary business English. Another weakness of using uncurated dictionaries is lexical ambiguity across domains. For example, financial terms such as "investor" and "financier" are classified as negative sentiment terms in some open-source sentiment dictionaries. MarketPsych has overcome lexical ambiguity with extensive business-specific customization and curation of lexicons.

Insensitivity to grammatical structures is perhaps the most significant weakness of the lexical approach. In order to address this weakness, MarketPsych engineers embedded a complex grammatical framework with traits specific to different text sources such as social media, earnings conference call transcripts, financial news and regulatory filings. The result is that customized lexicons, superior disambiguation, and optimized grammatical structures stand behind MarketPsych's textual analytics. For space reasons, the grammatical nuances of the natural language processing underlying the TRMI will not be described.

12.3.4 Entity Identification and Correlate Filtering

Consider that entities such as IBM may be referred to as "IBM", "Big Blue" or "International Business Machines" in the press. Additionally, international press may or may not use accent marks on common location names such as Düsseldorf. In order to identify entities such as IBM and Düsseldorf that have multiple spellings or reference names, MarketPsych prepared a list of over 60,000 entity names with aliases. This list has been improved by human review, and it is updated quarterly with new entities including IPOs such as GoDaddy (GDDY) and new location names such as South Sudan.

To improve entity name disambiguation, MarketPsych used supervised machine learning to identify correlate and anti-correlate words in the proximity of ambiguous entity references. For example, gold and silver are commonly spoken of as both commodities and constituents of jewellery, but every two years they are frequently mentioned as Olympic medals. To prevent entity identification errors, anti-correlate filters are utilized to eliminate Olympic references such as "gold medal" and "won a silver". Another example is the South Korean Won, which could be confused with a successful competition by a South Korean athlete who "won" an event. Anti-correlate filtering and case-sensitivity both improve precision of the scoring process and entity identification.

12.3.5 Sentence Level Example

When applied to text, the confluence of the various text processings described above generates over 4000 variables (Vars), each with the potential to be applied to a different entity. Using the principles outlined above, this sections describes how such software analyzes the following sentence:

"Analysts expect Mattel to report much higher earnings next quarter"

The language analyzer performs the following sequence of actions:
1. Associates ticker symbol MAT with entity reference "Mattel."
2. Identifies "earnings" as an *Earnings* word in the lexicon.
3. Identifies "expect" as a future-oriented word and assigns future tense to the phrase.
4. Identifies "higher" as an *Up-Word*.
5. Multiplies "higher" by two due to presence of the modifier word "*much*."
6. Associates "higher" (*Up-Word*) with "earnings" (*Earnings*) due to proximity.

The analysis algorithm will report:

Date	Time	Ticker	Var	Score
20110804	*15:00.123*	*MAT*	*EarningsUp_f*	*2*

In the example above, *2* is the raw score produced for EarningsUp_f.

12.3.6 Source Text

The TRMI are derived from a custom collection of premium news, global Internet news coverage and a broad and credible range of social media. The TRMI social media feed consists of both MarketPsych and Moreover social media content. Moreover Technologies' aggregated social media feed is derived from 4 million social media sites and is incorporated into the TRMI from 2009 to the present. MarketPsych social media content was downloaded from public social media sites from 1998 to the present.

The TRMI News indices are derived from live content delivered via Thomson Reuters News Feed Direct and two Thomson Reuters news archives: a Reuters-only one from 1998 to 2002 and one with Reuters and select third-party wires from 2003 to the present. In addition, the Moreover Technologies aggregated news feed which is derived from 40,000 internet news sites and spans 2005 to the present is incorporated. MarketPsych crawler content from hundreds of premium financial news sites is also included. The TRMI thus cover the period 1998 to the present. Currently all source text for the MarketPsych sentiment products is English-language.

12.3.7 Index Construction

Each TRMI is composed of a combination of Vars. First the absolute values of all TRMI-contributing Vars, for all asset constituents, over the past 24 hours are determined. These absolute values are then summed for all constituents. This sum is called the "Buzz," and it is published in conjunction with each asset's TRMIs. More specifically, where V is the set of all Vars underlying *any* TRMI of the asset class, where a denotes an asset, and where $C(a)$ is the set of all constituents[1] of a, we can define the Buzz of a as the following:

$$Buzz(a) = \Sigma_{c \in C(a), v \in V} |Var_{c,v}|$$

[12.1]

Each TRMI is then computed as a ratio of the sum of all relevant Vars to the Buzz. $V(t)$ is defined as the set of all Vars relevant to a particular TRMI t. Next a function is defined to determine whether a Var $v \in V(t)$ is additive or subtractive to a TRMI as the following: coincide

$$I(t, v) = \begin{cases} +1 \ if \ additive \\ -1 \ if \ subtractive \end{cases}$$

Thus the TRMI t of asset a can be computed as the following:

$$TRMI_t(a) = \frac{\sum_{c \in C(A), v \in V(t)}(I(t,v) \times PsychVar_v(c))}{Buzz(Asset)} \qquad [12.2]$$

It's worth noting that particularly for Equities where the assets all correspond to indices and sectors, an individual constituent may contribute to multiple assets. For example, Mattel is a constituent of both the Consumer Goods sector and the Nasdaq 100 index proxies. As a result, Mattel's Var scores will be incorporated into the TRMI for both.

Similarly, a single Var can contribute to multiple TRMI. For example, the EarningsUp_fVar noted in the "Sentence-level Example" section above is not only a constituent of EarningsForecast but also of the Sentiment, Optimism and FundamentalStrength TRMI.

12.3.8 Asset Classes Covered

The Thomson Reuters MarketPsych Indices cover tradable assets in five different asset classes. See an abbreviated list of coverage below:

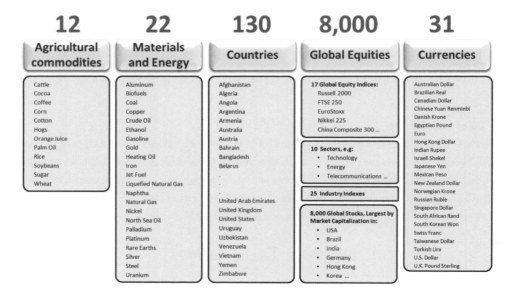

Figure 12.3.1: *Asset classes covered by the Thomson Reuters MarketPsych Indices.*

12.3.9 TRMI Content

The Thomson Reuters MarketPsych Indices consist of several different sentiments, fourteen of which are common to all five scored asset classes. Macroeconomic and topic TRMI vary by asset class. More documentation about the individual assets and indices covered is available in the Thomson Reuters MarketPsych Indices User Guide.

12.3.10 Visual Validation

One simple way to validate that the TRMI data reflects its intended output is to visualize actual events. One event with high psychological impact that has been in the news lately is social unrest. The SocialUnrest TRMI can be seen in the image below:

Figure 12.3.2: An image of average governmentInstability Thomson Reuters MarketPsych Indices values for countries in 2014.

12.4 ANALYZING SENTIMENT DATA

12.4.1 Nonlinear Characteristics

Extracting value from sentiment data requires an understanding of data dynamics, optimal statistical techniques and proper predictive hygiene.

The TRMI data is similar to other sentiment data in that is has nonlinear characteristics. For example, Fear periodically arises among investors in an asset. Fear does not arise on a smooth scale and with a normal distribution. Rather, fear occurs in sudden bursts. Price dynamics during such bursts – when Fear is in the top 10% of its historical range - are quite different from periods when Fear is in the lower 90% of its historical range.

For an example of the nonlinear characteristics of sentiment data, see the example of overall Buzz in news and social media about the Turkish Lira below:

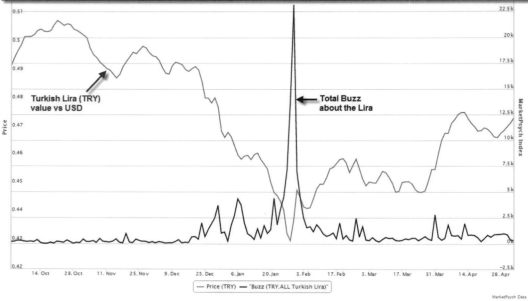

Figure 124.1: *An image of the Turkish Lira (TRY) price (blue line) versus the Buzz Thomson Reuters MarketPsych Index from October 1, 2013 to May 4, 2014.*

As you can see in this image, the Turkish Lira has a fairly low level of overall Buzz about it as an asset. However, when the Gezi Park and Taksim Square protests created economic and political instability in January 2014, the currency declined and the international business media increased coverage of the currency more than 20-fold.

12.4.2 Statistical Techniques

There are a variety of statistical techniques to extract value from sentiment data. This chapter demonstrates the use of cross-sectional rotation models, a statistical technique that can capture value from the nonlinear characteristics of sentiment data. Nonlinear predictive analytics techniques generally used with sentiment data include decision trees, moving average crossovers and cross-sectional rotation models.

The remainder of this chapter demonstrates interesting results derived from the use of cross-sectional rotation models. The best way to illustrate the models is to explain a simple equity curve derived in Figure 12.4.1. The top 20 stocks by buzz are selected for a given week. Those top 20 stocks are then ranked by their average value on the Sentiment TRMI over the study period. Absent sentiment values are not considered. The daily TRMI arrive at 3:30pm New York time, 30 minutes before the close of stock trading on the NYSE. The top quartile (five stocks) are bought, and the bottom quartile (five stocks) are shorted on Friday market close. Those positions are held for one week, until the following Friday close, when the operation is repeated. The prior week's picks are exited, and new positions are entered. Zero transaction costs are assumed, and there is up to 100 percent turnover each week.

The equity curve below represents the returns generated from a weekly rotational model using US stocks and the social media TRMI Stress. The x-axis is time in years, and the y-axis is the appreciation of 1 dollar (the starting value) equally distributed among the positions (20% in each stock if there are 10 positions in total). 100% of the portfolio is long, and 100% is short. At each iteration the entire portfolio value is re-invested. The model assumes zero transaction costs and excludes borrowing costs, which is obviously unrealistic.

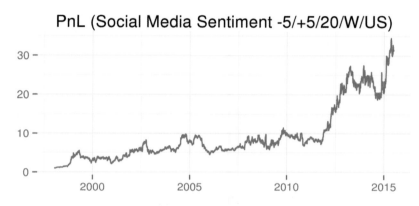

Figure 12.4.2: An equity curve derived by arbitraging the weekly average social media Sentiment Thomson Reuters MarketPsych Index for individual US stocks.

This equity curve demonstrates a 30-fold return using "emotional arbitrage" of social media sentiment. It appears that buying stocks which investors are negative about and shorting those high in positivity generates a "sentiment arbitrage" which may predict price mean reversion over time.

Each cross-sectional equity curve described in this chapter was constructed in a similar fashion, but with variations in the minimum buzz limit, holding period and the number of positions taken. The notation in the chart's title of "PnL (Sentiment -5/+5/20/W/US)" is aligned with a standard notation used in this chapter, where equity curve titles consist of Profit and Loss (PnL): (Source TRMI +long/-short/buzz filter/time period/country (2-letter ISO country code if equities). Note that when the source is news, the Source field indicates "News Media," and if social media, "Social Media" is written. If the source is the combination of both news and social media, as it is in Figure 12.4.1, no source is listed. TRMI refers to the single sentiment index tested. The next entries (-5/+5) refer to the direction and numbers of positions reweighted periodically. The leading –sign indicates the strategy shorts the five assets top ranked by average Sentiment TRMI. The buzz filter is the number of stocks ranked by buzz included in the analysis (20). The next field refers to the duration of both past TRMI averaging and future holding period, where durations are D for daily, W for weekly, M for monthly and Y for yearly.

The following sections describe various arbitrages which show promising results over different periods of time.

12.5 DAILY MOMENTUM

One of the common findings of sentiment data research is the presence of news momentum. That is, a sequence of positive or negative news events lead to similar movements in price in a predictable fashion.

The equity curves below demonstrate that such news momentum occurs in both the United States and Canada, and it occurs for both generic Sentiment as well as other specific indices.

12.5.1 US Daily Stock Momentum

The following equity curves depict the result of a cross-sectional rotation strategy which selects the top 20 stocks in the US news over the past 24 hours. The 24-hour data aggregation period stretches from 30 minutes before the NYSE close on the prior day to 30 minutes before the close on the current day. The positions are taken at the closing price on the current day and held until the close of the following day. Then the stocks are ranked on each TRMI, and an equity curve is derived by going long the top five and shorting the bottom five for 24 hours. The process is repeated every trading day. In this research, it appears that news optimism is generally accurate for the next 24 hours. Moreover, a specific type of optimism – an earningsForecast – is even more impressive in terms of its predictive power for the stock price.

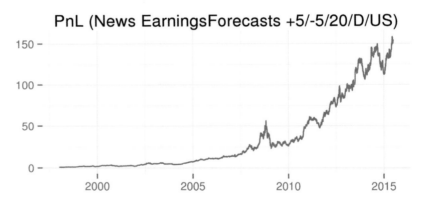

Figure 12.5.1: *An equity curve derived by arbitraging the daily average news earningsForecast Thomson Reuters MarketPsych Index for individual US stocks.*

The above equity curves demonstrate the value of quantifying verb tense. In each case expectations expressed in news media are positively correlated with the following 24 hours of price activity. In the short-term (24 hours), expectations are self-fulfilling.

12.5.2 Canadian Daily Stock Momentum

Similar to US stocks, Canadian stocks respond to news with momentum. In the following equity curves, the top 20 Canadian stocks in the news, traded only on the Toronto Stock Exchange, were selected; the selection was rotated daily.

The sentiment index is computed by quantifying the net difference between positive references to company versus negative references. Canadian stocks respond favourably to news sentiment over 24 hours. After a 24-hour period of positive (negative) news, stock prices drift in the positive (negative) direction over the following 24 hours:

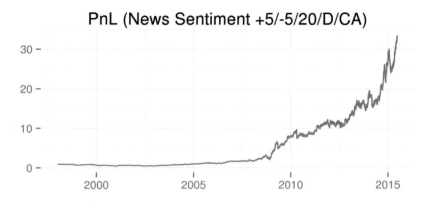

Figure 12.5.2: *An equity curve derived by arbitraging the daily average news sentiment Thomson Reuters MarketPsych Index for individual Canadian stocks.*

It appears that Canadian stocks incorporate positive and negative news over 24 hours or more, creating an opportunity for quick investors (excluding transaction costs).

12.6 ANNUAL MEAN REVERSION

The TRMI data also appear to show predictive relationships over annual time periods. In particular, contrarian (mean-reversion) patterns across countries and cross-sections of stocks are seen. In these cases, indexes of generally positive tone predict prices will decline, while negative indexes indicate prices are likely to rise.

Specific TRMI show value both across country stock indexes and within local stock markets. Specific emotions such as trust are correlated with longer-term mean-reversion patterns. High impact topics, such as those around leadership, also create significant opportunities. Importantly, TRMI that embody specific types of risk, such as environmental risks (naturalDisasters) and political risks (governmentInstability) inversely correlate with future returns.

The following results use an annual arbitrage model. The model first selects the 100 most talked-about US stocks in the media over the prior 12 months. Every stock is then ranked by the average level of the TRMI. The highest quartile of TRMI stocks are bought, and the five with the lowest TRMI value are shorted. Longs and shorts are held for 12 months. Every month one-twelfth of the portfolio positions are updated. The model assumes zero transaction costs. The equity curves from this absolute returns strategy follow each section.

12.6.1 Trust

Trust is a sentiment that shows value across stock markets, equity indexes, and currencies using the cross-sectional model. Many other sentiments do not show consistent returns. Trust is typically based on corporate fundamentals and management. When there is a problem at a company or in its management team, trust drops. Perhaps because trust is a prerequisite to economic activity and financial transactions, investors appear to overreact to violations of trust. They also appear to overvalue trusted companies.

The following image shows the hypothetical returns to investors from a simple trust-based dollar-neutral investment strategy in US stocks. This equity curve results from an arbitrage within the top 20 stocks in news media, buying the five lowest trust and shorting the five with the high trust in a given week.

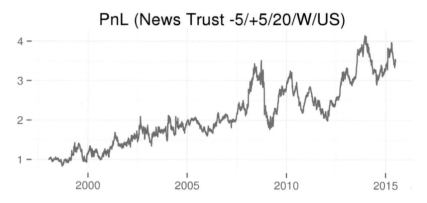

Figure 12.6.1: *An equity curve derived by arbitraging the weekly news average Trust Thomson Reuters MarketPsych Index for individual US stocks.*

12.6.2 Uncertainty

Now turning to uncertainty, there is evidence that uncertainty predicts overreaction and underreaction across US stocks. The following result was derived using an annual cross-sectional rotation model of the top 100 stocks by news Buzz. Buying stocks high in uncertainty, and shorting those low in uncertainty resulted in the equity curve in Figure 12.6.2.

Figure 12.6.2: An equity curve derived by arbitraging the annual average news and social media uncertainty.

Additionally, there appear to be positive effects of uncertainty for stock prices on shorter time horizons as well as for other assets, such as currencies (as described in Chapter 19).

Often when investors no longer trust a company, their ire is directed at the management team. The following section explores media-driven mistrust of corporate leadership and how this phenomenon may systematically predict stock price outperformance.

12.6.3 Leadership Psychology

They grumbled and complained of the long voyage, and I reproached them for their lack of spirit, telling them that, for better or worse, they had to complete the enterprise on which the Catholic Sovereigns had sent them. I cheered them on as best I could, telling them of all the honours and rewards they were about to receive. I also told the men that it was useless to complain, for I had started out to find the Indies and would continue until I had accomplished that mission, with the help of Our Lord.
~ Christopher Columbus, Wednesday, 10 October 1492

Christopher Columbus was nearly forced by his crew to prematurely end his first voyage to the New World. His crew had lost faith in his judgment. Such mutinies against leadership as Columbus experienced occur with some regularity at shareholder meetings and on earnings conference calls globally, where leadership teams serve as convenient scapegoats.

In the TRMI data, two of the most powerful annual predictors of stock returns appear to be the managementTrust index for individual stocks and the governmentInstability index for individual countries. Management trust is calculated by quantifying trusting versus mistrustful references to a company's corporate management team (Board, CEO, Directors, etc.). Mistrustful associations (scoundrels, criminals, etc.) were subtracted from trusting associations (reliable, trustworthy, etc.) to people on the management team. The final managementTrust TRMI index is a time series for each individual global stock.

Using the same style of annual rotation model as used previously for Anger, the equity curve for managementTrust in Figure 12.6.3 was produced. This equity curve is derived from the top 100 US stocks by Buzz over the past 12 months. Note that this curve is inverted – the model goes short the companies with the most trusted management and long those with the least trusted management:

Figure 12.6.3: An equity curve derived by arbitraging the annual average media managementTrust Thomson Reuters MarketPsych Index for individual US stocks.

The above equity curve is interesting, but is not the whole story. The managementTrust index has greater predictive power over monthly versus annual holding periods, implying that the mispricings due to such news impact on prices for a shorter period of time.

The nearest equivalent to the managementTrust index across countries is the governmentInstability index. To construct this index for a country, references to government instability versus stability are quantified for each country and converted into a time series.

The following result was derived using an annual cross-sectional rotation model. Instead of selecting the top 20 stocks by Buzz, the top 20 *countries* by news Buzz were selected. Countries without investable stock indexes were excluded. The countries were ranked by the average governmentInstability TRMI value over the past 12 months. The model went long the top quartile (5) of primary country stock indexes with the highest governmentInstability and went short the five stock indexes with the lowest. One-twelfth of the portfolio was rotated monthly. The resulting equity curve, showing an approximate eight-fold return, is found in Figure 12.6.4.

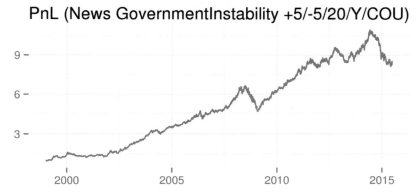

Figure 12.6.4: *An equity curve derived by arbitraging the stock indexes of the top 20 countries by buzz ranked by monthly average news (nws) governmentInstability Thomson Reuters MarketPsych Index.*

Based on the results above, it appears that investors overvalue management teams and governments. As a result they overreact to news about the trustworthiness of management and the stability of governments. Due to their collective overreaction, opportunities are available for savvy investors.

12.7 CONCLUSION AND DISCUSSION

The results exhibited in this chapter imply that some group-level information processing biases lead to patterns in prices. Significantly, these biases appear to originate in the human brain's common emotional circuitry. Because these biases appear to occur across assets and over various time horizons, they provide a robust and unique source of investment opportunity.

Using a novel source of information-derived psychological indices, it appears that specific emotions (anger, stress) and topics (prices, earnings and leadership) presage price patterns in assets over time. These patterns are rooted in human information processing and psychology, and they present opportunities for savvy investors who can remain unbiased in their risk assessments despite the pressure of the media and crowd psychology.

In the short term, over 24-hour periods, a contagion effect may emerge in which positive projections in news (specifically for US stocks) carry forward into 24-hour price action. For Canadian stocks, references to price momentum appear to carry over into price momentum. Over one-day periods the news media does appear to influence behaviour.

Over weekly periods, evidence of price overreaction can be associated with social media sentiments. On an annual basis, there is evidence of contrarianism. Using the cross-sectional analysis technique, trust appears to be a useful predictor of overvalued stocks. This effect occurs across stocks globally. Experiments on anger during financial transactions revealed that angry individuals reduced both their bid and offer prices for consumer items (Lerner et al., 2004; Lerner and Keltner 2001), which may, in part, contribute to mispricings based on mistrust.

Notably, an arbitrage of anger itself across stocks shows an outperforming equity curve, but it is less consistent across time periods than that of trust.

Investors may overreact when trust is broken, leading to selling shares and a similar reluctance to repurchase them. A study on the social media site Weibo found that anger disseminates faster through a network and farther across social connections than joy, disgust and sadness (Fan et al., 2014). Additionally, psychological research has found that venting anger (catharsis) increases innate feelings of anger (Bushman, 2002), thus creating a positive feedback loop in online environments where anger is vented. Ultimately prices - on average - drift higher as trust is rebuilt or bargain-hunters with less emotional sensitivity step in to buy discounted shares.

Some of the more interesting equity curves above are created by the excess returns of buying companies with mistrusted leadership and shorting companies with highly regarded leadership. This finding aligns with research performed by Ulrike Malmendier of Stanford and Geoffrey Tate of UCLA (Malmendier and Tate, 2009). In their 2009 paper "Superstar CEOs," the authors selected a sample of 283 companies whose CEOs had won prestigious nationwide awards from the business press. From 6 days following the award to three years later, they found that the stock of award winners underperformed those of predicted award winners (similar cohort in terms of business regard). In fact, the award-winners underperformed the predicted award winners by 20% over three years (Malmendier and Tate, 2009). Building on Malmendier and Tate's research, not only do celebrated management teams have *underperforming* stocks, but mistrusted management teams have *outperforming* stocks, leading to an excellent arbitrage opportunity.

Combining several sentiment indexes together appears to create more robust signals. Equity curves that appear smooth in-sample remain so in forward-testing. This preliminary result may indicate that specific sentiment indices contain orthogonal value.

Researchers on the MarketPsych team have also identified strategies for augmenting standard value and momentum strategies with sentiment indexes. For example, market fear – long touted as a timing tool by value investors – also appears to augment value strategy returns in studies of long-only portfolios.

Beyond cross-sectional models, in internal studies decision trees and moving average cross-overs appear to generate both in-sample and out-of-sample outperformance. Possibly due to the nonlinear nature of sentiment data, traditional linear modelling techniques such as regression produce inferior results. It is notable that the cross-sectional models above typically show more extreme returns (and more volatility) when more extreme quantiles are selected (such as deciles).

The results above are the tip of the iceberg. The study of quantified sentiment and topic data is in its early stages. In the following years there is likely to be an explosion in further research as additional academics and practitioners become aware of the vast untapped potential in news- and social media-derived data.

Notes

[1] For example, Mattel is a "constituent" of MarketPsych's Nasdaq 100 index proxy asset (MPQQQ).

12.8 REFERENCES

1. Andersen, T. G., Bollerslev, T., Diebold, F. X. and Vega, C. (2002). Micro Effects of Macro Announcements: Real-Time Price Discovery in Foreign Exchange. PIER Working Paper No. 02-011. Available at SSRN: http://ssrn.com/abstract=312158.

2. Andritzky, J. R., Bannister, G. J. and Tamirisa, N. T. (2007). The Impact of Macroeconomic Announcements on Emerging Market Bonds. *Emerging Markets Review, 8*(1), pp. 20-37.

3. Bartov, E., Mohanram, P. S. and Seethamraju, C. (2002). Valuation of Internet Stocks — an IPO Perspective. *Journal of Accounting Research, 40*(2).

4. Bjørnskov, C. (2012). How Does Social Trust Affect Economic Growth? *Southern Economic Journal, 78*(4), pp. 1346-1368.

5. Buffett, W. (1979). You Pay A Very High Price In The Stock Market For A Cheery Consensus. *Forbes Magazine*.

6. Bushman, B.J. (2002). Does Venting Anger Feed or Extinguish the Flame? Catharsis, Rumination, Distraction, Anger, and Aggressive Responding. *Personality and Social Psychology Bulletin, 28*(6), pp. 724-731.

7. Da, Z., Engelberg, J. and Gao, P. (2011). The Sum of All FEARS: Investor Sentiment and Asset Prices. Available at SSRN: http://ssrn.com/abstract=1509162.

8. Davis, A. K., Piger, J. M. and Sedor, L. M. (2011). Beyond the Numbers: Measuring the Information Content of Earnings Press Release Language. AAA 2008 Financial Accounting and Reporting Section (FARS) Paper. Available at SSRN: http://ssrn.com/abstract=875399.

9. Diamond, D.M., Campbell, A.M., Park, C.R., Halonen, J., and Zoladz, P.R. (2007). The Temporal Dynamics Model of Emotional Memory Processing: A Synthesis on the Neurobiological Basis of Stress-Induced Amnesia, Flashbulb and Traumatic Memories, and the Yerkes-Dodson Law. *Neural Plasticity*.

10. Doukas, J.A., Antoniou, C. and Subrahmanyam, A. (2012). Sentiment and Momentum. Available at SSRN: http://ssrn.com/abstract=1479197.

11.

12. Engelberg, J and Parsons, C. (2011). The Causal Impact of Media in Financial Markets. *Journal of Finance, 66*(1), pp. 67–97.

13. Engelberg, J., Sasseville, C. and Williams, J. (2010). Market Madness? The Case of Mad Money. Available at SSRN: http://ssrn.com/abstract=870498.

14. Erbas, S.N. and Abbas, M. (2007). The Equity Premium Puzzle, Ambiguity Aversion, and Institutional Quality. IMF Working Papers, 1-58. Available at SSRN: http://ssrn.com/abstract=1019684.

15. Fan, R., Zhao, J. Chen, Y. and Xu, K. (2014). Anger is More Influential Than Joy: Sentiment Correlation in Weibo. PLoS ONE 9(10): e110184.

16. Frank, M.Z. and Antweiler, W. (2001). Is All That Talk Just Noise? The Information Content of Internet Stock Message Boards. AFA 2002 Atlanta Meetings, Sauder School of Business Working Paper. Available at SSRN: http://ssrn.com/abstract=282320.

17. Garretta, I, Kamstra, M.J. and Kramer, L.A. (2005). Winter blues and time variation in the price of risk. *Journal of Empirical Finance, 12*, pp. 291– 316.

18. Guidolin, M. and La Ferrara, E. (2005). The Economic Effects of Violent Conflict: Evidence from Asset Market Reactions. Available at SSRN: http://ssrn.com/abstract=825889.

19. Hirschleifer, D. and Subrahmanyam, A. (1999). Investor Psychology and Security Under- and Overreactions. *Journal of Finance, 53*(6), pp. 1839-1885.

20. Knight, F.H. (1921). *Risk, Uncertainty, and Profit*. Boston, MA, USA: Hart, Schaffner & Marx, Houghton Mifflin Company.

21. Lerner, J. S. and Keltner, D. (2000). Beyond Valence: Toward a Model of Emotion-Specific Influences on Judgment and Choice. *Cognition and Emotion, 14*, pp. 473–493.

22. Lerner, J. S. and Keltner, D. (2001). Fear, Anger, and Risk. *Journal of Personality and Social Psychology, 81*, pp. 146–159.

23. Lerner, J. S., Small, D. A. and Loewenstein, G. (2004). Heart Strings and Purse Strings: Carry-over Effects of Emotions on Economic Transactions. *Psychological Science, 15*, pp. 337–341.

24. Loewenstein, G. and Lerner, J.S. (2003). The Role of Affect in Decision Making. In R. Davidson, H. Goldsmith, and K. Scherer (eds.), *Handbook of Affective Science*. Oxford: Oxford University Press.

25. Malmendier, U. and Tate, G. (2009). Superstar CEOs. *Quarterly Journal of Economics, 124(4)*, pp. 1593-1638.

27. Odean, T., Lin, S., and Andrade, E. (2012). Bubbling with Excitement: An Experiment. Available at SSRN: http://ssrn.com/abstract=2024549.

28. Russell, J. A. (1980). A Circumplex Model of Affect. *Journal of Personality and Social Psychology, 39*(6), pp. 1161-1178.

29. Schwabe, L. and Wolf, O.T. (2009). Stress Prompts Habit Behavior in Humans. *The Journal of Neuroscience, 3(29)*, pp. 7191-7198.

30. Sinha, N R. (2010). Underreaction to News in the US Stock Market. Available at SSRN: http://ssrn.com/abstract=1572614.

31. Stambaugh, R.F., Yu, J. and Yuan, Y. (2011). The Short of It: Investor Sentiment and Anomalies. *Journal of Financial Economics, 104,* pp. 288-302.

32. Tetlock, P. (2007). Giving Content to Investor Sentiment: The Role of Media in the Stock Market. *The Journal of Finance, 62(3).*

33. Tetlock, P.C., Saar-Tsechansky, M. and Macskassy, S. (2007). More than Words: Quantifying Language to Measure Firms' Fundamentals. 9th Annual Texas Finance Festival. Available at SSRN: http://ssrn.com/abstract=923911.

34. Trueman, B., Wong, F. M. H. and Zhang, X.J. (2003). Anomalous Stock Returns around Internet Firms' Earnings Announcements. *Journal of Accounting and Economics, 34(1),* pp. 249–271.

35. Winkielman, P., Berridge, K.C. and Wilbarger, J.L. (2005). Unconscious affective reactions to masked happy versus angry faces influence consumption behavior and judgments of value. *Personality and Social Psychology Bulletin, 31(1),* pp. 121-35.

36. Winkielman, P., Knutson, B., Paulus, M. and Trujillo, J. (2007). Affective Influence on Judgments and Decisions: Moving Towards Core Mechanism. *Review of General Psychology, 11(2),* pp. 179–192.

37. Yerkes, R.M. and Dodson, J.D. (1908). The relation of strength of stimulus to rapidity of habit-formation. *Journal of Comparative Neurology and Psychology, 18,* pp. 459–482.

38. Zak, P. J. and Knack, S. (2001). Trust and Growth. *Economic Journal, Royal Economic Society, 111(470),* pp. 295-321.

CHAPTER 13

An Impact Measure for News:
its use in (daily) trading strategies

Xiang Yu, *Researcher, OptiRisk Systems*

Gautam Mitra, *Visiting Professor, UCL, and CEO, OptiRisk Systems*

Cristiano Arbex-Valle, *Senior Software Engineer & Consultant, OptiRisk Systems*

Tilman Sayer, *Senior Quant Research Analyst, OptiRisk Systems*

ABSTRACT

We investigate how "news sentiment" in general and the "impact of news" in particular can be utilised in designing equity trading strategies. News is an event that moves the market in a small way or a big way. We have introduced a derived measure of news impact score which takes into consideration news flow and decay of sentiment. Since asset behaviour is characterised by return, volatility and liquidity we first consider a predictive analytic model in which market data and impact scores are the inputs and also the independent variables of the model. We finally describe the trading strategies which take into consideration the three important characteristics of an asset, namely, return, volatility and liquidity. The minute-bar market data as well as intraday news sentiment metadata have been provided by Thomson Reuters.

13.1 INTRODUCTION

13.1.1 Why sentiment analysis

A major plank in the development and application of behavioural finance is the consideration of bounded rationality as introduced by Nobel laureate Herb Simon (Simon, 1964). It follows from the theme of bounded rationality and later works of behavioural theorists/economists, Kahneman and Tverskey, Sheffrin, Shiller that human beings in general and retail investors in particular are influenced by various psychological imperatives of "fear, greed and exuberance". This is in sharp contrast with the postulates of neoclassical theories of rational economic behaviour and scrupulous application of logic in decision-making. Thus behavioural finance in many ways determines the risk attitudes and the investment goals of the (high net worth) individuals: so called HNIs who account for the majority of the invested wealth.

The neoclassical finance theory had embraced the efficient market hypothesis (EMH) which has become the cornerstone of investment science. The doubts about EMH and recent surge of interest in behavioural finance (Kahneman and Tversky, 1979; Kahneman, 2002; Shefrin, 2008) not only opened the debate and exposed the limits of EMH but also reinforced the important role of sentiment and investor psychology in market behaviour. The central tenet of EMH is information arrival, that is, news is rapidly digested by rational stakeholders; yet the work of Shiller (2000), Hais (2010), and Barber and Odean (2008) reinforce the irrational contrarian and herd behaviour of the investors. Today the availability of sophisticated computer systems facilitating high frequency trading (Goodhart and O'Hara, 1997) as well as access to automated analysis of news feeds (Tetlock, 2007; Mitra and Mitra, 2011) set the backdrop for computer automated trading which is enhanced by news. How investment strategies may harness sentiment of news events and also that of the market continue to be actively studied and reported by researchers in the investment community (Kahn, Dion, Brar, Hafez). Also see "Inside the Investor's Brain" (Wiley, 2007) by Richard Peterson. In this study we investigate how "news sentiment" in general and the "impact of news" in particular can be utilised in designing equity trading strategies.

13.1.2 Characterising Asset Behaviour

The majority of research on asset behaviour has focused on analysing historical market data and the construction of models which fit the data and best represent the true information held in such datasets. The key features studied in these models are return and volatility of stock price, which are considered in the decision-making stage of trading. In this report, however, we introduce two further (novel) concepts with a view to enhance these classical methods. Firstly, our model looks at three characteristics of an asset, namely return, volatility and liquidity. The consideration of liquidity, the additional feature, provides knowledge on the condition of markets and more importantly indicates whether a profitable signal can be successfully executed or not. Simply being able to determine a profitable position in the markets, through observation of stock price return and volatility, is not sufficient if in fact the actual trade is not available. Secondly, the investigational dataset is expanded with the incorporation of news sentiment metadata in addition to the historical market data. The datasets are fused together to form two intraday time series on a minute bar scale. This data fusion enables us to construct an enhanced predictive analytics model for three parameters which characterise asset price behaviour.

The asset price parameters have traditionally been represented by two methods: predictive modelling and explanatory modelling. One of the most well-known explanatory models is the factor model (Fama and French, 1992). They capture return by extending the Capital Asset Pricing Model (CAPM), which was independently proposed by Treynor (1961), Sharpe (1964), Lintner (1965), and Mossin (1966), to include market capitalisation size and book-to-market ratio as explanatory factors. Such types of models can be categorised in three groups, namely macroeconomic, fundamental and statistical factor models, depending on the choice and nature of these factors and how the respective models are calibrated. Although factor models have dominated this field of finance, a weakness is their failure to quickly update changes in market conditions. The structure of these models is only single-period, inhibiting the incorporation of relevant past information at a sufficient speed. Parameters are updated through calibration but only at a slow pace where the model adapts. Mitra, Mitra and diBartolomeo (2009) have shown how the incorporation of news enhances the results of factor models and leads to an early prediction of changes in volatility. We believe that news sentiment should also be considered as an explanatory factor in the pricing of assets and therefore return. However, our approach turns to another class of models that better predict volatility in a time-varying framework – generalised autoregressive conditional heteroskedasticity (GARCH) models.

By incorporating the additional factor of news sentiment in GARCH models, the near term volatility can be estimated using past news events over many periods. This near term estimation may be obtained using a number of alternative predictive models. Established models in this class are linear regression models (Stambaugh, 1999; Robertson and Wright, 2009), autoregressive (AR) models, moving average (MA) models and generalised autoregressive conditional heteroskedasticity (GARCH) (Bollerslev, 1986) models for volatility in particular. Our work utilises the family of AR and GARCH models within which news sentiment is introduced as an exogenous variable. Among the many applications of predictive modelling, the construction of preliminary stages to scenario generation is the most common practice. In the context of financial assets, scenario generators for possible movements in stock price are formed from a predictive model for stock price.

Research studies which address the relationship between stock price movements and news sentiment have been growing in recent years (Tetlock, 2007; Barber and Odean 2008; Mitra, Mitra and diBartolomeo 2009; Leinweber and Sisk, 2009; Sinha, 2011). The earliest work that incorporates news articles in the influence of stock prices dates back to Niederhoffer (1971), where the font size of news print was used to determine the relative importance of news events and measure how they affected the stock market. Later, news was categorised into scheduled and non-scheduled news with researchers exploring their effects on stock returns and volatility respectively (Lee, 1992; Engle, 1998). Tetlock (2007) was one of the first to use merely news sentiment data as a comparison to the movement in stock prices and trading activity.

13.1.3   Role of Liquidity in Asset Behaviour

Traditionally, research on asset behaviour has focused on the study of two main features, namely, stock price and volatility of stock prices. Since the financial crisis of 2008 with the collapse of Lehman Brothers and the subsequent banking crisis and bank bailouts in the UK and other European countries the importance of liquidity has become paramount and is widely acknowledged by the finance community. Another implication of the financial crisis has been that regulators have imposed stricter liquidity requirements for banks, especially those active in the low-latency trading activities (Gomber et al. 2011; AFM 2010). So for trading activities, the availability of liquidity to traders and brokers is of paramount importance. Hence many of the recent studies involving the impact of news consider the implication on liquidity. For instance, Gross-Klaussman and Hautsch (2011) use the bid-ask spread, trading volume and market depth as proxies for liquidity, with results showing greater increase of bid-ask spreads during news releases as opposed to market depth, which does not differ much. Furthermore, Riordan, Storkenmaier et al. (2013) found that liquidity increases with news releases that have positive or neutral sentiment whereas negative news sentiment gives a corresponding decrease in liquidity.

It is well accepted in the trading community that liquidity has the role of monitoring market conditions and assessing the viability of orders decided by trading algorithms by taking into consideration the spread and the depth of the market. Given that margin requirement is an important and defining aspect of trading it can be argued that liquidity is an important determinant in deriving trading strategies and should be introduced as a parameter in predictive models that characterise asset behaviour. There are a variety of definitions which explain the role and measure of liquidity mainly in the context of trading. Spread measures view liquidity from the point of the cost that one has to bear for immediate trade, in other words the viability of orders, and typical measures include the effective spread and the bid-ask spread. Depth measures consider liquidity as the effect of large orders on a particular asset, hence looking at market conditions, and are often measured using traded volume, order volume or Kyle's λ (Kyle, 1985). A short but comprehensive discussion of liquidity measures is given in chapter 13 of Mitra, Yu et al. (2015).

13.1.4   Modelling Architecture and Choice of Assets

In our investigation, two different datasets are used. We (i) consider the predictive models and investigate whether the additional information stream of news metadata improves the results of the predictive models. A selection of five assets from the Finance industry is used to test the models in an intraday setting for the year 2008. We then (ii) use the results of the predictive model to construct a daily trading strategy which uses the "Kelly Criterion". As we have already stated, according to earlier findings of one of the authors, Mitra and Mitra (2011), using news metadata leads to earlier and superior prediction of volatility. The Kelly Criterion uses volatility (see volatility pumping by Luenberger (1997)) to compute the "trading bets"; therefore we use this approach to determine our daily equity trading strategy. The FTSE100 index and its constituents are considered in our investigation for the years 2013 and 2014. The experimental platform can easily be adapted for higher-frequency lower-latency trading. It can equally be adapted for automated trading of other asset classes.

13.1.5   Outline of the paper

The rest of the paper is organised as follows: in section 13.2 we discuss the data instances that are used in our study. In section 13.3 we describe the key measures that we have used. First the return, volatility and liquidity measures are introduced. Then we define sentiment measures and in particular the positive and negative sentiment measures. Using accumulation and decay of sentiment we derive the positive and negative impact scores. Finally we introduce an approximation whereby we determine the number of past news items we may need to consider. In section 13.4 we set out the predictive models which describe price, volatility and liquidity of assets. Computational results for the predictive volatility model are also given. In section 13.5 we describe a daily trading strategy that is based on Kelly's betting formula. In this section we also report the results of applying the strategy to equities taken from the FTSE100 index. A summary of our findings and conclusions is presented in section 13.6.

13.2 DATA

Our modelling architecture uses two streams of time series data: (i) the market data which is given at the minute bar level as well as daily frequency, and includes bid price, ask price and the execution price, (ii) news metadata as supplied by Thomson Reuters.

13.2.1 Market Data

Both daily and intraday prices are used in this chapter, for testing the trading strategy and predictive models respectively. The data fields of the market data are set out in Table 13.2.1. The trading strategy (in section 13.5) is tested on the entire asset universe of FTSE100.

Table 13.2.1: Description of all the data fields for a company in the market data.

Data Field	Field Name	Description
1	13RIC	Reuters instrument code individually assigned to each company.
2	Date	In the format DD-MM-YYYY.
3	Time	In the format hh:mm:ss, given to the nearest minute.
4	GMT Offset	Difference from Greenwich Mean Time.
5	Type	Type of market data – in this case "Intraday 1 min"
6	Last	Last prices for the corresponding minute
7	Close Bid	Close bid prices for the corresponding minute
8	Close Ask	Close ask prices for the corresponding minute

The high frequency intraday market data, used for the predictive models, is compiled on a minute-bar scale for a selection of 5 assets from the Finance sector (AIG, Barclays, Bank of America, HSBC and JP Morgan). These companies have been chosen because of their large market capitalisation, which guarantees a wide coverage of news. As a consequence, we are able to generate a sufficient number of data points in the time series of news metadata.

We extract the data from 08:00 to 18:30 each day to make up a **trading day** such that pre-trade and post-trade hours are included; thus any news event (and the corresponding sentiment) captured outside of trading hours is incorporated into our predictive model and any loss of information is avoided (impact of news).

13.2.2   Sentiment and News Metadata

News analytics data is presented in the well established metadata format whereby a news event is given tags of relevance, novelty and sentiment (scores) for a given individual asset. The analytical process of computing such scores is fully automated from collecting, extracting, aggregating, to categorising and scoring. The result is an individual score assigned to each news article for each characteristic using scales from 0 to 100 or probabilities. Although we use intraday news data, for a given asset the number of news stories, hence data points, is variable and does not match the time frequencies of market data. The attributes of news stories used in our study are Relevance and Sentiment.

The news metadata for the chosen assets were selected under the filter of relevance score, that is, any news item that had a relevance score under the value of 70 was ignored and not included in the dataset. This ensured with a high degree of certainty that the sentiment scores to be used are indeed focused on the chosen asset and not simply a mention in the news for comparison purposes, for example.

The final preparation task for the data is to align the frequency of sentiment scores to the trading hours of 08:00-18:30. Any news item released before or after these trading times was summed and bucketed in the next time period, which may be the following day. As a consequence, there is no discarding of news sentiment which could be influencing the price and return thus, not a single piece of news data is ignored.

13.3   MEASURES: RETURN, VOLATILITY, LIQUIDITY, SENTIMENT AND IMPACT

13.3.1   Return, Volatility and Liquidity Measures

With the raw market data that is provided to us, we are able to calculate asset behaviour measures using close prices, bid prices and ask prices.

Bucket Size = 1 minute; Data Frequency = Minute Bar.

The **trading day** starts at 08:00 hours and ends at 18:30 hours, thus in a trading day the total number of buckets is 630.

Any news and sentiment retrieved overnight (between 18:31 and 07:59 the following day) is put in the first time bucket of the following day, i.e. 08:00. The same applies to weekend news, which is aggregated over both days and considered in the first minute when trading is resumed. This method of categorisation reflects our belief that reactions to news are reflected in stock price movements immediately or even days after release.

Return

The return measure that we use in the model is the log-return calculated by the following equation

$$R_t = Log(P_t) - Log(P_{t-1})$$ [13.3.1]

where is the close price at time t.

Volatility

The volatility measure used in the model is calculated as a rolling standard deviation of log returns for one **trading day** leading to 630 data points.

Liquidity

Liquidity is represented by the spread of the bid and ask prices, which measures the cost one has to bear for immediate trade. Equation 13.3.2 gives the expression for bid-ask spread.

$$Spread = \frac{Ask - Bid}{Mid}$$ [13.3.2]

where *Mid* is the mid-price between the bid and ask prices.

13.3.2 Sentiment Measure

In our analytical model we have introduced two concepts, namely (i) sentiment score and (ii) impact score. The sentiment score is a quantification of the mood (of a typical investor) in respect of a news event. The impact score takes into consideration the decay of the sentiment of one or more news events and how after aggregation these impact on the asset behaviour.

Sentiment Score

Thomson Reuters' news sentiment engine analyses and processes each news story that arrives as a machine-readable text. Through text analysis and other classification schemes the engine then computes for each news event: (i) relevance, (ii) entity recognition and (iii) sentiment probabilities, as well as a few other attributes (see Mitra and Mitra, 2011). A news event sentiment can be positive, neutral or negative and the classifier assigns probabilities such that

$$Prob(positive) + Prob(neutral) + Prob(negative) = 1.0$$ [13.3.3]

We turn these three probabilities into a single sentiment score in the range +50 to -50 using the following equation:

$$Sent = 100 * \left(Prob(positive) + \frac{1}{2}Prob(neutral)\right) - 50$$ [13.3.4]

where denotes a single transformed sentiment score. We find that such a derived single score provides a relatively better interpretation of the mood of the news item. Thus the news sentiment score is a relative number which describes the degree of positivity and negativity in a piece of news. During the trading day, as news arrives it is given a sentiment value. Given that

$$-50 \leq Sent \leq 50$$

for a given news item, k, at the time bucket t_k, we define $PNews(k,t_k)$ and $NNews(k,t_k)$ as the sentiment of the kth news (see following section).

13.3.3 Impact Score

It is well known from research studies that news flow affects asset behaviour (Patton and Verardo, 2012; Mitra, Mitra and diBartolomeo, 2009). Therefore, accumulation of news items as they arrive is important. Patton and Verardo (2012) noticed decay in the impact of news on asset prices and their betas on a daily timescale and further determine the complete disappearance of news effects within 2 to 5 days. This was also observed in Arbex-Valle, Erlwein-Sayer et al. (2013); Mitra, Mitra and diBartolomeo (2009) created a composite sentiment score in their volatility models after initial experiments revealed no effect on volatility predictions with sentiment alone; the decay period in this study was over 7 days.

In order to compute the impact of news events over time, we first find an expression which describes the attenuation of the news sentiment score. The impact of a news item does not solely have an effect on the markets at the time of release; the impact also persists over finite periods of time that follow. To account for this prolonged impact, we have applied an attenuation technique to reflect the instantaneous impact of news releases and the decay of this impact over a subsequent period of time. The technique combines exponential decay and accumulation of the sentiment score over a given time bucket under observation. We take into consideration the attenuation of positive sentiment to the neutral value and the rise of negative sentiment also to the neutral value and accumulate (sum) these sentiment scores separately. The separation of the positive and negative sentiment scores is logical, as this avoids cancellation effects. For instance, cancellation reduces the news flow and an exact cancellation leads to the misinterpretation of no news.

News arrives asynchronously; depending on the nature of sentiment it creates, we classify it in three categories, namely, positive, neutral and negative. For the purpose of deriving impact measures, we only consider the positive and negative news items.

Let

POS denote the set of news with positive sentiment value *Sent* >0;
NEG denote the set of news with negative sentiment value *Sent* <0;

and

PNews(k,t_k) denote the sentiment value of the kth positive news arriving at time bucket t_k, $1 \leq t_k \leq 630$ and $k \in$ *POS; PNews (k, t_k)< 0*.
NNews(k,t_k) denote the sentiment value of the kth negative news arriving at time bucket ,t_k, $1 \leq t_k \leq 630$ and $k \in$ *NEG; NNews (k, t_k)< 0*.

Let λ denote the exponent which determines the decay rate. We have chosen λ such that the sentiment value decays to half the initial value in a 90 minute time span. The cumulated positive and negative sentiment scores for one day are calculated as:

$$PImpact(t) = \sum_{\substack{k \in POS \\ t_k \leq t}} PNews(k, t_k)\, e^{-\lambda(t-1)} \qquad\qquad [13.3.6]$$

$$NImpact(t) = \sum_{\substack{k \in NEG \\ t_k \leq t}} NNews(k, t_k)\, e^{-\lambda(t-1)} \qquad\qquad [13.3.7]$$

In equations 13.3.6 and 13.3.7 for intraday *PImpact* and *NImpact*, t is in the range, $t = 1,\dots,630$. On the other hand for a given asset all the relevant news items which arrived in the past, in principle, have an impact for the asset. Hence, the range of t can be widened to consider past news, that is, news which is two or more days "old". We deal with this contingency by an approximation which is described in section 13.3.4. In Figure 13.3.1 we provide an illustration of how *PImpact (9,λ)* and *NImpact(9,λ)* are computed for the two positive news items (News.1 and News.3) and the negative news item (News.2) respectively.

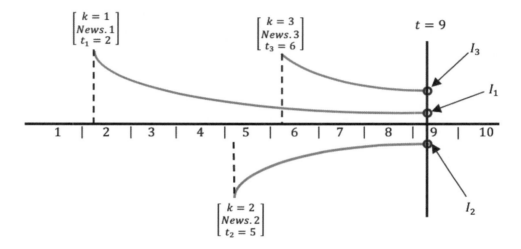

$$Impact\ of\ News.1 = I_1 = PNews(1,2)e^{-\lambda(9-2)}$$
$$Impact\ of\ News.2 = I_2 = NNews(2,5)e^{-\lambda(9-5)}$$
$$Impact\ of\ News.3 = I_3 = PNews(3,6)e^{-\lambda(9-6)}$$

Figure 13.3.1: *An illustration of how impact scores are calculated for individual news items that have positive or negative sentiment.*

The arrival of more news items leads to higher values of accumulation; this therefore takes into account the news intensity, that is, the news flow. The impact scores for JP Morgan during the month of August 2008 are illustrated in Figure 13.3.2 showing the positive and negative scores (with attenuation and accumulation).

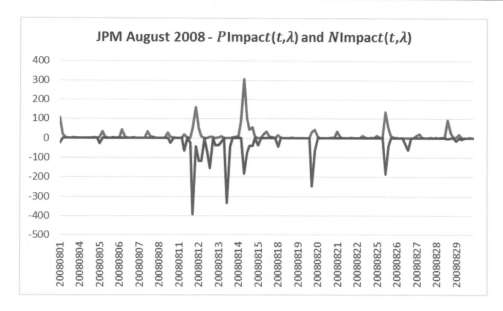

Figure 13.3.2: JP Morgan August 2008: News impact score (accumulated and aggregated) for positive (blue line) and negative (red line) sentiment respectively.

Moreover, the actual number of news volume across each time period can also be incorporated into the impact score, or a scaled-down measure of news volume. This impact measure is flexible to any number of variables being added to it, examples being news categories or market capitalisations. By incorporating these variables, more features about the news item and the particular asset are fed into the impact score to create a more informative measure.

13.3.4 Lookback Period: An Approximation

As set out in section 13.3.3, for a given asset all the past news items have an impact for the asset. Therefore, we define $T_{LBP}(t)$ as the number of past time buckets we need to consider looking back from the current time bucket t, such that the corresponding *PImpact* and *NImpact* computations will be an acceptable approximation controlled by threshold parameter θ. θ is the threshold expressed as the sentiment value that is considered large enough for inclusion in the impact computation for a given asset. This concept is illustrated in figure 13.3.3. The lookback period (LBP) is defined as the number of time buckets T_{LBP}.

Let

$$t_{LBP}^k = min(t - t_k)$$

[13.3.8]

where $PNews(k, t_k)e^{-\lambda(t-t_k)} \leq \theta$.
Therefore T_{LBP}^k is given by the expression

$$T_{LBP}^k = max_k\{t_{LBP}^k\}$$

[13.3.9]

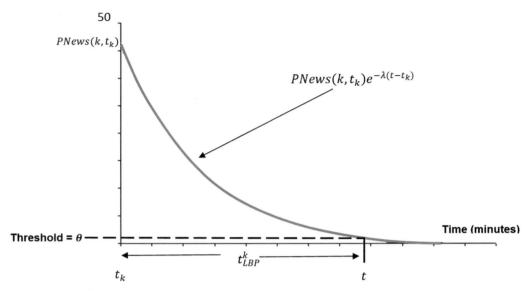

Figure 13.3.3: T_{LBP}^k *illustrated using a positive news item.*

In the case of negative sentiment value, the condition with respect to θ then becomes $NNews(k,t_k)e^{-\lambda(t-t_k)} \geq \theta$. So considering all the assets $i = 1,2,...,N$ in a given index we derive the LBP for the index as:

$$T_{LBP}^* = \max_i\{T_{LBP}(i)\}$$ [13.3.10]

where $T_{LBP}(i)$ is the LBP for asset i.

13.4 THE MODEL

13.4.1 Autoregressive and GARCH Models

Predictive analytical models for stock price return and volatility, such as the Autoregressive Conditional Heteroskedasticity ARCH model (Engle, 1982) and Generalised Autoregressive Conditional Heteroskedasticity GARCH model (Bollerslev, 1986), are well understood and extensively applied. These models utilise the techniques of time series analysis (Chatfield, 2009; Harvey, 1990) and are able to account for the correlation between each of the individual points in the time series of stock price returns by fitting them to models which are of Autoregressive (AR) nature. We have adopted this approach in the construction of our models for predicting return, volatility, and bid-ask spread. However, our method differs from ARCH/GARCH type models as it deals with two time series, (i) the first time series is that of market data and (ii) the second time series is the news metadata. ' T_{LBP}^k pproach can be seen as an extension of GARCH and AR models with the variable of news sentiment being the innovative addition. Another feature that distinguishes this from existing predictive models is the joint modelling of three key variables describing asset behaviour, namely return, volatility and liquidity, whereas the majority of existing literature focuses on only one variable, either return or volatility (Kothari,

Zimmerman 1995; French, Schwert, Stambaugh 1987). We believe that apart from the classic measures of return and volatility that need to be evaluated and monitored for risk control and trading strategies, it is now also imperative to include a liquidity measure as this reflects the conditions of the markets and the feasibility of trades. This can be determined from two perspectives: (i) the spread of the market, evaluated by the bid-ask spread, and (ii) the depth of the market, computed by the total volume of bids and asks. We set out below a detailed description of the model:

Asset Return

Taking into consideration the inclusion of two time series, we construct an AR(2) predictive model for return with the enhancement of a news impact score (see section 13.3.3).

Let R_t be the log return of stock prices at time period t

R_{t-i} be the log return of stock prices by lag i

$PImpact_{t-1}$ be the positive news impact score of the previous time interval

$NImpact_{t-1}$ be the negative news impact score of the previous time interval

θ_i be the weighting coefficients to be estimated

e_t be the error term

Therefore, the log-return is given by the expression,

$$R_t = \theta_0 + \theta_1 R_{t-1} + \theta_2 R_{t-2} + \theta_3 PImpact_{t-1} + \theta_4 NImpact_{t-1} + e_t \qquad [13.4.1]$$

Asset Volatility

The prediction model for volatility is an extended GARCH (1,1) model, as before with the addition of a news impact score.

Let σ_t^2 be the squared volatility at time t

ϵ_{t-1}^2 be the lagged log-return residuals

σ_{t-1}^2 be the lagged squared volatility

$PImpact_{t-1}$ be the positive news impact score of the previous time interval

$NImpact_{t-1}$ be the negative news impact score of the previous time interval

$\alpha_i, \beta_1, \omega_i$ be the weighting coefficients to be estimated

u_t be the error term

Therefore, σ_t^2 is given by the expression,

$$\sigma_t^2 = \alpha_o + \alpha_1 \epsilon_{t-1}^2 + \beta_1 \sigma_{t-1}^2 + \omega_1 PImpact_{t-1} + \omega_2 NImpact_{t-1} + u_t \qquad [13.4.2]$$

Asset Liquidity

We measure the liquidity of the chosen asset by the bid-ask spread by constructing an AR(3) model with the addition of the news impact score.

Let S_t be the bid-ask spread at time t

S_{t-1} be the bid-ask spreads at lag i

$PImpact_{t-1}$ be the positive news impact score of the previous time interval

$NImpact_{t-1}$ be the negative news impact score of the previous time interval

γ_i be the weighting coefficients to be estimated

n_t be the error term

The model for S_t is as follows:

$$S_t = \gamma_o + \gamma_1 S_{t-1} + \gamma_2 S_{t-2} + \gamma_3 S_{t-3} + \gamma_4 PImpact_{t-1} + \gamma_5 NImpact_{t-1} + \eta_t \qquad [13.4.3]$$

13.4.2 Computational Results

Extensive tests have been carried out on the predictive models for return, volatility and liquidity. Highly significant results were found for the extended GARCH model, some of which are displayed below (see Table 13.4.1). The performance of the autoregressive models for return and liquidity is not substantial enough to conclude that news sentiment certainly improves prediction. In this chapter, we only present results for volatility prediction because they are in line with later sections about trading strategies. In fact, the better performance of GARCH enhanced with news sentiment is utilised to create a profitable trading strategy. For results on asset return and liquidity, see Yu et al. (2013).

From the fitting of the models it can be seen that news sentiment does indeed have an effect on the prediction of volatility as all coefficient estimates are non-zero. The small magnitude of news impact coefficients does not mean that they are insignificant. This is due to the large magnitude of news impact scores which have been aggregated over time.

Table 13.4.1: *Estimated coefficients for the 5 chosen assets.*

Asset	Parameter	
AIG	α_0: -6.921e^{-6} α_1: 5.325e^{-2} β_1: 8.994e^{-1}	w_1: 1.126e^{-6} w_2: 6.311e^{-7}
Bank of America	α_0: -5.652e^{-7} α_1: 5.072e^{-2} β_1: 8.997e^{-1}	w_1: 1.021e^{-7} w_2: 1.625e^{-7}
Barclays	α_0: -7.561e^{-7} α_1: 5.278e^{-2} β_1: 9.233e^{-1}	w_1: 3.480e^{-7} w_2: 4.510e^{-7}
HSBC	α_0: -4.655e^{-7} α_1: 4.667e^{-2} β_1: 9.278e^{-1}	w_1: 1.329e^{-7} w_2: 1.753e^{-7}
JP Morgan	α_0: -1.543e^{-6} α_1: 5.059e^{-2} β_1: 9.002e^{-1}	w_1: 1.539e^{-7} w_2: 2.451e^{-8}

To understand the extent to which news impact enhances the results of these models, we use the fitted model to predict out-of-sample values. The out-of-sample period is taken as January to March 2009. The conclusions interpreted from out-of-sample results are that news-enhanced predictive models do better predict future values of liquidity and volatility but not for stock returns. Therefore, the inclusion of news sentiment to a predictive model, in the form of an impact score, does increase accuracy of predictions of volatility. Once again, only results for volatility are shown below. See Yu et al. (2013) for further results on liquidity and returns.

Table 13.4.2: *Out-of-sample statistics for the five chosen assets.*

Asset	RMSE	MAE
AIG	2.685e^{-3}	1.803e^{-3}
Bank of America	1.103e^{-3}	7.89e^{-4}
Barclays	1.419e^{-2}	9.89e^{-4}
HSBC	3.641e^{-3}	7.75e^{-4}
JP Morgan	6.431e^{-4}	5.11e^{-4}

As shown in Table 13.4.2, all assets performed better in the news-enhanced GARCH model. Therefore, the inclusion of news sentiment as an exogenous variable to the univariate GARCH model significantly reduces prediction errors and also estimates values far closer to the true values of volatility.

13.5 DAILY TRADING STRATEGY

We use the results of the predictive models to define and test a daily trading strategy. We first set out the motivation as well as the rationale of our approach. As already reported, including news (impact) as an additional independent variable in the prediction of volatility significantly improves the accuracy in prediction. This conclusion is also reported by a number of other researchers (Patton and Verardo, 2012; Arbex-Valle, Erlwein-Sayer et al, 2013; Mitra, Mitra and diBartolomeo, 2009). We have therefore set out to explore the effectiveness of applying the Kelly criterion, which is based on harnessing volatility in deriving betting strategies. The underlying principles are based on the concepts (i) log optimal growth and (ii) volatility pumping, as explained by Luenberger (1997). The mathematical methods underpinning the approach are presented in section 13.5.1, along with an example, and the results of our prototype (experimental) investigation are presented in section 13.5.2.

The fact that news and the included sentiment improve the estimation of the mean and volatility of the asset returns can be employed in various ways. Here, we want to focus on the log-optimal investment strategy, based on the Kelly criterion; see MacLean et al. (2011) and Luenberger (1997).

13.5.1 Log return and the Kelly Criterion

Kelly (1956) was one of the first to use logarithmic utility in gambling and repeated investment problems. The strategy maximizes the long run growth rate of the investment and is myopic in the sense that current investment decisions depend only on the current distribution of returns.

To understand the basic principle behind the strategy, consider the long run growth rate G which is defined as,

$$G = \lim_{N \to \infty} \frac{1}{N} \log\left(\frac{W_N}{W_0}\right),$$ [13.5.1]

where W_0 is the initial wealth and W_N is the wealth after N successive investments. Let p and $(1-p)$ denote the corresponding success and failure probabilities of the bets (trades). Then the terminal wealth of an investor after N trades, is

$$W_N = W_0(1+f)^M (1-f)^{N-M},$$ [13.5.2]

where f is the constant fraction of wealth wagered in each bet (trade) and M is the number of games won. Combining the two expressions, we obtain

$$G = \lim_{N \to \infty} \frac{M}{N} \log(1+f) + \frac{N-M}{N} \log(1-f),$$ [13.5.3]

which approaches $G = p\log(1+f) + (1-p)\log(1-f)$ almost certainly as n tends to infinity.

According to the independent nature of Bernoulli trials, maximising G is hence equivalent to maximising $E(W) = p\log(1+f) + (1-p)\log(1-f)$ that is, maximising the expected logarithmic utility of each bet (trade).

The optimal fraction f^* is calculated to be $f^* = 2p-1$, which is the expected gain per trial. Note that if the payoff is +b if the bet is won, the solution changes to $f^* = \dfrac{p(b+1)-1}{b}$

In contrast to maximising expected logarithmic utility, maximising simply the expected value of the game will lead to bankruptcy for the investor. This is because she is advised to invest all her capital in a game which is favourable. However, obviously, if this game is lost, all her money is gone.

Due to the constant fraction that is wagered in each game the absolute amount bet is monotone increasing in wealth and the investor never risks complete ruin. However, the fraction might be very large, especially if the wager is favourable and the risk is small. Besides, according to Thorp (1971), the Kelly portfolio does not necessarily lie on the efficient frontier in a mean-variance model.

13.5.2 Experimental Trading Results

We have investigated a daily trading strategy based on the "Kelly Criterion" for a subset of assets (equities) taken from the FTSE100 index for the two calendar years 2013 and 2014. The levels of news flow for the constituents of the FTSE100 were analysed and put on a ranking. The asset universe for the trading portfolio comprised of cash (at a risk free-rate of 2%), FTSE100 index future and four assets, namely, Barclays, Vodafone, BP and HSBC. These four constituents were chosen on the basis of ranked news flow intensity; they were also the most traded and had high capitalizations. In order to establish the advantages, or otherwise, of using news sentiment and news impact we have studied the results of applying this strategy for 'market data' only time series and 'market data' plus 'news metadata' time series.

In these experiments, rebalancing of the portfolio occurs daily, therefore, a new prediction of returns and volatility is computed every day using the previous 800 days (in-sample period) of daily returns and the corresponding 'news metadata'. The impact scores computed using the formula given in section 13.3.3 are incorporated in these predictions.

The FTSE100 index is chosen as the benchmark with which our trading strategies are compared. The period (2013-2014) for which we test the trading strategy is fairly lacklustre for FTSE100 index; it cannot be classified either as bull or bear regime. The two-year return was a meagre 11%. Additionally, a major criticism of Kelly is that the corresponding strategy tends to "bet" large amounts (in relation to the trade portfolio value). This approach is disliked by "risk-averse" investors. For this reason, a scaled down version is introduced, called partial Kelly. In the experiments we have compared and contrasted trade portfolios which

    i.   use full Kelly criterion with only market data
    ii.   use partial Kelly criterion with only market data
              -50% partial Kelly
              -30% partial Kelly
    iii.   use full Kelly criterion with market data and news impact measure
    iv.   use partial Kelly criterion with market data and news impact measure

        - 50% partial Kelly

        - 30% partial Kelly

The charts which display the behaviour of the benchmark and trading strategies (ii)...(v) are shown in Figures 13.5.1 and 13.5.2. Risk-averse approaches are covered with strategies (iii) and (v). The corresponding performance summaries are set out in Table 13.5.1. Use of news sentiment and the corresponding benefit of accurate early prediction of volatility is easily seen from the figures and tables.

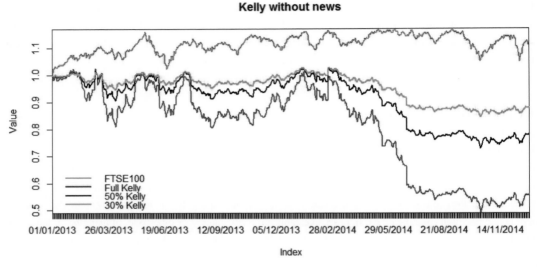

Figure 13.5.1: *Performance of FTSE100, full Kelly criterion and partial Kelly criterion strategies without the incorporation of news impact measures for the years 2013-2014.*

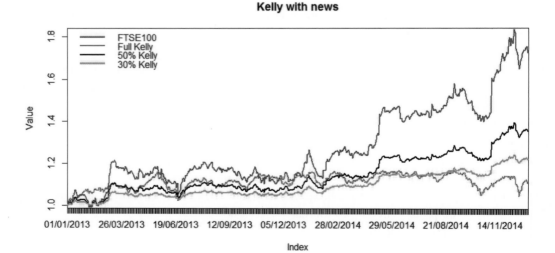

Figure 13.5.2: *Performance of FTSE100, full Kelly criterion and partial Kelly criterion strategies with news impact measures for the years 2013-2014.*

The mean and standard deviation of portfolio returns are presented for all seven strategies in Table 13.5.1. Maximum drawdown is computed as the maximum peak-to-trough decline during any time of the whole period. The drawdown is quoted as the percentage between the peak and the trough. For the strategies that do not include news sentiment data, the corresponding portfolio performances are far worse in terms of profitability and risk. On the other hand, the set of strategies which incorporate news sentiment metadata not only beat the performance of the benchmark, but also give better values for down-side risk. In particular, the partial Kelly strategies with news have the most favourable properties in terms of Sharpe ratio, Sortino ratio and maximum drawdown. Although the full Kelly strategy with news obtains the highest returns, due to the large positions suggested by the strategy, it also involves a high level of risk.

Table 13.5.1: Summary statistics for all the strategies tested from 2013-2014.

Portfolio	Final Value	Mean returns	St. Dev. Returns	Excess RFR (%)	Sharpe Ratio	Sortino Ratio	Max draw-down (%)	Max. rec. Days
FTSE100	1.11	-	-	3.46	0.28	0.39	11.86	195
Full Kelly, no news	0.56	-0.00096	0.0186	-26.79	-1.03	-1.36	52.03	465
50% Kelly, no news	0.78	-0.00044	0.0093	-13.44	-0.96	-1.28	29.12	241
30% Kelly, no news	0.88	-0.00023	0.0056	-8.04	-0.93	-1.25	18.00	241
Full Kelly with news	1.73	0.00116	0.0134	28.99	1.19	1.99	13.16	213
50% Kelly with news	1.36	0.00062	0.0067	14.25	1.24	2.09	6.43	102
30% Kelly with news	1.22	0.00040	0.0040	8.48	1.25	2.13	3.67	102

13.6 SUMMARY

Behavioural models and sentiment analysis are gaining momentum and acceptance within the investment community. Our study sets out to consider news sentiment and its impact on asset behaviour. We have introduced a novel concept of **news impact** which takes into consideration the volume of news and its decay over time.

We have (i) reported our study based on the predictive analysis of asset behaviour: return, volatility and liquidity. The main findings of this study are that by including news metadata as an additional time series and also treating it as an independent variable, the predictions of liquidity and volatility are improved, particularly the latter. Given that the **Kelly Criterion** uses asset volatility and that we are able to predict volatility both early and accurately, we have created our daily trading strategy using Kelly's formula.

(ii) The FTSE100 assets and the FTSE100 index futures were investigated for the 'lacklustre' regime of 2013 and 2014. In these investigations we used (a) market data only and (b) market data plus news metadata. The results for the latter dataset convincingly demonstrate the superior performance when we use news metadata in addition to market data.

ACKNOWLEDGEMENT

We would like to thank Zryan Sadik, our sponsored PhD researcher at Brunel University, Department of Mathematics, for his help in many of the experiments reported in this chapter.

13.7 REFERENCES

1.   Arbex-Valle, C., Erlwein-Sayer, C., Kochendörfer, A., Kübler, B., Mitra, G., Nzouankeu Nana, G.A., Nouwt, B. and Stalknecht, B. (2013). News-Enhanced Market Risk Management. Fraunhofer – OptiRisk whitepaper.

2.   Barber, B. M., and Odean, T. (2008). All that glitters: The effect of attention and news on the buying behaviour of individual and institutional investors. *Review of Financial Studies*, *21*(2), 785-818.

3.   Bollerslev, T., Engle, R., and Wooldridge, J. (1988). A capital asset pricing model with time-varying covariances. *Journal of Political Economy,96(1)*, 116-131.

4.   Bollerslev, T. (1986). Generalized Autoregressive Conditional Heteroskedasticity. *Journal of Econometrics*, *31(3)*, 307-327..

5.   Brar, G. (2013). Text mining for longer horizon investors. *[Presentation] Behavioral Models and Sentiment Analysis Applied to Finance, London, 2 July.* Available from: http://www.unicom.co.uk/quant-finance-course.html.

6.   Chatfield, C. (2009). The Analysis of Time Series: An Introduction. *Sixth Edition, Chapman & Hall Texts in Statistical Science.*

7.   Dion, M. (2013). Language recognition and news flow. *[Presentation]Behavioural Models and Sentiment Analysis Applied to Finance, London, 3 July.* Available from: http://www.unicom.co.uk/quant-finance-course.html.

8.   Engle, R. (1982). Autoregressive conditional heteroskedasticity with estimates of the variance of United Kingdom inflation. *Econometrica, 50(4),* 987-1007.

9.   Engle, R. (1998). Macroeconomic announcements and volatility of treasury futures.

10. Fama, E. F. and French, K. R. (1992). The cross-section of expected stock returns. *Journal of Finance, 47(2)*, 427-465..

11. French, K., Schwert, G.W., and Stambaugh, R.F. (1987). Expected stock returns and volatility. *Journal of Financial Economics, 19*, 3-29.

12. Goodhart, C.A., & O'Hara, M. (1997). High frequency data in financial markets: Issues and applications. *Journal of Empirical Finance, 4(2)*,73-114..

13. Groß-Klußmann, A., and Hautsch, N. (2011). When machines read the news: Using automated text analytics to quantify high frequency news-implied market reactions. *Journal of Empirical Finance, 18(2)*, 321-340..

14. Hafez, P. (2013). Market-level Sentiment for trading Forex and equity indices. *[Presentation]Behavioural Models and Sentiment Analysis Applied to Finance, London, 2 July.* Available from: http://www.unicom. co.uk/quant-finance-course.html, 131–156.

15. Harvey, A.C. (1990).Forecasting structural time series models and the Kalman filter. *Cambridge University Press*.

16. Kahn, R. (2013). Quant 3.0: Harnessing the mood of the web in alpha strategies. *[Presentation]Behavioural Models and Sentiment Analysis Applied to Finance, London 3 July.* Available from: http://www.unicom. co.uk/quant-finance-course.html.

17. Kahneman, D. and Tversky, A. (1979). Prospect Theory: An Analysis of Decision under Risk. *Econometrica, 47(2)*, 263 – 292..

18. Kahneman, D. (2002). Maps of bounded rationality: The [2002] Sveriges Riksbank Prize. *[Lecture] in Economic Sciences. Link:* http://www.nobelprize.org/nobel_prizes/economic-sciences/laureates/2002/ kahnemann-lecture.pdf.

19. Kelly, J. L. (1956). A new interpretation of information rate. *Bell System Technical Journal, 35*, 917-926.

20. Kothari, S.P. and Zimmerman, J.L. (1995). Price and return models. *Journal of Accounting and Economics, 20(2)*, 155-192..

21. Kyle, A. S. (1985). Continuous auctions and insider trading. *Econometrica: Journal of the Econometric Society*, 1315-1335..

22. Lattemann, C., Loos, P., Gomolka, J., Burghof, H. P., Breuer, A., Gomber, P., ...& Zajonz, R. (2012). High Frequency Trading. *Business & Information Systems Engineering, 4(2)*, 93-108..

23. Lee, C.M.C. (1992). Earnings News and Small Traders. *Journal of Accounting and Economics, 15,* 265-302.

24. Leinweber, D ., and Sisk, J.(2011). Relating news analytics to stock returns. Chapter 6 in Mitra, G. and Mitra, L. (2011). "The Handbook of News Analytics in Finance", *John Wiley & Sons*.

25. Lintner, J. (1965). The valuation of risky assets and the selection of risky investments in the portfolios and capital budgets. *Review of Economics and Statistics, 47,* 13-37.

26. Luenberger, D. (1997) Investment Science. *Oxford University Press*.

27. MacLean, L. C., Thorp, E. O. and Ziemba, W. T. (2011). The Kelly capital growth investment criterion: Theory and practice. *World Scientific, 3*.

28. Mitra, G., diBartolomeo, D., Banerjee, A. and Yu, X. (2011). Automated analysis of news to compute news sentiment: Its impact on liquidity and trading. Working paper. Available from: http://optirisk-systems.com/publications.asp#whitepaper.

29. Mitra, L., Mitra, G., and diBartolomeo, D., (2009). Equity portfolio risk (volatility) estimation using market information and sentiment. *Quantitative Finance, 9(8),* 887-895

30. Mitra, L., and Mitra, G. (2011). Application of news analytics in finance: A review. Chapter 1 of Mitra, G. and Mitra, L. (2011) "The Handbook of News Analytics in Finance", *John Wiley & Sons*..

31. Mossin, J. (1966). Equilibrium in a capital asset market. *Econometrica: Journal of the Econometric Society*, 768-783..

32. Niederhoffer, V. (1971). The analysis of world events and stock prices. *The Journal of Business, 44*(2), 193-219.

33. Patton, A.J. and Verardo, M. (2012). Does beta move with news? Firm-specific information flows and learning about profitability. *Review of Financial Studies, 25(9),* 2789-2839. .

34. Peterson, R.L. (2007). Inside the Investor's Brain. *John Wiley & Sons*.

35. Riordan, R., Storkenmaier, A., Wagener, M., & Sarah Zhang, S. (2013). Public information arrival: Price discovery and liquidity in electronic limit order markets. *Journal of Banking & Finance, 37,* 1148-1159.

36. .Robertson, D., & Wright, S. (2009). *The Limits to Stock Return Predictability*. mimeo.

37. Sharpe, W. F. (1964). Capital asset prices: A theory of market equilibrium under conditions of risk. *Journal of Finance, 19*(3), 425-442..

38. Shefrin, H. (2008). A Behavioral Approach to Asset Pricing. *Academic Press..*

39. Shiller, R. (2000). Irrational Exuberance. *Princeton University Press.*Riordan, R., Storkenmaier, A., Wagener, M., & Sarah Zhang, S. (2013). Public information arrival: Price discovery and liquidity in electronic limit order markets. *Journal of Banking & Finance, 37,* 1148-1159.

40. .Simon, H.A. (1964). On the concept of organizational goal. *Administrative Science Quarterly,* 1-22.

41. Sinha, N. (2010). Underreaction to news in the US stock market. *Available at SSRN 1572614.*

42. Stambaugh, R. F. (1999). Predictive regressions. *Journal of Financial Economics, 54*(3), 375-42

43. Tetlock, P. C. (2007). Giving content to investor sentiment: The role of media in the stock market. *Journal of Finance, 62*(3), 1139-1168

44. Thorp, E. O. (1971). Portfolio choice and the Kelly criterion. *Proceedings of the Business and Economics Section of the American Statistical Association,* 215-224.

45. Treynor, J.L. (1961). Toward a theory of market value of risky assets. Unpublished manuscript. A final version was published in "Asset Pricing and Portfolio Performance" (2009).

46. Yu, X., Mitra, G. and Yu, K. (2013). Impact of News on Asset Behaviour: Return, Volatility and Liquidity in an Intra-Day Setting. Available at SSRN: http://ssrn.com/abstract=2296855

CHAPTER 14

The Unbearable Lightness of Expectations
of the Chinese Investor

Eric Tham, *Thomson Reuters*

ABSTRACT

The Chinese equities markets witnessed wild swings in 2014-2015. The stock market's impact on the Chinese economy and in turn on the Federal Reserve's interest rate policy is indirect but significant. The high internet penetration of the Chinese population – about 670 million - and growth in its retail trading accounts reflect the importance of retail investor sentiment in the equity markets. In this paper, this investor sentiment is derived separately for rational arbitrageurs and retail noise traders through the textual analysis of newswires and social blogs. These are the general types of information fed to these investor groups respectively. Through a state space model of index returns on these sentiment types, it is shown that social blog sentiment and its time-varying sensitivities are most accountable for the index swings in 2014/15. This can be explained under Prospect Theory in Tversky and Kahneman (1979), with the blog sentiment reflecting the belief functions whilst the time varying sensitivities are due to the value functions.

14.1 INTRODUCTION

The Chinese equities markets have a major impact on the Chinese economy. Their impact on the global economy and in turn its impact on the Fed decision to raise rates cannot be understated.[1] During the 2014/2015 period, the benchmark Shanghai Stock exchange index doubled from 2400 to more than 5000, only to fall back to 3400 over nine months. The Shanghai and Shenzhen stock exchanges have a combined market capitalisation of more than $10 trillion that is second only to the United States. According to the World Federation of Exchanges[2], the trading volumes of the Shanghai and the Shenzhen stock exchanges were the highest in the world for the first eight months of 2015, with a peak of $3.3 trillion and $2.7 trillion in June, compared with the $1 trillion and $1.5 trillion for NASDAQ and NYSE. These trading volumes noticeably declined to less than $1 trillion after September 2015. All this occurred against the backdrop of the lowest China GDP growth at 7.0% since its economic boom started in 1978 when Deng liberalised agricultural output ownership laws. Government attempts to intervene in its financial markets illustrate the high priority placed on stock market price volatility. During this period, the Chinese Central Bank instituted a number of measures including cutting the reserve rate ratio six times since November 2014[3]. Other measures include the relaxation of security financing rules and the injection of funds into the stock markets to buy back shares. These initial measures had the stock indices responding by surging. The effects of these intervention measures, however, had muted market responses in the subsequent months. The investor sentiment somehow grew more "weary" and became more fickle, as we study in Sections 14.3 and 14.4.

Shanghai Stock Exchange index

Figure 14.1: SSE Index movements 2013-2015

The Chinese equity markets share unique peculiarities, with lower correlation with other financial markets and higher volatilities. Table 1 4 . 1 shows the correlation matrix of major equity indices from June 2013 to October 2015 and their annualised volatilities. The Shanghai Stock Index (SSE) has a lower correlation of about 0.14-0.20 with other major indices. Its average volatility over the past two years is also the highest amongst the major world indices, at 31%.

Table 14.1: *Correlations of the Shanghai Index with World Indices Jun2013 to Oct2015*

	Dow Jon sIndex	FTSE	Hang Seng Index	Shanghai Stock Ex-change30	FTSE Nikkei	S&P500
Dow Jones Index	1.0	0.61	0.28	0.14	0.29	0.97
FTSE	0.61	1.0	0.49	0.19	0.39	0.61
Hang Seng Index	0.28	0.49	1.0	0.54	0.44	0.31
SSE30	0.14	0.19	0.54	1.0	0.22	0.16
Nikkei FTSE	0.29	0.39	0.44	0.27	1.0	0.30
S&P500	0.97	0.61	0.31	0.16	0.30	1.0
Volatility	0.14	0.16	0.20	0.31	0.23	0.14

One of the prominent puzzles in finance, the equity home bias puzzle in French and Poterba (1991) is especially relevant for the Chinese equity market with its own-language media and cultural idiosyncrasies[4]. The Chinese investors mostly invest in their own domestic markets in spite of the direct Hong Kong-Shanghai connection that opened in November 2014. The direct connection allowed cross-border stock trading between investors in the two exchanges. This was set with an aggregate northbound quota of $2 billion for international investors to buy Chinese "A" shares and a southbound quota of $1.7 billion for mainland investors to buy Hong Kong "H" shares. The quota remained small in comparison with daily trading turnover of $161 billion at the time of writing, reinforcing the view of the isolation of the market.

14.1.1 The Rise of Chinese Investment Social Media

The 2014/2015 period also saw a surge of retail account interest. Figure 14.2 shows the number of new retail trading accounts opened since 2004. The surge in the stock markets appeared to stem more from retail interest than institutional interest, as the Wall Street Journal reported in November 2014[5]. In 2015, up to October, there were 50 million trading accounts. This represents almost 20% of aggregate account setups. This rate of opening has slowed noticeably since the stock market fall of June 2015.

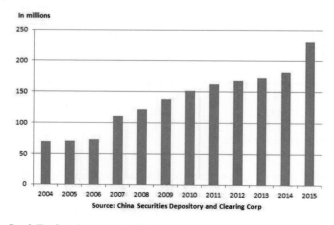

Figure 14.2: *Leap in Stock Trading Accounts in China*

During this period, China also witnessed the number of internet users rocketing to more than 670 million as of November 2015. This has spawned the rise of popular microblogging sites and stock blogging sites which gained immense following amongst retail investors. A website like Weibo has a monthly active user base of close to 180 million. The rise of social trading platforms like imaibo.net and xueqiu.com where experts offer stock advice and recommendations fed the information flow for the relatively inexperienced investor on the street[6]. This isolation of the stock markets of China makes for a conducive behavioural finance study of the impact of social media on financial sentiment.

14.1.2 What is Financial Sentiment?

Financial sentiment analysis is an area of behavioural finance which studies the effect of market psychology on market practitioners and its impact on the market. In academic literature, sentiment has been broadly understood from two angles - optimism and over-confidence. Optimism occurs when investors over-estimate future returns, whilst over-confidence under-estimates future returns volatility. Different measures of financial sentiment have been proposed over the past decade in the literature. These include the closed end funds discount in Thaler et al. (1991), sentiment surveys like the Yale-Shiller confidence index in Shiller (2000) and the Baker-Wurgler index in Baker and Wurgler (2006). The closed funds discount postulates that fluctuations in discounts of closed-end funds are driven by changes in investor sentiment. The Yale-Shiller index did a questionnaire survey to gauge crash expectations and investor confidence over time. The results of their survey have been well-cited on their website[7]. The Baker-Wurgler index did a Principal Component Analysis of six well-known market factors that reflect market sentiment. These include closed-end fund discount, NYSE share turnover, equity share in new issues, the number and average first-day returns on IPOs and the dividend premium. It used the first principal component as a proxy for sentiment.

In an article by Barone-Adesi et al. (2013), sentiment was obtained through taking the difference between option risk neutral densities and the GARCH econometric model. The idea is that the option risk neutral densities reflect the sentiment opinion of the representative investors while the GARCH econometric model reflects objective investors' pricing.

14.1.3 Prospect Theory and Social Media Sentiment

Recently, an increasing amount of literature has been devoted to obtaining financial sentiment from social media. Financial sentiment from social media can be seen in the context of the Prospect Theory in Tversky and Kahneman (1979) which is a seminal paper in behavioural finance. This postulates that investors make decisions based on their beliefs and their value functions in the equation.

$$V = \sum_{i=1}^{n} \pi(p_i)v(x_i)$$ [14.1]

- $\pi(p_i)$ as belief function
- $v(x_i)$ as value function

Sentiment information from social media may be seen as the investors framing beliefs that are evidenced from what they write or post online. In turn, their trading course of action is determined by their value functions, which in Prospect Theory are concerned with gains and losses from a frame of reference. One key finding in this paper is that social media sentiment has a time-varying correlation with the market index. This time-varying effect is postulated to be due to the value functions.

In the following sections, we first outline the data and methodology to quantify the daily sentiment scores of the Chinese indices. These sentiment scores are obtained by Natural Language Processing of the Chinese language separately from two different sources - the more informal social blogs and the newswire headlines. Next, we study the statistical relationships between these sentiment scores with the Shanghai stock index. We then use a state space model to model the time-varying relationships between the index and these sentiment scores where the time-varying sensitivity is underlined by an AR(1) state process. A discussion follows on the economic significance of the findings. A conclusion on its economic significance for trading and risk management ends the chapter.

14.2 THE DATA AND METHODOLOGY

In our study, sentiment data is obtained from the news headlines and the tweets from the more informal microblogging sites and stock forums from the Internet. This data is for the period 15 April 2013 to 21 October 2015. The news headlines come from the major Chinese news media, some of which are SINA, Yunvs, Eastmoney, jqka, Hexun and Caijing[8]. These websites carry more objective economic releases and fundamental company news reports. The other category of websites includes microblogging sites and stock forums, where netizens discuss stock prospects on a more informal level. These are frequently helmed by recognised stock experts who give stock advice and recommendations to their followers. The use of these websites has become increasingly popular over the last two years in line with interest amongst retail investors. Correspondingly, the number of websites in this category used for data analysis has expanded steadily from more than 100 in mid-2013 to over 300 at end-2015.

Generally, these websites tend to post more positive comments. This arises partly from the restriction that bans the shorting of stocks on the Chinese markets. This positive bias is also a characteristic of social investing websites where the followers generally do not like to follow "bad news". This is a phenomenon that is well-documented in Hong et al. (2000), which hypothesises that firm-specific information, especially negative publicity, tends to travel more slowly amongst investors. It is also interesting that the Chinese way of expression is more subtle or generally not-direct, using idioms and figures of speech. This requires a careful selection of reference corpus words.

14.2.1 Chinese Natural Language Processing

Chinese Natural Language Processing (NLP) is used to quantify sentiment from tweets and news headlines. There are a few steps to carrying out the NLP analysis successfully:

- Filtration of noisy posts
- Word segmentation
- Removal of stop words
- Classification of tweets into graduated sentiment scores
- Name Entity Recognition for weights

The filtration of noisy tweets and posts in the blogs to remove irrelevant tweets and posts is necessary given the laissez-faire nature of social media. These noisy posts constitute almost 80% of the total posts, and are generally identified by trivial word features and the shortness of the posts. Further, a major difference between English and Chinese NLP is the need for word segmentation as Chinese words are not separated from one another by spaces. A common issue with English language is word sense disambiguation, which refers to multiple meanings of the same word. This is less of an issue in the Chinese financial domain as characters are often bundled in pairs or triples for expressed meaning. Some open source NLP tool available for Chinese language include the Jieba and the excellent Stanford NLP program[9]. After the Chinese phrases are extracted by word segmentation, typical stop words are removed, referencing a standard corpus. Examples of stop words include '是', '以' which correspond to English words like 'is' and 'are'. The removal of stop words aids the classification process described in the next section.

14.2.2 Supervised Learning for Sentiment Analysis

The classification of the tweets and posts into graduated sentiment scores is done using a training corpus. This training corpus comprises words and idioms that are obtained through an examination of the most commonly used tweets and posts posted. The total number of words and idioms in this corpus is dynamic but at the time of the study is about 250. In the corpus, a most positive sentiment word like '暴涨' or translated 'skyrocket' is accorded the highest weight of 1.0, whilst on the contrary a most negative sentiment word like 'plummet'/'超跌' is weighted -1.0. Different levels of graduation are used in steps of 0.2 from -1 to 1.0 to manually annotate the corpus idioms. These weights are added up for the sentiment score of the sentence. Other semantic features for interaction amongst words like negation and conjunctive adverbs are factored into the sentiment classification. These include conjunctive words like '但是' or '当然' which translated are 'but' and 'certainly'. Conjunctive adverbs words that reinforce or negate the sentiment are considered in the manual score labelling. Negation words examples like '非' and '否' reverse the meaning of the sentences. Issues faced include unknown semantic words encountered in the testing phase, which can be further added to the training corpus. In particular, long tweets and posts can be split up by punctuation to separate phrases which are individually classified on sentiment scores.

14.2.3 Named Entity Recognition (NER)

Aside from training the model, it is also important to recognise the subject of discussion in the tweets and posts - Named Entity Recognition (NER). In this study, related stock symbols and names, and market words are identified as the named entities which are maintained in a separate corpus. A regular expression search through each tweet and post is done to filter out these entities. These are removed from the word vector before sentiment classification. The named entities are weighted to reflect the relevance of the tweet content to the market index sentiment. If for example the main market index '沪指' or '上海上证指数' (both forms refer to the SSE) is mentioned in the tweet, it is accorded a maximum weight of 1.0, whilst if a blue chip in the Shanghai Stock Exchange is mentioned, it is accorded a lower weight of 0.6. The rest of the smaller stocks are accorded weights of 0.1. This weighting scheme is necessary to segregate sentiment opinion on general market index, its blue-chip constituents or other smaller stocks. Tweets which do not mention any named entities in the corpus are weighted as zero and omitted from the analysis[12]. In this way, individual tweets and posts are weighted and assigned sentiment scores. The number of tweets and posts varies with the time of day and whether it is a trading date. On trading dates, the number of tweets is eight to ten times more than on non-trading dates. Almost 80% of the tweets are concentrated in the first hour and last hour of trading[13].The daily sentiment score is then calculated by:

$$Daily\_sentiment = \frac{\sum_{i=1}^{n} w_i s_i}{\sum_{i=1}^{n} w_i} \qquad [14.2]$$

- n total no of posts and tweets
- w_i weight of post or tweet
- s_i sentiment score of post or tweet

Two separate category scores of the more informal microblogging sites and the objective newswire headlines are obtained. These daily sentiment scores are plotted in two scatter graphs. Figure 14.3a below shows the empirical relation of the sentiment score of the newswire with the SSE index returns, while graph for Figure 14.3b shows the social blogs sentiment score with the SSE index returns. In both figures, there is a distinct positive relationship between the sentiment scores to the index returns. Relatively speaking, the scatter graph for Figure 14.3b for social blogs is observed to be noisier with a lower R-squared.

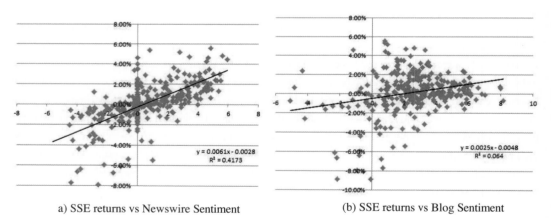

a) SSE returns vs Newswire Sentiment   (b) SSE returns vs Blog Sentiment

Figure 14.3: SSE returns vs Newswire and Blog sentiment

14.3 MODEL RESULTS

14.3.1 Statistical Tests

We first do an ordinary least squares regression between the daily index returns and the individual sentiment scores to establish a contemporaneous relationship. In Table 2, the R-squared is 0.47 with the F-statistic probability at a significant 0.001 with a sample data of 522 days from 15 April 2013 to 21 Oct 2015. We cannot reject the null hypothesis that sentiment changes are correlated with index changes. The observed negative coefficient c corrects the positive bias of the news and blog article sentiment mentioned in Section 14.2 for Data and Methodology. The t-statistic for the news sentiment and the blog sentiment are both significant, with a higher but noisier contribution from blog sentiment.

Table 14.2: Ordinary Least-Squares Regression of Index Returns against Sentiment

Variable	Coefficient	Std Error	t-Stat	Probability
Blog Sentiment	0.011	0.003	3.72	0.0002
News Sentiment	0.0047	0.000233	20.15	0.000
c	-0.0056	0.00105	-5.328	0.000

We test for Granger causality with lag 2. This is done at both daily and weekly intervals. For the daily interval, the results are:

Table 14.3: Granger Causality Tests of Daily Index Returns against Sentiment

Null Hypothesis	Obs	F-statistic	Probability	Significance 5%
SSERET does not Granger Cause NEWSSENT	566	3.929	0.0203	Rejected
NEWSSENT does not Granger Cause SSERET	566	3.161	0.0431	Rejected
BLOGSENT does not Granger Cause NEWSSENT	584	2.285	0.1027	Accepted
NEWSSENT does not Granger Cause BLOGSENT	584	4.729	0.0092	Rejected
SSERET does not Granger Cause BLOGSENT	566	4.991	0.007	Rejected
BLOGSENT does not Granger Cause SSERET	566	0.0231	0.9772	Accepted

At the daily interval, it is shown that there are two- way effects of the news sentiment and SSE returns on each other. This is a basis for momentum trading. Positive news sentiment gives rise to index returns which in turn feed back on the positive news sentiment. News sentiment also Granger- causes blog sentiment, but not the other way round. This is a logical conclusion, given that there is no reason for news fundamentals to follow what's happening at the informal blog level. On the contrary, stock experts follow the newswire headlines and respond correspondingly. Interestingly, blog sentiment does not Granger- cause the SSE returns though it was shown that they were contemporaneously related in the OLS regression. This indicates that blog sentiment tends to be forgetful and only mindful of existential market movements. Index trading purely on the blog sentiment is unlikely to yield results. On a weekly interval, none of the variables Granger-causes another. This substantiates the relatively short-term effect of sentiment decay reported in many studies.

14.3.2 State Space Model

Next, a state space model is used to time-varyingly model the relationships between the index returns and the blog and news sentiment. State space models are also known as stochastic parameter regressions and have been used in economics to study time-varying parameters like betas and risk premia. See Hamilton (1994) for an excellent technical introduction.

Two state space models are proposed to quantify independently the time-varying effects of the news sentiment and the blog sentiment. The left-hand set of equations models the time-varying sensitivity of the SSE returns to the blog sentiment by an AR(1) process. In order to prevent model bias, a similar state space model sets the sensitivity to the newswire sentiment instead. This is the model on the right-hand side of the equations below:

$$
\begin{aligned}
sse_t &= \alpha_t blog\_sent_t + c_1 news\_sent_t + \epsilon_{1,t} \\
\alpha_{t+1} &= c_2 \alpha_t + \epsilon_{2,t} \\
\epsilon_{1,t} &\sim N(0, \sigma_1) \\
\epsilon_{2,t} &\sim N(0, \sigma_2)
\end{aligned}
\quad \leftrightarrow \quad
\begin{aligned}
sse_t &= c_1 blog\_sent_t + \alpha_t news\_sent_t + \epsilon_{1,t} \\
\alpha_{t+1} &= c_2 \alpha_t + \epsilon_{2,t} \\
\epsilon_{1,t} &\sim N(0, \sigma_1) \\
\epsilon_{2,t} &\sim N(0, \sigma_2)
\end{aligned}
\qquad [14.3]
$$

Where:

sse_t :   SSE index returns

$blog\ sent_t$:   Sentiment score of social media blog

$news\ sent_t$: Sentiment score of newswire headlines

The first equation in [14.3] is the measurement equation that relates the index *returns* to the blog and newswire sentiment. It is similar to the ordinary least squares regression, except that its underlying coefficients are modelled by a recursive AR(1) equation. The latter is the transition equation which reflects the time-varying coefficients of the sentiment scores on the index returns. The $\epsilon_{1,t}$ and $\epsilon_{2,t}$ are Gaussian white noises for the measurement and transition equations, which are serially independent but contemporaneously correlated. The dataset used is fortnightly from 15 April 2013 to 21 October 2015 for 67 data points. A fortnightly interval is selected as a period where investor sentiment generally changes. It is also chosen for more tractability with less noise and convergence. All coefficients are significant and within statistical error, as seen from the results tables below for the two sets of equations.

Table 14.4: *Tabular Results of State Space Model for Time-Varying Blog Mood Sensitivity*

Coefficient	Values	Std Error	z-Statistic	Probability
$\sigma 1$	0.003	2.4e-06	1328	0.00
$\sigma 2$	0.003	2.7e-06	1156	0.00
$c1$	0.05	0.0099	253	0.00
$c2$	0.94	0.00027	3510	0.00
Log Likelihood	−6567			
Akaike info criterion	197			
Schwartz criterion	197			

On the same set of data, the log likelihood for the model with the blog sentiment is marginally higher at −6567 than the model with newswire sentiment at −7299. The AIC and Schwarz criterion are both lower at 197, rendering the blog sentiment a more probabilistic model. This implicitly means that the index returns are better explained by the fluctuations in the blog sentiment rather than the news sentiment.

Table 14.5: *Tabular Results of State space model for Time-Varying News Mood Sensitivity*

Coefficient	Values	Std Error	z-Statistic	Probability
$\sigma 1$	0.002	1.5e-06	1311	0.00
$\sigma 2$	0.0006	3.5e-07	1584	0.00
$c1$	0.10	0.0005	206	0.00
$c2$	0.99	0.0004	2423	0.00
Log Likelihood	−7299			
Akaike info criterion	218			
Schwartz criterion	218			

We further examine a time series of the filtered states $\hat{\alpha}_t$ for both the models seen in the graph below. The filtered states are the ex-post filtered estimates of the conditional sensitivities $\hat{\alpha}_t +1$ in the transition equations. The graph of the SSE index is overlaid on the graph. A couple of observations can be made on the graph.

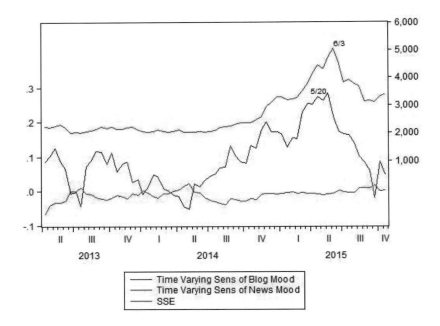

Figure 14.4: *Time Series of State Variables of the Social Blogs & Newswire Sentiment with the SSE*

• The news sentiment sensitivity had been relatively flat over the two-three year period, indicating sustained but consistent interest from institutional investors.

• In Q3 2014, the blog sentiment sensitivity had already begun to increase as interest from the new retail accounts grew. The sensitivity reaches a peak on 23 May 2015 before starting to wane. This precedes the index increase towards Q4 2014, reaching a bubble in June 2015. This bubble could be explained by an *informational cascade* or an investor herding phenomenon described in the next section.

14.4 DISCUSSION OF ECONOMIC SIGNIFICANCE

14.4.1 A Tale of Two Investors and Types of Information

In the paper "A Tale of Two Investors: Estimating Optimism and Overconfidence" by Barone-Adesi et al. (2013) and the book Hersh (2008), two types of investor were mentioned - rational arbitrageurs and the noise traders. The rational arbitrageurs are more rational, with objective beliefs, whilst the noise traders are representative traders who buy and sell based on "emotions" even though they may be incorrect. Prices are set by these noise traders. In Barone-Adesi et al. (2013), sentiment is defined as the difference in the mean probability density functions between the two investors. In our chapter, sentiment is exogenously derived from textual analyses of information that are read or posted by each category of investor.

We hypothesise the noise traders as the retail investors, whilst rational arbitrageurs refers to the institutional investors. The noise or retail investors follow the informal blogs presented in a more layman manner suited for them. This is an *availability* heuristic in Tversky and Kahneman (1974), where investors tend to make financial decisions based on feeling at ease with the information available to them. The institutional investors tend to follow relatively objective fundamental headlines from the official newswires.

We note in the following papers, Ammann et al. (2015) and Bollenetal (2011), that the two types of information could have a bearing on the stock market movements. In Ammann et al. (2015), newspaper headlines studied in German financial newspapers were found to have predictive power over the DAX returns. In Bollenetal (2011), Twitter mood was studied to predict the Dow Jones Industrial Average. In the rest of the chapter, retail and noise investors are mentioned synonymously.

14.4.2 Over-reaction, Investor Herding and Attention Cascade in the Chinese markets

Price over-reaction from the "fair" equilibrium price tends to result from exuberant sentiment. Trading strategies devised on sentiment analysis of news are usually short-term to capture this price mismatch inefficiency, as it moves back to equilibrium. This is one way rational arbitrageurs "make" profit. Due to the noise traders, however, the time to return to equilibrium could be longer than rational arbitrageurs can hold on to their positions for before their liquidity dries up. This scenario is a more pertinent case for the Chinese equity markets due to the large presence of "noise traders", which increased in the 2014-2015 period. This environment could make the Chinese equity markets a greater challenge for international institutional investors.

The increase in the sensitivity of the SSE returns to blog sentiment can also be explained by *attention cascade*. In this phenomenon, traders observe the actions of others and, despite their own beliefs or private information, follow the earlier actions of others. This can be evidenced in the graph below which shows a time series of the number of tweets posted on social media blogs used for the study. It shows a sharp increase of tweets and posts prior to the June peak indicating a cascade transfer of information via social media. The number of tweets and posts in April and May 2015 averaged about 30-50k a day, compared to less than 10k in the previous months. Attention cascade is synonymous with investor herding, a phenomenon first described by Banerjee (1992). In investor herding, informed traders make their decisions based on private information sequentially and copy other *informed* traders' actions. Only after a while is their own information considered. Both the attention cascade and the herding phenomena are exacerbated with social trading sites that deliberate the propagation of informed traders' actions. The increase in the number of posts and tweets in times of high sentiment potentially cascaded and contributed to the rise of the Shanghai stock index. It could have contributed to the increased sensitivity of the index to blog sentiment as studied in the previous section.

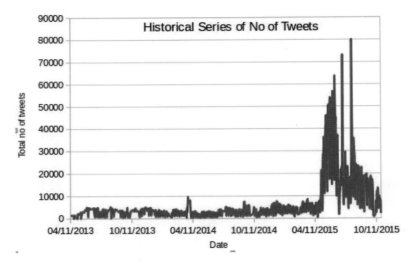

Figure 14.5: Time Series of Number of Tweets posted on Chinese social media

14.4.3 Time Varying Sensitivity Impact of Sentiment

The Chinese retail investors have light expectations in sentiment and expectations. Whilst what's communicated in the social blogs does not necessarily translate into actually buying or selling, it must be noted that blog sentiment showed a strong contemporaneous correlation with index returns.

Its impact on the index returns is hard to gauge solely at the level of text analytics. The blog sentiment and its time varying sensitivity on the index returns must therefore be carefully distinguished - it was not only the blog sentiment but also its secondary sensitivity effects that were largely responsible for the swings in the index movements. This is synonymous with traders' intuition in volatile markets - *that it is not just news that counts but how the markets react to news that matters*.

As described in the section 14.1.3 on Prospect Theory, this time-varying sensitivity function is postulated to be due to the value functions, whilst the blog sentiment reflecting beliefs or information is attributed to the belief functions.

14.5 CONCLUSION

Whilst both institutional and retail investors were responsible for the swings in the Shanghai stock exchange index in 2014/15, the swings could largely be attributed to the index sensitivity to blog sentiment reflective of retail investors. This increased sensitivity took place against the backdrop of a spike in retail trading accounts and rising use of the Internet in China that exacerbated investor herding and attention cascade. This phenomenon had never happened before in established markets, with implications for both risk management and trading.

In both cases, blog sentiment and newswire sentiment were obtained through textual analysis. This analysis needs to occur in the context of the risk environment of the index sensitivity to sentiment. Noticeably for the Shanghai stock markets, this sensitivity increased prior to the June peak and then decreased afterwards. This corresponded well with the number of tweets and posts online, which reinforced the idea of attention cascade contributing to the increase.

This strong dependence of the Shanghai stock market on the retail sentiment and its relative isolation from other world markets makes it a distinct challenge for international and institutional investors. However, its lack of correlation with world markets and liquidity makes Chinese equities an attractive addition to portfolio allocation whose benefits cannot be ignored.

ACKNOWLEDGEMENT

I would like to thank iMaibo for providing the sentiment data for this study.

Notes

[1] http://money.cnn.com/2015/09/18/news/economy/china-yellen-global-economy-worry/ Janet Yellen cited China sixteen times in global economic worries.

[2] Data is from http://www.world-exchanges.org/home/

[3] These six dates were 24 October 2015, 26 August 2015, 28 June 2015, 11 May 2015, 1 March 2015 and 22 November 2014, with the previous cut on 6 June 2012. On each date, the reserve ratio was cut by 25 basis points.

[4] This bias refers to the phenomenon where local investors tend to hold more home-based equity and less foreign-based equity. It was first documented by French and Poterta in 1991. This was puzzling in spite of the purported benefits of international diversification. Reasons cited include familiarity with the domestic markets, tax reasons, additional transaction costs and legal restrictions. The phenomenon is observed to be diminishing in recent years with the ease of flow of international capital and online trading.

[5] Retail Investors fuel China Stock Rally http://www.wsj.com/articles/retail-investors-fuel-china-stock-rally-1417173421

[6] These websites work on the basis of some renowned "expert" investment advisors who built up their follower base numbering in the hundreds of thousands. These popular websites help fuel an investor herding phenomenon as news and stock recommendations disseminate through unofficial channels and rumours. Similar websites exist in the United States and developed countries with examples like StockTwits and Trade Heroes. However, in these developed markets, there is also relatively stronger institutional interest compared to retail interest in the equity markets.

[7] http://som.yale.edu/faculty-research/centers-initiatives/international-center-finance/data/stock-market-confidence-indices/stock-market-confidence-indices

[8] In Chinese, these are 新浪财经,云财经, 东方财富网,同花顺,和讯网.

[9] http://nlp.stanford.edu/projects/chinese-nlp.shtml and https://github.com/fxsjy/jieba

[10] http://scikit-learn.org/

[11] Due to the graduated scale and non-binary nature of the score, Type I and Type II errors cannot be explicitly stated.

[12] It is possible to weigh the tweets according to how networked or influential the message source is. This would be a separate area of research.

[13] The trading hours for the Shanghai and Shenzhen stock exchanges are from 09.30 to 11.30 for the morning session and 13.00 to 15.00 hours for the afternoon session

14.6 REFERENCES

1. Ammann, M., Frey, R. and Verhofen, M. (2015). Do newspaper articles predict aggregate stock returns? *CFA Digest, 45(2)*.

2. Baker, M. and Wurgler, J. (2006). Investor sentiment and the cross-section of stock returns. *The Journal of Finance, 61(4)*, pp. 1645–1680.

3. Banerjee, A. (1992). A simple model of herd behavior. *The Quarterly Journal of Economics*, pp. 797–817..

4. Barone-Adesi, G., Mancin, L. and Hersh, S. (2013). A tale of two investors: Estimating optimism and overconfidence. Available at: http://ssrn.com/abstract=2319260.

5. Bollen, J., Huina, M. and Zhang, X. (2011). Twitter mood predicts the stock market. *Journal of Computational Science, 2(1)*, pp. 1–8.

6. French, K. and Poterba, J. (1991). Investor diversification and international equity markets. *American Economic Review, 2(4)*.

7. Hamilton, D. J. (1994). *Handbook of Econometrics*, Volume IV.

8. Hersh, S. (2008). *A Behavioral Approach to Asset Pricing*. Academic Press, Boston..

9. Hong, H., Lim, T. and Stein, J. (2000). Bad news travels slowly: Size, analyst coverage, and the profitability of momentum strategies. *The Journal of Finance, 55(1)*, pp. 262–295.

10. Shiller, R. (2000). Measuring bubble expectations and investor confidence. *The Journal of Psychology and Financial Markets, 1(1)*, pp. 49–60.

11. Thaler, R. (1999). Mental accounting matters. *Journal of Behavioural Decision Making, 3*, pp. 183–206.

12. Tseng, H., Chang, P., Andrew, G., Jurasky, D. and Manning, C. (2005). A conditional random field word segmenter. Sighan 2005.

13. Tversky, A. and Kahneman, D. (1974). Judgement under uncertainty: Heuristics and biases. *Science, 185,* pp. 1124–1131.

14. Tversky, A. and Kahneman, D. (1979). Prospect theory: An analysis of decision under risk. Econometrica, 47, pp. 263–291.

PART IV

Sentiment Analysis for other Asset Classes: Energy, Commodities, Green Commodities, Bonds, and Fx

CHAPTER 15

The Role of News in Commodity Markets

Svetlana Borovkova, *Vrije Universiteit Amsterdam*

ABSTRACT

In this chapter, we give a broad overview of how commodity-related news affects commodity markets. We examine the main commodity classes: energy, agriculturals and metals, as well as various ways markets respond to news: in terms of prices, returns, volatilities and price jumps. Market responses are analysed for different latencies, ranging from minutes to days to longer horizons. We discuss how these insights can be used in trading strategies, investment decisions and risk management.

In particular, we address the following questions:

- What are the distinguishing features of commodity-related news?
- How commodity prices react to positive and negative sentiment in news?
- How we can combine news signals from several commodity markets into an overall commodity news index? How does such a news index relate to the major commodity price indices?
- Can we improve volatility forecasts by including news variables in volatility models?
- Which characteristics of commodity price movements – volatility, positive and negative jumps – cause and are caused by news?

15.1 INTRODUCTION

Traditionally, the analysis of security returns has concentrated on responses to quantitative or *hard* measures such as corporate and economic statistics or, at most, a few ingeniously selected variables intended as proxies for some qualitative characteristic. Over the past decade, the IT revolution has provided us with a wealth of digitized text containing qualitative information and the processing power to apply algorithms that seek to quantify *soft* aspects of this text, such as sentiment, relevance and novelty.

Many studies, starting with the pioneering work by Tetlock (2007, 2008), investigated the effects of either market-wide or company-specific news announcements on stock prices (see e.g., *The Handbook of News Analytics in Finance* (2011), but also Mitra et al. (2009), Gross-Klussman and Hautsch (2011), Sinha (2010, Allen et al. (2013)). Research into the effects of new sentiment on commodity markets is, however, virtually non-existent (with some exceptions, including an article by Smales (2014) about gold futures). This is surprising for several reasons. First of all, commodity prices are primarily driven by news about supply and demand, such as OPEC or inventory announcements, geopolitical news, weather-related news and other external information. So we expect the effect of news on commodity markets to be even more profound than that observed for stock markets. Second, commodities have been at the centre of investors' attention for the past decade, as witnessed by a mass of non-traditional financial players such as hedge, investment and pension funds entering commodity trading. Finally, event-driven trading strategies in commodities and, in particular, energy have attracted a lot of interest recently, especially from the world of hedge funds, but also from large commodity-producing and trading firms. This chapter aims at closing this gap in the literature by providing an overview of the relationships between commodity-related news sentiment and various characteristics of commodity markets.

There are several challenges when dealing with commodities. First of all, in contrast to equities, for which the focus of attention is a single price, commodities trade in the form of futures contracts with monthly maturities that stretch several years into the future. So the object of interest is not just one price, but an entire forward curve, consisting of prices of futures with different maturities. News sentiment may affect futures returns for different maturities differently.

Furthermore, it is not immediately clear whether sentiment measures will work as well for commodities as they do for equities, as commodity prices are driven by supply and demand rather than by the present value of future cash flows. So while one would presume that just about any article with lots of positive words and a reference to Apple would correlate with upward pressure in its stock price, it is not clear whether an article with lots of positive words and a reference to crude oil would correlate with upward or downward pressure on the oil price. If the headline were "Stability in the Middle East and growth in rig counts leads to boom in crude supply", we would expect the price to go down, whereas the sentence "Boom in China and growth in the US makes oil soar" might lead us to expect prices to go up, while both articles may be classified as "positive". Thus, for sentiment measures to work effectively for commodities, they have to differentiate between sentiment with relation to factors that cause, or correlate with, supply and demand.

Finally, the sheer volume of news for commodities makes any quantitative research challenging. Given the huge amount of news about, for instance, crude oil (which is the world's biggest commodity), it is important to separate truly "new" news items, which would potentially move prices, from the so-called *momentum-related news*, where past price developments are discussed. Consider the following two recent examples. On 5 February 2015, a Bloomberg headline read: "Oil Caps Biggest 2-Week Gain in 17 Years Amid Volatility" (the full explanatory article can be found in Appendix 15.A.1). This headline was accompanied by the price chart shown in Figure 15.1.1. The headline obviously referred to the upward price development in the previous two weeks, clearly visible on the chart, and the volatility associated with it. This is typical "momentum" news, as any consequent price developments would reflect the price momentum rather than any new piece of information hitting the markets.

Figure 15.1.1: Oil price development around 5 Feb 2015.

Another illustrative example is the CNBC headline of 11 February 2015, which read: "Capex cuts will determine oil's bottom" (the price chart on that day is shown in Figure 15.1.2, and again, the associated article can be found in the Appendix 15.A.1). This, in contrast to the previous example, is a "forward-looking", supply-related piece of news, speculating on how cuts in capital expenditures will affect the declining trend in oil prices. So ideally we would like to separate these two types of news, or at least keep in mind that a large number of news about commodity markets is "momentum" news, i.e., is related to previous price developments.

Figure 15.1.2: Oil price development around 11 Feb 2015.

In this chapter we will address various aspects of commodity-related news and its effects on commodity prices. The chapter is organized as follows. Section 15.2 describes the commodity related news data and its aggregate characteristics. Section 15.3 presents event studies for various commodities and latencies. Section 15.4 addresses the decomposition of the forward curve into fundamental factors, the effect of news on these factors and in different market conditions. Section 15..5 presents the construction of commodity news sentiment indices and their relation to the major commodity price indices. Section 15.6 discusses news-augmented volatility models and causality effects between news, volatility and price jumps. Section 15.7 provides the conclusion.

15.2 COMMODITY-RELATED NEWS CHARACTERISTICS

15.2.1 Commodity news volumes

Many commercial and research companies are currently active in the area of news analytics. News analytics providers such as Ravenpack, Bloomberg and Thomson Reuters use sophisticated Natural Language Processing (NLP) techniques in their news analytics engines. These analyse thousands of news articles and determine whether each news item is relevant to a specific company, index or a commodity, and whether the tone of the item is positive, negative or neutral. Most news analytics engines focus specifically on companies (stocks) or general macroeconomic indicators; however, only a handful of news analytics providers also focus on commodities. One such provider is Thomson Reuters, whose News Analytics Engine (TRNA) for commodities and energy we use in our research.

The TRNA news sentiment historical database comprises commodity-related news from various news sources, time-flagged to the millisecond, from 2003 to the present day. As we already mentioned, the volume of commodity-related news is immense: for example, on an average working day we observe between 400 and 500 news items about crude oil, and on some days there may be up to 800–1000 oil-related items. When we compare this to the number of stock-related news items (also extracted from TRNA database), we find that, for liquidly traded stocks, we observe on average 40 news items per week.

On average, for all commodities we observe around 800 news items per (working) day; the histogram of the number of commodity-related news items per day is given in Figure 15.2.1.

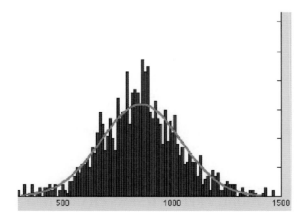

Figure 15.2.1: *Histogram of the number of commodity-related news items per working day.*

Commodity-related news flow steadily grew from 2003 to 2008, and has since stabilized with around 20,000 news items being produced each month.

Commodity-related news flow is relatively evenly spread over a working week, as Figure 15.2.2 shows. For oil, Wednesday is a particularly news-heavy day (lower bars in Figure 15.2.2), as weekly API inventory numbers are released at 10:30 am on Wednesdays, generating a lot of news activity around these announcements. For Natural Gas, such inventory numbers are released on Thursdays, making that a particularly news-busy day.

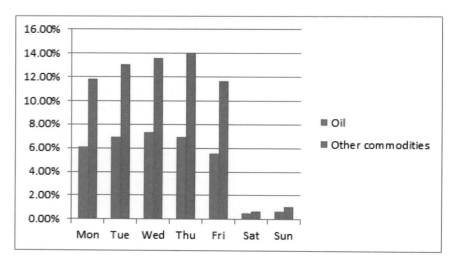

Figure 15.2.2: *Distribution of news volume over weekdays (higher bars: all commodities, lower bars: crude oil).*

Figure 15.2.3 shows the distribution of all energy-related news (oil, gas, oil products, coal, emissions) over a week. Due to the oil inventories release, Wednesday still dominates in terms of news volume, with 22% of all energy-related news appearing on Wednesdays.

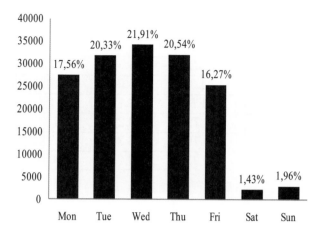

Figure 15.2.3: Distribution of energy-related news volume over weekdays.

The pattern of news arrival within a working day is shown in Figure 15.2.4. The peak in news volume corresponds to a few hours when both the European and US exchanges are open.

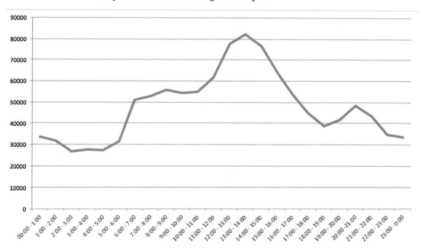

Figure 15.2.4: Aggregated news volume per hour of a working day.

The most newsworthy commodity is crude oil, accounting for over 34% of all news volume. Metals, being a large commodity class, account in total for approximately 44% of all news (this excludes gold, which alone accounts for nearly 9% of all news). The volume of news associated with agricultural commodities is rather modest, accounting for just a fraction of all commodity-related news. Table 15.2.1 presents the percentages of news items associated with various commodities. Percentages of news items interpreted as "positive", "negative" and "neutral" (for the commodity's price in question) over the entire historical period (2003–2014) are also given.

Table 15.2.1: Percentage of news volume per commodity.

	% of total	% pos	% neut	% neg
Crude Oil	34.31%	44.58%	14.27%	41.15%
Metals	44.35%	38.06%	23.03%	38.91%
Natural Gas	11.50%	42.13%	21.51%	36.36%
Gold	8.79%	43.29%	14.7%	42.00%
Corn	0.70%	46.30%	16.45%	37.25%
Soy beans	0.35%	42.97%	15.90%	41.13%

15.2.2 Quantitative news characteristics

News analytics engines "read" news items and interpret them using Natural Language Processing algorithms. This involves, first of all, identifying relevant entities in a news item (e.g., "crude oil" or "natural gas"). Then, various approaches of sentiment analysis are applied to the text of the news item to determine whether it conveys positive, negative or neutral opinion on each entity mentioned. One such approach is keyword identification (e.g., on the basis of Harvard IV Psychological Dictionary), where words are classified according to various (positive, negative or neutral) categories. To determine the sentiment in context, the grammatical relationships of words are used. Grammatical dependency relations are obtained e.g., by so-called deep parsing of the text. Furthermore, statistical methods that leverage elements from machine learning are employed, such as latent semantic analysis or "bag of words". At the next layer of complexity, concept-level approaches leverage elements from knowledge representation, such as semantic networks. These approaches are able to detect sentiment expressed in a subtle manner, for example, through a series of related (or implicitly linked) concepts. Finally, a human analysis component is important in sentiment analysis – this is particularly the case for commodity-related sentiment. Natural language processing algorithms are augmented by experts' opinions of commodity analysts, editors or other commodity specialists, by creating additional vocabulary or rules for assessing sentiment. This is because, for commodity sentiment measures to work properly, positivity and negativity of news must be assessed in relationship to supply and demand, rather than in terms of "human" interpretation of what is positive and negative.

The resulting output is a set of quantitative news characteristics for each news item, the main ones being relevance, sentiment and novelty measures. For Thomson Reuters News Analytics, the historical sentiment database covers the period from 2003 to the present day, and the database is frequently updated as new and more sophisticated NLP techniques become available (by regularly recalculating the sentiment scores for the entire database).

Figure 15.2.5 presents an extract from the Thomson Reuters News Analytic engine output. The first field is the time stamp of the news arrival, followed by the ticker corresponding to a particular commodity, a commodity class or a subset, such as grains. The relevance measure, between zero and one, indicates how relevant a news item is for a particular commodity. Relevance is determined, roughly speaking, by how often a particular commodity is mentioned in a news item, in relation to other commodities. For example, if "oil" and "gas" are mentioned equally often in a news item, the relevance scores assigned to this item in relation to "oil" and to "gas" are both equal to 0.5. However (in contrast to equities), for commodities the relevance measure is usually equal to one, unless an article addresses several commodities at once (such as in the above example, if an item discusses both crude oil and natural gas market developments).

IDN_TIME STOCK_RIC	RELEVANCE	SENTIMEN SENT_POS		SENT_NEUT	SENT_NEG	LNKD_CNT1	ITEM_TYPE BCAST_TEXT	
01:58.3 MTAL	1	0	0.191232	0.718185	0.0905829		0 ARTICLE	Hussey copper price Fall to 3.0885 -Decemb
02:54.3 COT	1	-1	0.201419	0.22755	0.571031		0 ARTICLE	NY Cotton No.2 Estimated Volume- 31 Dece
05:12.6 COT	1	0	0.0809842	0.849202	0.0698138		0 ARTICLE	ICE cotton stocks unchanged at 51,142 - De
13:42.4 LIV	0.816497	0	0.0880052	0.779822	0.132173		3 ARTICLE	CME estimated volumes - Dec 31
30:06.3 GRA	1	1	0.785536	0.0735535	0.140911		0 ARTICLE	CBOT rice deliveries - Jan 01
30:07.9 GRA	0.408248	1	0.785306	0.0738494	0.140844		1 ARTICLE	CBOT ethanol deliveries - Jan 01
30:09.1 MEAL	1	1	0.719192	0.128474	0.152334		1 ARTICLE	CBOT soybean deliveries - Jan 01
14:44.3 GOL	1	0	0.318323	0.421302	0.260375		0 ARTICLE	NY COMEX gold and silver delivery notices -
14:51.3 MTAL	1	1	0.416684	0.398823	0.184493		1 ARTICLE	NY COMEX high grade copper delivery notic
46:25.8 CRU	1	1	0.764544	0.0952038	0.140253		0 ARTICLE	S.Korea's Dec crude oil imports up 6.8 pct y,
17:28.4 COC	1	0	0.246601	0.451883	0.301516		0 ARTICLE	NY Cocoa delivery notices - Jan 01
55:52.7 PROD	1	1	0.776333	0.0752391	0.148428		0 ALERT	SAUDI ARAMCO SUSPENDS PLAN TO BUILD
20:23.0 CRU	1	-1	0.0841116	0.125463	0.790426		0 ARTICLE	INTERVIEW-Iran says Saudi Arabia should m
01:50.6 MTAL	1	-1	0.0855812	0.119604	0.794815		0 ARTICLE	Brazil to rework mining code stalled in Cong
53:26.6 CRU	1	1	0.463951	0.258316	0.277733		0 ALERT	U.S. CRUDE <CLc1> UP MORE THAN $1.50 A
53:50.7 CRU	1	-1	0.235173	0.123637	0.641191		1 ARTICLE	NYMEX-US crude up over $54 on stock fall;

Figure 15.2.5 An extract from the TRNA news sentiment database.

The next field is the overall sentiment classifier, where 1 stands for positive, -1 for negative and 0 for neutral. This field is calculated from the following three most important quantitative news characteristics, which are the sentiment scores: positive, neutral and negative. These are three numbers between zero and one, adding up to one, which should be interpreted as *probabilities that a news item conveys positive, neutral or negative outlook on this commodity's price.*

Another important indicator is novelty, measured by counting how many times a particular news item has been mentioned before (zero being the first time the news is reported). Many other characteristics are reported. Some of them can be quite useful, for example, whether a news item is an article or alert, or which other news items it is related to. The headlines of the news items are also given.

The overall impressions of such a news analytics engine's output are that the data is relatively high-frequency (which could be excellent for intraday traders), and that the sentiment grade is quite noisy: for example, very similar news items (containing essentially the same information) can be classified wildly differently (and hence incorrectly in some cases). This makes it questionable whether all this information is economically relevant.

One way to deal with this noise is to filter out a meaningful signal from noisy observations of sentiment. This can be done with the signal processing technique of Kalman filtering, which will be described shortly. Another way is to aggregate the sentiment scores into daily numbers.

15.2.3 Sentiment aggregation

Often it is informative to analyse how daily closing prices are related to/respond to news sentiment: the behaviour of returns over a longer period such as a trading day is arguably more economically relevant than that over milliseconds, which is largely due to the market microstructure and not fundamentals such as supply and demand. Furthermore, working on a longer time scale reduces complications caused by market microstructure, such as the bid-ask bounce and asynchronous trading.

To relate news sentiment to daily closing prices, we should aggregate the sentiment scores into daily numbers. This is also useful for dealing with a noisy signal, as aggregating sentiments over a day should reduce the noise.

To form the daily sentiment index for a particular commodity, we need to filter out all news items relevant to that commodity. Next, we must bear in mind the opening and closing times of the corresponding commodity exchange, where this particular commodity is traded. For the purpose of creating daily sentiment score, we define a "news day" as the time interval close-to-close of the corresponding exchange. For example, if working with WTI crude oil futures, we need to synchronise the time stamp of news to the time of New York Mercantile Exchange (NYMEX) in New York (its closing time would be 19:30 GMT or 14:30 EST, which is the same, given the 5-hour time zone difference). As the news data is usually stamped with a GMT or UTC time stamp, we also need to bear in mind daylight saving time. In other words, we should adjust the timestamps in such a way that each news item is stamped with the date indicating that it was available to traders before the market settlement on that day.

Daily aggregated news sentiments can be formed by averaging each of the three sentiment scores for all articles on each day, then normalizing the resulting scores so that the daily sentiment scores also add up to one. Often one would take into account only news items whose relevance for a particular commodity is higher than a certain threshold, e.g., 0.3 or 0.5. Alternatively, averages weighted by relevance can be taken.

A popular sentiment measure is the so-called net-positive score, obtained by subtracting the negative score from the positive one (this measure can be calculated for daily scores or per individual news item).

News is released also during weekends and bank holidays, which means that there are sentiment scores on non-trading days (whereas trading might be not available on those days). So we can create daily news sentiment scores only for trading days, using the following weighted scheme. First of all, we aggregate news that appeared on non-trading days into the score for the subsequent trading day. It is quite reasonable to assume that people have "short memory", meaning that, for instance, on Monday they remember news published on Sunday better than that published on Saturday and they remember the Monday's news the most vividly. So for Monday (and days following bank holidays) scores, we take the exponentially weighted average instead of an arithmetic average, with the weights being $0.9i$, where i is the number of days between the day of the news item and the subsequent trading day. For example, a normal Monday's score is

$$\frac{Score_{Monday} + 0.9 \times Score_{Sunday} + 0.9^2 \times Score_{Saturday}}{1 + 0.9 + 0.9^2} \qquad [15.2.1]$$

The same scheme can be used for news released during bank holidays. Finally, we can also employ a weighting scheme that weights news received during trading hours heavier than those which appeared outside trading hours.

Figure 15.2.6 shows the resulting positive and negative daily sentiment scores for crude oil, together with oil log-price, for the period 1/1/2003-1/1/2013. Already from these graphs the positive correlation of the price with the positive sentiment score is visible. It also appears that the daily sentiment series is much more stable (stationary) than either the price or the volatility.

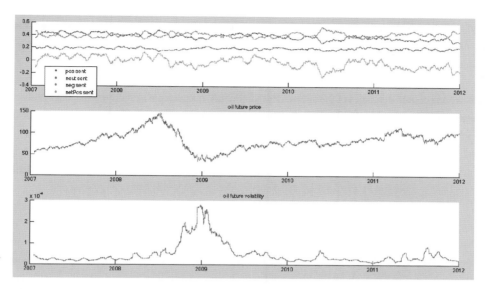

Figure 15.2.6 *Top graph: negative, positive, neutral and net positive daily sentiment scores; middle graph: WTI log-price, bottom graph: daily oil price volatility.*

In the next section, we will relate daily sentiment scores for various commodities to futures prices by means of event studies. But first we describe how a meaningful sentiment signal can be obtained from noisy sentiment observations in real time.

15.2.4 Intraday filtering of the news sentiment signal

Recall that the sentiment of a news item is defined as the triple (*pos,neut,neg*) representing probabilities that the item can be classified as positive, neutral or negative with respect to the relevant commodity price. (Because these three probabilities add up to one, it is sufficient to consider only two of them, e.g., positive and negative). News items arrive at irregular intervals and non-equispaced over time. What is needed for quantitative trading strategies, however, is a running sentiment indicator: a relatively smooth measure of the sentiment for a particular commodity at each point in time.

So we assume that such a sentiment measure exists, but is unobserved. We denote such a measure S_t – we assume that, at each point in time t, it is a two dimensional vector, containing probabilities that the time-t sentiment is positive or negative. What is observed is the aggregate of sentiments of all news items prior to t, which we consider a noisy measurement of the true signal S_t.

More precisely, we define the observed sentiment (positive and negative), which we denote with lower case letters, at time t as

$$s_t^{p,n} = \sum_{t_i < t} w_{t-t_i} \widetilde{s}_{t_i}^{p,n}, \qquad [15.2.2]$$

i.e., it is the weighted average of all news items' sentiments $\widetilde{s}$ prior to time t. We assume that people have "short memory" and weigh news items by hyperbolically decreasing weights. The weights are chosen in such a way that 90% of all the weight is on the latest 9 articles – the choice that follows from several cognitive studies showing that people remember well on average only the 9 last things that happened to them.

Next, we assume certain dynamics of the unobserved sentiments, for example a random walk, and the observation mechanism, both given by the so-called Local Level model (Durbin and Koopman (2001)):

$$S_{t+1}^{p,n} = S_t^{p,n} + \eta_t^{p.n}, \qquad \eta_t^{p,n} \sim N\left(0, \sigma_{\eta^{p,n}}\right)$$
$$s_t^{p,n} = S_t^{p,n} + \varepsilon_t^{p,n}, \qquad \varepsilon_t^{p,n} \sim N\left(0, \sigma_{\varepsilon^{p,n}}\right)$$

[15.2.3]

The discretization time interval can be chosen e.g., 1 or 5 minutes. The volatility of the signal $\sigma_{\eta^{p,n}}$ is much lower than the volatility of noise $\sigma_{\varepsilon^{p,n}}$, and their ratio is called signal-to-noise ratio. Now the unobserved sentiment series S_t can be filtered out by applying Kalman filter methodology, together with the assessment of the uncertainty (standard error) about this sentiment at each point in time. For technical details on this, including the technicalities on the application of Kalman filter, we refer the reader to Borovkova and Mahakena (2015).

We applied this procedure to the Natural Gas news sentiment and an example of the resulting sentiment indicator on a 5-minutes grid is shown in Figure 15.2.7 (solid red (positive) and green (negative) lines). The extracted signal is much smoother than the actual observed sentiment series for individual news items. It can also deal with no-news periods: in the absence of news, the sentiment stays the same but the uncertainty surrounding it (not shown) increases.

An even smoother signal can be obtained if we use the Kalman smoother instead of the Kalman filter. Such a Kalman smoother utilizes not only information observed prior to time t, but also some of the subsequent information, for example obtained in the next minute or next 5 minutes. For trading this is not very useful as this is a forward-looking procedure, but for a smooth measurement of the commodity market sentiment, it can be applied. In Figure 15.2.7, this Kalman smoothed sentiment indicator is shown in dotted lines, which are indeed even smoother than the filtered signal.

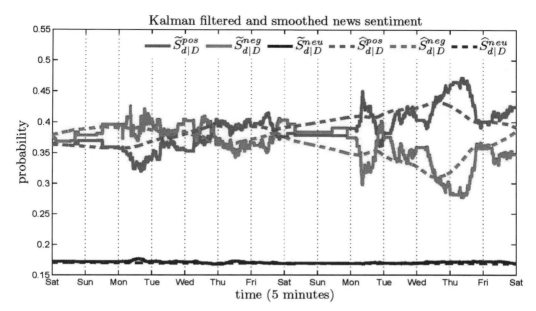

Figure 15.2.7 *Kalman filtered (solid) and smoothed (dashed) news sentiments for Natural Gas. Red: negative sentiment, green: positive sentiment, black: neutral.*

The procedure of filtering out a meaningful sentiment signal from noisy news sentiment observations can be applied to any commodity or a class of commodities. The resulting sentiment indicator can have many applications, for example, in trading or risk monitoring. Such a signal provides an excellent input to quantitative trading strategies, but can also be used for monitoring the overall sentiment of a particular commodity market.

15.3 EFFECTS OF NEWS ON RETURNS: EVENT STUDIES

We employ event studies as outlined in MacKinlay (1997) and used in Tetlock et al. (2007, 2008). We define an *event* (positive or negative) as a day in which positive resp. negative sentiment is in the top 10% of the positive resp. negative sentiment distribution. These would be the days that are "overwhelmed" by positive resp. negative news about a particular commodity. All other days are considered neutral. On each day, we use the empirical sentiment distributions obtained from the previous one year of data.

Now we describe the construction of our event studies. Note that commodities predominantly trade in the form of futures contracts with different maturities. So in the event studies presented in this section, we analyse the effects of extreme news days on a particular maturity's futures returns. The effects of news on the characteristics of the entire forward curve are analysed in the next section.

We select the specific maturity (e.g., 2nd nearby, i.e., two months to maturity) and the event window – how many trading days before and after the event we consider (e.g., 10 or 20 trading days). For each event day, we select the specific contract that has the selected maturity. For instance, on 17 March 2015, the 2nd nearby contract is May 2015. We analyse the returns of this specific contract (and not specific time to maturity) during the event window. So in the event study we are considering returns that are actually feasible – we can buy the May contract in February and sell it in March. We calculate the daily returns during the event window for the selected contracts, average the returns over all the observed events for each day before or after the event and depict the cumulative returns. The 95% confidence intervals (represented in all the plots as dashed lines) are based on the sample standard deviation of average returns.

Figure 15.3.1 shows the average cumulative returns of 2-months ahead WTI futures during the event window of 40 days. The top line shows the average cumulative returns for a positive event, the middle line – for neutral days and the bottom line – for a negative event.

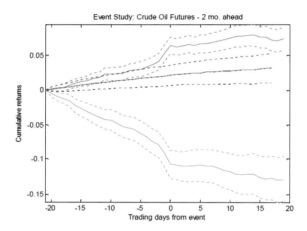

Figure 15.3.1 *Event study for WTI crude oil futures with 2 months to maturity; top: positive, middle: neutral, bottom: negative events.*

We see that, in the 20 days leading to a positive event, the overall average return on 2-month ahead crude oil futures is 6%, of which 2% are during the event day and in the day immediately prior to the event. In contrast, the overall average return is -11% leading up to a negative event, again with about -2% in the day immediately prior to the event and in the event day itself. This shows that either the news is providing stale information that has already been incorporated into the prices, or the news sentiment is correlated with the price momentum: articles about previous returns are likely rated as positive if past returns were high and negative if past returns were low – in this case, returns cause sentiment. In other words, we indeed to observe many news stories that are about past price developments, as noted in the introduction. However, it is likely that the emerging picture is the result of both stale information and correlation of news sentiment with the price momentum. Unfortunately, at present there is no indicator related to each news item signalling that this item is momentum news, neither is there a possibility of filtering out momentum-related news from the news analytics engine output. Currently our efforts, in collaboration with Thomson Reuters, are focusing on filtering out or flagging such news items and we expect to improve the TRNA output by adding such an indicator to each news item.

If there is no dramatic news (neutral days), returns are on average 2% per month; this is in line with the theory that, by buying commodity futures, you are essentially selling insurance (the return on the contract is your premium) to the commodity producer against a drop in price. For an insurance salesman, no news is good news. Equivalently, one can think of this in terms of normal backwardation: if the normal situation is for the price of the future to increase as it approaches maturity, that is what we expect to happen if there is no dramatic news.

Note that, in the 15 days after a positive event, cumulative returns rise further by 2–3%, then flatten out. It is unclear whether that is significantly more than the 2% returns observed in the absence of dramatic news. In contrast, cumulative returns drop another 3% after a negative event.

Looking at a more distant 1-year maturity in Figure 15.3.2, we see that returns fall only 8% preceding a negative event, and the post-event fall in returns is also smaller than in the 2-month case. By contrast, cumulative returns climb more than 3% after a positive event.

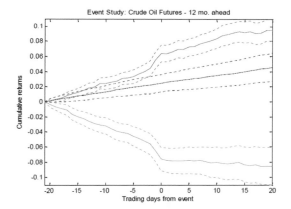

Figure 15.3.2 *Event study for WTI crude oil futures with 12 months to maturity; top: positive, middle: neutral, bottom: negative events.*

In all of the above graphs, the most distinctive feature is the asymmetry: although positive and negative events are both 10% of days, the negative events are accompanied by much greater losses than the gains surrounding positive events. So it seems that, overall, the oil futures market gives greater credence to negative news: positive news being seen to include self-serving statements from market participants.

Another explanation for this asymmetry can be found in behavioural aspects of finance: it has been observed in finance literature that bad earnings announcements have disproportionately large (negative) effects on stock prices (overreaction), compared to good earnings announcements. However, recall that the meaning of positive and negative news is different for crude oil than for stocks: news that sounds positive, can, in fact, have a negative effect on the price (and hence, will be classified as negative) and vice versa. One of the interesting conclusions of this study is that it is not negativity in terms of traditional human emotion that causes market overreaction, but negativity with respect to the price development of the considered asset or the asset class.

Similar pictures to those for oil are observed for many other commodities. Figure 15.3.3 shows event studies for NYMEX Natural Gas futures of two month maturity and an event window of 20 days. In this figure we show not only the cumulative returns surrounding the top 10% sentiment days, but also the top 30% for comparison. Note that the effects are greater for more extreme sentiment days, as expected. For top 10% sentiment days, the cumulative effect surrounding negative news events is even greater than for crude oil, while for positive events, the price increases prior to and on the event day and then reverts back to the normal level.

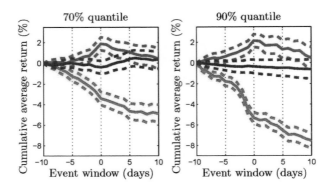

Figure 15.3.3 *Event study for NYMEX Natural Gas futures with 2 months to maturity; top: positive, middle: neutral, bottom: negative events.*

Figures 15.B.1, 15.B.2 and 15.B.3 in Appendix 15.A.2 show examples of event studies for other commodities: an industrial metal (copper) and two agricultural commodities (wheat and soy futures). All the same features – asymmetry and price momentum – are again observed. Same features are observed also for other metals such as aluminium and other agricultural commodities such as live cattle.

One commodity for which, surprisingly, we observe less asymmetry in the reaction to positive and negative news is gold (the corresponding event study is shown in Figure 15.3.4) – this is in contrast to what is observed by Smales (2014) for gold futures, which may be due to the chosen historical period. Also, here we did not use futures prices but the daily gold fixings at London Bullion Exchange.

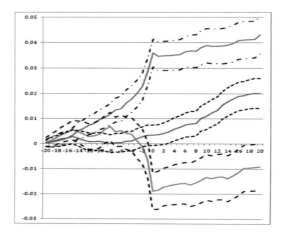

Figure 15.3.4 *Event study for gold prices at LBE; top: positive, middle: neutral, bottom: negative events.*

So to summarize the findings of the events studies, we can conclude that:

- The largest price move is observed on the event day (and in some cases one day before the event).
- For most commodities, we observe a great asymmetry: negative events are accompanied by much greater losses than the gains surrounding positive events (-12% for oil, -8% for NG; of these approximately 2–3% is post-event). Hence, commodity markets seem to give greater credence to negative news.
- News sentiment is correlated with price momentum: so news is either "old", i.e. provides stale information already incorporated into prices, or is about past price developments.

For completeness, Appendix 15.A.3 provides quantitative characteristics of event studies for different commodities, i.e. the tables of average cumulative returns.

For comparison, we present an event study performed on a higher frequency data. We take this time the first nearby WTI futures contract (the most liquid one) and define an event as a one-minute interval with the value of the running sentiment measure, described in the previous section, in the top 10% of the corresponding sentiment distribution (positive or negative). Figure 15.3.5 shows the cumulative returns for positive (upper) and negative (lower) events during an 8-hour window surrounding such an event. Again, we observe a significant price move prior to the event and price reversal in the subsequent hours. There is again a significant asymmetry in the reaction to positive and negative events: the price move accompanying a negative event is almost twice the size as the move accompanying a positive event.

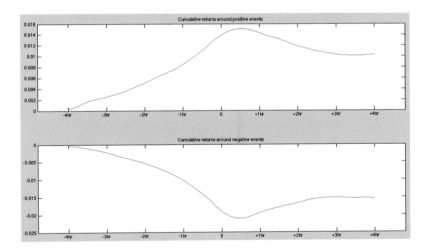

Figure 15.3.5 *An intraday event study for the first month WTI futures, 8-hour window.*
Top: positive sentiment, bottom: negative sentiment.

15.4 NEWS EFFECTS ON FORWARD CURVES

The main object in the study of commodity markets is the forward curve: a collection of futures prices for different maturities. Crude oil futures are traded up to 96 monthly maturities into the future, for natural gas, the number of available monthly maturities on NYMEX is 72. Other commodities are also traded for many maturities ahead. While futures for most commodities (energy, metals) expire monthly, agricultural commodity futures have irregular maturities, with more frequent maturities traded during harvest season.

Crude oil futures markets can be in two fundamental states: the so-called backwardation, when futures for longer maturities are cheaper than those expiring sooner, and contango, which is the opposite situation. These two states are shown in Figure 15.4.1. Backwardation is correlated with high oil prices and low inventories, and contango with low prices and high inventories; however, periods of contango with high oil prices and backwardation with low oil prices have also been observed. These two market states are very persistent and can last for months if not years. It takes approximately two weeks for the oil market to transit from one state to another. Many price features and market fundamentals are distinctly different in these two market states, so we expect the effects of news on the forward curve to be different in these two states.

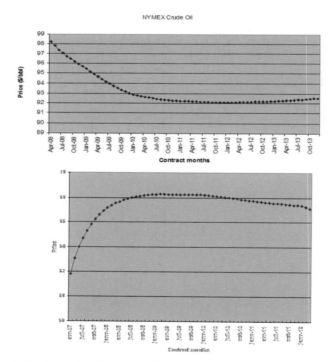

Figure 15.4.1 *Backwardation (upper) and contango (lower) market states.*

To study this, we separate backwardation and contango market states and analyse the effect of news separately for each one. We perform a similar event study to the one in the previous section (for the 2-month ahead WTI crude oil futures) separately for backwardated and contango markets. We observe that positive and, in particular, negative news events are accompanied by larger price moves in contango than in backwardated market (Figure 15.4.2).

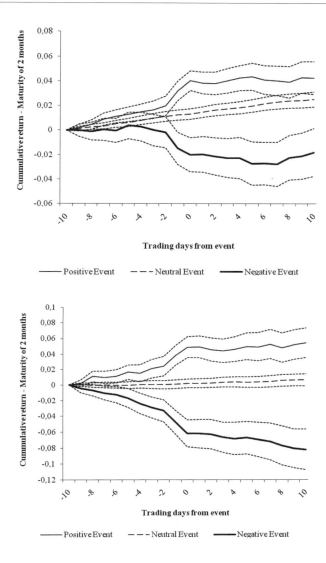

Figure 15.4.2 *Event studies for 2-month ahead WTI futures, backwardation (top) and contango(bottom).*

There could be several explanations for this phenomenon. First, in a contango market, the expectation of market participants is that the prices will rise. When a negative event occurs, it is not what the majority is expecting. Bearing in mind that the reaction to *negative news* is dominant, it appears that the market reaction to news is higher in contango. The second, and perhaps most plausible, explanation is that commodity investors, who invest predominantly in futures, earn money in a backwardated market just by rolling their contracts forward. In contango, on the other hand, they lose money by replacing their expiring contracts by the new ones, so any negative event occurring in this situation will exacerbate their losses, causing a stronger reaction to news. Finally, it can also be the case that the later period in our dataset coincided with a domination of contango, and also with heightened awareness of commodity-related news, so larger price effects in contango is partially also a coincidence.

When studying the evolution of the forward curve, it is not efficient to consider futures prices for different maturities separately, as these prices move, for a large part, together. Instead, we should define fundamental factors describing the forward curve's evolution and relate all futures prices to those factors. One such choice of the fundamental factors is described in Borovkova and Geman (2007, 2008) and it is inspired by the technique of Principal Component Analysis and study of interest rates yield curve. In Borovkova and Geman's model, the first fundamental factor is the level of the curve, defined as the *geometric average of futures prices of all maturities* (possibly liquidity-weighted). Another factor, describing the backwardation or contango shape of the curve, is its slope, defined as the *coefficient of the ordinary least squares regression of log-futures prices vs. time to maturity*. The model also allows for the stochastic forward premium (the third fundamental factor) and deterministic maturity-related seasonality, essential when modelling natural gas, electricity or agricultural forward curves. The seasonal nature of some energy and agricultural commodities is related to either harvest or heating season, and results in complex maturity-related seasonalities. As an example, observe a typical Natural Gas forward curve, shown in Figure 15.4.3; note significantly higher futures prices during winter months. This occurs due to the fact that natural gas is only partially storable and hard to transport, so these seasonal peaks are not completely smoothed out by transporting gas from warmer to colder regions, or by injection during summer months and extraction during winter months.

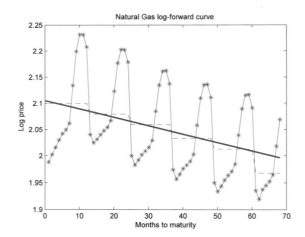

Figure 15.4.3 *Natural gas log-forward curve with the fitted regression line.*

For such seasonal commodities it is possible to extract maturity-related seasonalities by the procedure described in Borovkova and Geman (2007) and still describe the evolution of the forward curve by the level and the slope, defined above. Almost all possible movements of the forward curve (90–95%) can be explained by the movements of these two fundamental factors. So in this section we will investigate the effects of news sentiment on the movements of these two fundamental factors: the level and the slope.

Here we shall demonstrate the effects of news on forward curves in the example of crude oil; for other commodities, effects are similar. We perform event studies similar to those described in the previous section. The response variables are daily log-returns of the forward curve's level and daily changes in the forward curve's slope.

When we observe the effect of positive and negative news events on the forward curve's level, the same picture emerges as in the previous section (Figure 15.4.4). This is not surprising, as this effect is the "average" response of all individual maturities to significant positive or negative news.

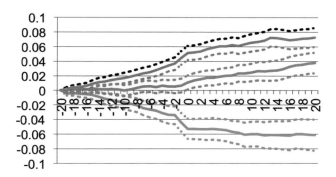

Figure 15.4.4 *The event study for the crude oil forward curve's level; top: positive, middle: neutral, bottom: negative events.*

The effect of news on the forward curve's slope, i.e., on the degree of backwardation or contango in the oil futures market, is not intuitively obvious. To assess this effect, we first fit a linear regression to the daily change in slope vs. daily sentiment, shown in Figure 15.4.5. This figure shows that, on average, positive sentiment decreases the slope, while negative sentiment does the opposite and increases the forward curve's slope (all linear regression coefficients are significant at 5% level). This is somewhat surprising, as it is the opposite of the effect of news on the level and on individual maturities' returns.

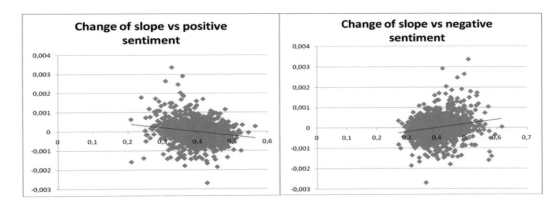

Figure 15.4.5 *Linear regression of slope changes vs sentiment.*

To investigate the cumulative effect of news on the slope through time, we again perform an event study. Figure 15.4.6 shows the event study results for the aggregated change in slope during 20 days surrounding a significant news event.

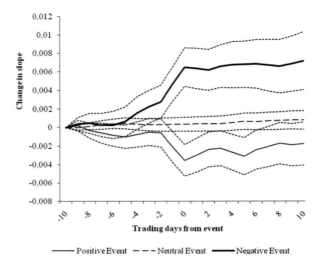

Figure 15.4.6 *The event study for the crude oil forward curve's slope; top (solid) line: negative event, bottom (thin solid) line: positive event, dashed line: neutral.*

Note that the above picture is indeed the reverse of those seen so far: remarkably, negative news is accompanied by a significant *increase* in forward curve's slope (accumulated increase of approximately 10% of the average slope); positive news is accompanied by a sharp *decrease* in the slope two days before the event, with little change afterwards (in the neutral case, the curve's slope stays, on average, the same). Again, asymmetry is clearly present: negative news events are accompanied by a greater change in the forward curve's slope than positive news events. This implies that contango deepens and backwardation flattens in the days surrounding a negative news event. The reason for this is the fact that, e.g., around a negative news event, prices for all maturities fall, but nearby futures fall in price more than distant maturities – the illustration of this effect is given in Figure 15.4.7. This observation gives rise to a relatively low-risk trading strategy: at a negative event, one can enter a short position in short-term futures and a corresponding long position in long maturity futures (and do the opposite at a positive event). By this, one can benefit from the subsequent price move, but at low risk, as such a short-long strategy is well hedged.

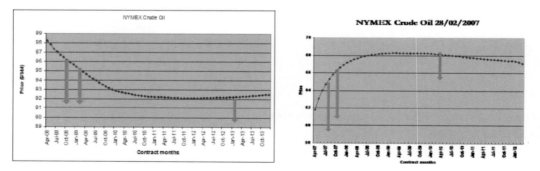

Figure 15.4.7 *Illustration of the negative event's effect on the crude oil forward curve's slope.*

To summarize the results of this section, we can note that the effects of news sentiment on commodity forward curves are complex and not obvious. Moreover, these effects depend on the overall state of the market. Analysing the effects of news sentiment on the fundamental factors of the forward curve can give rise to profitable and low-risk trading strategies, as trading in calendar spreads is much less risky than taking outright futures positions. For seasonal commodities, such as natural gas or agricultural commodities, maturity-related seasonalities should be taken into account.

15.5 COMMODITY NEWS SENTIMENT INDICES

In the first decade of the 2000s, surging interest in commodities has led institutional and private investors to enter commodity markets. Such non-traditional financial players invest in commodities predominantly by means of *commodity indices*, which are baskets of commodity futures. The three most popular indices are the DJ-UBS, S&P Goldman Sachs (GSCI) and Reuters/Jefferies CRB commodity indices. Each index has its advantages and disadvantages. For example, GSCI is the most-tracked index in the market — it has the most funds following, or tracking, its performance. However, the most closely *watched* index is the Reuters/Jefferies CRB Index. The CRB Index is a global benchmark for what the commodities markets are doing. The composition of the indices is also quite different, for example GSCI gives a relatively large weight (over 70%) to energy commodities. On the other hand, the DJ-UBS commodity index is more diversified, as no single commodity may constitute less than 2% and no related group of commodities (e.g., energy, precious metals, livestock or grains) may constitute more than 33% of this index.

Commodity-related news sentiment is measured in e.g., Thomson Reuters News Analytics (TRNA) for many specific commodities or commodity classes. However, if we want to investigate the sentiment of the commodity market as a whole and to relate it to commodity price indices such as GSCI, we need to construct a market-wide commodity news sentiment index. Such a news index can be constructed on the basis of any price index, or even independently of it, in the following way.

First, we need to determine the weights of each commodity, commodity class or group in such a news index. If the goal is to relate it to a price index such as DJ-UBS or GSCI, then the weights in the price index can be used for this purpose. For example, the weights of commodities in DJ-UBS commodity index (as of 2012) are given in Appendix 15.A.4. Note that sentiment measures are not available for all commodities in the price index. For example, there is no separate ticker in the news sentiment database for commodities such as live cattle, individual industrial or precious metals or for different grades of oil and oil products. So we assign the weights to those commodity groups equal to the aggregate DJ-UBS weights of the corresponding commodities in that group, also shown in Appendix 15.A.4.

The market-wide commodity news sentiment index can be constructed on a daily basis, using daily sentiment scores for individual commodities or commodity classes, or for higher frequencies, using commodity-specific running sentiments, whose construction we described in Section 15.2.2. Let $S_{k,t}$ be the sentiment for commodity (or commodity group) k at time/day t, and let be the commodity-k weight in the index. The overall commodity news sentiment index at time t is then the weighted average of the commodity-specific sentiments:

$$S_t^{Index} = \sum_{k=1}^{K} w_k S_{k,t},$$ [15.5.1]

where K is the number of commodities in the index and $\sum_{k=1}^{K} w_k = 1.$.

If for a certain day or time t there is no news about a particular commodity i (which can happen for smaller commodities such as some agricultural commodities), then we need to re-normalize the weights in the index so that the absolute weights remain the same but relative weights still add up to one $\widetilde{w}_k = \frac{w_k}{\sum_{j \neq i} w_j}$. For example, let the commodity news sentiment index consist of three commodities: oil (with the weight 0.6), gold (with the weight 0.3) and wheat (with the weight 0.1). If, on the day t, there is no news about wheat, then the sentiment index on that day is calculated as

$$S_t^{Index} = \frac{0.6}{0.6+0.3} S_{oil,t} + \frac{0.3}{0.6+0.3} S_{gold,t}.$$ [15.5.2]

If we wish to construct a commodity news sentiment index not related to any price index, we can define the weights as equal to the proportion of the average news volume about each commodity or commodity group provided by the news analytics engine. For example, for TRNA, such weights (for some commodities) are given in Table 15.2.1 (second column). Note that, for such a choice, agricultural commodities would be rather underrepresented, while energy and metals would receive quite a large weight, so such a news sentiment index would rather closely resemble that obtained on the basis of GSCI.

Having constructed an aggregated commodity news sentiment series, we can again employ event studies and vector autoregression (VAR) models to relate it to the corresponding commodity price index's returns and volatility. Furthermore, we can use the Granger Causality test to determine whether the market-wide news sentiment is driving the index returns and volatility or vice versa. Finally, we can employ cointegration analysis to test for long-term relationships between the commodity news sentiment and price indices. In this section, we report such findings for the example of the Goldman Sachs Commodity Index (GSCI), for daily closing prices and returns; the relationship between the news sentiment and the volatility will be dealt with in the next section.

First, we look at the relations between the returns and sentiment. We calculated the historical correlation between the daily returns of the commodity price indices and the daily changes in the corresponding news sentiment index. These are presented in Table 15.5.1.

Table 15.5.1: *Correlations between index returns and news sentiment daily changes.*

GSCI	DJ-UBS	CRB
0.0946	0.1243	0.2139

The event studies for commodity price indices at the daily frequency provide results that are very similar to the event studies presented in Section 15.3, as such an event study is just a weighted average of event studies for individual commodities. Hence, we do not present daily event study plots for commodity indices here, but only for price responses at a higher frequency. Figure 15.5.1 shows such an event study for an event window of +/- 4 hours for the CRB index; the time grid is 1 minute. Note again the same features as observed before: a significant price move prior to an event, but also a significant price move for an hour after an event (positive or negative), as well as asymmetry between the reaction to positive and negative news event.

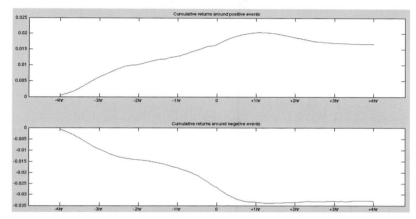

Figure 15.5.1 *Intraday event study for CRB, event window 8 hours. Top: positive sentiment, bottom: negative sentiment.*

We applied Vector Autoregression (VAR) to GSCI lagged returns and daily changes in the related net-positive sentiment index. From this analysis we observe a clear autocorrelation structure in the sentiment index, lasting up to four days. We also observe a slightly significant (at 10%) and positive effect of net positive sentiment on the next day's return. On the other hand, we also find a very significant (at 1%) effect of previous day return on the next day's sentiment. This means that if there is a positive return on the price index today, it increases the net positive sentiment tomorrow. This is again a manifestation of momentum-related news, i.e., news stories about previous returns.

If we separate the historical period into periods of bullish and bearish market (for example, the period August 2007–February 2009 is a clear example of a bearish, i.e., declining market) and apply VAR again, we observe that the effect of news sentiment on returns is higher when commodity markets fall, i.e., in bearish markets, and almost insignificant in bullish markets. The regression coefficient measuring the influence of net positive sentiment on the next day's return is almost three times higher during bearish markets than for the entire sample, while the adjusted R-squared for the regression is more than doubled. This indicates that investors pay more attention and trade more on the basis of news when markets are falling, and are rather ignorant of the news when commodity markets rise – a fact confirmed by many other behavioural finance studies. Furthermore, the reduction of the selected autoregression order from 4 to 1 during bearish markets indicates that investors need less time to incorporate news during bear periods.

The Granger causality test, applied to the same variables, shows results consistent with the VAR analysis: the news sentiment index Granger-causes the next day return (this is illustrated in Figure 15.5.2 by means of Impulse Response Function), and vice versa, i.e., the return causes sentiment. These causality relationships are again much stronger in bear than in bull markets. We also observe Granger causality relationships between sentiment and volatility, which we will elaborate on in the next section.

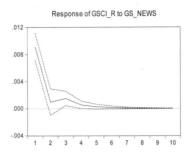

Figure 15.5.2: Impulse response function of GSCI return to net positive news sentiment (response to 1 S.D.)

Finally, we investigate long-term relationships between news sentiment and price indices. The daily sentiment score is a short-term measure, which is confirmed by the absence of any unit root in the daily sentiment series. So to measure long-term sentiment, we form moving average versions of the sentiment series, averaging the daily sentiment over a month, quarter or half a year. These series, together with the GSCI commodity index, are shown in Figure 15.5.3.

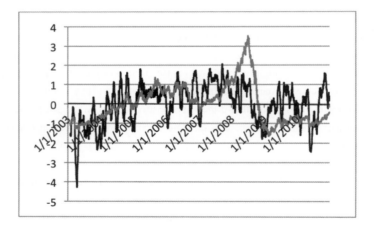

Figure 15.5.3 *Monthly (previous page), quarterly (top) and semi-annual (bottom) moving average news sentiment index (black) vs GSCI (grey).*

From the above figures it is clear that the series of long-term sentiment index and the GSCI closely follow each other in terms of long trends. Johansen's cointegration test confirms the existence of significant cointegrating relationships between long-term sentiment and commodity price index.

To summarize, the commodity market-wide sentiment indices, constructed on the basis of the corresponding price indices, both provide short-term forecasting power and reveal long-term relationships between sentiment and prices. They can be used for constructing trading and investment strategies (both short- and long-term) and for monitoring the overall state of commodity markets. In the next section, we will show how including sentiment indices in volatility models can help improve volatility forecasts and hence be used in risk-management applications.

15.6 VOLATILITY AND JUMPS VS. NEWS

15.6.1 News-augmented volatility models

For equities, significant relationships between volatility and news have been observed in the literature (see e.g., Mitra et al. (2009)). For commodities, we also expect to find significant relationships between news and its sentiment and volatility: when the volume of (particularly negative) news is high, volatility should rise, reflecting e.g., risk-aversion and other behavioural characteristics of market participants.

Time-changing volatility (also in commodity markets) is routinely modelled by GARCH models of the form:

$$\sigma_t^2 = \omega V_L + \alpha r_{t-1}^2 + \beta \sigma_{t-1}^2 \qquad [15.6.1]$$

where σ_t^2 is the conditional variance on day t, r_{t-1}^2 is the previous day's squared logreturn, V_L is the long-term variance and the positive model coefficients must add up to one to ensure stationarity of the resulting process: $\omega + \alpha + \beta = 1$.

Volatility responds asymmetrically to positive and negative returns, so the so-called leverage effect is often added:

$$\sigma_t^2 = \omega V_L + \big(\alpha + \gamma I(r_{t-1} < 0)\big) r_{t-1}^2 + \beta \sigma_{t-1}^2, \qquad [15:6.2]$$

where the sign of the leverage coefficient indicates the so-called normal ($\gamma > 0$) or inverse ($\gamma < 0$) leverage effect.

For equities, normal leverage effect is usually present. It has been a subject of a long debate in the literature whether the inverse or normal leverage effect is present in commodities. Many studies point out that the inverse leverage effect is persistent in agricultural commodities, as rising prices are often perceived as being bad for the economy and mankind. For metals and energy, however, evidence is mixed. Prior to the financial crisis of 2007–2008, the inverse leverage effect has also been documented for energy. Recently, however, more and more evidence has emerged in academic as well as in professional literature pointing to the disappearance of the inverse leverage effect and even a reversal towards the normal leverage for energy and metals. However, it is still important to include leverage terms in volatility models to take into account the possibility of asymmetric volatility.

To study the effects of news sentiment on volatility, we apply the so-called GARCH-X models, where we augment the variance equation with an external sentiment variable:

$$\sigma^2 = \omega V_L + \big(\alpha + \gamma I(r_{t-1} < 0)\big) r_{t-1}^2 + \beta \sigma_{t-1}^2 + \theta sent_{t-1}. \qquad [15.6.3]$$

We can include different sentiment variables into the GARCH model: positive and/or negative sentiment scores, or the net positive sentiment: $pos_{net} = sent_{pos} - sent_{neg}$. However, it might also be that high (in absolute value) sentiment (regardless whether it is positive or negative) causes volatility, so another choice of a sentiment variable would be the absolute net sentiment: $|sent_{pos} - sent_{neg}|$. It turns out that a slightly modified version of the absolute sentiment is also useful in volatility models: what we will call Absolute Sentiment:

$$AS = |sent_{pos} - sent_{neg}|/(1 - sent_{neut}).$$ [15.6.4]

It measures not just the strength of sentiment, but also "agreement" about today's sentiment (note that we can define $(1 - AS)$ as "disagreement" about the sentiment). We can illustrate this in the following simple example. Suppose we observed the following sentiment values on several days:

	pos	neut	neg	AS	net pos
Day 1:	0.5	0.4	0.1	2/3	0.4
Day 2:	0.5	0.1	0.4	1/9	0.1
Day 3:	0.8	0	0.2	0.6	0.6
Day 4:	0.6	0.4	0	1	0.6
Day 5:	0.9	0.1	0.3	2/3	0.6

The difference between Day 1 and Day 2 is that, although the positive sentiments are the same, the positive sentiment signal (as well as the overall agreement about this sentiment) is stronger on Day 1, which is captured by both net positive and absolute sentiment. However, if we consider Days 3, 4 and 5, we see that the Absolute Sentiment (AS) gives Day 4 the strongest score, as there is no negative sentiment at all on that day and hence, there is the highest "agreement" about the sentiment. So the Absolute Sentiment can also be included in the models, by itself or possibly combined with the net positive sentiment (e.g., weighting the net positive sentiment by AS).

We have fitted news-augmented asymmetric GARCH models to crude oil and natural gas futures (NYMEX first nearby contracts). The estimation results are presented in Tables 15.6.1 and 15.6.2. All reported parameters are significant at 5% (not significant parameters are not reported).

Table 15.6.1: Parameter estimates, asymmetric GARCH-X, crude oil.

Par.	GARCH	Sent_neg	Net pos	|pos-neg|	AS
Constant	0.0000	0.0000	0.0000	0.0000	0.0000
α	0.0198	0.0264	0.0205	0.0224	0.0206
β	0.9265	0.9111	0.9108	0.9258	0.9258
γ	0.0656	0.0631	0.0644	0.0640	0.0646
Θ	--	0.0002	-0.0002		
LogLik	5336.124	5338.691	5339.397	5337.257	5336.978

Table 15.6.2: *Parameter estimates, GARCH-X, natural gas*

Par.	GARCH	Sent_pos	Sent_neg	Net pos	|pos-neg|	AS
Constant	0.0000	0.0000	0.0000	0.0000	0.0000	0.0000
α	0.0285	0.0377	0.0263	0.0199	0.0008	0.0006
β	0.9617	0.9498	0.9666	0.9741	0.9817	0.9865
Θ	--	-0.0001	0.0001	0.0003	0.0002	0.0003
LogLik	1581.418	1582.171	1582.265	1583.094	1590.190	1589.175

From these tables we see that the best performance for crude oil is observed for the models that include negative sentiment, alone or in combination with positive sentiment (net positive). The coefficient of negative sentiment is highly significant and positive, indicating that high negative sentiment increases volatility, as expected. Significant normal leverage effect is observed for oil futures. For natural gas, the results are different: there is no significant leverage effect (hence, the results for the regular GARCH-X are reported) and the best models are the ones that include either absolute sentiment or AS. This shows that natural gas volatility increases when absolute sentiment is high, regardless whether it is positive or negative. Hence, the choice of the explanatory sentiment variables depends crucially on the commodity in question.

We also investigated the influence of news sentiment on commodity indices' volatility. As expected, negative sentiment significantly increases the next day's index volatility. This is illustrated by the impulse-response function of volatility to net positive sentiment, shown in Figure 15.6.1.

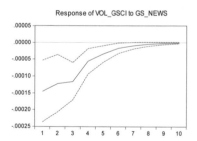

Response of VOL_GSCI to GS_NEWS

Figure 15.6.1 *Impulse response function of GSCI volatility to absolute positive news sentiment (response to 1 S.D.).*

We fitted a news sentiment-augmented asymmetric GARCH model to GSCI returns. The best explanatory power is obtained when including net positive sentiment in the model. Table 15.6.3 shows the estimated coefficients for such a model.

Table 15.6.3 *Estimated coefficients of asymmetric GARCH-X model fitted to GSCI returns.*

	Coefficient
Constant	0.0000
α	0.0246*
β	0.6242***
γ	0.4005***
Θ (net pos)	-0.0004***

The above table shows that GSCI exhibits the regular leverage effect, which is not surprising as this index is mostly used by long-only investors. Furthermore, the coefficient corresponding to the net positive sentiment is highly significant and negative, indicating that high positive sentiment decreases and high negative sentiment increases volatility.

In all, we find that sentiment measures are useful for improved volatility forecasting. Including carefully chosen sentiment variables in volatility forecasting models significantly improves model-fit and leads to superior forecasts.

15.6.2 Causality relationships between news, volatility and price jumps

Many commodity prices exhibit jumps, the extreme example of this being electricity prices. These price jumps occur due to unexpected supply interruptions, geopolitical and other external events, which are exactly the kind of information that appears in the news. If we were able to identify price jumps, we could relate them to the arrival and the sentiment of news. The technique of bi-power variation of Barndorff-Nielsen and Shephard (2004) allows us to do just that.

Suppose that the log-price process can be well described by the so-called *jump-diffusion*, that is, a stochastic process that consists of a diffusive component (typically modelled by the Brownian motion W_t with a drift) and a jump component J_t (usually taken to be a compound Poisson process):

$$dY_t = a_t dt + \sigma dW_t + dJ_t \qquad [15.6.5]$$

If, for each day t, we observe high frequency returns $r_{t,i}$, we can estimate the quadratic variation of this process on day t by the realized variance:

$$RV_t = \sum_{i=1}^{I} r_{t,i}^2 \qquad [15.6.6]$$

or by its alternative, the so-called *realized kernel RK*, which is an estimator more robust to microstructure noise (see e.g., Barndorff-Nielsen et al. (2008)). If jumps are present, then these estimates will contain both the diffusive component's variance and the jump variance. Can we separate these two components?

It turns out that it is possible, by calculating the so-called *bi-power variation*, which is a variant of the realized variance, robust to jumps (for details, we refer the reader to Barndorff-Nielsen and Shephard (2004)). Together, the jump variance and the jump-robust estimator of the diffusive component's variance (which is exactly the bi-power variation) must add up to the realized variance:

$$RV_t = BPV_t + JV_t \qquad\qquad [15.6.7]$$

Hence, we can use this equation to calculate the day-t estimate of the jump variance JV_t and to separate jumps from the diffusive price moves. Moreover, it is possible to separate up and down jumps, as well as up- and downside semi-variances, i.e., variances corresponding to the positive and negative price moves.

We applied the above procedure to the Natural Gas first nearby futures prices from NYMEX. The reason we chose Natural Gas is that this commodity clearly exhibits price jumps (unlike crude oil, where the presence of jumps has not been established with certainty), and for which there is enough news flow to relate this news to jumps in prices (unlike, e.g., electricity, for which there is no significant amount of news).

Figure 15.6.2 shows an extract from the historical dataset, with daily realized variance/realized kernel and jump variation extracted from it by means of the bi-power variation. It turns out that approximately 20% of all daily natural gas price moves can be classified as jumps, of which there are slightly more negative than positive jumps.

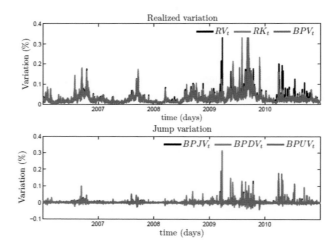

Figure 15.6.2 *Realized variation (top graph) and jump variation (bottom graph) for NG futures.*

Next, we applied the Granger causality test to establish whether the realized variance and its components (positive/negative jumps and semi-variances) cause and are caused by news. For news sentiment series, we use the running NG-related news sentiment series, whose construction we described in the Section 15.2. Tables 15.6.4 and 15.6.5 summarize the most important causality relationships. We adopt a convention that columns cause rows, "+" stands for significant at 10%, "++" significant at 5% and "+++" significant at 1% causality relationships.

Table 15.6.4 *Causality relationships between variance and sentiment measures.*

	RV/RK	NegVar	PosVar	SentPos	SentNeg	SentAbs
RV/RK				++	+++	
NegVar				+	+	
PosVar				++	+++	
SentPos	+++	+	++			
SentNeg	+++	+	+++			
SentAbs		++				

Table 15.6.5 *Causality relationships between price jumps and sentiment measures.*

	BPV	JV	NegJumpV	PosJumpV	SentPos	SentNeg	SentAbs
BPV					+	++	
JV					+++	+++	+++
NegJumpV					+++	+++	+++
PosJumpV					+++	+++	+++
SentPos			+++	++			
SentNeg			+++	++			
SentAbs		++	++				

Tables 15.6.4 and 15.6.5 show cross-causality relationships between positive and negative news sentiment, the realized variance and both semi-variances. We also see that negative sentiment causes the realized variance (as we have already observed in Section 15.6.1), but also that the variance measures cause news sentiment.

From the second table, it is clear that jumps (and especially negative jumps) cause absolute as well as positive and negative sentiment – so the sentiment is more sensitive to negative than to positive jumps. Most importantly, all news sentiment measures severely cause jumps. This confirms our hypothesis that jumps are predominantly caused by external information that arrives in the market in the form of news. As a result, market participants take futures positions (long or short) when news sentiment (either positive or negative) is high, causing large price moves that are identified as jumps.

To conclude this section, we argue that the findings of this section – volatility models augmented with sentiment measures, the causality relationships between news sentiment and up/down price moves – can help to devise better risk forecasting models for risk management and monitoring purposes.

15.7 CONCLUSIONS

In this chapter we gave an overview of news analytics for commodities. We described the main characteristics of commodity-related news, its effects on returns, volatilities and price jumps, and the construction of various news sentiment indices (commodity-specific and market-wide). However, this overview is by no means exhaustive, and commodity news sentiment applications are undoubtedly more numerous than those outlined here.

The overall conclusion of this chapter is that the responses of commodity markets to sentiment in news are complex: they depend on the state of the market and on the characteristics of a specific commodity. The exciting research area of commodity news analytics is relatively new, fresh and underdeveloped. Significant advances in quantitative trading, investment and risk management on the basis of commodity news are still much needed. In particular, investigating high-frequency reaction of prices to news sentiment and devising and testing corresponding trading strategies is an interesting research direction.

The main improvement in sentiment analysis for commodities would come from correctly identifying and filtering of momentum-related news (i.e., news discussing past price developments). Providing other characteristics of news such as whether a news item is supply- or demand-related would also greatly enhance any quantitative trading strategies, risk management or investment applications.

ACKNOWLEDGMENTS

The author would like to thank Alan Lammiman, Erszebet Toth, Nikki Be and Nawied Sawari for their invaluable input to this project. The hospitality and excellent working conditions at the Institute of Pure and Applied Mathematics at UCLA are also gratefully acknowledged.

15.8 REFERENCES

1.   Allen, D.E., McAleer, M. and Singh, A.K. (2013). Daily market news sentiment and stock prices. Working paper. Available from: http://eprints.ucm.es/33044/

2.   Barndorff-Nielsen, O. and Shephard, N. (2004). Power and bipower variation with stochastic volatility and jumps (with discussion). *Journal of financial econometrics*, 2(1), 1–37.

3.   Barndorff-Nielsen, O., Hansen, P., Lunde, A. and Shephard, N. (2008). Designing realised kernels to measure ex-post variation of equity prices in the presence of noise. *Econometrica*, 76(6), 1481–1536.

4.   Borovkova, S. and Geman, H. (2007). Seasonal and stochastic effects in commodity forward curves. *Review of Derivatives Research*, 9(2), 167–186.

5.   Borovkova, S. and Geman, H. (2008). Forward Curve Modelling in Commodity Markets. *Risk Management in Commodity Markets: from shipping to agriculturals and energy* (Wiley Finance, London), 9 – 32.

6.   Borovkova, S. (2011). News analytics for energy futures. Working paper. Available on SSRN: http://papers.ssrn.com/sol3/papers.cfm?abstract_id=1719582

7.   Borovkova, S. and Mahakena, D. (2015). News, volatility and jumps: the case of natural gas futures. *Quantitative Finance* (in press).

8.   Durbin, J. and Koopman, S.J. (2001). *Time Series Analysis by State Space Methods*. Oxford University Press.

9.   Gross-Klussmann, A. and Hautsch, N. (2011). When machines read the news: Using Automated text analytics to quantify high frequency news-implied market reactions. *Journal of Empirical Finance*, 18, 321–340.

10.   Mitra, L. and Mitra, G. (2011). *The Handbook of News Analytics in Finance*. John Wiley & Sons.

11.   MacKinlay, C. (1997). Event Studies in Economics and Finance. *Journal of Economic Literature*, 35, 13–39.

12.   Mitra, L., Mitra, G., and di Bartolomeo, D. (2009). Equity portfolio risk (volatility) estimation using market information and sentiment. *Quantitative Finance*, 9(8), 887–895.

13.   Sinha, N.R., 2010. Underreaction to news in the US stock market. Available on SSRN: http://ssrn.com/abstract=1572614

14.   Smales, L. (2014). News Sentiment in the Gold Futures Market. J*ournal of Banking and Finance*, 49, 275–286.

15.   Tetlock, P.C. (2007). Giving content to investor sentiment: The role of media in the stock Market. *Journal of Finance*, 62, 1139–1168.

16.   Tetlock, P.C, Saar-Tsechansky, M. and MacSkassy, S. (2008). More than words: quantifying language to measure firm's fundamentals. *Journal of Finance*, 63, 1437–1467.

15.A APPENDIX

15.A.1 News articles

<u>"Oil Caps Biggest 2-Week Gain in 17 Years Amid Volatility" (Bloomberg, February 5, 2015).</u>
Crude oil capped the biggest two-week rally in 17 years on speculation a falling rig count will curb U.S. production growth. Price volatility rose to the highest in almost six years.

Brent crude jumped 18 percent in the past 10 trading days, the most since March 1998. A volatility index gauging price fluctuations in West Texas Intermediate crude rose this week to the highest since 2009.

Oil has rebounded as companies including Statoil ASA, BP Plc and Royal Dutch Shell Plc have reduced investments in response to the market's collapse. U.S. drillers pulled more rigs off oil fields, according to data from Baker Hughes Inc. Friday. Saudi Arabia cut prices for March exports to Asia to the lowest in at least 14 years, signaling OPEC's largest producer may continue to fight for market share

"We are establishing a bottom," said Bill O'Grady, chief market strategist at Confluence Investment Management in St. Louis, which oversees $2.4 billion. "In the long run, probably $60 is going to be your pivot point. Usually you have high volatility when there is a disagreement on where the price should be."

Brent for March settlement increased $1.23, or 2.2 percent, to $57.80 a barrel on the London-based ICE Futures Europe exchange, up 9.1 percent this week. Even after the recent rally, Brent has still fallen about 50 percent from its June 19 high of $115.71.

<u>"Capex cuts will determine oil's bottom" (CNBC News, February 11, 2015).</u>
Despite the most-recent rally, oil prices will keep on dropping until capital expenditure cuts filter through the market, RBC Capital's head of commodities research said Wednesday.

"You had rig count reductions and people said this is a turn, but the problem is you're battling with very-high inventory levels, and the [capital expenditures] cuts are probably not going to filter through [until] the back half of the year," Helima Croft told CNBC's "Squawk on the Street."

Croft added other factors could also cause oil prices to bottom. "[Those] are not based on actual production," she said. "Those are more geopolitical factors." Croft also said some of these external geopolitical factors have yet to filter through the oil market.

"There's not a concern in the market right now about Nigeria," she said. "Their election was supposed to take place this weekend; it's been postponed. Historically, we've seen significant volumes of crude come off the market around Nigerian elections. In the 2003 elections ... we lost 850,000 barrels of production because of unrest around oil facilities."

Croft also said she expects oil to make a comeback as soon as early 2016, as long as capex cuts take effect. "This really should filter through 2016 and demand should recover," she said. "We should be looking at a much higher demand picture in 2016."

Nevertheless, Croft added that there will be a selloff on Wednesday if the rig count comes in higher than expected. U.S. crude inventories rose to 4.86 million barrels last week, topping analysts' estimates of 3.7 million. In early afternoon trading Wednesday, WTI was down 1.1 percent to about $49.50 per barrel, while Brent crude dropped 2.4 percent to $55.10 per barrel

15.A.2 Event studies for other commodities.

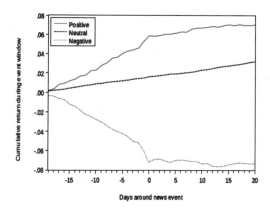

Figure 15.A.1 *Event study for copper futures with 2 months to maturity; top: positive, middle: neutral, bottom: negative events.*

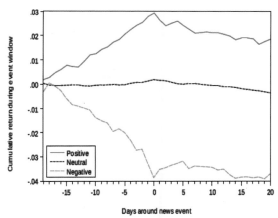

Figure 15.A.2 *Event study for wheat futures with 2 months to maturity; top: positive, middle: neutral, bottom: negative events.*

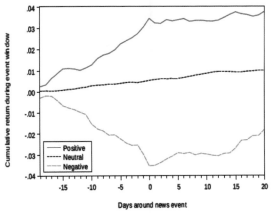

Figure 15.A.3 *Event study for soybean futures with 2 months to maturity; top: positive, middle: neutral, bottom: negative events.*

15.A.3 Cumulative excess returns for event studies

Commodity	Sentiment	Cumulative excess return during days				
		-60 to -6	-5 to 0	1 to 5	6 to 60	-60 to 60
Energy						
Natural Gas (US)	Positive	2,84%	1,84%	0,29%	-0,22%	4,75%
	Negative	-5,78%	-1,81%	0,13%	-8,14%	-15,60%
Natural Gas (Europe)	Positive	2,92%	1,09%	-0,13%	-1,12%	2,76%
	Negative	-3,49%	-1,79%	-0,22%	-6,02%	-11,52%
Agriculture						
Corn	Positive	2,13%	0,54%	-0,35%	0,06%	2,38%
	Negative	-5,56%	-1,36%	0,21%	-0,42%	-7,14%
Oats	Positive	4,59%	1,14%	0,41%	3,35%	9,50%
	Negative	-10,12%	-2,07%	-0,14%	-4,06%	-16,40%
Soybeans	Positive	1,88%	1,25%	-0,28%	1,50%	4,34%
	Negative	-6,28%	-1,65%	0,15%	-0,24%	-8,02%
Metals						
Copper	Positive	6,22%	1,68%	0,13%	-0,53%	7,50%
	Negative	-15,37%	-3,52%	-0,18%	-2,35%	-21,42%
Gold	Positive	-1,24%	0,92%	0,02%	-1,38%	-1,68%
	Negative	-0,74%	-1,29%	0,32%	0,81%	-0,90%
Silver	Positive	-0,01%	1,71%	-0,20%	-3,48%	-1,98%
	Negative	-5,28%	-3,01%	0,20%	1,42%	-6,67%

Commodity	Sentiment	Cumulative excess return during days				
		-20 to -6	-5 to 0	1 to 5	6 to 20	-20 to 20
Energy						
Natural Gas (US)	Positive	0,02%	2,01%	0,16%	2,43%	4,63%
	Negative	-1,35%	-2,15%	1,31%	1,05%	-1,14%
Natural Gas (Europe)	Positive	3,22%	1,04%	1,56%	1,46%	7,28%
	Negative	-0,29%	-0,96%	0,25%	0,05%	-0,95%
Agriculture						
Cocoa	Positive	0,13%	0,65%	0,28%	-0,93%	0,13%
	Negative	-0,38%	-1,53%	0,42%	0,48%	-1,00%
Coffee	Positive	0,58%	0,43%	-0,87%	-0,73%	-0,59%
	Negative	-0,57%	-0,95%	-0,07%	0,97%	-0,62%
Corn	Positive	0,91%	0,21%	-0,68%	-1,24%	-0,80%
	Negative	-1,46%	-2,07%	0,79%	0,16%	-2,57%
Cotton	Positive	0,12%	0,47%	-0,82%	-1,36%	-1,58%
	Negative	-0,80%	-1,94%	-0,22%	0,20%	-2,76%
Oats	Positive	2,85%	1,01%	0,04%	-1,11%	2,80%
	Negative	-3,49%	-2,13%	-0,20%	0,39%	-5,43%
Rough Rice	Positive	0,61%	0,14%	0,17%	0,33%	1,25%
	Negative	-2,78%	-1,92%	0,51%	-0,87%	-5,06%
Soybeans	Positive	1,62%	1,31%	-0,16%	-0,01%	2,76%
	Negative	-2,43%	-1,66%	0,53%	0,71%	-2,85%
Sugar	Positive	0,23%	0,20%	-0,94%	-1,89%	-2,40%
	Negative	-2,57%	-1,79%	0,76%	2,37%	-1,24%
Wheat Chicago	Positive	1,50%	0,84%	-0,28%	-0,03%	2,04%
	Negative	-1,77%	-2,36%	1,27%	-0,15%	-3,00%
Wheat Kansas	Positive	1,86%	0,89%	-0,34%	-0,21%	2,21%
	Negative	-1,83%	-2,23%	0,88%	-0,18%	-3,35%
Livestock						
Feeder Cattle	Positive	0,12%	0,06%	0,36%	0,51%	1,04%
	Negative	-0,66%	-0,50%	-0,03%	-0,14%	-1,34%
Live Cattle	Positive	0,07%	-0,37%	-0,13%	0,08%	-0,35%
	Negative	-0,41%	-0,64%	-0,25%	-0,58%	-1,88%
Metals						
Copper	Positive	2,51%	1,74%	-0,02%	-0,40%	3,83%
	Negative	-5,20%	-3,62%	-0,11%	-1,62%	-10,56%
Gold	Positive	0,59%	0,94%	0,05%	-0,39%	1,19%
	Negative	-0,38%	-1,25%	0,25%	-0,13%	-1,51%
Palladium	Positive	0,09%	0,13%	0,31%	-0,20%	0,33%
	Negative	-1,45%	-3,47%	-0,70%	-1,36%	-6,98%
Platinum	Positive	-0,39%	0,64%	0,47%	1,08%	1,80%
	Negative	-2,65%	-2,30%	-0,51%	-3,00%	-8,46%
Silver	Positive	1,30%	1,66%	-0,25%	-0,66%	2,05%
	Negative	-2,15%	-3,01%	0,22%	-0,30%	-5,23%

15.A.4 Composition of DJ-UBS index (2012) and the corresponding news sentiment index.

Commodity	Original weight	News data	Weight for analysis	RIC code
Natural gas	10.77	Natural gas	10.77	
WTI Crude oil	9.69			
Brent Crude oil	5.31	Crude oil	18.41	CRU
Unleaded/RBOB Gasoline	3.41			
Heating oil	3.46	Heating oil	3.46	HOIL
Live Cattle	3.63	Livestock	5.74	LIV
Lean hogs	2.11			
Wheat	4.96	Grains	4.96	GRA
Corn	6.67	Corn	6.67	COR
Soybeans	7.08	Oils	10.45	OILS
Soyabean oil	3.37			
Aluminium	5.88			
Copper	7.06			
Zinc	3.12	Metals	18.64	
Nickel	2.58			Met
Lead	0			
Tin	0			
Gold	9.79			
Silver	2.77	Gold	12.56	GOL
Platinum	0			
Sugar	3.76	Sugar	3.76	SUG
Cotton	2	Cotton	2	COT
Coffee	2.57	Coffee	2.57	COF

CHAPTER 16

Predicting Global Economic Activity with Media Analytics

Richard Peterson, *CEO, MarketPsych LLC*

Aleksander Fafula, *Chief Data Scientist, MarketPsych*

ABSTRACT

This chapter demonstrates how the incorporation of news and social media analytics into models of economic activity improves the accuracy of economic forecasts. Accurately quantifying economic growth in a timely fashion is an enduring challenge to economists. With the advent of big data and real-time information, data that reflects economic behaviour and intentions is now available via a variety of sources including internet search volume (Google Trends), credit card transaction histories (e.g. Visa transactions), and quantified news and social media content (e.g. Thomson Reuters MarketPsych Indices). The Thomson Reuters MarketPsych Indices (TRMI) - the subject of this chapter - are quantified sentiment and macroeconomic time series derived from the flow of news and social media information about individual locations and countries. In this chapter, we demonstrate how data derived from news and social media analytics can be used to model and predict daily economic activity in individual countries. Our research finds that predictive models built with the TRMI data show outstanding in-sample and forward-tested accuracy in predicting real-time economic activity (the PMI) for the G12 nations.

16.1 INTRODUCTION

All economic movements, by their very nature, are motivated by crowd psychology.
~ Bernard Baruch

Accurate and timely measures of economic activity are an integral component of economic forecasting. Policy-makers, businesspeople and traders seek to manage the economic, minimize economic risk, or profit from superior economic modelling. Bond-holders, bankers, and foreign exchange traders rely on economic activity to adjust asset allocation. As a result, each group seeks to have the most accurate and timely proxies for such activity.

Global economic activity is currently measured using a variety of techniques. The most widely followed metrics of economic activity include the Purchasing Managers' Indexes (PMIs) released by the Markit Group, the Institute of Supply Management (ISM) survey and quarterly GDP released by individual governments.

Unfortunately, the available data on economic activity is produced with a high degree of uncertainty. Many economic growth metrics are released following a delay; they are often subsequently revised. In addition, the process of producing economic data contains inherent biases. For example, PMI and ISM are released monthly, while GDP is published quarterly.

The construction of such indexes is also inherently fragile. The use of paper surveys and telephone interviews leads to delays in compilation, calculation or dissemination of the PMI and ISM indicators. Second, the surveys that underlie the PMI and ISM economic indicators are vulnerable to self-report bias and small sample sizes, both of which introduce noise into what is already an infrequent data release. Third, due to noise, significant revisions of these numbers are not uncommon on future release dates. Fourth, many countries are not covered by these commercial economic indicators. Finally, most economic indicators show a trivial correlation with future stock market, fixed income and currency valuations, thus diminishing their utility as forecasting tools. Nonetheless, despite their flaws, monthly economic indicators such as the PMI and ISM are watched closely by global traders, economists and central bankers, and they influence major asset allocation and monetary policy decisions.

Fortunately, economic information arrives rapidly and accurately via novel data sources. Researchers have explored the role of such real-time information in creating better forecasts of economic activity, which is called nowcasting, (Scott and Varian, 2014). Data that has been studied with the goal of improving existing economic time series includes sources as diverse as credit card transaction data, (Sobolevsky, 2015), satellite images of retail store parking lots, (Hope, 2014), ambient nocturnal light measured from space, (Mellander et al., 2013), credit spreads, (Faust et al., 2013), internet search data (Choi and Varian, 2012; Artola and Galán, 2012), and (theoretically) semantic analysis of news (Sakaji et al, 2008). Yet a source of social media data - Facebook - may not be predictive. In one sentiment at least, the Gross National Happiness index provided by Facebook, daily changes in happiness do not correlate with future economic activity (Karabulut, 2015). Given the mixed results in academic research, in this chapter we examine the potential of quantified news and social media flow to construct superior economic indicators. This chapter contributes to the literature in that no prior research has been published on predicting country-level economic activity using real-time news and social media-derived sentiment data.

This chapter is organised as follows. In Section 16.1 we introduce our data and objectives. In Section 16.2 we discuss data characteristics, cleansing, preparation and statistical methodology. In Section 16.3 we derive economic indicators and test their out-of-sample predictive power. In Section 16.4 we discuss the findings of the study and present our conclusions. The appendix includes charts for the remainder of modelled countries.

16.1.1 Quantifying News Flow

The 48-country TRMI used in this chapter are real-time quantitative time series of the provided sentiments and macroeconomic topics quantified in the news and social media flow about 130 countries. There are 48 TRMI country indexes available for research. Each is derived from textual analytics of global news and social media content referring to economic activity in specific locations such as cities, provinces and countries, and location-specific entities such as ministries and central banks.

Each day, up to 3 million articles from news (premium newswires and internet news aggregators) and social media (blogs, forums and tweets) are analysed and scored (quantified) in real-time by MarketPsych's text analytics software. Specific sentiment and macroeconomic references are identified in the text of the articles and, once aggregated, these scores form the TRMI. See Appendix 16.A.1 for a more detailed description of the country-specific TRMI and how the TRMI are constructed.

An example of the economicGrowth TRMI for the third quarter of 2015 is visible in the global map of Figure 16.1.1. Shading in a red hue indicates the balance of conversation is referring to increasing unemployment (and thus the Unemployment TRMI has a positive value), while countries shaded in green are experiencing a higher balance of conversation around increasing employment reflected in negative Unemployment values.

-0.022 ▮▮▮▮▮▮▮▮▮▮▮▮▮▮▮ 0.044

Figure 16.1.1: *Global heatmap displaying the economicGrowth TRMI for the third quarter of 2015, where green shading indicates positive economic growth, and red represents economic contraction mentioned in the media. No data is available for several countries in Sub-Saharan Africa, which are neutral grey.*

16.1.2 News Flow as a Leading Economic Indicator

In this chapter we introduce a predictive model of global PMI activity. We call the country-specific economic models the MarketPsych Manufacturing Indexes (MPMI), and they are derived from the country-level macroeconomic and sentiment TRMI as dependent variables, while Markit's PMI value is the independent variable. The MPMI are both highly correlated with and predictive of country-specific PMI changes.

This chapter reports on the second version of the MPMI. For the first version we statistically fit the TRMI indexes to prior PMI values from January 2008 to April 2013 using roll-forward learning models for the top 12 economies. From May 2013 to February 2015 the models were updated daily in forward-testing on our website www.marketpsych.com. The forward-tested models showed significant predictive power over flash PMI and end-of-month PMI values in the forward-testing period for the 12 countries studied. However, despite their predictive power, the first version of the MPMI models demonstrated significant noise. As a result, we produced a second version which we present in this chapter, MPMI 2.0.

16.2 TRMI DATA AND ANALYTICS ALGORITHMS

For the purpose of the research and modeling in this chapter, we investigate 48 country-level TRMI indexes as potential economic indicators. See Appendix 16.A.1 for a more detailed description of the TRMI data, including the country-specific TRMI available for our research. In this section of the chapter we examine the various indexes available and discuss the selection of appropriate statistical methods.

16.2.1 Professional News v Social Media

The TRMI data for social media and news media is qualitatively different both in terms of sources analysed and in terms of content. Social media sources include unstructured and ad hoc articles generated by anyone with a computer and an opinion, including finance-relevant tweets, comments, blog posts and forum postings. News media content is third-party edited and is derived from professional news sources. When news reporters express libellous statements, they are often disciplined. When social media authors post defamatory content, they may gain more readers. As a result, the information present in the separate news and social media TRMI is of significantly different credibility.

Sentiment data derived from professional news is generally superior for our purposes than that based on social media sources, and it is less susceptible to external manipulation. In 2014 the marketRisk TRMI for Russia showed a significant disparity between the values quantified in news and social media (Fig. 16.2.1). As a result of such a disparity, we found it important to explore the optimal techniques for handling such dissimilarities.

Figure 16.2.1: *Divergence between news and social media-based marketRisk TRMI for Russia following the ousting of Ukrainian President Viktor Yanukovych in late February 2015 and the subsequent sightings of Russian troops in Ukraine. In this case, social media about Russia was more positively emotional (reflected in higher values on the marketRisk TRMI).*

The greater accuracy of news versus social media in Figure 16.2.1 may represent institutionalized English-language trolling on social media websites. For example, the Russian state is reported to support English-language social media propaganda efforts in support of Russian markets and policies (Sindelar, 2014; Chen, 2015). Beyond the effect of paid propagandists and patriotic volunteers on social media tone, there are many other relevant differences between country-level social media and professional news feeds. Some topics are less frequently discussed in national news outlets versus social media, and some expressions - such as cursing and emoticons - are utilized by social media authors with regional variations but are entirely absent from news media. Fortunately, weighting algorithms can detect data nuances and adapt to data variability. In the model of economic activity we present today, we utilize inputs from both news and social media, and in some cases the differences between the two types of feeds turn out to be advantages.

16.2.2 Analysis of Single TRMI

Each TRMI has a different significance in forecasting economic activity. We compared each TRMI to established economic indicators, such as PMI values. We found that the PMI is very similar to the TRMIeconomicGrowth. This TRMI, when smoothed with a 200-day moving average, shows striking similarity to the PMI times series (Fig. 16.2.2). Such comparisons suggested that economicGrowth and similar TRMI may directly reflect economic activity with little latency.

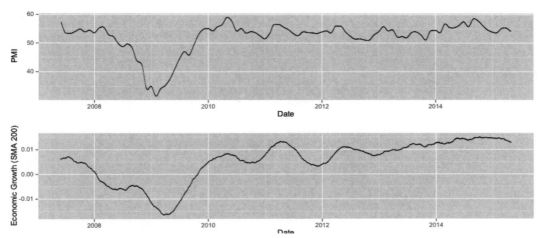

Figure 16.2.2: *Plots of the United States PMI (top) and the 200-day average of the EconomicGrowth TRMI (News_Social).*

In further testing, we found that higher values of the United States TRMI consumerSentiment are correlated with high values of the United States' PMI values. The consumerSentiment TRMI is smoothed with a 500-day average, and the results indicate that it may be a stable, long-term influencer on economic activity. We also identified that monthly deviations in the consumerSentiment TRMI have only a small correlation with monthly PMI.

The relationship between Markit's PMI and each TRMI varies by country. Some of the TRMI are correlated with PMI over time, while others show periods of correlation that later dissipate, depending on economic and political events in a country. Over time, different TRMI may emerge as influencers on the economic activity in each country.

For example, the United States TRMI that are positively correlated with the country's monthly PMI include EconomicGrowtheconomicGrowth, Optimismoptimism, InterestRatesinterestRates, and GovernmentCorruption governmentCorruption (perhaps surprisingly for the latter). The United States' US PMI is negatively correlated with short-term average values of the Unemploymentunemployment, EconomicVolatilityeconomicVolatility, Gloomgloom, and DebtDefault debtDefault TRMI. Long-term TRMI averages that are negatively correlated with monthly PMI including FinancialSystemInstability financialSystemInstability and Stressstress. As a result, an adaptive learning approach was utilized.

A correlogram presenting strength of individual United States TRMI correlations with PMI is presented in Fig. 16.2.3.

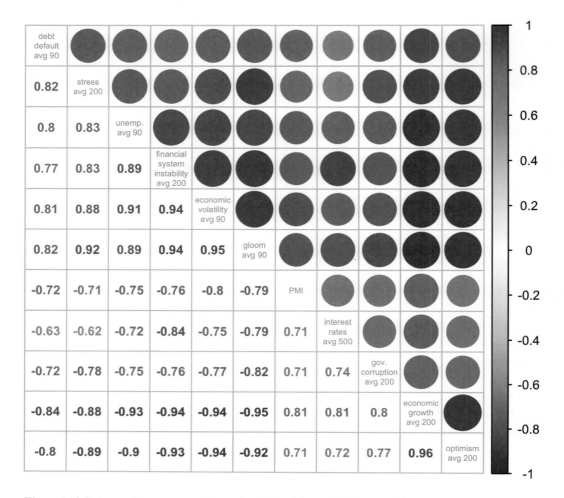

Figure 16.2.3: A correlogram comparing various United States TRMI to monthly PMI values.

16.2.3 Testing methodology

The data analysis procedures described thus far in this chapter were identical for all countries modelled. For the purpose of generating predictive learning models, the dependent variable was selected as the Manufacturing PMI. Twelve countries with large economies and developed markets were selected for modelling. In each model the longest possible data range was used for learning and testing of the models. Table 16.2.5 contains the list of economies and their number of monthly PMI observations used for training the models.

Table 16.2.4: *Number of monthly PMI observations used to train MPMI models, as of February 2015.*

	Country / Zone	***No. PMI in obs.***
1	Australia	90
2	Brazil	90
3	China	89
4	Euro Zone	92
5	France	87
6	Germany	87
7	India	86
8	Italy	87
9	Japan	91
10	Russia	139
11	United Kingdom	93
12	USA	95

We decided that a daily model of MPMI would be ideal, and in order to create a daily model using a monthly dependent variable - to merge interpolated daily PMI observations with daily TRMI data - a spline interpolation of PMI data points was performed. Various methods of interpolation were performed for testing, and based on initial results, the monotone Hermite spline (according to the method of Fritsch and Carlson (1980)) was chosen.

Now that a daily PMI data series was available for each country, we created a group of moving averages using each TRMI for each country. Based on our past experience, such smoothing decreases data variability and dampens the impact of sudden index changes. As a result of the averaging, a short-term surge in discussion about unemployment or national debt will have a moderated impact on the overall average. Based on testing of fit, we determined which indexes should have greater short-term responsiveness due to their more immediate effects on economic activity.

16.2.4 Selected models and algorithms tuning

It was initially unclear which statistical methods applied to TRMI would show superior results in order to model the PMI values. Four statistical techniques were tested to determine best fit: Generalized Linear Model (GLM), (Dobson, 1990), Supported Vector Machines (SVM), (Platt, 2000), the Lasso technique (LASSO), (Efron et al., 2004) and Linear Regression with Stepwise Selection (REGSEQ), (Miller, 2002).

Model learning was performed with the rolling forecasting technique described by Kuhn and Johnson (2013). For each model an initial window of 10% of the dataset was selected for in-sample testing. This process was repeated ten times with 30 observations within each window (10-fold). Based on average prediction quality in each fold, final modelling techniques were selected. The learning window was not fixed, which meant that the models were adaptive and expanded their window length with every 30 observations.

The results of cross-validation learning for the United States, based on these four techniques, are presented in Table 16.2.5 with Root Mean Squared Error (RMSE) and in Table 16.2.6 (R-squared). In theory, the average results of cross-validation should be similar to the real out-of-sample results, but there is also a risk of overfitting.

Table 16.2.5: RMSE for United States daily MPMI models using four statistical techniques.

Model	1st Qu.	Median	Mean	3rd Qu.
GLM	0.5875	**1.0470**	**1.4170**	1.6230
SVM	0.5182	**0.9250**	1.0300	1.4580
LASSO	0.5608	**0.9728**	1.0530	1.4470
REGSEQ	1.1180	**1.6040**	**1.6090**	2.2750

Table 16.2.6: R-squared for United States daily MPMI models using four statistical techniques.

Model	1st Qu.	Median	Mean	3rd Qu.
GLM	0.2017	**0.5609**	**0.5067**	0.7642
SVM	0.0487	**0.1802**	**0.2459**	0.4526
LASSO	0.1267	**0.4102**	**0.4264**	0.6826
REGSEQ	0.0875	**0.4002**	**0.4116**	0.7125

Based on these results, the Elastic Net model was selected as the optimal technique for modelling PMI activity using the TRMI data.

16.3 RESULTS

16.3.1 Out-of-sample results

For the true out-of-sample comparison, model learning was frozen and forward-tested results compared to actual PMI values for five months. Specifically, absolute predicted values and directional accuracy were compared to the absolute PMI values for 12 countries and the monthly change from the prior month's PMI value, respectively. This approach demonstrates a practical economic application of using the MPMI for predicting PMI changes. The MPMI values the day before the flash PMI release (the flash PMI is a draft monthly value released on the third week of the month) were compared. Additionally, the MPMI value at the end of the month was compared to the monthly PMI (released 1-3 days later). Figure 16.3.1 and Figure 16.3.2 present the United States MPMI fit to PMI with a shaded 5-month true out-of-sample period.

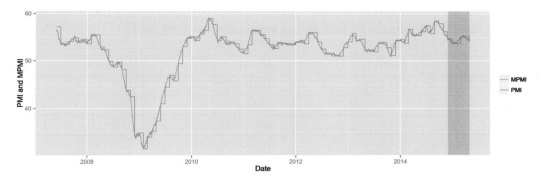

Figure 16.3.1: *PMI and MPMI with in-sample (light grey) and out-of-sample fit (shaded in darker grey), entire time series.*

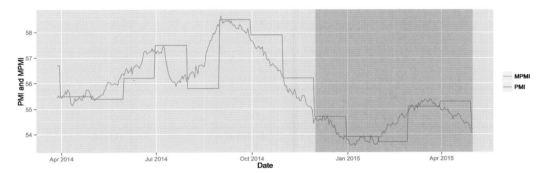

Figure 16.3.2: *PMI and MPMI – detailed view of out-of-sample period in darker grey.*

Based on Figures 16.3.1 and 16.3.2, the MPMI appears to capture significant turning points in the PMI's value. The flash PMI is a preliminary PMI value delivered three weeks into a month.

For all countries studied in the out-of-sample period, we collected the final results in Table 16.3.3. The overall directional accuracy of the MPMI in predicting the prior month's PMI to the current month's flash PMI values was 67% for all twelve countries. The average difference between prediction and the actual PMI was 0.68. In this case the model was not adaptive - it was not retrained monthly on the latest PMI release – however, that is a feature of the model that further improves accuracy. In the presented case, it operates for five months without feedback. Overall the quality of the predictions is stable.

Table 16.3.3: *MPMI vs Market's PMI – out-of-sample results in which the MPMI value on the final day of the month is compared to the beginning of month published PMI value.*

Date	PMI	MPMI	Country
31/01/15	53.7	53.65455	US
28/02/15	55.1	53.11644	US
31/03/15	55.3	51.70740	US
30/04/15	54.2	51.73934	US
31/01/15	51.0	51.45909	EZ
28/02/15	51.0	52.28469	EZ
31/03/15	52.2	54.03506	EZ
30/04/15	52.0	54.38422	EZ
31/01/15	50.7	50.09603	BR
28/02/15	49.6	50.51363	BR
31/03/15	46.2	51.16854	BR
30/04/15	46.0	52.16163	BR
31/01/15	49.0	47.73846	AU
28/02/15	45.4	47.03227	AU
31/03/15	46.3	46.44947	AU
30/04/15	48.0	44.88714	AU
31/01/15	49.7	49.65558	CN
28/02/15	50.7	49.75093	CN
31/03/15	49.6	49.74951	CN
30/04/15	48.9	49.70777	CN
31/01/15	52.9	53.22019	IN
28/02/15	51.2	51.69395	IN
31/03/15	52.1	52.00968	IN
30/04/15	51.3	51.53392	IN
31/01/15	53.1	54.53137	GB
28/02/15	54.1	54.91586	GB
31/03/15	54.4	55.91162	GB
30/04/15	51.9	55.54078	GB
31/01/15	47.6	48.74574	RU
28/02/15	49.7	49.11347	RU
31/03/15	48.1	49.64782	RU
30/04/15	48.9	49.64534	RU
31/01/15	52.2	51.89449	JP
28/02/15	51.6	53.26600	JP
31/03/15	50.3	53.24300	JP

30/04/15	49.9	53.77914	JP
31/01/15	49.9	49.06397	IT
28/02/15	51.9	49.27668	IT
31/03/15	53.3	49.69466	IT
30/04/15	53.8	50.13653	IT
31/01/15	50.9	52.30466	DE
28/02/15	51.1	50.95905	DE
31/03/15	52.8	50.60568	DE
30/04/15	52.1	49.45158	DE
31/01/15	49.2	46.08168	FR
28/02/15	47.6	45.62370	FR
31/03/15	48.8	46.42455	FR
30/04/15	48.0	45.73405	FR

16.3.2 Live Nowcasting

To facilitate its practical use, this MPMI model was implemented in a real-life decision support system. A dashboard consisting of interactive maps and charts can be used to quickly assess the current state of economic activity, based on the news and social media flow, in selected countries. Figure 16.3.4 demonstrates examples of the MPMI in a decision support system.

DAILY-UPDATED MANUFACTURING FORECASTS FOR THE TOP 12 ECONOMIES:

MPMI MarketPsych Manufacturing Index	Today's MPMI (2015-12-10) greater than 50 is expanding, less than 50 is contracting	Change from last day of prior month (2015-11-30)		Toolbox
United States (US)	54.40	⬆	0.00	[recent] [history]
Eurozone (EZ)	50.58	⬇	-0.31	[recent] [history]

Figure 16.3.4: MPMI implementation as dashboard in a decision support system (current-day view of selected countries).

DAILY-UPDATED MANUFACTURING FORECASTS FOR UNITED STATES: [VIEW ALL COUNTRIES]

MPMI MarketPsych Manufacturing Index	Today's MPMI (2015-12-10) greater than 50 is expanding, less than 50 is contracting	Change from last day of prior month (2015-11-30)		Toolbox
United States (US)	**54.40**	⬆	0.00	[recent] [history]

HISTORICAL VALUES, AT THE END OF THE MONTH:

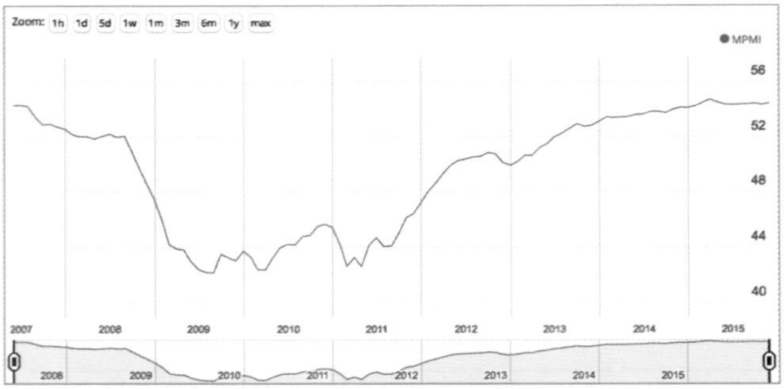

Date	Value
2015-11-30	54.40
2015-10-31	54.31
2015-09-30	54.39
2015-08-31	54.34
2015-07-31	54.33
2015-06-30	54.29
2015-05-31	54.32
2015-04-30	54.49
2015-03-31	54.69
2015-02-28	54.44
2015-01-31	54.22

Based on extraction of real-time manufacturing and sentiment data from news and social media articles, MarketPsych has created daily-updating predictive models for the top 12 economies.

Figure 16.3.5: *MPMI historical view for a single country (United States).*

16.4 DISCUSSION AND CONCLUSIONS

In this chapter we demonstrated how data derived from the business and financial news and social media about individual countries (the Thomson Reuters MarketPsych Indices, TRMI) may be used to generate a daily-updating predictive model of economic activity. This model complements existing models of economic activity such as the ISM and PMI by providing daily resolution and broad coverage of the unseen forces that drive the economy's "animal spirits" (specific sentiments, topics and outlooks embodied in text communications).

The MPMI model we created in this chapter shows stable performance in both training and out-of-sample periods. The increased resolution and higher frequency of such an economic model should be useful for policy-makers, currency traders, portfolio managers, banks and brokerages who need faster access to country-level economic activity.

There are at least four explanations for the role of media content in reflecting and, perhaps, forecasting economic activity. Economically-relevant information in the news flow – such as winter weather closing factories - may appear in the TRMI more rapidly than the data encountered by purchasing managers surveyed for the PMI and ISM indexes. A second possibility is that economic forecasters quoted in the media or who publish their opinions in financial news and social media are more informed about economic activity than the purchasing managers surveyed for the ISM and PMI indexes. A third interesting possibility is that sentiments relayed in the news flow predictably alter the economic activity of individuals. For example, individuals saddened or frightened by highly publicized news of a terrorist attack may be more reluctant to spend on consumer items. As a result of this media-inspired risk aversion, economic activity will fall slightly. And finally, there may be a "wisdom of the crowds" effect in which sampling millions of economic comments creates a more accurate composite picture of the current state of the economy than a limited survey of hundreds (400 plus) purchasing managers.

The MPMI model has several notable flaws, including the smoothing operations performed to improve stability - which may diminish the impact of sudden, important events. The MPMI model would further benefit from monthly recalibration using the latest PMI values. Furthermore, performance may benefit from periodic reshuffling of input TRMIs. Such rebuilding of the model would allow it to adapt more quickly to changes in media tone. Seasonal variations are another cyclical aspect of economic activity that was not considered in the MPMI. The TRMI are derived from English-language content only, and they would benefit from additional language capabilities.

On the positive side, the MPMI model provides readings in relatively high frequency, has a robust data history and can operate on more than 130 countries. By reviewing each TRMI that contributes to the MPMI, we can explain why and when the composite MPMI is likely to rise or decline by decomposing and plotting model variables (pointing to certain press trends, sentiments and topics). The MPMI model is not directly influenced by any political or financial institution, but rather by the flow of information in news and social media. However, media content may itself be motivating or demotivating human economic activity. Media both reflects in its reporting and stimulates through its messages human economic behaviour.

Like Google Trends and social media platforms, the MPMI model encapsulates a new way of understanding - and perhaps predicting - human behaviour by modelling the fundamental drivers of business activity. Based on research into data provided by Estimize, Google Trends and the TRMI, it appears that socially sourced and media-derived data can improve predictive models of fundamentals - including corporate earnings and economic activity - and stock prices.

16.5 REFERENCES

1.   Artola, C. and Galán, E. (2012). Tracking the Future on the Web: Construction of Leading Indicators Using Internet Searches. Banco de Espana Occasional Paper, (1203).

2.   Banbura, M., Giannone, D., Modugno, M. and Reichlin, L. (2013). Now-casting and the real-time data flow. Chapter 4 in G. Elliott and A. Timmermann, eds., *Handbook of Economic Forecasting SET 2A-2B*. Elsevier.

3.   Chen, A. (2015). The Agency. *New York Times* [online]. Available at: http://www.nytimes.com/2015/06/07/magazine/the-agency.html

4.   Choi, H. and Varian, H. (2012). Predicting the present with google trends. *Economic Record, 88(s1)*, 2-9.

5.   Dobson, A. J. (1990). *An Introduction to Generalized Linear Models*. London: Chapman and Hall.

6.   Efron, B., Hastie, T., Johnstone, I. and Tibshirani, R. (2004). Least angle regression. *The Annals of Statistics, 32(2)*, 407–499.

7. Faust, J., Gilchrist, S., Wright, J. H. and Zakrajšsek, E. (2013). Credit spreads as predictors of real-time economic activity: a Bayesian model-averaging approach. *Review of Economics and Statistics, 95(5),* 1501-1519.

8. Fritsch, F. N. and Carlson, R. E. (1980). Monotone piecewise cubic interpolation. *SIAM Journal on Numerical Analysis, 17,* 238–246.

9. Hope, B. (2014). Startups Mine Market-Moving Data From Fields, Parking Lots - Even Shadows. *Wall Street Journal.*

10. Karabulut Y. (2015). Can Facebook Predict Stock Market Activity? Working Paper. Received via personal communication with author.

11. Kuhn, M. and Johnson, K. (2013). *Applied predictive modeling*. New York: Springer.

12. Mellander, C., Stolarick, K., Matheson, Z. and Lobo, J. (2013). Night-time light data: a good proxy measure for economic activity. Royal Institute of Technology, CESIS and Centre of Excellence for Science and Innovation Studies.

13. Miller, A. (2002). *Subset Selection in Regression*. Chapman and Hall: CRC.

14. Platt, J. (2000). Probabilistic outputs for support vector machines and comparison to regularized likelihood methods. *Advances in Large Margin Classifiers, 10(3),* 61–74.

15. Sakaji, H., Sakai, H. and Masuyama, S. (2008). Automatic extraction of basis expressions that indicate economic trends. In *Advances in Knowledge Discovery and Data Mining* (pp. 977-984). Springer Berlin Heidelberg.

16. Scott, S.L. and Varian, H.R. (2014). Predicting the present with bayesian structural time series. *International Journal of Mathematical Modelling and Numerical Optimisation*, 5(1-2), 4-23.

17. Sindelar, D. (2014). The Kremlin's Troll Army. *The Atlantic* [online]. Available at: http://www.theatlantic. com/international/archive/2014/08/the-kremlins-troll-army/375932/

18. Sobolevsky, S., Massaro, E., Bojic, I., Arias, J. M. and Ratti, C. (2015). Predicting Regional Economic Indices Using Big Data Of Individual Bank Card Transactions. arXiv preprint arXiv:1506.00036.

16.A APPENDIX

16.A.1 Understanding the Thomson Reuters Marketpsych Indices

Country TRMI Indices

There are 48 TRMI indices for the for the country asset class. Each TRMI carries six significant digits past the decimal point. Negative numbers have a leading minus (-) sign. The table below summarizes these fields.

Index	Description: *24-hour rolling average score of references in news and social media to...*	Range
sentiment	overall positive references, net of negative references	-1 to 1
optimism	optimism, net of references to pessimism	-1 to 1
fear	fear and anxiety	0 to 1
joy	happiness and affection	0 to 1
trust	trustworthiness, net of references connoting corruption	-1 to 1
violence	violence and war	0 to 1
conflict	disagreement and swearing net of agreement and concilia-tion	-1 to 1
gloom	gloom and negative future outlook	0 to 1
stress	distress and danger	0 to 1
timeUrgency	urgency and timeliness, net of references to tardiness and delays	-1 to 1
uncertainty	uncertainty and confusion	0 to 1
emotionVsFact	all emotional sentiments, net of all factual and topical refer-ences	-1 to 1
loveHate	love, net of references to hate	-1 to 1
anger	anger and disgust	0 to 1
debtDefault	debt defaults and bankruptcies	0 to 1
innovation	Innovativeness	0 to 1
marketRisk	positive emotionality and positive expectations net of negative emotionality and negative expectations. Includes factors from social media found characteristic of speculative bubbles – higher values indicate greater bubble risk. Also known as the "Bubbleometer."	-1 to 1
budgetDeficit	a budget deficit, net of references to a surplus	-1 to 1
businessExpansion	businesses expanding, net of references to contraction	-1 to 1
centralBank	the central bank of a country	0 to 1
commercialRealEstateSentiment	positive references to commercial real estate, net of negative references	-1 to 1
consumerSentiment	positive consumer sentiment, net of references to negative consumer sentiment	-1 to 1

creditEasyVsTight	credit conditions being easy, net of references to credit conditions being tight	-1 to 1
economicGrowth	increased business activity, net of references to decreased business activity	-1 to 1
economicUncertainty	uncertainty about business climate net of confidence and certainty	-1 to 1
economicVolatility	increasing economic volatility, net of economic stability	-1 to 1
financialSystemInstability	financial system instability, net of references to financial system stability	-1 to 1
fiscalPolicyLooseVsTight	fiscal policy being loose, net of references to fiscal policy being tight	-1 to 1
governmentAnger	anger and disgust about government officials and departments	0 to 1
governmentCorruption	fraud and corruption in government, net of references to trust in government	-1 to 1
governmentInstability	governmental instability, net of references to governmental stability	-1 to 1
inflation	consumer price increases, net of references to consumer price decreases	-1 to 1
inflationForecast	forecasts of consumer price increases, net of forecasts of consumer price decreases (deflation)	-1 to 1
interestRates	interest rates rising, net of references to rates falling	-1 to 1
interestRatesForecast	forecasts of interest rates rising, net of forecasts of rates falling	-1 to 1
investmentFlows	investment inflows, net of references to investment outflows	-1 to 1
monetaryPolicyLooseVsTight	monetary policy being loose, net of references to monetary policy being tight	-1 to 1
naturalDisasters	natural disasters	0 to 1
regimeChange	regime change	0 to 1
residentialRealEstateGrowth	residential real estate expansion, net of references to contraction	-1 to 1
residentialRealEstateSales	residential real estate sales rising, net of references to sales decreasing	-1 to 1
residentialRealEstateSentiment	positive references to residential real estate, net of negative references	-1 to 1
residentialRealEstateValues	residential real estate values rising, net of references to declining values	-1 to 1
sanctions	sanctions or embargoes emanating from or against a country	0 to 1
socialInequality	social inequality	0 to 1
socialUnrest	social unrest and calls for political change	0 to 1
tradeBalance	exports, net of references to imports	-1 to 1
Unemployment	unemployment rising, net of references to unemployment falling	-1 to 1

Visual Validation

One simple way to validate that the TRMI data reflects its intended output is to visualize actual events. One event with high psychological impact that has been in the news following the Arab Spring and other revolutions against totalitarianism is social unrest. The SocialUnrest TRMI for the year 2014 is visible in Figure A.6.1below:

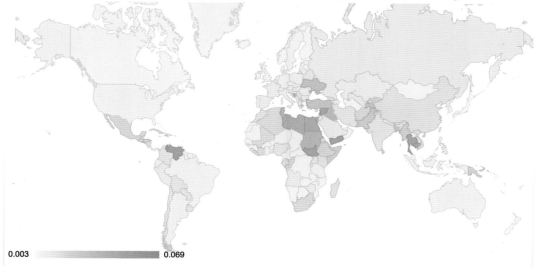

Figure 16.A.1: An image of average SocialUnrest TRMI values for countries in 2014.

Images such as that in Figure 16.A.1 validate the ability of the TRMI to track important global events.

16.A.2 APPENDIX 2: VISUALIZING GOODNESS OF FIT

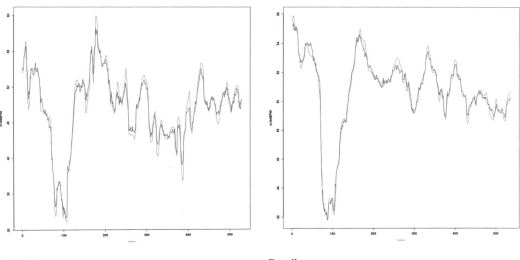

Australia   Brazil

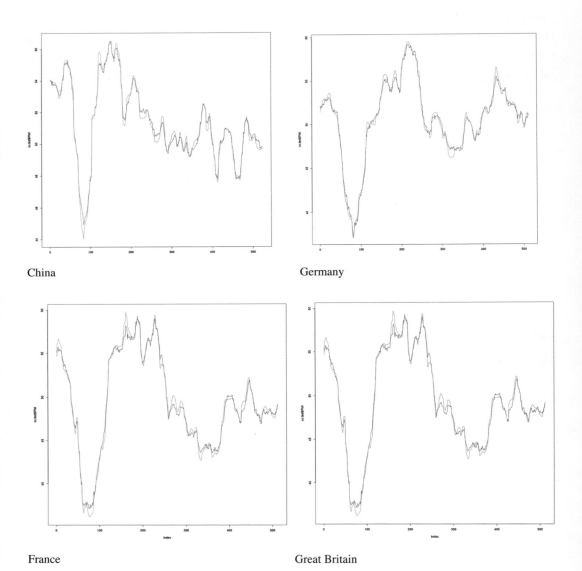

China

Germany

France

Great Britain

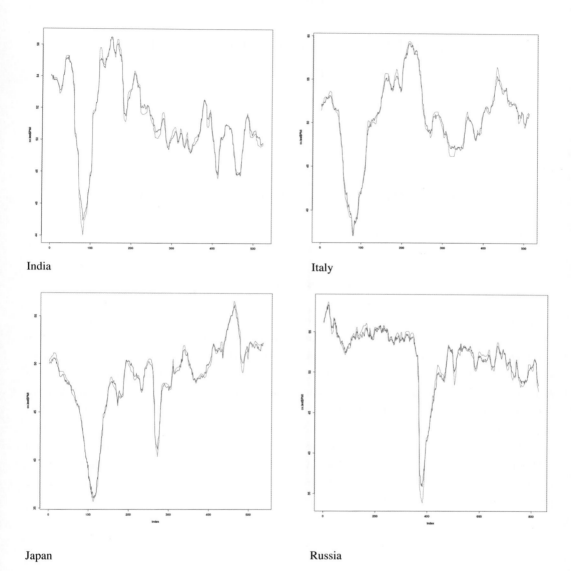

India

Italy

Japan

Russia

CHAPTER 17

Credit Risk Assessment of Corporate Debt using Sentiment and News

Dan diBartolomeo, *Founder, Northfield Information Services*

ABSTRACT

Since the Global Financial Crisis of 2007–2009, history has been marked by numerous failures to correctly assess the credit worthiness of financial instruments, financial institutions and governments. Institutional confidence in the traditional credit rating agencies has been greatly reduced. One of the largest rating agencies, Standard and Poors, recently agreed to pay a $1.4 billion fine to US regulators for alleged widespread negligence in the rating of certain complex financial instruments. As an alternative to the traditional rating process, this work will illustrate the potential use of sentiment statistics from quantified news to calibrate and update the credit risk of corporations and financial institutions in real time. A modified version of the Merton (1974) contingent claims model from diBartolomeo (2010, 2012) is used to break each corporate debt into two pieces, the first considered riskless debt and the second equity in the issuer. We utilize news flows and sentiment statistics to frequently update the expected volatility of the assets of the firm and hence the credit risk of the debt in terms of both the probability of default and loss given default.

17.1 INTRODUCTION

As an alternative to the traditional rating process, this work will illustrate the potential use of sentiment statistics from quantified news to calibrate and update the credit risk of corporations and financial institutions *in real time*. A modified version of the Merton (1974) contingent claims model from diBartolomeo (2010, 2012) is used to break each corporate debt into two pieces, the first considered riskless debt and the second equity in the issuer. We utilize sentiment statistics to frequently update the expected volatility of the assets of the firm and hence the credit risk of the debt in terms of both the probability of default (PD) and loss given default (LGD), which are the standard industry metrics for credit risk.

There is a great deal of information coming to investors about financial market conditions and the circumstances of specific firms in the form of "quantified news" and "sentiment" scores. To date most efforts by financial participants to use news flow information have attempted to obtain alpha (superior risk adjusted returns) in trading equity markets. Unlike use of sentiment statistics in the search for alpha within equity strategies, where "good" or "bad" news may already have been acted upon by other market participants, use of sentiment for credit risk has the advantage that it is largely unambiguous: "good" news is good (but not strongly) and "bad news" is bad for creditors (strongly).

17.2 PREVIOUS RELATED LITERATURE

There is a small but growing literature that strongly links news flows and sentiment into efficient volatility forecasting for equities (e.g. Mitra, Mitra and diBartolomeo, 2009). To effectively utilize this predictive power for analysing credit risk, we need to structure the forecasting of credit risk as a function of the volatility of the assets of an entity. It should be intuitive that if an entity has a positive net worth today, then the probability of having a negative net worth (technical default) is a function of balance sheet leverage (relative magnitude of assets and liabilities) and the volatility of the asset value. Since the leverage value can be readily observed from a corporate balance sheet, our challenge is to use news flows as a way to predict the volatility of the asset value of an entity.

Financial markets are driven by the arrival of information in the form of "news" (truly unanticipated) and the form of "announcements" that are anticipated with respect to time but not with respect to content. The time interval it takes markets to absorb and adjust to new information ranges from minutes to days. Such intervals are generally much smaller than a month, but up to and often larger than a day. That's why US markets were closed for a week after September 11th.

A key feature of traded financial markets is that much of the information coming forward to investors is in the form of the content of scheduled announcements (e.g. corporate earnings or government statistics). Several papers have examined the relative market response to "news" and "announcements" such as Ederington and Lee (1993), Kwag, Shrieves and Wansley (2000) and Abraham and Taylor (1993). The scheduled nature of such information flows (as opposed to unanticipated "news") allows market participants to anticipate the timing of announcements. Volume and volatility dry up as investors wait for the release of the information. Such anticipatory behaviour is contrary to the "random shock" assumption of widely used time series methods for estimating security return volatility (e.g. GARCH). When the announcement occurs, trading volume quickly spikes until the market clearing price is re-established, as market participants have made up their minds in advance what to do. This is conditional on the content of the announcement, after which trading conditions quickly return to normal. Such "trend in volatility" related models don't work well on announcements, as expected volatility is reduced going into the announcement due to the "quiet period" in front of the announcement. In addition, when volatility spikes as prices react to the information, such models will boost volatility forecasts for the next period, by which time things are back to normal.

Brown, Harlow and Tinic (1988) provide a framework of great importance with respect to credit risk. In their model, they assert the expectation of asymmetrical responses in security prices to "good" and "bad" news. In the context of the equity of a company, good news increases projected cash flows, while bad news decreases expectations of future cash flow. They suggest that asset prices are discounted present value of expected future cash flows. The discount rates are a combination of three components: the risk-free rate (time value of money), a risk premium for the actual uncertainty of the expected cash flows, and a second risk premium associated with whether the investor is confident (or not) in their understanding of the investment. *All new information is viewed as a "surprise", decreasing investor confidence* and increasing discount rates. Upward price movements are muted, while downward movements are accentuated. For bond investors, expected cash flows can't increase very much (they are bounded from above at a zero default probability), so nearly all news is bad news.

17.3 NEWS AND THE CALIBRATION OF FIRM LEVEL RISK ESTIMATES

The estimation of risk for any financial asset or portfolio is an explicitly forward-looking exercise. Risk is always in the future, yet almost all risk systems are exclusively based on statistical analysis of some sample of past observations of market data, upon which we overlay the explicit **assumption** that the future will be like the past. *What is missing from such constructs is news, which we define as the set of information that informs us how the present is different from how things usually are (i.e. the past captured in our sample).* The need is to treat news as a means to condition risk estimates on a rapid and on-going basis. For example, if news arrives that the well regarded CEO of a large company was killed in an automobile accident, that information would impact investor perceptions of the stability of the firm and hence the credit risk.

At the firm level, our functional form for risk is:

$$\text{Sit} = \text{Sim} * (a + b \, \text{Nit}^K) \qquad [17.3.1]$$

Where
Sit = the ex-ante risk estimate for firm i on day t
Sim = the long term risk estimate for firm i derived from historical data
Nit = the ratio of "news activity" in the recent past divided by the long term historical norm

We empirically estimate the parameters (a, b, k) from a pooled log regression over a universe of widely traded securities. The dependent variable in this regression is the ratio of observed security volatility over the desired time horizon (e.g. 10 trading days). One might think of the intercept a as the expected value of the security volatility in the absence of any news. The values of the parameters will depend on the ex-ante time horizon and the particular construction of the long-term estimate, Sim.

The functional form is similar to that of Kyle, Obizhaeva, Sinha and Tuzun (2012). This work shows that a theoretically predicted relationship between the frequency of news articles on companies and the volatility of stocks was fit almost perfectly by the empirical data over hundreds of companies and many years. They use a particularly clever construct, suggesting that a function of stock volatility and trading volume across stocks is constant when the rate of time passage is defined in "numbers of articles", which they call "business time".

The extent to which there is news on a particular topic or firm is captured in Nit. The numerator of the ratio is the amount of news over a recent time window (e.g. 5 trading days) while the denominator represents the "normal" state or average flow of news over a long window (e.g. 200 trading days). It should be noted that these values are not merely a count of the number of articles, but rather a weighted count. The weighting depends on numerous metrics including the "sentiment of the article" (good news/neutral/bad news). Another important indicator is "relevance". For example, an article about Verizon may peripherally mention Apple because Verizon sells IPhones. In this case, the relevance metric would be high for Verizon but lower for Apple. Other important factors include "novelty" (has similar news been previously reported recently?) and "event type" (news about a merger is probably more important than the announcement of a routine dividend payment).

To the extent that the long-term risk expectation Sim is formed by a factor model, we can use news to adjust separately condition risk arising from common factors from risk which is specific to a particular firm or security. diBartolomeo and Warrick (2005) show how adjustments to the security volatilities can be "fed back" into the model to adjust factor variances and specific volatility estimates for securities (see equations in paper).

A conceptual way to think about this process is to create a vector of coefficients which we will call "theta". For each important parameter of the risk estimation process, there will be a corresponding element in the vector theta. Each element has a default value of one. To update our model, we multiply each model parameter by its corresponding element. If there is no news from which we can infer that conditions that are different from the norm, the elements of theta remains one, and we just get our regular model back. For example, let's assume that the volatility of global prices is an element of our model (obviously impacting a broad range of firms). If there is news of a war breaking out in the Middle East that would threaten global oil supplies, there will be an unusual number of news stories on this topic.

The range of values that elements of theta can take may be subject to boundary conditions. For example, the implied covariance matrix of asset returns (see diBartolomeo, 1999) must be positive semi-definite. A Bayesian framework for weighting the historically observed relative to the "news implied" values for model parameters is presented in Shah (2008). Such a process typically allows for rapidly evolving short horizon risk forecasts to be estimated from relatively low-frequency historical observations, reducing many of the statistical complexities associated with high-frequency data (serial correlation, kurtosis, etc.).

17.4 CONTINGENT CLAIMS ANALYSIS (CCA) OF CREDIT RISK

Merton (1974) poses the equity of a firm as a European call option on the firm's assets, with a strike price equal to the face value of the firm's debt. Alternatively, lenders are short a put option on the firm assets. If the value of the firm's assets falls below the value of the firm's debt, the limited liability shareholders simply walk away, allowing the lenders to foreclose on the remaining assets. In the original Merton construct, default can normally occur only at debt maturity date. This option framework for analysing credit risk has been widely adopted in the financial community, with analyses provided by firms such as Moody's Analytics (KMV), Thomson-Reuters, Northfield and FactSet. Like all option valuation problems, the *most influential input parameter is the volatility of the "underlying", which in this case is the value of the firm's assets*.

Black and Cox (1976) provide a "first passage" model in which default can occur before debt maturity. Firm extinction is assumed if asset values hit a boundary value (i.e. specified by bond covenants) at any point in time before the maturity of the debt. This follows logically from the real world situation that many financial entities may have dozens or even hundreds of debt issuances. Leland (1994) and Leland and Toft (1996) further refined the contingent claims process to account for the fact that in most countries interest payments are tax deductible, and there may be significant legal and other frictional costs associated with a bankruptcy filing. They do so by adjusting the strike price of the shareholder options.

A key benefit of the contingent claims approach to credit risk is that the probability of default (PD) can be directly estimated. This likelihood value is simply the "percent moneyness" (closely related to option delta) of the shareholder put option. Such an immediate, direct and unambiguous estimate of default probability stands in stark contrast to the default probabilities associated with the long-term statistical studies of traditional credit ratings, subjectively chosen after some degree of fundamental financial analysis.

An alternative framing of the problem is presented in diBartolomeo (2010). In this version of CCA, we calculate the distribution of the implied life of the firm, rather than a probability of default per unit time. Obviously, if a firm has many bond issues outstanding, and has the ability to issue new bonds, we may wish to consider which bond issues will mature within the horizon of the firm's expected life and which will mature after we estimate the firm will cease to exist. This also allows us to consider the credit worthiness of the firms that currently have no debt, but may borrow in the future. Our option pricing exercise is now based on a perpetual American structure as described in Yaksick (1995).

This paper also frames the question of the volatility of the underlying (firm assets) in a simple way that allows us to use news to update estimates of corporate credit risk in "near" real-time. Put simply we ask ourselves, *"How volatile would the stock of a particular firm be, if the firm had no debt?"* which is equivalent to asking *how volatile the assets of the firm are*. Equity markets are transparent and liquid, and very sophisticated models of equity risk have been ubiquitous among institutional equity investors for decades. It is consequently possible for fixed income investors to efficiently parameterize a model of default risk and credit correlations, rather than relying on the traditional credit rating process that is widely perceived as "broken". To the extent that aforementioned process for rapidly conditioning risk estimates with news, we have the methodological recipe in place for estimating both probability of default (PD) and credit correlations across issuers in real time.

The remaining piece of our credit risk puzzle is to form expectations about the "loss given default" (LGD). Obviously, if a borrower defaults on a debt, this does not imply that the lender will recover zero. Lenders should recover the remaining value of the assets of the firm, minus frictional costs (e.g. legal expenses). An approximate expression for loss given default is provided in diBartolomeo (2012).

$$LGD = (-(T-B)/B) * (D_p / D_c) \qquad\qquad [17.4.1]$$

Where

T is the value of the bond if it were riskless

B is the market value of the bond

D_p = delta of the put option

D_c = delta of the call option

With this expression for LGD in place, we can think of each bond we hold as being divided into two portions: a riskless portion, the value of which we are assured of getting default, and a remainder, which is simply equity in the issuer.

An important feature of this construct is that both PD and LGD are increasing functions of the volatility of the underlying. This means that the probability of default and the loss given default will naturally have high positive correlation, which should be intuitive to lenders. The mechanism for addressing defaulted debts consists of bankruptcy courts, bank "work-out" officers and regulatory agencies, all of whom have finite resources. To the extent that those resources are called upon to resolve more defaults, the amount of attention given to each default must decline, resulting in less favourable deals for lenders (each borrower still only has to negotiate for themselves). A simple example would be home mortgages. The more houses in a given neighbourhood are subject to foreclosure, the greater the impact on house prices and hence the likely degree of lender loss on each default loan. This feature is consistent with the mathematical framework for LGD provided in Frye (2013).

17.5 AN EMPIRICAL EXAMPLE FROM THE GLOBAL FINANCIAL CRISIS

To illustrate the efficacy of our approach, we tested the ability of the credit model described here to address the events of the Global Financial Crisis of 2007–2009. The security universe studied was all US corporate bonds in the Northfield "Everything Everywhere" model, for which all required inputs were available with a minimum maturity of one year. The typical size of this universe was around 18,000 bond issues. The relationships between bond issues and the underlying issuers were updated at each year-end for mergers and acquisitions. Bonds that appeared to have obvious pricing errors in the information provided by our data suppliers eliminated. The study period ran from 31 December 2005 to 30 June 2011.

The analysis begins by matching each bond to the relevant firm-level risk estimate at each moment at the end of each month of the sample period. It should be intuitive that bonds with higher traditional credit ratings should be associated with issuers with longer expected firm lives and lower credit risk in our process. To test this basic intuition, we broke all bonds into 20 categories of traditional credit ratings (including "+" and "-") and replaced the letter ratings with an ordinal scale (i.e. 1,2,3, etc.). This average value and the average value of our credit measure were calculated for each grouping.

At 31/12/2005, the cross-sectional correlation was +.68 for a universe of 17445 issues. As we approached the GFC at 31/12/2007 (pre-bailouts), the correlation was -.35 for a sample size of 22069 issues, which is obviously counter-intuitive. The relationship between traditional credit ratings and our credit measure *is of the wrong sign*. By 31/12/2008, (post-bailouts) the correlation had returned to a positive value of +.27 for a sample of 20043 issues.

To further investigate the conflict between traditional ratings and our measure, we devised a simple trading strategy. At each year-end starting at 2005, we converted our credit measure into a Z-score *within* each traditional rating category. A negative Z-score indicated that our metric suggests that the firm is less creditworthy than the published rating. We then sorted the universe into quintiles by Z-score.

At 31/12/2006, in the bottom quintile of about 4400 bond issues, 2940 were from Wall Street firms that went bankrupt, were acquired in distress or needed major government assistance. The rogues gallery included Bear Stearns (534 issues), Merrill Lynch (868), Lehman Brothers (657), Morgan Stanley (257), CIT Financial (338), Countrywide (136) and Washington Mutual (24). Repeating the exercise at 31/12/2007 produced nearly identical results.

We also calculated returns to a simple trading strategy in which we simulated long positions in bonds that were in the top quintile of Z-scores, and short positions in the bottom quintile of Z-scores. The results are shown in Figure 17.5.1. US government intentions to mount the TARP bailout were announced on 3 October 2008, with most of the details filled in a couple weeks later. On 31 October 2008, the cumulative Q1/Q5 return spread was more than 1200 basis points in less than three years on widely diverse portfolios (1 bond from each issue). The cumulative return spread peaked in December 2008 and declined back to almost exactly zero by June 2011. *The implicit and explicit guarantees by the US Treasury and Federal Reserve had essentially driven the perceived creditworthiness of corporate bonds back to pre-GFC levels.*

While the unprecedented intervention of governments to stabilize the financial system was successful, we would assert that there is strong evidence that our approach to credit risk would have been helpful to investors during the GFC in dealing with both corporate bond risk and counterparty risk of financial institutions.

Figure 17.5.1: *Return spread for a long/short trading strategy in bonds based on Z-scores*

17.6 ANOTHER ROLE FOR NEWS IN CREDIT RISK CALIBRATION

One might wonder why CCA models of credit risk have not become the dominant method of credit analysis given their apparent advantages. The usual concern expressed by market participants is that such models will predict "fourteen out of every five defaults", essentially a tendency to produce upward-biased default estimates. This belief comes from several roots. The first is that some less sophisticated CCA models simply used equity volatility as a crude approximation of the volatility of a firm's assets. The second is that many financial economists (e.g. Shiller) have argued that equity markets prices are more volatile than is justified by underlying fundamentals.

A recent study by Govindaraj et al. (2014) sheds considerable light on this issue. They studied a large sample of traded stocks over the period 1982–2011. Each time a stock had a one-day return with absolute value greater than some threshold (e.g. 5%), they tracked what happened in the *subsequent* week to analyst estimates of the firm's future earnings and the value of the shares. In about 80% of the observations, nothing happened, suggesting that the price moves were "no information" transactions. For example, a large investor might choose to liquidate stocks to cash in order to meet a payment obligation, in which case it would be necessary to sell the stocks, temporarily depressing prices. This transaction illustrates how many financial market events may not carry any information about the investor's views. It is simply a "have to" rather than a "want to" transaction.

If a large magnitude return event were concurrent with or immediately subsequent to material news, we might assume with reasonable confidence that the observed price change carried information, and that such information was relevant to our estimates of the default risk of the firm. As such, the flow of news, timing of reports and the extent to which that news is classified as being related to fundamental activity (e.g. a merger) can all influence the extent to which we do (or don't) condition our estimates of credit risk.

17.7 BIG NEWS HAS LONG-TERM EFFECTS

Our final point of discussion is the long-term impact of very big "news" such as wars. If the market volatility associated with news has profound effects on credit risk and fixed income returns, this effect should manifest when in times of geopolitical instability. Put simply, if two countries go to war, it is unlikely that the loser will be in a position to pay their debts.

To test this hypothesis, we consider global bond market returns for the period from 1900 to 2010 using summary data from the Dimson, Marsh, Staunton data set compiled at London Business School (commercially available from Morningstar). We break the returns into eleven decade-long observations. Even though news delivery in 1900 was far slower than today's instantaneous dissemination of information online and on television, we assume that ten years is long enough for news to be distributed globally. Our measure of "news flow" is a Northfield proprietary data set, which estimates for each year the percentage of world population killed in armed conflict including war, revolutions, terrorism, genocides and induced famines over the same period of 110 years. The "news" included analysis of 32 major events, some of which extended over multiple years. For each event, a high, median and low estimate of casualties was established.

Across the "high", "median" or "low" estimate for conflict, the simple correlation between global bond returns and the conflict measure ranges from negative 63 to 71%. To address the potential impact of outliers (World Wars I and II), we also correlated global bond returns with the log of the casualty percentage, in which case the correlation extended to negative 86% (r-squared = .74). All correlations are statistically significant at conventional confidence intervals. It should be noted that highly negative correlations were also observed between casualty levels and global fixed income returns in the subsequent decade. Even with the two World Wars removed from the data entirely, bond market returns both in the contemporaneous and subsequent decades remained significantly negatively correlated with casualties. This result provides support for the old adage that, at least for fixed income investors, "No News is Good News".

17.8 CONCLUSIONS

Evaluation of credit risk for corporations and financial institutions (counterparty risk) has been demonstrated to be problematic in recent years. Use of news flows to calibrate a contingent claims model of credit risk can provide investors with efficient and transparent estimates of both key parameters, the probability of default (PD) and the loss given default (LGD). At an intuitive level, the use of quantified news and sentiment for credit risk has the advantage that it is largely unambiguous: "good" news is weakly good and "bad news" is strongly bad for creditors. Almost any news is bad news.

Our version of the Merton (1974) contingent claims model from diBartolomeo (2010, 2011) is used to break each corporate debt into two pieces: the first riskless debt and the second equity in the issuer. Existing methods for estimating equity risk expectations are then applied. We can utilize news flows and related sentiment statistics to update the calibration of the expected volatility of the equity portion and hence the credit risk of corporate debt in real time.

17.9 REFERENCES

1. Abraham, A. and Taylor, W.M. (1993). Pricing currency options with scheduled and unscheduled announcement effects on volatility. *Managerial and Decision Economics, 14(4),* 311–326.

2. Black, F. and Cox, J.C. (1976). Valuing corporate securities: some effects of bond indenture provisions. *Journal of Finance, 31,* 351–367.

3. Brown, K.C., Harlow, W.V. and Tinic, S.M. (1988). Risk aversion, uncertain information and market efficiency. *Journal of Financial Economics, 22(2),* 355–386.

4. diBartolomeo, D. (1999). Optimization of composite assets using implied covariance matrices. Northfield Working Paper.

5. diBartolomeo, D. and Warrick, S. (2005). Making covariance based portfolio risk models sensitive to the rate at which markets reflect new information. Chapter 12 in J. Knight and S. Satchell, eds., *Linear Factor Models.* Elsevier Finance.

6. diBartolomeo, D. (2010). Equity risk, credit risk, default correlation and corporate sustainability. *The Journal of Investing, 19(4),* 128–133.

7. diBartolomeo, D. (2011a). Use of news as a state variable in assessment of financial market risk. Chapter 10 in L. Mitra and G. Mitra, eds., *The Handbook of News Analytics in Finance.* Wiley.

8. diBartolomeo, D. (2011b). News analytics in a risk management framework for asset managers. Chapter 16 in L. Mitra and G. Mitra, eds., *The Handbook of News Analytics in Finance.* Wiley.

9. diBartolomeo, D. (2012). Equity factor models: estimation and extensions. In B. Scherer and K. Winston, eds., *The Oxford Handbook of Quantitative Asset Management.* Oxford University Press.

10. Ederington, L. and Lee, J. (1993). How markets process information: news releases and volatility. *Journal of Finance, 48,* 1161–1191.

11. Frye, J. (2013). Loss given default as a function of the default rate. Federal Reserve Bank of Chicago.

12. Govindaraj, S., Livnat, J., Savor, P.G., Zhao, C. and Blackrock, L.L.C. (2014). Large price changes and subsequent returns. *Journal of Investment Management (JOIM), Third Quarter.*

13. Kwag, A., Shrieves, R. and Wansley, J. (2000). Partially anticipated events: an application to dividend announcements. University of Tennessee Working Paper.

14. Kyle, A., Obizhaeva, A., Sinha, N. and Tuzun, T. (2012). News articles and the invariance hypothesis. Available at: http://papers.ssrn.com/sol3/papers.cfm?abstract_id=1786124.

15. Leland, H. (1994). Corporate debt values, bond covenants and optimal capital structure. *Journal of Finance*, *49*, 1213–1252.

16. Leland, H. and Toft, K.B. (1996). Optimal capital structure, endogenous bankruptcy and the term structure of credit spreads. *Journal of Finance*, *51*, 987–1019.

17. Merton, R.C. (1974). On the pricing of corporate debt: the risk structure of interest rates. *Journal of Finance*, *29*, 449–470.

18. Mitra, G., Mitra, L. and diBartolomeo, D. (2009). Equity portfolio risk (volatility) estimation using market information and sentiment. *Quantitative Finance*.

19. Shah, A. (2008). Short term risk from long term models. *Northfield News*, October 2008.

20. Yaksick, R. (1995). Expected optimal exercise time of a perpetual American option: a closed-form solution. In *Advances in Stochastic Modelling and Data Analysis* (pp. 29-56). Springer Netherlands.

CHAPTER 18

Trading Bond Futures (& FX) with News Meta Data

Saeed Amen, *The Thalesians*

ABSTRACT

Over the past few years, strategies which use news analytics have become more popular. Whilst the focus has been on equities, there is also significant news flow when it comes to macro assets. Here, we examine how macro news analytics data can be used to trade bond futures (& FX). We create news-based economic sentiment indices (NBESI) which mimic the behaviour of growth surprise indices. We discuss more broadly the relationship between growth surprise indices, NBESI and bond markets.

We use these news indices to create trading rules for bond futures. Our NBESI bond futures basket has risk-adjusted returns of 1.14 and drawdowns of 7.7% since 2001, outperforming a passive basket with risk-adjusted returns of 0.79. Our NBESI UST futures spreads basket has risk-adjusted returns of 0.90 which outperforms a passive strategy with risk-adjusted returns of 0.46.

We also apply the same approach to trading FX, using news data. Our combined filtered G10 FX carry and G10 FX NBESI basket has risk-adjusted returns of 1.11 and drawdowns of 6.7%.

18.1 INTRODUCTION

News analytics has emerged in the past few years as a rich new data source for traders to create systematic trading models. Much of the focus has been on equities over recent years. An example is Hafez (2009) which looks at how company-specific news impacts on equities. There has also been research on trading equity indices through the construction of sentiment indices (Hafez, 2013).

In this chapter, we seek to extend using news data for trading bond futures, an asset class, where traditionally there has been less news analytics research. We discuss the broad relationship between bond markets, economic surprise indices and news data. We construct a trading strategy for bond futures based upon our news-based economic sentiment indices (NBESI).

Later, we also examine using news analytics data to trade FX, an area where a larger body of news analytics research exists. Hafez and Xie (2013) use cross country news sentiment to trade FX. We shall also adopt a cross country approach for trading FX, albeit with differently constructed sentiment measures.

In Figure 18.1.1, we present returns for our news-based trading rule for bond futures and in Figure 18.1.2, for UST futures spreads. Our trading rules based on news, which we shall discuss later in more detail, significantly outperform the long only case, both in terms of risk-adjusted returns and the reduction of drawdowns.

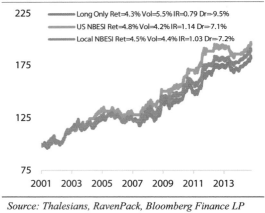

Source: Thalesians, RavenPack, Bloomberg Finance LP

Figure 18.1.1: Bond futures with news data

Source: Thalesians, RavenPack, Bloomberg Finance LP

Figure 18.1.2: Bond spreads with news data

18.1.1 The link between bonds and broader economic data

Before creating any sort of trading rule based on news data, we need to understand the relationship between markets and economic sentiment. It seems relatively intuitive that there should be a relationship between economic data and the price action in bonds. On a high frequency basis (Andersen et al., 2006) note how equity, bonds and FX markets react significantly to economic data releases. They suggest that the reaction can vary depending on where the economy is in the business cycle. Altavilla, Giannone and Modugno (2014) show how macroeconomic news can explain a reasonable proportion of low frequency fluctuations in US Treasury yields.

They define macroeconomic news as the difference between expectations and actual economic data releases, essentially the "surprise". Later we shall discuss the relationship more broadly between indices constructed from a large number of economic surprises and markets.

As economic data improves, we would expect central banks to adopt a more hawkish tone to keep inflation in check, which would be accompanied by rising yields as the market prices this in. By contrast, as economic data gets worse, we might expect central banks to become more dovish, which would be reflected in lower bond yields. There is the obvious caveat that there can be periods where high levels of inflation can occur during periods of poor growth, which is called stagflation. This broader relationship between growth and yields is discussed by Ang, Piazzesi and Wei (2004). To some extent we can think of bond yields as being a proxy for monetary policy expectations.

18.1.2 What does the data tell us about this link?

Can data confirm our hypothesis? We examine economic surprise indices to help answer this question. Economic surprise indices are popular amongst traders and economists. Many banks produce their own versions such as Citi, GS, JPM and Nomura (Amen, 2010). A surprise is defined as the difference between actual data and economist expectations. The data surprises are then standardised. This allows different sorts of economic data to be more easily compared. They are then aggregated to create a data surprise index, which is often smoothed. The final indices can be used as indicators of economic sentiment. Creating such indicators can be non-trivial from a data collection perspective. Scotti (2013) gives a detailed example of how a surprise index can be constructed.

In Figure 18.1.3, we plot Citi's US economic surprise index, which is the most well-known of the various surprise indices, against 3-month changes in UST 10Y yields. We find, at least on a stylized basis, that there is a strong positive correlation between changes in bond yields and changes in economic surprises. We note that broadly speaking, economic sentiment data has mean-reverting properties. This seems quite intuitive, if we consider how the market interprets economic data.

As data improves, the market updates its expectations higher. Eventually, the expectations become so elevated that data starts to miss expectations. We then see a peak in market sentiment with respect to economic data, which coincides with the medium-term peak in yields. At this point economic sentiment begins to mean-revert, as do yields. We see a similar process in reverse. When economic sentiment keeps worsening and it creates a trough, this coincides with the local low in yields.

In Figure 18.1.4, we look at the relationship in a more systematic manner, conducting a regression between daily changes in UST futures and Citi's US economic surprise index. We report T stats, which are statistically significant. This seems to tally with the findings of Altavilla, Giannone and Modugno (2014), who note how economic data can explain a reasonable proportion of the fluctuations in US Treasuries at lower frequencies. We note that the sign is obviously negative, because bond futures have an inverse relationship with bond yields. As we might expect, S&P500 has a positive correlation with US economic surprises, whilst EUR/USD has a negative correlation (the rationale is that worse data results in lower UST yields which tends to be bearish USD, thus pushing EUR/USD higher).

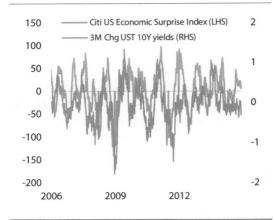

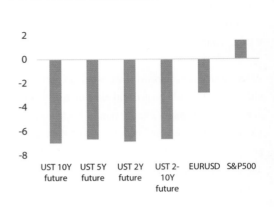

Source: Thalesians, Bloomberg Finance LP

Source: Thalesians, Bloomberg Finance LP

Figure 18.1.3: *UST 10Y yields vs Citi US ESI*

Figure 18.1.4: *Regressing macro (T stats)*

The idea behind creating news-based economic sentiment indices is that they will have a much richer dataset than economic data surprise indicators. Later, we shall discuss how we can use the relationship between economic sentiment and yields to enable us to create trading strategies to trade bond futures, using news-based economic sentiment indices.

On a broad basis, there are several ways we can trade economic sentiment indices. First, we can apply a momentum-based approach, which takes advantage of the fact that assets are correlated with economic sentiment. We can also take a longer-term approach, fading economic sentiment, given that over the longer term, sentiment is mean-reverting and it tends to be bounded.

18.1.3   What about the relationship between various bond markets?

So far we have only looked at UST futures. However, what is the relationship between USTs and other G4 bonds? In Figure 18.1.5, we plot the returns for UST 10Y, Bunds, long Gilts and JPN 10Y bond futures. We have adjusted for the differences in volatility. We see that there does appear to be a strong relationship between the various bond futures. In Figure 18.1.6, we compute weekly correlations between these various bond futures from 2001to present. We find that there are generally quite high correlations. This has been a feature of markets for a long time. Clare and Lekkos (2000) examine US, UK and German bond markets, noting how they can be influenced by international factors, which tallies with this point.

We shall later use the highly correlated nature of G4 sovereign bond markets to enable us to use both US-based and local news indicators. The rationale behind using US-based news indicators is that the US is likely to be a major driver for other bond markets.

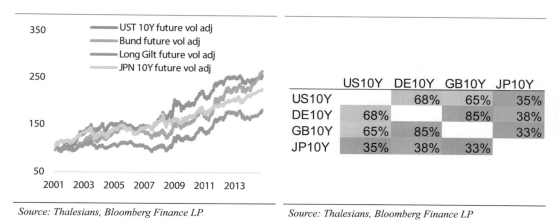

	US10Y	DE10Y	GB10Y	JP10Y
US10Y		68%	65%	35%
DE10Y	68%		85%	38%
GB10Y	65%	85%		33%
JP10Y	35%	38%	33%	

Source: Thalesians, Bloomberg Finance LP   *Source: Thalesians, Bloomberg Finance LP*

Figure 18.1.5: *G4 bond futures returns*   **Figure 18.1.6:** *G4 bond futures correlations*

18.2 DIFFERENCE BETWEEN UNSTRUCTURED AND STRUCTURED NEWS DATA

There are many different methods we can apply, when it comes to interpreting news data from a systematic viewpoint. The first step is to decide how we initially read news data. We have two choices:

- Unstructured news data – Read news articles, blogs etc. in their raw text form and then directly apply text-based analysis to gauge sentiment
- Structured news data – RavenPack processes a large amount of news from numerous sources into a more manageable dataset for us to explore. In their news analytics dataset, RavenPack include important additional fields which measure concepts such as the relative sentiment of news and its relative novelty.

Using unstructured news data can be hugely time consuming. Even before we have tried to interpret the news we have collected, we need to aggregate all our data sources and manage their storage. Once this has been done, the language needs to be analysed to gauge sentiment, using a natural language processing technique, which is non-trivial. This contrasts to structured news data, which can be accessible via APIs (on an intraday or daily basis) or CSVs produced on a daily basis, together with precomputed sentiment scores. Using structured news data therefore frees up a significant amount of time for traders. They can therefore concentrate on creating effective trading rules and running risk, rather than spending that time dealing with massive quantities of unstructured news and text analysis.

18.2.1 Description of RavenPack structured news analytics data

In this section, we briefly outline the structure of the RavenPack Macro 4.0 news dataset, which is available in three different sources listed below. We shall be using the Full Edition, which includes all three news sources (later, we shall also be using some elements of RavenPack's equity product):

- Dow Jones Edition – Dow Jones Newswires, regional editions of the Wall Street Journal and Barron's
- Web Edition – Business publishers, national and local news, blog sites, government and regulatory updates – 19,000 different sources
- PR Edition – 22 newswires and press release distribution networks – More than 100,000 press releases and regulatory disclosures processed every day

RavenPack classifies news events from these various sources using their own proprietary algorithms. For each news event analysed, a record is generated which includes 34 fields. Below, we give a small selection of the fields recorded for each news event. For full details, please read the RavenPack news analytics guide.

- Timestamp of publication – In UTC time with a millisecond timestamp
- Focus of the publication – Includes details on the country and the general subject of the news – We shall use these fields later to filter news (for example for US news related to the economy)
- Positive/negative nature of news – Scaled from 0 to 100, where >50 is positive, <50 is negative (and 50 is neutral) – We shall use this later for identifying the bullishness/bearishness of an article for trading purposes (Event sentiment score – ESS)
- Measures of the relative novelty of news – "Newer" news as opposed to repeated headlines scores higher (Event Novelty score – ENS)
- Prevalence of news – Identify the number of positive or negative events for a certain entity (Aggregate Event Sentiment – AES) and also the general news volume on an entity (Aggregate Event Volume – AEV)
- Source of the news and the RavenPack product edition

18.2.2 Aggregation of high frequency news data into daily news data

For every day, we have many thousands of records related to news events analysed by RavenPack, which are generated on a high frequency basis. Our objective is to create a daily trading rule. Hence we need to aggregate this high frequency data into daily chunks. This ability to aggregate high frequency data gives us control over the precise time of day we run our trading rule. This contrasts to daily data, where our trading time is determined by the availability of our daily signal. We shall be constructing our own aggregation of high frequency news data into daily data.

For example, if our daily signal is only available at New York close, and there is insufficient liquidity in the asset we wish to trade at that point, we would need to wait till the next day to trade (or potentially the entire weekend). In our analysis, we have solved this problem by creating different time based snapshots for our RavenPack derived indices, which are consistent with the assets we are trading. This avoids a large lag between the signal being generated and trading.

18.2.3 Subject aggregation of news data

Once we have created a scheme for aggregating high frequency data into daily data, we also need to direct our search to an appropriate subject within the news sample. This will enable us to focus on those news events which are most relevant for us. As mentioned above, we can use various fields to identify the focus of a news event. In the macro edition, RavenPack identify five "topics", which are used to classify some of the news events, which we list below. These classified events have a corresponding ESS[1] (event sentiment score).

- business
- economy
- environment
- politics
- society

These topics are further subdivided. The taxonomy structure goes from (broadest) topic to group, type, sub-type, property and category (narrowest).

At the beginning of the chapter, we discussed our hypothesis that there is a strong relationship between bond futures and economic sentiment. We later showed this using the underlying data. Hence our hypothesis suggests that we should focus our efforts on the "economy" topic, which has been classified by RavenPack. For most of the chapter, we shall use the entire "economy" topic in our aggregation. Later in the chapter, however, we shall also backtest other topics and groups of RavenPack news data to assess their value too.

18.3 CREATING NEWS-BASED ECONOMIC SENTIMENT INDICATORS

We have already applied both the daily and subject aggregations to the news data. However, our "raw" daily aggregation still exhibits a significant amount of noise (see Figure 18.3.1). We note that the volume of news data seems to rise over time, reflecting the general increase in news over the years. Hence we need to adjust our dataset for these factors in the construction of our news-based sentiment indicators. If a time series is too noisy, it can potentially generate far too many trading signals, resulting in excessive transaction costs eating away at returns. Noisy inputs can afflict all sorts of trading rules elsewhere, such as technical based approaches.

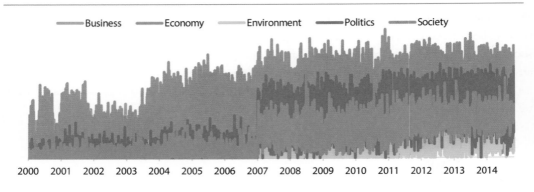

Source: Thalesians, RavenPack

Figure 18.3.1: *Daily aggregated data still needs to be de-noised and adjusted for volume*

Amen (2014) construct various "pressure" based indicators, which are broadly designed to create risk on/risk off signals. Volume of news data is also used as a signal, the rationale being that news volume tends to be correlated with market volatility. The use of news data to improve volatility modelling has been suggested by Yu (2014). Other forms of Big Data can also be correlated with market volatility. Kita and Wang (2012) discuss how investor attention, as measured by Google search volume for search terms related to FX, can be correlated to FX market volatility. In the FX section, we shall reuse this volume index to filter FX carry. The general approach is to reduce exposure to FX carry when news volume is high (and hence market volatility is also high). FX carry tends to perform poorly when market volatility is higher (Menkhoff et al., 2010).

In this chapter, we shall also be investigating turning points in sentiment and also the direction of this sentiment. Hence the construction of sentiment indices will be somewhat different to the approach adopted in Amen (2014). Here our resulting indicator is a slower moving and a less volatile indicator. For consistency, we adopt the same construction for nearly all the indicators we shall construct in this chapter.

In Figure 18.3.2, we plot our US news-based economic sentiment index (NBESI) against Citi's US economic surprise index. We note that there is a reasonable correlation between the Citi index and the US RavenPack news-based economic sentiment index (NBESI), which we have constructed. This should not be surprising given that the economy news topic we are selecting includes a large amount of information regarding economic data releases, alongside a plethora of other economic news, such as central bank meetings. In the appendix, we plot the various Citi ESI against our NBESI for G4.

Source: Thalesians, RavenPack, Bloomberg Finance LP

Figure 18.3.2: *Thalesians/RavenPack US news-based index (NBESI) vs Citi's US ESI*

The precise construction of our NBESI indicators is proprietary. However, using US NBESI as an example, we can summarise the basic steps we take to construct the index below. Our main objective is to create an indicator which is representative of medium-term sentiment, rather than having a very high frequency indicator.

- Data selection: Take all data for US and which are tagged with the "economy" topic, removing all other data
- Convert high frequency to daily: take the average hourly ESS score and aggregate these hourly scores to a daily reading using a cut off at NY close for the past day
- Reduce noise: Smooth the daily data to make the indicator less noisy
- Adjust for different levels of news volumes: Standardise score (excluding weekends)
- Reduce noise: Smooth the standardised score to make the indicator less noisy

18.4 THE RELATIONSHIP BETWEEN NEWS ECONOMIC SENTIMENT AND BOND FUTURES

Earlier, we discussed the broad relationship between bond yields, bond futures and economic data. We also showed that our US news-based economic sentiment index (NBESI) exhibited a strong relationship with the Citi US economic surprise index. However, do moves in news-based economic sentiment indices help us to understand returns in UST futures in the subsequent period?

To answer this, we look at UST 10Y futures returns in the subsequent month according to the level of US NBESI and conditioning on whether the index is rising or falling. We noted earlier that there tends to be a positive correlation between UST yields and US NBESI. When yields are falling, we would clearly prefer to be long bond futures and when yields are rising, we would prefer not to be long (flat or potentially short, although this would be a negative carry trade). In Figure 18.4.1, we report the total amount of returns in each case over our sample from 2001 to present. The y-axis reports a very large figure, given that it would imply repeatedly entering

a new position every day. The figure is also high because we are giving the total returns of these positions over
the entirety of our sample.

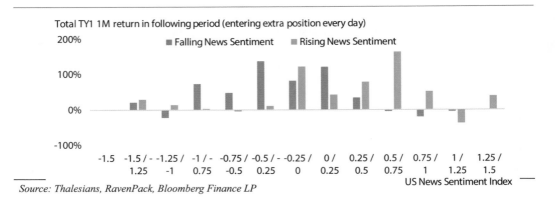

Source: Thalesians, RavenPack, Bloomberg Finance LP

Figure 18.4.1: *Total UST 10Y futures returns in subsequent month vs US NBESI*

We note that during extremes in our news sentiment indices, when sentiment is either very bad or very good,
bond futures returns are somewhat mixed. Part of the issue is of course that these are often turning points in
sentiment. Hence we have the choice of either developing an intuitive method of identifying these regions or
simply exiting exposure during these periods.

When data is merely bad, we see that bond future returns are better when sentiment is falling compared to rising.
By contrast, when data is good, although returns are positive, it seems difficult to discern whether this is more
for rising or falling sentiment. However, the most consistent returns appear to be for periods of falling news
sentiment and bad data. Ilmanen, Maloney and Ross (2014) examine how various asset classes have performed
over the past 40 years during various macro-economic environments. They note how during periods of poor
growth, bonds have outperformed, which tallies with our observations from Figure 18.4.1. This seems quite
intuitive, if we consider the relationship between bonds and economic data. This logic also fits into the general
idea that bonds (especially USTs) are perceived as "safer" instruments during times of market turbulence.

18.5   CREATING AN EXCESS RETURNS SERIES FOR BOND FUTURES

To backtest any strategy on bond futures, we need to take into account rolls in futures contracts. When a contract
expires, we need to roll it into the next active contract. This causes a jump in the price series as the expiring
contract will have a different price from the new active future. To avoid this problem, we could simply use
vendor-produced excess return indices to adjust for this to obtain a continuous time series. Alternatively, we can
back-adjust historical futures contracts prices for the most active contract to create a continuous time series. In
Figure 18.5.1, we plot S&P UST 10Y futures excess return series against our adjusted UST 10Y futures, when
both have been scaled to have the same volatility. We find that both series are very similar. S&P (2014) gives an
example of how to adjust for rolls in the context of bond futures.

Arguably, given that we are trying to compare returns to a long only benchmark, perhaps on a comparative basis it would not have made a lot of difference. However, from an excess returns basis, there is some difference between an ordinary futures time series and one which has been adjusted for rolls. Another way we can take account of roll is simply to exit the old contract at expiry and enter the new one, thus omitting the "jump" in the price from our time series.

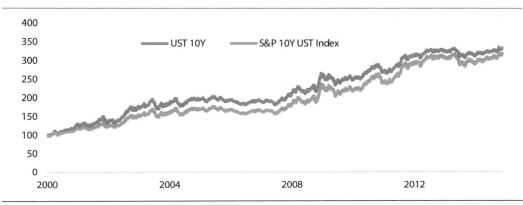

Source: Thalesians, Bloomberg Finance LP

Figure 18.5.1: *Comparing UST 10Y adjusted futures vs excess returns index*

18.6 APPLYING NEWS-BASED TRADING RULES TO BOND FUTURES

We have described the general approach which we have used to construct news-based economic sentiment indices (NBESI). We have used this to create indices for several countries (G4), which have a reasonably liquid bond futures market.

In this section, we create a trading rule which uses our news-based economic sentiment index (NBESI) as an input. In the previous section we also discussed the broader relationship between bond futures and NBESI. In particular, we suggested that periods of falling sentiment and poor data tend to be the best time to get into long exposure in bond futures, which also makes intuitive sense, whilst trying to exit exposure at extremes. Our NBESI trading rule encompasses some of these ideas and we give details below. We calculate the trading signal on a daily basis.

- Go long bond futures when
    - NBESI is bad (<0) **and** falling
- Go flat bond futures when
    - NBESI is at an extreme (>1 or <-1)
- Otherwise we do not adjust our existing exposure

For comparison, we also give the returns from long only strategies, focusing on liquid G4 bond futures (i.e. US, Germany, UK and Japan). Returns are given denominated in domestic currency. We present risk-adjusted returns in Figure 18.6.1 and drawdowns in Figure 18.6.2. Our sample is from 2001 to present. We include transaction costs[2] in our analysis.

We report results for long only, US NBESI and local NBSEI. We use US NBESI as a filter, given our earlier observation that bond futures tend to be highly correlated in G4. As the largest economy, the US is likely to be a major driver for other bonds in G4. The local indicators as their name suggests use local news. The main exception is Germany, where we have used a mixture of Eurozone (which includes news related to the ECB) and German news.

We find that in general, the lowest risk adjusted returns for US bond futures are from long only. Long only also has the worst drawdowns of nearly all the bonds in our sample. We find that the US NBESI filters have the best risk-adjusted returns on the whole, whilst also generally exhibiting the smallest drawdowns.

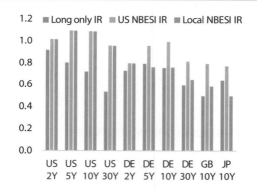

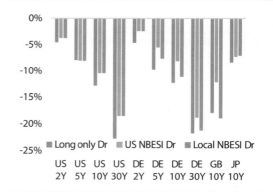

Source: Thalesians, RavenPack, Bloomberg Finance LP

Source: Thalesians, RavenPack, Bloomberg Finance LP

Figure 18.6.1: *G4 bond futures IR*

Figure 18.6.2: *G4 bond futures drawdowns*

We create baskets of all the bond futures. For simplicity, we have adopted equal weighting by notional. In practice, investors might consider other weightings, which take into account the varying liquidity of the bond futures and different volatilities. In all cases, we report the results in local currency. Obviously, these would most likely be reported in the investor's currency (e.g. USD) and would often have some element of currency hedging. In Figure 18.6.3, we plot the cumulative returns for the various trading rules.

We report results for long only, US NBESI and local NBESI-based baskets. We also show the returns on a year-on-year basis in Figure 18.6.4. We note that the US NBESI has the best risk-adjusted returns of 1.14. This is closely followed by the local NBESI filter, which has a risk adjusted return of 1.03. Long only has the worst risk-adjusted returns and drawdowns.

We need to bear in mind that in recent years, interest rates have been unusually low. Many analysts think the Fed is likely to hike relatively soon, which could see a normalisation of interest rates (at least in the US). We note that during periods when interest rates are more "normal", US NBESI generally performed better than long only. In recent years, local NBESI and long only outperformed US NBESI.

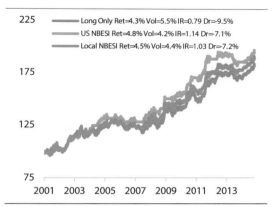

Source: Thalesians, RavenPack, Bloomberg Finance LP

Figure 18.6.3: *Bond futures basket*

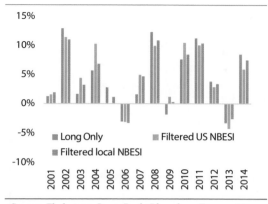

Source: Thalesians, RavenPack, Bloomberg Finance LP

Figure 18.6.4: *Bond futures basket YoY*

Trading bond future curve spreads using news data

We have seen that our news-based sentiment indicators generally outperform long only strategies in G4 space during our sample period 2001 to present. However, is the same true if we trade spreads via bond futures? One popular strategy in bond space, can be to buy longer-dated bond futures, which are generally higher yielding and funding these purchases with selling short-dated bond futures, which tend to be lower yielding. Clearly, for these strategies to work, traders are expecting a yield curve which isn't inverted. In an inverted yield curve, front end yields are higher than long end yields. In a sense, these curve trades can be seen as carry trades, which are common in other asset classes like FX. We have used the same notionals for both the short and long ends. There can be more complicated ways of constructing the trade, notably by vol adjusting the notionals. We focus on various UST bond spreads such as 2-10Y and present the risk-adjusted returns in Figure 18.6.5 and drawdowns in Figure 18.6.6. We find that generally long only has the lowest risk-adjusted returns, compared to US NBESI. US NBESI is the top performer, with both the highest risk-adjusted returns and the smallest drawdowns.

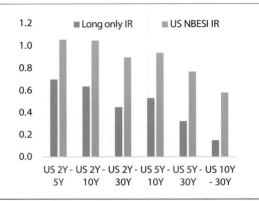

Source: Thalesians, RavenPack, Bloomberg Finance LP

Figure 18.6.5: *US bond futures spreads IR*

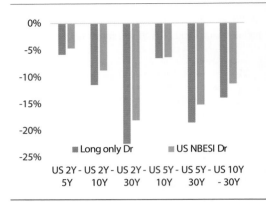

Source: Thalesians, RavenPack, Bloomberg Finance LP

Figure 18.6.6: *US bond futures spreads drawdowns*

Next, we create a basket of these various UST spreads, using our news-based trading rules. We present the cumulative returns in Figure 18.6.7 and the year-on-year returns in Figure 18.6.8 for our spread baskets.

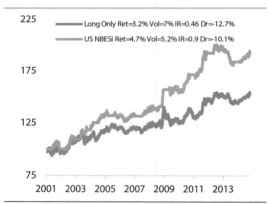

Source: Thalesians, RavenPack, Bloomberg Finance LP

Figure 18.6.7: *US bond futures spreads basket*

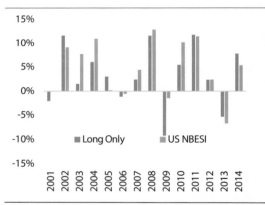

Source: Thalesians, RavenPack, Bloomberg Finance LP

Figure 18.6.8: *US bond futures spreads basket YoY*

We find that our US NBESI filtered basket has the best highest risk-adjusted returns (0.9) and the smallest drawdowns of the various strategies (especially in 2009). The worst performer is the long only benchmark again, whose risk-adjusted returns are 0.46.

We have noted that our trading rule is calculated on a daily basis. However, how often do we actually change our signal? In Figure 18.6.9, we plot the signal for US NBESI alongside the actual index to illustrate this.

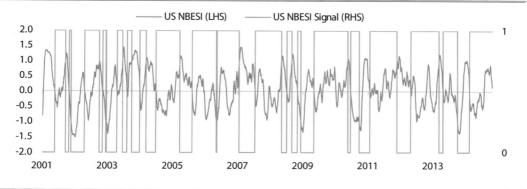

Source: Thalesians, RavenPack

Figure 18.6.9: *US NBESI alongside trading long/flat trading signals*

In Figure 18.6.10, we plot the number of trades which occur per year and also the number of business days when the signal is either long or flat. The trading rule spends more time long than it does flat. Note that we have not included rolls in this figure, which would also occur several times a year (these would also impact on long only, too, though). We find that on average we have a handful of trades a year.

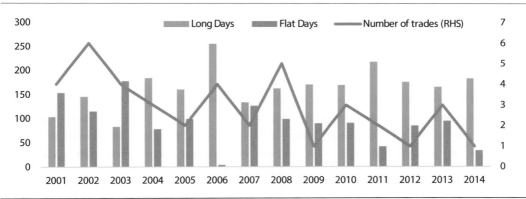

Source: Thalesians, RavenPack

Figure 18.6.10: *Trading frequency of US NBESI trading signal and distribution*

18.7 EXPANDING OUR FOCUS TO OTHER RAVENPACK TOPICS

So far we have primarily examined the "economy" topic from RavenPack's macro edition. However, as we noted earlier, there are several topics other than the "economy" topic which are captured by RavenPack and given sentiment scores.

Furthermore, there are also numerous groups beneath these topics that capture more nuanced news, such as employment and housing news. What type of results do we see with a selection of these? In this section, we shall be using pre-made RavenPack daily aggregations for these various topics and group. We have also included the "corporate" topic which is available from RavenPack's equity edition.

Using the daily pre-made aggregation of RavenPack data, we create sentiment indicators for these various extra topics. We adopt a similar methodology to their construction, as we did for all the other NBESI indicators earlier. In Figure 18.7.1, we present the risk-adjusted returns for trading UST 10Y futures using these topics. In Figure 18.7.2, we do the same for drawdowns.

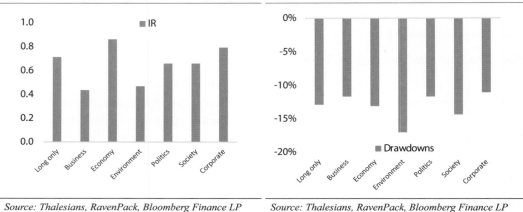

Source: Thalesians, RavenPack, Bloomberg Finance LP   Source: Thalesians, RavenPack, Bloomberg Finance LP

Figure 18.7.1: *UST 10Y futures with topics IR*   **Figure 18.7.2:** *UST 10Y futures with topics drawdowns*

We find that the "economy" topic has the best risk-adjusted returns, which confirms our original hypothesis that economic news is likely to be a major driver for bond futures. To any investor this is unlikely to be a surprise. The business and environment topics underperform long only. Most other topics have similar results to long only. As a next step we go beyond the topic section into events categorised as groups from RavenPack's macro and equity editions. Does our intuition about which news drives bond futures fit with backtested results?

In Figure 18.7.3, we show the risk-adjusted returns for trading UST 10Y futures using groups from RavenPack's macro edition. We do the same in Figure 18.7.4, but this time for groups from RavenPack's equity edition.

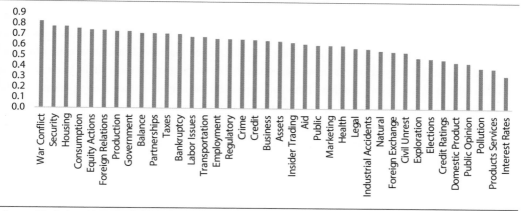

Source: Thalesians, RavenPack, Bloomberg Finance LP

Figure 18.7.3: *UST 10Y futures with groups from macro edition IR*

If we look at the macro groups, the top-performing trading rules are those related to "war conflict" and "security", which seems intuitive. During periods of significant geopolitical instability, we might expect investors to switch out of risky assets and into "safe haven" assets, such as USTs.

At the other end of the spectrum, the "interest rates" group appears to be the worst performer. One reason could be that a large number of events in this category tend be more backward-looking. For some of the other groups, we might consider adapting the trading rules to take into account the different interpretations of the various categories, although we would need to make this decision on a case-by-case basis.

In the equity edition, we find that bad news sentiment around acquisitions has the biggest IRs. This seems to make sense, if we consider that at times of risk-aversion, companies are less likely to engage in acquisitions. As we noted earlier, these tend to be times when "safe haven" assets such as USTs are more bid.

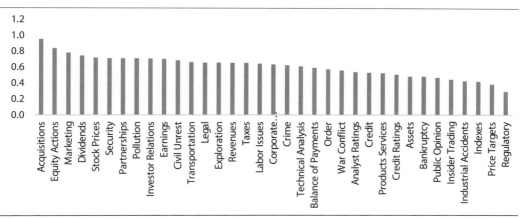

Source: Thalesians, RavenPack, Bloomberg Finance LP

Figure 18.7.4: *UST 10Y futures with groups from equity edition IR*

We can create portfolios of the best-performing groups. We create a geopolitical shock basket (based on an equally weighted portfolio of "war conflict" and "security" groups) and also a corporate shock basket (based on "acquisitions" and "equity action groups") for trading UST 10Y futures. We present cumulative returns for these baskets in Figure 18.7.5 and year-on-year returns in Figure 18.7.6. We have vol adjusted all the baskets, so their returns have the same long-term volatilities. Both the geopolitical and corporate shock baskets outperform the long only case on a risk-adjusted basis. Admittedly, there is some cherry-picking which has gone into selecting these groups to use in our shock baskets. However, it does illustrate there is some potential from narrowing down the news we use, although further work is necessary to fully answer this question.

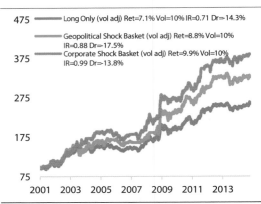

Source: Thalesians, RavenPack, Bloomberg Finance LP

Figure 18.7.5: *UST 10Y futures with combined groups IR*

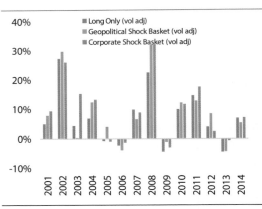

Source: Thalesians, RavenPack, Bloomberg Finance LP

Figure 18.7.6: *UST 10Y futures with combined groups year-on-year*

18.8 COMPARING TRADING RESULTS FOR ECONOMIC SURPRISE INDICES VERSUS NEWS-BASED ECONOMIC SENTIMENT INDICES (NBESI)

We earlier illustrated that NBESI can be used to mimic Citi's economic surprise indices. In this section we backtest strategies based on both for trading UST 10Y futures, to do a more quantitative comparison. We plot the results in Figure 18.8.1.

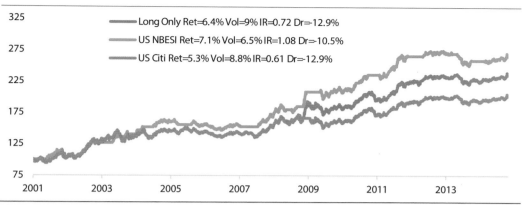

Source: Thalesians, RavenPack, Bloomberg Finance LP

Figure 18.8.1: *Comparing UST 10Y with US NBESI and Citi US economic surprise index*

We applied a similar trading rule to Citi's US economic surprise index[3] as the one we applied to US NBESI. We see that US NBESI outperforms the Citi Economic Surprise index and also long only. Admittedly, we might be able to improve the results from using the US Citi Economic Surprise index, using a trading rule which is specifically designed for it (given that Citi's indices exhibit less volatility than the US NBESI).

18.9   TRADING FX USING NEWS-BASED ECONOMIC SENTIMENT INDICES (NBESI)

So far, we have focused on using our news-based sentiment indices to trade bond futures. In this section, we use the same sentiment indices to trade individual FX crosses, albeit with slightly different trading rules. In FX, we are trading on a cross country basis. This contrasts to our bond futures trading rules, where we were trading single countries. It is also somewhat of a contrast to Amen (2014), which used news-based pressure indices to provide a broader-based risk on/risk off signal for FX carry. The approach also used news volume as a proxy for market volatility.

By contrast, Hafez and Xie (2013) use cross country news sentiment to trade EUR/USD. In this section, we shall also adopt a cross country news sentiment approach for trading a FX, albeit with differently constructed sentiment measures to Hafez and Xie (2013).

In this instance, we use a more mean-reverting style trading rule, to take advantage of the mean-reversion properties of economic sentiment. We illustrate our trading rule using EUR/USD. First we need to generate signals independently for EUR and USD, using their respective news-based economic sentiment indices (NBESI). Below we show how the EUR signal is constructed (the USD signal is computed in a similar manner):

- If EZ NBESI is rising, then create a bearish EUR signal.
- If EZ NBESI is falling, then create a bullish EUR signal.
- If EZ NBESI is extreme, then create a neutral EUR signal.

We then trade EUR/USD according to the following rules:

- If there are bearish EUR and bullish USD signals, we sell EUR/USD in a full unit.
- If there are bullish EUR and bearish USD signals, we buy EUR/USD in a full unit.
- When one currency out of the two has a neutral signal, we scale back exposure to a half unit.
- If both currencies are neutral, we keep holding our previous exposure.

As we did for Bunds, we have created a joint Eurozone/Germany NBESI for trading EUR. Of course this is only a rough proxy for Eurozone data. A more complicated proxy could involve GDP-weighting the individual Eurozone countries.

In Figure 18.9.1, we present the risk-adjusted returns for these strategies for the G10 USD crosses. In Figure 18.9.2, we show the drawdowns for these FX strategies. We find that this is profitable in every case, although the performance in USD/NOK is close to flat. One explanation could be that other drivers might be dominant in this cross (such as oil) and also because there are also fewer data events for the NOK leg. The relatively consistent risk-adjusted returns across all the other pairs, suggests that the trading rule we have used is relatively robust.

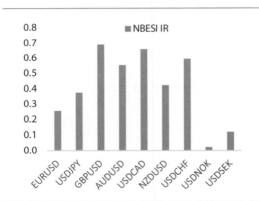

Source: Thalesians, RavenPack, Bloomberg Finance LP

Figure 18.9.1: *FX NBESI IR*

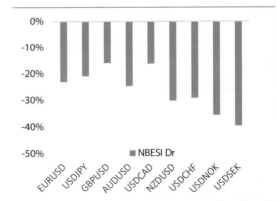

Source: Thalesians, RavenPack, Bloomberg Finance LP

Figure 18.9.2: *FX NBESI drawdowns*

Next, we create an FX basket, applying our various news-based trading rules used above for most of the above crosses tested. In Figure 18.9.5, we present the cumulative returns for this strategy, whilst in Figure 18.9.4 we show the year-on-year returns. We compare the returns with a generic G10 FX carry basket. We also show a generic G10 FX carry filtered by our RavenPack US news volume[4] index, constructed in Amen (2014). Lastly, we create an equally-weighted mixed portfolio of our G10 NBESI basket and G10 carry basket filtered by our RavenPack US news volume index.

We find that our FX NBESI basket has much better risk adjusted returns at 0.69 compared to unfiltered carry at 0.49. Notably the drawdowns are much smaller at 13.6% versus 35.5% for carry. Even once adjusted for volatility, FX NBESI still has far smaller drawdowns than a typical carry strategy. In general, the FX NBESI basket performed better following the financial crisis than before it. The filtered G10 FX carry basket has higher risk-adjusted returns at 0.87, than the G10 FX NBESI basket. However, the best performer is the mixed portfolio of G10 FX NBESI and filtered carry, with risk-adjusted returns of 1.11. Perhaps more importantly the drawdowns from the mixed portfolio are considerably lower. This illustrates that our FX NBESI and filtered G10 FX carry baskets do not exhibit significant correlation and hence complement each other well. For investors already invested in G10 FX carry, it suggests that adding a basket similar to our G10 FX NBESI basket can help to diversify their portfolio.

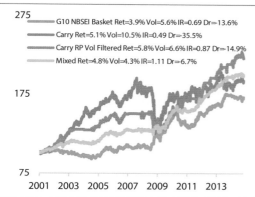

Source: Thalesians, RavenPack, Bloomberg Finance LP

Figure 18.9.3: *FX NBESI basket*

Source: Thalesians, RavenPack, Bloomberg Finance LP

Figure 18.9.4: *FX NBESI basket YoY*

As we did for bonds, we illustrate how signals of our NBESI FX trading rule change over time. In Figure 18.9.5, we plot the long/short signals for EUR/USD based upon NBESI. Note that the signal is always invested and frequently cuts exposure to half.

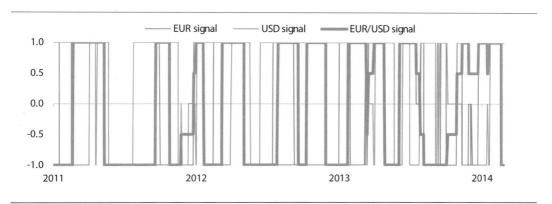

Source: Thalesians, RavenPack

Figure 18.9.5: *Trading signals for EUR/USD based on NBESI*

In Figure 18.9.6, we plot the distribution of EUR/USD NBESI signals by the number of days it is long or short EUR/USD. We also plot the number of trades which are executed per year on the same plot. We can see that generally it trades between 10-15 times a year, which is more often than the bond futures signals we generated earlier. The distribution of longs and shorts is fairly even from year to year.

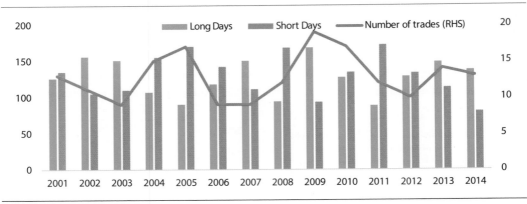

Source: Thalesians, RavenPack

Figure 18.9.6: *Trading frequency of NBESI EUR/USD trading signal and distribution*

18.10 CONCLUSION

We have discussed the relationship between economic data surprises and bond futures at length. We noted that better data is associated with higher yields (and worse data is associated with lower yields). This fits in with the broader relationship between growth and bond markets (Ang, Piazzesi and Wei, 2004).

We created news-based economic sentiment indices (NBESI) from RavenPack news analytics data using our own daily aggregation. We showed that these can be used as proxies for more commonly used economic data surprise indices, which are produced by many large banks. We refer the reader to Scotti (2013) for a detailed discussion of how a surprise index can be constructed. Our news-based economic sentiment indices (NBESI) are derived from high frequency data. Hence they can be snapped at any time of the day for generating a trading signal at the most appropriate time of day for liquidity purposes. Furthermore, they capture a richer data set of both news and economic events, compared to economic data surprise indices.

We used our various news-based economic sentiment indices (NBESI) to create trading rules for G4 bond futures and spreads. Our G4 bond futures basket had risk-adjusted returns of 1.14 outperforming a long only basket which had risk-adjusted returns of 0.79. Furthermore, our G4 bond futures spread basket also outperformed a passive strategy delivering both stronger risk-adjusted returns and smaller drawdowns. We also examined finer granularity news data, examining trading rules based upon RavenPack's group classification.

Hafez and Xie (2013) use cross country sentiment to trade FX and we adopt a similar approach to trading FX, albeit with our own sentiment aggregation (NBESI). Our FX news basket had risk-adjusted returns of 0.69 and annualised returns of 3.9%, whilst our combined filtered G10 FX carry and G10 FX NBESI basket has risk-adjusted returns of 1.11 and drawdowns of 6.7%.

ACKNOWLEDGEMENTS

With special thanks to Peter Hafez from RavenPack for his comments during the writing of the initial version of this chapter. This chapter has been kindly sponsored by RavenPack. Time series of the news-based sentiment indices (NBESI) constructed here are available on request. This work is based on an earlier paper by Amen (2015).

Notes

[1]   The ESS (Event Sentiment Score) is available for those news events which have classified. News events which have not been classified are not given ESSs.

[2]   We have assumed transaction costs of 3 bp bid/ask in this chapter. We have omitted the costs of rolling futures at expiry, although these would be incurred by all the different strategies.

[3]   Note: Citi ESI data starts in 2003 (hence we have assumed long only exposure before that point).

[4]   Data history starts in 2002.

18.11   REFERENCES

1.   Altavilla, C., Giannone, D. and Modugno, M. (2014). The Low Frequency Effects of Macroeconomic News on Government Bond Yields. *Feds (Finance & Economics Discussion Series)*, pp. 2014-52.

2.   Amen, S. (2010). Nomura Growth Surprise Indices. *Nomura Research*.

3.   Amen, S. (2014). Carry the news trade. *The Thalesians*.

4.   Amen, S. (2015). Bond over Big Data. *The Thalesians*.

5.   Andersen, T. G., Bollerslev, T., Diebold, F. X. and Vega, C. (2006, September). Real-Time Price Discovery in Global Stock, Bond and Foreign Exchange Markets. Retrieved from International Finance Discussion Papers No 871: http://www.federalreserve.gov/pubs/ifdp/2006/871/ifdp871.pdf

6.   Ang, A., Piazzesi, M. and Wei, M. (2004, August). What Does the Yield Curve Tell us about GDP Growth? Retrieved from NBER Working Paper No. 10672: http://www.nber.org/papers/w10672

7.   Clare, A. and Lekkos, I. (2000, December). An Analysis of the Relationship Between International Bond Markets. Retrieved from Bank of England Working Paper No. 123: http://www.bankofengland.co.uk/archive/documents/historicpubs/workingpapers/2001/wp123.pdf

8.   Hafez, P. (2009). Impact of News Sentiment on Abnormal Stock Returns. *RavenPack*.

9.   Hafez, P. (2013). Trading Relative Value Based on News Indicators. *RavenPack*.

10. Hafez, P. and Xie, J. (2013). Sentiment Derived from News Predicts EURUSD Movements. [Retrieved 7 July 2015] Available at: http://papers.ssrn.com/sol3/papers.cfm?abstract_id=2342247

11. Ilmanen, A., Maloney, T. and Ross, A. (2014). Exploring Macroeconomic Sensitivities: How Investments Respond to Different Economic Environments. *The Journal of Portfolio Management, 40*(3), pp. 87-99.

12. Kita, A. and Wang, Q. (2012). Investor Attention and FX Market Volatility. Available at SSRN: http://papers.ssrn.com/sol3/papers.cfm?abstract_id=2022100

13. Menkhoff, L., Sarno, L., Schmeling, M. and Schrimpf, A. (2010). Carry Trades and Global Foreign Exchange Volatility. Available at SSRN: http://papers.ssrn.com/sol3/papers.cfm?abstract_id=1342968

14. S&P (2014). S&P Global Bond Futures Index Series Methodology. Available at: http://us.spindices.com/documents/methodologies/methodology-sp-global-bond-futures.pdf

15. Scotti, C. (2013). Surprise and Uncertainty Indexes: Real-Time Aggregation of Real-Activity Macro Surprises. *FRB International Finance Discussion Paper No. 1093.*

16. Yu, X. (2014). Analysis of news sentiment and its application to finance. Retrieved from Brunel University: http://bura.brunel.ac.uk/bitstream/2438/9062/1/Full%20text%20Thesis.pdf

18.A   APPENDIX

We present the NBESI series for G4 below alongside Citi's economic surprise indices.

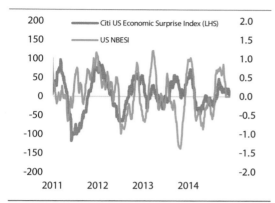

Source: Thalesians, RavenPack, Bloomberg Finance LP

Figure A1: *US NBESI vs. Citi US ESI*

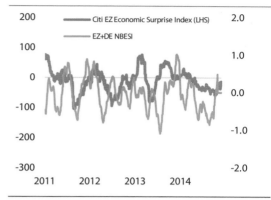

Source: Thalesians, RavenPack, Bloomberg Finance LP

Figure A2: *EZ+DE NBESI vs. Citi EZ ESI*

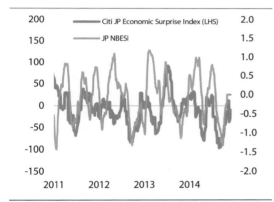

Source: Thalesians, RavenPack, Bloomberg Finance LP

Figure A3: *JP NBESI vs. Citi JP ESI*

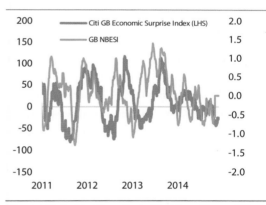

Source: Thalesians, RavenPack, Bloomberg Finance LP

Figure A4: *GB NBESI vs. Citi GB ESI*

CHAPTER 19

Currency Sentiment Analysis

Changjie Liu, *Chief of Analytics, MarketPsych*

Richard Peterson, *CEO, MarketPsych*

ABSTRACT

Alexander Hamilton identified that uncertainty irrationally debases a currency and trust inflates its value. Researchers have since found that monetary policy uncertainty adds a risk premium (an excessive discount) in currency values. Media sentiment gauges perceptions, and as such it holds promise towards the identification of currencies with relatively large risk premia. Using a unique array of media-derived currency sentiment data - the Thomson Reuters MarketPsych Indices (TRMI) - we demonstrate that colloquial wisdom about the drivers of currency valuations may be supported by such data. In particular, the Uncertainty TRMI shows significant historical predictive value over currency valuations in cross-sectional models at weekly and yearly horizons, most likely due to investor overreaction to uncertainty. Media price forecasts and expressed trust also appear to hold predictive value. Moving average crossovers (MACDs) may help time reversals in influential information flow, as in the case of the Japanese yen priceForecast TRMI. Using a combination of orthogonal TRMI boosts model returns in sample.

19.1 INTRODUCTION

There is no subtler, no surer means of overturning the existing basis of society than to debauch the currency. The process engages all the hidden forces of economic law on the side of destruction, and does it in a manner which not one man in a million is able to diagnose.
~ *John Maynard Keynes (Keynes, 1919)*

Over $5 trillion is traded in global foreign exchange markets every day, rendering currencies the most actively traded global asset class. Participants in the currency markets include central banks, multinational corporations, investment firms, banks and retail speculators, among others. These groups largely drive currency prices, and each party may have coordinating or competing goals in the markets. For example, governments may take monetary action to boost their own export-based industries (e.g. the Bank of Japan's efforts to depreciate the Japanese yen) or to undermine others (e.g. the 50 percent devaluation of the Iranian rial in 2013 following discussions about international sanctions). Retail and institutional investors may be pursuing a carry trade to earn higher yields in other nations' bonds. Speculators may trade based on macroeconomic announcements. Given these competing influences, and the difficulty of identifying both perception and reality in currency markets, how can investors determine the true equilibrium value of the dollar? This chapter explores how media sentiment and perceptions may drive currency prices in systematic patterns.

19.2 THE VALUE OF UNCERTAINTY

"[I]t is uncertainty - far more than disaster - that unnerves and weakens markets."
~ *Alexander Hamilton (Gordon, 1988)*

Alexander Hamilton was a founding father of the United States and served as the first US Secretary of the Treasury (1789–1795). Hamilton argued that a strong central government would serve to bolster business confidence, "[T]o give people faith in the financial structure of the country and in the soundness of the currency…." (ibid). As Secretary of the Treasury, Hamilton lobbied the US government to issue bonds to bolster the government's finances. The goal of this debt issuance was to reduce business uncertainty. Hamilton believed that a centralized and fiscally sound government would reduce uncertainty and thus boost economic activity following the US Revolutionary War.

Confirming Hamilton's belief in the value of strong governance to stabilize market values, researchers found that monetary policy uncertainty creates a risk premium in currencies (Mueller et al., 2014). A country's currency remains weak until policy uncertainty passes, after which the currency rises in value. This discount in currency value is larger when the country is economically weak.

Further academic research into the impact of uncertainty on bond prices finds that the bond risk premium rises (bond prices fall) as uncertainty about expected inflation rises (Bansal and Shaliastovich, 2012). Furthermore, price movements in currencies often occur as a result of sudden "flight to quality" (a euphemism for panic) among traders who engage in the same safety-seeking behaviour simultaneously (Brunnermeier and Pedersen, 2009). Such patterns in currency prices, based on changes in consensus price expectations and uncertainty may be modelled using a new and novel source of currency information flow.

19.3 CURRENCY SENTIMENT ANALYSIS

In order to statistically test Hamilton's hypothesis, it is first necessary to quantify the level of currency uncertainty. In partnership with Thomson Reuters, MarketPsych developed a text analytics engine to quantify references to uncertainty surrounding a currency in the media. The Thomson Reuters MarketPsych Indices (TRMI) - which are studied in this chapter - are quantified sentiment and macroeconomic time series derived from the flow of news and social media information about individual assets and countries.

Each day up to three million articles from news (premium newswires and internet news aggregators) and social media (blogs, forums, and tweets) are analysed and scored (quantified) in real-time by MarketPsych's text analytics software. Specific sentiment and macroeconomic references are identified in the text of the articles and, once aggregated, these scores form the TRMI. See Chapter 12 for a more detailed description of the country-specific TRMI and how the TRMI are constructed.

There are 21 currency-specific TRMI are a quantitative representation of commentary about currency-related technical, topics, sentiments and tones. Currencies are identified in macroeconomic and FX-related articles via direct references in text to the currency, a currency pair (e.g. JPY/USD) or to its aliases (e.g. "the Loonie" to describe the Canadian Dollar). TRMI derived from technical references to price include the priceDirection TRMI, an aggregate of all references to the currency's value rising versus falling. Topics such as violence (e.g. war) associated with a currency are quantified in the Violence TRMI. An example of a sentiment TRMI is Trust, which is the net difference between all trusting and mistrusting references to the currency. Tonal TRMI include the Uncertainty TRMI, which quantifies references to doubts and ambiguity associated with a currency including "doubt," "confusion" and "lack of clarity."

In many cases macroeconomic references are not associated with a currency directly in the media. Macroeconomic TRMI are typically associated with the country that hosts the currency. There are 48 TRMI country indexes available for research, many of which cover macroeconomic topics. Each is derived from textual analytics of global news and social media content referring to economic activity in specific locations and such as cities, provinces and countries and location-specific entities such as ministries and central banks.

19.4   CROSS-SECTIONAL ANALYSIS OF CURRENCY UNCERTAINTY

In an effort to test Hamilton's conjecture, one of the authors (CJ Liu) deployed a cross-sectional rotational model to analyze the relationship between media uncertainty and currency valuations for 32 currencies. The proxy for uncertainty studied is the Uncertainty index available in the Thomson Reuters MarketPsych Indices (TRMI) based on the news media flow for the currencies asset class in Figure 19.4.1

CJ performed a weekly analysis of uncertainty. His model first selected the top eight currencies in the news over the prior week and simulated going long the two with the highest uncertainty and going short the two associated with the most clarity (least uncertainty) at the open price on the first business day of the week. In order to prevent look-ahead bias, weekly models used prices opening on Monday and closing on Friday. The difference between the weekly price moves of each currency position were calculated as the overall growth (or loss) of equity. The ranking was repeated and positions were re-established on the following Monday. Rotating forward on a weekly basis, and plotting the long-short returns produces the equity curve seen in Figure 19.4.1.

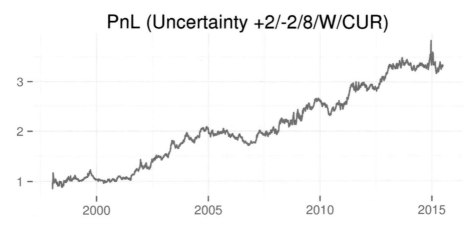

Figure 19.4.1: Equity curve derived from arbitraging currency uncertainty across the top eight currencies (top two long, bottom two short) in the media with 1-week look-back and prediction horizons.

On a weekly basis, currency-related uncertainty appears to provide an arbitrage opportunity. Over the course of an entire year, country-level uncertainty - a country's overall level of uncertainty (versus the uncertainty associated with the currency itself) – reveals an interesting arbitrage result. That is, similar to the weekly arbitrage, countries described with more uncertainty in the media have higher currency returns over the subsequent 12 months (and low uncertainty countries have lower relative currency returns). This result can be seen in the equity curve in Figure 19.4.2. This equity curve was derived by selecting the top eight countries in the news over the prior 12 months and buying the currencies of the two countries with the most uncertainty and shorting the currencies of the two countries with the least uncertainty and holding for 12 months. The strategy is rotated forward at the end of each month with one-twelfth of the portfolio redeployed.

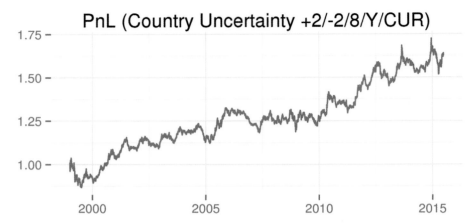

Figure 19.4.2 *Equity curve derived from arbitraging country uncertainty across the top eight currencies (top two long, bottom two short) in the media with 12-month look-back and prediction horizons.*

The value of the Uncertainty TRMI appears to be contrarian. When the media report uncertainty about a currency - such as its price direction, interest rates or government policy - investors may overreact and require a greater risk premium to hold it. Such uncertainty may distort yields between currencies and fuel carry-trade strategies. In general, currencies associated with uncertainty outperform those associated with a greater level of certainty.

19.5 CROSS-SECTIONAL ANALYSIS OF PRICE FORECASTS AND TRUST

When the Federal Reserve unexpectedly raises interest rates, the value of the US dollar may surge dramatically. When monetary policy deviates from expectations, prices adjust as expectations adjust. While uncertainty represents a lack of clarity about the future, it does not carry a directional expectation. That is, uncertainty has no valence. If a news article contains the statements, "Investors are unsure where the yen is headed," then it conveys uncertainty. If a journalist writes, "Analysts foresee a surge in the yen over the next week," then that reference contains a positive expectation for the currency's direction. One of the TRMI - the priceForecast TRMI - quantifies media expectations for the future direction of a currency's price. The TRMI priceForecast is the net balance of yen directional price forecasts in a given period of time, divided by the total volume of relevant yen references.

Using the same weekly cross-sectional analysis procedure described in the previous section, an arbitrage of the priceForecast TRMI across the top 10 currencies in the media was performed. The following week the model went long the currency with the highest price forecast and shorted the one with the weakest. Rotating forward weekly, this model developed the equity curve depicted in Figure 19.5.1.

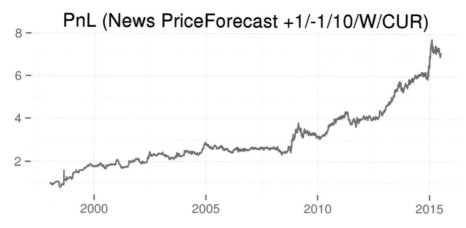

Figure 19.5.1 *Equity curve derived from arbitraging currency priceForecast across the top 10 currencies (top one long, bottom one short) in the media with one-week lookback and prediction horizons.*

The average news price forecast of a currency's value - at extreme levels (deciles) - was borne out over the following week. While uncertainty appears to fuel investor overreaction, the priceForecast appears to capture investor underreaction. Many of the weekly indexes demonstrating profitable arbitrage show similar results at monthly and yearly horizons, and like this index, more extreme average TRMI values have higher return/higher volatility equity curves.

Using the country Trust TRMI, it is possible to arbitrage across the prior year's national trust using that country's currency values. Buying the two most trusted and shorting the two least trusted currencies, year after year since 1999, yields the equity curve in Figure 19.5.2.

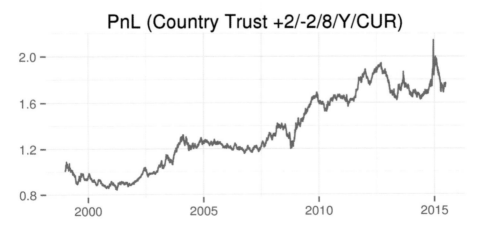

Figure 19.5.2 *Equity curve derived from arbitraging country-level Trust across the top eight currencies in the media (top two long, bottom two short) with 12-month lookback and prediction horizons.*

Equally, Hamilton's goal of restoring confidence (trust) in order to bolster the value of the nascent US government's securities is supported. High levels of trust in a country predicted outperformance of its currency over a 12-month horizon.

Importantly, high trust implies very little risk premium in a currency, while high uncertainty implies the opposite effect, yet the equity curves both capture arbitrage opportunities. It appears that trust and uncertainty contain orthogonal information for the prediction of currency values.

When looking across all of the historical currency sentiment data, it appears that currency investors should not only avoid countries with low levels of trust, but several sentiment indexes inversely-correlated with trust also defined arbitrage opportunities. For example, according to the data, investors should avoid currencies of countries with high levels of violence, government instability or social unrest, and they should prefer to hold the currencies of countries low on those indexes. Uncertainty was the only factor that contributed to an arbitrage-able risk premium.

Cross-sectional arbitrage allows the identification of opportunities at extreme values of sentiment or on macroeconomic metrics, which is useful as a simple directional indicator. In the final section of this chapter, we review a forward-tested model based on such cross-sectional arbitrage. Unfortunately, blunt cross-sectional models do not allow fine-tuning of timing. Moving average crossovers, applied to sentiment data, may be an elegant solution to the problem of timing major currency trends and reversals.

19.6 TIMING CURRENCIES WITH MOVING AVERAGE CROSSOVERS

Based on the above cross-sectional results, currencies may be driven, in part, by information flow, sentiments such as uncertainty and trust, and by media-embedded expectations. The effects of such information and sentiment impressions, through the process of over and underreaction, may contribute to price momentum (Menkhoff et al., 2012). Trading on price momentum in currency markets was found to earn surprisingly high excess returns, yielding an average annualized payoff of 4.4 percent, a standard deviation of 7.3 percent and a Sharpe ratio of 0.60 in one study (Burnside et al., 2011) and 10 percent annualized in another study (Menkhoff et al., 2012). In the foreign exchange markets, momentum strategies have demonstrated excess returns not only in the current period, but also back to the 1920s (Accominotti and Chambers, 2014). While price trends may be persistent, they are also, by their nature, lagging. If information flow is a leading indicator of price action, then changes in currency-related news might provide a useful signal on when to change directional bets.

Using moving averages of currency prices to indicate currency buy and sell signals was validated in one study as a technique for capturing price momentum (Schulmeister, 2008). Others found that adaptive systems founded using customer behaviour (order flows as an input appear to predict future currency price direction (Austin et al., 2004). Yet moving averages are lagging indicators, and they are susceptible to increased tail-risk as a result of extreme events (Gyntelberg and Schrimpf, 2011). Moving averages smooth out the noise in minutely and daily media flow. Amidst the whirl of thousands of contradictory opinions, the general average opinion is more evident, and the consensus opinion can be observed to shift over time. When a short-term moving average crosses over a longer-term moving average, it indicates that a trend has changed. In Figure 19.6.1 and the other MACDs profiled in this book, the colour green indicates when the short-term average crosses above the long-term average (often placing upward pressure on prices) and pink shading when the short-term average falls below.

In 2012, we visually identified that the yen's priceForecast MACD seemed useful for timing trends in the Japanese yen (versus the US dollar). Since first identified, that MACD has correctly forecast two major trends in the yen (both to the downside) in the intervening years. In order to explore this relationship further, MarketPsych's chief data scientist, Dr. Aleksander Fafula, used data-mining to identify the optimal TRMI-based MACDs for predicting the yen's direction since 1998. He added 10-fold cross-validation to ensure the findings were consistent over time (and weren't only catching two or three large trends).

According to this analysis, if one were to apply a constant position of either long or short, the JPY/USD - going long when the 90-day average of the yen priceForecast MACD crossed above the 200-day average, and short when the 90-day average crossed below the 200-day average, then a 6.7 percent average annual return with a Sharpe ratio of 0.6 was historically achieved. A one-dollar stake would have theoretically grown to $3.14 during the simulation, which covered the period from October 1998 to July 31, 2015. An image of that strategy in the recent period is visible in Figure 19.6.1.

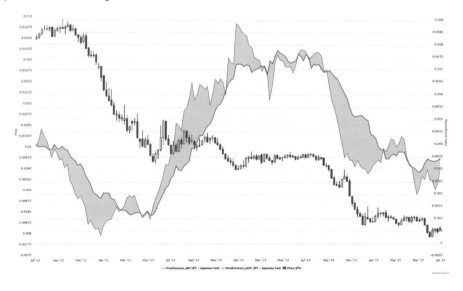

Figure 19.6.1 Japanese Yen PriceForecast MACD (90–200) versus the JPY/USD cross, July 2012 to July 2015.

The MACD in Figure 19.6.1 provides an unusually robust result. In order to understand this finding, several forex traders were asked their opinions on the relationship. One yen trader remarked that he sees more herding and news-following among traders of the Japanese yen. Another suggested that the Bank of Japan is leaking price forecasts to business reporters. The bank would do this to share with investors the risk of moving the yen in the Bank's desired direction. If the bank itself is buying or selling yen on the open market it may be more vulnerable to front-running or speculative attack.

Speculating on the motivations for an asset price move is inherently dangerous. Fortunately the priceForecast index is transparently constructed, and its role in predicting the yen's value since 1998, and especially during the premiership of Shinzo Abe, is interesting. When working with sentiment data, a dose of human discretion may improve the value of the TRMI in trading applications. If a new prime minister or head of the Bank of Japan changes monetary policy, it is possible that the historical value of the priceForecast index will remain a historical curiosity.

19.7 DISCUSSION AND CONCLUSIONS

Within our mandate, the ECB is ready to do whatever it takes to preserve the euro. And believe me, it will be enough.
~ Mario Draghi, ECB President, July 26, 2012

Since the Euro's launch in 2000, the optimal strategy for timing investments in the currency has been to await spikes in uncertainty about its future. Similarly, when the Mario Draghi at the European Central Bank asserted his leadership in organizing an effort to save the currency, the value of the currency rallied sharply. Amareos, a sentiment consulting and research provider, noted in a client report, "[I]t turned out to be "whatever it takes"; three words that marked a turning point in the Euro zone crisis..." With those words Draghi restored confidence in European central bankers, deflated uncertainty and kindled a months-long rally in the currency.

Before Mario Draghi, Alexander Hamilton noted that uncertainty irrationally debases a currency and trust inflates its value. Hamilton assumed that perceptions and expectations create a self-fulfilling prophecy during currency valuation. Hamilton's ideas were corroborated on both weekly (and yearly) horizons in examples of the Uncertainty TRMI generating opportunities for currency arbitrage. Other researchers similarly support Hamilton's conjecture, for example noting that monetary policy uncertainty increases the currency risk premium. Uncertainty may provoke risk-aversion and overreaction, and such uncertainty appears to generate opportunities for exploitation of currency price movements and perhaps for taking advantage of the carry trade.

Weekly TRMI that demonstrate appealing equity curves in cross-sectional models include priceForecast (a measure of expectations). The priceForecast momentum result may reflect investor underreaction on a weekly basis. Longer term, yearly TRMI including country-level trust appears to hold predictive power over the following year's currency price action, perhaps evidence of investor underreaction to brewing social instability.

Using moving average crossovers of sentiment data provides a potentially leading indicator for forecasting prices. In studying the viability and stability of simple TRMI moving average crossover models, we observed that many currencies are influenced by different TRMI. That is, there is no one single moving average crossover that shows value in forecasting currency prices. As in the case of the Japanese yen and the priceForecast TRMI, there may be unique local information that traders follow. When the widely-followed information rises or falls in intensity, currency prices follow.

While the yen MACD in Figure 19.6.1 is historically interesting, the rules it utilizes are not necessarily transferable to other currencies. Each currency appears to have its own optimal sentiment MACDs for forecasting. However, data-mining renders models vulnerable to historical overfitting. From our testing, data-mined MACDs do appear to have value going forward, in out-of-sample sets and forward-tested environments alike. Furthermore, cross-sectional models built on currency TRMI appear robust and generalizable.

When developing predictive models for currencies based on cross-sectional arbitrage, a combination of TRMI such as Uncertainty and priceForecast may offer superior returns to either one alone. In a simulation performed by CJ Liu, higher and more stable (less volatility) equity curves were observed when multiple TRMI were combined into a single predictive model. This finding suggests the news flow contains information with orthogonal value for predicting currency prices.

19.8 REFERENCES

1.   Accominotti, O. and Chambers, D. (2014). Out-of-sample evidence on the returns to currency trading. Available at: http://ssrn.com/abstract=2444873.

2.   Austin, M.P., Bates, G., Dempster, M.A., Leemans, V. and Williams, S. N. (2004). Adaptive systems for foreign exchange trading. *Quantitative Finance,4(4)*, pp. 37-45.

3.   Bansal, R. and Shaliastovich, I. (2012). A long-run risks explanation of predictability puzzles in bond and currency markets. *Review of Financial Studies, 26(1)*, pp. 1-33.

4.   Brunnermeier, M. K. and Pedersen, L. H. (2009). Market liquidity and funding liquidity, *Review of Financial studies, 22(6)*, pp. 2201-2238.

5.   Burnside, C., Eichenbaum, M. S. and Rebelo, S. (2011). *Carry trade and momentum in currency markets* (No. w16942). National Bureau of Economic Research.

6.   Gordon, J.S. (1988). The Scarlet Woman of Wall Street: Jay Gould. *Jim Fisk, Cornelius Vanderbilt, the Erie Railway Wars and the Birth of Wall Street (New York, 1988)*, p. 10

7.   .Ibid., p. 62..

8.   Gyntelberg, J. and Schrimpf, A. (2011). FX strategies in periods of distress. *BIS Quarterly Review, December*.

9.   Keynes, J.M. (1919). *The Economic Consequences of the Peace*. Chapter VI, pp. 235-236.

10. Menkhoff, L., Sarno, L., Schmeling, M. and Schrimpf, A. (2012). Currency momentum strategies. *Journal of Financial Economics, 106(3)*, pp. 660-684.

11. Mueller, P., Porchia, P. and Vedolin, A. (2014). Policy Announcements in FX Markets. Available at http://ssrn.com/abstract=2480131.

12. Schulmeister, S. (2008). Components of the profitability of technical currency trading. *Applied Financial Economics, 18(11)*, pp. 917-930..

PART V

Use of Sentiment Analysis in Weekly, Daily and High Frequency Trading

CHAPTER 20

Role of Options Markets in Price Discovery:
trading around news on Dow 30 options

Nitish Sinha, *Economist, Federal Reserve Board*

Wei Dong, *Credit Risk Analyst Lead, AIG Asset Management*

ABSTRACT

Using intraday data on stocks, options and firm-specific news events for Dow30 stocks, we find the volume of trading in the options increases almost seven times *an hour before* news, whereas the stock volume increases by 17%. Since the trading in the option market spikes prior to news, it is probably a venue for informed trading. Trading in the option market continues to be at an elevated level well after the news, suggesting that traders with disagreements also prefer to trade in the option market. The results suggest that options are important for price discovery due to informed as well disagreement-induced trading.

20.1 INTRODUCTION

What is the role played by the option market in price discovery? We answer this question by examining the effect of anticipated (and unanticipated) news events on trading patterns and price discovery in the options and equity markets. News affects price discovery in two ways in the option market. First, anticipation of news forces informed traders to trade aggressively. Foster and Viswanathan (1993) suggest that informed traders trade aggressively before the news comes out since their informational advantage or "edge" is likely to be depleted.[1] In such a setting, the trading volume before the news is likely to be driven by asymmetric information and hence contribute to price discovery. The second channel is suggested by Cao and Ou-Yang (2009), where difference of opinion induces trading in the option market *after* the news is available to all traders. We find evidence consistent with both channels. We find that the trading volume in the options market, indicated by the number of contracts, increases by a factor of nearly 7 *an hour before* the news arrives, whereas the volume in the equity market, indicated by number of stocks, increases by merely 17%. We also find that the option market trading volume sustains a higher level than usual even 200 minutes after the news arrives, whereas the trading volume in the stock market declines quickly after the news becomes public. While the trading volume prior to the news arrival indicates evidence of informed trading in the option market, a continued higher level of trading in the option market indicates the role played by difference of opinion trades in the option market. Our dataset allows us to identify surprise news items. We find the increase in the volume of the options market is substantially higher than the increase in the equity market even for surprise news. The unconditional information share of the option market is 14%, and almost 27% in the presence of news.

In this paper, we use two techniques to draw inferences. First, we conduct almost 70,000 event studies in which we observe the volume (option and stock) for 100 minutes before and 200 minutes after the news arrives. Second, we obtain the option-implied stock prices from at-the-money call and at-the-money put options before and after the news event. Once we have the option-implied stock price in the 200 minutes before and 400 minutes after the news event, we examine the information share of the options market using the Hasbrouck (1995) information-share measure, which represents the relative contribution of the option-implied price to the eventual price.[2] The information share measure takes into account the correlation structure of the lead-lag relationship between two markets as well. If the stock market is somehow very sensitive to prior changes in the option market, one could incorrectly interpret price changes in the stock market as higher price discovery, even though the chain of events originated in the option market. Hasbrouck (1995) shows information share is an internally consistent way of examining price discovery in two markets, unlike the popular lead-lag relationships. We also observe the nature of information in news articles. Using the timing information of news, we classify the news as scheduled or surprise. Volume in the option market increases before the news event even for surprise events. We employ an extensive dataset on firm-specific news. Prior studies have focused on specific kinds of news stories, such as earnings announcements in Amin and Lee (1997) and merger announcements in Cao, Chen and Griffin (2005). This paper includes all the news items electronically transmitted to Thomson Reuters's institutional customers. There are two distinct advantages to using all the news items. First, although examining the price-discovery process for specific types of news items such as mergers is informative, it also exposes the conclusions to sample-selection issues. Second, the database allows us to identify the content of each of these news items. We exploit this information by classifying each news item as scheduled or surprise news. We can therefore, quantify the role the options markets played in each of these events. We find the volume in the options markets increases to unusual levels almost an hour before the news arrives. The volume increase is more pronounced for news investors are less likely to anticipate, such as analyst upgrades, credit-rating changes, judicial proceedings, news alerts and merger announcements. The volume increase is less pronounced for scheduled news such as earnings announcements. We find the options market attracts traders who can predict surprise news as well as those who disagree with the interpretation of news.

Our information share methodology is closest to Chakravarty, Gulen and Mayhew (2004), who answer the question concerning the venue of informed trading by examining the information share of the options market. There are a few differences, though. First, Chakravarty, Gulen and Mayhew (2004) examine the daily information share for the option market, while we focus on the information share around the news events. We argue that not all trading days are equally informative, but some are more important than others. Intuitively, days with news are more important for the price discovery than days without news, hence we pay particular attention to days with news. Indeed, we find the information share of the option market around news events is almost two times the unconditional information share. Chakravarty, Gulen and Mayhew (2004) examine the information share in the time period prior to REG FD, whereas we examine the information share post REG FD.[3] Similarly, their study examined the information content of the options market prior to the decimalization of the equity market. Our sample period starts after the decimalization, thus we quantify the effect of a decrease in the transaction cost in the equity market on the information content of equity options. We observe that despite a much lower transaction cost in the equity market and reduced information asymmetry during our sample period compared with Chakravarty, Gulen and Mayhew (2004), the information content of the options market is similar. We find that the unconditional information share of the options market is 14%, similar to the 17% reported by Chakravarty, Gulen and Mayhew (2004). While prior literature, including Chakravarty, Gulen and Mayhew (2004), has extensively studied the role of informed traders in price discovery in options markets, this paper also sheds light on the nature of information that option market participants have an "edge" on. We condition the information share on different kind of news, and our findings suggest informed traders do trade in the options market. The findings are consistent with Aragon and Spencer Martin (2012), who report widespread use of options by hedge funds. Our findings are somewhat surprising, since we study Dow30 constituents, stocks with traditionally low information asymmetry; however, during the sample period of this study, the SEC was investigating five out of 30, suggesting that insider trading, one kind of informed trading, occurs within even the Dow30 stocks.

Our results on informativeness of the option market differ from Muravyev, Pearson and Broussard (2013), who examine the direction of quote revision every time the stock quote and the option-implied stock quote differ. Muravyev, Pearson and Broussard (2013) find the option-implied quote moving closer to the stock quote resolves the difference. They conclude that no price discovery exists in the options market. There are two methodological differences between our paper and Muravyev, Pearson and Broussard (2013). First, we consider news announcements as informative events, while Muravyev, Pearson and Broussard (2013) consider quote revisions as informative events. Second, we work with trade data, whereas Muravyev, Pearson and Broussard (2013) work with quote data. Trade data indicates prices at which options and stocks traded; the quote data, on the other hand, can suffer from staleness.[4] We have two reasons for choosing news announcements as informative events. First, news announcements force informed traders to trade aggressively since news lowers the value of private information.[5] For the purposes of examining informed trading, therefore, news provides a very useful way to identify periods of intense informed trading activity. Second, Mandelbrot and Taylor (1967), Clark (1973) and Hasbrouck (1999) suggest that some times are more informative than others and advocate the use of trading time instead of calendar time. While researchers have previously used volatility or volume as a proxy for more informative times or trading time, we use news events as a proxy for informative periods. An alternative explanation of the observed trading pattern could be the hedging motive of traders, but we find similar pattern for scheduled and unscheduled news, suggesting that hedging motives are not a likely driving factor. Similarly, we find a similar pattern in call and put options, once again weakening the argument for a hedging motive. Our method of detecting informed trading relies on the heuristic that informed traders can anticipate a news event. If we examine trading patterns occurring before and immediately after the news event, we are probably observing informed trading. We classify all news events as either scheduled or surprise. Market participants know well in advance the timing of news that includes earnings announcements, earnings forecasts and top performers (or under-performers) of the day, and therefore such news is scheduled news. Anticipating news about mergers and acquisitions, analyst upgrades (or downgrades), credit-rating changes, judicial outcomes, and criminal charges against the firms is difficult, and therefore such news is surprise news. We argue here that traders who can predict surprise news are informed traders. We do not claim they are insiders or that they are trading illegally, only that they can anticipate surprise news.[6]

20.1.1 Reasons for Preferring Options over Stocks

Black (1975) suggests two reasons informed traders prefer the options market over the equity market. First, options provide leverage, so participating in the options market is lucrative for informed traders. Second, the transaction cost in the options market is lower than in the equity market. Our sample period coincides with a low nominal interest environment, making leverage cheaper than ever. Our dataset also covers the period following the decimalization of prices when trading costs have also gone down substantially in the equity markets, making the transaction-cost-based explanation for preferring the options market less important. We find that, despite its relative illiquidity, the options market attracts informed traders. The findings surprise us since informed traders trade more intensely in a liquid market because the liquidity allows them to hide their presence, as in Kyle (1985). But the finding of a relatively illiquid market contributing to price discovery sheds light on another mechanism for informed trading.[7] Informed traders might prefer the options market because there are many instruments (contracts at multiple strikes) to trade anonymously, as in Easley, O'Hara and Srinivas (1998).

Another reason the options market might be informative about fundamental prices is that options provide an easy way to short stocks. Our data span the period in which a short-sale ban was in effect. Our study spans the SEC's ban on short sale for two of the stocks in our sample: Bank of America and J P Morgan. We use the ban as a natural experiment to understand the role of options in price discovery. The short-sale ban can influence the options market in two ways. On one hand, during the short-sale ban, investors who view the stock negatively could only trade in the options market, allowing the options market-maker to obtain monopoly rent and options prices to become less informative.[8] On the other hand, informed investors have only one place to trade ahead of negative news, which in turn makes options prices more informative. We find that during the short-sale ban, the information share of the financial stocks in our sample increased by almost 31% whereas that of other stocks in our sample did not change. The ban impacted on the ability of informed traders to trade in anticipation of negative news. Since the informed traders could not short the stock, the options market was the only venue for trading ahead of negative news. The information share of call options increased by almost 17% for those two stocks, without much change in the information share of call options for other constituents of the Dow30.[9] The increase in the information share for stocks under the short-sale ban suggests the ban pushed even more informed traders to an illiquid market.[10]

Cao and Ou-Yang (2009) suggest that information that is open to interpretation is more likely to induce disagreement, and will cause trading in the options market. We focus on the trading after the news is made public to test the predictions. We find that trading in the options market continues to be at heightened level *after* the news is made public and stock market volume has reduced to its usual level of volume. If one of the channels of price discovery in the options market is disagreement-induced trading, we should find that news that is open to interpretation is likely to have a higher information share of the options market. Consistent with the prediction of Cao and Ou-Yang (2009), we do find that the information share of the options market is higher for (1) news that is more relevant to the stock, (2) news that is not repetition of an existing story, and (3) news such as analyst rating changes. News that is less relevant for the stock is less likely to cause disagreement about the stock. News that repeats an existing story is also less likely to cause disagreement since it is essentially stale information. Extending the same argument to periods when there is no news, there is little to disagree about, which in turn can explain the low liquidity in the options market in general. We make four important contributions in this paper. First, we show that, despite reduction in liquidity and asymmetric information, the options market continues to contribute to price discovery. Second, we show that disagreement-induced trading is an important contributor to price discovery in the options market. Third, we show that the short-sale ban pushed more informed traders to the options market. Finally, we contribute to the emerging literature on news in finance, showing that public disclosure of information does force traders to trade aggressively.

We organize the rest of the paper as follows. Section 20.2 describes the data. Section 20.3 describes the patterns in volume around the news event. Section 20.4 describes the result on information share. Section 20.5 describes the effect of the short-sale ban. Section 20.6 concludes.

20.2 DATA

We base our analysis on two kinds of data: trading and news. We obtain the trading data for 29 of the Dow-30 stocks and the options series from 2003 through 2009. We use intraday transaction data divided into five-minute intervals, obtained from Thomson Reuters Tick History database.[11] Almost every Dow-30 company's option series is simultaneously traded on multiple options exchanges. To represent the full picture of the options price movements, we obtain the data from the Options Price Reporting Authority (OPQ).

We obtained the news data from Thomson Reuters NewsScope (RNSE) database, which contains all firm-specific news Thomson Reuters transmitted electronically its clients. Thomson Reuters provides firm-level tone information for all firms mentioned in a news item. The tone-score is derived from the text of the news item. If a news item mentions multiple firms, each firm receives a different score based on the words used to describe the firm. The database also contains information on the topics to which the news item pertains. Sinha (2015) describes the classification engine. Using the words and phrases in an article, RNSE can classify the news item along four major aspects: tone, relevance, novelty and topic code.

Tone of the article: Based on linguistic parsing and the words and phrases used in the news, RNSE estimates the tone of the news in terms of three probability scores: positive, negative and neutral. These three values add up to 1. For example, RNSE is likely to assign negative news such as "IBM's 3Q earnings disappoint" a higher value for the probability of the article being negative.

Relevance: The relevance score assesses how the targeted news is relevant to a particular company and ranges from 0 to 1. A high relevance score indicates a highly relevant story. A relevance score of 0.33 roughly corresponds to almost three firms being mentioned in the story. For example, RNSE can determine whether a named firm is the focus of the news item or whether it is simply mentioned in passing. The engine is able to provide relevance by tracking the mention of the firm across multiple lines in the news article.

Novelty : The novelty score measures the uniqueness of the news item compared to previously mentioned items. A novelty score of 1 indicates one similar story in last 24 hours. A higher score indicates a staler news article. News stories tend to develop over time. For example, when a company releases earnings, the first news is likely reported as a one-sentence alert. But because that alert is the first time that story has been released, its uniqueness is highest then and only decreases thereafter as other, newer, and more detailed stories surface. The engine produces the novelty score by matching the article to previous articles about the same firm within the last 12 hours.

Topic code: RNSE also contains information about the topic of a news item. This information is contained in the topic code. Journalists writing the articles provide the topic code. For example, journalists will tag with MRG any news related to changes of ownership, including mergers and acquisitions. The news data provides an opportunity to study the price-formation process conditional on the content of the news article. We want to avoid stale information and peripheral information about a stock. Seeing Intel mentioned in the discussion of any stock in the semi-conductor industry is not uncommon. Similarly, journalists follow up stories with more detailed information. Although each piece might contain new information, summary articles often outline the day's events. We select news articles with a relevance score of at least 0.75 and a novelty score of no greater than one.

News arrives at random time points during the day, whereas the trading data is obtained in five-minute intervals. We split the day into such intervals starting at 9:30 a.m. and ending at 4:00 p.m. If news arrives at 9:31 a.m., we map it to 9:30 a.m. We match the news data with the options data using the five minute intervals.[12] If the data arrives when the markets are closed, we match them to 9:30 a.m. the following day.

Table 20.2.1: *Summary of news – The table shows the total number of news items, total number of news events and trading periods The table shows of news items, total number of matching trading periods, and total number of alerts for each of the 29 firms in Thomson Reuters Newsscope database from 2003. The table also shows the total number of news items, matching trading periods, and total number of alerts as a percentage of the overall sample. The table shows that almost all of the firms in our sample have an average of two news items per trading period. The table also shows the ratio of alerts to non-alerts is similar across the 29 firms in our sample*

Firm Name	# of trading periods	% of observations	# of news	% of observations	# of alerts	% of observations
Alcoa	2,042	2.87%	3,797	2.81%	1,543	2.70%
American Express	1,708	2.40%	2,830	2.09%	985	1.72%
Boeing	3,954	5.55%	8,687	6.42%	4,708	8.22%
Bank of America	3,199	4.49%	6,805	5.03%	4,631	8.09%
Caterpillar	1,290	1.81%	2,426	1.79%	1,111	1.94%
Cisco	1,912	2.68%	3,174	2.35%	1,081	1.89%
Chevron	2,732	3.84%	5,262	3.89%	2,179	3.81%
Dupont	1,615	2.27%	2,996	2.21%	1,312	2.29%
Walt Disney	2,415	3.39%	4,273	3.16%	1,209	2.11%
General Electric	4,078	5.73%	8,539	6.31%	3,982	6.96%
Home Depot	1,802	2.53%	2,955	2.18%	820	1.43%
Hewlett Packard	2,299	3.23%	4,362	3.22%	1,655	2.89%
IBM	1,818	2.55%	3,568	2.64%	1,251	2.19%
Intel	2,530	3.55%	4,919	3.63%	1,884	3.29%
Johnson and Johnson	2,211	3.10%	3,869	2.86%	1,849	3.23%
J P Morgan	4,205	5.90%	8,466	6.26%	4,011	7.01%
Kraft Foods	1,450	2.04%	2,700	2.00%	1,045	1.83%
Kellogg	1,968	2.76%	3,235	2.39%	1,041	1.82%
McDonalds Corp.	1,935	2.72%	3,316	2.45%	1,138	1.99%
3M	1,091	1.53%	1,815	1.34%	642	1.12%
Merck & Co.	2,725	3.83%	5,313	3.93%	2,407	4.20%
Microsoft	3,662	5.14%	7,754	5.73%	2,995	5.23%
Pfizer	3,094	4.34%	6,029	4.46%	2,566	4.48%
Procter & Gamble Company	1,720	2.42%	3,028	2.24%	1,143	2.00%
AT&T	2,525	3.55%	4,512	3.33%	1,800	3.14%
United Technologies	1,495	2.10%	2,500	1.85%	1,066	1.86%
Verizon	2,659	3.73%	4,683	3.46%	1,865	3.26%
Walmart	3,193	4.48%	6,627	4.90%	2,816	4.92%
Exxon Mobil	3,889	5.46%	6,884	5.09%	2,507	4.38%

Table 20.2.1 describes our matched data. After matching the news data to the options trading data, we have 71,216 event periods and 135,324 news items. We have almost two news items per trading period that has a news item. Columns 3 and 4 show the number and proportion of trading periods for each of the 29 firms in our sample. Columns 5 and 6 show the number and proportion of news item for each of the 29 firms. Comparison of the third and fifth columns indicates that the clustering of news items within a trading period is common to all firms in our sample. Most of the firms contain two news items for each trading period. Two of our firms are financial firms that had a short-sale ban later in our sample period. We examine later the role of the ban and find that the change in the trading pattern for these firms is particularly informative.

Table 20.2.2: *Surprise and Schedule News: The table shows the dummy variables based on the topic code anditemtype.We use these dummy variables to decide whether the news is scheduled or surprise event. The "Scheduled News" column displays our classification of news as scheduled news, conditional on the news item containing a particular topic code. Y stands for yes (scheduled news), Q stands for questionable (hard to classify), and N stands for no (surprise news)*

Type of News	Scheduled News	Description
D_RES	Y	Dummy =1, whether news contained the topic code RES, i.e., news about an earnings announcement
D_RESF	Q	Dummy =1, whether news contained the topic code RESF, i.e., news about an earnings forecast
D_RCH	N	Dummy =1, whether news contained the topic code RESF, i.e., news about an analyst report
D_AAA	N	Dummy =1, whether news contained the topic code AAA, i.e., news about credit ratings
D_DBT	N	Dummy=1, whether news contained the topic code DBT, i.e., news concerning primary issuance and secondary trading of debt instruments; markets forecasts and analysis of debt markets
D_MRG	N	Dummy=1, whether news contained the topic code DBT, i.e., news about Mergers and Acquisitions (including changes of ownership)
D_CRIM	N	Dummy=1, whether news contained the topic code CRIM, i.e., Crime, Law Enforcement
D_JUDIC	N	Dummy=1, whether news contained the topic code JUDIC, i.e., Judicial processes, court cases or court decisions
D_STX	N	Dummy=1, whether news contained the topic code STX, i.e., Regulations, additions and deletions from indices, new listings, delistings
D_News	N	Dummy=1, whether news contained the topic code NEWS, i.e., Major breaking news
D_Hot	Y	Dummy=1, whether news contained the topic code HOT, i.e., News about stocks on the move
D_Alert	N	Dummy=1, whether news is an alert

Table 20.2.2 summarizes our classification of news as scheduled and surprise. The table shows the dummy variables based on the topic code and item type. We use these dummy variables to indicate whether the news is a scheduled or surprise event. We categorize news that contains the topic codes "RES", "RESF" and "HOT" as scheduled news. These topic codes imply earnings, earnings forecast, and stocks on the move, respectively. We classify news that contains the topic codes "RCH", "AAA", "DBT", "MRG", "CRIM", "JUDIC" and "NEWS" as surprise news. These codes refer to news regarding analyst updates, ratings, trading in bonds, mergers, criminal charges, judicial proceedings and breaking news, respectively. We also classify news items that are "Alert" as surprise news. Thomson Reuters disseminates news as follows: first, the reporters write a headline that contains important information. This headline-only item, that is, "Alert", is followed by a more substantial story called an article. Even for earnings announcements, the first item that arrives on the screen is an alert. Although the investor could well be anticipating a news event, he might not know the exact timing of news arrival. Our results are robust to the exclusion of alerts.

Table 20.2.3: *Correlation between Type of News Items: Panel A of the table shows Spearman correlation between different topic codes. Correlation above 0.30 is shown in bold font. The last row and column of Panel A shows the correlation between news topic codes and the news being an alert. Panel B shows the number of times each of these topic codes appears in our sample of news data.*

Panel A

	D_RES	D_RESF	D_RCH	D_AAA	D_DBT	D_MRG	D_CRIM	D_JUDIC	D_STX	D_News	D_Hot	D_Alert
D_RES	1											
D_RESF	**0.62**	1										
D_RCH	-0.03	0	1									
D_AAA	-0.05	-0.05	-0.03	1								
D_DBT	0.02	0.03	0.01	**0.44**	1							
D_MRG	0	0.02	-0.07	-0.03	0.04	1						
D_CRIM	-0.03	-0.03	-0.02	-0.01	0.02	0.03	1					
D_JUDIC	-0.04	-0.04	-0.03	-0.02	0.01	0.03	0.26	1				
D_Stx	-0.25	-0.21	-0.16	-0.11	-0.22	-0.27	-0.06	-0.1	1			
D_News	0.21	0.15	-0.06	-0.04	0.12	0.08	0.05	0.07	-0.13	1		
D_Hot	0.01	0.03	0.01	-0.02	-0.04	0	-0.01	-0.02	0.12	-0.01	1	
D_Alert	0.27	0.21	0.15	0.02	0.14	0.09	-0.01	0.03	**-0.57**	0.1	-0.02	1

Panel B

	D_RES	D_RESF	D_RCH	D_AAA	D_DBT	D_MRG	D_CRIM	D_JUDIC	D_STX	D_News	D_Hot	D_Alert
	16,338	13,095	6,735	2,818	12,974	18,648	997	2,512	47,659	10,367	3,905	57,242

Table 20.2.3 shows the correlation between different topic codes. Panel A shows Spearman's rank correlation between different topic codes. A correlation above 0.30 is shown in bold font. Notable correlations are between topic codes "RES" and "RESF", "DBT" and "AAA", and "ALERT" and "STX" of 0.62, 0.44, and -0.57, respectively. The last row and column of Panel A show the correlation between news topic codes and the news being an ALERT. Panel B shows the number of times each of these topic codes appears in our sample of news data. The largest news category is "ALERT", followed by "STX", "MRG", "RES", "DBT" and "NEWS".

20.3 PRICE DISCOVERY AND TRADING VOLUME

Increase in trading volume is often considered a proxy for new information. Correspondingly, when the same underlying asset is traded on different markets, we can infer the location of price discovery by examining which market leads the change in volume. Stephan and Whaley (1990) examine the volume changes in stock and options markets and find that stock market volume leads options markets. However, Easley, O'Hara and Srinivas (1998) observe that buying calls or selling puts conveys positive information about the stock otherwise not contained in the stock price. Similarly, selling calls or buying puts conveys negative information about the stock. Since we directly observe the news, our study is somewhat different from previous studies that have used volume as a proxy for information. We assume that when news appears on the Thomson Reuters screen, the information is made public.[13] Public revelation of private information forces informed traders to trade very aggressively. Informed traders also trade in anticipation of the public event, which we can observe by using the timestamp of news articles. In our setting, we observe which market responds to (and trades ahead of) the new information by conducting event studies on the volume in the stock and options market. We observe the trading volume for both stock and options for Dow30 constituents for 300 minutes around the news events: 100 minutes prior to and 200 minutes after the event. We consider the long periods before the news arriving as non-informative and call the volume in such periods the usual volume. For each Dow30 constituent, we obtain a measure of usual volume by averaging the trading volume (measured in number of contracts for options and number of stocks for stocks) that occurs in the interval between 100 minutes and 80 minutes prior to the news event. For each of the five-minute intervals in the 300 minutes around the event, we obtain the ratio of the trading volume over the usual volume. Our methodology ensures we control for the weekly trend in volume as well as the firm-specific information environment. For each of the almost 130,000 news events, we end up with 65 volume observations in five-minute intervals for both the stock and the option. We also end up with average volume around the news event for each of the Dow30 constituents in our study. Rather than reporting the average volume over the 130,000 observations, we first obtain the average volume number for each of the constituents and then take the average over 29 constituents.[14]

The news might have moved the stock price such that the at-the-money option before the event and the at-the-money option after the event are two completely different options. To get around this potential bias, we identify 10 option series at the time of the event. For each of our 61 data points (20 before, 1 at the event and 40 after the event), we find the most liquid option and document it as the comparable option for the purposes of the volume study. We obtain the average volume pattern in the event time for each stock using the following specification:

$$V_{jk} = d_{jk} + e_{jk},$$ [20.3.1]

where j is the firm, and k is the event time. $k \in (-100, 200)$. d_{jk} is the volume for either the stock or the option for stock j at event time k.

We further scale the raw volume to ensure that for each stock, the average of d_{jk} for $k = -100, -95, -90, -85$ and -80 is 1.[15] Figure 20.3.1 provides a schematic explanation of our methodology for findings of usual volume. The results we present use the average of 29 point estimates, one for each stock in our sample. Because the trading volume is not likely to be normally distributed, we also obtain bootstrap estimates for the volume as a proportion of its usual volume. Bootstrapped estimates provide similar estimates.

Figure 20.3.2 shows the volume in the stock and the options market around the event time. Each point on the plot represents a point estimate for volume for a Dow30 constituent. Each event time has two sets of points: one for option volume and another for stock volume. V is the option volume and VS is the stock volume. The volumes are normalized so the average trading volume during event time -100,-95,-90,-85, and -80 is 1. The volume in the options market increases substantially before the news arrives. The volume in the stock market also increases as news arrives; however, it picks up by a smaller amount. Any change in the volume is noticeable close to the news arrival for the stock market. Although the stock volume returns to its usual level within half an hour of the news, the volume in the options market stays at a high level well after the event is over. This observation suggests (1) trading in the options market is concentrated before and after the news emerges and (2) prior to the news arrival, informed traders trade in the options market.

Table 20.3.1: Trading volume around all news articles in the stock and options markets: The table shows the volume in the stock and options markets around the event time, from 100 minutes prior to 200 minutes after the event. The t-stat is for the volume not equal to 1, i.e., the volume not being equal to the usual volume. In both markets prior to the news announcement, the volume is lower than its usual level starting almost 80 minutes before the news event. The usual level is defined as the average volume of periods -100,-95,-90,-85 and -80 minutes for the respective market. Starting 80 minutes before the news event until 200 minutes after the news event, the option volume is unusually high. While the stock market volume falls to its normal level within 100 minutes following the news event, the options market volume stays at unusual level. Except for the first five minutes of observation, the scaled options market volume is higher than the scaled stock market volume.

Time w.r.t event	Stock Vol-ume	SE	t stat	Option Vol-ume	SE	t stat	Option >Stock
-100:-85	0.99	0.00	-3.05	0.77	0.06	-3.79	-3.68
-80:-65	1.06	0.01	10.52	3.02	0.19	10.83	10.5
-60:-45	1.17	0.01	23.78	7.07	0.48	12.72	12.36
-40:-25	1.35	0.01	32.26	10.19	0.62	14.85	14.28
-20:0	2.36	0.1	13.37	12.21	0.71	15.86	13.8
0:05	2.9	0.09	22.01	59.64	8.35	7.02	6.79
5:20	2.78	0.08	21.24	64.1	4.52	13.95	13.56
25-40	1.48	0.03	14.83	86.09	6.29	13.52	13.45
45-60	1.19	0.01	27.75	76.61	5.84	12.94	12.9
65:80	1.09	0.01	15.4	67.21	5.18	12.78	12.77
85:100	1.02	0.01	3.79	61.38	4.61	13.1	13.1
105:120	0.97	0.01	-6.25	63.39	7.24	8.61	8.62
125:140	0.91	0.00	-19.04	58.53	7.01	8.2	8.22
145:160	0.88	0.00	-29.34	58.03	7.1	8.03	8.05
165:180	0.84	0.00	-34.23	51.47	3.72	13.56	13.6
185:200	0.82	0.00	-38.81	49.23	3.77	12.78	12.83

Table 20.3.1 presents volume estimates in 20-minute intervals for the stock and options markets. Rather than showing 61 point estimates, one for each of the five-minute intervals of observation, we have collated the point estimates of volume as follows. We present the volume as the average of every 20 minutes of trading time sampled every five minutes except for the event time itself, which amounts to 16 estimates. For each of these time periods, we ask two questions: (1) Is the volume in the instrument, stock and option, different from 1 (normal volume)? (2) Is the volume in the options market unusually higher than in the stock market? The table shows the volume in stock and options markets around the event time, from 100 minutes prior to 200 minutes after the event. Column two shows the stock volume. Starting 80 minutes before the news event, the stock trading volume is higher than one. It increases monotonically up to 2.9 at the news-event interval, five minutes after the news arrives. It decreases to less than the usual volume 105 minutes after the news event. Column 5 shows the options volume. The options volume increases to nearly three times its usual volume almost 80 minutes before the news. It increases monotonically to 59 times its usual volume five minutes after the news. Unlike the stock volume, the options volume continues to increase to 86 times its usual volume in the interval between 25 minutes and 40 minutes after the news, before it begins to drop monotonically to 49 times its usual volume by the end of observation period. In both markets, prior to the news announcement, the volume is lower than its usual level starting almost 80 minutes before the news event. The t- statistics in column 4 and 7 indicate that starting 80 minutes before the news event until 200 minutes after the news event, the options volume is unusually high.

The stock market volume falls to its normal level within 100 minutes following the news event. The t-statistics columns, the stock volume (column 4) and the option volume (column 7), suggest informed traders trade in both the stock and options markets. The stock market volume falls below the normal level after 100 minutes. Except for the first five minutes of observation, the options market volume is higher than the stock market volume. Given the unusual amount of trading in the options market compared to the stock market, informed investors seem to prefer trading in the options market. Hedging activity by options market makers might induce some unusual levels of trading volume in the stock market. However, without the origin-of-trades data, obtaining the hedging demand in the options or the stock market is difficult.

Table 20.3.2: Trading volume around surprise news: The table shows the volume in the stock and options markets around the event time for the unanticipated events, from 100 minutes prior to 200 minutes after the event. The t-stat is for the volume not equal to 1, i.e., the volume not being equal to the usual volume. In both markets prior to the news announcement, the volume is lower than its usual level starting almost 80 minutes before the news event. The usual level is defined as the average volume of periods -100,-95,-90,-85 and -80 minutes for the respective market. Starting 80 minutes before the news event until 200 minutes after the news event, the option volume is unusually high. The stock market volume falls to its normal level within 120 following minutes after the news event. Except for the first five minutes of observation, the options market volume is higher than the stock market volume.

Time w.r.t event	Stock Volume	SE	t stat	Option Volume	SE	t stat	Option >Stock
-100:-85	0.99	0	-2.74	0.73	0.06	-4.45	-4.33
-80:-65	1.07	0.01	11.87	3.02	0.24	8.26	7.97
-60:-45	1.21	0.01	23.33	7.19	0.55	11.33	10.94
-40:-25	1.48	0.02	30.81	11.13	0.81	12.52	11.92
-20:0	3.24	0.18	12.52	13.47	0.9	13.83	11.13
0:05	4.43	0.15	23.4	224.27	44.04	5.07	4.99
5:20	2.93	0.07	28.3	202.85	18.73	10.78	10.68
25-40	1.68	0.03	22.59	213.27	20.28	10.47	10.43
45-60	1.33	0.01	35.71	176.86	15.21	11.57	11.54
65:80	1.2	0.01	27.34	154.01	13.23	11.56	11.55
85:100	1.1	0.01	18.13	136.47	11.15	12.15	12.15
105:120	1.02	0.01	4.87	177.46	52.38	3.37	3.37
125:140	0.95	0	-11.01	115.67	9.85	11.64	11.64
145:160	0.9	0	-21.4	112.39	10.27	10.84	10.85
165:180	0.85	0	-36.02	107.09	9.11	11.65	11.67
185:200	0.82	0	-51.24	101.93	9.13	11.06	11.08

We classify earnings news, earnings forecasts and momentum-oriented news as scheduled news. We classify news articles related to analyst updates, debt-rating changes, mergers, criminal charges and judicial proceedings as surprise news. We also classify alerts as surprise news. Table 20.3.2 presents volume estimates for surprise news in 20-minute intervals for the stock and options markets. The stock market trading volume is higher than usual, starting almost 80 minutes before the event and then increases monotonically to almost four times its usual volume within the first five minutes of the news event. Thereafter, the volume decreases monotonically to almost usual volume within 105 minutes after the event. The options volume increases to three times its usual volume almost 80 minutes before the event and then increases monotonically to almost 224 times its usual volume within five minutes of the news event. It then declines monotonically to 100 times its usual volume by the end of the observation period. For the stock market, the trading before surprise news is higher than trading before scheduled news. The trading in the options market before both surprise and scheduled news is not statistically different. The similarity of trading volume for surprise and scheduled news in the options market suggests that, for the options market participants, surprise news is similar to scheduled news.

20.4 PRICE DISCOVERY AND THE INFORMATION SHARE MEASURE

20.4.1 Information Share Measure

When the same asset is traded in two different markets, understanding the market in which the incorporation of new information occurs is important. Market participants observe prices from both the markets and assign higher importance to the market in which the new information is incorporated. As academics, when we study the impact of a firm's announcement, knowing which market we should use to examine the market reaction of the announcement is useful. When an enforcement agency examines insider trading prior to the announcement, knowing which market to examine is important. High-frequency data only exacerbates the problem. For example, Muravyev, Pearson and Broussard (2013) report needing more than terabytes of storage space to store the data from the stock and options markets for about 60 stocks. With the abundance of high-frequency data, the venue of price discovery is more important than ever.

Hasbrouck (1995) developed the information-share measure to analyse the problem of the location of price discovery. When the same asset is traded in multiple markets, the observed price in each market moves toward the unobserved true price. The unobserved true price follows a random walk. Because it is the true price and drives the observed prices in multiple markets, the observed prices in different markets are cointegrated. Suppose the hidden true price can be written as:

$$V_t = V_{t-1} + u_t, \; u_t \text{ is the innovation in prices at time } t. \qquad [20.4.1]$$

The asset is traded in two markets – stock and options. The stock price is Pt, whereas the prices implied in the options market are indicated by I_t. The cointegrated price vector is given by:

$$p_t = \begin{pmatrix} S_t \\ I_t \end{pmatrix} = \begin{pmatrix} V_t + e_{S,t} \\ V_t + e_{I,t} \end{pmatrix} \qquad [20.4.2]$$

where $e_{S,t}$ represents small random mispricing in the stock price and $e_{I,t}$ represents small random mispricing in the option-implied stock price. The cointegrated price series are not stationary, but the first difference, $\Delta p_t = p_t - p_{t-1}$, is a stationary process. We apply the Vector Error Correction Model (VECM) to the first difference of the cointegrated price vector:

$$\Delta p_t = A_1 \Delta p_{t-1} + A_2 \Delta p_{t-2} + \dots + A_m \Delta p_{t-m} + \gamma(z_t - \mu) + u_t, \qquad [20.4.3]$$

where z_t is the price difference between the stock price and the implied stock price at time t, μ is the long-term mean of z_t and the coefficients A_i, are two-by-two matrices that represent the m-order autoregressive (AR) process of the price changes. Similar to Simaan and Wu (2007), we use $m = 10$. The mean-reverting error-correction term $\gamma(z_t - \mu)$ reflects the idea that all transitory individual price movement converge to the true price. We estimate the coefficient matrices A_i using the ordinary least square (OLS) procedure.

The m-order AR process can also be interpreted as an infinite order of the moving average (MA) process. The VECM model can also be represented as:

$$\Delta p_t = u_t + \psi_1 u_{t-1} + \psi_2 u_{t-2} + \ldots \qquad [20.4.4]$$

We calculate the moving average coeffcients ψi by forecasting the system subsequent to a unit perturbation. Once we have the ψ, we can obtain the cumulative response function Ψ, defined as

$$\Psi = lim_{k \to +\infty} \Sigma_{t=1}^{k} \psi_t. \qquad [20.4.5]$$

We set k at 100. We observe that by k=100, ψ_t is almost always zero. If the covariance matrix Ω of the innovations in the equation 4 were diagonal, the Hasbrouck information share associated with the ith cointegrated price series is defined as:

$$IS_i = \frac{\psi_i^2 \Omega_{ii}}{\Psi \Omega \Psi^T}. \qquad [20.4.6]$$

In practice, the innovation covariance matrix is usually not diagonal; hence the information share is not uniquely defined. We can still compute the lower and upper bounds of information share by considering the Cholesky factorization of Ω with all possible rotations.

20.4.2 Implied Stock Price from the Options Market
We obtain the implied stock price using the implied volatility obtained earlier; we will get the same value as S_t.

We follow the Chakravarty, Gulen and Mayhew (2004) methodology, which uses the implied volatility from 15 minutes earlier to obtain the option-implied stock price. The option-implied stock price is I_t:

$$I_t = f^{-1}(V_t, \sigma_{t-\Delta t}, .) = f^{-1}[V_t, f^{-1}(V_{t-\Delta t}, S_t, .), .] \qquad [20.4.7]$$

where f is the option pricing operator. As mentioned earlier, we use $\Delta t = 15$ minutes.[16] Since the equity options are American, we use the binomial tree model.

20.4.3 Information Share of Options of Dow-30 Index Constituents

For almost 130,000 news events, we obtain the coeffcients of the VECM model, as in Equation 20.4.3. Based on these estimated models, we computed the information share of the options market for each news event. For the purpose of the VECM model estimation, we used an interval of 600 minutes, 200 before the event and 400 after the news event. We find that unlike the stock market, the options market does not have almost continuous trading. Finding many five-minute trading intervals in which no trading occurs in the options market is not unusual. We keep the option-implied stock price as constant while we change the stock price. Appendix 20.A shows how our approach understates the information share of the options market. Similar to our presentation of the trading volume, we obtain firm-wise averages of the lower and upper bounds of the information share.

Table 20.4.1: Information shares for the call option on each stock for different lag lengths: The table shows the information share for each of the 29 firms in our sample. The second column contains the information share for the call options conditional on any trade around the news event for the lag length of 15 minutes. The third column contains the information share for the call options conditional on any trade around the news event for the lag length of 30 minutes. To obtain the option implied stock prices, we lag the implied volatility by the lag length. The table shows that the average information share for call options is not very sensitive to lag length.

Firm Name	Call IS($\Delta = 15$ min)	Call IS ($\Delta = 30$ min)
AT&T	28% (1.80%)	25% (1.70%)
Alcoa	28% (0.50%)	29% (0.47%)
American Express	29% (0.50%)	28% (0.53%)
Boeing	27% (0.30%)	28% (0.34%)
Bank of America	30% (0.50%)	31% (0.52%)
Caterpillar	29% (0.70%)	29% (0.63%)
Cisco	28% (0.50%)	28% (0.52%)
Chevron	26% (0.40%)	26% (0.41%)
Dupont	29% (0.70%)	29% (0.66%)
Exxon Mobil	28% (0.30%)	29% (0.34%)
General Electric	22% (0.40%)	23% (0.36%)
Home Depot	25% (0.50%)	26% (0.56%)
Hewlett Packard	26% (0.50%)	27% (0.46%)
IBM	29% (0.50%)	29% (0.51%)
Intel	36% (1.00%)	34% (0.94%)
Johnson and Johnson	23% (0.50%)	24% (0.46%)
J P Morgan	29% (0.30%)	30% (0.32%)
Kraft Foods	29% (0.80%)	28% (0.76%)
Kellogg	24% (0.50%)	25% (0.52%)
McDonalds Corp.	25% (0.50%)	25% (0.50%)
3M	27% (0.80%)	29% (0.77%)
Merck & Co.	28% (0.50%)	27% (0.44%)
Microsoft	29% (0.40%)	28% (0.35%)
Pfizer	23% (0.40%)	23% (0.36%)
Procter & Gamble Company	24% (0.50%)	23% (0.51%)
United Technologies	25% (0.60%)	26% (0.63%)
Verizon	24% (0.50%)	23% (0.47%)
Walmart	26% (0.30%)	27% (0.35%)
Walt Disney	25% (0.50%)	25% (0.48%)
Average	27%	27%

We use the average of the lower and upper bounds of information share as our measure of information share, as in Blanco, Brennan and Marsh (2005). In Table 20.4.1, we present the information share for each of the 29 stocks in our sample. The second column shows the information share for call options for all constituents of the Dow. Figures in parentheses are the standard error. The highest information share for call options is 36% for Intel. The lowest information share for call options is 22% for General Electric. The average information share for similar stocks in the Chakravarty, Gulen and Mayhew (2004) study was 17%. Despite the increase in the liquidity of the stock market, the information share of stocks has gone up since the Chakravarty, Gulen and Mayhew (2004) study.

Column 3 shows the information share for call options for Dow30 constituents around surprise news. The highest information share is for Intel at 35%, while the lowest information share is 21% for General Electric, Johnson and Johnson, Pfizer and Proctor & Gamble.

Column 4 shows the information share for put options for Dow constituents. The highest information share is for United Technology at 32%. The lowest information share is 25% for Chevron. The average put options are more informative than the call options.

Column 5 shows the information share for put options for Dow30 constituents around surprise news. The most informative put options are for AT&T, with an information share of 35%. The least informative put options are for Cisco, with an information share of 24%.

Table 20.4.2: Information shares by the type of news: The table shows the results from regression analysis of the information share. The information share estimates for each event are regressed on the news categories. Panel A presents the analysis for call options. Panel B presents the analysis for put options. D_Surprise is a dummy variable indicating the news was a surprise event. D_Alert indicates the news was disseminated as an "Alert". Sentneg is a dummy variable indicating negative tone news. Other variables are defined in Table 20.2.2. Consistent with some informed trading in the options market, information share for time-sensitive information, for example, "Alerts" and "HOT", is higher in the options market.

	Call IS					Put IS				
Intercept	28%	30%	32%			28%	27%	29%		
	0.10%	0.40%	0.50%			0.10%	0.40%	0.60%		
D_Surprise	-3%	-3%	-3%			-2%	-2%	-1%		
	0.20%	0.20%	0.20%			0.20%	0.20%	0.20%		
D_Alert				2%	1%				1%	1%
				0.20%	0.20%				0.20%	0.20%
sentneg				0%	0%				0%	0%
				0.50%	0.50%				0.50%	0.50%
D_RES				4%	5%				1%	1%
				0.40%	0.40%				0.40%	0.40%
D_MRG				1%	1%				1%	1%
				0.30%	0.30%				0.30%	0.30%
D_RESF				0%	0%				1%	1%
				0.40%	0.40%				0.40%	0.40%
D_AAA				-3%	-2%				0%	0%
				0.70%	0.70%				0.70%	0.70%
D_DBT				1%	1%				0%	0%
				0.40%	0.40%				0.40%	0.40%
D_RCH				2%	1%				2%	2%
				0.40%	0.40%				0.40%	0.40%
D_Hot				5%	5%				5%	5%
				0.50%	0.50%				0.50%	0.50%
D_JUDIC				-2%	-2%				1%	1%
				0.70%	0.70%				0.70%	0.70%
Firm Fixed Effect	No	Yes	Yes	Yes	Yes	No	Yes	Yes	Yes	Yes
Year Fixed Effect	No	Yes	Yes	No	Yes	No	Yes	Yes	No	Yes

Table 20.4.2 presents a regression-based analysis of informativeness of the options market for different kind of news items. The information share from each event is regressed on news characteristics as follows:

$$IS_{it} = IS_{mean} + D_{year} + D_{Firm} + D_{News} \text{ Variables } + v_{it}.$$ [20.4.8]

We control for firm effect and year-fixed effect. Two classes of news variables exist – surprise news and scheduled news. In the first set of regressions, shown for call options in columns 2, 3 and 4, the news variable is a dummy variable for surprise news. The average information share of the call options is 28%. When we control for year and firm effect, the average information share for call options increases to almost 32%. Option trades around surprise news are 3% less informative than the average option trades. However, "Surprise News" lumps all non-earnings news and non-alerts into one category. We further decompose the information share for each of the common categories. Options trading around alerts has 1% more information share than the average trading in the call options. Alerts are also time-sensitive. Consistent with our claim of some informed trading in the options market, we find that the options market has higher price discovery around time-sensitive news. Call options trading around earnings is 4% more informative than the average call options trading. Options trading around mergers in call options is 1% more informative. Options trading around results forecasts is not particularly informative. Options trading around analyst rating changes and breaking news are 2% and 5% more informative, respectively. "Breaking News" category is associated with time-sensitive information. Consistent with informed trading in the options market, we find a higher information share for this category in the options market.

Similar patterns exist in the put options information share as well. Columns 6–10 present the results for put options. At 29%, the average information share of put options is statistically different from – and lower than – the average information share for call options. The information share of analyst-related news, however, is higher for put options.

20.4.4 Unconditional Information Share

We obtain information share using a procedure directly comparable to Chakravarty, Gulen and Mayhew (2004). Each day we obtain the information share for the options market. We find that the average information share for the options market is indeed lower than reported in the prior study. The information share is also lower than the conditional information share reported earlier. For example, Alcoa stock traded on 1,763 trading days during our sample. 800 out of these trading days had a news item about Alcoa – we denote these days as news days. The average information share across these news days was almost 25%, however, the average information share during the non-news days (963 days out of 1763) was only 10%.

Table 20.4.3: *Unconditional Information shares for each stock: The table shows the average information share for each of the 29 firms in our sample. The second column contains the daily average information share for the call options. The third contains the daily average information share for the put options. The average information share is almost 14% across all of the firms in our sample.*

Firm Name	Call IS		Put IS	
Alcoa	16%	0.54%	15%	0.52%
American Express	18%	0.61%	15%	0.58%
AT&T	2%	0.28%	3%	0.29%
Bank of America	13%	0.51%	13%	0.53%
Boeing	16%	0.57%	16%	0.55%
Caterpillar	16%	0.54%	16%	0.55%
Chevron	16%	0.55%	16%	0.58%
Cisco	16%	0.54%	15%	0.52%
Dupont	15%	0.58%	14%	0.59%
Exxon Mobil	19%	0.58%	17%	0.54%
General Electric	11%	0.43%	12%	0.50%
Hewlett Packard	12%	0.49%	14%	0.55%
Home Depot	14%	0.50%	15%	0.55%
IBM	17%	0.54%	16%	0.52%
Intel	6%	0.40%	10%	0.48%
J P Morgan	16%	0.55%	15%	0.52%
Johnson and Johnson	11%	0.47%	12%	0.52%
Kellogg	12%	0.50%	14%	0.57%
Kraft Foods	9%	0.48%	9%	0.49%
McDonalds Corp.	16%	0.57%	15%	0.58%
3M	14%	0.55%	12%	0.51%
Merck & Co.	14%	0.53%	15%	0.56%
Microsoft	14%	0.52%	15%	0.54%
Pfizer	13%	0.48%	13%	0.50%
Procter & Gamble Company	13%	0.50%	14%	0.56%
United Technologies	17%	0.60%	18%	0.64%
Verizon	13%	0.52%	15%	0.57%
Walmart	15%	0.52%	15%	0.54%
Walt Disney	14%	0.56%	14%	0.57%

Table 20.4.3 shows the average daily information share over the sample period for individual DOW stocks. The unconditional information share is 14%, almost half the information share of the options market conditional on news. The table shows that the information share is lower for the options market than the information share of the options market in presence of news.

20.5 SHORT-SALE BAN AND THE VENUE OF INFORMED TRADING

Our data span the period during which the SEC instituted a short-selling ban for select financial stocks. On 15 July 2008, SEC instituted a ban on shorting 19 financial stocks./footnote. The complete list of banned stocks is available at (SEC Release No. 58166 / July 15, 2008). Of the 19 banned stocks, B.N.P. Paribas and Daiwa

Securities Group are pink sheet companies and we could not locate option data for them. SEC banned shorting in two of 29 stocks in our sample – Bank of America and J P Morgan. The ban provides us with a natural experiment to quantify the magnitude of information share in the options market due to ease of shorting. We do not argue that the short-sale ban was a random treatment to these two stocks, instead we argue that the reasons for the short-sale ban were *independent* of the dynamics of the price-discovery process in the stock and options markets.[17] Later the SEC instituted a ban on other stocks as well, but by then there was some strategic incentive on the part of the firms to be included in the banned list. Hence we restrict our attention to the original list of stocks in the short-sale ban.

If options markets are informative due to the shorting opportunity, informed traders have only one market in which to trade in anticipation of negative news. The information share of options markets should increase during a short-sale ban. On the other hand, a short-sale ban provides monopoly power to the options market-maker. The monopoly power of options market-makers would let the market-maker set inefficient prices. Grundy, Lim and Verwijmeren (2012) observe violations of put-call parity during the short-sale ban, indicating that options prices became inefficient during this time. The inefficiency of the options market will lower the options market's information share. Ex-ante, how the overall effect of short-selling in stocks will play out in the options market is unclear. We use a difference-in-difference estimator as in Meyer (1995) to quantify the effect of the short-sale ban on the informativeness of the options market.

We measure the information share for Bank of America (BAC) and J P Morgan (JPM) options exactly one year before the SEC instituted the ban that included both companies. We therefore made these two stocks our "treatment group". Other members of Dow30 stocks are our "control group". We measure the information share for the "treatment group" and "control group" options during the short-sale ban. Measuring the information share for the "treatment" and "control" groups exactly one year prior to the short- sale ban ensures that we also control for calendar effects.

Table 20.5.1: Effect of Short-sale Ban on the Information Share: The table shows the effect of the short-sale ban instituted on Bank of America (BAC) and J P Morgan (JPM) from 15 July 2008 to 9 October 2008. The information share for the call options are shown in columns 2 and 3. The first row shows the information share for the options market one year before the short-sale ban was instituted. The second row shows the standard errors of the estimates. The third row shows the information share for the options market during the short-sale ban. The information share for the call options for BAC and JPM increased from 26% to almost 31% during the short-sale ban. The information share for BAC and JPM puts increased from 23% to almost 30% during the ban. The information share for the options for other Dow 30 constituents did not change significantly as a result of the ban.

	Call Options		Put Options	
	BAC and JPM	Other Firms	BAC and JPM	Other Firms
15th July, 2007 - 9th October 2007	26.14%	22.57%	23.01%	24.14%
	2.01%	0.57%	1.69%	0.69%
15th July, 2008 - 9th October 2008	30.69%	23.24%	30.22%	24.23%
	1.40%	0.61%	1.37%	0.59%

Table 20.5.1 provides the information share for BAC and JPM options as well as options on other Dow 30 components. The information share for call options of BAC and JPM from 26% a year before the ban was instituted to almost 31% during the short-sale ban. The information share for call options on other Dow30 options increased by less than 1%. The increase in information share for other Dow30 constituents is also statistically insignificant. The difference-in-difference estimate suggests an almost 4% increase in the information share of call options, an almost 15% increase.

The information share for put options of BAC and JPM increased from 23% a year before the ban to approximately 30% during the ban. The information share for put options for other constituents changed by 0.09% and was statistically significant. The difference-in-difference estimator suggests more than 7% increase in the information share, an almost 31% percent increase.

The evidence from the natural experiment suggests that the ban on short-selling increased the information share of options markets. Since the options markets are informative due to the presence of informed traders, the evidence also suggests that the short-sell ban affected informed trading in general.

20.6 CONCLUSION

We observe that, prior to the news arrival, the options market volume increases to well above its usual trading volume. Our result suggests that options market participants anticipate news. The findings hold even for news that by its nature cannot be anticipated, such as merger announcements, analyst updates, rating changes and breaking news. Stock market volume also increases to some extent; however, the increase in the stock market volume is far less pronounced than the options market volume.

We also obtain the information share for the options market. We find the information share increases to 27% in presence of news, whereas the unconditional information share of the option market is 14%. Our results on information share is somewhat surprising since we observe, like other researchers such as Muravyev, Pearson and Broussard (2013), that the options market is far more illiquid than the stock market. Despite its illiquidity, the options market has a higher information share than previously reported. Based on our results on the trading volume surrounding a news release, we ascribe the increase in the information share to trading by informed traders.

One reason the options market is lucrative for the informed traders is the ease with which one can short a stock. After the short-sale ban, we observe that the information share of the options market for financial stocks has increased by almost 31%, whereas the information share of all other stocks has barely changed. The increase in information share is consistent with our conjecture that informed traders prefer the options markets and the short- sale ban pushed even more informed traders in that direction.

Our results have three important implications. First, liquidity is not the only factor driving an informed trader's decision regarding trading venue. We find that such traders prefer a somewhat less liquid market. We conjecture that they might prefer the options market, placing a bet there by choosing any of the many available strikes, unlike the stock market where a buy or sell order can tip the informed trader's hand to smart traders. Second, the paper highlights the role of news events as interesting times to observe trading activity. Options markets are relatively low-volume markets, but we observe a different dynamic when we condition on trading surrounding news articles. Finally, the results are important for regulators who ban short selling in order to encourage the market to ignore bad news. Our results suggest that informed traders will simply move to the options market, which might become more inefficient, but nevertheless, more price discovery will occur in the options market.

Notes

[1]   Tetlock (2010) examines trading around news at the daily level and provides evidence that trading volume increases prior to the news release.

[2]   Chakravarty, Gulen and Mayhew (2004), Anand and Chakravarty (2007), Simaan and Wu (2007), Hendershott and Jones (2005) and Blanco, Brennan and Marsh (2005) have also used an information-share measure to identify the venue of price discovery. Chakravarty, Gulen and Mayhew (2004) document the average information-share of the option market for large stocks as 17 per cent. Anand and Chakravarty (2007) and Simaan and Wu (2007) identify the venue of informed trading across different option exchanges, whereas Blanco, Brennan and Marsh (2005) use the information-share methodology to identify the contribution of the CDS market in price discovery vis-à-vis the bond market. Our paper employs the information-share methodology conditional on an event – similar to Hendershott and Jones (2005).

[3]   Gintschel, A. and Markov, S. (2004) show that Reg FD decreased the price impact of analyst recommendation. Agrawal, A. and Chadha, S. and Chen, M.A. (2006) show analyst forecast became less informative post REG FD.

[4]   Battalio, R. and Schultz, P. (2006) discuss the possibility of stale quotes in the options (or the stock) market.

[5]   Foster and Viswanathan (1993) model trading around public information and suggest that public information like news make the value of private information lower. Foster and Viswanathan (1993) also suggest that the revelation of public information forces informed traders to trade aggressively.

[6]   Such traders could anticipate news either because of illegal information sharing from insiders or because of a deep understanding about a firm and its operating environment.

[7]   Our findings on significant price discovery in illiquid markets is in line with the evidence presented by Shastri, Thirumalai and Zutter (2008), Barclay and Hendershott (2003), and Chakrabarty, Corwin and Panayides (2011). Shastri, Thirumalai and Zutter (2008) observe significant price discovery at single stock futures despite low trading volume. Barclay and Hendershott (2003) show that price discovery occurs at Electronic Crossing Networks (ECN) after the market closure. Chakrabarty, Corwin and Panayides (2011) show that price discovery occurs at ECNs during trading halts at New York Stock Exchange.

[8]   The short-sell ban did indeed affect the efficiency of the option market. Battalio and Schultz (2011) document a dramatic increase in the bid-ask spread for the equity options of banned stocks. Grundy, Lim and Verwijmeren (2012) document violation of put-call parity.

[9]   We do not investigate price distortion effect of the short-sale ban, Harris, L.E. and Namvar, E. and Phillips, B. (2009) and Don, M. and Billingsley, R.S. and Kovacs, T. (2011) analyse the price distortion effects of the short-sale ban.

[10] The increase in the information share of put options during the short-sale ban also adds to our understanding of the short seller's source of profitability previously explored in Engelberg, Reed and Riggenberg (2011),

Piqueira and Hao (2010) and Ni and Pan (2011). Engelberg, Reed and Riggenberg (2011) find short sellers do not have private information but profit due to better interpretation of publicly available information. Piqueira and Hao (2010) find that, in general, short sales are more informative but that prior to earnings release put options are more informative. Our findings suggest short sellers are likely to be informed traders, and closing the short-sale channel forced some informed investors to the options market. Our findings are closest to Ni and Pan (2011) where they show that the short-sale ban drove a wedge between information in the options and stock market.

11   Altria, formerly known as Philip Morris, went through substantial corporate restructuring during our sample period. Data prior to 2007 for the same firm is not comparable to the data after 2007 for Altria, hence is excluded from our sample.

12   The mapping of news to the five minute interval following the news arrival has the potential of making the trades appear after the news appears on the screen. However, we are concerned about the relative speed with which options and stock volume respond to news and hence the aforementioned bias does not affect our study.

13   Newswires competing with Thomson Reuters might have broken the story first; however, we are concerned about the differential reaction by the stock and options markets. To the extent that we are observing both markets in the same interval, our methodology is not sensitive to the exact time at which the news becomes public.

14   By using the average of only 29 point estimates rather than the average of 130,000 estimates, we severely understate the precision of our estimates. We are calculating the average trading at event time k using N_2 (N_2 = 29) observations. These N_2 observations (firm-specific estimates) are average values over $r_1, r_2, \ldots r_m$ (m = 29) observations, such that $\sum_i^N r_i = N_i$. The average trading at event time k would have been the same, had we estimated by averaging over all 130,000 observations. If $N_1 >> N_2$, as it is in our case, the 1/2 precision of the average using the N_1 point estimates is higher by a factor of 1 whereas the point estimate of the average is unaffected. Hence our choice of first obtaining firm-specific trading activity and then providing average estimates does not change the value of the estimate but understates the statistical significance of the estimate.

15   The choice of normalization period does not alter the statistics qualitatively. We observe the same findings if we use k=-100, -95, and -90 instead.

16   Chakravarty, Gulen and Mayhew (2004) use $\Delta t = 30$ minutes. To ensure that our results on information share are not driven by the choice of lag length, we obtain news conditional information share for $\Delta = 30$ minutes as well.

17   Indeed Bris, A. (2008) finds that short selling accounted for 12% of all trades between January 1st and July 15th for the stocks on the ban list where for other similar US institutions the similar number was 13%.

20.7 REFERENCES

1. Agrawal, A., Chadha, S. and Chen, M.A. (2006). Who is afraid of Reg FD? The behaviour and performance of sell-side analysts following the SECs fair disclosure rules. *Journal of Business, 79(6)*, 2811–2834.

2. Amin, K. and Lee, C. (1997). Option trading, price discovery and earnings news dissemination. *Contemporary Accounting Research*, 14(2), 153–192.

3. Anand, A. and Chakravarty, S. (2007). Stealth trading in options markets. *Journal of Financial and Quantitative Analysis*, 42(1), 167–187.

4. Aragon, G.O. and Martin, J.S. (2012). A unique view of hedge fund derivatives usage: Safeguard or speculation? *Journal of Financial Economics, 105(2), 436–456*.

5. Barclay, M. and Hendershott, T. (2003). Price discovery and trading after hours. *Review of Financial Studies*, 16(4), 1041–1073.

6. Battalio, R. and Schultz, P. (2011). Regulatory uncertainty and market liquidity: The 2008 short sale ban's impact on equity options. *Journal of Finance, 66(6)*, 2013–2053.

7. Battalio, R. and Schultz, P. (2006). Options and the bubble. *Journal of Finance, 61(5)*, 2071–2102.

8. Black, F. (1975). Fact and fantasy in the use of options. *Financial Analysts Journal*, 31(4), 36–72.

9. Blanco, R., Brennan, S. and Marsh, I. (2005). An empirical analysis of the dynamic relation between investment-grade bonds and credit default swaps. *Journal of Finance, 60(5)*, 2255–2281.

10. Bris, A. (2008). Short selling activity in financial stocks and the SEC July 15th emergency order. Unpublished working paper. IMD.

11. Cao, C., Chen, Z. and Griffin, J. (2005). Informational content of option volume prior to takeovers. *Journal of Business, 78(3)*, 1073–1109.

12. Cao, H. and Ou-Yang, H. (2009). Differences of opinion of public information and speculative trading in stocks and options. *Review of Financial Studies*, 22(1), 299–335.

13. Chakrabarty, B., Corwin, S. and Panayides, M. (2011). When a halt is not a halt: an analysis of off-NYSE trading during NYSE market closures. *Journal of Financial Intermediation, 20(3)*, 361–386.

14. Chakravarty, S., Gulen, H. and Mayhew, S. (2004). Informed trading in stock and option markets. *Journal of Finance, 59(3)*, 1235–1258.

15. Clark, P. (1973). A subordinated stochastic process model with finite variance for speculative prices. *Econometrica, 41(1),* 135–155.

16. Don, M., Billingsley, R.S. and Kovacs, T. (2011). The 2008 short sale ban: Liquidity, dispersion of opinion, and the cross-section of returns of US financial stocks. *Journal of Banking & Finance, 35(9),* 2252–2266.

17. Easley, D., O'Hara, M. and Srinivas, P. (1998). Option volume and stock prices: Evidence on where informed traders trade. *Journal of Finance, 53(2),* 431–465.

18. Engelberg, J., Reed, A. and Riggenberg, M. (2011). How are Shorts Informed? Short-Selling, News and Information Processing. Unpublished working paper.

19. Foster, F. and Viswanathan, S. (1993). The effect of public information and competition on trading volume and price volatility. *Review of Financial Studies, 6(1),* 23–56.

20. Gintschel, A. and Markov, S. (2004). The effectiveness of Regulation FD.*Journal of Accounting and Economics,* 37(3), 293–314.

21. Grundy, B., Lim, B. and Verwijmeren, P. (2012). Do option markets undo restrictions on short sales? Evidence from the 2008 short-sale ban. *Journal of Financial Economics, 106(2),* 331–348.

22. Harris, L.E., Namvar, E. and Phillips, B. (2009). Price inflation and wealth transfer during the 2008 SEC short-sale ban. Unpublished Working Paper.

23. Hasbrouck, J. (1995). One security, many markets: Determining the location of price discovery. *Journal of Finance, 50(4),* 1175–1199.

24. Hasbrouck, J. (1999). The dynamics of discrete bid and ask quotes. *Journal of Finance, 54(6),* 2109–2142.

25. Hendershott, T. and Jones, C. (2005). Island goes dark: Transparency, fragmentation, and regulation. *Review of Financial Studies, 18(3),* 743–793.

26. Kyle, A. (1985). Continuous auctions and insider trading. *Econometrica, 53(6),* 1315–1335.

27. Mandelbrot, B. and Taylor, H. (1967). On the distribution of stock price differences. *Operations research, 15(6),* 1057–1062.

28. Meyer, B. D. (1995). Natural and quasi-experiments in economics. *Journal of Business & Economic Statistics,* 13(2), 151–161.

29. Muravyev, D., Pearson, N.D. and Broussard, J.P. (2013). Is there price discovery in equity options? *Journal of Financial Economics, 107(2),* 259–283.

30. Ni, S. and Pan, J. (2011). Trading puts and CDS on stocks with short sale ban. Unpublished Working Paper.

31. Piqueira, N. and Hao, X. (2010). Short sales and put options: where is the bad news first traded? Unpublished Working Paper.

32. Shastri, K., Thirumalai, R. and Zutter, C. (2008). Information revelation in the futures market: Evidence from single stock futures. *Journal of Futures Markets*, *28(4)*, 335–353.

33. Simaan, Y. and Wu, L. (2007). Price discovery in the U.S. stock options market. *Journal of Derivatives*, *15(2)*, 20–38.

34. Sinha, N. R. (2015). Underreaction to news in the US stock market. *Quarterly Journal of Finance*, forthcoming.

35. Stephan, J. A. and Whaley, R. E. (1990). Intraday price change and trading volume relations in the stock and stock option markets. *Journal of Finance*, *45(1)*, 191–220.

36. Tetlock, P. (2010). Does public financial news resolve asymmetric information? *Review of Financial Studies*, 23(9), 3520–3557.

20.A APPENDIX

The information share approach of Hasbrouck (1995) proposed is a fairly robust measure of price discovery. Here, we present results from a simulation in which the fundamental price is unobserved and the asset is being traded in two markets. To make our notations concrete, we will denote the fundamental value as f_t, the prices in market 1 as p_{1t}, and the prices in market 2 as p_{2t}.

The prices are related as follows:

$$f_t = f_t - 1 + e_{it}, \text{ where } e_{it} \quad N(0,1) \tag{20.A.1}$$

$$p_{1t} = f_t + 0.5n_{it}, \text{ where } n_{it} \ N(0,1), \text{ and} \tag{20.A.2}$$

$$p_{2t} = f_t - 1 + 0.5v_{it}, \text{ where } v_{it} \ N(0,1). \tag{20.A.3}$$

Prices in market 2 are stale prices with respect to the fundamental price and the prices in the market 1. We expect the information share of market 2 to be low. We obtain a time series of 620 observations using simulated data. We calculate information share for 1,000 such time series. The average information share for the second market from our simulation is 4.98%. The average lower bound of the information share for the second market is 2.85% and the standard error is 0.08%, whereas the average upper bound of the information share is 7.11% and the corresponding standard error is 0.27%. Figure 20.A.1 shows the distribution from the simulation exercise.

If we do not observe any trading in the options markets in a period, we use the prior period's option-implied price. In such a set up, although the stock price varies, the options price stays constant if no trading occurs in the options market. We would expect our procedure to show decrease in the information share for the options market. In our simulation, we set the prices in the second market such that every third price point is a stale price – price from the previous period. The average of the lower bound of the information share in the second market is 1.85%, and the standard error is 0.07%. The upper bound of the information share in the second market is 5.32%, and the standard error is 0.22%. Figure 20.A.2 shows the distribution of the information share from a simulation of lagged pricing scheme.

The simulation exercise confirms two important conjectures. First, the information share of a lagging market is much lower than the numbers we have presented for the options market. Information shares we report are unlikely to arise from a situation in which the options market-maker simply quotes off the stock market. Figure 20.A.1 suggests the information share would be in the vicinity of 5%. Second, the information share for a market with stale prices is even lower than the lagging market's information share. Figure 20.A.2 suggests the information share would be in the vicinity of 3% rather than the numbers we quote for the options market.

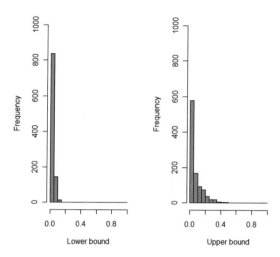

Figure 20.A.1: *Distribution of Information Share : The figure shows the distribution of information shares for a lagging market from a simulation. The plot on the left is the lower bound of the information share, and the plot on the right is the upper bound of the information share. The market lags by one time period. The average of the lower bound of the information share is 2.85%. The average of the upper bound of the information share is 7.11%.*

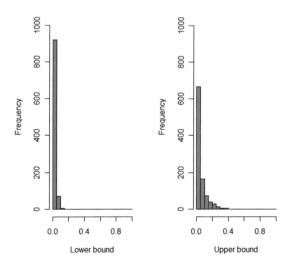

Figure 20.A.2: *Distribution of Information Share : The figure shows the distribution of information shares for a lagging market from a simulation. The plot on the left is the lower bound of the information share, and the plot on the right is the upper bound of the information share. The market lags by one time period and has stale prices in every third observation. The average of the lower bound of the information share is 1.85%. The average of the upper bound of the information share is 5.32%.*

CHAPTER 21

Abnormal News Volume and Under-reaction to Soft Information

Michał Dzieliński, *Researcher, Stockholm Business School*

ABSTRACT

News tone has been gaining popularity in the academic literature as a measure of "soft information" and numerous studies have explored its role for asset prices. However, as far as tone can give a good indication of whether the content was positive or negative, it does not tell anything about the importance of the announcement. I propose a measure of importance, abnormal news volume, and interact it with tone to examine subsequent stock returns. I find significantly more drift after highly publicized announcements, suggesting that important news takes longer to incorporate into prices. The results are stronger for negative than for positive stories.

21.1   INTRODUCTION

A considerable body of evidence exists to show that stock prices do not instantaneously adjust to new information but rather do so gradually, giving rise to some degree of post-announcement drift. Early studies of this phenomenon focused on accounting news, such as quarterly earnings, which was easy to quantify, e.g. (Bernard and Thomas, 1990). The main difficulty in extending the analysis to generic announcements was the lack of efficient ways to determine whether the news was good or bad. Researchers would thus either focus on certain types of announcements where the interpretation was unambiguous to begin with, e.g. share repurchases analysed by Ikenberry, Lakonishok and Vermaelencq (1995) are essentially always good news, or use the stock return on or around announcement days as a proxy for news content, as in the seminal paper by Chan (2003). Both workarounds were not without drawbacks. In the first case, the scope of any analysis was limited to just one or a handful of event types. The second approach involved using returns on both sides of the equation, as a measure of market response to news and of the news itself, raising concerns of endogeneity.

News analytics, the process of automatically evaluating text, was instrumental in overcoming these issues and providing arguably exogenous measures of news content based solely on language. This opened up a whole new field of research into the effects of what became known as "soft", textual – as opposed to "hard", numerical – information. The general approach would be to summarize text in a number representing its degree of negativity/positivity and use that as an explanatory variable, often labelled "news tone", for different financial outcomes. The ground-breaking results of Tetlock, Saar-Tsechansky and Macskassy (2008) documented the predictive power of tone for future earnings and short-term stock returns. Others, most notably Engelberg (2008), have argued that soft information takes longer to digest and is associated with higher post-announcement drift. More recent studies have applied the concept of news tone to other asset markets, such as currencies (Hafez and Xie, 2013) and commodities (Borovkova, 2011).

Parallel research has been underway to improve the way that news tone is measured. Generic dictionaries of positive and negative words borrowed from psychological research were replaced by word lists tailored specifically to finance, spearheaded by Loughran and McDonald (2011). Other researchers would pursue data-driven ways to identify the tonality but also the importance of specific words, as in Jegadeesh and Wu (2013). Such efforts were, however, not limited to university departments, and all major news providers have started developing their own analytical tools, which in turn became accepted sources of data for academic studies as well. A recent paper by Heston and Sinha (2014) argues that text-processing algorithms originating in the news industry offer superior performance compared to simpler dictionary-based methods.

At the same time, less attention was devoted to identifying which news matters most to investors and hence elicits the strongest overall response. This is a different objective from measuring tone, which is more about providing the direction of news rather than its magnitude. An announcement can have very pronounced tone but still be relatively immaterial to the future prospects of the company and vice versa. For instance, a clearly positive announcement about the opening of a company's new headquarters is unlikely to affect future returns. On the other hand, even slightly negative news signalling potential trouble with a key supplier can leave investors scrambling to determine its full impact on the prospects of the firm for a prolonged period of time. Unfortunately, based on just tone, one would reach the opposite conclusion about the size of the drift expected after each of these announcements. Ideally, one would like to have a separate measure of news importance that could be interacted with tone to provide a better prognosis of market impact. Boudoukh, Feldman, Kogan, and Richardson (2013) have suggested examining different news topics in an effort to distinguish those that systematically move prices. However, apart from the fact that any such categorization has to be derived from past market reactions and is thus backward-looking, the resulting categories are sufficiently broad (e.g. earnings news) to contain announcements of varying importance.

My contribution to the search for the best measure of importance begins with the simple observation that news publishing is driven by the demand for information. In other words, if news outlets expect, or observe, a high interest in a particular story, they will cover it more, providing updates and re-runs in order to capitalize on the readers' attention. Hence, the number of news items associated with a particular story should correlate well with its importance, especially if it is abnormally high in comparison to the coverage that a certain company typically enjoys. Consistent with this hypothesis, I find that abnormal news volume is a significant catalyst of under-reaction to soft information. Using panel regressions and portfolio analysis I show that the post-announcement drift is twice as large when abnormal news volume is high compared to when it is low. Intensive coverage appears to be a good proxy for the importance and perhaps also complexity of the news. This conclusion comes with a caveat that it performs better for negative than positive news. In the latter case, it could be that news coverage results more from publicity efforts by the company in question and less from the materiality of the announcement.

My results can be related to the studies of Chan (2003) and Tetlock (2010). The key difference is that, while they compare drift and reversal after periods with and without news, I focus only on weeks with news and explore the role of abnormal news volume in shaping post-news drift. Section 21.2 introduces the main data source followed by a detailed description of my empirical analysis. Section 21.4 offers some conclusions.

21.2   DATA

The main data source for my analysis is Thomson Reuters News Analytics. This extensive archive contains all news published either by the companies themselves (via direct outlets like the PR Newswire) or by Reuters about these companies in the period between January 2003 and December 2012. Reuters is one of the major financial news agencies, specializing in covering corporate events, and also one that is committed to impartial and factual reporting. This is important when relying on linguistic analysis to determine whether the actual events described in the news were positive or negative. On the other hand, it is well established that companies often "spin" their own announcements using favourable language, see e.g. Dzieliński (2012). Hence, I focus only on announcements attributed to Reuters.

The structure of the data is such that each time a company is mentioned in the news, its identifier (Reuters Instrument Code, or RIC) is recorded, together with a precise timestamp. In particular, it means that one record per company is created whenever a news announcement mentions several companies. This is a very useful feature, because the tone might differ for each company covered in the same news story (e.g. good news for a company might be bad news for its competitors). Similarly, the relevance of the news story for each company might be diffe re n t, with one of them being the main focus of attention, perhaps named in the headline, while the others are only briefly mentioned later in the text.

The linguistic analysis is performed by a proprietary algorithm developed by Reuters specifically for processing financial news. This is important because content analysis applications tend to be very context specific, which makes the use of generic tools difficult and potentially unreliable. The details are not publicly known but the basic structure combines the use of a syntactic parser with a neural network trained to recognize which expressions are positive or negative in the context of financial news. This combination allows the algorithm to work at the sentence level, identifying the subject (company) and any tone-relevant words related to it. The final output is delivered in the form of three "tone probability" scores, which show how likely each news item was to be positive, negative or neutral. Whichever probability is the highest determines the overall tone, represented as a discrete variable: +1 for positive, -1 for negative, and 0 for neutral tone. The last possibility means that no definite assessment as positive or negative could be made.

21.3 EMPIRICAL ANALYSIS

I construct my sample by matching tickers of common stocks from the Center for Research in Securities Prices (CRSP) database to Reuters Instrument Codes (RICs) in TRNA, yielding over 6.5mln matched news announcements[1] for 5,488 different stocks. To measure news tone, I use the same approach that has been suggested in earlier studies employing the TRNA dataset, e.g. Sinha (2010), and for every announcement define

$$tone = prob\ pos - prob\ neg \qquad [21.3.1]$$

In other words, the tone is the difference between the probability of the announcement being positive and it being negative. This measure can be easily extended to multiple news announcements and throughout the analysis I rely on tone computed at the weekly frequency for each firm as:

$$Tone_{i,t} = \frac{\sum^{n_{i,t}} tone}{n_{i,t}} \qquad [21.3.2]$$

where n is the number of announcements about company i in week t. This procedure results in close to 500,000 weekly observations. I further require data for market capitalization at the end of the preceding month and book equity from the preceding year to be available, which reduces the sample size to 387,559 observations. The higher the value of tone, the more clearly positive was the weekly news flow for a given firm. This also determines the expected direction of any potential under-reaction. Crucially, however, tone itself does not contain much indication about the importance of the news, which is going to matter for the magnitude of post-news drift. The underlying intuition is that news touching the very core of a firm's business will be more difficult to interpret, because more factors need to be considered to evaluate its implications for firm value. The TRNA dataset contains two variables that have been suggested for this purpose in earlier research: relevance and novelty. The first of these measures how prominently a firm has been featured in the news, e.g. mentioned in the headline or only in the last paragraph of an announcement. One could say that this better describes the importance of the company for the news rather than the other way round, since a story featuring just a single company will necessarily score high on relevance but could still cover a relatively unimportant event. Novelty, on the other hand, is mostly concerned with whether the current announcement has been preceded by textually similar ones, in order to identify stale news. Therefore, a news item will obtain a high novelty score if it mentions a new event or story, which might or might not turn out to be important, making it a rather noisy proxy for importance. My argument for using abnormal news volume is somewhat similar to the point made in Tetlock (2010) that news stories consisting of multiple messages are likely to be more thorough and hence more informative. However, controlling for some measure of average news flow is crucial to avoid bias towards news about larger, more visible stocks, which are more often cross-mentioned in news about other companies. With this in mind, I define abnormal news volume as the ratio of the number of news announcements about company i in week t to the average weekly number of announcements about company i in the calendar quarter preceding week t:

$$ln\ (AbCount_{i,t}+1) = \frac{n_{i,t}}{1 + AvgCount_{i,qtr(t)-1}} \qquad [21.3.3]$$

I add 1 to *AvgCount* to deal with cases where there was no news in the preceding quarter. One potential issue is that a higher number of news announcements in a given time period might reflect a higher number of separate firm events rather than increased coverage of a specific one. This is likely to become more of a concern as the time period in question becomes longer. On the other hand, very short time periods pose the risk of artificially "chopping up" what should in fact be a single story cycle. Using weekly intervals to aggregate news seems a reasonable compromise between these two objectives. Calculating *AbCount* requires me to sacrifice the first quarter of data and so the final sample used in the regressions consists of 382 603 observations.

Table 21.3.1 presents summary statistics of *Tone* and *AbCount* over my sample period. Average tone is close to zero, which seems reasonable for a period that featured an approximately equal share of bull and bear market. *AbCount* is on average close to 1, which suggests that most company stories are in fact "business as usual". On the other hand, the highly skewed distribution of *AbCount* indicates the presence of big "blockbusters" among them. Skewness can be problematic when computing correlations and running regressions, because it is usually associated with large outliers at one end of the distribution, which can distort the results. To alleviate this concern, I define a logarithmic transformation of the *AbCount* variable as $ln(AbCount_{i,t} + 1)$. This is a monotonic transformation, so it maintains the same order of values as the original variable. Adding unity to *AbCount* before taking the logarithm keeps the result positive. This plays an important role later on, when interacting *AbCount* with *Tone*, which can be either positive or negative. For similar reasons, I use $ln(Size)$ when computing correlations and running regressions.

Table 21.3.1: *Summary statistics.*

The table presents summary statistics across all weekly observations for the period Mar 2003 – Dec 2012. Size is given in $bln. For the purposes of computing correlations, natural logarithms of Size and AbCount are used.

	Univariate statistics					Correlations			
	Mean	StdDev	Skewness	p25	p75	AbCount	Size	BtM	AbTurn
Tone	0.09	0.40	-0.26	-0.15	0.36	-0.025	0.036	-0.025	0.003
AbCount	1.06	1.37	11.43	0.32	1.29		-0.095	0.004	0.208
Size	10.099	31.191	6.976	0.300	5.827			-0.198	0.000
BtM	0.69	0.81	10.03	0.29	0.84				-0.040
AbTurn	0.07	0.63	0.15	-0.29	0.39				

In my analysis I control for the size and book-to-market ratio of the company to isolate the influence of well-known asset pricing factors. I also include abnormal turnover because numerous studies have suggested that unusually heavy trading in a particular stock signals the arrival of new information[2]. Turnover is calculated as the natural logarithm of the ratio of shares traded in a given week to shares outstanding and abnormal turnover is the difference between turnover in week t and the average for the preceding 52 weeks. The correlations shown in the last four columns of Table 2 1.3.1 provide some initial insights into the relationships between the variables. *Tone* and (the logarithmic transformation of) *AbCount* are slightly negatively correlated, suggesting that negative news is more likely to receive high coverage, though the asymmetry is small. Furthermore, *AbCount* has only a small and, if anything, negative correlation with size, which shows that adjusting for average news volume in the preceding quarter is enough to separate the part of the newsflow not associated with how big and visible a particular firm is. Finally, *AbCount* has a significant positive correlation with abnormal turnover, underscoring the plausibility of using unusually high coverage as a proxy for important news.

The central question of the analysis is how *Tone* and *AbCount* combine to generate under-reaction to company news. I start by measuring the degree to which markets (on average) under-react to *Tone* itself. To this end, I regress excess return of stock i in week $t + 1$ on *Tone* in week t:

$$ExcessRet_{i,t} + 1 = \alpha + \beta 1 \cdot Tone_{i,t} + \beta 2 \cdot AbCount_{i,t} + \gamma \cdot X_{i,t} + E_{i,t} \qquad [21.3.4]$$

Excess return is measured as the difference (in percent) between the return of stock i and the CRSP value-weighted index. The matrix X contains control variables as described above. The result in the first column of Table 21.3.2 confirm that excess returns tend to drift in the direction of news tone. Specifically, a one standard deviation increase in *Tone* in week t is associated with an increase in excess returns of 12 basis points (0.40 × 0.31%) over the following week. The negative relationship between (the logarithmic transformation of) *AbCount* and future excess returns is surprising, given that *AbCount* is not intended to be a directional measure of news, as evidenced by its negligible correlation with news tone. One possible explanation, consistent with the findings of e.g. Solomon (2012), is that news coverage is a less reliable indicator of importance for positive news, because it can also result from deliberate efforts by companies to generate attention whenever something favourable happens.

Table 21.3.2: *Abnormal news volume and underreaction to tone.*

The table presents coefficients estimated from the following regression:

$$ExcessRet_{i,t} + 1 = \alpha + \beta_1 \cdot Tone_{i,t} + \beta_2 \cdot AbCount_{i,t} + \gamma \cdot X_{i,t} + E_{i,t}$$

Excess return is measured as the difference between the return on stock i and the value-weighted CRSP index. Column 2 additionally includes the interaction term between Tone and AbCount. Matrix X contains the contro variables AbTurn, Size and BtM (book-to-market ratio). Columns 3–6 repeat the original regression in four subsamples sorted on AbCount. Quartile breakpoints are calculated separately for each week. Weekly observations for the period Mar 2003 – Dec 2012 are used. t-statistics appearing in parentheses are based on standard errors clustered by stock.

	all	all	sorted on abnormal news volume			
	stocks	stocks	low	2	3	high
Tone	0.30	0.15	0.24	0.31	0.32	0.52
	(9.08)	(2.87)	(5.07)	(4.78)	(3.74)	(4.93)
AbCount	-0.17	-0.19	-0.61	-0.78	-0.31	-0.12
	(-4.98)	(-5.22)	(-2.12)	(-3.78)	(-1.78)	(-1.32)
Tone*AbCount		0.37				
		(3.36)				
AbTurn	0.15	0.15	0.11	0.14	0.26	0.10
	(5.62)	(5.54)	(1.80)	(2.65)	(5.23)	(1.78)
Size	0.08	0.08	0.06	0.06	0.09	0.09
	(10.02)	(9.97)	(3.44)	(4.35)	(6.05)	(5.62)
BtM	0.05	0.05	-0.03	0.11	0.06	0.04
	(2.03)	(2.08)	(-0.57)	(2.56)	(1.28)	(0.87)
Nobs	382 603	382 603	99 127	96 658	94 749	92 069
R2	0.09%	0.10%	0.07%	0.10%	0.13%	0.10%

In the next specification, I expand the regression to include an interaction term between *AbCount* week *t* and *Tone*:

$$ExcessRet_{i,t} + 1 = \alpha + \beta_1 \cdot Tone_{i,t} + \beta_2 \cdot AbCount_{i,t} + \beta_3 \cdot Tone_{i,t} \cdot AbCount_{i,t} + \gamma \cdot X_{i,t} + E_{i,t} \qquad [21.3.5]$$

The key coefficient of interest is β_3, which captures how abnormal news volume affects the relationship between *Tone* and future returns. As shown in the second column of Table 21.3.2, it is positive and highly statistically significant, suggesting a strong amplification effect. The standard deviation of the transformed *AbCount* variable is 0.43, which multiplied with β_3 means the coefficient on *Tone* doubles ($0.43 \times 0.37 = 0.16$) for every such increase in abnormal news volume. To explore the role of news volume further, I divide all weekly observations into 4 quartiles of *AbCount*. The quartile breakpoints are calculated separately for every week *t* to capture purely cross-sectional differences and avoid sorting observations into periods, when all stocks received unusually many (like the recent financial crisis) or unusually few news. I then repeat the regression in equation 21.3.4 for each subsample individually. The focus is now on comparing the coefficient on *Tone* when progressing from lowest to the highest quartile and one can see a pattern of monotonic increase. The coefficient on *Tone* in quartile 4 (=0.52) is more than twice the size as in quartile 1 (=0.24), meaning that weekly news with the same tone can be followed by under-reaction more than twice as large depending on news volume. Differences in the intermediate quartiles are smaller, which suggests that only very high abnormal news volume is a clear indicator of future under-reaction.

Is the effect of abnormal news volume consistent in time? Does it differ across positive and negative news? To explore these questions, I form long-short portfolios based on the values of *Tone* and *AbCount* in that week. Specifically, at the end of each week I select all stocks that had news volume above their average level (hence raw *AbCount* ≥1). The long leg of the portfolio then consists of those stocks that also had overall positive news tone (*Tone* >0), while stocks with overall negative news are shorted. Portfolios are equally weighted and held for one week.

Table 21.3.3: Long-short portfolio returns
The table summarizes the average performance of a long-short portfolio formed and the end of every week by filtering out stocks with news volume higher than the quarterly average (AbCount >1). Stocks that also had positive Tone are held long and those with negative Tone are shorted. Both legs are equally weighted and rebalanced weekly. Mean n(firms) refers to the average number of firms in each leg across all weeks. Median size refers to the median market capitalization (in $bln) of stocks held in each leg, averaged across all weeks. Hit rate refers to the fraction of observations with positive spread. Weekly observations for the period Mar 2003 – Dec 2012 are used.

		long leg	short leg	spread
Excess return		-0.15%	-0.37%	0.22%
t-stat		-1.58	-3.22	3.67
Mean n(firms)		204	111	
Median size		1.518	1.211	
Number of weeks	510			
Hit rate	59.0%			

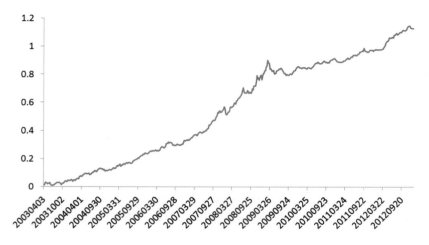

Figure 21.3.1: *Cumulative portfolio returns. The figure shows the cumulative performance of the strategy developed in Table 21.3.3. Weekly observations for the period Mar 2003 – Dec 2012 are used.*

The results in Table 21.3.3 demonstrate that the long-short spread is on average positive and statistically significant. It is positive in 59% out of total 510 weeks in the sample, indicating a fair degree of stability. The cumulative long-short returns shown in Figure 21.3.1 also do not experience any significant breakdowns, even during the financial crisis. However, the entire performance is generated by the short leg, while long returns are not significantly different from zero. This appears to confirm the suspicion raised by the regression results that abnormal coverage of positive news can be in part driven by PR efforts of the companies rather than the importance of the news. In this context, it is quite telling that in the average week there are twice as many companies with positive than with negative news flow.

Table 21.3.4: *Long-short portfolios for different parameter values*
The table summarizes the average performance of long-short portfolios formed according to the description of Table 21.3.3 for different values of the Tone and AbCount cutoff. Weekly observations for the period Mar 2003 – Dec 2012 are used.

		|Tone| > 0	|Tone| > 0.1	|Tone| > 0.2	|Tone| > 0.3
AbCount > 1	Spread	0.22%	0.26%	0.34%	0.40%
	t-stat	3.67	3.71	4.07	3.91
	Mean n(firms)	315	237	156	94
	Median size	1.375	1.358	1.337	1.222
	Hit rate	59.0%	57.3%	59.8%	58.0%
AbCount > 2	Spread	0.25%	0.38%	0.48%	0.55%
	t-stat	2.40	3.32	3.36	3.05
	Mean n(firms)	113	84	55	32
	Median size	1.522	1.482	1.447	1.258
	Hit rate	56.9%	56.7%	55.9%	56.9%

In Table 21.3.4 I consider a total of 8 different combinations of *Tone* and *AbCount* thresholds. In each case, stocks with weekly *Tone* below the threshold are held long and stocks with weekly *Tone* below minus the threshold are shorted. The first combination in the top-left corner is identical to the one in Table 21.3.3. The reasons for this exercise are twofold. First, applying more restrictive selection criteria could help reduce the number of stocks in the portfolios to a more manageable level. Secondly, if the selection variables truly capture important drivers of under-reaction, it should also lead to better performance. Indeed, focusing on stocks with more clearly pronounced news tone in a given week (i.e. moving from left to right in the Table) leads to a higher long-short spread. The number of stocks held decreases tenfold between the least and most restrictive approach but it is worth noting that this has little impact on their median size. The key takeaway is that additionally considering a more restrictive level abnormal news volume improves average portfolio performance for every single *Tone* threshold.

21.4 CONCLUSIONS

In this study, I argue that important news will only gradually be incorporated into stock prices as investors try to determine its full impact on firm value and propose using abnormal news volume as a proxy for importance. This approach makes use of the effort financial media puts into identifying topics most interesting to its audience. Consistent with this argument, I find more under-reaction to company announcements more intensively covered by financial media.

Notes

[1] This excludes announcements of order imbalances and items flagged as tables.

[2] See e.g. Tetlock (2010).

21.5 REFERENCES

1. Bernard, V., and Thomas, J. (1990). Evidence that stock prices do not fully reflect the implications of current earnings for future earnings, *Journal of Accounting and Economics, 13*, 305–340.

2. Borovkova, S. (2011). News analytics for energy futures. Available at: http://ssrn.com/abstract=1719582

3. Boudoukh, J., Feldman, R., Kogan, S. and Richardson, M. (2013). Which news moves stock prices? A textual analysis. NBER Working Paper.

4. Chan, W.S. (2003). Stock price reactions to news and no-news: drift and reversal after headlines. *Journal of Financial Economics, 70*, 223–260.

5. Dzieliński, M. (2012). The role of information intermediaries in financial markets. *Swedish House of Finance Research Paper,* (13-02).

6. Engelberg, J. (2008). Costly information processing: Evidence from earnings announcements. In *AFA 2009 San Francisco Meetings Paper.*

7. Hafez, P. and Xie, J. (2013). Intraday forex trading based on sentiment inflection points. RavenPack Data Science Paper.

8. Heston, S.L. and Sinha, N. (2014). News versus sentiment. Available at: http://ssrn.com/abstract=2311310

9. Ikenberry, D., Lakonishok, J. and Vermaelencq, T. (1995). Market underreaction to open market share repurchases. *Journal of Financial Economics, 39,* 181–208.

10. Jegadeesh, N. and Wu, D. (2013). Word power: a new approach for content analysis. *Journal of Financial Economics, 110,* 712–729.

11. Loughran, T. and McDonald, B. (2011). When is a liability not a liability? Textual analysis, dictionaries and 10-Ks. *Journal of Finance, 66,* 35–65.

12. Sinha, N. (2010) Underreaction to news in the US stock market. Available at: http://ssrn.com/abstract=1572614

13. Solomon, D.H. (2012). Selective publicity and stock prices. *Journal of Finance, 67,* 599–637.

14. Tetlock, P. (2010). Does public financial news resolve asymmetric information? *Review of Financial Studies, 23,* 3520–3557.

15. Tetlock, P., Saar-Tsechansky, M. and Macskassy, S. (2008). More than words: quantifying language to measure firms' fundamentals. *Journal of Finance, 63,* 1437– 1467.

CHAPTER 22

Automated Analysis of News to Compute Market Sentiment: its impact on liquidity and trading

Gautam Mitra, *Visiting Professor, UCL and CEO, OptiRisk Systems*

Dan diBartolomeo, *CEO Northfield Information Services, USA*

Ashok Banerjee, *Professor and Chairperson*

Financial Research and Trading Lab, IIM Calcutta, India

Xiang Yu, *Researcher, OptiRisk Systems*

ABSTRACT

Computer trading in financial markets is a rapidly developing field with a growing number of applications. Automated analysis of news and computation of market sentiment is a related applied research topic which impinges on the methods and models deployed in the former. In this review we have first explored the asset classes which are best suited for computer trading. We present in a summary form the essential aspects of market microstructure and the process of price formation as this takes place in trading. We critically analye the role of different classes of traders and categorise alternative types of automated trading. We introduce alternative measures of liquidity which have been developed in the context of bid-ask of price quotation and explore its connection to market microstructure and trading. We review the technology and the prevalent methods for news sentiment analysis whereby qualitative textual news data is turned into market sentiment. The impact of news on liquidity and automated trading is critically examined. Finally we explore the interaction between manual and automated trading.

22.1 INTRODUCTION

The neoclassical finance theory embraced the efficient market hypothesis (EMH) which became its central plank. The doubts about EMH and recent surge of interest in behavioural finance (Kahneman and Tversky, 1979; Kahneman, 2002, Shefrin, 2008) not only debated and exposed the limits of EMH but also reinforced the important role of sentiment and investor psychology in market behaviour. The central tenet of EMH was that information arrival, that is, news, is rapidly discounted by rational stakeholders; yet the work of Shiller (2000) and Haiss (2010) reinforce the irrational contrarian and herd behaviour of the investors. Today the availability of sophisticated computer systems facilitating high frequency trading (Goodhart and O'Hara, 1997) as well as access to automated analysis of news feeds (Tetlock, 2007; Mitra and Mitra, 2011[a]) set the backdrop for computer automated trading which is enhanced by news. The findings of this driver review may be summarized in the following way. Computer-mediated automated trading continues to grow in many venues where equities, futures, options and foreign exchange are traded. The research and adoption of automated analysis of newsfeed for trading, fund management and risk control systems are in their early stages but gaining in momentum. The challenge for the trading and the investment community is to bring the hardware technologies, software techniques and modelling methodologies together. The challenge for the regulatory authorities is to understand the combined impact of these technologies and postulate regulations which can control volatility, improve the provision for liquidity and generally stabilize market behaviour.

Over the last forty years there have been considerable developments in the theory which explains the structure, mechanisms and operation of financial markets. The classical economic theory of price formation through supply and demand equilibrium is too simplistic and does not quite apply to the evolving financial markets (O'Hara, 1995). Leading practitioners and specialists in finance theory, Garman (1976) and Madhavan (2000) amongst others, started to develop theoretical structures with which they could explain market behaviour. Indeed the field of market microstructure came to be established in order to connect the market participants and the mechanisms by which trading takes place in this dynamic and often volatile and tempestuous financial market. The players may involve a wide range of market participants, although not all types of players are found in every mechanism (O'Hara, 1995). **Firstly**, of course, **are customers** who submit orders to buy or sell. These orders may be contingent on various outcomes or they may be direct orders to transact immediately. The exact nature of these orders may depend upon the rules of the game. **Secondly**, there **are brokers** who transmit orders for customers. Brokers do not trade for their own account, but act merely as conduits of customer orders. These customers may be retail traders or they may be other market participants such as dealers who simply wish to disguise their trading intentions. **Thirdly** there **are dealers** who do trade for their own account. In some markets dealers also facilitate customer orders and so are often known as broker/ dealers. **Fourthly**, there **are** specialists, or **market makers**. The market maker quotes price to buy or sell the asset. Since the market maker generally takes a position in the security (if only for a short time waiting for an offsetting order to arrive), the market maker also has a dealer function. In many order-driven markets, there are no designated market makers. Limit order providers provide liquidity in those markets. From a commercial perspective there are other **tertiary market participants** such as **market data feed providers** and now **news data feed providers** whose influence can no longer be ignored and indeed they play important roles in automated trading.

We are now in a situation whereby trading takes place as orders placed by human agents and by computer automated (trade) algorithms appear side by side at the same trading venues. Here we make a distinction between computer-mediated communication of orders through Electronic Communications Network (ECN) and its execution and settlement, and orders generated by computer algorithms and their subsequent processing in the above sequence (Fig 22.1.1).

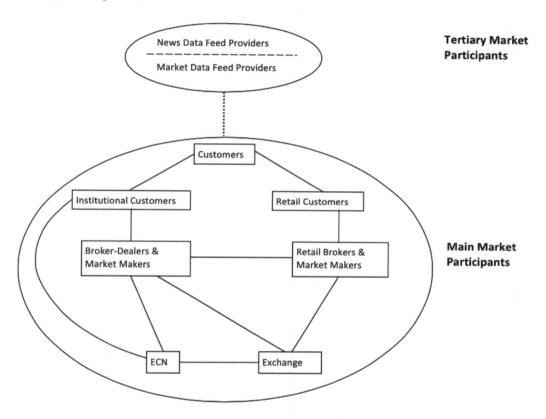

Fig 22.1.1:*Market participants and their connectivity.*

Structure of the Chapter

Automated trading has progressed and gained increasing market share in those asset classes for which the markets are highly liquid and trading volumes are large. In Section 22.2 of this chapter we consider briefly these asset classes; our review is, however, focused on equities as the automated news sentiment analysis is mostly developed for this asset class. A vast amount of literature has emerged on the topic of market microstructure and liquidity; the finance community, especially those concerned with trading, are very much involved in the development and understanding of the market mechanism which connect trading and liquidity. In Section 22.3 we provide a summary of the relevant concepts of market microstructure and liquidity and these serve as a back drop for the rest of the report. In Section 22.4 we first consider the different trader types, namely, informed, uninformed and value traders; we also analyse automated trading and break it down into five major categories. In Section 22.5 we provide an introduction and overview of news analytics in a summary form.

News analytics is an emerging discipline. It has grown by borrowing research results from other disciplines, in particular, natural language processing, text mining, pattern classification and econometric modelling. Its main focus is automating the process of understanding news presented qualitatively in the form of textual narratives appearing in newswires, social media and financial blogs and turning these into quantified market sentiments. The market sentiment needs to be measured and managed by an automated process which combines data feeds and news feeds. In turn this process automates trading and risk control decisions. In Section 22.6 we make the connection between earlier sections in respect of informed traders and news analytics. In this context, **news** is considered to be **an information event** which influences price formation, volatility of stock price as well as the liquidity of the market and that of a given stock. In short it impacts on the market microstructure. There are now a growing number of research papers (see Mitra and Mitra, 2011[a]) which connect News analytics with (i) pricing and mispricing of stocks and discovering alpha, (ii) fund management and (iii) risk control. However, very few research papers or studies are available in open literature which connect news analytics with automated trading; the two major vendors of news analytics data and market sentiment (RavenPack, 2011 and Thomson Reuters, 2011, see appendix in Mitra and Mitra 2011[b]) due to client confidentiality only reveal limited information about the use of these data sets. In Section 22.7 we consider the modelling and the information architecture by which automated analysis of news is connected to automated trading. In the final section of this review, Section 22.8, we give a summary discussion of the various findings and present our conclusions.

22.2   CONSIDERATION OF ASSET CLASSES FOR AUTOMATED TRADING

In this section we consider the criteria which make an asset class suitable for automated trading. These criteria are mainly associated with the market conditions of asset classes. Typically such market conditions include (i) sufficient market volatility and (ii) a high level of liquidity. This is so that firstly, changes in price are able to exceed transaction costs thereby making it possible to earn profits, and secondly, in order to make it feasible to move quickly in and out of positions in the market, which is a crucial criterion underpinning the strategies of high frequency trading. On top of this, the market needs to be electronically executable in order to facilitate the quick turnover of capital and harness the speed of automated trading. Currently, only spot foreign exchange, equities, options and futures markets fulfill such conditions of automated execution.

Set against these considerations, we examine the suitability of computer trading of the following asset classes: (i) Equity markets, (ii) Foreign exchange markets, (iii) Commodity markets, (iv) Fixed income markets.

To begin with, we study the trade-off between trading frequency and liquidity for the named asset classes (see Fig 22.2.1), using daily trading volume as a proxy for liquidity. It is observed that asset classes which are often traded at a frequency of less than a day tend to be accompanied with higher levels of liquidity in that market. This becomes an optimal trade-off for investors as it allows them to trade without the burden of worrying about transaction costs eating away at their profits, due to the presence of high liquidity and the ability to execute trades at favorable prices (offered by high trading frequencies). Furthermore, it can be noted that the more liquid asset classes are also those that are executable electronically and are traded on a more regular basis, supporting the capability of execution at high frequencies. In the markets today, we acknowledge that a sweeping but steady transition has occurred with the conversion of over-the-counter markets into electronic markets to keep up with the trading strategies of investors.

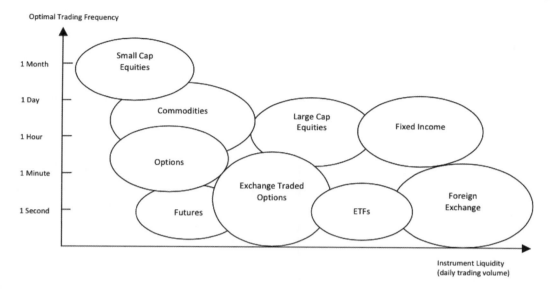

Figure 22.2.1: *The trade-off between optimal trading frequency and liquidity for various trading instruments.*

Now we assess each asset class individually, analysing the suitable properties present for computer trading.

Equity markets

This is the most favoured asset class for automated trading because of the large size and volume of the market; this is supported by the market's breadth of listed stocks. It is also popular for its diversification properties in portfolio investment with its possible positions to long and short stocks. In addition to stocks which are traded in the equity markets, the market also includes exchange-traded funds (ETFs), warrants, certificates and structured products. In particular, hedge funds are especially active in trading index futures. According to research conducted by Aite Group (2010), the asset class that is executed the most algorithmically is equities; by 2010 an estimated 50% or more of total volume of equities traded were handled by algorithms.

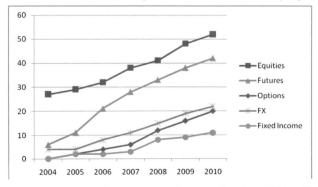

Figure 22.2.2: *Progress in adoption of algorithmic execution by asset class from 2004 to 2010. Source: Aite Group.*

Foreign exchange markets

The foreign exchange markets operate under a decentralised and unregulated mechanism whereby commercial banks, investment banks, hedge funds, proprietary trading funds, non-bank companies and non-US investment banks all have access to the inter-dealer liquidity pools. However, due to this decentralisation, the foreign exchange markets lack volume measures and the rule of "one price". This has beneficial implications for automated traders as there are substantial arbitrage opportunities that can be identified by their automated strategies. However, there are only a limited number of contracts that may be found on the exchange, restricting the variety of financial instruments available for traders in the foreign exchange market, namely foreign exchange futures and select options contracts. Over the years, there has been a swift transition from major trading in the spot foreign exchange markets to swaps.

Using the measure of liquidity as the average daily volume of each security, the foreign exchange market is ranked as the most liquid market, followed by US Treasury securities. There is no direct figure for traded volume to monitor developments in the foreign exchange market because of the decentralised structure for these markets. The main participants in this market are the large industrial banks. The financial instruments traded in foreign exchange markets include spot, forwards, swaps and futures contracts.

Commodity markets

The financial products in the commodity markets that are liquid and electronically traded are commodity futures and options, to allow viable and profitable trading strategies in automated trading. Futures contracts in commodities tend to be smaller than the futures contracts in foreign exchange.

Fixed income markets

The fixed income markets include the interest rate market and the bond market, with securities traded in the form of either a spot, a future or a swap contract. The interest rate market trades short and long term deposits, and the bond market trades publicly issued debt obligations. The fixed income feature of these markets comes from the pre-specified or fixed income that is paid to their holders, which in turn is what automated traders focus their strategies on to take advantage of short-term price deviations and make a profit.

In the interest rate futures market, liquidity is measured by the bid-ask spread. A bid-ask spread on interest rate futures is on average one-tenth of the bid-ask spread on the underlying spot interest rate. The most liquid futures contract in the interest rate market is short-term interest rate futures. Swap products are the most populous interest rate category, yet most still trade over the counter.

The bond market contains an advantageous breadth of products; however, spot bonds are still mostly transacted over the counter, which makes the market opaque. However, in the US, transparency in the bond market has improved since 2002 with the introduction of Transaction Reporting and Compliance Engine (TRACE) (Bessembinder and Maxwell, 2008). Bond futures contracts on the other hand are standardised by the exchange and are often electronic. The most liquid bond futures are associated with those bonds which are nearing their expiry dates compared to those with longer maturities (see Chapter 18 by Saeed Amen).

22.3 MARKET MICROSTRUCTURE AND LIQUIDITY

22.3.1 Market microstructure

A financial market is a place where traders assemble to trade financial instruments. Such trades take place between willing buyers and willing sellers. The market place may be a physical market or an electronic trading platform or even a telephone market. The trading rules and trading systems used by a market define its market structure. Every market has procedures for matching buyers to sellers for trades to take place. In quote-driven markets dealers participate in every trade. On the other hand, in order-driven markets, buyers and sellers trade with each other without the intermediation of dealers. Garman (1976) coined the expression "market microstructure" to study the process of market making and inventory costs. Market microstructure deals with operational details of a "trade" – the process of placement and handling of orders in the market place and their translation into trades and transaction prices. One of the most critical questions in market microstructure concerns the process by which new information is assimilated and price formation takes place. In a dealer-driven market, market makers, who stand willing to buy or sell securities on demand, provide liquidity to the market by quoting bid and ask prices. In a quote-driven market, limit orders provide liquidity. While the primary function of the market maker remains that of a supplier of immediacy, the market maker also takes an active role in price-setting, primarily with the objective of achieving a rapid inventory turnover and not accumulating significant positions on one side of the market. The implication of this model is that price may depart from expectations of value if the dealer is long or short relative to the desired (target) inventory, giving rise to transitory price movements during the day and possibly over longer periods (Madhavan, 2000). Market microstructure is concerned with how various frictions and departures from symmetric information affect the trading process (Madhavan, 2000). Microstructure challenges the relevance and validity of the random walk model.

The study of market microstructure started about four decades ago and it has attracted further attention in the past decade with the advent of computer-driven trading and availability of all trade and quote data in electronic form, leading to a new field of research called high frequency finance. Research in high frequency finance demonstrates that properties that define the behaviour of a financial market using low frequency data fail to explain the market behaviour observed in high frequency. Three events are cited (Francioni et al, 2008) as early triggers for the general interest in microstructure:

    a.   the US Securities and Exchange Commission's Institutional Investor Report of 1971;

    b.   the passage by the US Congress of the Securities Acts Amendment of 1975; and

    c.   the stock market crash of 1987

Market microstructure research typically examines the ways in which the working process of a market affects trading costs, prices, volume and trading behaviour. Madhavan (2000) classified research on microstructure into four broad categories:

    i.   price formation and price discovery;

    ii.   market structure and design issues;

    iii.   market transparency; and

    iv.   informational issues arising from the interface of market microstructure

The effect of market frictions (called microstructure noise) is generally studied by decomposing the transaction price of a security into fundamental component and noise component. Ait-Sahalia and Yu (2009) related the two components to different observable measures of stock liquidity and found that more liquid stocks have lower (microstructure) noise.

The knowledge of market systems and structure is essential for a trader to decide in **which market** to trade and **when** to trade. Such knowledge would also make it easier for a trader to assess the relative efficiency of the market and hence the arbitrage opportunities. In fact, the trading behaviour and trading costs are affected by market microstructure. We turn next to market liquidity.

22.3.2   Market liquidity

Liquidity is an important stylised fact of financial markets. Echoing the description put forward by cognoscenti practitioners, O'Hara (O'Hara 1995) introduces the concept in the following way: "liquidity, like pornography, is easily recognised but not so easily defined; we begin our analysis with a discussion of what liquidity means in an economic sense". A market is termed liquid when traders can trade without significant adverse affect on price (Harris, 2005). Liquidity refers to the ability to convert stock into cash (or vice versa) at the lowest possible transaction cost. Transaction costs include both explicit costs (e.g. brokerage, taxes) and implicit costs (e.g. bid-ask spreads, market impact costs). More specifically Black (1971) pointed out the presence of several necessary conditions for a stock market to be liquid:

a.   there are always bid-and-ask prices for the investor who wants to buy or sell small amounts of stock immediately;

b.   the difference between the bid and ask prices (the spread) is always small;

c.   an investor who is buying or selling a large amount of stock, in the absence of special information, can expect to do so over a long period of time, at a price not very different, on average, from the current market price; and

d.   an investor can buy or sell a large block of stock immediately, but at a premium or discount that depends on the size of the block – the larger the block, the larger the premium or discount.

Liquidity is easy to define but very difficult to measure. The various liquidity measures fall into two broad categories: trade-based measures and order-based measures (Aitken and Comerton-Forde, 2003). Trade-based measures include trading value, trading volume, trading frequency and the turnover ratio. These measures are mostly ex-post measures. Order-driven measures are *tightness/width* (bid-ask spread), *depth* (ability of the market to process large volumes of trade without affecting current market price), and *resilience* (how long the market will take to return to its "normal" level after absorbing a large order). A commonly used measure of market depth is called Kyle's Lambda (Kyle, 1985):

$$\lambda = \frac{r_t}{NOF_t}$$

where r_t is the asset return and NOF_t is the net order flow over time. The parameter λ can be obtained by regressing asset return on net order flow. Another measure of market depth is the Hui-Heubel liquidity ratio (Hui and Heubel, 1984).

Resilience refers to the speed at which the price fluctuations resulting from trades are dissipated. Market-efficient coefficient (MEC) (Hasbrouck and Schwartz, 1988) uses the second moment of price movement to explain the effect of information impact on the market. If an asset is resilient, the asset price should have a more continuous movement and thus low volatility caused by trading. Market-efficient coefficient compares the short term volatility with its long term counterpart. Formally:

$$MEC = \frac{Var(R_{long})}{T * Var(R_{short})}$$

where T is the number of short periods in each long period. A resilient asset should have a MEC ratio close to 1.

Literature also highlights another aspect of liquidity: *immediacy* - the speed at which trades can be arranged at a given cost. Illiquidity can be measured by the cost of immediate execution (Amihud and Mendelson, 1986). Thus a natural measure of illiquidity is the spread between the bid and the ask prices. Later, Amihud (2002) modified the definition of illiquidity. The now-famous illiquidity measure is the daily ratio of absolute stock return to its dollar volume averaged over some period:

$$ILLIQ_{iy} = \frac{1}{D_{iy}} \sum_{t=1}^{D_{iy}} \frac{|R_{iyd}|}{VOLD_{iyd}}$$

where R_{iyd} is the return on stock i on day d of year y and $VOLD_{iyd}$ is the respective daily volume in dollars. D_{iy} is the number of days for which data are available for stock i in year y.

The most popular indicator of liquidity is the bid-ask spread. Liquid stocks would have low bid-ask spread. The observed (traded) price of a stock (P_t) can be expressed as below:

$$P_t = P_t^* + \varepsilon_t$$

where P_t^* is the true (unobserved) price of the stock. The popular way to estimate the true price is to take the mid-point of the bid-ask spread (called "mid-quote"). The bid-ask spread denotes one of the important costs of trading. It is the cost of immediacy. For a fuller list of liquidity measures and examples adopting these measures in the Indian and UK markets, see Mitra et al. (2013).

The vast literature on liquidity studies the relationships of liquidity and the cost of liquidity with various stock performance measures, trading mechanisms, order-trader types and asset pricing. Acharya and Pederson (2005) present a simple theoretical model (liquidity-adjusted capital asset pricing model - LCAPM) that helps explain how liquidity risk and commonality in liquidity affect asset prices. The concept of commonality of liquidity was highlighted by Chordia et al. (2000) when the authors stated that liquidity is not just a stock-specific attribute given the evidence that the individual liquidity measures, like quoted spreads, quoted depth and effective spreads, co-move with each other. Later Hasbrouck and Seppi (2001) examined the extent and role of cross-firm common factors in returns, order flows and market liquidity, using the analysis of the 30 Dow Jones stocks.

Asset prices are also affected by the activities and interactions of informed traders and noise traders. Informed traders make trading decisions based on exogenous information and the true value of the asset. Noise traders do not rely on fundamental information to make any trade decision (Black, 1986). Their trade decisions are purely based on market movements. Thus noise traders are called trend followers.

22.4   CATEGORISATION OF TRADING ACTIVITIES

22.4.1   Trader types

Harris (1998) identifies three types of traders
   i.   liquidity traders, also known as inventory traders (O'Hara 1995) or uninformed traders
   ii.   informed traders and
   iii.   value-motivated traders.

The inventory traders are instrumental in providing liquidity; they make margins by simply keeping an inventory of stocks for the purpose of market making and making very small gains using limit orders through moving in and out of positions many times intra-day. Since the overall effect is to make trading in the stock easier (less friction) they are also known as liquidity providers. These traders do not make use of any exogenous information about the stock other than its trading price and order volume. The informed traders in contrast assimilate all available information about a given stock and thereby reach some certainty about the market price of the stock. Such information may be acquired by subscription to (or purchased from) news sources; typically FT, Bloomberg, Dow Jones or Reuters. They might have access to superior predictive analysis which enhances their information base. Value traders also apply predictive analytic models and use information to identify inefficiencies and mispricing of stocks in the market; this in turn provides them with buying or short selling opportunities. We note that the last two categories of traders make use of the value of information; such information is often extracted from anticipated announcements about the stock and is used in their predictive pricing models.

22.4.2   Automated trading

Automated trading in financial markets falls roughly into five categories:

   i.   Crossing Transactions
   ii.   Algorithmic Executions
   iii.   Statistical Arbitrage
   iv.   Electronic Liquidity Provision
   v.   Predatory Trading

Our first category, "crossing transactions" is the situation where a financial market participant has decided to enter into a trade and seeks a counterparty to be the other side of the trade, without exposing the existence of the order to the general population of market participants. For example, an investor might choose to purchase

100,000 shares of stock X through a crossing network (e.g. POSIT) at today's exchange closing price. If there are other participants who wish to sell stock X at today's exchange closing price, the crossing network matches the buyers and sellers so as to maximise the amount of the security transacted. The advantage of crossing is that since both sides of the transaction have agreed in advance on an acceptable price which is either specified or formulaic in nature, the impact of the transactions on market prices is minimised. Crossing networks are used across various asset classes including less liquid instruments such as corporate bonds.

It should be noted that our four remaining categories of automated trading are often collectively referred to as "high frequency" trading. The second category of automated trading is "algorithmic execution". If a market participant wishes to exchange 1000 GBP for Euros, or buy 100 shares of a popular stock, modern financial markets are liquid enough that such an order can be executed instantaneously. On the other hand, if a market participant wishes to execute a very large order such as five million shares of particular equity Y there is almost zero probability that there exists a counterparty coincidentally wishing to sell five million shares of Y at the exact same moment, or even within a very short time window. One way of executing such a large order would be a principle bid trade with an investment bank, but such liquidity provision often comes at a high price. The alternative is an "algorithmic execution" where a large "parent" order is broken into many small "child" orders to be executed separately over several hours or even several days. In the case of our hypothetical five million share order, we might choose to purchase the shares over three trading days, breaking the large order into a large number of small orders (r.g. 200 shares on average) that would be executed throughout the three-day period. Numerous analytical algorithms exist that can adjust the sizes of, and time between, child orders to reflect changes in the asset price, general market conditions or the underlying investment strategy. Note that like crossing, automated execution is merely a process to implement a *known transaction* whose nature and timing has been decided by a completely external process. However, this class of "algorithmic execution" will benefit from the inclusion of news analytics and predictive analysis of liquidity.

Our third category of automated trading is "statistical arbitrage". Unlike our first two categories, statistical arbitrage trading is based on *automation of the investment decision process*. A simple example of statistical arbitrage is "pairs trading" (Gatev, Goetzmann and Rouwenhorst, 2006). Let us assume we identify the relationship that "Shares of stock X trade at twice the price of shares of stock Z, plus or minus ten percent". If the price relation between X and Z goes outside the ten percent band, we would *automatically* buy one security and short sell the other accordingly. If we expand the set of assets that are eligible for trading to dozens or hundreds, and simultaneously increase the complexity of the decision rules and update our metrics of market conditions on a real-time basis, we have a modern statistical arbitrage strategy. The most obvious next step in improving our hypothetical pairs trade would be insert a step in the process that automatically checks for news reports that would indicate that the change in the monitored price relationship had occurred as a result of a clear fundamental cause, as opposed to random price movements such that we would expect the price relationship to revert to historic norms. Pairs trading may also benefit by taking into consideration market sentiment as determined by news.

The fourth form of automated trading is electronic liquidity provision. This form of automated trading is really a direct descendent of traditional over-the-counter market making, where a financial entity has no particular views on which securities are overpriced or underpriced. The electronic liquidity provider is *automatically* willing to buy or sell any security within its eligible universe at some spread away from the current market price upon counterparty request. Electronic liquidity providers differ from traditional market makers in that they often do not openly identify the set of assets in which they will trade. In addition, they will often place limit orders away from the market price for many thousands of securities simultaneously, and engage in millions of small transactions per trading day. Under the regulatory schemes of most countries such liquidity providers are treated as normal market participants, and hence are not subject to regulations or exchange rules that often govern market making activities. Many institutional investors believe that due to the lack of regulation, automated liquidity providers may simply withdraw from the market during crises, reducing liquidity at critical moments.

The final form of automated trading we address is "predatory trading". In such activities, a financial entity typically places thousands of simultaneous orders into a market while expecting to actually execute only a tiny fraction of the orders. This "place and cancel" process has two purposes. The first is an information gathering process. By observing which orders execute, the predatory trader expects to gain knowledge of the trading intentions of larger market participants such as institutional asset managers. Such asymmetric information can then be used to advantage in the placement of subsequent trades. A second and even more ambitious form of predatory trading is to place orders so as to artificially create abnormal trading volume or price trends in a particular security so as to purposefully mislead other traders and thereby gain advantage. Under the regulatory schemes of many countries there are general prohibitions against "market manipulation", but little if any action has been taken against predatory trading on this basis.

Some practitioners believe (Arnuk and Saluzzi, 2008) automated trading puts the manual trading of retail investors as well as institutional investors at a considerable disadvantage from the perspective of price discovery and liquidity. A number of financial analytics/consulting companies, typically Quantitative Services Group LLC, Greenwich Associates, Themis Trading LLC, have produced useful white papers on this topic (particular mention should be made of insightful white papers posted by Arnuk and Saluzzi (2008) and (2009)).

22.5 AUTOMATED NEWS ANALYSIS AND MARKET SENTIMENT

22.5.1 Introduction and overview

A short review of news analytics focusing on its applications in finance is given in this section; it is an abridged version of the review chapter in the handbook compiled by one of the authors (Mitra and Mitra, 2011[a]). In particular, we review the multiple facets of current research and some of the major applications.

It is widely recognised that news plays a key role in financial markets. The sources and volumes of news continue to grow. New technologies that enable automatic or semi-automatic news collection, extraction, aggregation and categorisation are emerging. Further machine-learning techniques are used to process the textual input of news stories to determine quantitative sentiment scores. We consider the various types of news available and how these are processed to form inputs to financial models. We consider applications of news, for prediction of abnormal returns, for trading strategies, for diagnostic applications as well as the use of news for risk control. There is a strong yet complex relationship between market sentiment and news. The arrival of news continually updates an investor's understanding and knowledge of the market and influences investor sentiment. There is a growing body of research literature that argues that media influences investor sentiment, hence asset prices, asset price volatility and risk (Tetlock, 2007; Da, Engleberg and Gao, 2009; diBartolomeo and Warrick, 2005; Barber and Odean; Dzielinski, Rieger and Talpsepp; Mitra, Mitra and diBartolomeo, 2009, (Chapter 7, Chapter 11, Chapter 13, Mitra and Mitra 2011ᵃ)). Traders and other market participants digest news rapidly, revising and rebalancing their asset positions accordingly. Most traders have access to newswires at their desks. As markets react rapidly to news, effective models which incorporate news data are highly sought after. This is not only for trading and fund management, but also for risk control. Major news events can have a significant impact on the market environment and investor sentiment, resulting in rapid changes to the risk structure and risk characteristics of traded assets. Though the relevance of news is widely acknowledged, how to incorporate this effectively, in quantitative models and more generally within the investment decision-making process, is a very open question. In considering how news impacts on markets, Barber and Odean note "significant news will often affect investors' beliefs and portfolio goals heterogeneously, resulting in more investors trading than is usual" (high trading volume). It is well known that volume increases on days with information releases (Bamber, Barron and Stober, 1997). It is natural to expect that the application of these news data will lead to improved analysis (such as predictions of returns and volatility). However, extracting this information in a form that can be applied to the investment decision-making process is extremely challenging. News has always been a key source of investment information. The volumes and sources of news are growing rapidly. In increasingly competitive markets, investors and traders need to select and analyse the relevant news, from the vast amounts available to them, in order to make "good" and timely decisions. A human's (or even a group of humans') ability to process this news is limited. As computational capacity grows, technologies are emerging which allow us to extract, aggregate and categorise large volumes of news effectively. Such technology might be applied for quantitative model construction for both high-frequency trading and low-frequency fund rebalancing. Automated news analysis can form a key component driving algorithmic trading desks' strategies and execution, and the traders who use this technology can shorten the time it takes them to react to "breaking" news stories (that is, reduce latency times).

News Analytics (NA) technology can also be used to aid traditional non-quantitative fund managers in monitoring the market sentiment for particular stocks, companies, brands and sectors. These technologies are deployed to automate filtering, monitoring and aggregation of news, in addition to helping free managers from the minutiae of repetitive analysis, such that they are able to better target their reading and research. NA technologies also reduce the burden of routine monitoring for fundamental managers. The basic idea behind these NA technologies is to automate human thinking and reasoning. Traders, speculators and private investors anticipate the direction of asset returns as well as the size and the level of uncertainty (volatility) before making an investment decision. They carefully read recent economic and financial news to gain a picture of the current situation. Using their knowledge of how markets behaved in the past in different situations, people will implicitly match the current situation with those situations in the past most similar to the current one. News analytics seeks to introduce technology to automate or semi-automate this approach. By automating the judgement process, the human decision maker can act on a larger, hence more diversified, collection of assets. These decisions are also taken more promptly (reducing latency). Automation or semi-automation of the human judgement process widens the limits of the investment process. Leinweber (2009) refers to this process as intelligence amplification (IA). As shown in Figure 5.1 news data are an additional source of information that can be harnessed to enhance (traditional) investment analysis. Yet it is important to recognise that NA in finance is a multi-disciplinary field which draws on financial economics, financial engineering, behavioural finance and artificial intelligence (in particular, natural language processing).

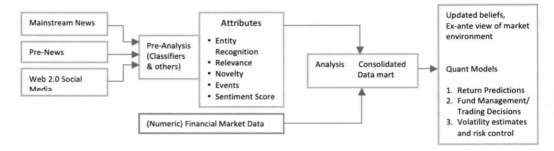

Figure 22.5.1: *An outline of information flow and modelling architecture*

22.5.2 News data sources

In this section we consider the different sources of news and information flows which can be applied for updating (quantitative) investor beliefs and knowledge. Leinweber (2009) distinguishes the following broad classifications of news (informational flows).

1. **News** This refers to mainstream media and comprises the news stories produced by reputable sources. These are broadcast via newspapers, radio and television. They are also delivered to traders' desks on newswire services. Online versions of newspapers are also progressively growing in volume and number.

2. **Pre-news** This refers to the source data that reporters research before they write news articles. It comes from primary information sources such as Securities and Exchange Commission reports and filings, court documents and government agencies. It also includes scheduled announcements such as macroeconomic news, industry statistics, company earnings reports and other corporate news.

3. **Web 2.0 and social media** These are blogs and websites that broadcast "news" and are less reputable than news and pre-news sources. The quality of these varies significantly. Some may be blogs associated with highly reputable news providers and reporters (for example, the blog of BBC's Robert Peston). At the other end of the scale some blogs may lack any substance and may be entirely fuelled by rumour. Social media websites fall at the lowest end of the reputation scale. Barriers to entry are extremely low and the ability to publish "information" easy. These can be dangerously inaccurate sources of information. At a minimum they may help us identify future volatility. Individual investors pay relatively more attention to the second two sources of news than institutional investors. Information from the web may be less reliable than mainstream news. However, there may be "collective intelligence" information to be gleaned. That is, if a large group of people have no ulterior motives, then their collective opinion may be useful (Leinweber, 2009, Ch. 10).

There are services which facilitate retrieval of news data from the web. For example, Google Trends is a free but limited service which provides an historical weekly time series of the popularity of any given search term. This search engine reports the proportion of positive, negative and neutral stories returned for a given search. In 1996, the Electronic Data Gathering, Analysis and Retrieval (EDGAR) system was introduced by the Securities and Exchange Commission (SEC) providing basic access to filings via the web (see http://www.sec.gov/edgar/searchedgar/companysearch.html). It covers all publicly traded companies in the US and is acknowledged to be a useful source of pre-news. Premium access gave tools for analysis of filing information and priority earlier access to the data. In 2002 filing information was released to the public in real time. Filings remain unstructured text files without semantic web and XML output, though the SEC are in the process of upgrading their information dissemination. High-end resellers electronically dissect and sell on relevant component parts of filings. Managers are obliged to disclose a significant amount of information about a company via SEC filings. This information is naturally valuable to investors. Leinweber introduces the term "molecular search: the idea of looking for patterns and changes in groups of documents." Such analysis/information is scrutinised by researchers/analysts to identify unusual corporate activity and potential investment opportunities. However, mining the large volume of filings to find relationships is challenging. Engleberg and Sankaraguruswamy (2007) note the EDGAR database has 605 different forms and there were 4,249,586 filings between 1994 and 2006. Connotate provides services which allow customised automated collection of SEC filing information for customers (fund managers and traders). Engleberg and Sankaraguruswamy (2007) consider how to use a web crawler to mine SEC filing information through EDGAR.

Financial news can be split into regular synchronous, that is, anticipated announcements (scheduled or expected news) and event-driven asynchronous news items (unscheduled or unexpected news). Mainstream news, rumours and social media normally arrive asynchronously in an unstructured textual form. A substantial portion of pre-news arrives at pre-scheduled times and generally in a structured form. Scheduled (news) announcements often have a well-defined numerical and textual content and may be classified as structured data. These include macroeconomic announcements and earnings announcements. Macroeconomic news, particularly economic indicators from the major economies, is widely used in automated trading. It has an impact in the largest and most liquid markets, such as foreign exchange, government debt and futures markets. Firms often execute large and rapid trading strategies. These news events are normally well documented, thus thorough back-testing of strategies is feasible. Since indicators are released on a precise schedule, market participants can be well prepared to deal with them. These strategies often lead to firms fighting to be first to the market; speed and accuracy are the major determinants of success. However, the technology requirements to capitalise on events are substantial. Content publishers often specialise in a few data items, hence trading firms often multisource their data. Thomson Reuters, Dow Jones and Bloomberg are a few leading content service providers in this space. Earnings are a key driving force behind stock prices. Scheduled earnings announcement information is also widely anticipated and used within trading strategies. The pace of response to announcements has accelerated greatly in recent years (see Leinweber, 2009, pp. 104–105). Wall Street Horizon and Media Sentiment (see Munz, 2010) provide services in this space. These technologies allow traders to respond quickly and effectively to earnings announcements.

Event-driven asynchronous news streams in unexpectedly over time. These news items usually arrive as textual, unstructured, qualitative data. They are characterised as being non-numeric and difficult to process quickly and quantitatively. Unlike analysis based on quantified market data, textual news data contain information about the effect of an event and the possible causes of an event. However, in order to be applied in trading systems and quantitative models they need to be converted to a quantitative input time-series. This could be a simple binary series where the occurrence of a particular event or the publication of a news article about a particular topic is indicated by a one and the absence of the event by a zero. Alternatively, we can try to quantify other aspects of news over time. For example, we could measure news flow (volume of news) or we could determine scores (measures) based on the language sentiment of text or determine scores (measures) based on the market's response to particular language. It is important to have access to historical data for effective model development and back testing. Commercial news data vendors normally provide large historical archives for this purpose. The details of historic news data for global equities provided by RavenPack and Thomson Reuters NewsScope are summarised in Mitra and Mitra (2011[b]).

22.5.3 Pre-analysis of news data: creating meta data

Collecting, cleaning and analysing news data is challenging. Major news providers collect and translate headlines and text from a wide range of worldwide sources. For example, the Factiva database provided by Dow Jones holds data from 400 sources ranging from electronic newswires to newspapers and magazines.

We note there are differences in the volume of news data available for different companies. Larger companies (with more liquid stock) tend to have higher news coverage/news flow. Moniz, Brar and Davis (2009) observe that the top quintile accounts for 40% of all news articles and the bottom quintile for only 5%. Cahan, Jussa and Luo (2009) also find news coverage is higher for larger cap companies.

Classification of news items is important for meaningful analysis. Major newswire providers tag incoming news stories. A reporter entering a story on to the news systems will often manually tag it with relevant codes. Further, machine-learning algorithms may also be applied to identify relevant tags for a story. These tags turn the unstructured stories into a basic machine readable form. The tags are often stored in XML format. They reveal the story's topic areas and other important metadata. For example, they may include information about which company a story is about. Tagged stories held by major newswire providers are also accurately time-stamped. The SEC is pushing to have companies file their reports using XBRL (eXtensible Business Reporting Language). Rich Site Summary (RSS) feeds (an XML format for web content) allow customised, automated analysis of news events from multiple online sources. Tagged news stories provide us with hundreds of different types of events, so that we can use these stories effectively. We need to distinguish what types of news are relevant for a given model (application). Further, the market may react differently to different types of news. For example, Moniz, Brar and Davis (2009) find the market seems to react more strongly to corporate earnings-related news than corporate strategic news. They postulate that it is harder to quantify and incorporate strategic news into valuation models, hence it is harder for the market to react appropriately to such news.

Machine-readable XML news feeds can turn news events into usable trading signals since they can be used relatively easily to back-test and execute event study-based strategies (see Kothari and Warner, 2005; Campbell, Lo and MacKinlay, 1996 for in-depth reviews of event study methodology). Leinweber (Chapter 6, Mitra and Mitra 2011[a]) uses Thomson Reuters tagged news data to investigate several news-based event strategies. Elementised news feeds mean the variety of event data available is increasing significantly. News providers also provide archives of historic tagged news which can be used for back-testing and strategy validation. News event algorithmic trading is reported to be gaining acceptance in industry (Schmerken, 2006).

To apply news effectively in asset management and trading decisions we need to be able to identify news which is both relevant and current. This is particularly true for intraday applications, where algorithms need to respond quickly to accurate information. We need to be able to identify an "information event"; that is, we need to be able to distinguish those stories which are reporting on old news (previously reported stories) from genuinely "new" news. As would be expected, Moniz, Brar and Davis (2009) find markets react strongly when "new" news is released. Tetlock, Saar-Tsechansky and Macskassy (2008) undertake an event study which illustrates the impact of news on cumulative abnormal returns (CARs).

Types of Score (meta data)

An array of information is covered in news analysis data, for example, date, time, novelty of news and sentiment scores. For a detailed description of the possible data fields and the types of scores covered, see Chapter 1.

22.6 NEWS ANALYTICS AND MARKET SENTIMENT: IMPACT ON LIQUIDITY

News influences and formulates sentiment; sentiments move markets. The crash of 1987 was one such sentiment forming event in the recent past. From 2003, equity markets grew steadily, but at the end of 2007 they started to decline and there was a dip in the sentiment. Over January 2008 market sentiment deteriorated further, driven by a few key events. In the US, George Bush announced a stimulus plan for the economy and the Federal Reserve made cuts in the interest rate by 75 basis points, the largest since 1984. In Europe, Societe Generale was hit by the scandal of the rogue trader Jerome Kerviel. In September-October 2008 further events in the finance sector impacted on the market: Lehman Brothers filed for bankruptcy, Bank of America announced the purchase of Merrill Lynch, the Federal Reserve announced the rescue of AIG, under the guidance of the UK Government, Lloyds Bank took over HBOS. These news events had a devastating **impact on market liquidity**.

22.6.1 Market sentiment influences: price, volatility, liquidity

Financial markets are characterised by two leading measures: (i) stock price returns and (ii) stock price volatility. In the context of trading, a third aspect, namely (iii) liquidity is seen to be equally important (Yu, 2014). There is a strong relationship between news flows and volatility. To the extent that a broad market or a particular security becomes more volatile, it can be expected that liquidity providers will demand greater compensation for risk by widening bid/ask spreads. This is confirmed in a research report by Gross-Klussmann et al. (2011) who conclude that by capturing dynamics and cross-dependencies in the vector autoregressive modelling framework they find the strongest effect in volatility and cumulative trading volumes. Bid-ask spreads, trade sizes and market depth may not directly react to news; but they do so indirectly through the cross dependencies to volume and volatility, and the resulting spillover effects. There is a strong distinction between "news" and "announcements" in terms of liquidity. If information comes to the financial markets as an "announcement" (e.g. the scheduled publication of an economic statistic, or a company's period results), market participants will have anticipated the announcement and formulated action plans conditional on the revealed content. Since everyone is prepared for the announcement, market participants can act quickly and liquidity is maintained. On the other hand, if a "news" item (fully unanticipated) is revealed to financial market participants, they will need some time to assess the meaning of the announcement and formulate appropriate actions. During such periods of contemplation, traders are unwilling to trade and liquidity dries up. If the news item is of extreme importance (e.g. 9/11), it may take several days for conditions to return to normal. Regulators and exchanges respond to such liquidity "holes" by suspending trading for short periods in particular securities or markets. There is a vast literature on the impact of anticipated earnings announcements; in contrast there are very few studies on the intraday firm-specific news. Berry and Howe (1994) in a study link intraday market activity to an aggregated news flow measure, that is, the number of news items. Kalev et al. (2004) and Kalev and Duong (2011) report a positive relationship between the arrival of intraday news and the volatility of a given stock, the market index and the index futures respectively. Mitchell and Mullherin (1994) and Ranaldo (2008) consider the impact of news on intraday trading activities.

22.6.2 News enhanced predictive analytics models

Mitra and Mitra (2011[a]) reports studies which cover stock returns and volatility in response to news; however, none of these studies are in the context of high frequency or consider the impact on liquidity. We therefore turn to the study by Gross-Klussmann et al. (2011) as they consider the impact of intra-day news flow. These authors consider an interesting research problem: "Are there significant and theory-consistent market reactions in high-frequency returns, volatility and liquidity to the intra-day news flow?" The authors set out to answer this question by applying a predictive analysis model (in this case an event study model) and use the news data feed provided by Thomson Reuters News analytics sentiment engine. These authors conclude that the release of a news item significantly increases bid-ask spreads but does not necessarily affect market depth. Hence liquidity suppliers predominantly react to news by revising quotes and not by order volumes. This is well supported by asymmetric information based market microstructure theory (Easley and O'Hara, 1992) where specialists try to overcompensate for possible information asymmetries. Although there are no designated market makers in an electronic market, the underlying mechanism is similar to that of a non-electronic market: liquidity suppliers reduce their order aggressiveness in order to avoid being picked off (that is, selected adversely) by better informed traders. For earnings announcements, such effects are also reported by Krinsky and Lee (1996). Overall, the authors find that the dynamic analysis strongly confirms the unconditional effects discussed above, and that volatility and trading volume are most sensitive to news arrival.

We generalise this approach and propose a modelling framework that closely follows the paradigm of event studies and is shown in Figure 22.6.1.

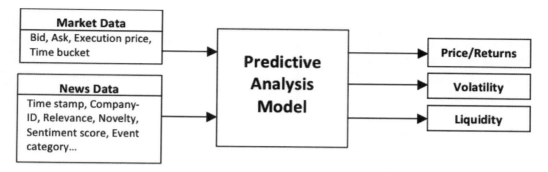

Figure 22.6.1: *Architecture of predictive analysis model*

The **input** to the Predictive analytics model is made up of

   i.   **Market data** (bid, ask, execution price , time bucket)

  ii.   **News data** suitably pre-analysed and turned into **meta data**

        (time stamp, company-ID, relevance, novelty, sentiment score , event category...)

The **output** is designed to determine **state** of the stock/market (returns, volatility, liquidity).

22.7 NEWS ANALYTICS AND ITS APPLICATION TO TRADING

The automated sentiment scores (computed by using natural language processing, text mining and AI classifiers, see Section 22.5) are finding applications in investment decisions and trading. In this section we consider the growing influence of news analytics on investment management and manual trading as well as automated, that is, computer-mediated algorithmic trading. In the discussions and conclusions presented in Section 22.8 we provide a critical evaluation of the issues surrounding the interaction between manual and automated trading.

22.7.1 Trading by institutional investors and retail investors

Barber and Odean in their landmark paper (Barber and Odean, 2011) report on the buying behaviour of individual (retail) investors as well as those of professional money managers. The study is based on substantial data (78,000 households' investment activities between 1991 and 1996) collected from a leading brokerage house. The authors observe that retail investors show a propensity to buy attention-grabbing stocks (impact of news stories). They conclude that this is more driven by the emotional behaviour of the investor than based on a rational analysis of investment opportunities. By and large such trades lead to losses for the retail investors. The institutional investors in contrast tend to make better use of information (flowing from news), in particular they use predictive analysis tools thus enhancing their fundamental analysis. Leinweber and Sisk (2011) describe a study in which they use pure news signals as indicators for buy signals. Through portfolio simulation of test data over the period 2006–2009 they find evidence of usable alpha using news analytics. The quantitative research team at Macquarie Securities (see Moniz et al, 2011) report on an empirical study where they show how news flow can be utilised in existing momentum strategies by updating earnings forecast ahead of analysts' revisions after news announcements. Cahan et al. (2010), who use Thomson Reuters news data, report similar results; these studies have many similarities given that Cahan and the team moved from Macquarie securities to Deutsche Bank in 2009. Macqauarie securities and Deutsche Bank offer these news enhanced quant analysis services to their institutional clients. Other examples of applying NA in investment management decisions such as identifying sentiment reversal of stocks (see Kittrell, 2011) are to be found in Mitra and Mitra (2011ª).

22.7.2   News analytics applied to automated trading

The topic of automated algorithmic trading is treated as a "dark art" by its practitioners, that is, hedge funds and proprietary trading desks. As we stated earlier (Section 22.1), even the content vendors are unwilling to reveal information about organisations which utilise NA in algorithmic trading. Given a trade order, the execution of this by a strategy such as volume-weighted average price (VWAP) is designed to minimise the market impact (see Kissell and Glantz, 2003). Almgren and Chriss (2000) in a landmark paper discuss the concept and the model for optimal execution strategies. In these models for execution the implicit assumption is that for a stock there is no price spike which often follows some anticipated news (announcements) or an unexpected news event. Aldridge (2010) in her book introduces the following categories of automated arbitrage trading strategies: event arbitrage and statistical arbitrage including liquidity arbitrage. Of these the first: event arbitrage is based on the response of the market to an information event, that is, a macro-economic announcement or a strategic news release. Event arbitrage strategies follow a three-stage development process:

i.   identification of the dates and times of past events in historical data

ii.   computation of historical price changes at desired frequencies pertaining to securities of interest and the events identified in step-1 above

iii. estimation of expected price responses based on historical price behaviour surrounding past events

The event arbitrage strategy is based on events surrounding news release about economic activity, market disruption or anything else that impacts on the market price. A tenet of efficient market hypothesis is that price adjusts to new information as soon as this becomes available. In practice market participants form expectations well ahead of the release of the announcements and the associated figures. For the FX market the study by Almeida, Goodhart and Payne (1998) find that for USD/DEM, new announcements pertaining to the US employment and trade balance were significant predictors of the exchange rates. Taking into consideration the above remarks we have encapsulated the information flow and computational modelling architecture for news enhanced algorithmic trading in Figure 22.7.1.

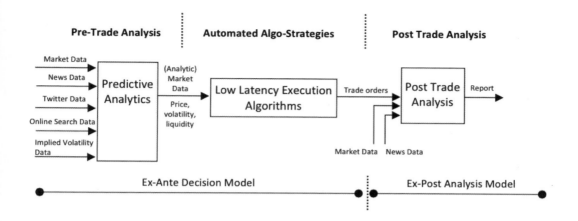

Figure 22.7.1: *Information flow and computational architecture for automated trading*

In the pre-trade analysis the predictive analytics tool brings together and consolidates market data feed and the news data feed. The output of the model goes into automated algorithm trading tools; these are normally low latency automatic trading algorithms (algos). Finally the outputs of these algorithms take the form of automatic execution orders. Whereas pre-trade analysis and the algos constitute ex-ante automatic decision tool, the results are evaluated using a paradigm of ex-post analysis. Finally, we note that Brown (2011) suggests use of news analytics for "circuit breakers and wolf detection" in automated trading strategies, thereby enhancing the robustness and reliability of such systems.

22.8 DISCUSSION

As the saying goes, the genie is out of the bottle and cannot be put back. Automated trading is here to stay and increasingly dominate the financial markets; this can be seen from the trends illustrated in Figure 22.2.2. In this report we first examined the asset classes which are suitable for automated trading and conclude these to be primarily equity, including ETFs and index futures, FX and to a lesser extent commodities and fixed income instruments. We then considered in a summary form market microstructure and liquidity and their role in price formation. We examined the role of different market participants in trading and types of automated trading activities. Set against this backdrop, we explored how automated analysis of informational contents of anticipated news events as well as unanticipated extraordinary news events impact on both "manual" and automated trading activities. Automated algorithmic trading and news analytics alike are recently developed technologies. The interactions of these technologies are uncharted and rely upon artificial intelligence, information and communication technologies as well as behavioural finance. Computer-mediated automated trading continues to grow in many venues where equities, futures, options and foreign exchange are traded. The research and adoption of automated analysis of newsfeed for trading leads to the enhancement of performance, yet should there be a positive feedback effect due to inclusion of news sentiment, this will lead to increase in market instablility; thus uncontrolled automated trading may become one of the drivers of extreme behaviour such as "flash crashes". The challenge for the regulatory authorities is to understand the combined impact of these technologies and postulate regulations which can control volatility, improve the provision for liquidity and generally stabilise market behaviour.

22.9   REFERENCES

1.   Acharya, V.V. and Pedersen, L.H. (2005). Asset pricing with liquidity risk. *Journal of Financial Economics, 77(2)*, pp. 375–410.

2.   Aitken, M. and Comerton-Forde, C. (2003). How should liquidity be measured? *Pacific-Basin Finance Journal, 11*, pp. 45–59.

3.   Ait-Sahala, Y. and Yu, J. (2009). High Frequency Market Microstructure Noise Estimates and Liquidity Measures. *The Annals of Applied Statistics, 3(1)*, pp. 422–457.

4.   Aldridge, I. (2010). *High Frequency Trading: A Practical Guide to Algorithmic Strategies and Trading Systems*. John Wiley & Sons, New Jersey.

5.   Almeida, A., Goodhart, C. and Payne, R. (1998). The effect of macro-economic news on high frequency exchange rate behavior. *Journal of Financial and Quantitative Analysis, 33*, pp. 1–47.

6.   Almgren, R. and Chriss, N. (2000). Optimal Execution of Portfolio Transactions. *Journal of Risk, 12*, pp. 5–39.

7.   Amihud, Y. and Mendelson, H. (1986). Asset Pricing and the Bid-Ask Spread. *Journal of Financial Econometrics, 17*, pp. 223–249.

8.   Amihud, Y. (2002). Illiquidity and Stock returns: cross-section and time-series effects. *Journal of Financial Markets, 5*, pp. 31–56.

9.   Arnuk, S.L. and Saluzzi, J (2008). Toxic equity trading order flow on Wall Street: the real force behind the explosion in volume and volatility. Available at: http://www.thetradingmesh.com/pg/blog/Admin/read/38009/toxic-equity-trading-order-flow-on-wall-street-the-real-force-behind-the-explosion-in-volume-and-volatility-pdf

10.   Arnuk, S.L. and Saluzzi, J. (2009). Latency Arbitrage: the real power behind predatory high frequency trading. Available at: http://blog.themistrading.com/2009/12/latency-arbitragethe-real-power-behind-predatory-high-frequency-trading/

11.   Bamber, L.S., Barron, O.E. and Stober, T.L. (1997). Trading volume and different aspects of disagreement coincident with earnings announcements. *The Accounting Review, 72*, pp. 575–597.

12. Barber, B.M. and Odean, T. (2011). The behavior of individual investors. Available at SSRN: http://ssrn. com/abstract=1872211.

13. Berry, T.D. and Howe, K.M. (1994). Public information arrival. *The Journal of Finance, 49(4)*, pp. 1331–1346.

14. Bessembinder, H. and Maxwell, W. (2008). Markets: Transparency and the Corporate Bond Market. *Journal of Economic Perspectives, 22(2)*, pp. 217-234.

15. Black, F. (1986). Noise. *The Journal of Finance, 41(3)*, pp. 529-543.

16. Black, F. (1971). Towards a fully automated exchange, part I. *Financial Analysts Journal, 27*, pp. 29–34.

17. Brown, R. (2011). Incorporating News Analytics into Algorithmic Trading Strategies: Increasing the Signal-to-Noise Ratio. In G. Mitra and L. Mitra, eds., *The Handbook of News Analytics in Finance*, Chapter 14. John Wiley & Sons.

18. Cahan, R., Jussa, J. and Luo, Y. (2009). Breaking news: how to use sentiment to pick stocks. MacQuarie Research Report.

19. Cahan, R., Jussa, J. and Luo, Y. (2010). Beyond the Headlines: Using News flow to Predict Stock Returns. Deutsche Bank Quantitative Strategy Report, July 2010.

20. Campbell, J.Y., Lo, A.W. and MacKinlay, A.C. (1996). The econometrics of financial markets. In *Event Study Analysis*, Chapter 4. Princeton University Press, Princeton, NJ.

21. Chordia, T., Roll, R. and Subrahmanyam, A. (2000). Commonality in liquidity. *Journal of Financial Economics, 56(1)*, pp. 3–28.

22. Da, Z., Engleberg, J. and Gao, P. (2009). In search of attention. SSRN Paper. Available at: http://papers.ssrn. com/sol3/papers.cfm?abstract_id=1364209

23. diBartolomeo, D. and Warrick, S. (2005). Making covariance based portfolio risk models sensitive to the rate at which markets reflect new information. In J. Knight and S. Satchell, eds., *Linear Factor Models*. Elsevier Finance.

24. Dzielinski, M., Rieger, M.O. and Talpsepp, T. (2011). Volatility, asymmetry, news and private investors. In G. Mitra and L. Mitra, eds., *The Handbook of News Analytics in Finance*, Chapter 11. John Wiley & Sons.

25. Easley, D. and O'Hara, M. (1992). Time and the process of security price adjustment. *Journal of Finance, 47*, pp. 577–605.

26. Engleberg, J. and Sankaraguruswamy, S. (2007). How to gather data using a web crawler: an application using SAS to research EDGAR. SSRN Paper. Available at: http://papers.ssrn.com/sol3/papers.cfm?abstractid=1015021&r

27. Francioni, R., Hazarika, S., Reck, M. and Schwartz, R.A. (2008). Equity Market Microstructure: Taking Stock of What We Know. *Journal of Portfolio Management, 35(1)*, pp. 57.

28. Garman, M. (1976). Market Microstructure. *Journal of Financial Economics, 3*, pp. 257–275.

29. Gatev, E., Goetzmann, W.N. and Rouwenhorst, K.G. (2006). Pairs trading: Performance of a relative-value arbitrage rule. *Review of Financial Studies, 19(3)*, pp. 797-827.

30. Goodhart, C.A.E. and O'Hara, M. (1997). High Frequency Data in Financial Markets: Issues and Applications. *Journal of Empirical Finance, 4*, pp. 73–114.

31. Greenwich Associates (2009). High-frequency trading: lack of data means regulators should move slowly. Available at: http://www4.greenwich.com/WMA/greenwich_reports/show_reports/1,1624,,00.html?prodCatId=1&regionId=6&rtOrigin=S&vgnvisitor=equenqWKnpc=

32. Gross-Klussmann, A. and Hautsch, N (2011). When machines read the news: using automated text analytics to quantify high frequency news-implied market reactions. *Journal of Empirical Finance, 18*, pp. 321–340.

33. Haiss, P. (2010). Bank Herding and Incentive Systems as Catalysts for the Financial Crisis. *The IUP Journal of Behavioural Finance 7 (Nos. 1 &2)*, pp. 30–58.

34. Harris, L. (1998). Optimal dynamic order submission strategies in some stylized trading problems. *Financial Markets, Institutions & Instruments, 7(2)*, pp. 1-76.

35. Harris, L. (2005). *Trading and Exchanges: Market Microstructure for Practitioners*. Oxford University Press.

36. Hasbrouck, J. and Schwartz, R.A. (1988). Liquidity and execution cost in equity markets. *The Journal of Portfolio Management, 14*, pp. 10–16.

37. Hasbrouck, J. and Seppi, D.J. (2001). Common factors in prices, order flows, and liquidity. *Journal of Financial Economics, 59(3)*, pp. 383–411.

38. Hui, B. and Heubel, B. (1984). Comparative liquidity advantages among major U.S. stock markets. Technical Report, DRI Financial Information Group Study Series No. 84081.

39. Kahneman, D. and Tversky, A. (1979). Prospect Theory: An Analysis of Decision under Risk. *Econometrica, 47(2)*, pp. 263–292.

40. Kahneman, D. (2002). Maps of bounded rationality: The [2002] Sveriges Riksbank Prize [Lecture] in Economic Sciences. Available at: http://www.nobelprize.org/nobel_prizes/economic-sciences/laureates/2002/kahnemann-lecture.pdf

41. Kalev, P.S., Liu, W.M., Pham, P.K. and Jarnecic, E. (2004). Public information arrival and volatility of intraday stock returns. *Journal of Banking and Finance, 28(6)*, pp. 1441–1467.

42. Kalev, P.S. and Duong, H.N. (2011). Firm-specific news arrival and the volatility of intraday stock index and futures returns. In G. Mitra and L. Mitra, eds., *The Handbook of News Analytics in Finance*, Chapter 12. John Wiley & Sons.

43. Kissell, R. and Glantz, M. (2003). Optimal Trading Strategies. American Management Association, AMACOM.

44. Kittrell, J. (2011). Sentiment reversals as buy signals. In G. Mitra and L. Mitra, eds., *The Handbook of News Analytics in Finance*, Chapter 9. John Wiley & Sons.

45. Krinsky, I. and Lee, J. (1996). Earnings announcements and the components of the bid-ask spread. *Journal of Finance, 51(4)*, pp. 1523–1535.

46. Kothari, S.P. and Warner, J.B. (2005). Econometrics of event studies. In B. Espen Eckbo, ed., *Handbook of Empirical Corporate Finance*. Elsevier Finance.

47. Kyle, A. (1985). Continuous auction and insider trading. *Econometrica, 53*, pp. 1315–35.

48. Leinweber, D. (2009). *Nerds on Wall Street*. John Wiley & Sons.

49. Leinweber, D. and Sisk, J. (2011). Relating news analytics to stock returns. In G. Mitra and L. Mitra, eds., *The Handbook of News Analytics in Finance*, Chapter 6. John Wiley & Sons.

50. Madhavan, A. (2000). Market Microstructure: A Survey. *Journal of Financial Markets, 3*, pp. 205–258.

51. Mitchell, M.L. and Mulherin, J.H. (1994). The impact of public information on the stock market. *Journal of Finance, 49*, pp. 923–950.

52. Mitra, L., Mitra, G. and diBartolomeo, D. (2009). Equity portfolio risk (volatility) estimation using market information and sentiment. *Quantitative Finance, 9(8)*, pp. 887–895.

53. Mitra, L. and Mitra, G. (Editors) (2011)[a]. *The Handbook of News Analytics in Finance*. John Wiley & Sons.

54. Mitra, L. and Mitra, G. (2011)[b]. Applications of news analytics in finance: a review. In G. Mitra and L. Mitra, eds., *The Handbook of News Analytics in Finance*, Chapter 1. John Wiley & Sons.

55. Mitra, G., Yu, X., Banerjee, A. and diBartolomeo, D. (2013). Automated Analysis of News to Compute Market Sentiment: Its Impact on Liquidity and Trading. Available at: http://ssrn.com/abstract=2605049.

56. Moniz, A., Brar, G. and Davies, C. (2009). Have I got news for you. MacQuarie Research Report.

57. Moniz, A., Brar, G., Davies, C. and Strudwick, A. (2011). The impact of news flow on asset returns: an empirical study. In G. Mitra and L. Mitra, eds., *The Handbook of News Analytics in Finance*, Chapter 8. John Wiley & Sons.

58. Munz, M. (2010). US markets: earnings news release - an inside look. Paper presented at CARISMA Annual Conference. Available at: http://www.optirisk-systems.com/papers/MarianMunz.pdf

59. O'Hara, M. (1995). *Market Microstructure Theory*. Blackwell Publishing, Malden, Massachussetts.

60. Quantitative Services Group LLC (2009). QSG® study proves higher trading costs incurred for VWAP algorithms vs. arrival price algorithms, high frequency trading contributing factor. Available at: http://www.qsg.com/PDFReader.aspx?PUBID=722

61. Ranaldo, A. (2008). Intraday market dynamics around public information disclosures. In *Stock Market Liquidity*, Chapter 11. John Wiley & Sons, New Jersey.

62. RavenPack white papers (2011). Available at: http://www.ravenpack.com/research/resources.html

63. Schmerken, I. (2006). Trading off the news. *Wall Street and Technology* [online]. Available at: http://www.wallstreetandtech.com/technology-risk-management/showArticle.jhtml

64. Shefrin, H. (2008). *A Behavioral Approach to Asset Pricing*. Academic Press.

65. Shiller, R. (2000). *Irrational Exuberance*. Princeton University Press.

66. Tetlock, P.C. (2007). Giving content to investor sentiment: the role of media in the stock market. *Journal of Finance, 62,* pp. 1139–1168.

67. Tetlock, P.C., Saar-Tsechansky, M. and Macskassy, S. (2008). More than words: Quantifying language to measure firms' fundamentals. *Journal of Finance, 63(3),* pp. 1437–1467.

68. Thomson Reuters (2011). Machine Readable News and Algorithmic Trading. Thomson Reuters and Market News International, White Paper.

69. Yu, X. (2014). *Analysis of news sentiment and its application to finance*. PhD Thesis, Brunel University. Retrieved from: http://bura.brunel.ac.uk/handle/2438/9062

PART VI

Applications of Sentiment Analysis:
Case Studies

CHAPTER 23

Twitter Sentiment Analysis Applied to Finance:
a case study in retail industry

Thársis T. P. Souza, *PhD Researcher, UCL*

Olga Kolchyna, *PhD Researcher, UCL*

Tomaso Aste, *Professor of Complexity Science, UCL*

ABSTRACT

This chapter presents a financial analysis over Twitter sentiment analytics extracted from listed retail brands. We investigate whether there is statistically-significant information between Twitter sentiment and volume and stock returns and volatility. Traditional newswires are also considered as a proxy for market sentiment for comparative purposes. The results suggest that social media is indeed a valuable source in the analysis of the financial dynamics in the retail sector sometimes carrying larger prior information than mainstream news such as *The Wall Street Journal* and *Dow Jones Newswires*.

23.1   INTRODUCTION

Major news announcements can have a high impact on the financial market and investor behaviour, resulting in rapid changes or abnormal effects in financial portfolios. As human responsiveness is limited, automated news analysis has been developed as a fundamental component in algorithmic trading. In this way, traders can shorten reaction time in response to breaking stories. The basic idea behind these news analytics technologies is to predict human behaviour and automate it, so traders can anticipate asset movements before making an investment or risk management decision.

Twitter data has also become an increasingly important source of information for financial dynamics. It provides a fine-grained real-time information channel that includes not only major news stories but also minor events that, if properly filtered and modelled, can provide ex-ante information about the market even before the main newswires. Recent developments have reflected this prominent role for social media in the financial markets. One major example is the U.S. Securities and Exchange Commission report allowing companies to use Twitter to announce key information in compliance with Regulation Fair Disclosure (SEC, 2013). Twitter has also shown that can cause fast and drastic impact. In 2013, in the so-called *Hash Crash*, a hacked Twitter account of the American news agency Associated Press falsely disclosed a message about an attack on the White House, causing a drop in the Dow Jones Industrial Average of 145 points in minutes (WSJ, 2013).

In Chapter 5 of this book, we introduced a new model for sentiment classification using Twitter. We combined the traditional lexicon approach with a support vector machine algorithm to achieve better predictive performance. In the present chapter (Souza et al., 2015), we use this sentiment classification technique to investigate the interplay between the Twitter sentiment extracted from listed retail brands, and financial stock returns and volatility. We verify whether there is statistically significant information in this relationship and also compare it to a corresponding analysis using sentiment from traditional newswires. We consider volatility and log-returns as financial endogenous variables and we take Twitter sentiment and volume as exogenous explanatory variables in the financial dynamics of the selected stocks. We also consider traditional newswires as a data source for comparative purposes. Therefore, the main objectives are: (i) to verify whether there is statistically significant information between the Twitter sentiment and stock returns and volatility; and (ii) to compare this interplay while using mainstream news as a proxy for market sentiment. The main contribution of this chapter is empirical evidence that supports the use of Twitter as a significant data source in the context of financial markets in the retail industry even when compared to traditional newswires.

23.2   LITERATURE REVIEW

The investigation of the market impact of news has been studied since the seminal work of Cutler et al. (1989), where the authors investigate the extent to which macroeconomic news explain stock's return variance and the market moves following major political and world events. More recently, Tetlock (2007) provided the first evidence that news media content can predict movements in broad indicators of stock market activity. The authors found correlation between high/low pessimism of media and high market trading volume. They further analysed the relation between the sentiment of news, earnings and return predictability (Tetlock et al., 2008). Since then, with the availability of machine readable news and the use of sentiment analysis, several works have found news as a significant source for financial applications: Alanyali et al. (2013) found positive correlation between the number of mentions of a company in the *Financial Times* and its stock's volume; Lillo et al. (2015) investigated the effect of news on the behaviour of traders; Mitra et al. (2013) analysed the Thomson Reuters News Analytics (TRNA) and found a causality between sentiment and, volatility and liquidity.

Recent research supports the hypothesis that Twitter data also contains statistically significant information related to financial indicators. One of the first investigations of Twitter in the context of financial markets was carried out by Bollen et al. (2011). They analysed the text content of daily Twitter feeds to identify two types of mood: (i) polarity (positive vs. negative) and (ii) emotions (calm, alert, sure, vital, kind and happy), increasing the accuracy in the prediction of the DJIA index. Similar work by Zhang and Skiena (2010) was able to predict not only the DJIA index but also the NASDAQ-100 index; the authors measured the agreement of sentiment between messages in addition to the market mood. More recently, Zheludev et al. (2014) combined Information Theory with sentiment analysis to demonstrate that Twitter sentiment can contain statistically significant ex-ante information on future prices of the S&P500 index and also identified a subset of securities in which hourly changes in social media sentiment do provide lead-time information. As a contribution to the field of event study research, Sprenger et al. (2014) introduced a methodology to analyse market reactions to combinations of different types of news events using Twitter to identify which news is more important from the investor perspective. In a similar way, Ranco et al. (2015) combined sentiment analytics with the identification of Twitter peaks in an event study approach to imply directions of market evolution. Further, exploring the social network structure from Twitter users, Yang et al. (2014) provided empirical evidence of a financial community in Twitter in which users' interests align with the financial markets.

Similar to the present chapter, Smailovi et al. (2013) investigated the causality between polarity measures from Twitter and daily return of closing prices. The authors also use sentiment derived from a Support Vector Machine model to classify the tweets into positive, negative and neutral categories. In this chapter, we not only investigate the causality with returns but also with stock's volatility, providing also a comparison between Twitter and traditional newswires. Moreover, we concentrate the analysis on retail brands that can provide meaningful insights for applications in that domain.

Further examples of social media applications in the stock market are: the use of StockTwits sentiment and posting volume to predict daily returns, volatility and trading volume (Oliveira et al., 2013); the extraction of features from financial message boards for stock market predictions (Sehgal and Song, 2007) and approaches combining Twitter with other sources such as blogs and news (Zhang and Skiena, 2010; Shi et al., 2014; Crone and Koeppel, 2014).

23.3 DATASET

Our analysis is conducted on a set of five listed retail brands with stocks traded on the US equity market, which we monitored during the period from 1 November 2013 to 30 September 2014. The name of the investigated stocks with respective Reuters Instrument Codes (RICs) are: ABERCROMBIE & FITCH CO. (ANF.N), NIKE INC. (NKE.N), HOME DEPOT INC. (HD.N), MATTEL INC. (MAT.N) and GAMESTOP CORP. (GME.N).

Given the companies selected, we consider three streams of time series data: (i) the market data, which is given as the daily stock price; (ii) news metadata supplied by Ravenpack (2015), which consists of 10,949 news stories from *Dow Jones Newswires*, *The Wall Street Journal* and *Barron's*, and (iii) the social media data from Chapter 5, which is based on 42,803,225 Twitter messages. The choice of companies is bounded by the Twitter dataset from (iii).

23.3.1 News Analytics

The news analytics data supplied by Ravenpack (2015) are provided in a metadata format where each news story receives scores quantifying characteristics such as relevance and sentiment according to a related individual stock. Table 23.3.1 shows a sample of the news sentiment analytics data provided. The relevance score (*Relevance*) of the news ranges between 0 and 100 and indicates how strongly related the company is to the underlying news story, with higher values indicating greater relevance. Usually, a relevance value of at least 90 indicates that the entity is referenced in the main title or headline of the news item, while lower values indicate references further down the story body. Here we filter out the news stories with a relevance of 100. This increases the likelihood of the story considered being related to the underlying equity. Besides relevance, we also consider the Event Sentiment Score (*ESS*), which measures the short-term positive or negative financial or economic impact of the news on the underlying company. It ranges between 0 and 100, where higher values indicate more positive sentiment while lower values, below 50, indicate negative sentiment.

Table 23.3.1: *Example of News Sentiment Analytics. Each line represents a news story related to a company. The metadata consists of the relevance and sentiment scores and a timestamp.*

Story	Company	Date	Hour	Relevance	Event Sentiment Score (ESS)
1	NIKE INC.	20140104	210130	33	64
2	MATTEL INC.	20140105	41357	100	50
3	NIKE INC.	20140105	145917	93	88
4	NIKE INC.	20140105	150523	100	61
5	GAMESTOP CORP.	20140105	193507	44	50
6	GAMESTOP CORP.	20140106	170040	99	44
7	MATTEL INC.	20140106	222532	100	61
8	GAMESTOP CORP.	20140107	32601	100	50
9	MATTEL INC.	20140107	172628	55	40
10	NIKE INC.	20140110	204027	100	67

Given this metadata information, we first normalize the Event Sentiment Score (*ESS*) of a given story at a timestamp τ so that it ranges between -1 and 1, and we label it as $\widehat{ESS}(\tau) \in [-1, 1]$. Then, we define the sentiment and volume analytics for each company as:

- $G_{News}(t)$: *daily number of positive News, i.e., daily total number of News with* $\widehat{ESS}(\tau) > 0$;

- $B_{News}(t)$: daily number of negative News, i.e., daily total number of News with $\widehat{ESS}(\tau) < 0$;

- $V_{News}(t)$: daily total number of News;

- $SA_{News}(t)$: daily absolute sentiment from News:
$$SA_{News}(t) = G_{News}(t) - B_{News}(t);$$ [23.3.1]

- $SR_{News}(t) \in [-1, 1]$: daily relative sentiment from News as the daily mean of sentiment score $\widehat{ESS}(\tau)$, $\tau \in [t, t+1)$.

23.3.2 Twitter Analytics

For the Twitter data, we applied the classification technique from Chapter 5 to compute the sentiment and volume metrics of tweets related to a company. Also successfully applied in a different context (Kolchyna et al., 2015), the algorithm in Chapter 5 combines the traditional lexicon approach with a support vector machine model to achieve better predictive performance, which outperformed standard benchmarks. We then compute the following analytics:

- $G_{Twitter}(t)$: daily number of positive English tweets;

- $B_{Twitter}(t)$: daily number of negative English tweets;

- $V_{Twitter}(t)$: daily total number of messages regardless of the language.

Table 23.3.2 shows an example of the Twitter sentiment analytics for the company MATTEL INC. Notice that the number of positive, negative and neutral messages do not sum up to the total volume, as the former consider only English tweets and the total volume covers the total number of messages regardless of the language. Also, although provided, we do not use the number of neutral messages as we believe that the extreme polarities (positive and negative) may be more informative.

Table 23.3.2: Example of Twitter Sentiment Analytics. Sample of analytics for the company MATTEL INC. It shows the number of positive, negative and neutral English Twitter messages related to the company and the total number of messages regardless of the language.

Date	CompanyID	Volume	#Positive	#Negative	#Neutral
01/11/2013	MATTEL INC.	1,980	8	4	485
02/11/2013	MATTEL INC.	1,750	12	2	339
03/11/2013	MATTEL INC.	1,700	8	1	518
04/11/2013	MATTEL INC.	2,720	19	2	429
05/11/2013	MATTEL INC.	1,980	11	8	793
06/11/2013	MATTEL INC.	1,580	11	4	470
07/11/2013	MATTEL INC.	1,770	7	1	498
08/11/2013	MATTEL INC.	1,900	5	4	288
09/11/2013	MATTEL INC.	1,260	16	2	236
10/11/2013	MATTEL INC.	1,700	7	8	313

We hence compute the variables:

$SA_{Twitter}(t)$: daily absolute sentiment from Twitter:
$$SA_{Twitter}(t) = G_{Twitter}(t) - B_{Twitter}(t);$$ [23.3.2]

$SR_{Twitter}(t) \in [-1, 1]$: daily relative sentiment from Twitter as

$$SR_{Twitter}(t) = \frac{G_{Twitter}(t) - B_{Twitter}(t)}{G_{Twitter}(t) + B_{Twitter}(t)}.$$ [23.3.3]

Notice that $SR_{Twitter}(t_0) = +1$, represents a day t_0 with the highest positive sentiment for the company considered; conversely $SR_{Twitter}(t_0) = -1$ indicates the highest negative sentiment, whereas we consider neutrality when $SR_{Twitter}(t_0) = 0$.

Although Twitter and News are distinct data sources, notice that we have computed sentiment and volume analytics in such way that we have comparable time series between those sources[1]. This allows us to make a comparative study between them while analysing the financial data.

Table 23.3.3 reports a summary description of the selected companies with the total number of news related to the each company; the number of relevant news, i.e., those in which the news story has a *Relevance* score equals to 100, and the total number of tweets related to each company. Notice that the Twitter dataset does not have any relevance score, therefore we use this score only to filter news.

Table 23.3.3: *Summary table of selected companies. The five retails brands selected for the analysis along with their market capitalization. Also, we present the total number of news and tweets in the selected period. The relevant news represent the news filtered with the highest relevance score (100).*

Company	RIC	Market Cap.* ($Billions)	Total No. of News	Relevant News	No. of Tweets
ABERCROMBIE & FITCH CO.	ANF.N	2.86	1,608	174	1,352,643
NIKE INC.	NKE.N	67.39	2,881	178	38,033,900
HOME DEPOT INC.	HD.N	111.57	3,835	241	1,593,204
MATTEL INC.	MAT.N	15.02	1,508	125	613,798
GAMESTOP CORP.	GME.N	6.41	1,117	167	1,209,680

(*) Market Capitalization as in October 31, 2013. Source: Thomson Reuters Ikon.

23.4 FINANCIAL VARIABLES

Let $P(t)$ be the closing price of an asset at day t and $R(t) = \log P(t) - \log P(t-1)$ its daily log-return. We consider the Excess of Log-return[2] of the asset over the log-return of the market index R as:

$$ER(t) = R(t) - \hat{R}(t) \qquad [23.4.1]$$

We consider the S&P500 daily returns as the market index as all companies analysed are listed in the US market. As a proxy for the daily volatility of a stock, we define:

$$VOL(t) = 2 \; \frac{P_{high}(t) - P_{low}(t)}{P_{high}(t) + P_{low}(t)} \qquad [23.4.2]$$

where $P_{high}(t)$ and $P_{low}(t)$ are the highest and the lowest price of the stock at day t, respectively.

Fig. 23.4.1 shows a sample of the calculated variables from Twitter for the company Home-Depot Inc. It is interesting to note a spike in volume and decrease in sentiment at the end of the period which follows a corresponding drop in excess of log-return. Further, Fig. 23.4.2 depicts the distribution of values of the relative sentiment obtained from Twitter and news for each company. We observe that both present a skewed distribution while news has a more neutral-centred distribution compared to Twitter. The Twitter sentiment seems to be much more polarized with heavy-tailed distributions. NIKE's Twitter sentiment, for instance, is highly positive while the news' sentiment has a mean around a neutral point.

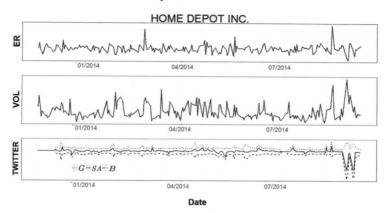

Figure 23.4.1: *Twitter's Sample Descriptive Analysis for Home-Depot Inc. Variables: Excess of log-return, ER; volatility, V OL; absolute sentiment, $SA_{Twitter}$; number of positive messages, $G_{Twitter}$ and number of negative messages, $B_{Twitter}$. Notice the spike in volume and decrease in sentiment at the end of the period, which follows a corresponding drop in excess of log-return.*

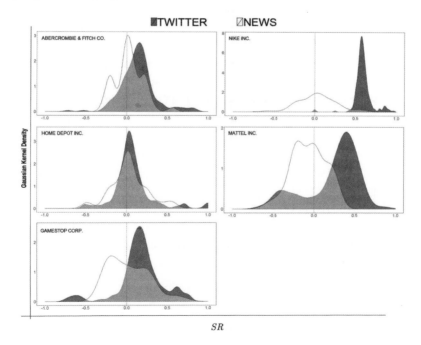

Figure 23.4.2: *Distribution of relative sentiment from Twitter $SR_{Twitter}(t)$ and News $SR_{News}(t)$ for the companies: ABERCROMBIE & FITCH CO., GAMESTOP CORP., HOME DEPOT INC., MATTEL INC. and NIKE INC. It is clear that the sentiment provided by Twitter is a distinct proxy for market sentiment compared to News as each company analysed depicts different distributions of sentiment.*

23.5 METHOD: QUANTIFICATION OF CAUSAL RELATIONS

23.5.1 Granger Causality

We are interested in investigating the statistical causality between sentiment and financial variables. The definition of causal relation introduced by Granger (1980) is based on a concept of cause-effect dependence where the cause not only should occur before the effect but also should contain unique information about the effect. Therefore, we say that X Granger-cause Y if the prediction of Y can be improved using both information from X and Y as compared to only utilizing Y.

In a Vector Auto-Regressive (VAR) framework, we can assess the Granger causality performing a F-test to verify the null hypothesis that Y is not Granger-caused by X and measure its probability of rejection within a confidence level. Specifically, assuming the VAR model:

$$Y_t = \gamma_0 + \gamma_1 Y_{t-1} + \ldots + \gamma_k Y_{t-k} + \theta_1 X_{t-1} + \ldots + \theta_k X_{t-k} + \hat{\varepsilon}_t \qquad [23.5.1]$$

we take the null hypothesis in equation (23.5.2) and test it against its alternative one in equation (23.5.3). Thus, a rejection of the null hypothesis implies that X Granger-cause Y.

$$H_0 : \theta_1 = \theta_2 = \ldots = \theta_k = 0 \qquad [23.5.2]$$
$$H_1 : \exists\, \theta_\tau,\ 0 \le \tau \le k : \ \theta_\tau\, I \neq 0 \qquad [23.5.3]$$

For both News and Twitter, we test the Grange-causality between the Excess of Log-return *ER* and the number of positive stories *G*, the number of negative stories *B*, the relative sentiment *SR* and the absolute sentiment *SA*. For the volatility *V OL*, we consider the total volume of stories *V* in addition to previously mentioned variables. Furthermore, we perform the Granger-causality test over the normally standardized versions of the time series analysed such that they have zero mean and standard deviation 1. To perform the F-statistics of the Granger-causality tests, we perform an ANOVA test using the function anova.lm from the package stats of the R Project for Statistical Computing (R Core Team, 2014).

For the purpose of visualization of the Granger-causality results we create a Granger-causality graph $G = [V, E]$, where V is a node set, and E is an edge set. A node $u \in V$ represents a variable in the causality test and an edge $e = (u, v)$ indicates that u Granger-causes v within a pre-defined significance level. Further, we label the edge with the set of companies C. Fig. 23.5.1 shows an example of a Granger-causality graph that indicates that u Granger-causes v for the set of companies C.

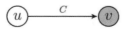

Figure 23.5.1: *Granger-causality graph. The variable u Granger-causes the variable v for the set of companies C.*

23.5.2 Predictive Analysis

In the Granger-causality test we verify whether or not each individual sentiment analytics variable from Twitter or News has significant causality with a financial variable. Moreover, we are also interested in the combined predictive power of sentiment analytics, i.e., to what extent the inclusion of several sentiment analytics covariates improves the prediction of volatility or excess of log-returns.

Hence, the regression models for the excess of log-return prediction are:

$$\mathcal{M}_0 : ER(t) = \alpha + \beta_1 ER(t-1) + \beta_2 ER(t-2) + \epsilon_t,$$
$$\mathcal{M}_1 : ER(t) = \alpha + \beta_1 ER(t-1) + \beta_2 ER(t-2)$$
$$+ \gamma_1 G(t-1) + \gamma_2 B(t-1) + \gamma_3 SR(t-1) + \widehat{\epsilon}_t$$

[23.5.4]

[23.5.5]

As the absolute sentiment $SA(t)$ (of both News and Twitter) is already a linear combination between positive $G(t)$ and negative stories $B(t)$, we will not consider it in the linear regression for any dataset. Moreover, we consider only 1-day lag for the sentiment variables and a lag of 2 days for the financial variables[3]. Again, we consider the normally standardized versions of the time series analysed.

For the volatility prediction using news as data source we will not include the volume time series $VNews(t)$ as an explanatory variable in the regression because of its high correlation with the number of positive and negative news already taken into account in the model. Notice that, for the Twitter case, the volume time series consider also non-English messages, which are not taken into account by the time series in $GTwitter$ (t) and $BTwitter$ (t). Therefore, we keep $VTwitter$ (t) as an explanatory variable in the Twitter model. As a result, we have for news:

$$\mathcal{M}_0 : VOL(t) = \alpha + \beta_1 VOL(t-1) + \beta_2 VOL(t-2) + \epsilon_t,$$
$$\mathcal{M}_1 : VOL(t) = \alpha + \beta_1 VOL(t-1) + \beta_2 VOL(t-2)$$
$$+ \gamma_1 G_{News}(t-1) + \gamma_2 B_{News}(t-1) + \widehat{\epsilon}_t$$

[23.5.6]

[23.5.7]

and for Twitter:

$$\mathcal{M}_0 : VOL(t) = \alpha + \beta_1 VOL(t-1) + \beta_2 VOL(t-2) + \epsilon_t,$$
$$\mathcal{M}_1 : VOL(t) = \alpha + \beta_1 VOL(t-1) + \beta_2 VOL(t-2)$$
$$+ \gamma_1 G_{Twitter}(t-1) + \gamma_2 B_{Twitter}(t-1) + \gamma_3 V_{Twitter}(t-1) + \widehat{\epsilon}_t.$$

[23.5.8]

[23.5.9]

Forecasting accuracy is measured by comparing the standard error of the two residuals ε_t and $\widehat{\varepsilon}_t$:

$$\hat{\sigma} = \sqrt{\frac{\sum\limits_{i=1}^{T}(y_i - \widehat{y}_i)^2}{n}} = \sqrt{\frac{\sum\limits_{i=1}^{T}\widehat{\epsilon}_i^2}{n}}$$

[23.5.10]

where, T is the total number of points, n is the number of degrees of freedom of the model, $\widehat{y}_i$ are the predicted values and y_i are the observed ones.

23.6 RESULTS AND DISCUSSION

Here we present the results from the Granger-causality tests and the predictive analysis between the financial variables and sentiment data from Twitter and News. The sentiment predictive power and its Granger-causality tests are fulfilled in 1-step ahead fashion. We investigate the statistical significance of the sentiment variables with respect to movements in returns and volatility and we compare the Twitter results with news. We provide empirical evidence that Twitter is Granger-causing the excess of log-returns for a subset of stocks. Also, we show that Twitter presents a stronger relationship with stock returns compared to news. On the other hand, the Twitter sentiment analytics show a weaker relationship with volatility compared to news.

23.6.1 Excess of Log-Returns

We analyse the dynamics of excess of log-returns of the stocks considered in relation to absolute and relative sentiments and also with the number of positive and negative stories.

Fig. 23.6.1 shows the Granger-causality graph that summarises the significant Granger-causalities (p-value < 0.05) between the excess of log-return and the sentiment variables for both news and Twitter. See Table 23.6.2 for the detailed results. We observe that the Twitter's sentiment analytics present more significant links compared to news. The Twitter's relative sentiment and its number of positive messages Granger-cause excess of log-returns, respectively, for the companies GAMESTOP CORP. and MATTEL INC. The Twitter's absolute sentiment also Granger-causes excess of log-returns for MATTEL INC. while having a two-way significant (p-value < 0.01) Granger-causality for the company HOME DEPOT INC. Notice that the number of negative stories alone has no significant relationship with returns but, combined with the number of positive stories in the form of relative and absolute sentiment, it is shown to be an important measure. The News analytics have only one significant relationship, which is observed in the number of positive news Granger-causing the excess of log-returns for the company GAMESTOP CORP.

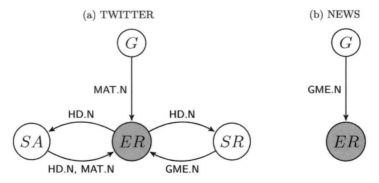

Figure 23.6.1: *Granger-causality graph for (a) Twitter and (b) News. It shows the significant links (p-value < 0.05) in the Granger-causality test between excess of log-returns (ER) and the sentiment analytics: number of positive stories (G), number of negative stories (B), absolute sentiment (SA) and relative sentiment SR. Sentiment variables that presented no significant causality are not shown in the graph.*

The solution of the multiple regression analysis in Table 23.6.3 agrees with the Granger-causality tests as it shows Twitter with a higher number of significant sentiment coefficients compared to news. The company MATTEL INC. particularly presents all sentiment coefficients with high significance (p-value < 0.01), suggesting that the Twitter sentiment analytics is indeed relevant in the prediction of the next-day excess of log-return. The companies HOME DEPOT INC. and GAMESTOP CORP. also present significant sentiment coefficients. For the News analytics, the sentiment results were significant only for the company GAMESTOP CORP. Further, analysis of the Residual Standard Error of the models with and without the sentiment variables in Table 23.6.1 shows that the use of the Twitter sentiment variables reduces the error of the model with only market data for the companies MATTEL INC., HOME DEPOT INC. and GAMESTOP CORP. while the News sentiment improved the prediction only for the company GAMESTOP CORP.

In sum, the Twitter analytics surprisingly showed a stronger causality with stock's returns compared to news. It is interesting to note that we did not perform any explicit filtering process in the Twitter analytics. However, we only considered the extremes of polarity (positive and negative categories), i.e., we did not consider the neutral tweets. This suggests that the sentiment classification itself is indirectly filtering the noise in the data in the sense that the non-neutral tweets are really informative. Moreover, the increased causality compared to news indicates a prominent role for Twitter in the retail industry. We believe that Twitter acts as a feedback channel for the retail brands in a timely fashion fine-grained way compared to News.

Table 23.6.1: *Standard error relative change in the prediction of excess of log-return ER(t) using SR(t), G(t) and B(t) (Equation 23.5.5) compared to the model with only market data (Equation 23.5.4). Negative values indicate an improvement in prediction, whereas positive ones show that sentiment analytics have not led to improvement.*

Company	Prediction Error Relative Change (%)	
	NEWS	TWITTER
NIKE INC.	+2.41	+0.58
ABERCROMBIE & FITCH CO.	+1.26	+0.60
HOME DEPOT INC.	+0.99	-1.23
MATTEL INC.	+0.48	-2.82
GAMESTOP CORP.	-8.34	-1.10

Table 23.6.2: *Statistical significance (p-values) of Granger-causality analysis between excess log-return and SA(t), SR(t), G(t) and B(t) for the companies: ABERCROMBIE & FITCH CO. (ANF.N), NIKE INC. (NKE.N), HOME DEPOT INC. (HD.N), MATTEL INC. (MAT.N) and GAMESTOP CORP. (GME.N).*

	TWITTER ANALYTICS					NEWS ANALYTICS				
	HD.N	MAT.N	GME.N	NKE.N	ANF.N	HD.N	MAT.N	GME.N	NKE.N	ANF.N
$SA \rightarrow ER$	0.003***	0.046**	0.140	0.888	0.477	0.303	0.411	0.140	0.621	0.707
$ER \rightarrow SA$	0.006***	0.404	0.231	0.354	0.937	0.423	0.451	0.230	0.546	0.281
$SR \rightarrow ER$	0.449	0.497	0.032**	0.680	0.591	0.747	0.977	0.696	0.816	0.814
$ER \rightarrow SR$	0.024**	0.855	0.196	0.995	0.875	0.942	0.314	0.162	0.564	0.213
$G \rightarrow ER$	0.182	0.016**	0.885	0.400	0.685	0.203	0.228	0.014**	0.304	0.231
$ER \rightarrow G$	0.050*	0.305	0.957	0.380	0.197	0.388	0.382	0.171	0.199	0.518
$B \rightarrow ER$	0.327	0.559	0.267	0.344	0.763	0.681	0.976	0.920	0.796	0.398
$ER \rightarrow B$	0.219	0.792	0.538	0.166	0.480	0.855	0.646	0.894	0.769	0.863

Significance codes: p-value < 0.01: ***, p-value < 0.05: **, p-value < 0.1: *

Table 23.6.3: *Summary statistics of multiple regression. Prediction of excess of log-return (ER) using sentiment (SR, G, B) for the companies: ABERCROMBIE & FITCH CO. (ANF.N), NIKE INC. (NKE.N), HOME DEPOT INC. (HD.N), MATTEL INC. (MAT.N) and GAMESTOP CORP. (GME.N).*

	TWITTER ANALYTICS					NEWS ANALYTICS				
	HD.N	MAT.N	GME.N	NKE.N	ANF.N	HD.N	MAT.N	GME.N	NKE.N	ANF.N
$SA \rightarrow ER$	0.003***	0.046**	0.140	0.888	0.477	0.303	0.411	0.140	0.621	0.707
$ER \rightarrow SA$	0.006***	0.404	0.231	0.354	0.937	0.423	0.451	0.230	0.546	0.281
$SR \rightarrow ER$	0.449	0.497	0.032**	0.680	0.591	0.747	0.977	0.696	0.816	0.814
$ER \rightarrow SR$	0.024**	0.855	0.196	0.995	0.875	0.942	0.314	0.162	0.564	0.213
$G \rightarrow ER$	0.182	0.016**	0.885	0.400	0.685	0.203	0.228	0.014**	0.304	0.231
$ER \rightarrow G$	0.050*	0.305	0.957	0.380	0.197	0.388	0.382	0.171	0.199	0.518
$B \rightarrow ER$	0.327	0.559	0.267	0.344	0.763	0.681	0.976	0.920	0.796	0.398
$ER \rightarrow B$	0.219	0.792	0.538	0.166	0.480	0.855	0.646	0.894	0.769	0.863

Significance codes: p-value < 0.01: ***, p-value < 0.05: **, p-value < 0.1: *

23.6.2 Volatility

We further analysed the interplay between message volume and sentiment with stock's volatility. As volume measures we consider: the number of positive and negative English stories and also the total volume of stories, regardless of the language. As sentiment analytics we consider: absolute sentiment and relative sentiment. Fig. 23.6.2 shows the significant links (p-value < 0.05) of the Granger-causality test between the volatility and the sentiment variables. See Table 23.6.5 for the detailed results. Overall, there are more significant links of causality for the News sentiment analytics compared to Twitter. We observe that the number of positive stories and the total volume both Granger-cause volatility for news and Twitter; more companies are affected by news. The absolute sentiment Granger-causes volatility only for news, observed in the company ABERCROMBIE &

FITCH CO. (ANF.N). The relative sentiment and the number of negative stories are not causing volatility, on the other hand volatility is Granger-causing negative news for the company GAMESTOP CORP. (GME.N).

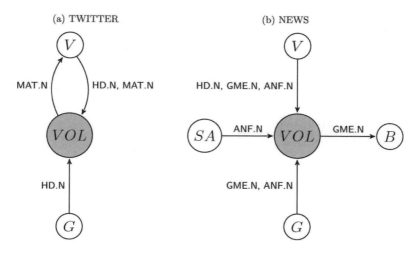

Figure 23.6.2: *Granger-causality graph for (a) Twitter and (b) news. It shows the significant links (p-value < 0.05) in the Granger-causality test between volatility (VOL) and the sentiment analytics: total number of stories (V), number of positive stories (G), number of negative stories (B), absolute sentiment (SA) and relative sentiment (SR). Sentiment variables with no significant causality are not shown in the graph.*

The solution of the multiple regression analysis in Table 23.6.6 shows that the number of positive stories is a significant variable for both News and Twitter, being more significant for the former. The number of negative stories showed, instead, no relevance in both regressions. The total volume of Twitter was relevant only for the company NKE.N. Moreover, analysis of the Residual Standard Error of the models with and without sentiment variables in Table 23.6.4 shows that both Twitter and News were able to reduce the error in prediction for a subset of the companies. In the cases where the model was improved with sentiment, News provided a higher reduction of error compared to Twitter.

Overall, the News analytics showed a higher causality relation with volatility compared to Twitter. This confirms the predictive power of News with volatility as described in the literature (diBartolomeo et al., 2009; Mitra et al., 2013; Date et al., 2014; Kalev and Duong, 2011). Further improvements in entity detection in the sentiment classification algorithm used in the dataset provided (Kolchyna et al., 2015b) may improve the Twitter results.

Table 23.6.4: *Standard error relative change in the prediction of volatility V OL(t) using G(t), B(t) and V (t) (Equations 23.5.7 and 23.5.9) compared to the model with only market data (equations 23.5.6 and 23.5.8). Negative values indicate an improvement in prediction, whereas positive ones show that the sentiment analytics have not led to improvement.*

	Prediction Error Relative Change (%)	
Company	NEWS	TWITTER
NIKE INC.	-1.36	1.08
ABERCROMBIE & FITCH CO.	-4.03	+0.52
HOME DEPOT INC.	-2.46	+1.10
MATTEL INC.	+2.21	+0.36
GAMESTOP CORP.	-14.99	-0.20

Table 23.6.5: *Statistical significance (p-values) of Granger-causality analysis between volatility (V OL(t)) and G(t), B(t), SA(t), SR(t) and V (t) for the companies: ABERCROMBIE & FITCH CO. (ANF.N), NIKE INC. (NKE.N), HOME DEPOT INC. (HD.N), MATTEL INC. (MAT.N) and GAMESTOP CORP. (GME.N).*

	TWITTER ANALYTICS					NEWS ANALYTICS				
	HD.N	MAT.N	GME.N	NKE.N	ANF.N	HD.N	MAT.N	GME.N	NKE.N	ANF.N
$V \to VOL$	0.025**	0.004***	0.751	0.976	0.729	0.029**	0.320	0.020**	0.846	0.001***
$VOL \to V$	0.228	0.016**	0.980	0.611	0.924	0.307	0.453	0.053*	0.462	0.560
$G \to VOL$	0.004***	0.072*	0.678	0.397	0.228	0.060*	0.341	0.031**	0.961	<0.001***
$VOL \to G$	0.560	0.273	0.668	0.330	0.690	0.146	0.390	0.211	0.859	0.615
$B \to VOL$	0.053*	0.118	0.720	0.636	0.884	0.522	0.301	0.204	0.526	0.540
$VOL \to B$	0.420	0.477	0.363	0.729	0.967	0.484	0.620	0.026**	0.391	0.801
$SR \to VOL$	0.539	0.305	0.489	0.786	0.220	0.416	0.925	0.510	0.441	0.056*
$VOL \to SR$	0.944	0.867	0.791	0.611	0.623	0.854	0.352	0.590	0.184	0.340
$SA \to VOL$	0.274	0.736	0.437	0.142	0.216	0.435	0.194	0.497	0.652	0.010**
$VOL \to SA$	0.458	0.900	0.747	0.120	0.950	0.173	0.352	0.187	0.707	0.996

Significance codes: p-value < 0.01: ***, p-value < 0.05: **, p-value < 0.1: *

Table 23.6.6: *Summary statistics of multiple regression. Prediction of volatility (V OL) using sentiment (G, B) and volume (V) for the companies: ABERCROMBIE & FITCH CO. (ANF.N), NIKE INC. (NKE.N), HOME DEPOT INC. (HD.N), MATTEL INC. (MAT.N) and GAMESTOP CORP. (GME.N).*

| | TWITTER ANALYTICS | | | | |
	HD.N	MAT.N	GME.N	NKE.N	ANF.N
$VOL_{(t-1)}$	2.305851e-01***	2.211374e-01***	1.019004e-01	1.893666e-01***	1.308395e-01*
$VOL_{(t-2)}$	1.250733e-01*	1.238580e-01*	-6.173133e-02	4.307688e-02	8.735957e-02
$G_{(t-1)}$	1.845026e-01*	1.073941e-01	-2.807417e-01*	-1.586209e-03	3.533443e-02
$B_{(t-1)}$	1.420223e-03	-7.759929e-02	4.461084e-02	-2.181354e-03	-8.569212e-02
$V_{(t-1)}$	-1.468387e-03	-1.862391e-02	1.920558e-01	1.901394e-01**	5.742508e-02

| | NEWS ANALYTICS | | | | |
	HD.N	MAT.N	GME.N	NKE.N	ANF.N
	3.891e-01*	6.265e-02	9.587e-02	3.785e-01**	3.792e-01**
	-9.120e-02	-4.451e-03	5.092e-02	3.093e-02	1.054e-01
	3.018e-01**	2.772e-03	6.046e-01***	1.274e-01	-3.329e-01*
	9.294e-02	-1.105e-01	1.184e-01	-1.400e-01	-1.300e-01
	N/A	N/A	N/A	N/A	N/A

Significance codes: p-value < 0.01: ***, p-value < 0.05: **, p-value < 0.1: *

23.7   CONCLUSION

We showed that measures of Twitter sentiment extracted from listed retail brands have a statistically significant relationship with stock's excess of log-returns and volatility. While analysing the interplay between the excess of log-return and the Twitter sentiment variables we conclude that: (i) Twitter presented a stronger Granger-causality with stocks' returns compared to news; (ii) positive tweets and Twitter sentiment Granger-cause excess of log-returns for a subset of companies;(iii) Twitter's sentiment analytics reduce the prediction error of the next-day excess of log-return performing better than traditional newswires. Moreover, in the volatility analysis we found that: (i) Twitter analytics showed a weaker relationship with volatility compared to the one observed with returns; (ii) the number of positive tweets and the total volume Granger-cause volatility for some companies but present reduced Granger-causality compared to news; (iii) the number of positive tweets is a significant variable for the 1-step ahead prediction of volatility while the number of negative messages showed no relevance. Overall, Twitter sentiment analytics showed to be a distinct and complementary proxy of market sentiment compared to news in the analysis of the financial dynamics of retail brands' stocks. Surprisingly, Twitter sentiment presented a relatively stronger relationship with stocks' returns compared to traditional newswires. The results suggest that social media analytics have a prominent role in the dynamics of the retails sector in the financial markets.

ACKNOWLEDGMENTS

We thank the valuable feedback from the two anonymous reviewers. This work was supported by OptiRisk Systems which provided the news sentiment analytics from RavenPack. T.A. acknowledges support of the UK Economic and Social Research Council (ESRC) in funding the Systemic Risk Centre (ES/K002309/1). T.T.P.S. acknowledges financial support from CNPq - The Brazilian National Council for Scientific and Technological Development. O.K. acknowledges support from the company Certona Corporation.

Notes

[1] We may refer to a time series independently to a specific data source, in such cases we will represent it as its original symbol but without the text subscript, e.g., the number of positive will be represented as $G(t)$ when discussing both News $G_{News}(t)$ and Twitter $G_{Twitter}(t)$ in the same context.

[2] An alternative approach is to examine the alpha generation as the excess return of the underlying stock relative to its benchmark adjusted for a given level of risk as in the market model described in Fama (1970).

[3] A model selection approach can be also used in order to find an optimal lag for the explanatory variables, examples of selection's criteria are: the Akaike information criterion (AIC), the Bayesian information criterion (BIC) and Mallow's Cp. See Box and Jenkins (1976).

23.8 REFERENCES

1.   Alanyali, M., Moat, H.S. and Preis, T. (2013). Quantifying the relationship between financial news and the stock market. *Sci. Rep.*, *3*.

2.   Bollen, J., Mao, H. and Zeng, X. (2011). Twitter mood predicts the stock market. *Journal of Computational Science, 2(1)*, 1–8.

3.   Box, G. and Jenkins, G. (1976). *Time series analysis: forecasting and control*. Holden-Day series in time series analysis and digital processing. Holden-Day.

4.   Crone, S. and Koeppel, C. (2014). Predicting exchange rates with sentiment indicators: An empirical evaluation using text mining and multilayer perceptrons. In *Computational Intelligence for Financial Engineering Economics*. IEEE Conference, pp. 114–121.

5.   Cutler, D.M., Poterba, J.M. and Summers, L.H. (1989). What moves stock prices? *The Journal of Portfolio Management, 15(3)*, 4–12.

6. Date, P., Sidorov, S.P. and Balash, V. (2014). Garch type volatility models augmented with news intensity data. In *Chaos, Complexity and Leadership 2012*. Springer Proceedings in Complexity 2014, pp. 199–207. Springer Netherlands..

7. diBartolomeo, D., Mitra, G. and Mitra, L. (2009). Equity portfolio risk (volatility) estimation using market information and sentiment. *Quantitative Finance, 9(8),* 887–895..

8. Fama, E.F. (1970). Efficient capital markets: A review of theory and empirical work. *The Journal of Finance, 25(2),* 383–417.

9. Granger, C.W. (1980). Testing for causality: a personal viewpoint. *Journal of Economic Dynamics and control, 2,* 329–352.

10. Kalev, P.S. and Duong, H.N. (2011). Firm-specific news arrival and the volatility of intraday stock index and futures returns. In: L. Mitra and G. Mitra, eds., *The Handbook of News Analytics in Finance*. John Wiley & Sons, pp. 271–288.

11. Kolchyna, O., Souza, T.T.P., Treleaven, P. and Aste, T. (2015). In Quest of Significance: Identifying Types of Twitter Sentiment Events that Predict Spikes in Sales. arXiv preprint. Available at: http://arxiv.org/abs/1508.03981.

12. Lillo, F., Miccich, S., Tumminello, M., Piilo, J. and Mantegna, R.N. (2015). How news affects the trading behaviour of different categories of investors in a financial market. *Quantitative Finance, 15(2),* 213–229..

13. Oliveira, N., Cortez, P. and Areal, N. (2013). On the predictability of stock market behavior using stocktwits sentiment and posting volume. In *Progress in Artificial Intelligence*. Springer Berlin Heidelberg, pp. 355–365.

14. R Core Team (2014). *R: A Language and Environment for Statistical Computing*. R Foundation for Statistical Computing, Vienna, Austria.

15. Ranco, G., Aleksovski, D., Caldarelli, G. and Mozetič, I. (2015). Investigating the relations between twitter sentiment and stock prices. arxiv preprint. Available at: http://arxiv.org/abs/1506.02431.

16. Ravenpack (2015). Ravenpack official website. http://www.ravenpack.com/. [Accessed 29 January 2015]. SEC (2013). SEC says social media ok for company announcements if investors are alerted. *U.S. Securities and Exchange Commission*. Available at: http://1.usa.gov/1zFxUPa. [Accessed 29 January 2015].

17. SEC (2013). SEC says social media ok for company announcements if investors are alerted. U.S. Securities and Exchange Commission. Available at: http://1.usa.gov/1zFxUPa. [Accessed 29 January 2015].

18. Sehgal, V. and Song, C. (2007). Sops: Stock prediction using web sentiment. In *Proceedings of the Seventh IEEE International Conference on Data Mining Workshops*. IEEE Computer Society, pp. 21–26..

19. Shi, B., Ifrim, G. and Hurley, N. (2014). Be in the know: Connecting news articles to relevant twitter conversations. arXiv preprint. Available at: http://adsabs.harvard.edu/abs/2014arXiv1405.3117S.

20. Smailovi, J., Grar, M., Lavra, N. and Nidari, M. (2013). Predictive sentiment analysis of tweets: A stock market application. In A. Holzinger and G. Pasi, eds., *Human-Computer Interaction and Knowledge Discovery in Complex, Unstructured, Big Data*. Springer Berlin Heidelberg, pp. 77–88.

21. Sprenger, T.O., Sandner, P.G., Tumasjan, A. and Welpe, I.M. (2014). News or Noise? Using Twitter to Identify and Understand Company-specific News Flow. *Journal of Business Finance & Accounting*, *41(7-8)*, 791–830..

22. Tetlock, P.C. (2007). Giving content to investor sentiment: The role of media in the stock market. *The Journal of Finance*, *62(3)*, 1139–1168.

23. Tetlock, P.C., Saar-Tsechansky, M., and Macskassy, S. (2008). More than words: Quantifying language to measure firms' fundamentals. The Journal of Finance, 63(3), 1437–1467.

24. WSJ (2013). False AP twitter message sparks stock-market selloff. *Wall Street Journal*. Available at: http://on.wsj.com/12ms85v. [Accessed on 29 January 2015].

25. Yang, S.Y., Mo, S.Y.K., and Zhu, X. (2014). An empirical study of the financial community network on twitter. *2014 IEEE Conference on Computational Intelligence for Financial Engineering & Economics*..

26. Yu, X., Mitra, G. and Yu, K. (2013). Impact of news on asset behaviour: return, volatility and liquidity in an intra-day setting. Available at SSRN: http://ssrn.com/abstract=2296855.

27. Zhang, W. and Skiena, S. (2010). Trading strategies to exploit blog and news sentiment. In *Fourth International Conference on Weblogs and Social Media*..

28. Zheludev, I., Smith, R. and Aste, T. (2014). When Can Social Media Lead Financial Markets? *Scientific Reports*, *4*.

CHAPTER 24

Financial Prediction from Hetrogenous Streams of Online Lead Indicators

Abby Levenberg, *Research Scientist, WorkFusion*

Edwin Simpson, *Postdoctoral Research Fellow, University of Oxford*

Stephen Roberts, *Professor of Machine Engineering, University of Oxford*

Stephen Pulman, *Professor of Computational Linguistics, University of Oxford; Co-founder, TheySay Ltd*

Karo Moilanen, *Co-founder & CTO, TheySay Ltd*

Georg Gottlob, *Professor of Computing Science, University of Oxford*

ABSTRACT

Learning to predict trends of financial and economic variables is a hard problem with a large body of literature devoted to it. Further, companies and sources that provide financial and economic data do so at a premium. As such, there is a significant amount of work on using freely available sources of *big text data* from the WWW to learn from. Much of this work has relied on some form or other of superficial sentiment analysis to generate the text features for the learners. In this project report we extend the current literature and present a framework for learning from Streams of Online Lead Indicators (*SOLID*). We describe a novel approach for economic prediction using heterogeneous streams of Web data. We incorporate different data types into our model – such as time series and text – by treating each data stream as an independent source with its own features and posterior distribution. For the text data streams we use a novel approach to prediction using a sentiment composition model to generate features that can operate over much lower levels of granularity than in the prior literature. We then use a Bayesian classifier combination model to combine the suite of independent "weak" predictions into a single prediction of the primary economic and financial variables. We report experiments over multiple instruments and time frames including daily versus monthly trends. Our results show that the *SOLID* can achieve high predictive accuracy for a variety of leading indicators.

24.1 INTRODUCTION

The World Wide Web (WWW) is a collection of data produced from a very large number of distinct sources. While the WWW already contains a vast amount of data, the *rate* at which the data store is growing is increasing exponentially year over year. This data provides a continually growing source of information on a myriad of diverse topics. Currently there is significant interest in both academic and industrial research that aims to utilise this abundant big data source to gain insights into and learn about dynamic aspects of human society. Topics from the recent literature in this field span diverse areas including, for example, public health monitoring, economic prediction, sports prediction, retail trends, and food and entertainment preferences (Dredze et al., 2014; Xu et al., 2012; Preis et al., 2013; Sinha et al., 2013; Choi and Varian, 2012; Jurafsky et al., 2014; Joshi et al., 2010). However, due to the overwhelming amount of data freely available, structured extraction and efficient learning from *multiple* online sources of data is a nontrivial, challenging problem that spans the big data, machine learning, and information extraction communities.

In this work we contribute to the current literature in this area and present a novel *streaming*- based approach for learning from freely available big data from the WWW. We combine state-of-the-art information-extraction algorithms within a Bayesian modelling framework to obtain an efficient and accurate predictive framework to learn from heterogeneous streams of Web data. While our approach is general enough to use for many predictive scenarios, our experimental domain is predicting economic and lead financial indicator variables. Here we are interested in using WWW data to learn trends about monthly economic variables as well as daily stock market trends for various instruments.

Over the past few years there has been a sharp increase in the literature that uses *text* data from the WWW to learn predictions of a financial nature. The overriding goal is to find correlations between human- written text data and the direction of lead economic indicators such as the stock market. Most of this work (reviewed in Section 24.2) is limited to using only a single source of data. Further, even if multiple sources are accounted for, the models in the literature thus far are unable to incorporate data of differing types. In contrast, the framework we present is well suited for efficient processing of heterogeneous data streams, which allows us to use a single model to learn from both text and time-series data obtained from any number of sources.

To process heterogeneous data types within a single prediction framework, we rely on a state-of-the-art machine learning algorithm called *Independent Bayesian Classifier Combination* (IBCC) (Ghahramani and Kim, 2003). As explained in Section 24.3, our framework treats each data stream from the WWW as an independent classifier with its own predictive posterior distribution. IBCC then operates over the posterior distributions from each separate input stream. This allows us to access and combine features from arbitrary data streams from multiple sources in a principled manner. In particular we are able to combine features generated from both *text* and *real-valued time series* data streams.

Using features from multiple WWW streams for financial prediction is a contribution to the current literature and presents a number of challenges that we address in the following sections. First we review a selection of the recent relevant literature that uses WWW data to make predictions of economic and financial variables. In Section 24.3 we present our *SOLID* framework, which allows us to mine and learn from multiple heterogeneous data streams. We discuss in detail our data extraction methods for given data types and describe the IBCC model for binary trend prediction. In Section 24.4 we touch briefly on the sentiment composition algorithm we made use of in this work to produce high-quality sentence-level sentiment analysis for text-based prediction.

The remainder of this report focuses on the data we obtained and experiments conducted to test the efficacy of the *SOLID* framework. We report on trend prediction experiments at varying levels of granularity ranging from monthly economic variables to daily commodity future markets. Our experiments make use of varying data types from daily market data, monthly economic time series, news and opinion pieces from newspapers and magazines, and Twitter data specific to commodity futures. We show predictions that are state-of-the-art and analyse our results in detail.

24.2 LITERATURE REVIEW

In this section we present an overview of some of the related literature in the area. While in this work we combine heterogeneous data streams within a single predictive framework, previous work has concentrated on learning from (possibly multiple sources of) a single data type. Our review is therefore divided into two broad categories of prior work: time series and text data.

24.2.1 Time Series Prediction

There is a vast body of literature on the field of quantitative financial analysis. This literature describes models and methods with the ability to detect signals within and between multiple time series data. Over the last many decades scores of textbooks have been and continue to be published that describe a huge number of techniques for finding correlations between various financial and economic time series (see, for examples, Chatfield (1975), Hamilton (1994) and, Mills and Markellos (2008)). Techniques and strategies are too broad to fit into the scope of this review and range from simple historical heuristics based on intuition and market knowledge to a plethora of regression based techniques to more complex algorithms such as genetic algorithms and deep learning neural networks.

Today numerous journals and conferences are devoted to disseminating the latest approaches for financial time-series prediction and regression for analysts, traders, quants and academics. For examples, the *Journal of Time Series Econometrics* and the *Journal of Time Series Analysis* are journals devoted entirely to publishing the latest findings in this area.

24.2.2 Text Prediction

Here we review the relevant prior literature that uses text data for prediction. While there are a number of potential uses for text prediction, utilizing the information implicit in market news and opinion to predict the direction of the economy is of obvious interest to many. As such there has been significant amount of work that uses text from various online sources for prediction of economic indexes, company earnings and stock market trends (Mitra and Mitra, 2011; Lavrenko et al., 2001; Schumaker and Chen, 2009; Fan, 2010; Mittermayer and Knolmayer, 2007; Nikfarjam et al., 2010; Kogan et al., 2009)

In general the methodology of the work reviewed is to obtain a body of text (usually from the WWW in the form of company filings, reports, news stories or message board data) and to extract natural language text features (most often sentiment based). These documents are aligned with historical market trends and a classification algorithm is trained to predict the future direction or value of the index/market. Learning algorithms range from simple two-class Naive Bayes and Support Vector Machines to more sophisticated algorithms with varying results and claims.

While some of the work describes trading strategies based on their system's predictions that reportedly outperform the market, most of the work suffers from a lack of rigorous testing and unrealistic market expectations. Consequently in this work we concentrate only on reporting the robustness of the *SOLID* framework and the accuracy of our models. As well, most of the systems reviewed that use sentiment analysis apply a "bag-of-words" model to compute the features for the document-level classification. We agree with the authors of Nikfarjam et al. (2010), who argue that this approach is too general and prediction accuracy is impacted due to the loss of context within documents. In contrast, in this work we use a sentence-level sentiment analysis approach intended to capture the context of text at a fine granularity.

More recent work has focused on the use of other sources of online data to predict economic and market trends, specifically using aggregated online search queries via Google Trends or social media text streams via Twitter to learn correlations between the big data produced by the "crowd" and lagged market trends (Choi and Varian, 2012; Bollen et al., 2011; Mao et al., 2011; Preis et al., 2010; Preis et al., 2013). In general, there is an active and growing interest in techniques and methods for using textual WWW data to predict financial variables.

24.3 *SOLID* FRAMEWORK

Our goal is to efficiently use the big data freely available on the WWW to make predictions of economic and financial variables of interest. However, for a given domain there is an overwhelming amount of data available from any number of sources. A simplifying conceptual approach for making sense of the abundance of WWW data is to treat each online source of data as a separate *stream* of data. Each data stream has its own underlying distribution and throughput, the rate at which the source produces raw data, and hence its own independent level of predictive accuracy. If we treat each stream as a classifier in its own right we can make use of ensemble-like methods to combine the independent predictions into a single best prediction. As well, since each stream is considered independently this approach enables us to fuse multiple heterogeneous sources of differing data types together into a single combined model of prediction. In this section we describe a framework for data stream extraction and aggregate prediction using IBCC from independent "weak" classifiers built from multiple WWW streams.

Figure 24.3.1 depicts our framework for stream-based prediction. It is divided into three parts:
1. Extracting the relevant streams from the WWW in a structured and efficient manner.
2. Training an ensemble of base classifiers – one for each data stream – using features and models specific to each stream's data type.

3. Aggregate multiple, stream-specific classifications into a single globally optimised prediction. Below we describe in detail each part of this framework.

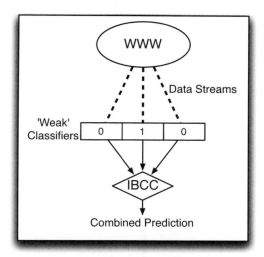

Figure 24.3.1: *Framework for prediction. We aggregate independent predictions from multiple heterogeneous data streams from the WWW into a single combined trend prediction using a Bayesian combination framework.*

24.3.1 Structured Stream Extraction

When considering the WWW as the source of data from which we plan to learn, an immediate question we must answer is how to find and extract *only* the data relevant to the predictive task at hand from the massive amount of data already available online and constantly growing. Consider that even within a stream from a single source there may be data that pertains to an arbitrary number of domains. Most of these will be irrelevant to the predictive domain of interest. For example, a stream of text from a website that broadcasts real-time news will contain stories ranging from the economy to celebrity gossip and everything in between. We may want to use the pertinent articles on the economy from such a source but indiscriminate collection of the stream will mean most of the text we collect will be irrelevant to our predictive task.

To solve this problem we use a mechanism based on *Oxpath*, a query language for web data extraction that enables the automation of user-driven queries of a given source and then structured retrieval of the returned data (Furche et al., 2012). For instance, suppose we aim to collect articles pertaining to a specific economic indicator, say nonfarm payrolls, from the websites of various newspapers and magazines. Using Oxpath we can set up an automated process to periodically query multiple sources for particular terms over specific dates, daily for instance, and save the data returned as structured entries into a local repository. This enables us to capture details present on a web page such as the author, title, date, etc., of an article. This means we do not have to download, process, and classify raw HTML pages from the web, which is a tedious and error-prone process. Instead we have direct structured access to the desired content of the stream.

24.3.2 Stream-specific Weak Classifiers

The above approach allows us to access a pertinent data stream from any data source on the WWW. We now describe how we train a predictive model specific to that stream. Since we train a suite of these classifiers, one for each input stream, we consider each independent model a *weak* classifier that need only provide a posterior distribution of nominal accuracy. We rely on the final combination model (described in Section 24.3.3) to aggregate the weak classifier's predictions into a final accurate prediction. For the weak classifiers, any of the standard machine learning models in the literature are viable. For example, since we are predicting the trends of economic and financial variables, we make use of simple binary logistic regression models where a class of 1 means "up" and 0 means "down".

To use any predictive models we first must derive features from the raw streams to use as training data for our classifier. In this work we use both real-valued time series and text data streams. For the time series data we use standard multivariate features such as binary trend indicators, smoothed moving averages, etc. For the text data we use a novel approach. First we use sentiment composition to score individual sentences with a distribution over positive, negative or neutral sentiment (Moilanen and Pulman, 2007). Afterwards we combine these sentence-level sentiment features in some informative way as input into our training algorithms. We find that using the sentiment over each sentence provides a deeper level of context than a bag-of-words model allows, so we get a better representation of the text. Further detail of how we extract and use text features via a sentiment composition model is given in Section 24.4. Next we describe how we can use a principled combination approach to aggregate the predictions of the stream-specific weak classifiers via IBCC.

24.3.3 Binary IBCC Model

Due to the differences in their underlying distributions, each of the individual data stream's predictive accuracies may vary enormously in reliability. Classifier combination methods are well suited to situations such as these and serve to make best use of the outputs of an ensemble of imperfect base classifiers to enable higher accuracy classifications. Using a *Bayesian* approach to classifier combination provides a principled mathematical framework for aggregation where poor predictors can be mitigated and in which multiple data streams, with very different distributions and training features, can be combined to provide complementary information (Ghahramani and Kim, 2003). Here we describe a binary, two-class variation of the IBCC model of Simpson et al. (2013).

We want to predict the trend of the dependent variable(s) (DV) over some number of *epochs*, usually days or months, indexed from $i \in \{1, \ldots, N\}$. We assume the trend T of the DV is generated from an underlying binomial distribution with parameters $\varkappa$. Each epoch has a value $t_i \in \{0,1\}$ where the ith epoch has a label $t_i = 0$ if the trend decreased from the prior epoch and $t_i = 1$ if it increased. The prior probabilities of the trends t_i are given by κ : $p(t_i = j | \kappa) = \kappa j$, where j iterates over the class labels $\{0,1\}$.

We denote the number of base classifiers, or data streams, as K. Each stream's base classifier $k \in \kappa \{1, \ldots, K\}$ produces a real-valued output matrix $\hat{C}^k$ of size $N \times j$. The output vector $\hat{c}_i^k \in [0, 1]$ for epoch i denotes the probabilities given by classifier k of assigning a discrete trend label $c_i^k \in \{0, 1\}$. The jth element of the trend label, $c_{ij}^k = 1$, while all other elements are zero, indicates that classifier k has assigned label j to epoch i. We assume the vector c_i^k is drawn from a Binomial distribution dependent on the true label t_i, with probabilities π_{j}^{k} $= p(c_i^k | t_i = j, \pi_j^k)$. Both parameters π_j^k and κ have Beta-distributed priors.

The joint distribution over all variables for the binary IBCC model is

$$p(\kappa, \Pi, T, C | A_0, \nu) = \prod_{i=1}^{N} \{\kappa_{t_i} \prod_{k=1}^{K} \pi_{t_i}^k \cdot c_i^k\} p(\kappa | \nu) p(\Pi | A)$$

[24.3.1]

where $\Pi = \{ \pi_j^k \ | j \in \{1, 0\}, k = 1 \ldots K\}$ denotes all base classifier probabilities, $A_0 = \{\alpha_{0j}^k \ | j \in \{1, 0\},$ $k = \{1,...,K\}$ the corresponding set of hyper-parameters, and $\nu_0 = [\nu_0, \nu_1]$ are the hyper-parameters for κ. A graphical model of IBCC is shown in Figure 24.3.2.

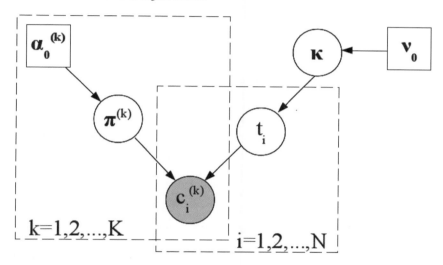

Figure 24.3.2: *Graphical model for IBCC. The arrows indicate dependencies while the shaded node represents observed variables, and the square nodes are hyper-parameters. All other variables must be inferred. Here the predictions c_i^k of each base classifier k are generated dependent on the confusion matrices π^k and the true label t_i.*

The probability of a test point t_i at epoch i being assigned class j is given by

$$p(t_i = j) = \frac{\rho_{ij}}{\sum_{y=1}^{J} \rho_{iy}}$$

[24.3.2]

where

$$\rho_{ij} = \kappa_j * \prod_{k=1}^{K} (\pi_j^k \cdot c_i^k)$$

[24.3.3]

which accounts for the probability of the class κ_j weighted by the combined prediction probabilities π_j^k of each stream's independent predictions c_i^k.

A key feature of IBCC is that each base classifier k is modelled by π^k, which intuitively represents a *confusion matrix* that quantifies the decision-making abilities of the individual base classifier k. The goal of inference for

the model is to optimise the distributions over the unknown variables T, Π and κ such that the probability of t_i for each epoch i is maximized for epochs with true increases in the DV and minimised for epochs i where the trend of the DV decreases.

IBCC has been shown to outperform a number of baseline ensemble and combination methods for classification tasks (Ghahramani and Kim, 2003; Simpson et al., 2013; Venanzi et al., 2013). In later sections of this report we describe how we combine independent predictions from multiple heterogeneous data streams within the *SOLID* framework using IBCC to achieve high predictive accuracy for a range of financial indicators. First we discuss how we generate features for our text streams using a sentiment composition model.

24.4 SENTIMENT COMPOSITION

The majority approach towards the task of sentiment analysis is to treat it as a supervised classification task. Given a corpus of data that is annotated to reflect sentiment polarity, you train a statistical classifier on this data, typically using word n-grams as features. These classifiers will usually give good results, and have the advantage of being language-independent in the sense that all one needs to do to move to a new language is to find a sufficiently large annotated corpus.

Positive Sentiment Example

"The Governor noted that despite jobs being down, there was a surprising bright spot: construction added 1,900 jobs in November - its largest gain in 22 months."

positive: *0.925* negative: *0.0*   neutral: *0.075*   confidence: *0.69*

Negative Sentiment Example

"When I drive down the main street of my little Kansas City suburb I see several dark empty storefronts that didn't used to be that way."

positive: *0.0* negative: *0.973*   neutral: *0.027*   confidence: *0.67*

Mixed Sentiment Example

"We continue to do far better than the nation – our rate has been at or below the national rate for 82 out of the past 83 months – but we must also recognize that there were 102,000 jobs lost at the same time."

positive: *0.372* negative: *0.591*   neutral: *0.037*   confidence: *0.73*

Figure 24.4.1: *Examples of sentiment distributions accounting for the positive, negative and neutral dimensions at the sentence level.*

The disadvantage of such approaches is that they typically fail to deal well with classification at a level below that of a whole document, such as sentences or entities. They also – unless specific examples happen to fall within the n-gram range used – fail to deal with the compositional aspects of sentiment described in Polanyi and Zaenen (2004), Moilanen and Pulman (2007) and, Choi and Cardie (2008), where, for example, the fact that "unemployment" in general is judged as a negative word, whereas "lower unemployment" is generally a positive attribute, but "failed to lower unemployment" is again negative. Another good example is the word "clever", which in isolation is positive, but "too clever" is negative, whereas, unpredictably, "not too clever" is again negative.

Various approaches have been advocated to deal with these surprisingly frequent phenomena, a very recent example being Socher et al. (2013). However, we use the language-specific compositional techniques described in Moilanen and Pulman (2007) and available to us via a commercial API supplied by TheySay Analytics Ltd. This system carries out part-of-speech tagging followed by chunking and dependency parsing, and uses the resulting syntactic analysis to apply a large set of recursive compositional sentiment polarity rules to assign sentiment scores to each relevant linguistic unit.

We chose to use a compositional approach because it gives us control over the granularity at which we get sentiment distributions, at any linguistic level from individual words up to whole documents, and because the results of analysis for particular examples are transparent and open to justification or challenge, a valuable property if we want to fine-tune the system to a particular domain or to justify its findings in the context of an application. In this work we capture sentiment at the sentence-level, which provides a fine level of granularity for us to work with. Figure 24.4.1 shows some example results returned from the sentiment composition model.

At the sentence-level, sentiment is expressed in terms of a three-dimensional distribution over positive, negative and neutral sentiment probabilities with an additional confidence score. The sentiment scores derived from the compositional analysis reflect the scope and intensity of the sentiment assigned, normalised to behave like a true probability. The associated confidence score is derived from properties of the linguistic analysis and reflects the model's belief that the underlying syntactic analysis (and hence corresponding sentiment assignment) is correct. Next we report on experiments using sentiment composition to generate features for a real-world prediction problem.

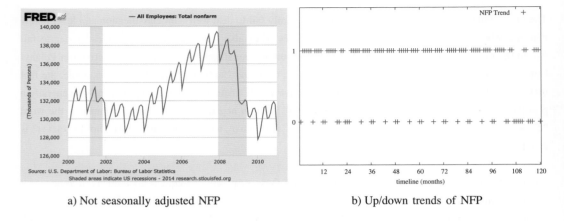

a) Not seasonally adjusted NFP   b) Up/down trends of NFP

Figure 24.4.2: *The NFP shown in Figure (a) is the (not seasonally adjusted) reported values from 2000 through 2010. In Figure (b) the same timeframe is shown as up/down (0/1) trends.*

24.5 PREDICTING NONFARM PAYROLLS

Thus far we have described the *SOLID* framework for extracting heterogeneous data streams from the WWW, drawing type specific features for each stream, building a suite of weak learners and combining their posterior distributions via a principled Bayesian framework. In the following sections we describe sets of experiments conducted to verify the efficacy of our framework. We used the *SOLID* framework in an online setting to extract data from the WWW and predict trends in various economic and financial variables. In this section we report on prediction of a monthly economic variable, the nonfarm payrolls (NFP). In the following section we report experiments conducted on daily market trends.

24.5.1 Nonfarm Payrolls

The NFP is a monthly economic index that measures employment growth (and conversely decay) and is considered one of the most significant indicators of the welfare of the U.S. economy. The NFP index is part of the Current Employment Statistics Survey, a comprehensive report released by the United States Department of Labor, Bureau of Labor Statistics, on the state of the national labour market. Released on the first Friday of each month, the index is given as the *change* in the number of (nonfarm) employment compared to the prior month. Besides indicating the state of the economy, the NFP is an index that "moves the market" upon its release (Savor and Wilson, 2013) with the market reacting positively to an increase in the index and negatively to a decline. It is therefore of obvious interest to anyone with an stake in the market – such as banks, hedge funds, prop traders, etc. – to try to make accurate and timely predictions of the NFP trend. As such, as the NFP release data nears, there is a significant amount of speculation in the media from economists attempting to forecast its direction and value. Here we are interested in seeing whether we can use data freely available on the WWW to automatically make quality predictions of the trend of the next NFP release.

Table 24.5.1: *Example source-specific statistics for words and sentences contained in six of the text streams.*

	Training		Testing	
Source	Sentences	Words	Sentences	Words
Associated Press	46K	385K	8K	53K
Dow Jones	182K	2.45M	54K	630K
Reuters	122K	1.28M	47K	427K
Market News Intl.	304K	2.22M	81K	583K
Wall Street Journal	61K	660K	15K	150K

24.5.2 Data and Experimental Setup

Here we briefly describe the specifics of the data streams collection and the experimental setup we used for testing.

Using the methods described in Section 24.3, we collected time series data online from a variety of online sources, including the Federal Reserve Economic Data website, a Federal Reserve bank resource that compiles and maintains a large number of economic time series and data sets. Other sources included the Bureau of Labor Statistics and the Conference Board, which both publish various economic indexes. We collected 33 different time series from such online sources to use as independent variables for predicting the NFP.

We also ran pointed queries against a large news database and collected archived test data from nearly 700 distinct online text sources such as the Associated Press, Dow Jones, Wall Street Journal, etc. Altogether we collected over 6.6 million sentences of raw text from the streams. Statistics from some of the data streams are given in Table 24.5.1. After we collected the text data, we processed the individual sentences for sentiment analysis using the model in Section 24.4. As shown in Figure 24.4.1, after analysis each sentence is represented only as a distribution over three dimensions of sentiment: positive, negative and neutral.

We use the above time series and text data via a straightforward experimental setup. We collected data over a timeline of 13 years from 2000–2013, which contained 156 monthly epochs. We used the last 24 epochs as test points and the rest of the epochs in the timeline as training points. However, as the economy normally tends to grow outwith periods of recession, there is an over representation of 109 (70%) positive cases compared to only 47 (30%) negative instances in the NFP index since 2000. This can be seen clearly in Figure 24.4.2. So to ascertain whether our approach is valid for learning good predictions (rather than just optimising for the overrepresented class) we *subsampled* randomly from the positive class to obtain a balanced training set with equal class representation.

Our experiments are then conducted as follows. For each online source, we extracted a relevant data stream and associated features to feed into an independent base classifier. Since the NFP is a monthly economic indicator, we grouped data from the online sources from the day after the first Friday of each month until the Thursday of the following month. We used *rolling* predictions so that the features associated with a given test point became part of the training data for the next test epoch. The posterior distributions of each independent weak classifier were then used as base inputs for IBCC. Note that the stream-specific classifiers need not give good individual prediction results as long as each contain useful information for the IBCC model. In fact, base classifiers with poor performance may be useful as IBCC can account for negative results so long as there is consistent information encoded in the posterior distributions.

Table 24.5.2: *Baseline results for predicting the NFP index.*

Source	AUC
Random	0.52
Always Up	0.50
Back Returns	0.54
Bag of Words Sentiment	0.61

We measure our results using the standard metric Area Under the Receiver Operating Characteristic Curve (AUC) (Spackman, 1989). The AUC is the preferred metric when posterior probability distributions are being learnt for binary classification models as it measures the *strength* of the predictions for each test point on top of the overall accuracy of the model. Hence models that learn to predict with higher confidence will score higher compared to models that predict all test points closer to 50-50. This means that we get an accurate measure of how well the model accounts for the input features. AUC also accounts for true and false positive predictions. For completeness, in the results that follow we show the AUC scores for the individual streams as well as the combined results using the IBCC model for each data type. First we describe some industry standard baselines that we used to compare the goodness of our results against.

24.5.3 Baselines

Table 24.5.2 reports some baseline measures of prediction standard for the NFP. For example, to compare our models against chance predictions we built a pseudorandom model shown in the *Random* row of Table 2. We compare this to a an *Always Up* strategy which always predicts an upwards NFP trend with a probability of 1 and serves as a measure of volatility for the NFP. We also used the industry standard of *Back Returns* and predict each epoch will follow the trend of the last. Each of these achieve a low score of around 0.5 AUC which is expected since subsampling makes the empirical priors of up and down equal.

The final row of Table 24.5.2 shows the results of processing the text streams using features from the standard bag-of-words approach to sentiment classification (Section 24.4). To do this we trained a support vector machine (SVM) classifier using the *n*-grams from training examples from standard gold labelled data sets such as the MPQA Opinion Corpus, Senseval 2007, and others (Agirre, 2007; Wiebe, 2005). Then for each text stream we extracted a bag-of-words per epoch and drew sentiment features using this SVM classifier for the weak logistic regression classifiers. Table 24.5.2 shows only the single best individual text stream result using the SVM classifier. With an AUC of 0.61 this approach clearly outperforms the other baselines. However, the IBCC model was unable to improve upon this result when combining all the streams. This is in sharp contrast to the results reported below. This indicates that there is little diversity in the per-stream predictive distributions when ignoring low level context for sentiment classification. To address this issue we tested using multidimensional, context heavy features obtained from the sentiment composition model at the sentence level.

24.5.4 Text Streams Results

Our general approach to multi-stream prediction is to aggregate the sentence-level sentiment distributions in some way over all sentences in a given epoch to use as feature input into the weak logistic regression classifier models. We first directly compare the *sentiment composition* model with the bag-of-words baseline. To accomplish this we assigned a *single* discrete label to each sentence, "positive", "negative" or "neutral", by selecting the sentiment dimension with the highest probability in each sentence's distribution. Then we correlate the ratio of the positive versus negative sentences within an epoch to the NFP's up/down trend. The results for using only a single sentiment feature per sentence are shown in the first results column of Table 24.5.3.

Table 24.5.3: Stream-specific and combined results for predicting the NFP index. We get better prediction accuracy using multiple sources (starred) with IBCC. Using these starred sources resulted in the overall best predictions from all the stream combinations we tested.

Source	1-Dimension Averages	2-Dimension Averages	Trends
Associated Press*	0.59	0.69	0.37
Dow Jones	0.45	0.44	0.25
Reuters News	0.50	0.46	0.36
Market News Intl.*	0.66	0.70	0.23
Other Sources*	0.58	0.63	0.63
Wall Street Journal	0.44	0.63	0.53
IBCC	0.67	0.81	0.85

To test the IBCC model using this basic strategy, we compared numerous combinations of the various text sources. We found the starred sources in Table 24.5.3 consistently resulted in the best accuracy obtained over all combinations tested. We report only on this best combination in the IBCC row of Table 24.5.3. Using this simple approach of a single feature per sentence and correlating the maximum sentiment per epoch with the NFP trend beats the baseline results by a margin. We see that using the sentiment composition model gives better results than using the bag-of-words classifier due to the context of each sentence being accounted for. Still here, however, the IBCC model is unable to improve much upon the best base classifier's results with AUC scores of 0.67 versus 0.66 respectively.

We then accounted for *multiple* dimensions of the per-sentence sentiment distributions. For each sentence, we treated the probability scores for each dimension of the sentiment, positive or negative, as a count that we aggregate over in some manner for each epoch. We then use the aggregated totals as feature input into a logistic classifier. For example, the second results column in Table 24.5.3 shows the results when we use the percentages of word-weighted positive versus negative sentiment for each epoch for NFP trend prediction.

Clearly this approach has better accuracy than using a single dimension of sentiment per sentence when used in conjunction with the IBCC model.

The third results column of Table 24.5.3 shows another approach using all the dimensions of sentiment available but using the *differences* in the counts between epochs as features. The idea behind this approach is intuitive and assumes the trends of sentiment implicit in the text should correlate with the trends of the economy. A raised level of negativity in the news media compared to normal would reflect a period of economic difficulty and vice versa for positive sentiment in the news. We can see this approach achieves a good measure of correlation between the text sentiment and the trends of the NFP.

From Table 24.5.3 it is clear not all sources give improvement over the baseline results individually. However, as the final line of Table 24.5.3 shows, we can achieve significantly higher accuracies than the baselines or from any single source using a combination of streams within the IBCC framework provided there is useful, complementary information from each source. We note again, we tested many combinations of the text streams as weak inputs into IBCC. We found our predictive results varied widely depending on which text sources were used. Here we only report the results using the stream combination that resulted in the highest prediction accuracy.

24.5.5 Time Series Results

Using the same methodology as above, we build a suite of independent classifiers based on the time series data we collected. We collected over thirty different economic indexes but here we report only on the four series with the best independent prediction results: the Consumer Price Index (CPI), the Institute for Supply Management Manufacturing Index (ISM), the JOLTS Nonfarm Index (JOLTS), and the Labor Force Levels (LFL). Each of these is directly or indirectly related to the unemployment rate and hence the NFP. As with the text streams, for each time series we trained a logistic regression classifier using multivariate features from the data. The features consisted of the point value plus a number of indicators of the trend – both binary and smoothed moving averages – for various time frames.

As can be seen from Table 24.5.4, each individual time series gives significantly better results than the baselines and improves upon the text sentiment results. When we combine each of these weak classifiers using the IBCC model, we get an improved overall AUC of 0.90.

Table 24.5.4: *Stream-specific and combined AUC results for predicting the NFP index using time series data. Here again accuracy is improved when using IBCC.*

Source	AUC
CPI	0.70
ISM	0.85
JOLTS	0.66
LFL	0.71
IBCC	**0.90**

Table 24.5.5: *The AUC results when we combine heterogeneous data types with the IBCC model.*

Source	AUC
Time Series + Text Averages	**0.94**
Time Series + Text Trends	0.91

24.5.6 Combined Heterogeneous Prediction

Finally we tested combining the different data types – time series and text stream data – into a single prediction. This extension is straightforward since each data source is already treated as an independent base classifier by the *SOLID* framework. Since only the posterior distributions of each weak classifier are used as inputs to the combination model, IBCC cannot distinguish between differing types of data input. As Table 24.5.5 shows, using both data types together provides significantly improved prediction accuracy, indicating that the sentiment within the text streams contained distribution information that is complementary to the real-valued time series.

Figure 24.5.1 depicts the AUC results between the baselines and the IBCC results. Clearly we are learning something of interest using our streaming framework and associated combination model. The improvements we get by combinations of data streams is not that surprising given previous work on ensemble methods and classifier combination. Where base classifiers provide complementary information or have uncorrelated random errors, a combination can reduce errors. Therefore, we believe the improvement when using IBCC is not due to including any single strong base classifier, but due to using a combination of streams. As well, when we use the text and time series data streams together, we observe that the text data is providing us with a source of knowledge that is not present in the time series and, when used in a classifier combination setting, provides extra useful information that improves prediction.

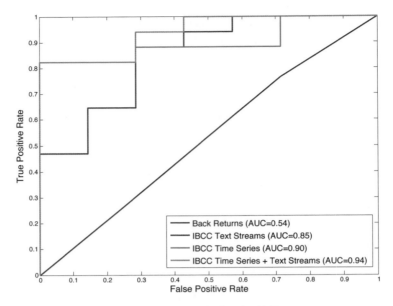

Figure 24.5.1: *Sentiment and baseline prediction results for the NFP.*

24.6 PREDICTING COMMODITY FUTURES

In Section 24.5 we reported results predicting the trend of a monthly economic indicator. In this section we examine whether the *SOLID* framework can be useful for prediction of *daily trends* within the commodity futures markets. As with the experiments in Section 24.5, we show that incorporating heterogeneous streams of data into a model for trend prediction in the commodity futures space may lead to improvements compared to strong baselines that only use more traditional time series data. Specifically, we do this by adding text from the Twitter stream to models that use correlated time series for prediction of commodity futures. We consider three different commodities – corn, gold and crude oil – and analyse the effect of adding the Tweet stream to models for daily trend predictions.

24.6.1 Commodity Futures

Commodity futures are widely traded instruments with high levels of volume and volatility. Prediction of market direction within the commodity futures space is a challenging problem due partly to the diversity and number of real-world variables that individual futures markets respond to (weather, policy, acts of nature, etc.). Normally prediction within the commodity futures space requires analysts to have highly specialised, domain-specific knowledge. Our work asks whether we can automatically learn to match analyst predictions by aggregating the "wisdom of crowds" via the Twitter stream. We describe our methods and experiments below.

24.6.2 Data and Experimental Setup

As we aim to discover if using heterogeneous data streams from the WWW can be utilised for high accuracy trend predictions in the commodity futures space, as before with the NFP, we built models from both time series and test data streams. Time series data available on the Web in this domain is abundant and we mined freely available correlated market data from the API provided by the Open Financial Data Project. We also want to use sources of human-generated text that generate enough daily volume to learn from. Nowadays when one considers sources of such data, Twitter is the obvious forerunner for consideration. Twitter's users generate a massive volume of public "Tweets" continuously. A Tweet is an individual document posted by a user that is restricted to 140 characters. Each Tweet is available publicly or restricted to the author's specifications. Twitter's usage statistics are impressive with half a billion Tweets posted each day written in more than 35 languages from over 250 million global users. In the last few years a significant amount of research has been conducted that has used Twitter to build models of prediction over a myriad of academic and business topics (see Dredze et al. (2014), Bollen et al. (2011), Mao et al. (2011), Yano et al. (2013), Sinha et al. (2013) for just a few examples).

Table 24.6.1: *The correlated time series data streams for commodity futures.*

CBOT	Oats Futures
CBOT	Wheat Futures
CBOT	Soybeans Futures
CBOT	Corn Futures
LBMA	Gold Futures
SPX	Index Futures
Brent	Crude Futures

Here we aim to use the Twitter stream within the *SOLID* framework as a weak classifier of commodity futures' market trend prediction. We mined the Twitter stream for Tweets relevant to our three commodities of interest. Here we treat each Tweet as its own document. That is, for each Tweet considered relevant to the instrument under consideration we extracted its associated sentiment score. For each daily epoch we collected up to 50 Tweets and, as with the NFP, used the trends of the extracted sentiment distributions as features for our weak classifiers.

Our experimental setup for daily trend prediction was setup as follows. We collected the Twitter and time series streams shown in Table 24.6.1 for a time period of January 2013 – April 2014. For robustness, we varied the training and testing subsets of the data. For all models we report on the average results from multiple experiments over 20, 40 and 60-day test periods. Taking the average over multiple testing timeframes for each commodity allowed us to ascertain whether our approach worked in a generalised setting. Again, we report results using AUC as our metric.

24.6.3 Baselines

For each commodity future we built multiple baseline models for comparison. The first was a basic *back returns* approach. Here the forecast trend is predicted to go in the same direction as the last move. So within a daily forecasting system, today's trend would follow yesterday's. We also built a standard regression model using standard features from the time series in Table 24.6.1. These features included the open price, close price and daily volume of each instrument plus the same standard time series features used for the NFP, such as smoothed moving averages, binary trends, etc. Baseline results can be seen in Table 24.6.2 and Figure 24.6.1. While back returns is a poor description of market movements, the regression results for all three instruments perform better than random and, for some futures, achieve quite good results.

24.6.4 Adding the Twitter stream via IBCC

After obtaining our regression baseline we tested incorporating features from the Twitter streams for each commodity futures model using IBCC. To build the weak classifier for the Twitter stream we used recent results from Levenberg et al. (2014), which reported strong correlation between the trends of positive and negative *sentiment* and the trends of the economy. After significant testing, we found this to be the case here too reaffirming the results from Section 24.5. Our features for the Twitter data are thus the daily deltas of aggregate sentiment, both positive and negative, over all Tweets posted between given days.

We then used IBCC to combine the predictions of the time series baselines with our Tweet-based model. Results are shown in Table 24.6.2 and Figure 24.6.1. Recall that these results are the averages of multiple runs of each model spanning different test periods. The results suggest that including user sentiment is beneficial for some commodities futures, such as corn and crude, where we achieve a notable improvement in the average prediction accuracy. However, adding the text data did not improve the (already high) baseline regression model for gold. We analyse why this is the case next.

Table 24.6.2: AUC results for each model.

Future	Back Returns	Time Series	+Twitter
Corn	0.45	0.55	**0.64**
Gold	0.40	**0.72**	0.71
Crude	0.33	0.55	**0.60**

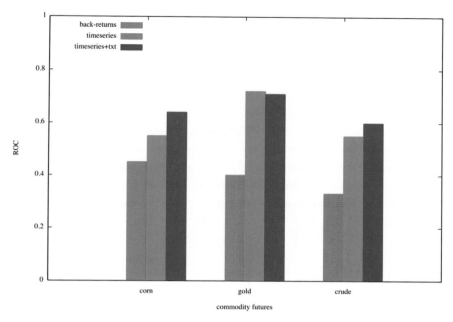

Figure 24.6.1: *Results of the three models for daily prediction of commodity futures trends. Shown are the average results of 20, 40 and 60-day experiments. For certain instruments, adding user sentiment via the Twitter stream improves model performance.*

24.6.5 Analysis

For two of three of our target commodity futures we see clearly that adding extra information by way of streams of text from Twitter improves model accuracy. For corn we get an absolute improvement of 9% AUC by adding sentiment features to daily trend prediction. For crude the accuracy of our model also improves from 0.55 to 0.60 AUC. These results serve to further enhance our previous work in this area and support the claim that there is latent information content included within natural language data that is orthogonal but complementary to standard models of prediction for financial variables.

However, in the case of gold futures we see that adding the same sentiment features from the Twitter stream does not enhance model prediction. Why would this approach work well for some commodity markets but not for others? After examining the data we found that even the filtered Tweet stream for gold contains a high percentage of well-formed but completely irrelevant messages. This is due to the word "gold" having a large number of meanings and colloquial uses within English. Obviously using uncorrelated sentiment features within our model will only generate noise.

For instance, consider the following example Tweets:

gold,silver,diamond,platinum,rings,jewelry | Precious Metal Determinants: Rarity and high economic value

Owners of Health and Medicat biz in Gold Coast City Queensland Australia get FREE business listings at WomTown

Stevie Ray Vaughan gold record award \"Texas Flood\" for sale at: http://t.co/G8Ini6ea

Each of the above Tweets uses the word "gold" with different semantics and, more importantly, all unrelated to the gold futures market. Only one of the Tweets references gold as a precious metal. The other Tweets use gold as part of a proper noun ("Gold Coast City") and as part of an industry specific sales certification ("gold record award"). Note that each of these Tweets is correctly scored with an extremely high positive sentiment value but this sentiment score only serves as feature noise for our classifier. A finance-specific filter would have trouble classifying these Tweets as unrelated to gold markets without including rules specific to each case separately. Building better filters specific to each market, specifically gold, is ongoing current work.

24.7 CONCLUSION

In this report we have described the research done on the *SOLID* framework. We've reported experiments that demonstrate the framework is capable of learning from heterogeneous data streams mined from the WWW to make high quality predictions for daily and monthly trends of lead economic and financial indicators. Using news streams and other text sources to make economic predictions is an area that has generated significant interest in the last decade. The results we've described in this report show clearly there is predictive information within text data that we can access via selecting intuitive features from the sentiment analysis of the text. Using these sentiment features in a state-of-the-art machine learning framework gives good prediction results of financial trends and variables of interest such as the NFP and commodity futures. However, our results show that combining these text streams with more standard time series data within a classifier combination framework such as IBCC produces highly accurate predictions. Clearly there is information within the text that is complementary to the information contained in the time series data. Using IBCC allows easy integration of multiple classifiers of arbitrary data types from a variety of sources and allows us to model the complementary information to obtain better results.

The scope of this type of lead indicator prediction has many potential applications in both further academic research and more direct financial and market- oriented work, with a host of directions for future work. For example, extending the classifier combination model to produce bucketed, real-valued predictions instead of just predicting binary trends is research that we are current conducting. While there is large scope for future work on using the sentiment of big WWW text data for economic predictions, we believe the research we have reported in this paper is a step forward in the current literature in this area.

Notes

[1] www.theysay.io

[2] All data used in this work (including the raw news text as well as its sentiment analysis results) are freely available by emailing the authors.

[3] http://research.stlouisfed.org/fred2/series/PAYNSA?cid=32305

[4] http://research.stlouisfed.org/fred2/

[5] http://www.bls.gov/

[6] http://www.conference-board.org/

[7] http://www.dowjones.com/factiva/index.asp

[8] The text streams were collected using two queries against the Factiva database: "nonfarm payroll near20 (employ)" and "nonfarm payroll near20 (predictORforecast)". The first query searched for documents with any word having the stem word "employ" ("employment", "unemployment", "employed", etc.) within 20 words before or after the NFP term. Similarly, the second search term searches for words with the stem "predict" or "forecast" and occur within 20 words of the term "nonfarm payroll".

[9] www.quandl.com/OFDP

[10] Special thanks to FSWire (www.fswire.com) for their help in the mining and text analysis of the Twitter stream.

24.8 REFERENCES

1.   Agirre, E., M`arquez, L. and Wicentowski, R. (2007). In *Proceedings of the Fourth International Workshop on Semantic Evaluations*. Association for Computational Linguistics, Prague, Czech Republic.

2.   Bollen, J., Mao, H.N. and Zeng, X.J. (2011). Twitter mood predicts the stock market. *Journal of Computational Science, 2(1),* 1–8.

3.   Chatfield, C. (1975). *The Analysis of Time Series: An Introduction.* CRC Press.

4.   Choi, H.Y. and Varian, H.R. (2012). Predicting the present with google trends. *Economic Record, 88(1),* 2–9.

5.   Choi, Y.J. and Cardie, C. (2008). Learning with compositional semantics as structural inference for sub-sentential sentiment analysis. In *Proceedings of the 2008 Conference on Empirical Methods in Natural Language Processing*, pp. 793–801. Association for Computational Linguistics.

6.   Dredze, M., Cheng, R.Y., Paul, M. and Broniatowski, D. (2014). Healthtweets.org: A platform for public health surveillance using twitter. In *AAAI Workshop on the World Wide Web and Public Health Intelligence*.

7.   Fan, D.P. (2010). Predicting the index of consumer sentiment when it isn't measured. In *JSM Proceedings, AAPOR, (Alexandria, VA)*.

8.   Furche, T., Gottlob, G., Grasso, G., Schallhart, C. and Sellers, A. (2012). Oxpath: A language for scalable

data extraction, automation, and crawling on the deep web. *The VLDB Journal*, pp. 1–26.

9.   Ghahramani, Z. and Kim, H.C. (2003). Bayesian classifier combination. *Gatsby Computational Neuroscience Unit Technical Report GCNU-T., London, UK.*

10.   Hamilton, J.D. (1994). *Time Series Analysis*. Princeton University Press.

11.   Joshi, M., Das, D., Gimpel, K. and Smith, N.A. (2010). Movie reviews and revenues: An experiment in text regression. In *Human Language Technologies: The 2010 Annual Conference of the North American Chapter of the Association for Computational Linguistics*, pp. 293–296. Association for Computational Linguistics.

12.   Jurafsky, D., Chahuneau, V., Routledge, B. and Smith, N. (2014). Narrative framing of consumer sentiment in online restaurant reviews. *First Monday, 19(4)*.

13.   Kogan, S., Levin, D., Routledge, B.R., Sagi, J.S. and Smith, N.A. (2009). Predicting risk from financial reports with regression. In *Proceedings of Human Language Technologies: The 2009 Annual Conference of the North American Chapter of the Association for Computational Linguistics*, pp. 272–280. Association for Computational Linguistics.

14.   Lavrenko, V., Schmill, M., Lawrie, D., Ogilvie, P., Jensen, D. and Allan, J. (2001). Mining of concurrent text and time series. In *Proceedings of the 6th ACM SIGKDD International Conference on Knowledge Discovery and Data Mining Workshop on Text Mining*, pp. 37–44.

15.   Levenberg, A., Pulman, S., Moilanen, K., Simpson, E. and Roberts, S. (2014). Predicting economic indicators from web text using sentiment composition. In *International Journal of Computer and Communication Engineering*. IACSIT Press.

16.   Mao, H.N., Counts, S. and Bollen, J. (2011). Predicting financial markets: Comparing survey, news, twitter and search engine data. *arXiv preprint, arXiv:1112.1051*.

17.   Mills, T.C. and Markellos, R.N. (2008). *The Econometric Modelling of Financial Time Series*. Cambridge University Press.

18.   Mitra, L. and Mitra, G. (2011). *The Handbook of News Analytics in Finance*. The Wiley Finance Series. Wiley.

19.   Mittermayer, M.A. and Knolmayer, G. (2007). Text mining systems for market response to news: A survey. In *Proceedings of the IADIS European Conference Data Mining*.

20.   Moilanen, K. and Pulman, S. (2007). Sentiment composition. In *Proceedings of Recent Advances in Natural Language Processing*, pp. 378–382.

21.   Nikfarjam, A., Emadzadeh, E. and Muthaiyah, S. (2010). Text mining approaches for stock market

prediction. In *The 2nd International Conference on Computer and Automation Engineering*. Vol. 4, pp. 256–260. IEEE.

22. Polanyi, L. and Zaenen, A. (2004). Contextual lexical valence shifters. In *Proceedings of the AAAI Spring Symposium on Exploring Attitude and Affect in Text: Theories and Applications*.

23. Preis, T., Moat, H.S. and Stanley, H.E. (2013). Quantifying trading behaviour in financial markets using google trends. *Scientific Reports*, *3*.

24. Preis, T., Reith, D. and Stanley, H.E. (2010). Complex dynamics of our economic life on different scales: insights from search engine query data. *Philosophical Transactions of the Royal Society A: Mathematical, Physical and Engineering Sciences*, *368*(1933), 5707–5719.

25. Savor, P. and Wilson, M. (2013). How much do investors care about macroeconomic risk? Evidence from scheduled economic announcements. *Journal of Financial and Quantitative Analysis, 48*, 1–62.

26. Schumaker, R.P. and Chen, H.C. (2009). Textual analysis of stock market prediction using breaking financial news: The azfin text system. *ACM Transactions on Information Systems, 27(2)*, 12:1–12:19.

27. Simpson, E., Roberts, S., Psorakis, I. and Smith A. (2013). Dynamic bayesian combination of multiple imperfect classifiers. *Decision Making and Imperfection. Intelligent Systems Reference Library*, *474*.

28. Sinha, S., Dyer, C., Gimpel, K. and Smith, N.A. (2013). Predicting the nfl using twitter. *CoRR*, abs/1310.6998.

29. Socher, R., Perelygin, A., Wu, J., Chuang, J., Manning, C., Ng, A. and Potts, C. (2013). Recursive deep models for semantic compositionality over a sentiment treebank. In *Conference on Empirical Methods in Natural Language Processing*. Association for Computational Linguistics.

30. Spackman, K.A. (1989). Signal detection theory: valuable tools for evaluating inductive learning. In *Proceedings of the sixth international workshop on Machine learning*, pp. 160–163. Morgan Kaufmann Publishers Inc.

31. Venanzi, M., Guiver, J., Kazai, G. and Kohli, P. (2013). Bayesian combination of crowd-based tweet sentiment analysis judgments. *Proceedings of the Crowdscale Shared Task Challenge*.

32. Wiebe, J., Wilson, T. and Cardie, C. (2005). Annotating Expressions of Opinions and Emotions in Language. *Language Resources and Evaluation, 39(2-3)*, 165–210.

33. Xu, W., Li, Z. and Chen, Q. (2012). Forecasting the unemployment rate by neural networks using search engine query data. In *Proceedings of the 2012 45th Hawaii International Conference on System Sciences*, pp. 3591–3599. IEEE Computer Society.

34. Yano, T., Yogatama, D. and Smith, N.A. (2013). A penny for your tweets: Campaign contributions and

capitol hill microblogs. In E. Kiciman, N.B. Ellison, B. Hogan, P. Resnick, and I. Soboroff, eds, *ICWSM*. The AAAI Press.

PART VII

Directory of Service Providers

ALEXANDRIA TECHNOLOGY

About company: Alexandria Technology (www.alexandriatechnology.com) employs advanced machine learning techniques to replicate the decisions of domain experts when classifying critical information in unstructured content. Alexandria's Contextual Text Analytics (ACTA) engine was first used to classify DNA and now decodes the subject matter and sentiment in financial news.

The company's unique approach allows for relevant classification of virtually any unstructured content set, in any language, which currently includes native Japanese. In its current form, analyzing financial news, ACTA matches the decision of a research analyst with extremely high accuracy for multiple asset classes in real time.

Head office location: Los Angeles, CA

Other sites: New York, NY

Chief executive officer or Managing Director: Dan Joldzic, *CFA, FRM*

Marketing and sales director: Rowan Pritchard

Key services provided by the company:
The Alexandria ACTA engine classifies financial news for entities, events, and sentiment for multiple asset classes including global equities, economies, commodities, currencies and government debt instruments.

ACTA's breakthrough technology avoids the accuracy and flexibility problems inherent in standard word- and rule-based approaches, while classifying articles at much lower latencies.

While ACTA's engineering goal is to match the analyst, Alexandria's research finds their data is predictive of price and volatility, and uncorrelated to traditional factors.

Contact: dan.joldzic@alexability.com; rowan@alexability.com; 323-461-8500

AMAREOS LTD.

About company: Amareos is a financial services company, which specializes in financial news & sentiment analytics. Established in 2015 by a small team of financial market veterans with experience in large sell-side and buy-side financial institutions Amareos is a trusted partner of Thomson Reuters and Market Psyche - longstanding innovators in the field of news analytics.

Amareos provides several types of services to a wide range of clients (large financial organizations, private banks, hedge fund, insurance companies and official institutions) via its web-based platform www.amareos.com.

Head office location: 1102, Lee Garden One, 33 Hysan Avenue, Causeway Bay, Hong Kong.

Other sites: Paris and London

Chief executive officer or Managing Director: Jerome Favresse (CEO)

Chief Technology Officer: Jacques Labbaci

Chief Business Development Officer: Philippe El-Asmar

Key services provided by the company:
- Research: Amareos' research is the best way to comprehend sentiments on a topic. We build analytics & tools that are truly useful to your business. In addition to high quality fundamental macroeconomic analysis we provide indicators and metrics to sharpen the decision making process. We go beyond what the data providers usually deliver. We provide you high value content through advanced analytics & indicators... And all of this in one single interface.
- Consulting: Implementing News analytics & sentiment indicators into trading systems, risk monitoring or any other in-house system is not trivial. We can help you in the process. Amareos provides advisory on data sources, implementation and the use of sentiment analytics.
- Asset management solutions: At Amareos we develop and manage sentiment augmented proprietary strategies leveraging our own research. Our in-house strategies cover all asset classes and geographical zones.

Contact: info@amareos.com; +852 3959 8691

BLOOMBERG L.P.

About company: Bloomberg, the global business and financial information and news leader, gives influential decision makers a critical edge by connecting them to a dynamic network of information, people, and ideas. The company's strength—delivering data, news, and analytics through innovative technology, quickly, and accurately—is at the core of the Bloomberg Professional® service, which provides real-time financial information to more than 320,000 subscribers globally. With over 15,000 employees in 192 locations, including more than 151 news bureaus globally, we deliver business and financial information, news and insight around the world.

Head office location: 731 Lexington Avenue, New York, NY 10022

Other sites: More than 192 Bloomberg News bureaus and offices, including London, Tokyo, Beijing, Hong Kong, Singapore, Dubai, San Francisco, Sydney, Frankfurt, Mumbai, and Sao Paulo.

Chief executive officer: Michael R. Bloomberg

Head of Bloomberg for Enterprise: Gerard Francis

Head of Event-Driven Feeds: Don Huff (Business), Daniel Caporaletti (Product)

Key services provided by the company:
Bloomberg Event-Driven Feeds balance speed and precision to enable more effective coordination and execution of your trading strategies. Each feed is highly structured and specifically designed to deliver real-time, machine-readable data—including breaking headlines, exclusive global coverage, structured financial data, news analytics and global economic indicators—for black box applications.

Key products:
- **Textual News** aggregates breaking news from 151 Bloomberg bureaus worldwide—generating 10,000+ headlines and stories daily—plus other valuable third-party sources, including web and social media content. This amounts to more than 500,000 items per day, paired with granular metadata covering companies, topics and people.
- **News Analytics** delivers an informative second layer of processing for our industry-leading textual news feed at both the story and company levels. These analytics include sentiment analysis, novelty scores, readership heat, social velocity, and more.
- **Global Macroeconomic Indicators (ECO)** provides timely, accurate, and comprehensive global coverage for economic, central bank, and industry datasets.
- **Corporate Events Calendar (EVTS)** delivers 300,000 event notifications from more than 48,000 companies in 100-plus countries, including earnings release dates, sales results, and shareholder and board meeting information.

- **Corporate Actions Calendar (CACS)** covers 50 unique corporate-action types on millions of instruments, providing unsurpassed insight into spin-offs, bankruptcies, and class-action events, as well as breaking news on dividends, splits, IPOs and acquisitions.

Contact: Web: http://www.bloomberg.com/enterprise/content-data/event-driven-feeds/

Email: eventfeeds@bloomberg.net

Bloomberg Terminal: EDF <GO>

DELTIX

About company: Deltix is a leading provider of software and services for quantitative research, algorithmic and automated systematic trading. Deltix software enables a complete straight through processing environment for the development and deployment of closely-integrated alpha generation and/or execution strategies.

Our clients are both buy-side and sell-side firms. On the buy-side, we work with hedge funds, CTA's, proprietary trading firms, investment management firms and banks. In those firms, we work with professional "quants", quantitative traders, portfolio managers and technologists. On the sell-side, we provide solutions to banks and brokers for algorithmic execution of orders for equities, futures and FX. More recently, we have deployed a full FX market making solution for banks.

The common theme across our solutions for both buy-side and sell-side clients is our ability to deploy our own highly advanced product componentry in a customized deployment in a collaborative manner.

Wholly owned by employees, Deltix was founded in 2005 by a group of computer scientists and mathematicians who held key technology positions at several successful software companies, including PTC, HighRoads, and Transdecisions with extensive expertise in sophisticated quantitative and event-driven solutions.

Deltix is headquartered in Natick, Massachusetts, and has offices in New York, Minsk and St. Petersburg, Russia. There are currently over 50 staff in the company, mostly engineers with advanced degrees in mathematics or computer science.

Head office location: Boston, MA

Other sites: New York, London, Saint Petersburg, Minsk

Chief executive officer or Managing Director: Ilya Gorelik

Marketing and sales director: Stuart Farr

Key services provided by the company:
Intelligent Collaboration is in our DNA Deltix ("**D**evelopment **L**aboratory for **T**echnology and **I**nformatics") was founded to develop **Open Intelligence Software**. The main characteristic of **Open Intelligence Software** is that it allows the **end user client** to modify and extend the functionality of the resulting solution. Open Intelligence Software development requires a very close partnership with clients: the development of software based on end-user requirements is in our DNA. We developed and tuned our software development processes specifically to ensure that the resulting solutions not only meet the requirements of end users, *but at the same time are flexible and extendable*.

History

Since 2005, Deltix has worked with over 120 financial firms, including banks, brokers, ECNs, energy producers and small proprietary trading firms. We have an organization of highly qualified software engineers and analysts, holding MS and PhDs degrees, with hundreds of years of combined software development experience, creating high-performance, robust, multi-tiered, cross-platforms computational systems and applications. Out teams can work on project independently, or, embedded in the development organization of our clients.

Proficiency in the development of enterprise-wide information and decision management systems, especially processing large sets of heterogeneous time-series data. From its inception, Deltix focused on solving generic problems of information management especially on tasks related to the processing of large volumes of heterogeneous time-series data. We created and refined our software and in parallel developed in-house expertise and software engineering skills to cover the entire workflow of an advanced information management, from data acquisition, cleansing and validation, to advanced decision support, visualization and reporting. We applied this know-how to the development of solutions in the field of quantitative finance, but our software for systematic trading is only an example of how our technology could be utilized.

During the first years of Deltix's growth we developed software for advanced content management, insurance procurement, data center wellness management and generic knowledge management. Today Deltix has dedicated teams specializing in various horizontal software engineering domains including enterprise-wide data management and warehousing, complex event processing, real-time mathematics, decision support systems, automatic code generation, dynamic data visualization and reporting. We possess deep vertical knowledge of financial markets, including market data aggregation and connectivity, strategy development and backtesting, advanced order execution and management.

Our QuantServer and QuantOffice solution is an illustration of how our software development expertise in the field of quantitative finance could be utilized for the development of broader spectrum of information management systems utilizing time-series data.

Diversity of in-house expertise allows us to solve the most advanced technical problems

Not only do we work with the majority of standard technologies (.NET, Java, C++ etc.), we have a talented team with deep hands-on knowledge and demonstrable results in the broad area of generic enterprise-wide information management and dynamic decision support.

Contact: Phone: 1-617-273-2540, 1-617-273-2540; Global Sales enquiries: sales@deltixlab.com
Toll Free: 1-800-856-6120, 1-800-856-6120 FREE

IMAIBO.NET

About company: Founded in 2013 by a group of financial & media veterans, Imaibo.net is a pioneer in financial social network services in China, with a mission to create an investment ecosystem encompassing retail investors, portfolio managers and financial institutions. As of June 2015, there were over 2 million Chinese users on iMaibo.net.

iMaibo.net is offering three pillars of services, namely, (i) Chinese equity sentiment indices and scores (ii) investment portfolio sharing platform and (iii) real time chat room and market commentary.

The ultimate goal of iMaibo.net is to become a disruptive alternative to traditional mutual fund products by offering retail investors a low cost, transparent and interactive investment experience.

Head office location: China

Chief executive officer: Gilbert Tse

Chief operating officer: Jonathan Cai

Key services provided by the company:

- Sentiment indices and scores:
  iMaibo offers the iMaibo China Equity Sentiment Indices. The indices comprises the sentiment scores for the 4 major equity indices in China, 26 major sector indices and individual 'A' stocks. These indices are obtained through a Natural Language processing of the Chinese language from the domestic social media with over 3000+ websites and up to 80k incoming messages a day. The sentiment data is planned to be available on the Reuters Elkon platform by 2Q 2016.

- Portfolio sharing platform:
  On iMaibo.net, there are currently over 10,000 investment portfolios contributed by investment advisors, fund managers, financial bloggers as well as retail investors. Our users can review the track record of the portfolios, follow every trade of the strategies and portfolios they like, post questions and even enter into real-time dialog with the portfolio contributors. While most of the portfolios are free to review, iMaibo.net has started offering paid services on selected portfolios, allowing our portfolio contributors to capitalize on their contents and services.

Contact: Tel: +86-20-87385050-820; Email: gilbert.tse@ijinzhuan.com, jonathan.cai@ijinzhuan.com, eric.tham@ijinzhuan.com ; Website: http://www.imaibo.net/

LAMPLIGHT ANALYTICS

About company: A social media analytics platform for Asia

More than half of all active social media users live in Asia, home to the world's largest and most engaged social media audience. It is the most dynamic and complex place to do business today, requiring a level of cultural and linguistic fluency that not all businesses have.

Lamplight was built to account for the diversity of the region. As Asia's premier social media intelligence platform, Lamplight gives business leaders brighter insights into the world of online conversations. Lamplight's advanced Asian language software and analytics capabilities provide the most accurate and authentic data on Asian social media audiences.

Head office location: Hong Kong

Chief Executive Officer: Sam Olsen (Co-Founder)

Chief Operating Officer: Fergus Clarke (Co-Founder)

Chief Technology Officer: Nathan Pacey (Co-Founder)

Key services provided by the company:

The advent of social media services has impacted the way people think, communicate, behave, learn, and conduct their activity. For anyone seeking independent information, social media represents a wealth of public information that provides great insights into topics, regions and target audiences. Information contained in social media, can often reflect the offline world more closely than official news sources and provide shifts in opinion in real-time.

Lamplight lets you harness social data to make quicker, more informed decisions that allow you to create better products and services for your customers. With Lamplight, you can monitor, analyze, and gather insights and multilingual social media data to effectively understand and expand your brand/services and generate global revenue opportunities and connections with multilingual customers.

Most of the existing social media analytics platforms and research in this domain are mainly focused on monolingual data. Therefore, it is hard to connect their analysis/insights to real world outcomes. Lamplight helps you cut through the noise to illuminate the multilingual conversations that matter most for your business. It provides analysis and insights to plan your strategy, optimize your tactics, and tie social activity to larger business outcomes.

Lamplight's online, multilingual analytics platform is intuitive and fully customizable, so users can access and share the social media data that is most relevant to them as they need it. We capture online conversations from 20+ million sources, including major social networking sites, and independent blogs and bulletin boards from all over the world. Our proprietary natural language processing technology enables users to drill down into the data for behavioural and demographic analysis in over 15 languages. It includes topic modelling and its temporal evaluation, identifying topic specific spatio-temporal influence, engagement patterns, sentiment analysis by extracting opinions placed on social media, and semantic intelligence capabilities.

How businesses are using Lamplight:

Marketing/PR Effectiveness	Monitoring buzz and real-time responses to campaigns and initiatives.
Crisis Management	Tracking overall sentiment, and identifying conversation drivers during times of crisis.
Influencer Identification	Pinpointing the key influencers in conversations, and measuring their reach
Reputation Monitoring	Staying on top of how the business is perceived by consumers and the media.
Audience Research	Understanding the texture of conversations, and knowing exactly where they occur.
Competitor Benchmarking	Measuring how they compare to competitors in their industries.
Market Research	Better target traditional consumer research using real-time unfiltered data, saving money and time.
Equity Research	Identify consumer trends and insights ahead of the rest of the market. Get the edge & turn real-time commentary into critical analysis.

Contact: +852 2780 0708, info@lamplight.me, https://www.lamplight.me

MARKETPSYCH DATA

About company: MarketPsych Data provides news and social media-derived sentiment and macroeconomic data through Thomson Reuters. The co-branded Thomson Reuters MarketPsych Indices distribute data on over 8,000 companies, 30 currencies, 35 commodities, and 130 countries. The data is delivered in minutely, hourly, and daily formats, and it spans from 1998 to the present. The data is derived from tens of thousands of global business and finance-related news and social media sources. The data delivers quantified time series of dozens of granular categories of emotion (fear, anger, joy), expectations (optimism, earningsForecast, interestRateForecast), political risk (governmentInstability), and macroeconomic (inflation, unemployment) factors, among many others. MarketPsych began work on financial text analytics in 2004. MarketPsych aims to provide the global standard in financial sentiment data.

Head office location: California, USA

Chief executive officer or Managing Director: Richard L. Peterson

Marketing and sales director: The product is provided exclusively through Thomson Reuters.

Key services provided by the company:
The company's primary business is the creation and distribution of sentiment data.

Contact: +1.323.389.1813

NORTHFIELD

About company: Established in 1987, Northfield provides investment managers models to identify, measure and control risk for both absolute and relative return strategies. Our models cover traded securities worldwide including bottom up alternative assets.

Head office location: Boston, MA USA

Other sites: Chicago, London, Tokyo and soon Sydney

Chief executive officer or Managing Director: Dan diBartolomeo

Marketing and sales director: Nick Cutler

Key services provided by the company:
Risk modelling for institutional money managers, asset owners of all kinds and large retail and/or wealth management firms. Our service applications enable users to manage risk for both taxable and tax-exempt portfolios. These applications are used at both the enterprise-wide level and one portfolio at a time.

Contact: Sales: Sean Leger, 617 208 2050, sales@northinfo.com

OPTIRISK SYSTEMS

About company: OptiRisk Systems specializes in optimization and risk analytics and is renowned for its research and development of models and software systems in these domains. In the domain of Sentiment Analysis, OptiRisk is a partner of Thomson Reuters, Bloomberg, RavenPack and TheySay. The company pursues a committed research program in this domain and has developed trading products that apply news sentiment data. The other specialisation of OptiRisk Systems is Stochastic Optimisation. The company is a certified (global) partner of IBM in Optimisation Modelling. In the domain of optimization, the company has further developed a family of Algebraic Modelling Language (AML) tools which are specifically designed for modelling and solving a wide range of stochastic optimisation and robust optimisation problems. In the area of AML the company is a technology partner and a sub-contractor of AMPL Optimization Inc. In the general field of Business Intelligence (BI) the company has a track record of successfully delivering tailored applications in finance, logistics and enterprise risk management systems.

Head office: London, UK

Other sites: Kolkata and Chennai, India

Managing director: Professor Gautam Mitra

Head of Business Development: Dr Xiang Yu

CEO (India): Bala Padmakumar Pillai

Key services provided by the company:
- **Products**:
  Financial Analytics: OptiRisk offers two trading products in this field

    i.   Sentiment Analysis Toolkit (SAT)
         SAT combines market data and news (meta) data and applies predictive analytic models to describe the behaviour of (equity) asset prices. The approach is fairly generic and the product has been tested on FTSE 100, Hang Seng, Eurostoxx 50, and Nifty 50.

    ii. SSD Signals
         SSD Signals uses the technique of second order stochastic dominance to achieve portfolio selection. Back testing results have been produced for FTSE 100, Hang Seng, Eurostoxx 50, and Nifty 50 for daily trading.

    iii. LDIOpt
         LDIopt is an asset and liability management (ALM) optimisation modelling software for

pension funds, insurance companies, and banks. The tool enables the user to analyse their current investment portfolio, rebalance it to a new portfolio using advanced stochastic optimization models which take into account future uncertainties of the assets and liabilities.

Optimisation: We develop as well as resell Algebraic Modelling Language Family of Products that are used in Mathematical Modelling and Optimization. Our in-house products include AMPLDev (IDE for AMPL), FortMP and FortSP. FortMP is a solver which has sparse LP, MIP and QMIP features. The Stochastic solver FortSP uses Benders Decomposition or Level Decomposition and regularisation and is built around embedded solvers: CPLEX or Gurobi or FortMP.

* **Services:**

OptiRisk offers training (including bespoke in-house courses), solver tuning, advisory and outsourced modelling services in a wide range of domains such as optimization, risk management, financial mathematical modelling, data management and more,

Contact: *Tel*:   +44 1895 819483; +91 9094532918
      Email   gautam@optirisk-systems.com
             bpadmakunar@optiriskindia.com
      Website   www.optirisk-systems.com

PSYCHSIGNAL

About company: PsychSignal is a provider of real time Trader Mood, data, analytics and indices for financial institutions & investment professionals seeking an edge. We datamine the global online conversation, so that you know which way the mood is trending for specific securities. We created a natural language processing engine, which correctly interprets social media text in the context of stock prices. Our technology parses millions of online conversations every day in order to quantify the public's mood about specific stocks and other securities.

The concept behind PsychSignal's technology is that we have created a smart way for computers to correctly interpret and understand text content of a financial nature. We have built a sentiment engine which is able to parse through online conversations to analyze and quantify the public's bullish or bearish mood about specific stocks and other securities. Our system outputs are valuable because they tell professional trading firms what the underlying market perception is behind their investments, which in turn enables them to have an additional set of indicators as inputs to their investment strategies.

By understanding the underlying mood behind each stock, we enable our customers to generate powerful trading strategies by being able to proactively time their positions in response to mood shifts, rather than being limited to trading reactively based on pure algorithmic and event-trigger strategies. In short, other news sentiment and event detection systems tell you the news, whereas we tell you how the market is likely going to react in the event of news coming out.

We license our sentiment platform for delivering highly predictive sentiment data and analytics to institutional investors globally. PsychSignal covers over 10,000+ stocks, ETFs and other assets.

Head office location: Miami, Florida, USA

Other sites: Rio De Janeiro, New York City, Amsterdam, London, Hamburg, Santa Barbara, Austin, Los Angeles, Chicago

Chief Executive Officer or Managing Director: James Crane-Baker (CEO)

Marketing and Sales Director: Bjorn Simundson (CMO) Marketing, Malik Corbett (CRO) Sales

Key services provided by the company:
Our smart filtering, natural language processing engines, and quantification algorithms are built to recognize and specifically quantify the meaning behind each word communicated in the nuanced language used on professional trading floors, giving us a critical advantage over others using standard language processing technology.

This highly-tuned precision to generate two continuous scales of Bullishness and Bearishness, trends, alerts with a full spectrum continuous flow of information in much greater detail than a simple red or green view found on other platforms.

Our signals deliver market mood to algos, just like Squawk-Boxes gave professional traders the ability to listen to the trading pits from their desks, back during the open-outcry analog trading days. (pre-2000's)

PsychSignal's technology delivers the same critical market information as the VIX, AAII, NAAIM and TRIN, but does so for over 10,000+ specific symbols every minute, instead of for a half-dozen sectors once per week. We achieve these results because we have spent the past 5 years building a custom programmed specialized natural language processing engine built to recognize, categorize, and quantify the sentiment of the language being used by financial professionals in online conversations.

We can zero-in on the "Trader Mood" specifically, because our system uses a linguistic-based natural language processing approach trained to look for the subtle yet specific language nuances used by professionals on the trading floors. This makes our technology much more powerful and reliable than comparable machine-learning based approaches mining the general public.

This more powerful technology allows us to correctly interpret meaning of statements that other platforms would fail to recognize because our system knows the inside language used only in professional trading environments that other language engine cannot decipher. As a result, our system can correctly score messages like: "$MSFT is ripping rite now", "…dead cat bounce on $NFLX", or "loading the boat with $SPY ", giving our system the ability to filter through the noise with far greater accuracy than any other engine available.

In addition to being the only engine built to process mood in the native language of traders, we set ourselves apart from other companies in that we have access to and/or process the full 100% firehose datafeeds from our partners like Twitter, StockTwits, T3Live and a variety of other private chatrooms, instead of the smaller "Gardenhose" or "Faucet" feed that other platforms use from a single-source.

According to 3rd party studies, our data-stream consistently generates much stronger Alpha, Sharpe and Sortino than any other sentiment platform. Other companies claim that they "process the Twitter feed", but leave out the fact that they only process the "Decahose " which is in fact only 10% of the Twitter data stream. In contrast, we not only have access to the whole 100% "Firehose Feed" Data-stream for Twitter at the same level of access as Google & Yahoo, but we also process the entire firehoses for more than a half dozen public and private chatrooms focused purely on the financial industry, with some through exclusive contract.

Learn more at: www.psychsignal.com.

Contact: Mr. James Crane-Baker (CEO)   Mr. Bjorn Simundson (CMO / Marketing)
+1805.284.8654   +1.805+678.0602 office
james@psychsignal.com   bjorn@psychsignal.com

Mr. Malik Corbett (CRO / Sales)
+1.718.637.3703 mobile
malik@psychsignal.com

RAVENPACK

About company: RavenPack was founded in 2003 and launched the first version of RavenPack News Analytics (RPNA) in 2007. Since then RPNA has evolved based on client feedback and quantitative research to be a leading provider of Big Data Analytics for financial applications.

RavenPack has the longest-serving data science team in the business.This award-winning team maintains RavenPack's thought leadership in big data analytics through its own quantitative research and partnerships with independent researchers, sell-side banks and academics.

Financial firms rely on RavenPack to abbreviate the tasks of categorizing and managing unstructured content, turning it into structured data for ease of analysis and deployment. RavenPack has proven applications across financial services firms, from quantitative trading to retail broking, from risk management to market surveillance. The company's clients include some of the best performing hedge funds, banks and investment managers in the world.

Head office location: Marbella, Spain

Other sites: New York City / London, UK

Chief executive officer or Managing Director: Armando Gonzalez, CEO

Chief Data Scientist: Peter Hafez

Key services provided by the company:
RavenPack transforms unstructured big data sets, such as traditional news and social media, into structured granular data and indicators to help financial services firms improve their performance.

The product serves to overcome the challenges posed by the characteristics of Big Data - volume, variety, veracity and velocity - by converting unstructured content into a format that can be more effectively analyzed, manipulated and deployed in financial applications.

Whether your objective is generating more alpha, managing risk more effectively, cutting false positives in market surveillance or generating trading ideas, RavenPack Analytics can improve your performance.

Use Cases:
- Asset Management: Build or subscribe to factors that deliver orthogonal alpha across all asset classes.
- Brokerage & Market-Making: Detect and instantly react to unscheduled events that may impact your performance.
- Risk & Compliance: Monitor accumulation of adverse sentiment, detect headline risk, or reduce false positives from market abuse alerts.

- Research: Provide unique aspects to quantitative and fundamental research; control for news and social media in academic research.
- Software / Data Vendor: Build an innovator position by adding powerful Big Data analytics to your offering.
- Media: Attract attention to your content by adding unique analytics to your website or article.

Contact: Americas Sales: +1 (646) 277 7339; EMEA / APAC Sales: +44 (0) 20 3714 8788;
Head Office: +34 952 90 73 90
Email: info@ravenpack.com
Web: www.ravenpack.com

STOCKTWITS, INC.

About company: StockTwits is the largest social investment network, globally. StockTwits is an open, community-powered idea and information service for investments. Users can eavesdrop on traders and investors, or contribute to the conversation and build their reputation as savvy market participants. The service takes financial related data and structures it by appending ticker stream, user behavior, reputation, etc.

Head office: New York, NY, USA

Other sites: San Diego, CA, USA

Managing director: Justin Paterno

Marketing and sales director: Pierce Crosby (New York)

Key services provided by the company:
Tools and services: **StockTwits API**
    StockTwits Sentiment API
    StockTwits Firehose

Tools and services description:

> **Products**: In addition to the consumer-facing applications, StockTwits specializes in raw data extraction as a basis of quantitative investing and signal generation.
> Applicable to:

> i.   Low latency sentiment modelling, sentiment signal extraction, directional and momentum modelling.
> ii. Risk mitigation, portfolio optimization, decision tree processing.
> iii. Raw volatility trading.

Contact: *Tel*   +1 (707) 223-6100
         Email   pierce@stocktwits.com
         Website   www.stocktwits.com

THEYSAY LIMITED

About company: TheySay is a UK-based leader in language analytics based on cutting-edge research from the University of Oxford. The Company has developed a proprietary technology suite based on a complex set of natural language processing algorithms and machine learning solutions. The technology is capable of analysing high volumes of text data in real time and detecting rich emotion signals about products, people, organisations, events, and issues.

The Oxford academics who invented the TheySay software are linguists and logicians by background which has led them to take a completely new and much more serious approach to text analytics. Unlike the majority of technology providers who use shallow statistical approaches, TheySay's technology is based on a deep understanding of language, its structure, patterns, and rich nuances that form human communication. This enables sophisticated understanding and analysis of large volumes of text in real time to generate insight and business intelligence signals.

Head office location: Oxford Centre for Innovation, New Road, Oxford OX1 1BY

Other sites: 24 Cornhill, London EC3V 3ND

Chief executive officer or Managing Director: David Morgan

Marketing and sales director: Jon Halestrap

Key services provided by the company:
The Company has created two products to help develop and deliver its technology, namely

1. a language-analytics-as-a-service API product (called PreCeive) that allows clients to plug our complex analytics services into their existing workflows and services without any heavy development or R&D work, and

2. a real-time opinion streaming platform (called MoodRaker) that monitors large-scale public opinion around various topics for customer-driven applications.

It is through these plug-and-play solutions that the Company has built up a customer base of leading blue-chip names enabling real-world validation and crucial development feedback pertaining to the core language analytics technology.

Contact: david.morgan@theysay.io

THOMSON REUTERS

About company: Thomson Reuters connects and powers the global financial community through our open and trusted news, data, analytics and insight, tools and applications, trading capabilities, and infrastructure and services – enabling discovery, liquidity and compliance.

We help our customers uncover critical insights and market opportunities and connect to the largest network of financial professionals – enabling better decisions and more confident actions.

We create efficiencies that drive profits with scalable infrastructure and services that enable faster and smarter performance. Our trading applications and venues provide access to liquidity that connects customers and markets. Through our regulatory insight and workflow tools, we enable our customers to manage compliance and mitigate risk.

With headquarters in New York and major operations in London and Eagan, Minnesota, Thomson Reuters employs more than 55,000 people and operates in over 100 countries. Thomson Reuters shares are listed on the Toronto and New York Stock Exchanges.

Head office location: New York City, London

Chief executive officer: Jim Smith, CEO

Marketing and sales director: James Canterella, Global Business Manager of Machine Readable News

Key services provided by the company:
Thomson Reuters Elektron is a suite of trading and data propositions that power the enterprise and connect global markets, whether deployed or hosted as a managed service.

Contact: Keesa Schreane, Senior Marketing Manager, Enterprise Platform and Analytics
646.223.4447
Keesa.schreane@thomsonreuters.com

INDEX